PERSONALITY AND PLACE
IN RUSSIAN CULTURE

PERSONALITY AND PLACE IN RUSSIAN CULTURE

Essays in Memory of Lindsey Hughes

Edited by
Simon Dixon

Modern Humanities Research Association
for the
UCL School of Slavonic and East European Studies

2010

Published by

The Modern Humanities Research Association,
1 Carlton House Terrace
London SW1Y 5AF
for the
UCL School of Slavonic and East European Studies

This collection also appeared as Volume 88:1/2 (2010) of
The Slavonic and East European Review

First published 2010

ISBN 978-1-907322-02-0 hardback
ISBN 978-1-907322-03-7 paperback

Copies may be ordered from www.seer.mhra.org.uk

CONTENTS

INTRODUCTION

Personality and Place

SIMON DIXON

In what must surely be one of the most evocative recreations of a sense of place in any language, Richard Cobb (1917–96) conjured up an English childhood of the 1920s and 1930s in the Royal Borough of Tunbridge Wells. *Still Life* recalls a favourite gate, associated with a particular birthday; a small boy's fantasies about the giant ferns near the town centre ('The Congo, Java, Borneo, the Gran Chaco lay, for those in the know, within a few hundred yards of the Pantiles and of [the church of] King Charles the Martyr'); mental snapshots, captured on teenage cycle-rides, to be savoured in a bleak moment (there were many) at Shrewsbury School.[1] Above all, however, Cobb recovers 'a society based on elaborate, if unstated, hierarchies of class relations of considerable subtlety'.[2] Mount Ephraim — home to 'the best dentists (but not the best doctors, less ostentatious) and elderly retired female courtiers' — sat comfortably enough alongside aspirant, respectable, snobbish Mount Sion. But neither sensed much fellow feeling for 'the ill-defined population of Monson Road and Calverley Road', still less for the menacing inhabitants of neighbouring High Brooms — 'not a *place*, just a sordid word'.[3] 'I did not know anything about the Russian Revolution', Cobb admitted, 'though there were flag-days and collections in King Charles for the Relief of the Famine in the Ukraine. But I certainly *did* know about class antagonism and class fear.'[4]

Swanscombe, where Lindsey Hughes (1949–2007) was born, and nearby Dartford, where she went to school, lay in an altogether less prosperous part of Kent than the Royal Borough. Increasingly

Simon Dixon is Sir Bernard Pares Professor of Russian History at UCL SSEES.

I am grateful to my friend Jim Cutshall for helping me with this essay in so many ways, both spoken and unspoken.

[1] R. Cobb, *Still Life: Sketches from a Tunbridge Wells Childhood*, London, 1984 edn, pp. 9 and passim.
[2] Ibid., p, xiii.
[3] Ibid., pp. 6, 7, 18, 30 (p. 18).
[4] Ibid., p. 32.

indistinguishable from the sprawling suburbs stretched out along London's eastern edge, they could boast none of Mount Ephraim's fading Regency charm; their shops were no match for the fashionable Pantiles; their air was not so clean (until the 1990s, Swanscombe was a centre of the cement industry).[5] Yet behind the ubiquitous net curtains, 'the minutely defined frontiers separating middle class from lower middle class'[6] were just as valiantly defended in the flatlands of the post-war Thames estuary as they had been thirty years earlier in Tunbridge Wells. Matched by anguish about lower-middle-class security among a generation haunted by memories of the Great Depression, such frontiers were still the crucial fault-lines of English society.[7] Language was one obvious signifier in this status-obsessed culture — 'a mutual recognition of the right sort of accent, the emission and reception of a verbal semaphore in a recognised code that would exclude others'.[8] Costume was another. At one level, it took historical imagination of a very high order for the adult Lindsey Hughes to reconstruct the dress codes of the Muscovite elite.[9] At another, such distinctions had been with her all her life. In Dartford, as in Tunbridge Wells — indeed, anywhere in England in the middle decades of the twentieth century — 'clothes called to clothes, cutting out words and greetings'.[10]

Lindsey first encountered Russian language and culture at Dartford Grammar School for Girls, where Marjorie Vanston taught her a crash-course 'O'-level in her first year in the Sixth Form and 'A'-level in the second. Only an extraordinary pupil would have been capable of the achievement; only an outstanding school would have offered her the chance. (It is some index of the commitment and flexibility of the best grammar schools, already under pressure from a Secretary of State determined to 'destroy' them,[11] that Mrs Vanston should have returned from maternity leave to teach Lindsey in the upper sixth, having been allowed to bring the baby into school provided she

---

[5] Elementary statistical comparisons can be attempted through <http://www.visionofbritain. org.uk>, a digital resource supported by the University of Portsmouth and the Joint Information Systems Committee.

[6] Cobb, *Still Life*, p. 121.

[7] See, generally, R. McKibbin, *Classes and Cultures: England, 1918–1951*, Oxford, 1998, and B. Harrison, *Seeking a Role: The United Kingdom 1951–1970*, Oxford, 2009, pp. 199–209.

[8] Cobb, *Still Life*, p. 17.

[9] L. Hughes, 'From Caftans into Corsets: The Sartorial Transformation of Women during the Reign of Peter the Great', in P. Barta (ed.), *Gender and Sexuality in Russian Civilization*, London, 2001, pp. 17–32, is merely the most explicit engagement with this subject in Lindsey's *oeuvre*. For a bibliography of her work, see Part Three, below.

[10] Cobb, *Still Life*, p. 18.

[11] See S. Crosland, *Tony Crosland*, London, 1982, p. 148.

kept the pram with her during lessons.)[12] At first hearing, the school's motto — 'In quietness and confidence' — sounds an echo of the hushed, mildly repressive temple remembered by Joan Bakewell from Stockport High School for Girls in the late 1940s.[13] Dartford Grammar was indeed a purposeful place, reinforcing Lindsey's lifelong capacity for industry and self-discipline (much of her prolific writing was done before breakfast; she rarely worked at weekends). Yet while some of her contemporaries rebelled against a passing world of berets and indoor shoes, Lindsey was happy to make the most of gifted teaching in what was, by the early 1960s, a far from repressive institution under its remote but enlightened headmistress, Kathleen Janes.[14] When Lindsey's mother died in 1965, it was Miss Janes who helped to resolve the tensions that plagued so many lower-middle-class households in less acute form — intellectual opportunity versus alien social values and urgent economic need.[15] Lindsey was permitted to remain at school and eventually to pursue her new-found passion for Russia at university.

Turned down by an unimaginative Oxford college — her teachers were unsure whether to attribute the rebuff to her estuary accent (which soon evaporated) or to a determination to do things her own way (which did not) — Lindsey went to Sussex in 1967. That was the year in which the new university at Brighton (f. 1961) reached its initial target of something over 3,000 students, taught by 197 members of faculty.[16] Asa Briggs, the newly-appointed vice-chancellor, had been determined to ensure that rigid departmental divisions (and with them professorial power) were dissolved in a network of multi-disciplinary schools. Yet in Beryl Williams, Sergei Hackel and especially Robin Milner-Gulland, Lindsey found three mentors whose commitment to interdisciplinary innovation needed no stimulation from on high. A sense of the connections between history, spirituality, literature and the visual arts was as integral to much of their work on Russia as it subsequently became to hers. Though she understandably looked back on her undergraduate dissertation on seventeenth-century church

[12] *The Independent*, 18 May 2007. Mrs Vanston and her former colleague, Angela Norton, generously talked to me about the school.
[13] J. Bakewell, *The Centre of the Bed*, London, 2003, pp. 60–67, esp. p. 67.
[14] See L. Hughes, 'The 1960s', in *A Hundred Years On: Dartford County School, 1904–2004*, Dartford, 2004, pp. 70–88. I owe this reference to Angela Norton, who taught Lindsey German in the Sixth Form.
[15] Compare L. Heron (ed.), *Truth, Dare or Promise: Girls Growing Up in the Fifties*, London, 1993; J. Street-Porter (b. 1946), *Baggage*, London, 2004.
[16] A. Briggs, 'The Years of Plenty, 1961–1976', in *The Sussex Opportunity: A New University and the Future*, ed. R. Blin-Stoyle in association with G. Ivey, p. 15. (Still relatively small, Sussex now has over 10,000 students, of whom almost 3,000 are postgraduates.)

architecture as 'rather naïve', the kernel of her intellect had already
formed by 1971, when she left for Cambridge to develop this early
work into a doctoral thesis under the supervision of Nikolay Andreyev.
By the time she took up her first academic job at Queen's University
Belfast three years later, her interest in the 'seventeenth-century "age
of transition" had spread beyond architecture to encompass virtually
every aspect of the era, including its leading personalities'.[17] Long after
her research had ranged back and forth for several centuries beyond
the 1670s, 1680s and 1690s, its centre of gravity remained firmly in the
decades that originally sparked her imagination.[18]

Sussex gave Lindsey, as it gave others, as much social as intellectual
freedom. Buildings were at the heart of its sense of community. As
the architect, Basil Spence, had told the BBC in 1963, his modernist
designs were intended to 'give the student a feeling of confidence',[19]
and it was in the distinctive environment he created that a group of
bright young things over the following decade helped to turn Sussex,
however fleetingly, into the most fashionable university in England.
Sex, drugs and rock and roll were a crucial part of their culture — 1967
was also the year in which two former Dartford schoolboys, Keith
Richards (b. 1943) and Mick Jagger (b. 1946), were imprisoned on drugs
charges. Lindsey always believed that people of her generation were
deep-down either Rolling Stones or Beatles: she was the former.[20] The
official history of Sussex University prefers to concentrate on the excitement of technological advance. But then, as Lindsey observed in her
biography of Sofiia Alekseevna, 'One should never assume that lack of
explicit reference to sexual activity indicates its absence'.[21]

The same cool, sceptical interrogation of the sources was to remain
the defining characteristic of Lindsey's work throughout her career.[22]

---

[17] L. Hughes, *Sophia: Regent of Russia, 1657–1704*, London and New Haven, CT, 1990,
p. ix.
[18] To take only one example, the icon-painter Simon Ushakov (1629–86), who appears
in many of Lindsey's works, first figured in an essay on 'The Moscow Armoury and
Innovations in Seventeenth-Century Muscovite Art', *Canadian-American Slavic Studies*, 13,
1979, 1–2, pp. 207–08, 214, eventually merited articles of his own — 'The Age of Transition:
Seventeenth-Century Russian Icon Painting', in S. Smyth and S. Kingston (eds), *Icons 88*,
Dublin, 1988, pp. 63–74; 'Simon Ushakov's Icon "The Tree of the Muscovite State"
Revisited', *Forschungen zur osteuropäischen Geschichte*, 58, 2001, pp. 223–34 — and was due to
be the focus of a chapter in her uncompleted *Landmarks in Russian Culture*.
[19] <http://www.basilspence.org.uk/learning/buildings/sussex-university> [accessed 1
September 2009].
[20] She was delighted to learn that Jagger was presenting the prizes at Dartford Grammar
School for Boys in the year in which she returned to present them at the Grammar School
for Girls.
[21] Hughes, *Sophia*, p. 50.
[22] From Belfast (1974–77), she moved to the University of Reading (1977–87) and London
University's School of Slavonic and East European Studies (1987–2007), now part of UCL.

'For the most part', she commented in her *magnum opus* on the tsar reformer, 'Peter's correspondence is very concrete and lacking in sustained metaphysical musings'.[23] The same might be said of her own scholarship. There is no point in searching her *oeuvre* for reflections on the philosophy of history. Neither did she make overt use of the binary models that were to prove so fertile in the hands of Russian scholars working on the eighteenth-century transformation of Muscovite culture. Indeed, it sometimes exasperated Lindsey's Russian friends that she should have remained so immune to their lure.[24] Hers, however, are not concept-driven books. Occasionally, critics hinted, she veered towards Cobb's temptation never to give fifteen examples where fifty would do. Yet the vast majority of her work is written with ruthless economy and characterized by a self-denying empiricism intended to strip away accumulated myth. As she pointed out in her study of Peter I's half-sister, 'If we base our knowledge on reliable contemporary sources alone, we know rather less about certain aspects of Sophia's life than previous writers would have us believe'.[25]

As so often happens, social class proved an unreliable indicator of future scholarly interests.[26] While Richard Cobb went on from Tunbridge Wells, Shrewsbury and Oxford to immerse himself in the *petit peuple* of Revolutionary France, exposing 'the lowest, most private, and most obscure' levels of their seedy lives,[27] Lindsey Hughes's intellectual journey took her via Dartford, Brighton and Cambridge to the study of public imagery and ceremonial at the apex of the Russian Court. While Cobb became 'a local historian, not a national one',[28] the heart of Lindsey's historical world remained in the power-houses of Moscow and St Petersburg. While Cobb was determined to write 'history from below', Lindsey unashamedly offered 'history from above'.[29] Yet the contrasts must not be stretched too far. Though her

---

[23] L. Hughes, *Russia in the Age of Peter the Great*, London and New Haven, CT, 1998, p. 378.

[24] She did, however, acknowledge the binary models developed by Iu. M. Lotman and B. A. Uspenskii as 'particularly fruitful' in L. Hughes, 'Cultural and Intellectual Life', in M. Perrie (ed.), *The Cambridge History of Russia, 1: From Early Rus' to 1698*, Cambridge, 2006, p. 640.

[25] Hughes, *Sophia*, p. 274.

[26] At the launch of David Bates's *Regesta regum Anglo-Normannorum: the Acta of William I, 1066–1087*, Oxford, 1998, the late Patrick Wormald remarked that while he had given the Anglo-Saxon peasantry an accent from Eton, the king now spoke through the vowels of Nuneaton.

[27] R. Cobb, *Reactions to the French Revolution*, Oxford, 1972, p. 131.

[28] R. Cobb, *The Police and the People: French Popular Protest, 1789–1820*, Oxford, 1970, p. xvi.

[29] L. Hughes, *The Romanovs*, London, 2008, p. 4.

books incorporated painstaking discussions of foreign and economic policy, Lindsey was the first to admit that her heart was not quite in it. As Robin Milner-Gulland suggests in this volume, she was fascinated, like Cobb, above all by quirks of personality (though hers was markedly less eccentric than his); an acute sense of place made her as conscious as he was that 'history should be walked, seen, smelt, eavesdropped as well as read';[30] and she would surely have agreed with him that 'the endless fascination of history, its justification as a discipline, as a field of inquiry, as a form of culture, is the exploration of the wealth and variety of human motivations, the myriad variations of individual lives'.[31]

Cobb delivered this last verdict in 1971, the year of Lindsey's graduation from Sussex, as a riposte to the impersonal forms of history then dominant in a profession which held its collective nose at the thought of admitting biography to the scholarly canon.[32] Nine years later, Derek Beales still felt impelled to argue, in a celebrated inaugural lecture, that biography had been 'too much disparaged': 'When a great historian can mistake a person for a trend [he was speaking of Braudel], when it is thought more important to analyse social backgrounds than opinions, then the time has come for a reaction.'[33] Lindsey, too, sensed this need, for although Peter the Great had never lacked biographers, the tsar who emerged from most twentieth-century scholarship was an improbably Herculean figure concerned almost entirely with driving the socio-economic development of his expanding secular empire. 'Pig-iron figured strongly', Lindsey remarked of this literature in her own inaugural lecture in 1998.[34]

The prevailing consensus was all the odder since abundant evidence was available to fashion a more convincing portrait. As Lindsey recognized in her biography of Prince V. V. Golitsyn, 'one of the many developments of the Petrine age was the gradual emergence of the individual personality and its expression in personal writings'.[35] Peter I

---

[30] R. Cobb, 'Maigret's Paris', in *Tour de France*, London, 1976, p. 179.

[31] R. Cobb, 'History by Numbers', in ibid., p. 8.

[32] Despite a revival since the 1980s, the author of an outstanding recent study deliberately 'intended to recognize the plurality of "histories" and the interests embodied in them', excluded biography and memoirs while acknowledging that the decision was 'at least in some measure arbitrary and the line of demarcation is a wavering one'. See J. Burrow, *A History of Histories: Epics, Chronicles, Romances and Inquiries from Herodotus and Thucydides to the Twentieth Century*, London, 2007, p. xvi.

[33] D. Beales, 'History and Biography: An Inaugural Lecture', in T. C. W. Blanning and D. Cannadine (eds), *History and Biography: Essays in Honour of Derek Beales*, Cambridge, 1996, p. 282.

[34] L. Hughes, *Playing Games: The Alternative History of Peter the Great*, London, 2000, p. 1.

[35] L. Hughes, *Russia and the West: The Life of a Seventeenth-Century Westernizer, Prince Vasily Vasil'evich Golitsyn (1643–1704)*, Newtonville, MA, 1984, p. 99.

epitomized the change, bequeathing to posterity an unprecedented cache of personal papers. Beales points out that 'one of the principal uses of a biography is to help us appraise the evidence left by the subject'.[36] But Lindsey never confined herself to the textual record. As she reminded readers of one of her most successful and distinctive books, 'probably no Russian ruler left and inspired so many physical reminders of his life and activities' as Peter the Great.[37] It was this material legacy that Lindsey made her own, not only in her biography of the tsar but also in a series of studies devoted to 'Petrine places', and especially to the 'little houses' that this master of parody and inversion preferred to his grander Baroque palaces. 'Like Christ, who was born in a stable and brought up in a carpenter's cottage, Peter exalted himself by making himself humble.'[38] This was scarcely the prototype of the New Soviet Man who emerged from modern historiography before the 1980s. On the contrary, it was the artist Valentin Serov's image of Peter that Lindsey chose to highlight — a freakish giant 'on weak, spindly little legs and with a head so small in relation to the rest of his body that he must have looked more like a sort of dummy with a badly stuck on head than a living person'.[39]

Lindsey, as James Cracraft explains in this volume, had come to Peter by way of Golitsyn and Sofiia, products of an earlier, less readily recoverable age. A biography of the latter — 'ambitious and daring above her sex'[40] — posed particular challenges. 'While late seventeenth-century England enjoyed the "age of the pin-up", with prints of royal mistresses and assorted actresses (sometimes nude) widely available for sale, most Muscovite women remained faceless.'[41] One of the pleasures to be derived from reading Lindsey's chapter on Sofiia's early years is the sense one gains of her ability to manipulate fragmentary and indirect evidence into a plausible reconstruction of the part the girl played in a household in which she 'aroused little interest as an individual'.[42] The secular name-day ceremonies and multiple religious rituals, whose fate Lindsey would later trace in the Petrine era, offered

---

[36] Beales, 'History and Biography', p. 281.

[37] L. Hughes, *Peter the Great: A Biography*, London and New Haven, CT, 2002, pp. xiii–xiv.

[38] Ibid., p. 235. See, in particular, Hughes, '"Nothing's Too Small for a Great Man": Peter the Great's Little Houses and the Creation of Some Petrine Myths', *SEER*, 81, 2003, 4, pp. 634–58.

[39] Quoted in Hughes, *Russia in the Age of Peter*, p. 357, the opening paragraph of the chapter on 'Peter: Man, Mind and Methods'.

[40] L. Hughes, '"Ambitious and Daring above her Sex": Tsarevna Sophia Alekseevna (1657–1704) in Foreigners' Accounts', *Oxford Slavonic Papers*, New Series, 21, 1988, pp. 65–89.

[41] Hughes, 'Cultural and Intellectual Life', p. 652.

[42] Hughes, *Sophia*, pp. 23–51 (p. 29).

one clue to the mystery; others were found in the wider environment of the royal Court.[43] No less crucial to Lindsey's sense of place were interiors reconstructed with a sharp eye for detail. Her own house in London is full of expertly chosen Russian silver, porcelain, paintings and engravings, sought out on treasured weekend shopping trips with her partner and husband, James Cutshall. No wonder that the catalogue of Golitsyn's possessions compiled, after his exile, in 1689–90 allowed her to recapture the Janus-faced meanings of his mansion on Okhotnyi Riad. Its interior was 'fitted out with a fascinating mixture of traditional and foreign trappings' including a portrait of the owner himself:

> The centrepiece of the main bedroom was a German four-poster bed, lavishly carved with birds, plants and human faces. The occupants of the bedroom could look at both icons and five maps. The list of curiosities continues: the walls of one passageway were covered with red English cloth, there were clocks (as many as seven in one room), Indian and Persian carpets, German jugs, chests, stained glass, Venetian plates and dishes.[44]

By the same token, the Palladian architect Prince N. A. L'vov caught Lindsey's attention because he applied 'his skills not only to bricks, stone and wood, but also to the smallest details of furnishings, the installation of modern heating, ventilation, and plumbing systems'.[45] It was in an unerring eye for the 'smallest details' that the key to her own achievement may be found.

*   *   *

When Lindsey Hughes died from cancer, shortly before her fifty-eighth birthday, obituarists praised not only the excellence of her scholarship, but also the warmth of her friendships.[46] Members of the Study Group on Eighteenth-Century Russia, whom she regarded as an extended family, held a commemorative international workshop as a mark of

---

[43] L. Hughes, 'The Petrine Year: Anniversaries and Festivals in the Reign of Peter the Great', in K. Friedrich (ed.), *Festival Culture in Germany and Europe from the Sixteenth to the Twentieth Century*, Lewiston, NY, 2000, pp. 148–68; ead., 'The Courts of Moscow and St Petersburg, c. 1547–1725', in J. Adamson (ed.), *The Princely Courts of Europe: Ritual, Politics and Culture under the Ancien Régime, 1500–1750*, London, 1999, pp. 295–313, 336–38.

[44] Hughes, *Russia and the West*, p. 95.

[45] Hughes, 'N. A. L'vov and the Russian Country House', in R. P. Bartlett, A. G. Cross and K. Rasmussen (eds), *Russia and the World of the Eighteenth Century*, Columbus, OH, 1986, p. 290.

[46] *The Independent*, 4 May 2007 (Anthony Cross); *The Guardian*, 16 May 2007 (Robert Service); *The Times*, 10 May 2007 (the late John Klier, who himself met a tragically early death on 23 September 2007). See also Roger Bartlett, 'Professor Lindsey Hughes, 1949–2007', *SEER*, 85, 2007, 3, pp. 560–65, and Janet Hartley, 'Lindsey Hughes (1949–2007), *Kritika: Explorations in Russian and Eurasian History*, 8, 2007, 3, pp. 705–08.

their special affection.[47] However, to mark Lindsey's wider scholarly interests, which stretched from medieval Rus´ to the twenty-first century, a further tribute seemed both appropriate and necessary. From everything I have so far said, it will be obvious why 'Personality and Place' stood out as themes for this volume, which incorporates essays by leading scholars in Britain, Italy and the United States. (It is very much to be regretted that financial considerations have precluded the participation of Lindsey's many Russian friends, colleagues and admirers.) Contributors were encouraged to develop any of the approaches featured in Lindsey's work — pointillist or panoramic, playful or morbid, quotidian or bizarre — and they have responded with a rich collection of essays ranging from the sixteenth century to the present day. Pig-iron is conspicuous by its absence. Religion, by contrast, looms large, as befits a volume devoted to a scholar who consistently emphasized its resilience in the face of what was, for much of her lifetime, an overwhelmingly secular historiography on both sides of the Iron Curtain.[48]

Following a critical appreciation by James Cracraft of Lindsey's contribution to Petrine studies and an introduction by Robin Milner-Gulland to her uncompleted project on *Landmarks in Russian Culture*, the first substantive piece in the volume is a hitherto unpublished essay by Lindsey herself, originally destined for *Landmarks* and tracing the history of Cathedral of SS Peter and Paul in St Petersburg.[49] The essay discusses in turn the origins of the building, the vagaries of its construction and repair, and its subsequent fate as both mausoleum and museum. The emphasis throughout, however, is on the shifting meanings and responses the cathedral has evoked among successive generations of Russians and foreign observers. Here, it might seem, personality takes a back seat to place. But in Lindsey's mind it was sometimes hard to distinguish between them: 'All buildings have two characters — internal and external. This one has lived with an almost split personality.'[50]

The next two essays take up Lindsey's interest in royal symbolism and imagery in the sixteenth and seventeenth centuries. Peter I,

---

[47] The proceedings have been published as A. Cross (ed.), *Days from the Reigns of Eighteenth-Century Russian Rulers*, Study Group on Eighteenth-Century Russia Newsletter, 2 parts, Cambridge, 2007.

[48] L. Hughes, 'Restoring Religion to Russian Art', in G. Hosking and R. Service (eds), *Reinterpreting Russia*, London, 1999, esp. pp. 42–46. Among other passages on the limits of secularization, see ead., *Russia in the Age of Peter*, pp. 292 ff.; ead., 'Cultural and Intellectual Life', pp. 658–62.

[49] For a parallel essay, conceived as 'research in progress' for *Landmarks in Russian Culture*, see L. Hughes, 'St. Basil's Cathedral through British Eyes', in A. B. Davidson (ed.), *Rossiia i Britaniia, 4: Sviazi i vzaimnye predstavleniia*, Moscow, 2006, pp. 71–80 (p. 72).

[50] See below, p. 25.

she believed, 'was certainly the first [Russian] ruler whose image was produced in three dimensions. (The art of carving human figures in marble and casting them in metal was unknown in Muscovite Russia)'.[51] She evidently had in mind the tradition of classical sculpture, which was indeed absent in Russia before 1700. However, as Sergei Bogatyrev shows here, a partial exception to the rule is to be found on the Tsar Cannon, cast by the renowned Russian gun founder Andrei Chokhov in 1586. This incorporated a three-dimensional depiction of Tsar Fedor Ivanovich, which Bogatyrev compares with the image of Ivan the Terrible on a Livonian gun produced by the German master Karsten Middeldorp in 1559. Royal symbolism is equally central to Simon Franklin's essay on the illustrated title page and the elaborate woodcut frontispiece of the bible published in Moscow in 1663. Lavish though it was, the 1663 Bible made a negligible impact on subsequent Russian print culture. But it was innovative in the context of books printed in the Russian capital. Included among 'the extraordinary list of its "firsts"' were 'the first Moscow-printed portrait of a Russian ruler, or indeed of any living person' and 'the first Moscow-printed map of any kind' — significantly, a map of Moscow itself.[52]

Moscow is also the subject of Maria Di Salvo's contribution, which takes us into the period studied most intensively by Lindsey Hughes. While some textbooks still portray the Nemetskaia Sloboda as the nursery of Western-inspired modernization, Di Salvo paints a more nuanced picture of the suburb's social life, drawing on a range of Italian sources including the unpublished memoirs of a young castrato from Pisa, Filippo Balatri, himself closely linked to Peter I and his mistress Anna Mons. Remaining in the Petrine era, Gary Marker examines the controversial figure of the Ukrainian hetman, Ivan Mazepa, through the prism of accounts written in the early 1720s by Pylyp Orlik, the hetman of the Ukrainian forces in exile, and the archbishop of Novgorod, Feofan (Prokopovich). As the Great Northern War came to an end, ideologists on all sides began to craft rival versions of Mazepa's 'betrayal' of the tsar in 1708–09. Whereas Prokopovich regarded Mazepa as an irredeemable traitor to his faith, Orlyk portrayed him as a flawed political actor, 'a real human being, mistaken and conflicted rather than demonic and evil'. However, focusing on the rhetorical strategies of these two myth-makers, Marker shows that, for different reasons, they agreed that 'the rights and freedoms of the Cossacks were larger than the man himself and that they were important to maintain'.[53]

[51] L. Hughes, 'Images of Greatness: Portraits of Peter I', in Hughes (ed.), *Peter the Great and the West: New Perspectives*, London, 2001, p. 260.
[52] See below, p. 88.
[53] See below, p. 133.

The next three contributions focus on the early history of Peter I's new capital and its environs, an area traversed time and again by Lindsey in the company of guidebooks old and new.[54] Paul Keenan, one of her last research students, compares the St Petersburg Summer Gardens, a symbol of the tsar's 'Europeanizing' aims for the city, with contemporary palace gardens elsewhere on the continent, focusing on their role as a social space for the ruler, the Court and the elite, particularly in the 1750s under Elizaveta Petrovna. Roger Bartlett shows that the suburban estate of Ropsha, notorious as the place where Peter III was assassinated, had a more interesting existence, both before and after 1762, not least as the site of Enlightened social experiments by the Livonian Pastor Johann Georg Eisen in the 1760s. That was the decade when the young scholar-monk Platon (Petr Georgievich Levshin, 1737–1812) first attracted the attention of Catherine II. In her analysis of three of Platon's celebrated sermons at Court, Elise Kimerling Wirtschafter highlights another crucial aspect of the Enlightenment in Russia: 'The Russian Enlightenment, an enlightenment to be lived, stressed the spiritual development and moral perfectibility of the individual human being.'[55]

David Moon broadens the geographical focus of the volume by discussing the Academy of Sciences expeditions to the steppes in the reign of Catherine II. In an essay which reaches back in time to Herodotus on the Scythians and forward to the nineteenth-century soil scientist, Vasilii Dokuchaev, Moon emphasizes the reactions of the expeditions' German-educated leaders to the unfamiliar conditions they discovered in the treeless steppe. A similar preoccupation with differences recurs in Peter Waldron's discussion of Nikolai Przheval'skii, the nineteenth-century explorer of Central Asia, though, lionized by society and by Alexander II himself, Przheval'skii was a far more glamorous personality than Peter Simon Pallas and his Enlightened colleagues.

Between these contributions on the empire come three which illuminate a period crucial to the development of the self in Russia. In a study of life-writings by three noblewomen, Wendy Rosslyn shows that while Varvara Sheremeteva (1786–1857) remained within traditional prescriptions of femininity wherever she was, being more concerned with others' perceptions of her self than with its inner essence, Varvara Bakunina (1773–1840) was powerfully affected by place. By contrast, Anastasiia Kolechitskaia's (1800–71) self was cultivated to be largely

[54] L. Hughes, 'Petrine St Petersburg in the works of Pavel Svin´in (1787–1839)', in A. Cross (ed.), *St Petersburg 1703–1825: A Collection of Essays to Mark the Tercentenary of the City*, Basingstoke, 2003, pp. 148–64.
[55] See below, p. 180.

immune to changes of circumstance. Patrick O'Meara focuses on male sociability at the Second Army HQ at Tul´chin, where the youthful chief-of-staff between 1819 and 1829, P. D. Kiselev (1788–1872), risked losing an already brilliant career through potentially compromising friendships with several of his staff officers who were Decembrists, in particular with Pavel Pestel´, the republican ideologist of the Southern Society. O'Meara's forensic examination of Kiselev's motives shows the extent to which Pushkin's generation were capable of developing, revealing and concealing a sophisticated sense of self. That this capacity sometimes came at a heavy price is suggested by Robin Aizlewood, whose essay adds a further dimension to our subject by exploring disorientation of the person in Russian culture. Pushkin's poem 'Besy' is shown to be a primary text for this theme, providing one of the epigraphs of Dostoevskii's novel of the same name and informing agonized reflections on the revolution in *Iz glubiny* (1918). Beginning with this volume of essays and its predecessor *Vekhi* (1909), Aizlewood discusses conceptualizations of the person (*lichnost´*) in relation to place in Russian thought, from Chaadaev through to Bakhtin, drawing finally on Bakhtin's notion of 'outsideness' to cast light on the disorientation of the person in Pushkin's poem, alongside that which is conveyed symbolically through spatial disorientation.

Anglo-Russian contacts were a subject of particular interest to Lindsey Hughes, who studied relevant archival sources in both countries.[56] The essays on this subject in the present volume exemplify the two cultures' capacity to survive as if in a sealed vacuum when transferred to foreign parts. Anthony Cross tells the story of a house built on St Petersburg's Palace Embankment in the 1780s by Quarenghi, purchased soon afterwards by N. I. Saltykov, and partially occupied by his descendants even while the front portion of the building served as the British Embassy from 1863 to 1918. While Foreign Office officials agonized about the state of the drains, successive British residents tried to domesticate their cavernous neo-classical palace. As Meriel Buchanan recalled in 1932, once 'the pictures and prints had been hung up, the arm-chairs covered with bright chintzes, some of the more heavily ornate pieces removed and replaced by Queen Anne cabinets, old Dutch chests of drawers, Wedgwood or Empire chairs, the rooms took on a more homelike appearance, so that sometimes with the curtains drawn, one could almost imagine oneself in some old London Square'.[57]

---

[56] See, in particular, L. Hughes, 'V. T. Postnikov's 1687 Mission to London: Anglo-Russian Relations in the 1680s in British Sources', *SEER*, 68, 1990, 3, pp. 447–60.

[57] Quoted by Anthony Cross, below, p. 347. Compare the mischievous remark of William Gerhardi on the tastes of Nicholas II's consort, 'whose idea of decorating their "ordinary decent life" was a suburban English villa with furniture which might have come — and perhaps did come — from the Tottenham Court Road'. W. Gerhardi, *The Romanovs: Evocation of the Past as a Mirror for the Present*, London, 1940, p. 502.

Robert Service shows that the Russian political émigrés who inhabited such squares thanks to uniquely generous British immigration legislation, barely noticed their surroundings. So impervious were they to local influences that 'their colony might just as well have been in Africa'.[58] Oblivious to virtually every aspect of British political culture, they arrived and left London with their doctrines intact. Here was a case where 'intellectual formation' was indeed 'far more important than social or geographical origin or physical location'.[59]

Place, on the other hand, certainly mattered in the case of our last personality — the 'mad monk' Iliodor (Sergei Mikhailovich Trufanov, 1880–1952), who died in New York only months before Lindsey Hughes's third birthday. When Sergei Bulgakov complained in his contribution to *Vekhi* that 'the concepts of *personal* morality, *personal* self-perfection, the elaboration of the *personality* are extremely unpopular among the intelligentsia (and, on the contrary, the word *social* has a special, sacramental character)', he knew that he was swimming against the tide.[60] By the beginning of the twentieth century, a preoccupation with celebrity — a subject of great interest to Lindsey and one of the liveliest issues in current scholarship on the individual[61] — had gone beyond heroes such as Przheval'skii to penetrate even the most ascetic intellectual circles. Outside their ranks, no one attracted more attention than Iliodor, who exploited the patronage of Rasputin and Nicholas II (and a variety of mass media) to undermine P. A. Stolypin in one of his former stomping grounds, the traditionally rebellious province of Saratov, where Iliodor repeatedly defied the government in the name of the Russian people, paradoxically contributing in the process to the desacralization of the monarchy he purported to defend.

This, then, is a collection of essays intended to emphasize the significance of personality and place in Russian culture. Some are directly inspired by the work of Lindsey Hughes; each of them echoes her interests in the kaleidoscopic variety of individual motivations and the shifting meanings attributable to particular settings. We offer them in respectful memory of a creative scholar, an inspired teacher and a dearly-loved friend.

---

[58] See below, p. 368.
[59] Beales, 'History and Biography', p. 273.
[60] Quoted by Robin Aizlewood, below, p. 293.
[61] Among a rapidly growing literature, see, for example, M. Postle (ed.), *Joshua Reynolds: The Creation of Celebrity*, London, 2005, and T. Mole (ed.), *Romanticism and Celebrity Culture, 1750–1850*, Cambridge, 2009.

PART ONE

Lindsey Hughes on Peter the Great: A Personal Memoir

JAMES CRACRAFT

WELL KNOWN as she is for her work on Peter the Great, Lindsey Hughes was drawn to intensive study of his reign only gradually, and then reluctantly. As an undergraduate at Sussex University and a postgraduate at Cambridge she majored in Russian studies, as we would say in the United States, with concentrations in language, literature and visual art. Her Cambridge thesis (1976), a pioneering work in English, was devoted to late seventeenth-century 'Moscow Baroque' architecture seen as an instance of early 'Westernization' in Russia. Portions of the thesis were soon published as articles, which served in turn as my introduction to her work; in my own monograph on architectural developments in Petrine Russia I cited four of these articles as well as the dissertation while quoting from them several times. She was now the unique authority on Moscow Baroque architecture outside Russia and I was pleased to claim a convergence of views on the subject's historical significance.[1] She had made an impressive debut as an early modern Russian architectural or more broadly cultural historian, and I was in her debt.

But that was scarcely the end of it. Researching the transmission of Baroque architectural forms from Europe to Russia had immersed Lindsey (as I soon came to know her) in the simultaneous transmission of the new (post-Renaissance) graphic art and in the roles of the local people involved, both artists and patrons. An article (1982) and then book (1984) on Prince Vasili Vasil'evich Golitsyn ensued. Golitsyn was a Westernizing patron second in importance only to Russia's 'regent' in the 1680s, Grand Princess Sofiia Alekseevna, the subject of another series of articles (including a seminal one in this journal) that culminated in a major monograph published in 1990. The impact of this

James Cracraft is Emeritus Professor of Russian History at the University of Illinois at Chicago.

[1] James Cracraft, *The Petrine Revolution in Russian Architecture*, Chicago, IL and London, 1988, pp. 99, 100, 106–07, 345 (nn. 30, 32, 44), 346 (n. 47), 359–60.

thoroughly researched, engagingly written and judiciously feminist study remains, I think, incalculable. Sofiia Alekseevna was thereby not simply restored to Russian history but given at long last her rightfully prominent place in it.[2]

At some point after leaving Cambridge, possibly while she was lecturing at the University of Reading (1977–87), Lindsey began toying with the idea of writing a biography of Peter the Great, the undeserving winner (as she might well have thought of him) in the struggle for power with his elder half-sister Sofiia that issued in the latter's deposition and virtual imprisonment and the beginning of Peter's (or his party's) de facto rule. A touch of revenge playfully fueled her motivation here, I suspect: the debt the crass upstart owed to his Westernizing half-sister would be revealed together with his quite shabby post-coup treatment of her, and the Petrine 'cult' would be thereby eviscerated for all to see. But an admirable professional restraint held Lindsey back from taking the plunge. She was neither excessively committed, like so many historians, to the period of her debut, determined to defend its importance at all costs; but nor was she as yet confident that she could master the massive documentation and controversial historiography of the Petrine era sufficiently to satisfy her own high standards. And then there were the many repugnant aspects of Peter's long reign to consider. At any rate, I seem to recall a conversation along some such lines in the course of my first, very pleasant meeting with Lindsey over lunch at a restaurant in the shadow of the British Museum (then also the British Library), our mutual workplace in London, in 1979. She told me about her shift in focus from the architectural history of the Moscow Baroque to biographical study of Golitsyn and Sofiia. And I assured her, in response to her cordial inquiry, that I had no intention of writing a biography of Peter while rather needlessly observing that to do so successfully would be a daunting task.

Probably the crucial factor in Lindsey's decision in this respect was her move in 1987 to the School of Slavonic and East European Studies in London (SSEES), where she taught Russian history (including art and architectural history) instead of language or literature, and from where her distinguished senior colleague, Isabel de Madariaga, had retired three years earlier. Professor de Madariaga had published, in 1981, with Yale University Press in London, her monumental *Russia in the Age of Catherine the Great*, which was immediately recognized as the most important such work in English (nor was there anything at

---

[2] Lindsey Hughes, *Sophia, Regent of Russia 1657–1704*, London and New Haven, CT, 1990; also Hughes, 'Sofiya Alekseyevna and the Moscow Rebellion of 1682', *SEER*, 63, 1985, 4, pp. 518–39.

all recent to match it in Russian). Lindsey conceived the notion of producing a parallel volume on Peter, as she readily acknowledged in her own magnum opus, *Russia in the Age of Peter the Great* (New Haven, CT, 1998), where she states (p. xv) that de Madariaga's study of Catherine 'was an inspiration and a model for my own work'. That such had in fact been the case was affirmed for me in a letter of April 1991 from Robert Baldock, her editor at Yale. Baldock was pleased with Lindsey's recently published biography of Regent Sofiia and asked me to comment on her still 'preliminary' proposal for a new book on Peter 'based on the template of Isabel de Madariaga's similar project on Catherine'. I was happy to reply that there could be 'no doubt she is eminently well qualified to undertake the project outlined in her proposal' — indeed, that 'whatever Lindsey Hughes comes up with here, I for one will read it with the utmost interest and enthusiasm'.

And so I did. But it should be noted at once that notwithstanding Lindsey's typically generous acknowledgement of her debt to Professor de Madariaga, the similarity between her volume on Catherine and Lindsey's on Peter does not go very far. Overall structure and scope are comparable, perhaps, the two titles obviously resonate, and the publisher is the same. Yet in the range of topics covered, the approaches taken, and the style in which it is written Lindsey's book stands fully on its own. Nor do the subjects themselves of the two volumes have much in common beyond the fact that they ruled for comparable stretches of time over the place called Russia. Adam was not Eve, as Lindsey's book makes abundantly clear.

I was asked to review *Russia in the Age of Peter the Great* immediately on its appearance for the Sunday Book Review section of the *New York Times*, a fact that in itself testifies to the importance attached to its publication by media well beyond the specialized scholarly journals.[3] There I promptly announced, in the way of academic reviewers speaking to a larger audience, that Lindsey's big book was most timely, as it drew a parallel of sorts between Peter the Great, recently restored to superhero status in Russia, and Mikhail Gorbachev, the prospective hero of a Soviet revival that would never, it was now certain, come to pass: each man, she suggested, 'challenged old orthodoxies, broke down walls, changed his titles, acknowledged the need to learn from the West, and travelled there himself, creating a new image for [Russia's] leader. But whereas Peter presided over the consolidation and expansion of empire, Gorbachev precipitated its collapse'. This was but

---

[3] James Cracraft, 'Russia's Cultural Revolution: A New Study of Czar Peter I and his Campaign to Modernize and Westernize his Country', *The New York Times Book Review*, Sunday 20 September 1998, pp. 14–15.

one small sample of the fluency and liveliness of Lindsey's prose, rare in books produced by academic historians, whose inaccessibility to readers living in the real world is of course a matter of common complaint. On the other hand, such quickly dated 'presentism', I hastened to assure her fellow scholars, was not a prominent feature of her book, as witness the ongoing validity of its final sentence, which I also quoted in the review: 'The day when Peter the Great and his reforms cease to be a live issue in Russia will be the day when Russia finally resolves the "cursed question" of its true identity and its relationship with the outside world.' The judgement was true then, is true now, and will be true, surely, for a long time to come.

Russia in the Age of Peter the Great is most remarkable, for specialist and general reader alike, for the quality as well as the scope of its coverage. In this respect, as in others, it had only two possible rivals in English, both written as it happens by Americans: Eugene Schuyler's two-volume *Peter the Great, Emperor of Russia: A Study of Historical Biography*, first published in 1884 and the first such work to be based on Russian sources; and Robert K. Massie's *Peter the Great, His Life and World*, first published in 1980 and based to a considerable extent on Schuyler's volumes. But neither effort, in fact, rivals Lindsey's book except in its ambition. Both have been seriously outmoded by subsequent research and publication, Russian and Western. Both also plainly reflect, in temper and style, the times in which they were written: that by Schuyler, a professional diplomat, the America of the Gilded Age, gingerly stepping onto the world's stage; that by Massie, a popular historian, the America of Hollywood and the Cold War. And both authors clearly evince great admiration for their subject and his achievements as well as a certain reluctance, perhaps as outsiders, to criticize or condemn.

Not so Lindsey Hughes. Her exhaustive research in an unprecedentedly large number of Russian and Western repositories, including official archives and major libraries in Russia itself along with art galleries, building sites and historical museums, yielded an unprecedentedly detailed, complex and often dark portrayal of the great tsar — 'great', she sometimes seems to say, mainly or even solely because of all the commotion he caused. Her book leaves its readers, at Peter's death, with a Russia that is exhausted, confused and fearful — not unlike the immediately post-Soviet Russia in which she conducted much of her research. And it leaves us with a Peter, for all the incredible colour and drama of his life, who is at once glamorous but crude, neurotic, bad-tempered to the point of cruelty, and faintly ridiculous; a figure heroic at times, it may be, generous and kindly on occasion, remarkably bright despite his lack of formal education, but ultimately a lonely man, this in part because he was a reformer steadfastly pursuing his modernizing agenda within a tradition-bound society, in part because of the 'uncomfortable traits of his personality', which are fully documented. Indeed this is a Peter for the chastened political tastes of survivors of the twentieth century — for readers, both Russian and Western, who have followed Solzhenitsyn among other witnesses and investigators into the hellhole of Stalin's regime. Lindsey's *magnum opus* exhibits a certain partiality to the view of Peter as the forerunner of Stalin advanced by the leading Petrine historian in Russia today, Evgenii Anisimov, who gave her, when she was working in Russia, 'generous advice, inspiration, and encouragement, as well as materials from his own library'.[4] But ample reference is certainly also given in her volume to the views of Peter and his historical significance published by a huge number of other historians, publicists and contemporary witnesses — a feature of the book that naturally heightens its impression of complexity, definitiveness and, in the end, ambiguity.

Russia in the Age of Peter the Great succeeds, and succeeds brilliantly, through its pointillist accumulation of detail (470 pages of text supplemented by another ninety-two pages of notes), its many vividly descriptive passages, its regular flashes of wit (e.g., a passage on Peter's gardening endeavours ends with the observation that he 'is famed less for green fingers, however, than for bloody hands'),[5] and its always stimulating if not provocative interrogation of the historical record. Concentrated attention is paid, often for the first time in such a format, to Peter's opponents as well as his allies, to his mock Court in addition to the real one, and to the women around him as well as the men (her discussions of women in Petrine Russia are unique in the literature). Sex, music, food, medicine, dress, manners and hair codes all take their turn, as do architecture and the figurative arts, science and religion, book publishing and language, not to mention the more conventional subjects of war and diplomacy, economics and government. Much within Russia itself as well as in Russia's standing in the world had changed under Peter, Lindsey grants in her book's concluding chapter, 'But did change mean "progress," and did progress mean improvement? Was Russia better or worse off as a result of Peter's reforms?'.[6] She does not really answer these fundamental questions, in effect thus reflecting, once again, the times in which she wrote: the years of uncertainty about Russia's future following the collapse of the Soviet Union, on the one hand, but also the era of a relativistic 'new historicism' in the Western academy. Put otherwise, readers emerge from her

[4] Lindsey Hughes, *Russia in the Age of Peter the Great*, London and New Haven, CT, 1998, pp. xv, 465; see also pp. 80, 88, 94, 137, 138, 154–55, 157, 356.
[5] Ibid., p. 371.
[6] Ibid., p. 462.

volume — so I have found — roundly invigorated rather than merely sated or dully convinced, ready to argue with any or all of the commentators she quotes and eager to advance their own views. My published response to her questions, which involves a cautiously favourable appraisal of Peter's cultural revolution, a subject she moots but does not pursue, could hardly forego citing *Russia in the Age of Peter the Great* half a dozen times, while recommending it among further reading suggestions as indisputably the most comprehensive scholarly account of Peter's reign in English.[7]

During the last decade of her life Lindsey continued to publish on Peter's reign as author, editor, or translator. My favourite among these later works is *Playing Games: The Alternative History of Peter the Great*, her inaugural lecture of October 1998 as professor of Russian history at SSEES, which was subsequently published as a pamphlet.[8] This is the best short treatment available (twenty-five densely printed pages, eighty-nine footnotes, a dozen appended documents) of the variously elaborate and generally rebarbative entertainments staged by Peter the Great throughout his reign but hitherto largely ignored, the rich documentary record notwithstanding, by his baffled if not embarrassed biographers.[9] It is also, perhaps, the best short introduction we have to Lindsey the inimitable historian: to her ever present, now playful, now mordant, sense of humour; to her fluent, readily accessible prose and pointed contemporary asides; to her sound judgement and scrupulous attention to detail; and to her practice, at the end of her story, of leaving her audience free 'to ponder and draw their own conclusions'. One might even say that this work, particularly for students of a postmodernist bent, is the best introduction yet to the 'other' or conventional history of Peter the Great.

Lindsey's many kindnesses to her colleagues also continued apace during those last ten years of her life, as I can personally testify. She was always ready to offer sound professional advice, the loan of rare research materials, and ever charitable criticism of one's work, whether published, under consideration for publication, or still in draft. She had become the leading British authority on the whole Petrine era, with important secondary fields in Russian art and architectural history — interests she had never abandoned. Probably her most

---

[7] James Cracraft, *The Revolution of Peter the Great*, London and Cambridge, MA, 2003, p. 186; also pp. 28 and n. 25 (p. 175), 176 (n. 21), 181 (n. 1), 182 (n. 5), 183 (n. 2).

[8] Lindsey Hughes, *Playing Games: The Alternative History of Peter the Great*, London, 2000.

[9] Ernest A. Zitser's more extended study of the same phenomena had yet to appear: Zitser, *The Transfigured Kingdom: Sacred Parody and Charismatic Authority at the Court of Peter the Great*, London and Ithaca, NY, 2004.

important publication of this period, certainly the most widely disseminated apart from her posthumously published *The Romanovs*, is the
book entitled *Peter the Great: A Biography*. It represents, following her
magnum opus, her 'second bite at the cherry', as she says in its preface;
and, as indicated there as well as in its title, it is a much shorter and
more straightforwardly chronological rather than topical study of its
subject's life and reign. It is also more clearly aimed at students and
general readers, offering, especially for the latter, an attractive alternative to M. S. Anderson's textbook on Peter first published in 1978. Her
model, once again, was Isabel de Madariaga, who late in her own
career published a short history of Catherine the Great that distilled
for students the wisdom and knowledge of her well-earned authority.
But other than that, as before, Lindsey's short history of Peter the
Great is entirely her own. And if to a considerable extent it was
digested from her *magnum opus*, two whole chapters of 'Peter the Little'
(so she jocularly called it) contain new information relating to the
visual monuments in Russia of the great tsar's reign, thus highlighting
her persistent fascination with such material as well as his role as the
perdurable ghost of Russian greatness.[10]

In fact, Lindsey's *Peter Biography* complements rather than digests her
larger volume, its predictably lively narrative filled, as promised in its
preface, with the 'personal drama and bizarre incident' of its subject's
life. The dark portrait of Peter painted earlier is somewhat tempered,
and, in accord with a long line of Russian publicists as well as historians, his legacy is framed in more positive terms: 'Ultimately, the
sacrifices made by all sections of the population were justified by international success. Peter made Russia a great power.' But the book is no
more decisive than its predecessor with respect to Peter's overall place
in history. The current 'fragmentation of opinion' on this point in
Russia itself, in Lindsey's own words, and the fact that 'many of the
issues he grappled with still await a resolution', left her, she seemed to
say at last, no real choice.[11]

As the bibliography of her published work makes clear, Lindsey's
scholarly interests were not limited to the pivotal Petrine era in Russian

---

[10] Lindsey Hughes, *Peter the Great: A Biography*, London and New Haven, CT, 2002; M. S.
Anderson, *Peter the Great*, 2nd edn, London and New York, 1995; Isabel de Madariaga,
Catherine the Great: A Short History, London and New Haven, CT, 1990. Also notable among
shorter comprehensive histories of Peter's reign is Evgenii Anisimov's *The Reforms of Peter the
Great: Progress through Coercion in Russia*, trans. John T. Alexander, Armonk, NY, 1993, a
somewhat condensed version of a book first published in Russia and Russian in 1989 and
reflective of late Soviet historiography in its attention to class conflict and the development
(or not) of capitalism in Petrine Russia; similarly its recurrent allusions to Stalin.

[11] Hughes, *Peter the Great: A Biography*, pp. xii–xiv, 214, 250.

history. Her early training as a Russianist, her debut as a specialist in art and architectural history, and her indefatigable curiosity insured that she would continue to range widely in her search for suitable subjects to investigate. But the focus on Peter remained. Her initial hesitations triumphantly overcome, sundry Petrine myths briskly eviscerated, the hero's warts fully restored, his turbulent life laid bare: Lindsey Hughes could have no successor, anywhere, as a historian of Peter the Great. Her legacy is secure.

Lindsey Hughes's *Landmarks in Russian Culture*

ROBIN MILNER-GULLAND

LINDSEY HUGHES is remembered doubtless by all professional Russianists, and also by a wider public, as a meticulous traditional historian: chronicler in the first place of Peter the Great, and of other lives too — of Sofiia, Golitsyn and of the Romanovs (in her last volume). Such a perception, however understandable, reflects only part of her ambitions and achievements: if we look a little further into her copious published work, we get a rather different picture. Conventional investigation of biography and historico-political processes retreats from view. In her many shorter articles, we find a tireless enthusiast for generally disregarded corners of history — all the more significant in shedding an oblique, maybe discomfiting, light on the bigger, more public events. She clearly relished not just historical oddity for its own sake, but the multivalent, disparate strands that make up the texture of human culture. She had a special eye for the ephemera of social life — old guidebooks, prints, cards and the like. We detect her interest not only in ceremony and ritual but in the off-guard moments of the great — in quirky topics like Peter's decree against beards or the cult of his various 'domiki', the houses he stayed in; and on a broader front in the development and meanings of Court portraiture in an age of massive cultural change.

Several clues to Lindsey's interests and their motivation can be found in her inaugural lecture at SSEES, published in 2000 as *Playing Games: The Alternative History of Peter the Great*. It opens thus:

> People often ask me how I became interested enough in Peter the Great to spend several years writing a 600-page book about his reign. Here is a partial answer: a seed of interest was sown at Sussex University when, as a student of Russian Studies in the early 1970s taking a course on 'Russian Ornamentalism and the Grotesque in the 20th Century', I read a novel by Iurii Tynianov called 'The Wax Effigy' [...] Early eighteenth-century Russia sounded like a sort of freak-show of waxworks, which I found intriguing.

Unlike, she adds, the textbook version, full of 'sensible, concrete things'. She came to her great work on Peter a 'natural sequel' to her 'examination of the life and regime' of his half-sister Sophia — the other way

Robin Milner-Gulland is Research Professor of Russian and East European Studies at the University of Sussex.

round to how one might expect. She was always excited by that which was off-centre, distinctive, diverse, involuntarily indicative — the qualities that made her a cultural (rather than political, social or whatever) historian. It began with her doctoral work (though she had left Sussex for Cambridge, I remember it well, talked or corresponded about it often, and – such was academic life then — found myself appointed one of her examiners). It was on the 'Moscow Baroque', a strange, idiosyncratic, yet memorable period of architectural and maybe general culture, squeezed between the Old and New Russia, hard to discuss in terms of either. Never thereafter did her intense interest in the processes and achievements of the visual arts leave her.

She was also extremely responsive to Russia as a place, having (I believe) been galvanized into academic achievement by the experience of an undergraduate third year there, at a time when this was very unusual. Not only did buildings, pictures and so on as they now exist interest her, but their shifting cultural meanings through the generations and for people of varied circumstances. All this naturally gave rise to her great, uncompleted project on *Landmarks in Russian Culture*. She took it characteristically seriously, producing a document setting out her plans and making it the subject of discussion at a professional study-group in the late 1990s; so she saw it to some degree as a collaborative enterprise. It is worth quoting her aims as set out in this document:

> *Landmarks in Russian Culture* will focus on about twenty extant Russian buildings, paintings and statues which, in my view, have a particular resonance for the history of Russian culture, from the time of their creation to the present day. Individual chapters on each work or group of works will include, as appropriate, [1] history of creation; [2] formal analysis; [3] comparative aspects (sources, influences and analogies); [4] social, political and economic background; and [5] spatial context (significance within architectural and cultural systems); in each case, however, the major attention will be paid to [6] resonances and response up to the present day.

Already at this stage, she had a provisional shortlist, though she was ready to modify it if persuaded. It included: Vladimir Mother of God icon (12th c.); Old Testament Trinity icon (*c.* 1420); Kremlin Dormition Cathedral (1475–79); St Basil's Cathedral (1555–60); Tree of the Muscovite state icon (1668); the Cathedral of SS Peter and Paul in St Petersburg (1712–); portraits of Peter I (?Ivan Nikitin, 1720s); Church of the Transfiguration, Kizhi (1714); Rastrelli's stone Winter Palace in St Petersburg (1754–64); Falconet's 'Bronze Horseman' (unveiled in 1782); Briullov's 'Last Day of Pompeii' (1822–33); Ivanov's 'Appearance of the Messiah' (1837–57); the Cathedral of Christ the Saviour in Moscow (1839–83; rebuilt 1997); Repin's 'Volga Bargehaulers' (1870–73); Vasnetsov, 'Three Epic Warriors' (1898); Malevich's 'Black Square' (?1914); Mukhina's 'Worker and Collective Farm Woman' (1937);

Moscow State University (1949–53); Tsereteli's 'Statue of Peter the Great', i.e. his monument to the 300th anniversary of the Russian fleet (1990s).

Though well aware that literary and musical works could equally be classed as 'cultural landmarks', and herself well-grounded in Russian literature, she decided to stick to the visual arts: the project was already a most ambitious one, and twenty illustrated articles the length of the one which follows here — on the Cathedral of SS Peter and Paul — would have made for a very weighty volume, not to mention a huge intellectual task. She made study visits to Russia, and worked on the project in London, in 1999–2000 and subsequently, but broke off in view of a commission to write her (posthumously-published) volume on the Romanovs. She would, if spared, assuredly have taken it up again. A great deal remains on disk, with a few chapters almost complete. 'The Cathedral of SS Peter and Paul', published here in edited form, is an excellent specimen chapter of Lindsey's projected book, displaying her particular interest in the shifting fates and images of cultural landmarks through history. What cannot, alas, now be recaptured is the full scope of her great and discriminating knowledge of 'original graphics; photographs; guidebooks; travel literature and memoirs (Rossica)', as well as press articles and often obscure monographs; also her long teacher's experience of what makes people from another culture excited or puzzled by that of Russia.

The Cathedral of SS Peter and Paul

LINDSEY HUGHES

edited by Robin Milner-Gulland *and* Simon Dixon*

The Peter-Paul belfry is the same for St Petersburg as the tower of St Mark's for Venice, or its cathedral for Strasbourg, or Ivan the Great for Moscow. Take them away, and the 'face' of the city immediately changes.[1]

ALL buildings have two characters — internal and external. This one has lived with an almost split personality: the view from the outside, with the golden spire glistening in the sun, is very upbeat; inside, it is a mausoleum, containing the tombs of all the rulers of Russia from the time of Peter I, slightly gloomy and cold, even on a bright day. The Peter Paul Cathedral takes a little effort to visit on foot, as the fortress in which it stands is slightly off main transport routes, and any visitors have probably arrived by tourist buses. With its thrusting spire the cathedral seems a masculine, essentially Petersburgian building, redolent of multi-national Rossiia — 'otets' as opposed to the 'matushka' of ethnic Rus´.[2] It was also particularly meaningful to the imperial family. In April 1834, a week before his son's coming of age, Nicholas I accompanied the future Alexander II on a walk around the fortress, stopping at the cathedral to kiss the tombs of Paul, Alexander I, their wives and Grand Duke Konstantin Pavlovich.[3]

The foundation of the first church of SS Peter and Paul, dedicated to Peter I's patron saints, is closely associated with the founding of St

---

Lindsey Hughes was Professor of Russian History at UCL SSEES.

* Editors' note: On the one hand, Lindsey Hughes left this essay more or less complete, and meticulously footnoted. On the other, her text remained a first draft: parts, particularly at the beginning and end, were in note form, or interspersed with Russian words, and there were stylistic roughnesses that the author would have smoothed out. In making a readable and useful version, we have tried not to add any ideas that were not in the original, occasionally adding a note of our own in square brackets. We have checked all accessible references, amending them where necessary. We have corrected a few obvious mistakes and filled out many incomplete sentences, dropping occasional passages whose full sense could not be retrieved. Much the greater part of the text, however, remains as Lindsey left it.

[1] I. E. Grabar´, *Istoriia russkogo iskusstva*, 6 vols, Moscow, 1909–13, 3, p. 64.
[2] On the opposition of Moscow and St Petersburg, see G. Vdovin, *Obraz Moskvy 18 veka: gorod i chelovek*, Moscow, 1997, Introduction.
[3] R. S. Wortman, *Scenarios of Power: Myth and Ceremony in Russian Monarchy, I: From Peter the Great to the Death of Nicholas I*, Princeton, NJ, 1995, pp. 358–59.

Petersburg in 1703, about which concrete facts are few, legends many. According to one account, Peter saw an eagle hovering over Hare Island. He grabbed a bayonet, cut two strips of turf, laid one on top of the other in the shape of a cross, then made a cross from pieces of wood which he erected in the turf, with the words: 'In the name of Christ Jesus on this place shall be a church in the names of the apostles Peter and Paul.' The anonymous author records the legends that Constantine the Great was led to Byzantium by an eagle and that the Apostle Andrew, en route from Kiev and Novgorod, planted his staff in a spot not far from St Petersburg and blessed the region.[4] Thus Peter's city was placed in the context of Christian world history. It was to be the new city of St Peter, a new Rome. The wooden fortress church was consecrated on 29 June, the feast of SS Peter and Paul, the tsar's name-day.[5]

The original church's most striking feature — its spire — was repeated and emphasized in its stone successor. The cathedral which survives today was one of the many major buildings in the city begun in the wake of the Russian victory at Poltava in 1709. Its designer, the Swiss-Italian Domenico Trezzini, came to Russia at Peter's invitation in 1703 and died there in 1734. He was master of works, 'lieutenant-colonel of fortification and architect' for much of Peter's reign, in charge of fortification work in the Peter-Paul fortress, Peter's summer palace, the Alexander Nevsky monastery, and countless administrative buildings, as well as drawing up plans for individual residences and whole districts and squares. He was also in charge of the first architectural training brigade.[6]

Peter laid the foundation stone of the new cathedral on 8 June 1712, as recorded in the official journal, followed by all chief officials.[7] There is some confusion in the records, however, with certain sources recording the beginning of May[8] (when Peter himself was actually on the way home from Vyborg on board the ship *St Catherine*), or even 30 May 1714, an error still found in some modern guide-books.[9] The date of 8 June makes more sense when calculations indicate that in 1712 it

[4] 'O zachatii i zdanii tsarstvuiushchego grada Sanktpeterburga', in Iu. Bespiatykh (ed.), *Peterburg Petra I v inostrannykh opisaniiakh*, Leningrad, 1991, pp. 258–62.

[5] *Pis'ma i bumagi Imperatora Petra Velikago*, 2, St Petersburg, 1889, pp. 173, 560–61.

[6] See J. Cracraft, *The Revolution in Petrine Architecture*, Chicago, IL, 1988, pp. 155–60, and L. Hughes, 'Domenico Trezzini', in J. Turner (ed.), *The Dictionary of Art*, 34 vols, London, 1996, 31, pp. 317–18.

[7] *Pokhodnyi zhurnal*, St Petersburg, 1913, p. 56.

[8] *Zhurnal ili Podennaia zapiska*, 1770, 1.

[9] See *Pokhodnyi zhurnal*, p. 105; E. N. El'kin, 'Stroitel'stvo Petropavlovskogo sobora (1712–1733)', in *Kraevedcheskie zapiski: Issledovaniia i materialy, vyp. 2: Petropavlovskii sobor i velikokniazheskaia usypal'nytsa*, St Petersburg, 1994, pp. 56–86; B. Brodskii, 'Igla Petra i Pavla', *Novaia Rossiia*, 1995, 3, pp. 24–26.

coincided with the movable feast of Holy Trinity (in Russian Piatidesi-atnitsa, i.e. fifty days after Easter), which in 1703 fell on 16 May.[10] It made sense to postpone the event from Peter's birthday on 30 May, for Trinity in the Russian church coincided with Pentecost (Whitsun), the day on which the Church was founded in that the Holy Spirit descended upon the Apostles, including Peter (Acts: 2, i–iv) and hence an appropriate day for the dedication of a church. The Holy Trinity already had associations for Peter through the Trinity St Sergius monastery at Sergiev Posad, where he sought refuge in 1689, and was to assume special significance in the new city with the dedication of its main cathedral and the square around it to the Trinity. The new brick walls of the Peter-Paul cathedral went up around the old wooden church, which continued to function until 1718–19, when it was removed. Like the rest of the city, the church was built by conscripted workers, soldiers and convicts.

Originally devised as a fortress church (a fortress in the thick of military operations was unthinkable without a chapel, regarded as essential a defence as guns and troops), there is evidence that Peter came to regard the new building as something to be viewed more from the outside, a very visible landmark, a sign of Russia's presence on the Baltic, of the new city's predominance over Moscow (also a city of spires, but all lower than that of the new fortress cathedral). It was the 'new Ivan the Great', the bell-tower in the Moscow Kremlin. It was also a sort of symbolic ship, its boat-like nave and exterior (both of the old and the new church) decorated with pennants, like ships of the fleet, its outline echoed in the masts of ships on the Neva below. The tall spire and bell-tower overshadow the modest dome at the east end; hence the Orthodox tradition was not abandoned, but minimized. The basilica design (an elongated, rather than compact and centralized, nave) and large windows depart from older Muscovite traditions. Three aisles are covered with cross vaults, supported by piers clad in imitation marble with gilded capitals.

Early documents concentrate on the bell tower. Peter demanded that 'the bell tower which is in the fortress be made as quickly as possible, in order that the clock can be mounted in it by 1716, but the church can be built in a more leisurely fashion'.[11] The tower was started in

---

[10] E. I. Lelina, 'Novoe o khorosho izvestnom. (K voprosu o nachale stroitel´stva Petropav-lovskogo sobora)', *Peterburgskie chteniia*, 96, St Petersburg, 1996, pp. 65–68. [For more on these matters, see R. R. Milner-Gulland, '16 May 1703: The Petersburg Foundation-Myth', discussing a later comment by Hughes, in A. Cross (ed.), *Days from the Reigns of Eighteenth-Century Russian Rulers*, Study Group on Eighteenth Century Russia Newsletter, 2 parts, Cambridge, 2007, 1, pp. 37–48. Editors' note.]

[11] Quoted by El´kin, 'Stroitel´stvo', p. 60, original at Rossiiskii gosudarstvennyi istoricheskii arkhiv, f. 466, op. I, d. 476 (1706–1714), ll. 9–10.

March 1716 and completed as far as the third Corinthian order, 140 feet from the ground, by September. Clearly at this point Peter viewed the tower primarily as a repository for the clock, an essential device the installation of which could not be delayed, for, in his own words, 'wasted time, like death, cannot be reversed'.[12] In fact, the chiming clock, brought from Holland at a cost of 45,000 roubles, was not in itself an innovation but recalled Tsar Aleksei's famous chiming clock on the Saviour Tower in Red Square, subsequently destroyed by fire. It was also a vantage point for viewing the expanding city and the coming and going of ships. Peter intended that the tower should have a lift (*pod"emnyi stul*, or 'a machine on which one can go up and down from floor to floor'), an example of which the tsar first saw in Dresden in 1711 in the workshop of the mechanic Andreas Gertner. This device, upholstered in green cloth, was first mentioned by Trezzini in 1720.[13] It must have perished in the fire of 1756, which also claimed the clock and bells.

Were there identifiable foreign sources for the cathedral's design? A drawing of the Church of St Peter in Riga (1690–95) — the chief candidate — survives in Trezzini's archive (Museum of the Academy of Arts, no. 224). It is dated 5 February 1714, two years after the foundation of the St Petersburg cathedral. The question therefore remains open.[14]

The spire was designed by the Dutchman Harman van Boles (who signed himself Bolios). When it began to go up it caused amazement (it remains today the tallest structure in St Petersburg, at 122.5 metres), but in fact it had its Muscovite predecessors from the late 1690s and early 1700s, notably Alexander Menshikov's Moscow church of the Archangel Gabriel which had a similarly tall, slim spire. In September 1718 the ball (*iabloko*) was hoisted up by Russian carpenters and captive Swedes, who 'for their brave work when they raised the ball onto the spire were given a bucket of wine worth 44 altyns'.[15] That same year the bell tower was the scene of a curious incident involving Bolios and his family. After Tsarevich Aleksei's death in June 1718, a letter written by the Dutch ambassador De Bie was apprehended in which rumours about Aleksei's death were reported. These were traced to the cook Maria von Gussen, a relative of Bolios, who was arrested with his wife and children. He admitted that 'while working on the new tower in the fortress, on the eve of the tsarevich's death, I remained there for the

[12] *Pis'ma i bumagi Imperatora Petra Velikago*, 11:1, Moscow-Leningrad, 1964, p. 281 (1711).
[13] El'kin, 'Stroitel'stvo', p. 82.
[14] See A. I. Nekrasov, 'K voprosu o vozniknovenii Petropavlovskogo sobora v Leningrade', *Peterburgskie chteniia*, 96, St Petersburg, 1996, pp. 78–79.
[15] El'kin, 'Stroitel'stvo', p. 62.

night unobserved and in the evening saw from up above in the torture chamber the heads of some people and I talked about this to my mother-in-law, the kitchen woman of the Dutch resident'.[16] Bolios's sighting seems rather vague, but naturally the authorities did not wish to publicise evidence of torture (the last session of which took place after sentence had been passed) or identification of individuals involved.

In November 1719 the chimes (*kuranty*) were installed in the tower, and Peter went to hear them playing.[17] One of the last details to be added was the 'flying angel of copper [. . .] which will hold a cross in its hands' (Trezzini, 28 May 1722), made by the silversmith Lazar Zadubskii and the peasant Ivan Menshii.[18]

Work on the main body of the church was slower, despite Peter's growing demands that 'the church of stone construction must be finished with all haste'.[19] The roof started going on in 1722 but was completed only in 1727. Work on the interior decoration began only in April 1725, i.e. after Peter's death. A large group of wooden statues of saints and cherubs (*kheruvimy*, first mentioned in 1721) was apparently projected for the exterior. Makhaev indicates some on the east façade but they do not feature in the earliest descriptions of the cathedral. Perhaps they decayed and were not replaced, or were even removed as a result of clerical disapproval.[20] Feofan Prokopovich took an interest in the final work and advised Anna to gild capitals and other details in order to augment the cathedral's grandeur.[21]

Only later, when attention switched to the interior, did Peter see the church as a mausoleum, and even then not so much as a 'replacement' for the Archangel Cathedral in the Kremlin, rather an extension of it. There were no plans, for example, to transfer the remains of the tsar's Muscovite predecessors to St Petersburg. As it turned out, his brother Ivan, buried in the Archangel Cathedral in 1696, provided a sort of end-stop to the Muscovite period, while the new mausoleum would provide 'one of many proofs of the new era of Russian history which Peter had begun and that he wanted to break the link with Muscovite antiquity (old ways)'.[22]

---

[16] Ibid., p. 63.

[17] [On the cathedral's bells, see I. A. Chudinova, *Penie, zvony, ritual: Topografiia tserkovno-muzykal'noi kul'tury Peterburga*, St Petersburg, 1994, p. 34. Editors' note.]

[18] The angel figure survived until 1777, when it was broken in a storm. Antonio Rinaldi designed a new one and a lightning conductor was fitted in the following year.

[19] Quoted by El'kin, 'Stroitel'stvo', p. 67.

[20] [The Holy Synod of the Russian Orthodox Church pronounced against religious sculpture in 1722. Editors' note.]

[21] El'kin, 'Stroitel'stvo', p. 78.

[22] V. Rusakova, *Usypal'nitsa russkikh gosudarei: Petropavlovskii sobor i ego tsarskie grobnitsy*, n.p., n.d., p. 1.

Inside the designers seemed to break with tradition just as radically, and nowhere more than in the iconostasis, created by Trezzini and Ivan Zarudnyi, which used sculpture for the images of the Prophets and Apostles rows rather than painted icons, which make up only a partial Festivals row. An inscription running along the base of the iconostasis records that Peter ordered the church to be built and began the altar in 1722 and that it was completed under Catherine I in 1726.[23] The programme of the iconostasis was based on the themes of War and Peace, heavenly intervention and divine retribution: on the left stands the Archangel Gabriel, the messenger of God, with olive branches, on the right his militant counterpart Michael, fighting a serpent. Under Gabriel is the Annunciation (the first coming); under Michael, the Apocalypse (the second coming). At the foot of the arch of the gates stand Peter and Paul to the left, Solomon (peace and wisdom), to the right are David (the Church Militant), Moses (lawgiver) and Elijah (lightning). Above are the combined symbols of Trinity and Transfiguration. The overall effect of the iconostasis is reminiscent of the triumphal arches which decorated the streets during victory parades.[24] The forty-three icons seem dwarfed, but they are there, in a combination of old and new. Panels on the dominant right side were associated with Peter and male saints; those on the left with Catherine and female saints. Thus the icon of St Peter, to the right of the Saviour, is flanked on both sides by four smaller images, of Boris and Gleb, Alexander Nevsky and Tsarevich Dimitry, to make the link with Muscovite royal saints. The Saviour is flanked by the prophets Ioasaf, David, Ezekiel and Solomon. The icon of St Paul to the left of the Mother of God is flanked by holy women — Pulcheria, Bathsheba, Solomonia, Jael — while the Mother of God is flanked by female family saints — Paraskeva, Anna, Natalia and Elizabeth, and above them Catherine and Esther. The former novel composition has been interpreted as an 'apologia' for Catherine I who was a foreigner (like Jael) and not Peter's first wife (as Bathsheba was not David's first wife).[25] At the far right and far left respectively are icons of St Samson and Constantine the Great, Ezekiel and Helena. The icon of the Emperor Constantine

[23] S. Novoselov, *Opisanie kafedral'nago sobora vo imia svyatykh Pervoverkhovnykh Apostolov Petra i Pavla*, St Petersburg, 1857, pp. 90–91.

[24] E. B. Mozgovaia, 'Tvorchestvo I. P. Zarudnogo', unpublished candidate dissertation, State University of Leningrad, 1976, pp. 108–10. [See now, E. A. Tiukhmeneva, *Iskusstvo triumfal'nykh vrat v Rossii pervoi poloviny XVIII veka*, Moscow, 2005. Editors' note.]

[25] N. A. Naryshkina, *Petropavlovskii sobor (1712–1733): Pamiatnik morskoi slavy*, St Petersburg, 1997, p. 48. [On the iconography of St Catherine in St Petersburg, see now a study dedicated to the memory of Lindsey Hughes: G. Marker, *Imperial Saint: The Cult of St Catherine and the Dawn of Female Rule in Russia*, DeKalb, IL, 2007, pp. 160–62 and passim. Editors' note.]

alluded not only to Constantine's role as the first Christian emperor, but also to his foundation in Constantinople, his new capital, the successor to the old capital Rome, of the mausoleum church of the Holy Apostles.[26] Likewise, an icon of the Holy Wisdom ('Wisdom has built herself a temple') seems to pick up both the Solomon theme and the theme of building a temple. In this case, wisdom is identified not as a female allegory but as a male, i.e. Christ.[27]

Most of the icons follow traditional iconographic types, treated in the 'Moscow Baroque' manner. Several icons, however, are taken directly from Western religious paintings. These include the Presentation of Christ in the Temple, after Rubens, the Nativity of Christ after Hyacinthe Rigaud, and the Resurrection of Christ by Jean-Paul André (1711).[28] In all four cases, the Russian artists used engravings of the originals (now in the Hermitage) to trace their icons and produce more or less exact copies of the originals, treating them rather like templates (podlinniki), albeit taken from Western sources. There was still no question of producing original biblical compositions. There were, by contrast, many contemporary references, not least to St Samson, whose feast coincided with the battle of Poltava, metonymically also referring to the Swedish lion.

It is sometimes mistakenly believed that the Peter Paul Cathedral was the main church of Petrine St Petersburg. But because it remained unfinished and because of its designation as a mausoleum and its location, during Peter's reign the cathedral was rarely used. His main Court church was the Trinity Cathedral, adjacent to the main government buildings, which the tsar generally used for Sunday worship when he was resident in the new capital, for major festivals such as Easter, and also for national celebrations.[29] Nevertheless, it was the Peter Paul rather than the apparently more traditional Trinity which attracted the attention of foreign visitors. An anonymous German predicted in his 'Description of the City of St Petersburg' dating from 1718–19: 'This will be something fine, the like of which one cannot as yet find

[26] V. B. Gendrikov and S. E. Sen´ko, Petropavlovskii sobor: Usypal´nitsa imperatorskogo doma Romanovykh, St Petersburg, 1998, p. 24; Novoselov, Opisanie, pp. 85–89.

[27] Iu. V. Gerasimova, 'Vizantiiskie istochniki skul´ptory kompozitsii tsarskikh vrat kionostasa petropavlovskogo sobora v Leningrade', in G. L. Kurbatov (ed.), Iz istorii Vizantii i Vizantinovedeniia, Leningrad, 1991, pp. 124–37. See the engraving by Mikhail Shiriaev (1715) for Peter in the temple of Wisdom, at p. 133.

[28] J. [Iu. V.] Gerasimova, 'Western Prints and the Panels of the Peter and Paul Cathedral Iconostasis in St. Petersburg', in J. Klein, S. Dixon and M. Fraanje (eds), Reflections on Russia in the Eighteenth Century, Cologne, 2001, pp. 204–17; ead., The Iconostasis of Peter the Great in the Peter and Paul Cathedral in St Petersburg, Leiden, 2004.

[29] See, for example, Easter 1723, when from 14 April (Easter day) to 21 April, Peter attended at least once a day. A. N. Filippov, Odin iz neizdannykh 'iurnalov' Petrovskago tsarstvovaniia za 1723–1724, Kiev, 1912, pp. 13–14.

in Russia. The tower is already completed as far as the rafters; it is unusually tall and built of good stone masonry, with pilasters of good proportions and high vaults.' He expected the tower to exceed the height of German equivalents.[30] Bergholz, the Holstein envoy, writing in 1721, thought it 'the biggest and most beautiful cathedral in St Petersburg, with a tall bell tower in the new style, but as yet undecorated inside'. As he stressed, it was 'not in the Byzantine but in the new taste', and he found it natural to describe it using Western terms — portico, columns, vaults and so on.[31]

In the eighteenth and nineteenth centuries the cathedral's chief role was to house the spectacle of royal endings and beginnings (the emperor/empress is dead; long live the emperor/empress). The first burial in the old fortress church was of Tsarevna Ekaterina Petrovna, who died in 1708 aged eighteen months. The first funeral in the territory of the new church, only just being constructed, was of Peter I's daughter-in-law, Charlotte, buried in Western style in October 1715 despite being a Lutheran. Peter's small daughters Natalia and Margarita were also laid there in 1715, followed by a stillborn son, Pavel, in 1717, Aleksei in 1718,[32] Peter Petrovich (d. 1719 and initially buried in the Alexander Nevsky Monastery) in 1724, and Natalia Petrovna in 1725. The tsar's sisters-in-law, Martha Matveevna and Praskovia Fedorovna, were buried in 1716 and 1723 respectively, the latter having been granted a particularly sumptuous funeral, including the display of royal symbols, trimmings of white and violet satin, and a torch-lit procession.[33] In 1722, Trezzini measured the tombs of Peter's five children to calculate how much material was needed to make covers, and in 1732 Anna ordered replacements for the old tombs, but by 1736 the author of the first (apparently unpublished) description of the cathedral indicated that the places were no longer marked at floor level.[34]

---

[30] Arkhimandrit Avgustin, *Pravoslavnyi Peterburg v zapisiakh inostrantsev*, St Petersburg, 1995, pp. 54–55.

[31] Ibid.; O. A. Ageeva, 'Vospriiatie russkogo zodchestva Petrovskoi epokhi zapadno-evropeiskimi diplomatami', in Iu. S. Borisov et al. (eds), *Rossiia i vneshnii mir: Dialog kul'tur: Sbornik statei*, Moscow, 1997, pp. 113–14.

[32] In 1906 a crack was discovered in the floor under the staircase of the bell tower, where Alexis, Charlotte and Tsarevna Maria Alekseeva were buried. In order to repair the subsidence under the stairwell, which would cause some disturbance to the tombs, permission had to be obtained from the palace authorities and a requiem was said. In May 1909 the outer tombs were reconstructed, with three horizontal slabs and three vertical slabs on the wall in white marble, with crosses and inscriptions. See E. El'kin, 'Nadgrobiia na tsarskikh mogilakh', in *Kraevedcheskie zapiski*, p. 167. But apparently in 1911, the commandant of the fortress reported that no lamps were lit over the three graves: see S. V. Trofimov, 'Tserkovno-sluzhebnaia zhizn' Petropavlovskogo sobora', in *Kraevedcheskie zapiski*, p. 278.

[33] [See O. G. Ageeva, 'Peterburgskii traurnyi tseremonial Doma Romanovykh v nachale XVIII v.', in Iu. N. Bespiatykh (ed.), *Fenomen Peterburga*, St Petersburg, 2001, pp. 495–99; L. Hughes, *Peter the Great: A Biography*, New Haven, CT, 2002, pp. 181–82. Editors' note.]

[34] El'kin, 'Nadgrobiia', p. 161. First description in Gosudarstvennaia publichnaia biblioteka, Pogodin 1751, l. 23.

The most spectacular event was Peter's funeral within the temporary structure.[35] The tsar's coffin stood in the centre of the church for six years, where it was joined in 1727 by that of Catherine I. Their tombs stood together until 29 May 1731, when both were lowered into a vault (*sklep*) by order of Empress Anna.

The present white Italian marble gravestones over fifteen of the tombs (marking the appropriate place in the vaults below) were designed by the architect A. A. Puaro in 1865–67 on the orders of Alexander II, who had the fabric covers removed and discovered that the tomb stones underneath were unpolished, cracked and chipped. The old tombs were encased by the new ones, which were fitted with new metal plaques.[36] But Peter was the first, himself a new beginning for the Romanovs, all of whom, male or female, to a greater or lesser extent acknowledged his legacy and followed in his footsteps.

On 30 April 1756, disaster struck: lightning set the spire on fire and the clock burnt. Collapsing masonry damaged the main roof. The interior suffered some damage, with wall paintings darkened in places by smoke and heat. The damage was repaired, with some wooden structures replaced by metal. The cathedral was reconsecrated on 23 June 1756.[37] Following the fire, Lomonosov proposed a project for a monument to Peter in the form of mosaic panels to be completed in time for the fiftieth anniversary of the battle of Poltava. The Senate accepted the project and set aside 148,682 roubles. The architects I. Schumacher and I. Dunker produced plans, but everything was delayed [presumably by the Seven Years' War, which delayed all prestige projects including Rastrelli's stone Winter Palace, eds] and Elizaveta Petrovna gave her approval only on 26 October 1760. Not until May 1762 (after further delays and another competition for the architectural and sculptural plan) did Lomonosov begin to assemble his Poltava mosaic. A month later, Catherine II came to the throne and the scene was set for a new style and a quite different monument to her glorious predecessor.[38]

In between funerals, the cathedral provided a site for sustaining and renewing patriotic sentiments or (in the case of foreigners) for reflecting on the frailty of human existence. One such was the Swede Count

[35] [This paragraph, and those both preceding it and following it, left in relatively staccato form by Lindsey Hughes, have been reconstructed by the editors using material from her essay, 'The Funerals of the Russian Emperors and Empresses', in M. Schaich (ed.), *Monarchy and Religion: The Transformation of Royal Culture in Eighteenth-Century Europe*, Oxford, 2007, pp. 395–419, where further references may be found. Editors' note.]

[36] El'kin, 'Nadgrobiia', pp. 162–63.

[37] Novoselov, *Opisanie*, pp. 9-10.

[38] E. F. Krasheninnikov, 'O proekte pamiatnika Petru Velikomu', in *Kraevedcheskie zapiski*, pp. 174–77. On Falconet's 'Bronze Horseman', see below.

Johann Hård, released from captivity in the fortress by Peter III in 1762 having been taken prisoner in Prussian service during the Seven Years' War: 'The cathedral aroused my curiosity; in its architecture it is one of the most splendid churches in existence. I saw in the church, by the light of an ever-burning lamp, two splendid tombs, of Emperor Peter I and Empress Anna. I sat in the space between these tombs and gave myself up to thoughts about the vicissitudes of human greatness.' The cathedral was never used for baptisms or weddings or, indeed, regular celebrations of the liturgy. Other than funerals and requiem services for departed members of the imperial family, its main purpose was for requiems and Te Deum services in association with other national events. During the reign of Catherine II, it was identified as the natural temple in which to celebrate naval victories.[39] On 29 August 1770 (the feast of the decolletation of John the Baptist, the traditional day for remembering the fallen in battle), Catherine II brought naval trophies from the Turkish war. At the end of a general requiem for the fallen, the empress took the standard captured at the battle of Chesme from Count I. G. Chernyshev, vice-president of the Admiralty College, approached Peter I's tomb, knelt down and lowered the flag to the base of the tomb with the words: 'Tvoia ot tvoikh prinoshu' ('I bring to Thee that which is thine from Thy people') to the accompaniment of drum beats, cannon fire and the peal of church bells. Then Archbishop Platon (Levshin) delivered a discourse in Peter's memory, which began with a stirring call to the late tsar delivered in a booming voice: 'Arise now, Great Monarch, Father of Our Fatherland. Arise and look upon your handiwork; it has not decayed with time and its glory has not dimmed.' He recounted the victories in the Mediterranean, where the proud Porte had been humbled.

Despite the cathedral's relative youth, it housed ancient relics more or less requisite for a church of its status. These included a part of the Robe of Christ, taken from the piece of fabric brought to Moscow in 1626,[40] and part of the head of the Great Martyr James the Persian, associated with curing children's illnesses. In the tour recommended in his celebrated early-nineteenth-century guide-book, Pavel Svin´in mentioned first the iconostasis ('in old taste, i.e. high-relief carving amazingly richly gilded'), then the relics, before directing the visitor to 'the objects made by the hand of the immortal Founder of this church'.[41]

[39] [See S. Dixon, 'Religious Ritual at the Eighteenth-Century Russian Court', in Schaich (ed.), *Monarchy and Religion*, p. 222. Editors' note.]

[40] [For this and other relics in the Dormition Cathedral in Moscow, see A. M. Lidov (ed.), *Khristianskie relikvii v Moskovskom kremle*, Moscow, 2001. Editors' note.]

[41] P. Svin´in, *Dostopamiatnosti Sanktpeterburga i ego okrestnostei*, 5 parts, St Petersburg, 1816–28, 3, p. 16. [On the author, see L. Hughes, 'Peter the Great's St Petersburg in the Works of Pavel Svin´in (1787–1839)', in A. G. Cross (ed.), *St Petersburg 1703–1825*, Basingstoke, 2003, pp. 148–64. Editors' note.]

There were five icons said to be carved from ivory by Peter himself: a Crucifixion with Saints Peter and Paul, Catherine and Andrew, grouped together in the shape of a cross, and Peter's chandelier.[42] Svin´in also noted the battle standard laid on Peter's tomb by Catherine II and a poem commemorating the event:

> Come Peter from the heavens; look down on your city
> And on Catherine now reigning there,
> Holding sacred your labours for the good of all
> To you as the founder of the Russian fleet be glory
> And attributes to you the start of her own glory
> Regarding you as the cause of Russia's blessings
> And lays the flag taken from the enemies
> Fervently at your feet. (Ruban, 1772?)[43]

As the visitor turns his gaze to the 'cold granite holding all that remains of Peter and Catherine', he is to recall the words of Prokopovich's funeral sermon, and will cry out with Bobrov: 'No gde Velikii Chelovek?//Gde Tsar mudrets? Gde voin mochnyi?' ('But where is the Great Man? Where is the wise Tsar? Where the mighty warrior?'). But the next moment he will recall Peter's deeds (*podvigi*) on behalf of the happiness and glory of millions and will feel love flame up. 'The monuments are even more precious for the Russian, even more sacred, even more than for the foreign visitor, when he gazes on the trophies.' Emotions of respect and reverence (*blagogovenie*) were sustained as the visitor next made a pilgrimage to the little '*botik*' [Peter's first boat, now in the Naval Museum, eds] in its pavilion beside the cathedral, then proceeded out of the fortress to visit Peter's little house.[44]

Despite these gushing sentiments, the cathedral was poorly maintained. By the beginning of Nicholas I's reign it no longer represented 'that splendour appropriate to a church so dear to the heart of Russia'.[45] Frescoes were flaking, lacquer cracking, gilding blackened, icons covered with dust and candle grease. Part of the iconostasis was suffering from subsidence to the extent that in 1829 services had to be suspended at the main altar. The emperor financed a restoration programme, completed only in 1842, of which the most famous incident related to the repair of the angel on the tip of the steeple in 1830. A. Olenin was able to witness the 'amazing bravery' of the Russian steeplejack Teleshkin from his windows and decided to write it down when the press failed to report it. Apparently Teleshkin, a man of

---

[42] Rusakova, *Usypal´nitsa*, pp. 11–12.

[43] Svin´in, *Dostopamiatnosti*, 3, pp. 19–20.

[44] Ibid., pp. 23–24. [On the *domik*, see L. Hughes, '"Nothing is Too Small for a Great Man": Peter the Great's Little Houses and the Creation of Some Petrine Myths', *SEER*, 81, 2003, 4, pp. 634–58. Editors' note.]

[45] Novoselov, *Opisanie*, p. 43.

medium height weighing about 13 puds [since a pud is around 35 pounds, if this is not a mistake he sounds rather stockily built! Eds], offered to save the huge cost of erecting scaffolding by attaching ropes and then easing himself up the spire until he could reach the cross: he worked suspended from a sort of rope ladder for about six weeks, repairing the angel's wing and replacing torn panels. To anyone who asked whether Teleshkin did a good job, Olenin said Teleshkin would be happy to show his work to anyone who agreed to climb up there to take a look.[46] The Russian's brave deed became legendary.

Nicholas I's promotion of Official Nationality (whose slogan was Orthodoxy, Autocracy and National Feeling) prompted a revival of pre-Petrine Russia, which included the veneration of monuments such as the Kremlin cathedrals, somewhat neglected in the eighteenth century, as well as the neo-Russian style, in the church of Christ the Saviour in Moscow. But it was not difficult to integrate Petrine monuments into the new scheme of things. Thus a guide to St Petersburg for children, published in 1838 by V. Bur´ianov, takes the young visitors to the cathedral and tells them to look up at the angel and cross and to tell the story of the courageous Russian workman, Petr Teleshkin, before leading them first to the lectern from which Feofan Prokopovich delivered his funeral oration to Peter and the imperial pew with its Russian coat of arms, then to the cathedral's relics ('A sort of inexpressible, wonderful feeling fills our soul when we approach such a great reliquary'). Two chandeliers made by Peter's own hands bring them to his tomb: 'Get down on your knees, children, before the tomb of Peter, with hot tears let us bedew (*srosim*) this monument and recall the deeds of the one who is hidden beneath this stone.' Reference to a battle standard placed on Peter's tomb by Catherine II and a medal laid there by Alexander in 1803, followed by the excerpt from Metropolitan Platon's sermon, quoted above, allow the writer to make the link with Peter's current successor: 'We too ask him to rise up and view the achievements of his successors who try to imitate him.' (In Bur´ianov's itinerary, as in Svin´in's, visitors were advised to continue the Petrine theme by visiting the 'grandfather of the Russian fleet', i.e. the 'botik'.)[47] In the same vein, I. Pushkarev wrote:

> How many holy thoughts and reminiscences well up in the soul with a single glance at the sarcophagi, made from simple stone without any decoration and clad in brocade covers; beneath them rest the wearers of

---

[46] A. Olenin, *O pochinke kresta i angela [bez lesov] na shpitse Petropavlovskago sobora v S. Peterburge*, St Petersburg, 1831.
[47] V. Bur´ianov, *Progulka s det´mi po S.-Peterburgu*, 3 parts, St Petersburg, 1838, 1, pp. 83–99.

our crown. Walking past a long row of graves of ordinary people one feels dejection and with involuntary sadness you look into the distance at the empty plot which, perhaps, will receive your own dust and your passions; but standing above the tomb of the ruler of millions of subjects, who encompassed in his designs all the world, the father of the fatherland, you are struck by a strange sensation, which you experience fully but cannot express in words.[48]

Despite its role in the life of the nation, the cathedral failed to attract serious studies in the nineteenth century and much remains unknown. One of the better documented events was the replacement of the wooden framed spire with a metal one on a ribbed carcass in 1858 under the design and direction of the engineer D. V. Zhuravlev. This was new technology not only for Russia and significantly Zhuravlev was an expert on the construction of railways and bridges — thus one of the city's oldest buildings became the beneficiary of the latest modern discoveries. The basic components of the new carcass were produced at the Votkinsk works in Eastern Russia, which did the job for half the price asked in St Petersburg; there the workers laboured through public holidays to complete the commission and the machines broke down under the strain of producing such large components. The whole spire was loaded onto barges along the Kama and Volga rivers, thence by train from Tver´ to St Petersburg where it was assembled. It took two months to raise the 207-ton, 122.5-metre spire. A staircase was installed in the lower part and an external ladder on the upper. The chimes playing 'God Save the Tsar' and 'Kole slaven' also date from that time, as does the new angel.[49]

In the words of S. Novoselov, commandant of the fortress and author of the first substantial guide to the cathedral: 'Every Russian considers it his sacred duty to visit the mausoleum of our Royal House; foreigners visiting St Petersburg also hasten to pay their respects to the tombs of the Lofty Departed, then often experience disappointment that no modern description of the cathedral is available.'[50] His 'Description', the work of a self-confessed amateur, remains one of the fullest compendia of information, especially on the cathedral in the mid-nineteenth century. 'The bell tower of the Peter Paul cathedral has a special character and anyone seeing it once will never forget it and will always recognize it in a true reproduction.' In churches one usually describes the interiors, the painting and so on,

[48] I. Pushkarev, *Kafedral'nyi sobor sv. apostol Petra i Pavla*, [reprinted from?] *Sankt Peterburgskiia vedomosti*, otdel vtoroi, chast´ neoffitsial'naia, n.d. (after 1830?), p. 39.
[49] E. Andreeva, 'Preobrazhenie shpilia', *Sankt-Peterburgskaia Panorama*, 1992, 3, pp. 24–25.
[50] Novoselov, *Opisanie*, p. xi.

but every Russian on entering and bending his knee before the altar, will hasten to bend with deep emotion before the tombs of the benefactors of his fatherland, his ancestors and himself and pray for the rest of the souls of the lofty departed, before those holy visages to which they themselves once prayed and which now guard their last resting place.

Therefore Novoselov begins his 'Description' with the tombs, starting with 'the founder of a new life for our fatherland'.[51] In 1857 at the foot of Peter's tomb was the flag from Chesme, laid there by Catherine II in 1770, the 1803 medal, the icon of SS Peter and Paul in gold casing. Of the two chandeliers made by Peter only one was still in the cathedral, hanging before the icon of St Peter. (A scroll inside the central globe reads: 'This object was brought here as a sign of gratitude to the Lord God for the healing waters [at Olonets] and made there. March 14 1724. Peter.')[52] Another candelabrum, which hung in the centre of the cathedral in front of the royal doors, was removed by order of Nicholas I. This one had four discs on the globe, featuring medals on Peter's death, the battles of Poltava and Hangö and an inscription: 'The work of the hard-working hands of Peter the First the Great Emperor and Autocrat of All Russia. 1723.' As Novoselov remarked, these objects 'arouse wonderment in an artistic context, both by the creative idea and also by the sophistication of the handiwork. Peter was great in everything'.[53]

Novoselov also celebrated modern advances. In 1855, for example, it was observed that the cross had leaned from the vertical and the spire was slightly crooked. This time not Teleshkin (who was still alive, both in person and folk memory) but modern science came to the rescue in the shape of scaffolding designed by the engineer Pauker. (The spire, Novoselov informed his readers, was the seventh tallest in the world.) But his main focus was on the liturgical life and contents of the cathedral, as a testimony of national religious sentiment. In his view, the huge number of offerings made and candles lit in a church that was open day and night bore witness to Russian patriotic feelings, as 'a source of good heartfelt convictions among the people, of their respect for the God-Anointed rulers'. Ordinary people watched over the graves — the brigade of soldiers who looked after cleanliness and security, the old watchman who, according to anecdote, prevented Baroness de Staël from stealing a piece of the cover from Peter's tomb. Moreover, the many trophies which decorated the interior aroused another affecting thought which makes the Russian heart beat faster — that here

---

[51] Ibid., p. 21.
[52] Ibid., p. 105.
[53] Ibid., pp. 105–07. See also V. N. Vasilev and V. M. Glinka (eds), *Pamiatniki russkoi kultury pervoi chetverti XVIII veka v sobranii gos. ordena Lenina Ermitazha: Katalog*, Leningrad, 1966, p. 182.

'enemy banners guard the last resting-place of the those who glorified the Fatherland with a wonderful series of their miraculous feats'.[54] (Given the date, in the immediate aftermath of Russia's defeat in the Crimean war, past glories were all the more worth dwelling on.) Novoselov ends his book with prayers of gratitude and good wishes to Alexander II: 'Where but here would it be more appropriate to do this, while visiting the church in which everything speaks of Holy Rus and our great Autocrats?' On behalf of the Guards and the nobility, he says to the emperor: 'He is with us, we are with him. The dvorianstvo will always be in the full sense a real noble estate and the source of all good.'[55] Thus the book ends with a confirmation of the loyalty of that noble estate which in 1856–57 was already being prepared for a sacrifice to the greater good.

Despite its 'cathedral' status, the Peter Paul was never really regarded as the central city church in terms of use, and was inaccessible to most when the Neva was dangerous. In the eighteenth century, the Trinity Cathedral and the cathedrals in the Alexander Nevsky Monastery were more important. State occasions were generally commemorated at the Kazan′ Church, consecrated in 1737, and its magnificent stone successor, the Kazan′ Cathedral, consecrated in 1812. In 1858, St Isaac's became the main diocesan cathedral in the capital and the Peter Paul was officially designated a Court church under the authority of the palace administration.[56]

Another reason for its demise as a 'regular' cathedral was that its liturgical life was unlike that of other churches. No weddings or baptisms were held there. Though regular services were conducted, these had to make way for the programme of requiem masses which naturally expanded over the course of two centuries, reaching its height (before terminating completely in 1917) in the reign of Nicholas II. In the 1850s, a programme of requiem offices was fixed and printed.[57] Departed emperors and empresses merited services on their birthdays, name-days and the anniversaries of their deaths. Members of the Holy Synod conducted requiems for Peter I and rulers from Nicholas I; other requiems were conducted by lesser-ranking bishops. The printed programme by no means included all requiem services. Sometimes special memorial services for departed royals were ordered and paid for by organizations or individuals. There were services for the recently departed, usually for a year after the funeral, when each

[54] Novoselov, *Opisanie*, p. 158.
[55] Ibid., pp. 296–97.
[56] See Trofimov, 'Tserkovno-sluzhebnaia zhizn′', pp. 272–81.
[57] *Tabel′ pominovenii v sem sobore, povsegodno sovershaemykh v raznykh mesiatsiakh i chislakh po Velikikh gosudarekh imperatorekh i imperatritsekh i po vysokoi ikh familii* (various dates of publication, including 1877 and 1895).

liturgy included versicles and responses, and afterwards a short litany at the tomb of the deceased. Clergy had to ensure that lamps were always alight over the tombs.

Here Protoierei A. A. Dernov, a prominent priest in the diocese of St Petersburg at the end of the nineteenth century, describes a name-day requiem for Tsars Alexander I, II and III on 28 August 1895: 'Thousands of worshippers, people of various callings and ranks surrounded the cathedral on all sides, which was filled with a crowd of worshippers — factory workers who had come to pay their respects at the tombs of our tsars buried in the cathedral.' A procession of the cross entered, with two rows of banners stretching from the royal doors to the centre and two rows of icons 'like two solid walls'. On the left stood a choir of factory choristers, men, women and children. The liturgy was led by the choir of the Life Guards of the Grenadiers, then nine priests and four deacons served the office. All the emperors and empresses buried there were mentioned. 'It was moving to see how during the singing of "rest with the saints" and "eternal memory", the whole church fell to its knees and above this kneeling mass of people the banners waved and the icons could be seen.'[58]

Although the number of 'regular' services was limited, this was nevertheless a hard-working church. Vespers were sung on the eve of festivals, on Saturday and 'high imperial' days, and after each liturgy all the rulers buried in the cathedral were mentioned. There were also services for the fortress garrison, workers in the Mint and fortress prisoners, including annual confessions for all. It was calculated that the annual workload of each priest was ninety liturgies, twenty vespers, twenty major and 140 everyday services.[59] As well as accommodating funerals and requiems, the cathedral remained a prime site for national anniversaries and acts of remembrance — wars, treaties and the birth of heirs — as well as for more personal acts of commemoration (for example, rulers were supposed to take their leave of their forefathers and ask their blessing for their journey before leaving the capital).[60] Alexander II was particularly adept at harnessing the possibilities offered by the cathedral. A famous lithograph shows him, half-kneeling, head in hand, with his right arm resting on the tomb of Nicholas I on the night before the publication of the manifesto for the emancipation of the serfs in February 1861. The pose conveys both the anticipation of a momentous act and also his homage to his father

[58] Quoted in Trofimov, 'Tserkovno-sluzhebnaia zhizn'', pp. 276–77. [On workers' choirs in this period, see P. Herrlinger, *Working Souls: Russian Orthodoxy and Factory Labor in St. Petersburg, 1881–1917*, Bloomington, IN, 2007. Editors' note.]
[59] Trofimov, 'Tserkovno-sluzhebnaia zhizn'', p. 279.
[60] Novoselov, *Opisanie*, p. 157.

The Cathedral of SS Peter and Paul, St Petersburg. Nineteenth-century photochrome print (1890–1900)
Library of Congress Prints and Photographs Division, Washington, DC

whose wishes he believed he was following.[61] The wider context for
Alexander's subsequent reforms was the emulation of Peter I. On 30
May 1872 a twenty-one gun salute from the fortress signalled the start
of the day of commemoration of the Petrine bicentenary. Delegations
of urban representatives and priests bearing the icon of the Saviour
from the 'domik', joined by others from the Trinity Cathedral,
converged on the Peter Paul. Here on three gold cushions were laid
out Petrine memorabilia: the tsar's uniform, breast plate and hat, and
sword from Poltava; his order of St Andrew. A scroll bore an extract
from Peter's (probably apocryphal) speech to the troops before the
battle: 'Of Peter, know only this that he does not value his life; if only
Russia will live, in glory and prosperity for your well-being.' On
another cushion was a medal issued in Peter's honour which Alexander
would place on his tomb. Lined up were representatives of Peter's army
and navy. A requiem was held over Peter's tomb, after which the
medal was brought by Alexander. Then a procession set off for the
Nevsky gates and quay of the fortress, where a flotilla was waiting to
escort the icon and memorabilia across the river to the statue of the
'Bronze Horseman'.[62]

The cathedral had two main festivals — 29 June (St Peter, in the
main cathedral, from its foundation in 1704) and 24 November (St
Catherine, in the chapel, from 1779). Also there were feasts to com-
memorate the two main relics: 10 July (Deposition of the Robe) and 27
November (St James the Persian), and from 1908, when the mausoleum
of the grand dukes was consecrated, the patronal festivals of Alexander
Nevsky on 30 August and 23 November.[63] The Peter Paul was also the
starting point for a number of processions of the cross which were so
much part of city life in the nineteenth and early twentieth centuries.
The major fortress festival was Prepolovenie, when a procession of all
the priests of the city, clad in gold vestments, went round the walls
along the Neva, stopping to pray at each gate, and visiting also
the boathouse where Peter's dinghy was stored before returning to the
cathedral. People threw bread and money into the courtyard for the
prisoners. This always attracted large, colourful crowds, both on land
and on boats on the water, providing both 'a magnificent sight' and
'a feeling of reverence'. At the beginning of the Dormition Fast on
1 August, there was another blessing of the waters, again at the Neva
via the boathouse, just one of sixteen such processions held in the city
that day.[64]

[61] Gendrikov, *Petropavlovskii sobor*, p. 24.
[62] *Prazdnovanie v S.-Peterburge 200-letiia so dnia Rozhdeniia Petra Velikago*, St Petersburg, 1872.
[63] Trofimov, 'Tserkovno-sluzhebnaia zhizn'', p. 280.
[64] Novoselov, *Opisanie*, pp. 155–56.

On the eve of the First World War the cathedral must have been overflowing with objects. On and around Peter I's tomb alone the following items were recorded: four icon lamps, six medals (from 1803, 1872, 1903, 1904 and 1909 [two]), and seventeen silver wreaths. On the wall there was a bas-relief of the statue to Peter in Taganrog, dating from 1898.[65]

What happened after 1917? In fact, in the autumn of that year, it was the Provisional Government which ordered that the many icons, medals and wreaths decorating the graves be packed up and sent to Moscow, after which their fate is apparently unknown.[66] Already in 1918, the cathedral was more or less closed as a working church 'for reason of inconvenience to the work of the administration of the fortress'. The first excursions were organized in the same year, twice a day with a guide only.[67] In May 1919, the cathedral was locked and sealed and in 1922 the 'remains of church treasures' were sold to help the starving. In 1921 a telephone was installed in the bell tower.[68] From 1922, the building was under the auspices of Glavnauka, when it was subjected to 'museumization' under the direction of O. M. Rabitskova. From 1926 it was a branch of the Museum of the Revolution. In 1954, the Museum of the History of Leningrad took it over.[69] There were also symbolic changes. In the words of a later Soviet guide-book, in the nineteenth century the cathedral chimes played 'God Save the Tsar', 'but Revolutionary Petrograd did not want the sound of the tsarist anthem ringing out over the city', so the chimes were silenced and not restored until 1937, when they played the International. In the Second World War, bombs falling nearby made the bells ring. Then, in 1952, the Soviet national anthem was installed, to play at 6, 12, 16 and 24.00 hours. The spire 'symbolized Russia's entry onto the expanses of the Baltic sea'.[70]

Despite B. S. Arakcheev's assurance in the preface to a recent guide-book that the cathedral, as a national holy place (natsional'naia sviatynia) remained unscathed even during the years of 'militant atheism',[71] in the interwar years it could not have functioned very well, with no heating and no repairs. In 1935 sufficient funds were found to erect scaffolding, but an inspection declared it to be in a 'catastrophic state'.

[65] M. S. Verekin, *Kratkoe opisanie pridvornogo petropavlovskogo sobora v petrogradskoi kreposti*, Petrograd, 1913, pp. 15–17.
[66] Gendrikov, *Petropavlovskii sobor*, p. 28.
[67] L. V. Andrianova, 'Iz istorii Petropavlovskogo sobora i Velikokniazheskoi usypal'nitsy 1920–1940-kh godov', in *Kraevedcheskie zapiski*, pp. 316–19.
[68] Gendrikov, *Petropavlovskii sobor*, p. 28.
[69] Andrianova, 'Iz istorii Petropavlovskogo sobora', pp. 316–19.
[70] I. E. Bartenev (ed.), *Gorod na Neve: Dostoprimechatel'nosti Leningrada*, Leningrad, 1967, pp. 163, 160.
[71] Gendrikov and Sen'ko, *Petropavlovskii sobor*, preface by B. S. Arakcheev.

In the words of a report by the director of the Museum of Revolution: 'The cathedral is included in excursions around the fortress but its external state of repair constitutes a danger to the workers who visit it. Outside the plaster work is falling off in many places, bricks sometimes come loose, pieces of cornice become detached; inside, paint and stucco are peeling'; and so on.[72] The building was fenced off and closed, but on the outbreak of war with Nazi Germany in 1941, money allocated for renovation had to be used for camouflaging the building. The grand princely mausoleum fared even worse. Almost all the internal decorations and fittings were removed in 1922 on the grounds that they and the building 'constituted no artistic or historical value'. In 1932 the building was again declared to be of no interest and even to have spoiled the silhouette of the fortress. It was taken over by the state book industry, sealed off from the main church and used as a book store.[73]

With the advent of war in 1941, thoughts initially turned to saving monuments: part of the iconostasis was dismantled and hidden, sand put on the floor. The camouflaging of the spire needed mountain climbers, sportsmen and steeplejacks, in exploits reminiscent of Teleshkin's feat in 1830. Steeplejack Mikhail Bobrov from the 'Progress' factory climbed through the spire and worked on a harness, onto which Aloizii Zemba, a lighting man with Lenfilm, then climbed. At one point they had to secure the figure of the angel which got caught up in their ropes. Bobrov was injured in the course of duty when an incendiary bomb landed in front of the cathedral. 'Protecting the monument of the heroic past, these men performed new feats of its heroic present. The spire of the Peter-Paul cathedral became the measure of their courage.'[74] The cathedral came back into its own on the initiative of none other than Stalin in the autumn-winter of 1942–43. On 28 October 1942, an 'Act on the carrying out of repair works and the design of Peter I's tomb' was issued, in time for the anniversary of the October Revolution on 7 November. The tombs of Alexander Nevsky, Suvorov and Kutuzov were also hurriedly tidied up and embellished as rallying points in the struggle against the fascists. A special design for Peter's tomb was prepared by Ia. O. Rubanchik, who imported a sculptured head of Peter designed perhaps for the 'Bronze Horseman'. New recruits came to Peter's tomb, where they read the words allegedly spoken by Peter to his troops before Poltava [see above]. Damage caused by the shelling eventually amounted to 69,514,000 roubles.[75] Two years after the war, the camouflage paint was removed,

[72] Quoted in Andrianova, 'Iz istorii Petropavlovskogo sobora', p. 317.
[73] Ibid., pp. 317–18.
[74] Naryshkina, *Petropavlovskii sobor*, p. 132.
[75] Ibid., p. 134.

an even more difficult task than its application, again with help of mountaineers. The gilding was restored for the first time since 1858.

Guidebooks generally reflected the current political climate. For example, a guide to the fortress published in 1947, while characteristically giving the lion's share of attention to the fortress as a 'bulwark of autocracy for dealing with the revolutionary movement in Russia', does include a dozen pages on the cathedral with the fairly standard facts and figures. But it also adds an unexpected section as commentary on the tomb of Tsarevich Aleksei Petrovich (omitted from standard guides partly because it is not generally on view) with a brief summary of the 'plot against Peter's progressive reforms' organized by the conservative boyars and clergy who, with the help of foreign aid, intended to turn Russia back 'along its old path'. This seems to mimic scenes in Part I of Eisenstein's 'Ivan the Terrible', featuring plots by power-hungry boyars and clerics, with foreign aid, against Ivan, which in turn reflects the ideological gloss on Stalin's position regarding conspiracy, sabotage and treachery as viewed in the immediate post-war years. The Aleksei case also has the added feature of culminating in a 'show trial' in which the tsarevich 'confessed himself guilty of devising a treasonous scheme to kill Peter and named his fellow-conspirators'.[76]

Meanwhile, around the cathedral itself and its significance there reigned a 'conspiracy of silence', as N. A. Naryshkina wrote in a pioneering study published in 1997.[77] Her own work suffers from some imprecision (for example, the claim that this is the first example in world architecture where a church was added onto a bell tower rather than vice-versa, not strictly true) and a tendency to sentimentality and excessive patriotism. Between 1956 and 1959 a general restoration was undertaken, under difficult conditions of cold and humidity. The colour of the façades and interior was much discussed and attempts made, from documents and scientific probes, to establish the original scheme. The earliest paint found under layers inside was a turquoise, with pinkish-green columns and pillars. It was decided to revert to this, using imitation marble effects in red and green on the pillars. The interior decoration was completed in July 1957, when the cathedral opened for visitors. The exterior was finished in a 'pinkish cream and sand tone' and completed in 1959.[78]

In 1972, for the tercentenary of Peter's birth (a low-key affair compared with the bicentenary), Peter's tomb was restored to its original appearance with copies of medals and a copy of a bronze bust by Carlo Albagini made in Peter's lifetime. Banners were restored,

[76] *Petropavlovskaia krepost': Putevoditel'*, Leningrad, 1947, pp. 33–35.
[77] Naryshkina, *Petropavlovskii sobor*.
[78] Ibid., pp. 139–44.

including the flag of St Andrew. But Peter's was the only tomb in the cathedral thus honoured, and the only one (as will be recalled by readers who visited the cathedral in the 1970s and 1980s) regularly supplied with fresh flowers. A manual for tour guides published in 1980 listed the themes of an excursion around the fortress as: (i) The historical necessity of the struggle of the Russian state for access to the Baltic; (ii) history of the fortress as a unique example of fortification architecture and as monument of art; (iii) a political prison. No mention was made of its significance for the Romanov dynasty. The approved route, starting from the Ioann gates, was: Petrovsky gates, central square, commandant's house, mint, boathouse, cathedral, Zotov bastion and, as a culminating objective, the prison whose inmates had included Radishchev, the Decembrists, Dostoevskii and so on.[79]

A measure of the cathedral's new symbolism in post-Soviet Russia may be gauged through the revived fortunes of a part of the building neglected in Soviet times, its initial function glossed over. This is the purpose-built mausoleum of the grand dukes which, in the words of a recent guide, can now be added to 'the famous list of generally known buiding-monuments, building symbols in St Petersburg such as the Admiralty, the Hermitage, Smolny, the Mikhailovsky castle, the Peter-Paul cathedral, and many more'.[80] The project was commissioned by Alexander III, but the project lay dormant until 1896 and was completed only in 1909 (the architects were D. I. Grimm, A. O. Tomishko, and L. N. Benois). The mausoleum was dedicated to Alexander Nevsky. After 1917, of course, it was particularly unfavourably regarded, in view of the generally negative appraisal of the grand dukes of the late imperial period. As we have seen, it was declared to be 'of no historical or artistic interest' and all the brass objects, including grave plaques, were removed and disappeared. Following a period of use as a book store, it was converted to an exhibition hall in the 1960s. It is now being restored as part of the rehabilitation of Romanov history. In 1992, Grand Duke Vladimir Kirillovich was buried there. The funeral service actually took place in St Isaac's with Patriarch Aleksii on 29 April; the burial followed in the Peter Paul on 29 May. More recently, the remains considered to be those of Nicholas II were buried: his tomb, in a chapel to the right of the entrance, is hardly marked. In the 1990s the old chimes were restored, as was the angel, which was brought down to earth following an inspection in 1987, which revealed a fault in the mechanism on which the figure turns, and damage as a result of strong winds, acid rains, and a 'general deterioration' of the environment.[81]

[79] *Metodicheskoe posobie k ekskursii v Petropavlovskuiu krepost'*, Leningrad, 1980.
[80] Iu. V. Trubinov, *Velikokniazheskaia usypal'nitsa*, St Petersburg, 1997.
[81] Gendrikov, *Petropavlovskii sobor*, p. 28.

On 26 May 1991 a prayer of thanksgiving was said in the fortress of St Peter for Alexander Nevsky, Kseniia of St Petersburg and John of Kronstadt. On 12 June that year (Peter I's birthday), a service commemorating his foundation of St Petersburg was held on the same day as the referendum on restoring the city's name.[82] But apparently these services were held outside, rather than in the cathedral, which remains a museum.[83] Like several great Russian buildings, it was 'sui generis': only one clear (if not wholly successful) architectural imitation is known — the Church of SS Peter and Paul (1734–42) in the developing district of the Great Manufactory at Iaroslavl', whose industrialists seem to have wished to emphasize their up-to-dateness, and — since they produced sailcloth for the Russian fleet — their closeness to Peter's own concerns.[84]

[82] *Smena*, no. 132, 11 June 1991.
[83] See Avgustin, *Pravoslavnyi Peterburg*, p. 63.
[84] [See E. Dobrovol'skaia and B. Gnedovskii, *Iaroslavl', Tutaev*, Moscow, 1971, pp. 167–68. Editors' note.]

PART TWO

Bronze Tsars: Ivan the Terrible and Fedor Ivanovich in the Décor of Early Modern Guns

SERGEI BOGATYREV

VISUAL material was one of Lindsey Hughes's favourite subjects. Lindsey often used portraits, paintings and buildings as historical sources in her studies. An inspiring teacher, she also generously shared the results of her research with her students. In a course on Russian history, which I was fortunate to teach together with Lindsey at SSEES, she asked the students to compare two portraits of Russian royalty, those of Aleksei Mikhailovich (1672) and his son Peter the Great (1717). In one such class Lindsey told me that she was working on an article about those portraits. Published posthumously in 2008, her article deals with them as manifestations of the Russian 'monarchical myth'. In the article, Lindsey examines the symbolism and historical contexts of the portraits. She concludes that they serve the same purpose, to represent the power and dignity of the Russian rulers. At the same time, they reflect profound cultural changes in the conception of Russian rulership that occurred during the reign of Peter the Great.[1]

This paper is based on Lindsey Hughes's method of comparative analysis of royal portraiture. What follows is an interpretation of two images of Muscovite royalty on early modern guns. One of them can be found on a gun produced by the German master Karsten Middeldorp in 1559. As will be shown below, that image represents Ivan the Terrible. Another image, which depicts Tsar Fedor Ivanovich, is on the Tsar Cannon, which was cast by the renowned Russian gun founder Andrei Chokhov in 1586.

Sergei Bogatyrev is a Senior Lecturer in Early Russian History at UCL SSEES.
  This work would not have been possible without the help of Dorena Caroli, A. I. Filiushkin and I. A. Komarov who have provided me with copies of rare publications. I am also grateful to Ann Kleimola and Charles Halperin for their comments and suggestions. Special thanks are due to Martyn Rady for his help in translating German inscriptions.

[1] Lindsey Hughes, 'From Tsar to Emperor: Portraits of Aleksei and Peter I', in Valerie A. Kivelson and Joan Neuberger (eds), *Picturing Russia: Explorations in Visual Culture*, New Haven, CT, London, 2008, pp. 51–56.

Both images were made possible by a technological revolution in weapons production, casting in bronze. Previously guns were manufactured from wrought iron. Cast bronze guns involved smaller labour costs; they offered better military characteristics at less weight, though the cost of their material, bronze, was higher.[2] The new technology was brought to Muscovy by Italian masters in the late fifteenth century. The impact of foreign specialists on Muscovite artillery is usually studied in terms of Muscovy's technological backwardness and the pace of Muscovy's catching up with the West. However, historians of knowledge transfer challenge the view that knowledge and expertise were spread across the world through a simple process of diffusion. In the fifteenth and sixteenth centuries, there was a common international pool of gun makers working in Spain, France, England, Venice, the Ottoman Empire and Muscovy.[3] This is why in recent studies of technology exchange in the early modern world, Western triumphalism and local nationalism give way to a more complex picture of diverse contacts and mutual relations.[4] Thus, Yves Cohen, who studies Russian and Soviet technology, notes that Russia was not just an importer of Western technology. Thanks to a variety of institutional, human and material agents, imported knowledge was profoundly transformed in Russia. The Russian locale itself also changed as a result of knowledge transfer.[5]

Casting in bronze gave guns a new cultural dimension because the technology permitted decorations to be added to the gun barrel. Bronze guns thereby functioned not only as weapons, but also as means of political propaganda. In this paper I will study the images of tsars on the above-mentioned guns in a historical and cultural context. A word of caution about attribution is in order. The images under discussion are attributed in this work to the masters of corresponding guns, Karsten Middeldorp and Andrei Chokhov. These attributions are to an extent conventional because in the sixteenth century gun founders often employed professional sculptors and artists to execute decorations

---

[2] See Thomas Esper, 'Military Self-Sufficiency and Weapons Technology in Muscovite Russia', *Slavic Review*, 28, 1969, 2, pp. 185–208 (p. 188). On Muscovite artillery, see also B. A. Svetlosanov (ed.), *Istoriia otechestvennoi artillerii*, 1, Moscow, 1959; Richard Hellie, *Enserfment and Military Change in Muscovy*, Chicago, IL, 1971, pp. 151–57; Gustave Alef, 'Muscovite Military Reforms in the Second Half of the Fifteenth Century', *Forschungen zur Osteuropäischen Geschichte*, 18, 1973, pp. 73–108; Vladimir Volkov, *Voiny i voiska Moskovskogo gosudarstva*, Moscow, 2004, pp. 427–37; Carol B. Stevens, *Russia's Wars of Succession, 1460–1730*, London, 2007, pp. 47–48.

[3] Gábor Ágoston, *Guns for the Sultan: Military Power and the Weapons Industry in the Ottoman Empire*, Cambridge, 2005, pp. 46–47.

[4] Susan Gross Solomon, 'Circulation of Knowledge and the Russian Locale', *Kritika*, 9, 2008, 1, pp. 9–26 (pp. 13, 18).

[5] For a review of Cohen's published works and announcement of his forthcoming publications, see Solomon, 'Circulation', pp. 18–19.

on barrels. Whether Middeldorp and Chokhov worked on their images alone or in collaboration with somebody else, their barrels are important but often overlooked sources on the representation and perception of the Muscovite monarchy.

I

In the sixteenth century, both in the West and in Muscovy, gun décor often included various animalistic, floral and anthropomorphic motifs. The latter were especially typical of German masters, who decorated their guns with images of rulers.[6] In line with this tradition, the German master Karsten Middeldorp cast a gun called the 'Lion' (also known as the 'Lion of Reval', 2,375 kg) in 1559. The barrel was commissioned by the city council of Reval (Tallinn). In 1800, together with other cannon, Middeldorp's gun was removed from Reval to St Petersburg where it is now kept in the Artillery Museum.[7]

The iconographic programme of the barrel was defined by the commissioner, as becomes apparent from the inscription on the gun:

> A Council of Reval had named me the 'Lion',
> to tear apart his enemies
> should they not wish to live in peace.
> Karsten Middeldorp cast me in the year 1559,
> that is true.[8]

The décor of the cannon develops the themes outlined in the inscription. Thus, we can see the great and small coats of arms of Reval and a lion on the barrel. There is also a sculptural image of a human head at the rear of the barrel (Fig. 1). The depicted person can be identified with the help of the reference to an enemy in the inscription and the production date, 1559. The enemy of Reval was then Ivan the Terrible. After the beginning of the Livonian war Ivan's troops reached the suburbs of Reval in September 1558, but they failed to take the city. Muscovy and Livonia concluded a truce in early 1559. Both parties used this pause' to build up their military strength before military operations resumed in the autumn of 1559.[9]

---

[6] Heinrich Müller, *Deutsche Bronzegeschützrohre, 1400–1750*, Berlin, 1968, p. 149.

[7] The Military-Historical Museum of Artillery, Engineer and Signal Corps, no. 09/27.

[8] DEN LOWEN EIN RADT LET // NOMEN MICH VAN REVEL DAT // TO SPALDE ICH ERE FIENDE // SOL DE DAR NICHT WOLLEN // DAT SE IM FREDE LEVEN SOL//LEN ANNO 1559 IAR GOET // MI KARSTEN MIDDEL//DORP DAT IS WAR. N. E. Brandenburg, *Istoricheskii katalog S-Peterburgskogo Artilleriiskogo muzeia*, 3 *Prilozhenie*, St Petersburg, 1889, no. 87, pp. 64–65 (checked *de visu* against the original inscription).

[9] *Polnoe sobranie russkikh letopisei*, 13 (hereafter, PSRL), Moscow, 2000, p. 312; Alexander Filjushkin, *Ivan the Terrible: A Military History*, London, 2008, pp. 166–68.

FIGURE 1: Portrait of Ivan IV on the 'Lion of Reval' cannon by Karsten
Middeldorp of Lübeck (1559)
The Artillery Museum, St Petersburg. Author's photo

Commissioning the gun from Middeldorp was thus part of strengthening the defence of Reval in anticipation of new Muscovite attacks. The city also ordered a number of guns from the renowned local master Kort (Cordt, Cort, Korth) Hartmann (active 1544–70), including the 'Red Lion' (1559) and the 'Bitter Death' (1560), now also in the Artillery museum in St Petersburg.[10] The guns commissioned by the city are decorated with politically charged symbols. Reval obviously wished to represent two sides of the unfolding conflict in the décor of their cannon. The 'Bitter Death' features a figure of a city councillor (*Ratmann*) holding the coat of arms of Reval in his hand. The *Ratmann* on Hartmann's gun symbolizes the elective municipal authority of Reval, whereas the head on Middeldorp's barrel represents the autocratic power of the city's enemy, the tsar of Muscovy. This is why the image on Middeldorp's gun features several symbols of Muscovite royalty (on which, see below). A convergence of evidence, including the inscription on the barrel, the historical context of its production and the symbolism of Middeldorp's sculptural portrait indicates that the master depicted Ivan the Terrible.[11]

Karsten Middeldorp was from Lübeck, as evidenced by an inscription on a bell cast by the master for a church in Denmark. Three bells manufactured by Middeldorp between 1548 and 1554 have survived in Denmark.[12] John Lind has noticed that these bells can be found in churches scattered across the country. Lind has thus suggested that Middeldorp received orders from different clients, including the citizens of Reval, while working from Lübeck.[13] The fact that Middeldorp's name does not appear in the city registry of Reval seems to corroborate Lind's suggestion that the master worked from Lübeck.[14]

---

[10] L. Anting, *Tallinskie oruzheiniki i ognestrel'noe oruzhie XIV–XVI vekov*, Tallinn, 1967, pp. 37–39. Kort Hartmann and his son Hinrich also took orders for bells. Two of their bells, which were commissioned for churches in Finland, can be seen now in the National Museum in Helsinki: Kort's bell of 1554 and Hinrich's one of 1572. The former is misdated in the museum tag to c. 1590. One of Hinrich's bells (1586) is still hanging on the City Hall of Tallinn.

[11] Recently several scholars have independently identified Middeldorp's image as a portrait of Ivan IV. V. M. Krylov et al. (eds), *The Military Historical Museum of Artillery, Engineer and Signal Corps: History and Collection*, St Petersburg, 2004, p. 4; Sergei Bogatyrev, 'Lestnitsa v nebo: Simvolika vlasti Ivana Groznogo', *Rodina*, 12, 2004, pp. 9–13 (pp. 9, 12); K. V. Shmelev, 'Ob izobrazhenii "moskovita" na revel'skoi pushke epokhi Livonskoi voiny' <http://www.nwae.spb.ru/?o-600> [accessed February 2007]. Nothing supports L. Anting's interpretation of the image as the master's self-portrait (Anting, *Tallinskie oruzheiniki*, p. 35).

[12] Hans Nyholm, *Kirkeklokker i Danmark* <http://www.hikuin.dk/kirkeklokker/klokkestoebere_kronologisk2.htm> [accessed 9 November 2008].

[13] John Lind's email of 10 February 2007.

[14] Anting, *Tallinskie oruzheiniki*, p. 37. The website of the cannon tower Kiek in de Kökin (Tallinn) erroneously identifies Middeldorp as a local master <http://www.linnamuuseum.ee/kok/index.php?&id=171> [accessed 15 February 2009].

Lübeck was famous for its sculpture traditions which explains why Middeldorp's portrait is so individualized and expressive. The master demonstrates perfect command of three-dimensional space. At the same time, human figures on items produced by local masters from Reval often look flat, conventional and somewhat archaic for the middle of the sixteenth century.[15] A further study in the archives of Lübeck will probably yield more information about the master and the place of his work.

Middeldorp's barrel is an important example of cultural traffic in the Baltic region. Lübeck traditionally had close cultural contacts with Denmark, the Netherlands, as well as the German and Italian lands. However, in the sixteenth century the Lübeck economy stagnated.[16] The shrinking of local markets may explain why Middeldorp actively sought commissions from abroad, including Reval, in the late 1540s and 1550s.

Middeldorp's image is one of the earliest examples, if not the earliest, of revived interest in the figure of Ivan the Terrible in north-western Europe during the Livonian war. By the middle of the sixteenth century the Western tradition of depicting the ruler of Muscovy was still rather limited. The interest of Western artists in Muscovite royalty was stimulated by Sigismund Herberstein's missions to Russia in 1517 and 1526. Erhard Schoen of Nuremberg seems to be the first Western artist to create images of Muscovite royalty in the late 1520s. Schoen produced two woodcuts representing Vasilii III in profile, one half-length and another equestrian full-length (Fig. 2).[17] In both woodcuts, Vasilii's head, including his face and headgear, is executed almost identically. Schoen's prints are typical Renaissance representations of an 'exotic' ruler and hardly contain any reliable historical information. His Vasilii wears a combination of a fur-brimmed hat and a Western-type circlet with triangular rays all round (similar to the German *Zackenkrone* and the English heraldic 'antique crown'). Similar fanciful crowns also appear in many images of Muslim rulers in Sebastian Münster's *Cosmographia*.

---

[15] Compare images of noble men and women on Kort Hartmann's gun 'Bitter Death', Hinrich Hartmann's bell from Helsinki and in a fresco from the Castle of Turku (c. 1530) reproduced in Martti Puhakka (ed.), *Turun linna*, Vammala, 1999, p. 29.

[16] Alexander Cowan, 'Cultural Traffic in Lübeck and Danzig in the Sixteenth and Seventeenth Centuries', *Scandinavian Journal of History*, 28, 2003, 3–4, pp. 175–85 (p. 180).

[17] Max Geisberg, *The German Single-Leaf Woodcut: 1500–1550*, revised and edited by Walter L. Strauss, 4, New York, 1974, nos. 1235 G. 1287, 1236 G. 1288. See also Ursula Mende, *Westeuropäische Bildzeugnisse zu Russland und Polen bis 1700: ein Beitrag zur historischen Bildkunde*, Bamberg, 1968, pp. 6–13; [A. L. Khoroshkevich], 'Izdaniia "Zapisok o Moskovii"', in Sigizmund Gerbershtein [Sigismund Herberstein], *Zapiski o Moskovii*, Moscow, 1988, pp. 355–78.

FIGURE 2: Portrait of Ivan IV by Hans Weygel (1563), based on the portrait of Vasilii III by Erhard Schoen (late 1520s). From D. Rovinskii, *Dostovernye portrety Moskovskikh gosudarei Ivana III, Vasiliia Ivanovicha i Ivana IV Groznogo i posol'stva ikh vremeni*, St Petersburg, 1882

A crown with rays has been a symbol of rulership in Western art since the classical period. Circlets with triangular rays can be seen in some portraits of Roman emperors, for example, on the coins of Claudius II Gothicus (268–70 AD) and Aurelian (270–75 AD). At the same time, there is no reason to believe that the headgear of the Muscovite ruler was deliberately reminiscent of a Western crown. It is true that Ivan IV wears a crown with rays in many miniatures in the *Illustrated Chronicle Compilation* (*Litsevoi letopisnyi svod*, 1570s–early 1580s). However, these miniatures are not reliable because they had been heavily influenced by Western prints.[18]

Some scholars of Muscovite regalia tend to accept Schoen's images uncritically and even use them for reconstructing the crown of Muscovite rulers.[19] Schoen's image is obviously a misinterpretation of the design of the Cap of Monomakh, which combines elaborate metalwork and fur brim. Such combinations of metal and fur in headgear was unusual for Westerners and made them think that the Muscovite ruler was wearing a fur hat and a metal crown on his head.

In 1547 another artist, Augustin Hirschvogel, who worked, among other places, in Nuremberg and Vienna, prepared an engraved portrait of Vasilii III (Fig. 3). Part of his series of prints depicting various rulers, Hirschvogel's image was intended as an illustration for verses glorifying Herberstein.[20] Unlike Schoen, Hirschvogel did give his Vasilii some features which can be considered Muscovite, like a cone-shape cap with fur brim (no fanciful rays), a long garment with a fur neckpiece, and boots with curved toe-caps without heels. Hirschvogel's Vasilii is sitting on a throne; a heraldic shield leaning against the throne bears an image of a horseman beating a dragon. This is obviously an attempt to reproduce the famous Muscovite symbol (on its meaning, see below). Hirschvogel's rendering of the symbol suggests that his image was influenced by Herberstein, who describes in his travel account a Muscovite seal with a naked horseman (*homo nudus*). In accordance with Herberstein, the master also depicted the Muscovite horseman naked.[21] Western artists, however, did not always closely follow Herberstein. Thus, despite his account of Vasilii III shaving his beard in order to please his young wife, both Schoen and Hirschvogel consistently pictured Vasilii III bearded.

---

[18] Iu. A. Nevolin, 'Novoe o kremlevskikh khudozhnikakh-miniatiuristakh XVI v. i sostave biblioteki Ivana Groznogo', *Sovetskie arkhivy*, 1982, 1, pp. 68–70.

[19] N. V. Zhilina, *Shapka Monomakha: Istoriko-kul'turnoe i tekhnologicheskoe issledovanie*, Moscow, 2001, pp. 146, 147, 158; Iakob Ul'fel'dt, *Puteshestvie v Rossiiu*, Moscow, 2002, p. 428, note 231 (commentary by A. L. Khoroshkevich).

[20] D. Rovinskii, *Dostovernye portrety Moskovskikh gosudarei Ivana III, Vasiliia Ivanovicha i Ivana IV Groznogo i posol'stva ikh vremeni*, St Petersburg, 1882, no. 7.

[21] Gerbershtein, *Zapiski*, pp. 225, 351 note 801.

Ruſſorum Rex & Dominus ſum,iure paterní
Sanguinis, imperij titulos a n mine,quauis
Mercatus prece vel precio,nec legibus vllis
Subditus alterius,ſed CHRISTO credulus vel
Emendicatos alijs,aſpernor honores.

FIGURE 3: Portrait of Vasilii III by Augustin Hirschvogel (1547). From D. Rovinskii, *Dostovernye portrety Moskovskikh gosudarei Ivana III, Vasiliia Ivanovicha i Ivana IV Groznogo i posol′stva ikh vremeni*, St Petersburg, 1882
© *British Library Board. All Rights Reserved (L.22.a.18). Reproduced by permission*

Schoen and Hirschvogel set the standards for depicting the ruler of Muscovy in Western Europe. Their vision of Muscovite royalty was based on a mixture of exoticism and elements of Western court culture, like a crown with rays and a heraldic pattern. Typical facial features of Western 'portraits' of the Muscovite ruler included a beard and a prominent nose. Schoen's and Hirschvogel's prints were very influential, although for different reasons. Hirschvogel's image became well known due to the close connections between the artist and Herberstein (both of them also worked with the same printer in Vienna). Hirschvogel's 'portrait' was reproduced in numerous editions of Herberstein's account of Muscovy from 1549. Schoen's woodcut gained popularity for political reasons. Ivan IV's military victories at the beginning of the Livonian war generated numerous *Flugschriften* and prints devoted to the fearsome ruler of Muscovy.[22] Some of them capitalized on Schoen's prints. The best known example of this trend is the portrait of Ivan IV printed by Hans Weygel in Nuremberg 1563, which is in fact a straightforward and flat reproduction of Schoen's image (Fig. 2).[23]

Like Weygel, Middeldorp relied on Schoen's prints, but in a very specific way. Middeldorp obviously borrowed the chequered pattern of the collar and the handlebar moustache of the Muscovite ruler from Schoen's 'portrait' of Vasilii III. Where Middeldorp differs from Shoen is the striking historical accuracy of the ceremonial hat. N. E. Brandenburg misinterpreted the hat in Middedorp's image as an Eastern turban.[24] In fact this is a very early and in many respects unique representation of the Cap of Monomakh.

The Cap of Monomakh was a major instrument of legitimization of the power of Muscovite rulers. According to the legend, it was a gift from a Byzantine emperor to Vladimir Monomakh of Kiev (r. 1113–25), but the actual date and place of its production remain unclear. It is usually dated to the fourteenth century, but it is possible that it was compiled under Vasilii III (r. 1505–30) of different earlier components.[25] It was precisely the reign of Vasilii III when the cap became a symbol of continuity of power from Constantinople to Kiev and to Moscow. The cap was demonstrated to Herberstein who left us the earliest description of it. He does not say whether he saw the hat during his

---

[22] Andreas Kappeler, *Ivan Groznyj im Spiegel der ausländischen Druckschriften seiner Zeit. Ein Beitrag zur Geschichte des westlichen Russlandbildes*, Bern and Frankfurt, 1972.

[23] Kappeler, *Ivan Groznyj*, p. 274; Gerbershtein, *Zapiski*, pp. 214, 373–74; S. P. Orlenko (ed.), *Rossiia i Britaniia. K 450-letiiu ustanovleniia diplomaticheskikh otnoshenii*, Moscow, 2003, p. 35.

[24] Brandenburg, *Istoricheskii katalog*, 3 *Prilozhenie*, no. 87, p. 64.

[25] Zhilina, *Shapka*; Nancy Shields Kollmann, 'The Cap of Monomakh', in Kivelson, *Picturing Russia*, pp. 38–41; Sergei Bogatyrev, 'Ceremonial Headgear and Dynastic Politics under Ivan the Terrible'. Paper delivered at the BASEES conference at Fitzwilliam College, Cambridge, 29 March 2009.

first (1517) or second (1526) visit to Moscow, but his account confirms that the headgear surely existed by 1526. In 1547, the Cap of Monomakh became a central element in the ritual of Ivan IV's coronation as tsar.

The design of the cap changed over the course of time, and we know little about how the Cap of Monomakh actually looked in the sixteenth century. Foreign descriptions of the cap, including that given by Herberstein, are very short.[26] Visual material is not a great help either. The earliest known depiction of the cap can be found in the panels of the throne of Ivan the Terrible in the Dormition Cathedral of the Moscow Kremlin (1551), which illustrate the legend about obtaining the cap from Byzantium. However, these Muscovite renderings are very conventional.[27] So, as we have seen, are sixteenth-century Western images of the Muscovite crown.

In this context, Middeldorp's representation of the Cap of Monomakh becomes an important historical source because the master reproduced many details of the cap as exactly as the technology of casting allowed. We can see over half of the total surface of the hat in the image. The back part of the hat is at the place where the sculpture joins the back side of the barrel (the so-called cascable plate). The headgear has three parts: fur brim, semi-spherical middle part and a tip. This composition fully corresponds to that of the Cap of Monomakh which can be seen now in the Armoury of the Kremlin. Both caps have fur brims (Fig. 4, section 1). The middle part of the hat in Middeldorp's sculpture is divided by recesses into several segments. The master thereby rendered the structure of the Cap of Monomakh, which is composed of segmental plates covered with filigree (Fig. 4, section 2).

The tip of the hat in Middeldorp's portrait has a round base, almond-shaped elements and a pommel on top of them. Similar components can be detected in the Cap of Monomakh. The round base corresponds to the cup crowning the plates of the Cap of Monomakh (Fig. 4, section 3); the almond-shape parts obviously represent the precious stones and pearls on top of the hat from the Kremlin (Fig. 4, section 4); the pommel denotes the actual hat's holder for a cross (Fig. 4, section 5).

We can only speculate where Middeldorp received such detailed information about the actual design of the Muscovite cap from. One possible source is his clients from Reval. He could also have learned

---

[26] Gerbershtein, *Zapiski*, pp. 82–83; Lloyd E. Berry and Robert O. Crummey (eds), *Rude and Barbarous Kingdom: Russia in the Accounts of Sixteenth-Century English Voyagers*, Madison, WI, 1968, p. 55.
[27] I. M. Sokolova, *Tron tsaria Ivana Groznogo v Uspenskom sobore*, Moscow, 2006, pp. 44, 45, 47, 50, 55.

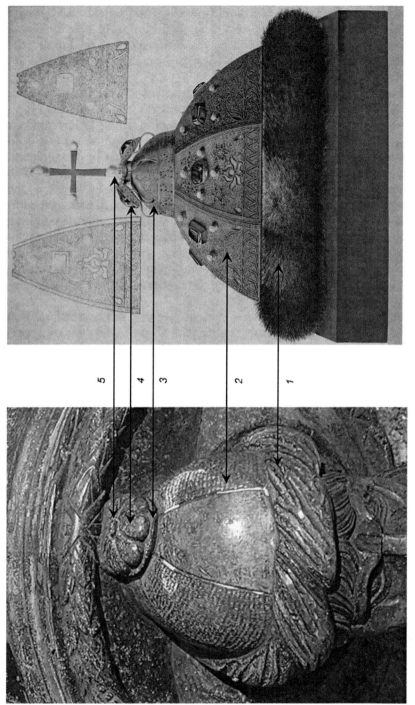

FIGURE 4: Ceremonial headgear: Sculpture on the 'Lion of Reval' by Middeldorp and the Cap of Monomakh

about the cap from other German founders who frequented Muscovy. Usually trained as engineers and designers, they were able to give a professional account of how the Cap of Monomakh looked. Finally, the possibility that Middeldorp visited Moscow himself cannot be ruled out either.

Missing from Middeldorp's image is the cross which crowns the real Cap of Monomakh. The dating of the present cross is unclear. N. V. Zhilina dates it to the thirteenth century, but I. A. Bobrovnitskaia seems to be closer to the truth when she writes that the cross should be dated to the seventeenth century.[28] It is likely that in the sixteenth century the cross was not a permanent feature of the headgear. The images on Ivan IV's throne, which illustrate the legend about how the cap was obtained from Byzantium, present the cap both with and without a cross. The cross appears in the scene of coronation, something which is quite natural given the religious character of the ceremony. In other situations, like the scene of transporting the cap in a ship, the cross is missing.[29] Even in the Muscovite image of Tsar Fedor on the Tsar Cannon (on which more later), the ruler wears the Cap of Monomakh with no cross.

On the basis of Middeldorp's 'portrait' we can safely conclude that in the middle of the sixteenth century the Cap of Monomakh generally had the same design as that which we can see today. At the same time, such components as the cross and the massive precious stones on the hat's plates are missing from Middeldorp's image; the design of the fur brim and the tip of the cap in his sculpture look slightly different in comparison with the cap from the Kremlin (Fig. 4). It is hard to say whether these differences reflect artistic conventionality or the evolution of the actual cap's design.

Apart from the headgear, the master made a reference to another element of Muscovite ceremonial dress. The complex collar around the head's neck is highly reminiscent of *barmy*, another item of Muscovite royal regalia which was allegedly received together with the cap from Byzantium. The head adorning Middeldorp's barrel thus represents Ivan the Terrible in full regalia.

Unlike the ceremonial gear, the face of Middeldorp's image presents greater problems for historical analysis. It is of course tempting to see it as a realistic portrait of Ivan the Terrible. Some traits of the image, like hair divided in the middle, are highly individual and are not attested by any other images of the tsar. However, it is important to remember that we have no authentic portraits of Ivan the Terrible.

[28] Zhilina, *Shapka*, p. 113; I. A. Bobrovnitskaia, *Regalii rossiiskikh gosudarei*, Moscow, 2004, p. 6.
[29] Sokolova, *Tron*, pp. 50, 55.

Sixteenth-century Muscovite images of Ivan lack individual facial features. Miniatures of the official chronicle represent Ivan through a set of conventional symbols typical of medieval art. Thus, the appearance of a beard indicates changes in his age (young Ivan is depicted clean shaven). Changes in Ivan's status as a monarch are indicated through different designs of his headgear. A princely hat, similar to that depicted by Hirschvogel, corresponds to the title of grand prince, while the above-mentioned Western-type crown with rays symbolizes the title of tsar which Ivan assumed in 1547. Various modes of communication between the tsar and his courtiers, like order or discussion, are represented with various gestures of the tsar's hands. However, his face always remains the same and in fact does not differ from thousands of other faces appearing in the numerous chronicle miniatures.[30] The famous portrait of Ivan which is now kept in Copenhagen was obviously painted long after his death, probably in the seventeenth century, and still bears many features of conventional Muscovite icon painting.[31] Even the anthropological reconstruction of Ivan's face carried out by M. M. Gerasimov is based on a method that is not entirely free from artistic imagination.[32] Without reliable points of reference, it is hard to verify the accuracy of Middeldorp's rendering of Ivan's face. However, his 'portrait' is the only known contemporary sculptural image of the tsar.

II

In Muscovy, the first master to use royal imagery in gun décor was the famous gun maker Andrei Chokhov. He was active from 1567/68 to 1628/29, which means that he managed to survive the turmoil of

---

[30] A. V. Artsikhovskii, *Drevnerusskie miniatiury kak istoricheskii istochnik*, Tomsk, Moscow, 2004, pp. 164–73; V. V. Morozov, 'Ivan Groznyi na miniatiurakh Tsarstvennoi knigi', in *Drevnerusskoe iskusstvo. Rukopisnaia kniga*, 3, Moscow, 1983, pp. 232–40; S. O. Shmidt, *Rossiiskoe gosudarstvo v seredine XVI stoletiia: Tsarskii arkhiv i litsevye letopisi vremeni Ivana Groznogo*, Moscow, 1984, pp. 216–55; O. Iu. Klautova, 'Zhest v drevnerusskoi literature i ikonopisi XI–XIII vv. K postanovke voprosa', in *Trudy Otdela drevnerusskoi literatury*, 46, St Petersburg, 1993, pp. 256–69.

[31] Frank Kämpfer, 'Die "parsuna" Ivans IV. in Kopenhagen — Originalporträt oder historisches Bild?', in Daniel Clarke Waugh (ed.), *Essays in Honor of A. A. Zimin*, Columbus, OH, 1985, pp. 187–204.

[32] See *Mikhail Gerasimov, The Face Finder*, trans. Alan Houghton Brodrick, London, 1971; M. M. Gerasimova, K. M. Gerasimova, Mikhail Gerasimov, *Ia ishchu litsa. O vosstanovlenii vneshnego oblika istoricheskikh lits*, Moscow, 2007, pp. 137–49 (reconstruction of Ivan IV's face), 149–57 (Fedor Ivanovich's face). Gerasimov's follower, Sergei Nikitin, who has recently reconstructed the faces of Muscovite royal women, acknowledges that his method includes the 'animation' of a portrait (*odushevlenie portreta*). Natal´ia Davydova, 'Sergei Nikitin: "Chtoby poluchilos´ zhivoe litso, nuzhno iz sebia polovinu krovi vykachat´"', *Izvestiia*, 14 August 2008, p. 9.

the Oprichnina and the Time of Troubles. Thanks to his expertise, Chokhov's service was requested by practically all Russian rulers from Ivan the Terrible to the False Dmitrii I to Mikhail Romanov. Like his Western colleagues, Chokhov cast both guns and bells. Two bells bearing the name of the master have survived in the Moscow Kremlin: 'Glukhoi' (1620/21) and 'Reut' (1621/22). A number of other bells have been attributed to Chokhov on the basis of circumstantial evidence.[33]

Chokhov's main specialization, however, was gun making, as becomes apparent from the inscription on his 'Reut' bell which identifies the master as 'gun founder' (*pushechnoi litets*). He began his career as an apprentice to the renowned German master at the tsar's service Kashpir (Caspar) Ganusov in the late 1560s. By 1575 Chokhov's apprenticeship was completed and he acted as an independent master. In 1589/90 he already had his own apprentices. In the 1590s Chokhov became the leading specialist of the Artillery Office (Pushechnyi prikaz) with the highest annual salary of 30 rubles (the administrative head of the Office received 20 rubles).[34] Inscriptions on Chokhov's gun reflect his leading position in the profession by systematically referring to him as *master*.[35]

Chokhov was much indebted to the German tradition of gun founding. He picked up, among other things, the Western practice of decorating gun barrels with floral motifs and political symbols. The earliest of his known guns, a piece of 1567/68 which he produced during his apprenticeship, already bore images of plants and the double-headed eagle.[36] The double-headed eagle was used on the seals of the princes of Moscow long before Chokhov, only beginning to appear on gun barrels in the 1560s. Muscovites borrowed the practice of depicting heraldic emblems on guns from Poland and Lithuania, apparently

---

[33] I. D. Kostina, 'Kolokola Andreia Chokhova', in S. A. Beliaev and I. A. Vorotnikova, *Pravoslavnye sviatyni Moskovskogo Kremlia v istorii i kul'ture Rossii*, Moscow, 2006, pp. 277–79; E. L. Nemirovskii, *Andrei Chokhov, okolo 1545–1629*, Moscow, 1982, pp. 70–81. On Russian bells in general, see Edward V. Williams, *The Bells of Russia: History and Technology*, Princeton, NJ, 1985.

[34] Nemirovskii, *Andrei Chokhov*, pp. 67, 68.

[35] The earliest survived gun with an inscription identifying Chokhov as *master* is a mortar commissioned by the first False Dmitri in 1605. V. P. Vyshenkov et al. (eds), *Katalog material'noi chasti otechestvennoi artillerii*, [1], Leningrad, 1961, p. 76, no. 106. According to a survey of Pskov in 1699, Chokhov was also called *master* in an inscription on the gun 'Egup', which he produced in 1586/87. Nemirovskii identifies the 'Egup' with Chokhov's mortar of 1586/87 from the Artillery museum. This identification is questionable because, contrary to Nemirovskii, there are significant differences between inscriptions on two guns. The inscription on the 'Egup', as it is quoted in the survey, calls the gun *pishal'*. The inscription on the piece from the Artillery museum uses *pushka* instead of *pishal'*, does not call Chokhov *master* and does not mention the name 'Egup'. Nemirovskii, *Andrei Chokhov*, p. 48; Vyshenkov, *Katalog*, p. 76, no. 105.

[36] *Dopolneniia k Aktam istoricheskim, sobrannyia i izdannyia Arkheograficheskoiu komissieiu*, 5, St Petersburg, 1853, p. 300.

through Ruthenian masters captured by Ivan the Terrible after the taking of Polotsk in 1563.[37]

Chokhov took the tradition of using political symbols in gun décor much further by including images of royalty. An anthropomorphic image appeared on a Muscovite barrel cast by certain Ignatii as early as 1499/1500, but it was probably a mere decoration deprived of any political meaning.[38] By contrast, human figures on Chokhov's guns symbolize power, dignity and military might. In 1586 he cast the magnificent Tsar Cannon (Tsar'-pushka, 38,400 kg) which is decorated with a 'portrait' of Tsar Fedor Ivanovich (Figs 5, 6).[39] Later Chokhov created images of classic personages, apparently under the influence of the East Slavic adaptations of Guido de Columnis's *History of the Destruction of Troy*.[40] Adaptations of Columnis's narrative provided a cultural model for sixteenth-century monarchs.[41] This may explain why the classic figures executed by Chokhov have attributes of royal power (crown, throne, staff, orb).

There is still much uncertainty as to why Chokhov manufactured the massive Tsar Cannon. Most historians believe that it had a military purpose, though they disagree about what type of missile it could fire.[42] If the Tsar Cannon was created as a weapon, by all standards it was hopelessly obsolete for the 1580s. In Europe the production of gigantic pieces was abandoned by the beginning of the sixteenth century. The

---

[37] The earliest known Muscovite gun with the double-headed eagle was produced by the Ruthenian master Bogdan in 1562/3. See A. P. Lebedianskaia, 'Ocherki iz istorii pushechnogo proizvodstva v Moskovskoi Rusi', in *Sbornik issledovanii i materialov Artilleriiskogo istoricheskogo muzeia Krasnoi Armii*, 1, Leningrad and Moscow, 1940, pp. 77–78; Vyshenkov, *Katalog*, p. 118, no. 202.

[38] A. N. Lobin, 'Pushechnaia izba i proizvodstvo artillerii v 1480–1500-e gg.', in *Trudy Kafedry istorii Rossii s drevneishikh vremen do XX veka [Sankt-Peterburgskogo gos. universiteta]*, 1, St Petersburg, 2006, p. 161.

[39] The image is identified with the following inscription: 'By the grace of God Tsar and Great Prince Fedor Ivanovich, Sovereign and Autocrat of All Great Russia'. Nemirovskii, *Andrei Chokhov*, pp. 40–41.

[40] 'Troil' (Troilus), 1590; 'Akhilles' (Achilles), 1617. See Nemirovskii, *Andrei Chokhov*, pp. 61–63; 82–89; L. K. Makovskaia, 'Artilleriiskie orudiia XV–XVII vv. — pamiatniki kul'tury Moskovskoi Rusi', in *Materialy mezhdunarodnoi nauchnoi konferentsii 'Victoria, Gloria, Fama', posviashchennoi 300-letiiu Voenno-istoricheskogo muzeia artillerii, inzhenernykh voisk i voisk sviazi*, 4, St Petersburg, 2003, pp. 52–70 (pp. 58–59); I. A. Komarov, 'O khudozhestvennom oformlenii russkikh bronzovykh artilleriiskikh stvolov kontsa XV–XVII vekov', in *Dekorativno-prikladnoe iskusstvo* (Gos. istoriko-kul'turnyi muzei-zapovednik 'Moskovskii Kreml'', Materialy i issledovaniia, 9), Moscow, 1993, pp. 122–37 (pp. 130–33).

[41] Susan Doran (ed.), *Henry VIII: Man and Monarch*, London, 2009, p. 71, no. 60.

[42] N. Gordeev, *Tsar'-pushka*, Moscow, 1969, pp. 14, 16 (special type of mortar for firing case shot); Nemirovskii, *Andrei Chokhov*, pp. 36–47 (mortar, fired cannon balls); G. M. Zakharikov, 'O boevom naznachenii Tsar'-pushki', in N. K. Gavriushkin and A. A. Kuzin (eds), *Pamiatniki nauki i tekhniki, 1984*, Moscow, 1986, pp. 31–45 (siege weapon for destroying fortress walls with stone cannon balls); M. Portnov, *Tsar'-pushka i Tsar'-kolokol*, Moscow, 1990, p. 21 (special type of cannon close to mortars, fired case shot).

FIGURE 5: Image of Fedor Ivanovich on the Tsar Cannon by Andrei
Chokhov (1586)
The Moscow Kremlin. Author's photo

Ottomans manufactured large pieces for a slightly longer period, but
in very limited numbers.[43] The development of Muscovite gigantic
artillery largely followed this common pattern. A huge piece (16,380 kg)
was cast by the Italian master Paolo (Pavlin) Dubosis in Moscow in
1488.[44] In the middle of the 1550s, large guns were also manufactured
by Chokhov's tutor Kashpir Ganusov (19,657 kg, 1554) and the master
Stepan Petrov (16,708 kg, 1555). The production dates allow one to link
the appearance of these guns with Ivan IV's triumph over Kazan' in
1552 and with the end of the dynastic crisis of 1553. By commissioning
these super guns Ivan celebrated his military victory and the restoration
of stability in his realm. In this respect it is important that Ganusov's
gun featured an inscription which mentioned the name of the tsar

---

[43] Ágoston, *Guns*, p. 196.
[44] See *Ioasafovskaia letopis'*, Moscow, 1957, p. 126; PSRL, 18, Moscow, 2007, p. 272
(Simeonovskaia); PSRL, 8, St Petersburg, 1859, p. 217 (Voskresenskaia); PSRL, 12, Moscow,
1965, p. 219 note 'ch' (Illustrated Chronicle Compilation); PSRL, 26, Moscow, Leningrad,
1959, p. 279 (Vologodsko-Permskaia); Alef, 'Muscovite Military Reforms', p. 80; Nemirovskii,
Andrei Chokhov, pp. 37–38.

FIGURE 6: Image of Fedor Ivanovich on the Tsar Cannon. Outline. Adapted from A. V. Viskovatov, *Istoricheskoe opisanie odezhdy i vooruzheniia rossiiskih voisk s risunkami, sostavlennoe po vysochaishemu poveleniiu*, St Petersburg, 1899, part 1, plate 2

and his long title, including his newly conquered possession, Kazan'.
Ganusov's and Petrov's guns, however, were not just show pieces. Ivan
the Terrible used them in his campaign against Polotsk in 1562–63.[45]

Why did the Muscovites revitalize the tradition of massive cannon
in the mid-1580s? Why did the Tsar Cannon remain unfinished,
making it unsuitable for firing?[46] Technological backwardness is
obviously irrelevant here because even such a critical observer as Giles
Fletcher highly praised Russian artillery during the 1580s.[47]

Like any powerful weapon, gigantic guns performed not only military but also political functions.[48] Under Fedor, artillery was actively
used during ceremonies associated with royal power.[49] Together with
Ganusov's and Petrov's pieces, the Tsar Cannon was put on public
display near the Frolovskie gates in Red Square (then called the Site of
Fire, *Pozhar*) as if to guard the fords over the Moskva river and the
entrance to the Kremlin. The three guns remained there until 1701
when Peter I ordered that Ganusov's and Petrov's barrels be recast
into new guns needed for the Northern war. Peter, however, saved
Chokhov's Tsar Cannon, as well as another mortar by the master,
which can now be seen in the Artillery museum.

It was important that the Muscovite super guns could be observed
by many people, including foreign diplomats visiting Moscow. Like the
large guns of Ivan the Terrible, the Tsar Cannon was commissioned
during the period of unrest which engulfed Moscow after the death of
Ivan in March 1584. The beginning of the reign of Ivan's son Fedor
was marred by two uprisings instigated by competing boyar factions.
During the first uprising in April 1584, the rebels tried to turn one of
the large guns (Ganusov's or Petrov's) against the Kremlin.[50] The
unrest of 1584 was followed by another upheaval in 1586. In this
context adding Chokhov's huge piece to the guns of Ivan the Terrible,
which guarded the royal residence in Moscow, symbolized the continuity of power in the dynasty and the (alleged) stability of Fedor's
regime.

The creation of the Tsar Cannon in 1586 also had a diplomatic
dimension. With Ivan the Terrible defeated in the Livonian war and
the tame Fedor on the throne, Polish-Lithuanian magnates believed

[45] Nemirovskii, *Andrei Chokhov*, pp. 13–14.
[46] The vent on the barrel remained undrilled; the barrel's interior was not fully cleaned
after casting. See Zakharikov, 'O boevom naznachenii', pp. 31, 44.
[47] Berry, *Rude and Barbarous Kingdom*, p. 186.
[48] Ágoston, *Guns*, p. 196.
[49] Jerome Horsey, 'The most solemne and magnificent coronacion of Pheodor Ivanowich,
Emperour of Russia . . .', in Edward A. Bond (ed.), *Russia at the Close of the Sixteenth Century*,
London, 1856, pp. 268–87 (p. 274).
[50] A. A. Zimin, *V kanun groznykh potriasenii: Predposylki pervoi krest'ianskoi voiny v Rossii*,
Moscow, 1986, pp. 113–16.

that the Russian tsar was not prepared to fight again. During negotiations about renewing a truce in 1586, Muscovite diplomats tried to dispel the dismissive perception of Fedor in Poland-Lithuania. According to them, the tsar was a mature (*dorodnyi*), sensible (*razumnyi*) and happy (*schastlivyi*) sovereign who governed his domains with his father's blessing; the tsar reigned himself and he was ready to stand against his enemies like his ancestors did; the number of his people had doubled because he was kind to them and generously paid their wages.[51] The huge piece produced by Chokhov was supposed to visualize the military might of the Russian tsar, which was questioned in Poland-Lithuania.

The Tsar Cannon was thus deliberately created to attract publicity. In this respect its iconographic programme, which features an equestrian figure of Tsar Fedor Ivanovich, becomes especially significant. Chokhov's 'portrait' of Fedor is based on the Byzantine iconography of a triumphant emperor and the Muscovite emblem of a horseman.[52] In her recent study of Russian political symbols, Magdolina Ágoston offers a balanced and inclusive interpretation of this emblem. A horseman was a symbol of grandeur, power and victory since antiquity. In the Middle Ages it was widely used in political imagery across Eastern and Central Europe. A horseman occasionally appeared in the seals of East Slavic princes, including Alexander Nevsky, since the thirteenth century. At the turn of the fifteenth century a horseman became a dominant motif in grand princely seals, probably under the influence of Lithuanian practice. This horseman usually has a crown, which is an attribute of a secular ruler, and lacks a halo. This means that the figure symbolizes not a saint, but a prince, something which is often corroborated by accompanying inscriptions. Sixteenth-century Muscovite sources systematically identify the equestrian figure on coins and seals as the ruling prince. There were many variants in the design of the horseman on seals and coins, including figures with a sabre, a spear and a falcon in hands, with and without a dragon under the horse. Starting from Ivan III, a horseman beating a dragon became a symbol of the ruling prince defeating the Devil.[53] As we have seen above, Western artists also linked the image of a horseman with the prince of Moscow in the first half of the sixteenth century.

[51] L. E. Morozova, *Dva tsaria: Fedor i Boris*, Moscow, 2001, p. 93. See also Zimin, *V kanun*, pp. 142–43.

[52] Frank Kämpfer, *Das russische Herrscherbild von den Anfängen bis zu Peter dem Grossen: Studien zur Entwicklung politischer Ikonographie im byzantinischen Kulturkreis*, Recklinghausen, 1978, p. 199.

[53] M. Agoshton [Magdolina Ágoston], *Velikokniazheskaia pechat' 1497 g.: K istorii formirovaniia russkoi gosudarstvennoi simvoliki*, Moscow, 2005, pp. 318–75.

Chokhov's rendering of Fedor is distinctively Muscovite in style. Fedor's face and body are turned in three quarters, but his horse is depicted in profile. Anatomically unrealistic, Fedor's posture represents royal majesty. His figure is less dynamic than the horseman on Muscovite royal seals. Thus, the horseman's cloak on seals is dramatically twisted in the wind, whereas Fedor's cloak is only slightly bagging. The tsar's long ceremonial robe, rather unsuitable for riding, emphasizes his dignity. The figure of the tsar is thus solemn and majestic. However, his horse is galloping, which is unusual for Byzantine royal iconography, but typical of images of holy warriors slaying dragons or heathens.[54] In Chokhov's 'portrait', the swiftly moving horse counterbalances the static figure of the rider by adding internal dynamism to the whole composition. Like the Muscovite horseman, Fedor is riding to the right from the viewer. In Muscovite iconographic tradition, this direction of movement is associated with the commencing and active phase of action.[55] Fedor is moving towards the gun's muzzle, i.e. in the shooting direction. His figure thereby echoes the potential power of the massive gun. The charge of the tsar is unstoppable like the Tsar Cannon projectile.

Fedor's regalia mark his royal status. He wears the Cap of Monomakh, which is shown very schematically, very much like Ivan IV's princely cap in the miniatures of his official chronicle. For some reason, as in Middeldorp's image, Fedor's cap has no cross. In his right hand Fedor holds a sceptre. This may seem a departure from the traditional representation of the Muscovite horseman who, according to standard interpretation, holds a spear in his right hand. Ágoston, however, plausibly argues that in Muscovite seals the horseman beats the dragon not with a spear, but with a staff or a long sceptre. According to Metropolitan Zosima, the sceptre was the prince's invincible weapon for defeating the enemies of God.[56] In Byzantium, staffs of various lengths symbolized the executive authority and jurisdiction of the emperor. A short version of the royal staff called *narthex* was used during the ceremony of coronation. In sixteenth-century Muscovy it became known as sceptre (*skipetr*). Ivan IV started using a sceptre after his coronation in 1547. Frank Kämpfer thinks that Muscovites borrowed a short staff from Byzantium through books and pictures whereas a long staff (*posokh*) came to Moscow from Novgorod.[57] However, the sceptre was not originally mentioned in the legend about

---

[54] Kämpfer, *Das russische Herrscherbild*, p. 199.
[55] Agoshton, *Velikokniazheskaia pechat'*, p. 369.
[56] Ibid., p. 367.
[57] Frank Kämpfer, '*Dikanikion — Posox*: Some Considerations on the Royal Staff in Muscovy', in *Forschungen zur Osteuropäischen Geschichte*, 24, 1978, pp. 9–19.

imperial regalia received in Rus´ from Byzantium. It is possible that the sceptre was introduced into Muscovite royal ritual as a result of dynastic competition between Ivan the Terrible and Gustav Wasa of Sweden who used a sceptre during his coronation. In Muscovy, the sceptre was used for the first time in the coronation ritual in 1584 when Fedor ascended the throne.[58]

Muscovite royal staffs were usually of Western origin. Thus, Ivan IV bought a staff, allegedly made of a unicorn's horn, from Augsburg in 1581.[59] It was later inherited by Fedor who used it, along with the sceptre, during his coronation. Fedor's sceptre in Chokhov's image also looks like the sceptres of Western kings.

Chokhov's image differs from the traditional rendering of the Muscovite horseman in two important respects. First, it lacks the dragon, probably to avoid distracting the viewer's attention from the figure of the tsar. Second, unlike the traditional representations of Muscovite horsemen in seals, Chokhov's Fedor has a halo, which is here a symbol of royal power blessed by God. Chokhov followed a pattern of royal imagery which was established under Ivan the Terrible. In particular, haloes can be seen in the images of princes commissioned by Ivan for the Archangel Cathedral in the Kremlin.[60]

The horsegear in Chokhov's image is a peculiar mixture of Eastern and Western elements. Fedor's saddle is of a distinctive Mongol type.[61] It has short stirrups which allowed the rider to stand when riding and shooting (something Fedor hardly ever did). The saddle also features two belly bands (cinches) and front and crupper straps which prevented the saddle from slipping (this is what Fedor obviously needed). The horsegear is lavishly decorated, including a massive rattling chain lying on the horse's neck. Muscovites ordered such chains, which were part of ceremonial horsegear, from Lübeck.[62]

---

[58] Horsey, 'The most solemne and magnificent coronacion', p. 272. The first reference to the use of a sceptre during a Muscovite coronation can be found in the formulaic redaction of the coronation of Ivan IV in 1547. Pierangelo Catalano and Vladimir T. Pašuto (eds), *L'idea di Roma a Mosca secoli XV–XVI. Fonti per la storia del pensiero sociale russo*, Roma, 1989, pp. 79, 85. However, this description is anachronistic. It was compiled in 1557–60 and reflects the growing contacts of Muscovy with Sweden and Constantinople. See Sergei Bogatyrev, 'Ivan the Terrible Discovers the West. The Cultural Transformation of Autocracy during the Early Northern Wars', in *Festschrift for Richard Hellie*, part 1, *Russian History*, 34, 2007, 1–4, pp. 161–88 (p. 168). Judging by the chronicle redaction of Ivan IV's coronation, no sceptre was used in 1547. PSRL, 13, pp. 150–51. On Fedor's coronation, see Catalano, *L'idea*, pp. 106, 107, 112.

[59] Horsey, 'The most solemne and magnificent coronacion', p. 272.

[60] T. E. Samoilova, *Kniazheskie portrety v rospisi Arkhangel'skogo sobora Moskovskogo Kremlia*, Moscow, 2004.

[61] On the use of the Mongol saddle in Muscovy, see Donald Ostrowski, 'Sixteenth-Century Muscovite Cavalrymen', in Kivelson, *Picturing Russia*, pp. 28–32 (pp. 28, 29).

[62] L. P. Kirillova, *Starinnye ekipazhi. Sokrovishcha Oruzheinoi palaty*, Moscow, 2000, p. 197.

The décor of the Tsar Cannon thereby makes a powerful political statement: Fedor is a capable ruler; he is invested with royal regalia; his power is sanctioned by God; he masters both a galloping horse and weapons technology that can produce a super gun. This is in line with the official image of Tsar Fedor which was created in the Faceted Chamber of the Kremlin during his reign. Judging by later descriptions and murals based on original paintings, Fedor was depicted sitting on the throne, with the Cap of Monomakh on his head and a halo around it, holding a sceptre in his right hand. The imagery of the Faceted Chamber put the prince of Moscow in the context of sacred rulership originating in Ancient Israel and culminating in the figure of Fedor.[63] Next to Fedor the masters of the Faceted Chamber depicted Fedor's brother-in-law Boris Godunov, who acted as regent under the weak tsar.

Chokhov also made a reference to the Godunov family in one of the inscriptions accompanying the equestrian figure of Fedor on the Tsar Cannon. Very unusually for Muscovite weaponry, the inscription glorifies not only the ruler, but also his wife Irina Godunova.[64] On the basis of this reference, I. A. Komarov, the Keeper of the Tsar Cannon (Kremlin museums), thinks that the gun was a symbolic response to Godunov's opponents, who tried to divorce Fedor and Irina in 1586 on the pretext of her barrenness.[65] While this factor might have played a role, it is important to point out that Irina Godunova became a prominent figure in dynastic politics from Fedor's coronation in 1584. According to Horsey, Irina, wearing a crown and rich clothes, made a public appearance during the ceremony.[66] This was a novelty in the Muscovite ritual of coronation because previous princes (Dmitrii Ivanovich the Grandson and Ivan IV) were crowned while they were still unmarried. In this respect, the mentioning of Irina in the inscription on the Tsar Cannon can be seen as part of the new public image of the tsaritsa under Fedor Ivanovich. Uncertainty about dynastic continuity resulted in a very specific, masculine image of Irina in official propaganda. She was presented as a decisive, independently acting

---

[63] Aida Nasibova (ed.), *The Faceted Chamber in the Moscow Kremlin*, Moscow, 1978, images 75–77; Daniel Rowland, 'Architecture and Dynasty: Boris Godunov's Uses of Architecture, 1584–1605', in James Cracraft and Daniel Rowland (eds), *Architecture of Russian Identity, 1500 to the Present*, Ithaca, NY and London, 2003, pp. 34–47 (pp. 44–45).

[64] 'This gun was cast on the order of the blessed (*blagovernyi*) and Christ-loving Tsar and Great Prince Fedor Ivanovich, Sovereign and Autocrat of All Great Russia under his pious (*blagochestivaia*) and Christ-loving Tsaritsa Great Princess Irina in the glorious reigning city of Moscow in the year of 7094, in the third year of his reign. The gun founder Andrei Chokhov made this gun'. See Nemirovskii, *Andrei Chokhov*, pp. 40–41.

[65] I. A. Komarov, by phone, 17 April 2007.

[66] Horsey, 'The most solemne and magnificent coronacion', p. 273.

woman who could execute governmental functions without restrictions imposed by her sex and who could become successor to her husband.[67] In terms of court politics, the public promotion of Irina helped Boris Godunov to consolidate his power as regent through propagating his kin ties with the Riurikid dynasty.[68]

III

Like the portraits of Aleksei and Peter studied by Lindsey Hughes, the images discussed in this paper represent father and son, Ivan IV the Terrible and Fedor Ivanovich. Furthermore, like the portraits of Aleksei and Peter, the 'portraits' created by Middeldorp and Chokhov belong to different cultural traditions, Western and Muscovite. Middeldorp's and Chokhov's representations of Muscovite royalty reveal similarities and contrasts between Western and Muscovite perceptions of the tsar's power in the sixteenth century. The commissioners of both guns shared common ideas about the political function of gun décor. Both representations are based on the symbolism of dynastic culture, including the figure of the ruler and royal regalia, which was generally common in the West and in Muscovy.

Chokhov also utilized religious symbolism by depicting a halo around Fedor's head. By contrast, Middeldorp's image makes no references to the religious aspect of the tsar's power. This may be explained by the fact that during the Livonian war Ivan IV's opponents in the West presented him as an enemy of Christianity.

Coincidentally, both images represent Ivan and Fedor at the same age (they were twenty-nine in 1559 and 1586 respectively). However, their appearance is very different. Middeldorp shows Ivan as a mature man with a severe frown and a prominent beard. Chokhov's Fedor is very young and clean shaven. This artistic difference reflects different perceptions of Ivan and Fedor as political leaders. By 1559 Ivan became known in the West as a powerful monarch who conquered Kazan´ and Astrakhan´ and who was waging a victorious campaign in Livonia. Despite the official representation of Fedor as a capable monarch, Chokhov's 'portrait' does not fully dispel the common perception of Fedor as a young person. Such dualism in the official imagery of Fedor served the political interests of Boris Godunov.

[67] Isolde Thyrêt, *Between God and Tsar: Religious Symbolism and the Royal Women of Muscovite Russia*, DeKalb, IL, 2001, pp. 81–103.
[68] Godunov's dynastic propaganda culminated in an inscription on the 'Swan' bell (1594) which Nemirovskii attributes to Chokhov. The inscription mentions Fedor, Irina, their newly born daughter Feodosiia, Boris Godunov, his wife Maria and his son Fedor. Nemirovskii, *Andrei Chokhov*, p. 73.

The location of royal portraits on the barrels also has a political con-
notation. Ivan's head in fact serves as the rear button at the extremity
of Middeldorp's barrel (the so-called cascable button or *vingrad*). The
cascable button was used as a leverpoint for elevating the gun. In this
sense, the location of Ivan's head at the rear of the barrel is somewhat
insulting, because this part of the barrel was supposed to be pulled and
pushed when the gun was employed against the tsar's troops. On the
contrary, the image of Fedor occupies a very prestigious place on the
Tsar Cannon, in the front part of the barrel, on its right side when seen
from the gun's rear. This placing was a 'signature' of Chokhov's. The
different locations of royal images on the barrels reflect the opposing
attitudes of their commissioners to the tsar of Moscow. For the citizens
of Reval, Ivan the Terrible was an aggressor who did not want to
live in peace with them. At the same time, the Tsar Cannon was an
official Muscovite project which propagated the power of Tsar Fedor
Ivanovich.

Despite all the stylistic peculiarities and different political connota-
tions, Middeldorp's and Chokhov's images of Muscovite royalty are
part of the same process of cultural exchange between Western Europe
and Muscovy. Muscovites utilized the Western technology of gun
decoration casting for political purposes. In turn, the Muscovites
'exported' a public image of the Russian monarchy which was associated with the solemn representation of the Russian tsar in full regalia.
Perceptive Westerners like Middeldorp actively drew on this official
image of the Russian ruler in their works. Dynastic politics, Russia's
military aggression and the growing interest in the figure of the tsar
required the visualization of the tsar's power both in Muscovy and in
the West. Royal 'portraits' created by Middeldorp and Chokhov were
intended not only for the elite, but also for wider circles of the population. They could be seen by townspeople, commoners, artillerymen,
soldiers, foreigners. Cast in bronze, the 'portraits' of Ivan the Terrible
and Fedor Ivanovich on guns expanded the cultural image of the
Russian monarchy. The Muscovite tsar became a recognizable, public
figure who embodied the military might of Muscovy.

Printing Moscow: Significances of the Frontispiece to the 1663 Bible

SIMON FRANKLIN

ON 12 December 1663 the Moscow Printing House published a complete bible. It was a deliberately impressive production both in scale and in presentation. It was designed to look and to be, on several levels, significant. Although, as Lindsey Hughes noted, 'the "print revolution" in political discourse that burgeoned in Europe — for example in England during the Civil War — was quite alien to Russia',[1] nevertheless a political dimension could still figure even in the largely monologic, devotional and edificatory print-culture of pre-Petrine Muscovy.[2] The 1663 Bible was a monument of ideology as well as piety.

The present study starts with a consideration of just the first two leaves of the 1663 Bible: the title page (including the text on the reverse), and — in particular — the remarkably elaborate woodcut frontispiece (Fig. 1). These preliminary leaves frame the book as an object of significance, to the glory not only of God but of Moscow and the tsar. Significance, of course, is a slippery quality, changing according to perspective and criteria. Here I will consider four types of significance that might be claimed for the 1663 Bible. The first type of significance relates to implied intention: a reading of the preliminaries as statements by those who commissioned and produced them, so as to address the question of what the production was designed to signify. The second type of significance is contextual in relation to the object's prehistory, sources and precedents, so as to address the question of what it signifies as a new phenomenon in Moscow print culture. The third type of significance is contextual in relation to its early consumers, addressing the question of what it may have signified to buyers, owners and readers, as indicated in sales, responses and imitations, in the half-dozen years or so after its publication. The fourth type of significance is contextual over a longer span, relating to the resonances (or lack

Simon Franklin is Professor of Slavonic Studies at the University of Cambridge and a Fellow of Clare College.

[1] Lindsey Hughes, *The Romanovs: Ruling Russia 1613–1917*, London and New York, 2008, p. 42.

[2] For the classic analysis of seventeenth-century Muscovite printing as merely ecclesiastical, see N. P. Kiselev, 'O moskovskom knigopechatanii XVII veka', *Kniga. Issledovaniia i materialy*, 2, 1960, pp. 123–86; for more emphasis on its contemporary political, ideological and polemical relevance, see I. V. Pozdeeva, 'The Activity of the Moscow Printing House in the First Half of the Seventeenth Century', *Solanus*, 6, 1992, pp. 27–55.

FIGURE 1: The frontispiece to the 1663 Bible

thereof) of the 1663 Bible in Muscovite print culture over the next several decades. Thus, though the narrow focus is on just a couple of leaves of one book, the concerns of this study extend into wider areas of seventeenth-century print (and manuscript) cultures in Moscow and beyond.

I

The frontispiece of the 1663 Bible is arranged in three unequal tiers, and in three unequal columns.[3] The central and largest image is the double-headed eagle, with three crowns, with outspread wings, with a sceptre and orb in its talons, and with a representation of a dragon-slaying horseman on its breast. The dragon-slaying horseman, the focal point of the entire composition, is superficially reminiscent of St George, except that this particular rider is bearded, and capped not with a halo but with a crown. He is not a saint but an earthly ruler who, as we shall see, was readily identified as Tsar Aleksei Mikhailovich himself. Above the eagle, the Lord of Hosts, wearing a crown strikingly reminiscent of its earthly counterparts, and likewise holding an orb, peers down and gestures his blessing from his seat in the clouds. Below the eagle is a map, recognizably of Moscow. Red Square is at the centre; St Basil's and the Kremlin churches are shown as if side-on and in partial perspective; surrounding this is a street-plan roughly as far as the modern Boulevard Ring, which is in turn encircled by clusters of houses, again in partial perspective, out as far as the modern Garden Ring. The hierarchical vision is plain: from heavenly ruler down to earthly ruler down to earthly realm; the heavenly king blesses the earthly tsar; the tsar, in his triple-crowned emblem, protects his city. This main composition is flanked by biblical scenes: top left, the Fall; top right, the Crucifixion; centre left, Moses and the brazen serpent; centre right, the Descent into Hell; bottom left, the expulsion from Eden; bottom right, the Transfiguration. Thus Moscow and its tsar are associated with — enveloped within — sacred history (as narrated in the very book which this frontispiece prefaces).

Interpretation does not have to depend on the images alone. The visual clues are reinforced by verbal clues. The four main inscriptions on the frontispiece are not just captions, but biblical quotations,

---

[3] See illustration, from *Bibliia sirech' knigi vetkhago i novago zaveta po iazyku slavensku*, Moscow, 1663 (hereafter, *Bibliia* 1663); detailed description in A. A. Sidorov, *Drevnerusskaia knizhnaia graviura*, Moscow, 1951, pp. 210–20; readings of the principal elements in Iu. E. Shustova, 'Geral'dicheskie kompozitsii kak element pechatnoi knigi v rossiiskikh izdaniiakh vtoroi poloviny XVII v.: traditsiia i semantika', in I. V. Pozdeeva (ed.), *Traditsionnaia kniga i kul'tura pozdnego russkogo srednevekov'ia. Chast' 1: Kirillicheskaia kniga v russkoi istorii i kul'ture*, Iaroslavl', 2008, pp. 281–84.

helpfully referenced by book and chapter. The banner above the eagle contains two citations: 'Песнь песней глава 3. Дщери сиони изыдите и видите в царе Соломоне в венце в нем же венча мати в день женитбы. Се царь правдивый царствуетъ и началницы судом владети начнут. Исаиа 32' ('Song of Songs, chapter 3: 'Go forth, ye daughters of Sion, and behold king [*tsar*] Solomon, with the crown wherewith his mother crowned him, on the day of his espousals', followed by 'behold, a righteous king [*tsar*] shall reign, and princes shall govern with judgment; Isaiah 32'.[4] The side-banners flanking the eagle display a further quotation from Isaiah: 'Азъ поставихъ царя с правдою и вси путие его прави. Исаиа глава 32' ('I have raised him up to be a king [*tsar*] with righteousness, and all his ways are right; Isaiah, chapter 45' (=Isaiah 45:13). Finally, the banner above the Moscow map reads: 'Градъ царя великаго. Богъ въ тяжестех его знаемъ есть. Псалом 47' ('The city of the great king [*tsar*]. God is known in its burdens. Psalm 47.'[5] Aleksei Mikhailovich is Solomon, the 'great tsar'; Moscow, city of the great tsar, is Jerusalem. At the base of the page the whole composition is dated: 'лета от воплощениа слова Божиа 1663' ('In the year 1663 from the Incarnation of the Divine Word').

More cryptically, some of the spaces around the eagle are filled with a smattering of individual letters which at first sight seem random: В, Г, Ц, В, К, А, М, В, В, М, Б, Р, С. This is a more veiled, less declarative statement; but for those who understood, it was no less weighty: it is deciphered as 'Великий Государь, Царь и Великий Князь Алексей Михайлович Всея Великия и Малыя и Белыя России Самодержец' ('Great Sovereign, Tsar and Grand Prince Aleksei Mikhailovich, Autocrat of All Great, Little and White Rus'). The letters thus stress that the emblem refers not just to the Muscovite State, but to Aleksei Mikhailovich personally as its ruler. Iu. E. Shustova affirms this interpretation with reference to the tsar's 1667 decree concerning his titles and his seal,[6] but in fact, the decipherment would have been plain without a four-year wait for an official decree. The same

---

[4] Song of Solomon 3:11; Isaiah 32:1. For the English I use Lancelot Brenton's 1851 version of the Septuagint. Note that 'princes' in the quotation from Isaiah renders *nachalnitsy*, though the text of the 1663 Bible (following the Ostrog Bible) has *kniazi*.

[5] Psalm 47:2–3. Note that 'in its burdens' — '*v tiazhestekh ego*' implies a (mis)reading of the Greek '*en tais baresin*' (from *baris* — palace) as '*en tois baresin*' (from *baros* — weight, burden); compare Brenton's version 'in its palaces'.

[6] See Iu. E. Shustova, 'Gosudarstvennaia simvolika v geral´dicheskikh kompozitsiiakh knig kievskoi i moskovskoi pechati 60-kh godov XVII v.', in *Chelovek v kul´ture russkogo barokko. Materialy mezhdunarodnoi konferentsii*, Moscow, 2006, available on *Elektronnaia biblioteka Tsentra izucheniia pravoslaviia i drevnerusskoi kul´tury* <http://barocco2006.narod.ru/shustova.htm> [accessed 19 February 2009]; also Shustova, 'Geral´dicheskie kompozitsii', p. 283.

formula is articulated several times on the pages immediately preceding and following the frontispiece: on the title page, in the prefatory prayer, and in the main preface.

The title page provides the name and publication details of the book: the Bible, with the Old Testament following the Septuagint version, in a Slavonic translation following the Ostrog version, printed by order of Aleksei Mikhailovich, with the blessing of the metropolitans and arch-bishops and bishops (though with no mention of the patriarch),[7] issued in Moscow, the ruling city (*tsarstvuiushchii grad*), on 12 December 7172 from the creation of the world, or 1663 from the Incarnation. Again the central panel is set in a frame of images. At the base of the page is the Dormition, captioned with four verse couplets on the Theotokos as intermediary and intercessor. In the upper part of the page, closest to the book-title, are roundel portraits of Old Testament prophets and kings: Moses and Aaron, David and Samuel. In the lower part of the page, closest to the Dormition, are roundel portraits of metropolitans of Moscow: Petr, Aleksei, Iona, Filip (again we note the absence of the patriarch). Though less dramatic than the frontispiece, the title page, too, projects images of Moscow in the line of sacred history.

On the verso of the title page — that is, directly opposite the frontis-piece, on the left-hand side of the double-page spread — we find another set of texts, all of which serve as commentaries on the double-headed eagle. The first gives a response to the question 'why does Moskovia have a three-crowned emblem?'. The second is a quotation from the Psalter: 'thy youth shall be renewed like that of the eagle'.[8] The third and longest is a set of heraldic verses (*stikhi na gerb*): six rhymed couplets praising and explaining the double-headed eagle as emblem of the rule of Tsar Aleksei Mikhailovich:

Орла сугубоглавство, образ сугубодержавства,
   Алексия царя, над многими странами началства.
В десней скиптръ, знамение царствия,
   В шуей же, держава его самодержствия.
Выспрь глав, трегубии венцы,
   Тройцы содержащия земли концы
Посылаемии на главы побеждающихъ враги,
   Просящихъ от нея помощи крепкия руки.
Успевай и царствуй, великий царю в новом Израиле,
   Наставляй и управляй и, во Христе спасителе.
Побеждай копием сопротивнаго ти змия,
   Найпаче же мечем симъ духа еретики злыя.

---

[7] Nikon, in dispute with Aleksei Mikhailovich, had withdrawn from his duties five years previously, but had not been replaced.
[8] *Obnovitsia iako orla iunost' tvoia*: Psalm 102:5.

. The verses make the visual clues explicit. The first four couplets decode the emblem: the double-headed eagle is a symbol of Aleksei Mikhailovich's rule; the sceptre signifies tsardom, the orb is a sign of Aleksei's autocracy, and the triple crowns are for the vanquishing of enemies. In the final two couplets the anonymous versifier addresses Aleksei; or rather he addresses Aleksei in the person of the dragon-slaying horseman depicted in the frontispiece: 'Thrive and rule, great tsar, in the new Israel [. . .] Conquer with the spear your enemy the serpent, and the heretic with this sword of the spirit . . .' Thus the verses make it clear that the mounted figure was indeed the tsar. This intended reading is confirmed by the archive of the Moscow Printing House, which records that a certain Zosima, from the Novinskii monastery, was paid for making the pear-wood plate for this portrait (*persona*) of the tsar.[9]

The preliminary leaves of the 1663 Bible are a flourish of visual and verbal ideology, a paean, in words and pictures, to Moscow and its ruler.[10] This was their first significance, the significance of intention and production.

II

Both as a whole and in many of its constituent elements the 1663 Bible was unprecedented in the history of printing in Moscow. We turn now to contexts and precursors, first with regard to the book itself, then with regard to the details of its preliminary leaves.

The 1663 version was the first complete Moscow-printed bible. Textually it was unambitious. It followed the East Slav *editio princeps*, Ivan Fedorov's Ostrog Bible of 1581, as stated on the title page, as reiterated and justified at length in the preface.[11] Its publication was a special event in Moscow printing, the end of a major project which had taken three years to complete. Commissioned by a decree of 1 September 1660, work progressed first on two presses, then three, then four, for a total of 635 days, allowing for a period of several months in 1662 when the presses were idle owing to a financial crisis. Over a dozen

---

[9] L. N. Gorbunova and E. V. Luk'ianova (eds), *Moskovskie kirillovskie izdaniia v sobraniiakh RGADA. Katalog. Vypusk 3 1651–1675*, Moscow, 2003, p. 121. The title page was commissioned separately, from the *rezets* (engraver) Aleksei Nefed'ev.

[10] The eulogizing theme is also taken up in the preface, which (*Bibliia* 1663, fol. 2, cols. 1–2) includes a section on the Tsar's great merits as initiator of the project. Clearly, these leaves can be seen as a declaration of the 'triumph of the secular power over the ecclesiastical' that was 'crucial in the symbolic clash between tsar and partiarch' after Nikon abstained from active duty in 1658: see Hughes, *The Romanovs*, p. 37.

[11] See Francis Thomson, 'The Slavonic Translations of the Old Testament', in Jože Krašovec (ed.), *The Interpretation of the Bible: The International Symposium in Slovenia*, Journal for the Study of the Old Testament, Supplement Series 289, Sheffield, 1998, pp. 686–92.

compositors were involved. We know their names: Grigorii and Evsevii Semenov, Ivan Khristianinov, Leontii Vasilev, Fedor and Ivan Fedorov, Daniil Artemev, Fedka Isaev the Younger, Tikhon Fefilov and others. Between them they produced a 'double' print-run: that is, 2,400 copies (the Printing House's normal print-run was 1,200), plus a further twelve copies on special 'Alexandrine' paper for presentation to the tsar.[12]

The 1663 Bible was an unusually big book by the normal standards of the Printing House. Any complete folio bible has a certain monumentality. Beyond that, comparisons of size may be based on a range of different criteria.[13] If we merely count the pages, the 1663 Bible (with 550 leaves) is not as fat as the calendrical compilations of services and saints' lives such as the Synaxarion (*Prolog*) for March to August, or the General Menaion, or the Lenten Triodion, all of which were also being printed between 1661 and 1663, and all of which had upwards of 800 leaves. In overall dimensions, however, the 1663 Bible was bigger. With a column height of *c.* 275 mm, it was among the tallest folio volumes produced by the press, on a par with — though thicker than — an altar gospel. Regular Moscow Printing House folios of the time (the Gospel Homiliary, the Synaxarion) had a column height of *c.* 225 mm. The column height of quarto volumes (Psalters, Menaia) was around 130 mm, and of octavos such as the Canons (*Kanonik*) or Horologion (*Chasoslov*) about 105 mm.[14] The sheer weight of the book was to some extent kept under control by the use of the press's recently-introduced small typeface (with fifty-six lines to the page, in double columns, rather than the normal twenty-six to twenty-seven), but still it was an exceptionally solid and imposing object, a landmark.

The size of the book, and the labour involved in its production, also made the 1663 Bible exceptionally expensive. The use of the small typeface reduced paper costs, but the compositors on the presses with the smaller typeface received double wages (wages constituted a far higher proportion of total outlay on the Bible than on any other book of the period).[15] After allowing for a hundred or so free copies for the Palace Department, the proofreaders and others, the unit cost per volume was 3 rubles, 17 altyns, 4 dengas and 1 polushka per copy, and

[12] Gorbunova and Luk'ianova (eds), *Moskovskie kirillovskie izdaniia v sobraniiakh RGADA. Katalog. Vypusk 3*, p. 120.
[13] On large English Bibles of the seventeenth and eighteenth centuries, see Simon Franklin, 'How High is a Bible?', *The Book Collector*, 44, 1995, pp. 339–45.
[14] Figures extrapolated from the statistics presented in Table 2 of V. P. Pushkov, '"Knizhnoe delo" na Moskovskom pechatnom dvore po otchetam tseloval'nikov za pervuiu polovinu 1660-kh godov', in I. V. Pozdeeva, A. V. Dadykin and V. P. Pushkov, *Moskovskii pechatnyi dvor — fakt i faktor russkoi kul'tury. 1652–1700 gody. Issledovaniia i publikatsii. Kniga 1*, Moscow, 2007, pp. 218–19.
[15] Ibid., pp. 218–19.

the sale price was 5 silver rubles.[16] Five silver rubles in 1663 would have bought fifteen bullocks, or more than a year's supply of bread.[17] The gross annual pay (basic pay plus the subsistence allowance) of the Printing House employees was 7 rubles for a custodian, 20 rubles for a compositor, 43½ rubles for a senior official (*pod'iachii*) in the Printing Department.[18] The Bible was issued at more than double the price even of the majority of the press's other 'fat' books, and five or six times the price of its normal output.

The monumental preliminaries were appropriate for — and as unaccustomed as — the monumentality of the book. For the first hundred years or so, Moscow-printed books generally lacked any kind of title page. Fedor Burtsev's experiment with a title page, with woodcut decorative borders, for his 1641 Canons (*Kanonik*), found no imitators.[19] In January 1649 Grigorii Blagushin was paid 1½ rubles for his design of the extraordinary copper-engraved title page of Johann Jacob von Wallhausen's *Kriegskunst zu Fuss*, a manual of infantry formations, printed in translation (as *Uchenie i khitrost' ratnago stroia pekhotnykh liudei*) two years earlier at the Moscow Printing House. However, though the design was Muscovite, the engraving itself was commissioned from a foreigner (*nemchin*) and may have been printed abroad.[20] Only from 1660 did the Printing House begin to use title pages at all regularly. A woodcut 'architectural' border for title pages was used in four of the Printing House's books in 1660 and 1662, and title pages with typeset borders began to be produced in the same year.[21] None was as

[16] That is, 3 rubles, 53¼ kopeks: 1 altyn = 3 kopeks; 1 denga = ½ kopek; 1 polushka = ¼ kopek.

[17] See S. P. Luppov, *Chitateli izdanii Moskovskoi tipografii v seredine XVII veka. Publikatsiia dokumentov i issledovanie*, Leningrad, 1983, p. 29; see idem, *Kniga v Rossii v XVII veke*, Leningrad, 1970, pp. 40–41, on the case of six people who clubbed together to buy a 1½-ruble book: one of them indeed contributed by selling a bullock. On payment for the press workers — part in wages, part in food allowances, and sometimes part in books, see Pushkov '"Knizhnoe delo"', pp. 180–85.

[18] See I. V. Pozdeeva, 'Istoriko-kul'turnoe znachenie deiatel'nosti Moskovskogo pechatnogo dvora v pervoi polovine XVII veka', in I. V. Pozdeeva, V. P. Pushkov and A. V. Dadykin, *Moskovskii pehatnyi dvor — fakt i faktor russkoi kul'tury. 1618–1652*, Moscow, 2001, p. 37. These figures relate to 1634, so the comparisons with 1663 prices are not exact, but they have some credibility since the Bible was put on sale at precisely the time when Printing House wages and prices returned to their mid-century norms after an inflationary financial crisis of the early 1660s.

[19] See A. A. Sidorov, *Istoriia oformleniia russkoi knigi*, Moscow and Leningrad, 1946, pp. 98–100, and p. 87, fig. 16.

[20] Sidorov, *Graviura*, pp. 252–55 and fig. 108; also the image in <http://www.kreml.ru/en/main/exhibition/visit/2005/AlMihandNikon/hall02/exhibit/> [accessed 19 February 2009]; see E. V. Luk'ianova (ed.), *Moskovskie kirillovskie izdaniia XVI–XVII vv. v sobraniiakh RGADA. Katalog. Vypusk 2. 1626–1650*, Moscow, 2002, pp. 249–50 (no. 108). Note that the thirty-five copper engravings illustrating the main text were printed from the same plates as were used for the second edition of the original, printed in Holland in 1615.

[21] Kiselev, 'O moskovskom knigopechatanii', pp. 154–56.

elaborate as the woodcut frame for the title page of the 1663 Bible, with its iconographic scene and its portrait roundels.[22]

If the title page was exceptional, the frontispiece was unique. Traditional frontispieces had been limited to full-page portraits of the Evangelists (in a Gospel book) or St Luke (in the Acts and Epistles) or King David (in the Psalter), or occasionally the most celebrated patristic writers. The frames were normally architectural. The complex, florid, largely emblematic composition (though with a portrait at its centre) of the 1663 Bible frontispiece was an entirely new phenomenon in Moscow printing.[23]

What was new to Moscow was not necessarily new to the wider print-culture of the East Slavs. The closest parallel and most likely model for the frontispiece had been issued just two years previously, as a frontispiece to the first printed edition of the *Paterikon* (*Paterik*) of the Monastery of the Caves in Kiev, produced in 1661 at the monastery's own press.[24] The *Paterik* frontispiece is composed in four tiers: at the top a winged figure of Christ crowned, spreading out his arms in blessing and protection over the figure in the second tier, the Theotokos — also winged and crowned — who in turn spreads out her robe to protect the third-tier figure of the double-headed, triple-crowned (and of course winged) eagle with the dragon-slayer on its breast (but with empty talons). Crowns and wings echo each other visually and the banner inscriptions, though less verbose than those of the 1663 frontispiece, reinforce the message. The banner above the crowned heavenly figure at the top proclaims: 'Яко орелъ покры гнездо свое. Второзак. 32' ('as an eagle he sheltered his nest. Deut. 32') (cf. Deut. 32:11). For the Theotokos in the middle the inscription is: 'И даны быша жене две крыле орла велика. Апок 12' ('and to the woman were given two wings of a great eagle. Rev. 12' (Rev. 12:14). To the left of the eagle itself a curling banner bears the message 'Покры нас кровом крылу твоею' ('you sheltered us in the shelter of your wings') (cf. Psalm 60:4) and on an equivalent banner on the right are the words 'Во кровех крылу твоею возрадуемся' ('in the shelter of your wings we will rejoice') (Psalm 62:7). Thus a cascade of winged, eagle-like protection

[22] See A. S. Zernova, *Ornamentika knig moskovskoi pechati XVI–XVII vekov*, Moscow, 1952, p. 25, and fig. 440 on plate 61.
[23] On seventeenth-century title pages and frontispieces, see Sidorov, *Graviura*, pp. 160–249. Note, among very few 'non-standard' specimens, the 1659 frontispiece of Iakov Borovitskii printed at Partiarch Nikon's press at the Iverskii monastery: ibid., p. 207; and the double-sided representation of the 'ladder' (*Lestvitsa*, published in 1647 (ibid., pp. 192–94).
[24] A. A. Guseva, T. N. Kameneva and I. M. Polonskaia (eds), *Ukrainskie knigi kirillovskoi pechati XVI–XVIII vv. Vypusk II, Tom 1. Kievskie izdaniia 2-i poloviny XVII v.*, Moscow, 1981, no. 107 and fig. 1119, pp. 14, 137.

descends from Christ in heaven, through the Theotokos, to the Muscovite emblem, and thence by visual implication to the fourth and lowest tier of the composition: to the Monastery of the Caves itself, as represented by a picture of its church of the Dormition and an assemblage of monks. The 1661 *Paterik* frontispiece differs from that of the 1663 Moscow Bible in detail and in emphasis: it lacks the narrative border scenes; it is less explicit about the person of the ruler; the dominant motif — visually and verbally — is of the protective wings, rather than the tsar and his city. Nevertheless, in structure and in principle the two compositions are identical. The 1661 Kievan *Paterik* provided a visual model for the 1663 Bible's representation of the divinely protected and protecting Muscovite state.

The 1661 Kiev *Paterik* was the immediate precedent for the frontispiece as a whole (and possibly, we should note, for the title page as well),[25] but what of the individual components? We should consider briefly the precedents for five elements in particular: the eagle, the mounted portrait on the eagle's breast, the heraldic verses which form its articulate commentary, the map of the city and the mode of dating.

In emblems of Muscovite authority the combination of double-headed eagle and dragon-slaying horseman had first appeared in the late fifteenth century.[26] In 1625 Tsar Mikhail stipulated that, in place of a depiction of the Cross, a third crown should be shown above the eagle's heads, and under Aleksei Mikhailovich the eagle acquired its sceptre and orb. In 1667, in the context of truce negotiations with Poland and Lithuania, Aleksei Mikhailovich issued a detailed decree concerning his titles and seal, including instructions about the eagle.[27] The idea of reproducing the eagle in print, indeed on a title page of a printed book, pre-dates the frontispieces of the early 1660s by more than a decade. A plainer version (with a single crown, and lacking the

[25] Framed title pages with portrait roundels were frequent in books printed in Lvov and Kiev throughout the first half of the seventeenth century: see, e.g., Ia. Zapasko, Ia. Isaevych, *Pamiatky knyzhkovoho mystetstva. Kataloh starodrukiv, vydanykh na Ukraini. Knyha persha (1574–1700)*, Lvov, 1981, nos 76, 120, 121, 138, 193, 204, 220, 253, 256, etc. The title page of the 1661 *Paterik* was a prominent example, with the Dormition at the top, the Caves monastery's church of the Dormition at the bottom, flanked by Antonii and Feodosii, and with roundel portraits of five of the revered monks down each side of the frame: see also Guseva, Kameneva and Polonskaia (eds), *Ukrainskie knigi kirillovskoi pechati XVI–XVIII vv. Vypusk II, Tom 1*, figs 1673–1675, pp. 302–04.

[26] For the history of both components, see M. Agoshton, *Velikokniazheskaia pechat' 1497 g. K istorii formirovaniia russkoi gosudarstvennoi simvoliki*, Moscow, 2005, pp. 318–447; N. A. Soboleva, *Ocherki istorii rossiiskoi simvoliki. Ot tamgi do simvolov gosudarstvennogo suvereniteta*, Moscow, 2006, pp. 99–169.

[27] *Polnoe sobranie zakonov Rossiiskoi Imperii. Sobranie pervoe*, St Petersburg, 1830, pp. 706–09, no. 421; see also A. G. Silaev, *Istoki russkoi geral'diki*, Moscow, 2002, pp. 170–73.

orb, sceptre and dragon-slaying horseman) figures in a small roundel at the top of Blagushin's engraved title page for Wallhausen's *Kriegskunst zu Fuss*. The Kievan *Paterik* turns it into a focal point of the composition, and the 1663 Bible is its first fully articulated printed version from Moscow.

If a definition of printing were to include all techniques of 'impression', then printed representations of horsemen, with and without halos or crowns, had been produced in Rus´ from at least the thirteenth century (on seals). The dragon appears at the horse's feet on coins from the late fourteenth century. The origin of such images is contentious, and on occasion their 'readings' can be ambiguous: the iconography is strongly reminiscent of traditional images of St George, but there was a strong local tradition of treating the horseman as a representation (though not necessarily a portrait) of the ruler.[28] However, if our definition of 'print' is limited (as it is) to that which was produced from a printing press, then for precedent we look to the Ruthenian lands,[29] where mounted dragon-slayers appeared in heraldic devices in several books from the late sixteenth and early seventeenth centuries, starting with the version (of St George, with halo) on the arms of Konstantin of Ostrog, in Ivan Fedorov's 1578 primer.[30] A version strikingly similar to that of the 1663 frontispiece appeared in the armorial device of the Sviatopolk-Chetvertinskii princes, in a book printed in L´vov in the very same year.[31]

In the Moscow version, as we noted above, the mounted figure was definitely intended to be the tsar. Printed portraits of Muscovite rulers (together with the mounted dragon-slayer device) had appeared in

[28] See esp. Agoshton, *Velikokniazheskaia pechat´*, pp. 318–75; A. A. Molchanov, 'Predystoriia moskovskogo gerba', in *Drevneishie gosudarstva vostochnoi Evropy. 2005 god. Riurikovichi i rossiiskaia gosudarstvennost´*, Moscow, 2008, pp. 457–64; also N. A. Soboleva, *Rossiiskaia gosudarstvennaia simvolika. Istoriia i sovremennost´*, Moscow, 2003, pp. 42–43; Silaev, *Istoki*, pp. 80–137; G. A. Fedorov-Davydov, *Monety Moskovskoi Rusi*, Moscow, 1981, pp. 131–35. In a different medium and on a different scale, note the mounted 'portrait' (without dragon) of Tsar Fedor Ivanovich on the 'Tsar Canon' of 1586, as analysed by Sergei Bogatyrev in the present volume.

[29] 'Ruthenia', 'Ruthenian lands' refers, approximately, to Ukrainian and Belorus territories in the Polish-Lithuanian Commonwealth. 'Ruthenian' refers to the vernacularized version of the of the written language.

[30] Silaev, *Istoki*, p. 119, fig. 42; see also, for example, T. N. Kameneva and A. A. Guseva (eds), *Ukrainskie knigi kirillovskoi pechati XVI–XVIII vv. Vypusk I. 1574 g. — I polovina XVII v.*, Moscow, 1976, figs 761, 775, 782, in books from 1623–24, 1632, 1641.

[31] A. A. Guseva and I. M. Polonskaia (eds), *Ukrainskie knigi kirillovskoi pechati XVI–XVIII vv. Vypusk II, ch. 2. L´vovskie, novgorodo-severskie, chernigovskie, unevskie izdaniia 2-i poloviny XVII v.*, Moscow, 1990, no. 180 and fig. 2354, p. 282. Shustova, 'Geral´dicheskie kompozitsii', p. 281, asserts (without argument) that the somewhat sketchy version on the frontispiece to the 1661 Kievan *Paterik* depicts the tsar's son, Aleksei Alekseevich.

West European printed books from Herberstein onwards.[32] 'Impressed' portraits of East Slav rulers go right back to the very earliest coins depicting 'Vladimir on the throne' at the turn of the eleventh century, and equestrian portraits of Aleksei Mikhailovich had appeared on coins from 1654.[33] On our narrower definition of printing, however, there is no local precedent. The mounted dragon-slayer of the 1663 Bible frontispiece is the first Muscovite printed portrait of a tsar. Indeed, it is the first Moscow-printed portrait of a living person.

The praise of the tsar in the preliminaries to the 1663 Bible echoes sentiments and phrases which had become traditional in Moscow printing,[34] except that Muscovite prefaces and afterwords had traditionally been in prose rather than in verse.[35] Senior staff at the Printing Department were among the earliest regular Muscovite writers of verse, prominent in what A. M. Panchenko has labelled the 'chancellery school' of versifiers,[36] yet their versifying and their printing remained separate: Moscow verse culture in the first half of the seventeenth century was almost entirely confined to manuscript culture, and did not tend to leak into print culture. The 1663 Bible does include a prose preface — indeed, two prose prefaces — but the eulogy linked to the frontispiece is in the form of a set of heraldic verses (*stikhi na gerb*).[37]

In the Muscovite context this was exceptional. In the wider context of East Slav Cyrillic printing, it was commonplace. Again the precedents are from Ruthenia, and again it was the 1663 Bible which brought the practice to Moscow. Emblem books, combining allegorical pictures and verses, were popular throughout Western Europe in the sixteenth and seventeenth centuries. Heraldic verse, elaborating the symbols on personal devices and coats of arms, was a distinct but related genre. Emblems became fashionable in Russia in the late seventeenth and

[32] See the portrait of Vasilii III, with the inset device of a dragon-slaying horseman, in the suite of illustrations accompanying the second (=first Italian) edition of Herberstein, *Commentari della Moscovia*, Venice, 1550; also reproduced in Cynthia Hyla Whittaker (ed.), *Russia Engages the World, 1453–1825*, Cambridge, MA and London, 2003, p. 13.

[33] M. P. Sotnikova, *Drevneishie russkie monety X–XI vekov*, Moscow, 1995, pp. 26–38; Franz Kämpfer, *Das russische Herrscherbild von den Anfängen bis zu Peter dem Grossen*, Recklinghausen, 1978, pp. 212–13, 223–24 and figs 131, 132. See also B. N. Floria, 'Nekotorye dannye o nachale svetskogo portreta v Rossii', *Arkhiv russkoi istorii*, 1, 2002, pp. 132–41.

[34] See, for example, A. S. Eleonskaia, 'Russkie staropechatnye predisloviia i poslesloviia vtoroi poloviny XVI — pervoi poloviny XVII v. (patrioticheskie i panegiricheskie temy)', in A. S. Demin et al. (eds), *Tematika i stilistika predislovii i posleslovii*, Moscow, 1981, pp. 71–99 (esp. pp. 76–77).

[35] Prefatory verses appear in, for example, the 1637 edition of Burtsev's primer, the 1644 *Kirillova kniga*, the 1648 *Kniga o vere*, but are vary rare in Moscow until the latter decades of the century. See, for example, V. K. Bylinina and A. A. Iliushina (eds), *Virshevaia poeziia (pervaia polovina XVII veka)*, Moscow, 1989, pp. 230–37.

[36] A. M. Panchenko, *Russkaia stikhotvornaia kul'tura XVII veka*, Leningrad, 1973, pp. 34–77.

[37] I focus here specifically on heraldic verses, but note that the preliminary leaves of the 1663 Bible also contain other elements of verse: two couplets on the Theotokos on the title page; three couplets on the eagle's triple crown on the title page verso (before the heraldic verses proper), and ten couplets 'to the reader' at the end of the main preface.

early eighteenth centuries. Personal devices, and heraldic verses thereon, appeared in Cyrillic printed books from the 1580s. Ivan Fedorov's 1581 Ostrog Bible includes verses on the device of his patron, Konstantin of Ostrog.[38] Vernacular (Ruthenian) heraldic verses appear to have been a specialty of the poet Andrei Rymsha, whose compositions were printed at the Mamonichi press in Vilno to accompany the devices of various patrons.[39] Heraldic verses on the arms of L'vov appear in the first book printed by the L'vov Brotherhood, the *Adelfotes* (a grammar book) of 1591, and verses on the Brotherhood's own device first appear in 1609.[40] Through the first half of the seventeenth century armorial devices together with explanatory or laudatory verses (usually headed *stikhi na gerb*) appear frequently in books printed in Ruthenia, even at the institutional presses, which took external commissions.[41] Moscow printers did not have a variety of patrons, only the tsar and the patriarch. The first heraldic verses to be printed in Muscovy (though not in Moscow) are four lines of matter-of-fact description of Patriarch Nikon's device in a small monastic miscellany, *The Spiritual Paradise (Rai myslenyi)* printed for him in 1659 — after he had withdrawn from active duty as patriarch — at the press which operated occasionally at his own Iverskii Monastery.[42] The heraldic verses opposite the frontispiece of

[38] *Ostrozhskaia Bibliia. Fototipicheskoe pereizdanie teksta s izdaniia 1581 goda*, Moscow and Leningrad, 1988, verso of title page.
[39] V. I. Luk'ianenko (ed.), *Izdaniia kirillicheskoi pechati XV–XVI vv. (1491–1600). Katalog iz sobraniia GPB*, St Petersburg, 1993, nos 90, 96, 103, in books published in 1585, 1588 and 1591 respectively. For an English translation of the last of these, see M. L. Gasparov, *A History of European Versification*, trans. G. S. Smith and Marina Tarlinskaja, Oxford, 1996, pp. 224–25.
[40] Iu. E. Shustova, 'Simvolika L'vovskogo stavropigiiskogo bratstva', *Gerboved"*, 2, 2005, 80, pp. 94–104; also at <http://www.bractwo.narod.ru/Libraries/JES/JESSymbolika. htm> [accessed 19 February 2009]; see also Iu. E. Shustova, 'Problema kompleksnogo istochnikovedcheskogo issledovaniia predislovii i posviashchenii izdanii l'vovskoi bratskoi tipografii kontsa XVI–XVII veka', *Fedorovskie chteniia 2005*, Moscow, 2005, pp. 231–47.
[41] For example, on the devices of: Konstantin of Ostrog in a translation of Meletios Pegas (Derman, 1605); the Sheptitskii device in Domzhiv-Liutkovich's edition of the Gospels and Acts (Ugortsy, 1620); Konstantin Bogdanovich Dolmat in a translation of homilies of John Chrysostom (Kiev, 1624); on the Balaban device in Pamvo Berynda's *Leksikon* (Kiev, 1627); on the device of Petr Mogila in the translation of the sermons of Dorotheos of Gaza (Kiev, 1628), and so on: Kameneva and Guseva, *Ukrainskie knigi kirillovskoi pechati XVI–XVIII vv. Vypusk I* (above, note 30), nos 15, 33, 37, 48, 51. See also, more broadly, L. I. Sazonova, 'Ukrainskie staropechatnye predisloviia kontsa XVI–pervoi poloviny XVII v. (osobennosti literaturnoi formy)', in *Tematika i stilistika*, pp. 153–87.
[42] I. V. Pozdeeva, I. D. Kashkarova and M. M. Lerenman, *Katalog knig kirillicheskoi pechati XV–XVII v.v. nauchnoi biblioteki Moskovskogo Universiteta*, Moscow, 1980, nos 523–25, p. 216. For Nikon's emblem and accompanying verses, see S. V. Lobachev, *Patriarkh Nikon*, St Petersburg, 2003, p. 238; for a transcription of these and the verses from the 1663 Bible, see Sazonova, *Literaturnaia kul'tura*, p. 312. Note that the printers and press at the Iverskii monastery were brought in by Nikon from Kutein, so this heraldic verse may be another example of a directly imported habit or fashion: see Panchenko, *Stikhotvornaia kul'tura*, p. 106.

the 1663 Moscow Bible are more ambitious and grandiloquent in their glorification of their patron and his rule. One could regard them as the first printed specimens of Russian Court poetry.

The heraldic verses in the 1663 Bible may reflect a more specific influence. In the 1581 Ostrog Bible, as in the 1578 primer, the device in the upper left segment of the arms of Konstantin of Ostrog is a mounted dragon-slayer, in this instance clearly St George, with halo rather than crown. The second stanza of the 1581 heraldic verses is addressed to this figure, and includes elements analogous to the final couplet of the 1663 heraldic verses (Въоруженъ воинъ змия поправъ мужественно, // копиемъ сего посреде проньзе явственно, // Яко древняго враждебника человеческого рода // [...] Боди в князех избранный мысльнаго супостата).[43] There is no direct quotation here, but we know that the compositors and proofreaders of the 1663 Bible worked from a copy of the 1581 edition, so the analogy in the preliminaries is suggestive.

And so to the plan of the city. The earliest printed map of Moscow appears to be that which is attributed to Herberstein and which first appeared the 1556 edition of his description of Muscovy (the book was first published in 1549).[44] Willem Blaeu printed his first plan of Moscow in 1614, from an original by the cartographer Hessel Gerritsz, and various versions derived both from Herberstein and from Gerritsz appeared in West European atlases through the middle of the seventeenth century. Copies may well have made their way to Moscow,[45] and the direct influence of West European printed cartography is therefore plausible.[46] However, for a closer context we again look to Ruthenia. The first cartographic woodcuts printed in Kiev were published by the Caves Monastery Press in 1638. The *Teratourgema* of Athanasius Kalnofoyskii, an account of miracles worked at the monastery, published in Polish, included a plan of the city and two schemes of sections of the monastery.[47] The 1661 *Paterik* picked up the topographic theme. Among its copious woodcuts are two detailed plans of the monastery, which constitute not only the first maps in an East Slav Cyrillic printed book, but also, in a sense, the only 'proper'

---

[43] *Ostrozhskaia Bbliia*, title page verso.

[44] See Leo Bagrow, 'At the Sources of the Cartography of Russia', *Imago mundi*, 16, 1962, pp. 33–68, esp. 45–48; also Stéphane Mund, *Orbis russiarum. Genèse et développement de la représentation du monde 'russe' en Occident à la Renaissance*, Geneva, 2003, pp. 254–56.

[45] Note, for example, a printed map of Muscovy in the library of Artamon Sergeevich Matveev, listed in 1677: Luppov, *Kniga v Rossi*, p. 105.

[46] For convenient comparisons, see V. S. Kusov, *Moskovskoe gosudarstvo XVI–XVIII veka. Svodnyi katalog russkikh geograficheskikh chertezhei*, Moscow, 2007, pp. 59–62, figs 34–36.

[47] Kusov, *Moskovskoe gosudarstvo*, nos 939–41; see ibid., p. 51, fig. 26 for the plan of Kiev; for the other two schemata, see the facsimile of the *Teratourgema* in *Seventeenth-Century Writings on the Kievan Caves Monastery*, Cambridge, MA, 1987, pp. 139, 145.

seventeenth-century East Slav Cyrillic printed maps, for they include indications of scale, compass points and a key to places depicted.[48]

In one respect, however, the 1663 Moscow map was distinctive: in its orientation. The Herberstein map faces north, with the river in the foreground. The plans of the monastery in the *Paterik* also face north, and are clearly influenced by West European cartography: the scale motif of compass-dividers along a measured strip closely matches an equivalent motif in Ortelius.[49] All the seventeenth-century West European maps of Moscow face west: that is, with the river on the left and the Kremlin on the right. The Moscow map in the 1663 Bible is unique, in that it faces east: with the river on the right and the Kremlin on the left. Since printed cartography was new to Moscow, one might be tempted to explain this as merely an anomaly, an error, perhaps even a mistake by Zosima, the engraver. Yet it is more likely to be a deliberate cultural adaptation to local cartographic custom: the standard orientation of *manuscript* maps in seventeenth-century Muscovy (and there were many of them) is to the east. Some face south, a few face north, but there was apparently no Muscovite tradition of west-facing maps.[50] Thus Zosima, in making the plate for the first Muscovite printed map of Moscow, adapted his foreign models to local cartographic habit.

Finally we come to the dates. As we saw in the description above, the preliminary leaves to the 1663 Bible are dated in two places: on the title page, and on the frontispiece. The title page gives the date according to two styles, both *anno mundi* and *anno domini*, while at the base of the frontispiece the *anno domini* date stands by itself. Again we can suspect the borrowing of Ruthenian custom. Dual dating became habitual in Moscow print culture in the latter part of the seventeenth century, but single *anno domini* dating was exceptional. By contrast, in the Ruthenian lands single *anno domini* dating had been standard since the beginnings of printing, starting with Ivan Fedorov's afterword to his 1574 Lvov Acts and Epistles (*Apostol*). Indeed, Fedorov shows an intriguing awareness of the cultural difference in dating habits. In his afterword to the 1564 Moscow edition he uses only the *anno mundi* date; in the 1574 Lvov afterword he uses an *anno mundi* date when referring back to his Moscow press, but an *anno domini* year when dating the Lvov edition![51]

[48] Guseva, Kameneva and Polonskaia (eds), *Ukrainskie knigi kirillovskoi pechati XVI–XVIII vv. Vypusk II, Tom 1* (above, note 24), figs 1121, 1123 (pp. 139, 141).
[49] V. S. Kusov, *Kartograficheskoe iskusstvo Russkogo gosudarstva*, Moscow, 1989, pp. 40–42 and fig. 29.
[50] Ibid., p. 27.
[51] See both afterwords in *Biblioteka literatury Drevnei Rusi. Tom 12. XVI vek*, St Petersburg, 2003, pp. 526, 528, 532–34.

Thus, in the context of Moscow-printed books, the 1663 Bible was remarkably innovative. It was the first Moscow-printed complete bible, and the grandest single volume hitherto produced at the Moscow Printing House. Its preliminary leaves were correspondingly adventurous. They include: the first Moscow-printed heraldic verses (arguably, the first Moscow-printed Court poetry); the first fully-fledged (so to speak) Moscow-printed representation of the double-headed eagle as the tsar's emblem; the first Moscow-printed portrait of a Russian ruler, or indeed of any living person; the first Moscow-printed map of any kind (appropriately, a map of Moscow); the first Moscow-printed non-biblical or non-patristic frontispiece; perhaps the first Moscow-printed example of single dating from the Incarnation. None of this arose *ex nihilo*. The book and its preliminaries were a complex adaptation of local and imported (Ruthenian and West European) visual and textual practices. Nevertheless, on account both of its exceptional scale and of the extraordinary list of its 'firsts', the 1663 Bible can be represented as an important landmark in the history of printed books in Russia.

III

There are, however, other measures of importance. Having 'read' the 1663 Bible as a statement by those who produced it, and as a departure from Muscovite printing habits which preceded it, we turn to the third type of 'significance': to the Bible's reception by its early consumers, those who acquired or read or perused it in the period immediately following its publication.

Despite its price, the 1663 Bible initially sold quite well. Among the published documents from the Printing Department archive is the full list of purchasers, day by day, month by month, from March to mid July 1664.[52] This is no mere record of copies sold, but a rich source of data on book-consumption and distribution. Thus, for example — to pick a few lines more or less at random — on 9 March:

> Two books to the priest Iov. A book to Avramii, elder of the monastery of St Andrew. A book to the unattached priest Ivan. A book to the compositor Danil Artem´ev. A book to the merchant Semen Levashev. A book to Fedor, priest of the church of Nicholas the Wonderworker. A book to Mikhail Semenov the printer. A book to Prince Semen Nikitich Bonkhovskii. A book to Lazar Dorofeev´.

And so on. Sometimes we find a cluster of out-of-town purchasers: buyers on the first couple of days included people from Voronezh, Ustiug, Vologda, Kargopol, Iaroslavl´ and Tver´. By no means all purchasers limited themselves to a single copy: the list records multiple

---

[52] Luppov, *Chitateli*, pp. 132–57; see also the analysis of the figures, ibid., pp. 29–36.

purchases of two, three, five or seven copies, and even of ten copies to the Novgorod trader Kostiantin Kharlamov.[53] Not surprisingly, a relatively high proportion of the buyers were clergy (31.6 per cent), merchants (12.4 per cent), or government officials (23.3 per cent), and 17.3 per cent of the books went to Printing House workers (who often bought for resale), with only a small proportion (3.5 per cent) going to 'lower' groups such as guards, monastic servants, or grooms.[54] The sales list suggests that the book served its purpose, reached its audience, lay in churches and monasteries and houses of the great and the good of the capital city, and carried the word and the accompanying image out into the provinces. The publication of the 1663 Bible appears to have been treated as a success, as an event of some significance.

Purchasers, too, appear to have appreciated what they had. A less systematic — though no less eloquent — source for early distribution is provided by owners' and donors' inscriptions. Very few of the surviving published inscriptions are precisely dated, but, such as they are, they tend to confirm the evidence for wide distribution, and indeed for a lively secondary market in resale and relocation. Thus inscriptions record that, for example, on 21 February 1666 the clerk (*pod'iachii*) Larka Poretskoi donated a copy to the Monastery of the Intercession near Uglich; on 16 September 1665 Gavrilko Tomilov, from the Solovetskii monastery, signed a copy associated with a Muscovite named Foma Semenov; on 9 December 1680 the *pod'iachii* Sidor Rodionov sold a copy to another *pod'iachii*, Stepan Sofronov; on an unspecified 7 May the deacon Filip Petrov sold his copy to the monk Feolog Pustynnyi from the Chudov monastery; the priest Gerasim sold a copy to the priest Ivan Eremeev for five rubles.[55]

Distribution may be informative with regard to demand for the book, but tells us nothing about perceptions of its frontispiece. Most unusually, however, we do have one very articulate response, from no less a figure than Patriarch Nikon himself. In his voluminous polemical *Refutation* of questions addressed by the boiar Semen Streshnev to Paisios Ligarides, Nikon provides a curious *ekphrasis* of the 1663 frontispiece, on which, he tells his readers, 'есть написан орел двоеглавый, на орле же царь на коне в гордости велицей зело, а свыше его на таблице написано, еже Соломон о Христе пророчествова, то царь на себя преписа [. . .] Увы, увы! Люте, люте! В каковы времена достигохом! Збышася писанное: "Измениша бо славу Божию в славу человеческую, и четвероногих скот, и птиц"' ('is depicted a

---

[53] Ibid., p. 146.

[54] See the summary table, ibid., p. 30.

[55] *Moskovskie kirillovskie izdaniia v sobraniiakh RGADA. Katalog. Vypusk 3 1651–1675* (above, note 9), nos 62.1, 62.5, 62.6 (from the RGADA collections); A. I. Kopanev (ed.), *Korpus zapisei na staropechatnykh knigakh. Vypusk 1: Zapisi na knigakh kirillovskogo shrifta, napechatannykh v Moskve v XVI–XVII vv.*, St Petersburg, 1992, pp. 113–14, nos 530, 536 (from the Academy of Sciences collections).

double-headed eagle, and on the eagle the tsar on horseback, in excessive pride, and above is inscribed that which Solomon prophesied
about Christ, but which the tsar ascribed to himself [. . .] Alas, alas!
Woe, woe! to what times have we descended! That which was written
has come to pass: "[They] changed the glory of God into the glory of
man, and of four-footed beasts, and birds"").[56] True, Nikon was by this
stage raging from the outside. From 1658 he had withdrawn from per-
forming any duties as patriarch, in his disagreement with the tsar over
the relationship of the Church to the State, and by 1663 he was fighting attempts formally to condemn him, so he is hardly an impartial
witness. But the point here is not whether or not Nikon approves, but
the fact that Nikon's remarks attest to the contemporary authenticity
of readings which we otherwise merely infer. He confirms the perception of the mounted dragon-slayer as a portrait of the tsar; he confirms
the overall reading of the frontispiece as the glorification not only of
Moscow as God-protected city but of Aleksei Mikhailovich personally
as God-protected ruler; he confirms the inference that this configura-
tion of words and images prefatory to a bible might also be intended
and perceived as a projection of the tsar's authority in relation to the
Church. And Nikon also confirms the prominence, for a contemporary
reader, of the compositional component which is perhaps less immediately striking for the modern viewer — the inscriptions. For Nikon
the inscribed quotations are not secondary incidentals. Quotation is at
the core of his own mode of exposition and argument, and for him it
is the quotations as much as the images which expose the frontispiece
as the epitome of the tsar's blasphemous arrogance. Above all, Nikon
confirms that the frontispiece mattered, that it was not a decorative
frill, but was indeed striking, innovative, controversial.[57]

Despite Nikon's disapproval, some of the key visual components
were coming into Muscovite fashion in the 1660s, and the 1663 Bible
may well have had a role in their dissemination. For example, we have
seen the possible influence of West European and/or Ruthenian precedent on the frontispiece's map, but the map must also be seen in the
context of the intensive development of cartography in the Muscovite
administration itself from the mid-seventeenth century. Whether this
preoccupation was prompted by a sense of imperial mission, or for
use in local litigation, map-making proliferated,[58] acquiring notable

[56] Valerie A. Tumins and George Vernadsky (eds), *Patriarch Nikon on Church and State*. *Nikon's 'Refutation'*, Slavistic Printings and Reprintings 300, Berlin, New York and Amsterdam, 1982, pp. 609–10, 615. The 'quotation' is adapted from Romans 1:23.

[57] Nikon's response is evidence against the assertion of Kämpfer, *Herrscherbild* (above, note 33), p. 231, that the ruler-portrait here 'ist aber noch kein Beispiel für das Gebrauch des Buchschmuckes zur Verbreitung politischer Anfassungen'.

[58] Valerie Kivelson, *Cartographies of Tsardom: The Land and its Meanings in Seventeenth-Century Russia*, Ithaca, NY and London, 2006; Kusov, *Moskovskoe gosudarstvo*.

impetus in Aleksei Mikhailovich's administration precisely in the 1660s.[59] Although ruler-portraits were not in themselves new, the 1663 frontispiece can be seen in the context of their proliferation in several media in the 1650s and 1660s, from Aleksei Mikhailovich's coins, through to the sequence of Riurikid portraits in the manuscript *Titulary* (*Tituliarnik*) of 1672 and including Simon Ushakov's famous 1668 icon of *The Tree of the Muscovite Realm*.[60] Similarly with regard to the double-headed eagle, and to associated verses, the 1663 Bible appears to be in tune with the times. We have already noted Aleksei Mikhailovich's 1667 decree concerning his titles and seal. In the same year Aleksei's Court poet, Simeon Polotskii, produced his *Orel rossiiskii* (*Russian Eagle*) the epitome of heraldic verse on the theme of this emblem.[61] An ornate presentation manuscript of the work includes, among several elaborate graphic devices, a picture of the eagle remarkably similar to that on the 1663 frontispiece, right down to the distinctive portrait version of the crowned and mounted dragon-slayer (except that here the eagle holds a sword instead of the orb).[62] Other splendid manuscript versions of the eagle with accompanying accoutrements can be found, for example, in copies of the *Tituliarnik* of 1672.[63] Meanwhile, back in Kiev, multi-tiered woodcut frontispieces, including double-headed eagles, continued to be produced for a range of publications through to the early 1680s.[64]

---

[59] A. V. Postnikov, *Karty zemel' rossiiskikh: ocherk geograficheskogo kartografirovaniia nashego otechestva*, Moscow, 1996, p. 18.

[60] On portraits in the age of Aleksei Mikhailovich, see Kämpfer, *Herrscherbild*, pp. 212–33, and E. S. Ovchinnikova, *Portret v russkom iskusstve XVII veka*, Moscow, 1955, pp. 58–85; also Lindsey Hughes, 'Images of the Elite: A Reconsideration of the Portrait in Seventeenth-Century Russia', *Forschungen zur osteuropäischen Geschichte*, 56, 2000, pp. 167–85; on Aleksei in the *Tituliarnik*, see Lindsey Hughes, 'From Tsar to Emperor: Portraits of Aleksei and Peter I', in Valerie A. Kivelson and Joan Neuberger (eds), *Picturing Russia: Explorations in Visual Culture*, New Haven, CT and London, 2008, pp. 51–56.

[61] See Anthony Hippisley, *The Poetic Style of Simeon Polotsky*, Birmingham, 1985, pp. 44–48; extracts in P. Berkov (ed.), *Virshi. Sillabicheskaia poeziia XVII–XVIII vekov*, Leningrad, 1935, pp. 99–100.

[62] Illustrated in *Pamiatniki literatury Drevnei Rusi. XVII vek. Kniga tret'ia*, Moscow, 1994, unnumbered illustration (15th in sequence; compare other illustrations from the same MS, 12, 16, 19, 23 in sequence).

[63] See I. M. Kudriavtsev, '"Izdatel'skaia" deiatel'nost' Posol'skogo prikaza (K istorii russkoi rukopisnoi knigi vo vtoroi polovine XVII veka)', *Kniga. Issledovaniia i materialy*, 8, 1963, pp. 179–244: see pp. 183–89 on MSS copies of the *tituliarnik* and the illustration p. 190.

[64] For subsequent double-headed eagles, see Guseva, Kameneva and Polonskaia (eds), *Ukrainskie knigi kirillovskoi pechati XVI–XVIII vv. Vypusk II, Tom I* (above, note 24), nos 109, 126, 127 and figs 1280, 1431 (pp. 14–15, 19–21, 175, 197), various editions (1666, 1674) of works by Lazar Baranovych; no. 115 and fig. 1285 (pp. 16–17, 178), teachings on penitence, edited by Abbot Innokentii Gizel' of the Caves; no. 140 and fig. 1564 (pp. 24, 253), a Menaion of 1680, with a preface by Innokentii addressed to Tsar Fedor Alekseevich; see also figs 1668–69 (pp. 298–99), esp. fig. 1668a, from the third edition (1681?) of Innokentii's *Sinopsis*. All of these editions include verses on the tsar's emblem, but not identical to those in the 1663 Bible. For an overview see Shustova, 'Geral'dicheskie kompozitsii', pp. 284–94.

IV

Such apparent resonances — among purchasers and readers, cartographers and versifiers, panegyricists and printers — are eloquent, but also to some extent misleading. The fourth type of significance comes into view when we step back and view the impact and reception of the 1663 Bible over a longer period.

Textually, the 1663 Bible is uninteresting. In a milieu preoccupied by and in some instances spectacularly polarized by the 'correction' of received texts, the text of the 1663 Bible stands out for its conservatism.[65] Technically it was as mediocre as most Moscow printing of the mid-seventeenth century, with uneven inking and slapdash alignment: an ordinary book produced by a rather ordinary printing house. However, textual historians and scholars of fine typography were not its target audience. It was produced because of a perceived greater need. The preface addresses the problem directly: correction and collation would have been an enormously lengthy task, so the tsar decided that the priority was to get the book printed, on account of 'the severe shortage of these divine books in the realm of his tsardom; for nothing in manuscript could be found, and scarcely any copies anywhere even of the Ostrog printed version'.[66] In retrospect, the shortage turns out not to have been as critical as the preface suggests. We have seen that initial sales were fairly brisk, but they were not brisk enough to warrant a reprint. In 1668, five years after the Bible's publication, nearly 400 copies still lay unsold.[67] Indeed, the 1663 Bible was apparently sufficient to fill the need for not far short of a century. After the eighty-two years from the Ostrog Bible to the Moscow Bible, there followed a gap of a further eighty-eight years before the *next* complete bible printed in Russia, the St Petersburg 'Elizabeth' Bible of 1751. Although in Western Europe, too, impressive folio bibles could be produced more for display than for practical use, Latin and vernacular quarto bibles for reading and interpretation were printed in their hundreds of thousands over the equivalent period.[68] In Russia the 2,400 copies of the 1663 Bible remained the entire local printed output in the pre-modern age. Doubtless it was prized by those who initially acquired it; but there it lay, admired, unneeded, unimitated, mostly unopened, unspoiled for

---

[65] See Thomson, 'The Slavonic Translations' (above, note 11), pp. 686–92.

[66] *Bibliia* 1663, fol. 2v, of the preface, col. 2: видя и велий недостатокъ сихъ божественныхъ книгъ в державе царствия своего, ниже бо рукописныя отнюдъ обретахуся, в мале же и едва где уже печатнымъ острозскимъ обрестися.

[67] Luppov, *Kniga v Rossii*, pp. 62, 65.

[68] See Paul Saenger, 'The Impact of the Early Printed Page on the Reading of the Bible', in Paul Saenger and Kimberly Van Kampen (eds), *The Bible as Book: The First Printed Editions*, London, 1999, p. 32.

posterity;[69] a 'top-down' initiative that led nowhere, at least in its own time.

As with the book as a whole, so with many of the constituent elements of its bombastic preliminaries. Cartography and equestrian ruler-portraits and heraldic verses and elaborate tributes to Muscovite eagles remained in manuscript culture, but did not at this stage become features of Moscow book-printing. Just as, earlier in the century, the 'chancellery school' poets had confined their versifying to manuscript even while employed in the Printing Department, so the 'heraldic verses' of the 1663 preliminaries sparked no fashion in Muscovite printing to match the Ruthenian equivalents. Simeon Polotskii's *Orel rossiiskii* remained a monument of elite manuscript production, and there was no analogous development in print culture until Magnitskii's lengthy acrostic verse in his *Arifmetika* of 1703.[70]

The eagle reappeared regularly in the woodcut headpieces to the printed charters which began to be produced from around 1680, but much diminished in scale, and lacking the mounted dragon-slayer and even the third crown.[71] The representation on the eagle's breast was unstable both in form and in signification. In the subsequent Kievan frontispieces, in place of the equestrian portrait we also find the Theotokos, and the Crucifixion. Samuel Collins, who spent several years at the Muscovite Court in the 1660s, reported to his English readers that the figure on the tsar's armorial device was St George.[72] The tsar himself, in his 1667 decree, specified that on his seal the horseman should represent his heir.[73]

---

[69] The 1663 Bible is not a rare book in major modern libraries, whether in Russia and Ukraine, or in Britain and the Unites States: see, for example, Gorbunova and Luk'ianova (eds), *Moskovskie kirillovskie izdaniia v sobraniiakh RGADA. Katalog. Vypusk 3 1651–1675* (above, note 9), pp. 120–24; S. O. Petrov et al. (eds), *Slavianskie knigi kirillovskoi pechati XV–XVIII vv.. Opisanie knig, khraniashchikhsia v Gosudarstvennoi publichnoi biblioteke USSR*, no. 220; Pozdeeva, Kashkarova, Lerenman (eds), *Katalog knig kirillicheskoi pechati XV–XVII v.v. nauchnoi biblioteki Moskovskogo Universiteta* (above, note 42), nos 546, 547; Ralph Cleminson et al., *Cyrillic Books Printed Before 1701 in British and Irish Collections: A Union Catalogue*, London, 2000, no. 126, pp. 121–25; Houghton Slav 395.8* F; SMU Library BRA2390.

[70] See Sazonova, *Literaturnaia kul'tura*, pp. 796–803.

[71] See, for example, the 1686 version reproduced in Whittaker, *Russia*, p. 176. On the production of early printed charters, see E. V. Luk'ianova, 'Listovye izdaniia Moskovskogo pechatnogo dvora vo vtoroi polovine XVII v. (po dokumentam Prikaza knigopechatnogo dela)', *Fedorovskie chteniia 2003*, Moscow, 2003, pp. 214–24. The double-headed eagle, of course, was still used in many media other than print: see, for example, Soboleva, *Ocherki*, pp. 308–15, for the eagle on banners in the second half of the seventeenth century.

[72] [Samuel Collins], *The Present State of Russia*, London, 1671, p. 56. Collins (who frequently castigates the Muscovites for their ignorance) also reports here the view that the device may have been adopted after Queen Elizabeth granted Ivan IV the Order of the Garter.

[73] *Polnoe sobranie zakonov* (above, note 27), p. 709. This was topical, for the tsar's son was proclaimed heir in the same year, and the presentation manuscript of Simeon Polotskii's *Orel rossiiskii* was produced to mark the occasion.

Map-making, likewise, may have been modish in the later seventeenth century — but not in print. The map on the 1663 frontispiece was the first *and only* Russian printed map of Moscow until 1741![74]

Despite the continuing Kievan tradition of multi-tiered laudatory frontispieces, no Moscow-printed book of the later seventeenth century was issued with a frontispiece or title page comparable in scale or design to that of the 1663 Bible.[75] In 1663 a range of visual and verbal idioms from Ruthenian print-culture were translated into a grand Muscovite experiment. The idioms were not assimilated into the vocabulary of Moscow print culture of the second half of the seventeenth century, even though some comparable elements flourished in manuscript culture. In a sense, therefore, the 'translation' failed.

A generation later, substantially the same idioms were, so to speak, retranslated, in a different context, with different functions, and with notably improved success. The sequence of multi-tiered woodcut frontispieces printed at the Caves monastery in Kiev was crowned by a florid copper-engraved variant, as a frontispiece to the 1683 edition of Lazar Baranovych's *Blagodat′ i istina* (*Grace and Truth*), published in Chernigov. The engraver signs his work: *Ioannes Szczyrski sculpsit.*[76] Eight years later, in 1691, the same engraver, working in Kiev, was responsible for a remarkable transposition: he used a similarly structured multi-tiered image (God looking down on the double-headed eagle protecting the city), no longer as a frontispiece in a book but as a separate engraving of the genre known as *konkliuziia* — that is, an announcement of a philosophical disputation, including quite wordy texts of some of the theses.[77] In this context the compositional form was more successfully transplanted to Moscow, and indeed to St Petersburg. In 1693 an unidentified engraver produced an equivalent *konkliuziia* for Karion Istomin.[78] Increasingly fanciful versions of multi-layered *konkliuzii* appeared in a more or less continuous Russian tradition for three decades, but the early versions are obviously related to the Kievan

[74] L. A. Gol′denberg and A. V. Postnikov, *Petrovskie geodesisty i pervyi pechatnyi plan Moskvy*, Moscow, 1990; note also, however, a 1711 engraved map of Muscovy (see ibid., p. 15).

[75] Simon Ushakov's designs for copper-engraved frontispieces of the early 1680s were perhaps as innovative in the Muscovite context, but were on a less monumental scale: see Sidorov, *Graviura*, pp. 256–76.

[76] Guseva and Polonskaia (eds), *Ukrainskie knigi kirillovskoi pechati XVI–XVIII vv. Vypusk II, ch. 2* (above, note 31), no. 212 and fig. 1981a, p. 145.

[77] M. A. Alekseeva, 'Zhanr konkliuzii v russkom iskusstve kontsa XVII–nachala XVIII v.', in T. V. Alekseeva (ed.), *Russkoe iskusstvo barokko*, Moscow, 1977, pp. 7–29; see esp. figs 2, 3, juxtaposing the 1683 engraved frontispiece and the 1691 engraved *konkliuziia*. Note that here the representation on the eagle's breast is no longer a St George-like equestrian dragon-slayer, but a straightforward portrait bust.

[78] Ibid., fig. 4.

tradition and share significant features with the 1663 Moscow frontispiece. The two traditions (of frontispiece and *konkliuziia*) briefly merged
in the multi-tiered, eagle-centred frontispiece to Magnitskii's *Arifmetika*
of 1703 (engraved by Mikhail Karnovskii, whose background was also
Kievan).[79] There is no clear evidence that the culture of printed *konkliuzii* from the end of the century reflects to any appreciable extent a
secondary influence of the 1663 frontispiece. It is more likely that the
visual stimulus for *konkliuzii* was entirely due to the re-import of its
components from Kiev. Thus, if we view the landscape from an eagle-
high perspective, then the path chosen by those who produced the 1663
frontispiece, despite their trail-blazing flourish, turns out to have been
just a side-road, a dead end: monumental for those interested in mid-
seventeenth-century Muscovite printing and its Ukrainian models, irrelevant for those interested in the equivalent flow of cultural influence
in the Petrine age.[80]

The survey of four types of significance leads to very different assess-
ments of the 1663 Bible. None is correct in isolation, all are necessary.
This monumental undertaking of the Moscow Printing House can be
seen as behind its time, or as a radical innovation ahead of its time, or
as epitomizing its time, or as stranded outside a meaningful time-chart.
It was behind the times partly because, in the larger European context,
big printed Bibles had been around for over two hundred years before
this Muscovite *editio princeps*, and partly because even in the East Slav
context all the principal elements — double-headed eagles, armorial
pictures of mounted dragon-slayers, ruler-portraits, Moscow maps,
heraldic verses, bibles — had been around for some while. It was
innovative, in that all these elements, plus the composition of the multi-
tiered frontispiece itself (and of the title page with portrait roundels),
were new to the print culture of Moscow. It epitomized its time in the
extent to which it reflected mid-1660s preoccupations with mapping,
and with visual and verbal representations of the Muscovite tsardom.
It was ahead of its time, since its innovations were taken up again in
Moscow's print culture several decades later. Or, in a harsher version,
it was none of the above, but merely an untimely grand experiment of
little consequence.

[79] See M. A. Alekseeva, *Graviura petrovskogo vremeni*, Leningrad, 1990, pp. 64–67; the frontispiece is also reproduced in Whittaker, *Russia*, p. 165.
    [80] Thus, for example, the discussion of graphic art in James Cracraft, *The Petrine Revolution
in Russian Imagery*, Chicago, IL and London, 1997, pp. 149–90, makes no mention of the
1663 Bible.

The 'Italian' Nemetskaia Sloboda

MARIA DI SALVO

'ONE of Moscow's main quarters is Kakui; the houses there are made of wood but are so elegantly built that they look like caskets.'[1] This is how the Bolognese nobleman Ercole Zani described the Nemetskaia Sloboda — or German Quarter — created less than twenty years earlier by Tsar Aleksei Mikhailovich. Zani had come to Moscow in December 1671 in the train of a large Polish delegation (led by J. Gniński and C. P. Brzostowski), one of the many that testified to the rapprochement between Poland and Muscovy — due to their common struggle against the Turks — in the second half of the seventeenth century. He had already travelled extensively all over Europe and was neither a superficial nor an excessively prejudiced observer. His words betrayed his admiration, shared later by other travellers, for the quality of the Sloboda buildings and for the good care that the capital's foreigners took of their homes, especially if compared with those of the Russian common population. The quarter was beginning to take on an air of its own, although Zani evidently witnessed a moment of transition: up until a few years earlier, in 1665, foreigners' houses had not been entirely moved there from other parts of Moscow and were not yet clearly distinguished by any particular style.[2]

The Italian visitor was intrigued by the fact that artisans were often concentrated in the same streets according to their craft (although they were also so concentrated in other European cities, at least in the Middle Ages, as the names of many roads and quarters still testify),[3] but he did not seem to be surprised by the existence of a whole quarter inhabited by foreigners. In Moscow, there were numerous *slobody*, and the mention of 'Kakui' (or 'Kukui', as the name sounded in Russian) was part of a brief description of the topography of the capital, where,

Maria Di Salvo is Professor of Slavic Philology at the University of Milan.

[1] 'Relazione e viaggio della Moscovia del sig. cavaliere Ercole Zani', in *Il Genio vagante. Biblioteca curiosa [. . .] raccolta dal Signor Conte A. degli Anzi*, 1, Parma, 1691, p. 155.

[2] V. A. Kovrigina, *Nemetskaia Sloboda Moskvy i ee zhiteli v kontse XVII–pervoi chetverti XVIII veka*, Moscow, 1998, p. 28. The author refers to the 1665 census and to drawings by A. Meyerberg, dating to 1661.

[3] This phenomenon also struck Filippo Balatri: 'The Muscovite merchants' shops are all together in various streets in the inner city, known as *Kitài*, and you won't find a single cloth merchant in the goldsmiths' street, or a furrier in the shoemakers' street, *et sic de singulis*', *Vita e viaggi di Filippo Balatri* (further reference will be given in the text), MS of the Russian State Library in Moscow (RGB), f. 218, N. 1247, t. 5, l. 124. I am currently editing the full text of this nine-volume manuscript, which is to appear in print by the end of 2010.

as almost everywhere in Europe, foreigners tended to congregate in ethnic communities. Thus the adjacent 'Basmanik' quarter was inhabited by 'those re-baptized Christians that had adopted the Moscovites' Ruthenian rite,[4] while outside the city there were 'the Tatars, with the mosque that had been granted to them'; the list of the capital's guests also included the Georgian prince and a diplomatic Resident of the king of Persia.[5]

In this context, the 'Novoinozemskaia' or, as the more common name, 'Novonemetskaia' Sloboda suggested, could rightly be considered not a generally 'foreign quarter', but a 'German' settlement given the objective prevalence of German and Dutch residents: 'Kakui', Zani recalled, had been granted 'to the German nation' by the tsar. The presence of Lutheran and Calvinist churches (although devoid of bells and subjected to government control) in some way matched the mosque granted to the Tatars; being Muslims, however, the latter were held in less esteem and were not allowed to kiss the hand of the tsar, but only his knee. However, shortly afterwards this situation was increasingly depicted by foreign (often Catholic) sources as being unfairly biased. Ever closer relations with Poland rekindled in the church of Rome (and especially among the Jesuits) the hope that they would be allowed to proselytize in Muscovy; the opening of trade with Europe and the ever-increasing presence of Western men of arms swelled and diversified the population of the quarter, where the Catholic minority began to gain visibility. Some twenty years after Ercole Zani, between 1699 and 1701, a young Italian castrato, Filippo Balatri (1682–1756), took up residence in Moscow. In his memoirs, written after 1725, he recalled his first visit to the Nemetskaia Sloboda:

> In a secluded place in the outskirts of Moscow there is a group of houses that could be likened to a fairly large town, and this place is called *Slobotta*. There foreigners can attend three different churches, one *Roman Catholic*, another *Lutheran* and the third *Calvinist*, since the place is inhabited entirely by the English, Dutch, Flemish and Germans. Some of these are H. M.'s officers, some merchants and others artisans and trades people. The Muscovites (and especially the lower classes, who are always less inclined to follow reason) consider them little more than dogs, but the Roman Catholics are the most despised. The two churches of the mentioned heretics are made of stone and lime, but the Roman Catholic one is made of wood, and can hardly hold above three hundred people. (*Vita e viaggi*, t. I, ll. 149–50)[6]

[4] By 'Ruthenian' Zani obviously meant, as on other occasions, 'Orthodox'.
[5] *Il Genio vagante*, p. 156. J. Reutenfels, who had been staying in Muscovy at approximately the same time, describes the suburb in almost identical terms.
[6] To get an idea of the figures, V. A. Kovrigina's calculations may be useful; according to her, in 1702 the population of the quarter numbered some 2,000 people, excluding the servants, who by then were mostly local. See Kovrigina, p. 36.

The question of the various confessions had become a somewhat thorny issue within the quarter and the Posol´skii Prikaz had had to deal with it on several occasions, especially when the imperial ambassadors repeatedly pressed for a Catholic church to be built and the Jesuits allowed to stay in the Sloboda. Italians living there or passing through Moscow often found themselves involved in such questions.

In his essay on the origins of the Nemetskaia Sloboda, Samuel H. Baron suggested that all aspects of the suburb should be taken into account, including 'its social and ethnic composition, its internal organization and life, and its position vis-à-vis the Russian community'.[7] Since then, numerous contributions have been published (in particular, well-informed books by V. A. Kovrigina and S. P. Orlenko,[8] based on hitherto unpublished archival sources) while accounts by foreign travellers have been more thoroughly and systematically researched. This article aims to provide additional information about the presence of Italians in the Nemetskaia Sloboda.

Initially, Moscow's foreign colony had consisted mainly of soldiers but, like the sailors and carpenters that flocked from Italy to Russia during Peter's reign,[9] little trace of them survives except in lists of names, both in the Venice archive, and in that of the Posol´skii Prikaz in Moscow. One of the most successful was undoubtedly Giorgio Lima, a Venetian who arrived in Russia in 1678 and rose to the ranks of colonel and vice-admiral of the Russian fleet. Several of Lima's letters, written both in Russian and in rather uncouth Italian to Franz Lefort, have been preserved: they date to the time of the second Azov campaign and, a little later, to that of the Grand Embassy, when among other things Lima wrote about the work in progress on building the Lefort palace in the Sloboda, which he was evidently charged with supervising.[10]

Another, rather different, character — who could have come straight out of the Commedia dell'Arte — was the self-styled 'Capitano Lominso'. His adventurous story, narrated with a hint of satire by Filippo Balatri, can, however, serve as a paradigm of the diverse and contorted ways in which various Western European stragglers ended up in Moscow. A native of north-eastern Italy, he had run away from home in his youth and embarked in Venice on a ship bound

---

[7] S. H. Baron, 'The Origins of Seventeenth-Century Moscow's Nemeckaia Sloboda', *California Slavic Studies*, 5, 1970, repr. in S. H. Baron, *Muscovite Russia: Collected Essays*, London, 1983, p. 2.

[8] S. Orlenko, *Vykhodtsy iz Zapadnoi Evropy v Rossii XVII veka (pravovoi status i real'noe polozhenie)*, Moscow, 2004.

[9] The most famous among them was Captain Luca Molino, but their stay was spent working in the shipyards in Voronezh.

[10] F. Lefort, *Recueil de documents / Sbornik materialov i dokumentov*, Moscow, 2006, esp. letter n. 175, pp. 305–06.

for Holland. From there, having made a fortune thanks to an English merchant, he had moved to Archangel and then to Moscow. In the capital he had enrolled in the Russian army, but following the outbreak of war with Sweden had given up his military career, thanks also to a conspicuous inheritance that allowed him to live comfortably in the Sloboda, 'dressed like a parrot' and addicted to womanizing, cavorting and gambling. He had converted to Lutheranism to gratify his patron but, 'one day he was a Lutheran and the next a Calvinist, always steering clear of the Roman Catholic church, because the few Catholic ladies of Slobotta were both ugly and humbly born' (*Vita e viaggi*, t. IV, ll. 74–74v).

Equally complicated routes had brought another man to Muscovy, one who was surely to become the most representative of the Italian community, and for a considerable length of time: the noble Florentine merchant Francesco Guasconi.[11] Born in 1640, he had worked in the family business, based on a trading company with branches in various busy ports (Amsterdam, Venice, Madrid, Smyrna); according to Paul Pierling, who mentions documents from the Vienna State Archives, Guasconi was widely travelled and versed in several languages, including Turkish, and had reached Moscow around 1666[12] with references from the Austrian emperor.[13] Francesco Guasconi can rightly be considered one of the Nemetskaia Sloboda's historical figures, because he remained there until his death some time around 1708 and accompanied its growth in a position that frequently went beyond simple commercial interests.

Already in the first half of the seventeenth century, the tsar had granted Tuscan merchants a concession to trade in caviar, and the arrival in Tuscany of various Russian ambassadors (in 1656, 1660 and 1663) had consolidated economic relations, gradually opening the way to new prospects also on the cultural front: Russian emissaries to Italy enjoyed visits to the theatre and soirées where the ladies danced and played cards, and they increasingly became the bearers of requests not only for merchandise, but also for technological expertise. Of the numerous merchants keen to import caviar into Italy, only the

---

[11] On this subject, see M. Di Salvo, 'Florence, Amsterdam, Moscow: An Italian Merchant in Peter the Great's Time', in E. Wagemans (ed.), *Russia and the Low Countries in the Eighteenth Century/ Rossiia i Niderlandy v XVIII veke*, Gröningen, 1998, pp. 87–95. Further information about Guasconi can be found in S. Villani, 'Ambasciatori russi a Livorno e rapporti tra Moscovia e Toscana nel XVII secolo', *Nuovi studi livornesi*, 15, 2008, pp. 37–95.

[12] The date, indicated by G. David, *Status modernus Magnae Russiae seu Muscovye*, 1690, repr. The Hague, 1965, pp. 44–45, was confirmed by I. S. Sharkova on the basis of documents from RGADA: see I. S. Sharkova, *Rossiia i Italiia. Torgovye otnosheniia XV–pervoi chetverti XVIII v.*, Leningrad, 1981, pp. 58–59.

[13] P. Pierling, *La Russie et le Saint-Siège. Etudes diplomatiques*, Paris, 1907, repr. The Hague, 1967, vol. 4, pp. 100–01.

Guasconis appear to have created a stable base in Muscovy,[14] thanks also to the fact that one of Francesco's brothers, Giovacchino, lived in Amsterdam, from where he ran a shipping business involving Dutch vessels. Goods were shipped from Archangel to Tuscany via the English Channel and the Straits of Gibraltar and regular exchanges over such a distance depended on the association of far-reaching trading networks such as that of the British (John Hebdon operated out of the port of Leghorn) and above all of the Dutch. This close relationship is reflected in an archival document, which curiously defines Guasconi as 'gollandskii kupets ital′ianets'.[15] The Florentine merchant did his best to satisfy his Italian customers' demands, shipping carefully selected hides and caviar, a delicacy relished by the Italians: the ships were sometimes so laden with caviar that there was little or no room for anything else. In turn, in Muscovy, Francesco sold luxury fabrics from various Italian towns, spices and other goods to order: Giovacchino Guasconi's letter-books, preserved in the State Archives in Florence,[16] also tell of Armenian books which, if necessary, could be procured via another brother living in Smyrna, and in one instance Giovacchino asks 'as I have already done many times in the past, what has happened to the six Bibles, four New Testaments, four Histories and twenty cosmographic books that I sent you in 1673'.[17] The books could have been supplied to Russian customers or to foreigners living in the Sloboda: these certainly included Andreas Winius, and we also have information about Francesco Guasconi's close ties with General Patrick Gordon;[18] perhaps we can add the name of Franz Lefort who, on his arrival in Archangel at the end of 1675, penniless and without employment, would have found himself 'en tres mauvais estat si le dit Monsr [François] Gascogne marchand en cette ville ne mavoit fait la grace de maccomoder de dix escu'.[19] The acquaintance continued in the Nemetskaia Sloboda too: apparently, it was Guasconi who introduced Lefort to Paul Menzies and to Patrick Gordon, thus opening the way to a lightning career; but even earlier, when Lefort was struggling to find his feet in Russia, Guasconi had introduced him to John

---

[14] At the end of the century, J.-G. Korb indicated the presence of just one Italian in the Sloboda: namely Guasconi.

[15] Rossiiskii Gosudarstvennyi Arkhiv Drevnikh Aktov (hereafter, RGADA), f. 159, opis′ 2, n. 1618, ll. 1–20.

[16] I have only been able to examine part of the as yet uncatalogued Guasconi papers, which the family donated to the Florence archive after the damage suffered in the 1966 flood.

[17] Archivio di Stato di Firenze, Carte Guasconi, filza 7–8, 9 April 1680.

[18] His wife Louise was the godmother of one of Gordon's children, George, on 17 September 1693: see M. S. Posselt (ed.), *Tagebuch des Generals Patrick Gordon [...] vom Jahre 1661 bis 1699*, St Petersburg, 1851, vol. 2, p. 417.

[19] Lefort, p. 42. It is his first letter after his arrival in Muscovy, written from Archangel on 15 November 1675.

Hebdon, with whom the Swiss émigré planned to return to Western Europe.

Francesco Guasconi himself probably never returned to Italy, but in the 1680s he was joined for a while by his brother and a nephew; he married a German woman, the only daughter of the rich merchant for whom he had worked in Holland, and had at least two children.[20] He never lost touch with his native country, however, and as time went by he also acted as an informer and go-between for all matters concerning Tuscany's commercial, political and religious interests. His time in Moscow coincided with the Grand Duchy of Cosimo III Medici, who, by means of intense European diplomacy, was trying to ensure the survival of his state, wracked by serious dynastic squabbles and an even more serious economic crisis. A fairly regular flow of information on the political situation in Russia reached Florence through Giovacchino's good offices and the events of 1682 in particular were the subject of quite detailed letters addressed to the Grand Duke's secretary.[21] The power struggle in Moscow, however, made it difficult to identify precise contacts, and only in 1688, pre-announced by Francesco's letters, did a Russian ambassador, V. T. Postnikov, return to Tuscany at the end of his mission in Europe. In 1684, Guasconi asked the tsars — on behalf of the Grand Duke — to promote direct commercial trade exchanges between the ports of Archangel and Leghorn, as they did for other countries; but Guasconi's request failed to achieve immediate consideration because, as often happened, the tsars' titles had been written incorrectly and their patronymic had not been stated in the letter; after the necessary corrections, Francesco Guasconi delivered it to V. V. Golitsyn. But, as a report in the Posol´skii Prikaz archive reveals, Guasconi seems to have been indulging in a little wishful thinking: he in fact mentioned the possibility of establishing a diplomatic delegation in Moscow, to be headed by himself, despite never having been fully authorized by his sovereign to conduct negotiations of the kind.[22]

Any information coming from Muscovy was naturally close to the heart of other Italian states too: thus, in 1696–97 another Guasconi brother, Alessandro, based in Venice, told the State Inquisitors of the imminent departure of a large delegation made up of prominent figures in incognito, who planned to visit various European capitals, including

---

[20] Two daughters, Laura and Costanza, are mentioned by F. Balatri, *Vita e viaggi*, t. IV, f. 67; Gordon, II, p. 354, speaks about the funeral of a Carlo Guasconi, probably one of Francesco's sons, who died prematurely.

[21] Fairly lengthy excerpts from these letters are given in F. Bacci, 'Cosimo III e Pietro il Grande', in *Giornale di bordo*, 3, 1969–71, pp. 326–28.

[22] Bacci, pp. 435–36; RGADA, f. 88, 1684 g., n. 14. Dopros florentiiskomu urozhentsu Frantsu Karlovu Gvaskoniu.

Venice. He also reported on the Azov campaign, a subject that would surely interest the Republic, as did anything concerning the Turkish front.[23]

However, it was above all in religious affairs that the Florentine merchant in the Sloboda appears to have played an increasingly important role. On the one hand, the bigoted Cosimo III urged him to help the Catholic missionaries as they crossed Russia on their way to China, entrusting him with an ampoule for Tsar Peter containing a miraculous liquid from the church of San Nicola in Bari, and asked him to ensure that the young Filippo Balatri — whom he was dispatching to Moscow with P. A. Golitsyn — did not neglect his prayers. On the other hand, both the Viennese and the Roman Courts increasingly relied on Guasconi and Patrick Gordon to consolidate and expand the Catholic colony in the Sloboda. In 1685, with money brought by the imperial emissary Johann Kurtz, a house was purchased, in Guasconi's name, to serve as a place of worship. This is the best-known episode of his biography, since it gave rise to a great deal of suspicion and to an intense investigation, especially when it became clear that the owners had begun to build annexes and to turn the building into a church proper. In July 1695 Guasconi was interrogated at the Posol'skii Prikaz, and had trouble convincing those examining the case that the building in question was not a church, but a family chapel for General Gordon. Building work was suspended and forbidden 'po ikh velikikh gosudarei ukazu', but the Florentine merchant does not appear to have suffered any serious consequences:[24] on the arrival of the imperial extraordinary envoy Ignaz von Guarient und Rall, in 1698, he was in a pre-eminent position among the Catholic representatives of the Sloboda, and the diary of the mission of Johann-Georg Korb recalls, among other things, a magnificent dinner that he organized in honour of the envoy. Guasconi and Gordon continued to be entrusted with the economic affairs of the Sloboda church and after the general's death Guasconi still figured as a reliable intermediary for money to be sent to the Jesuits, when the latter were readmitted to Russia by Peter the Great.[25] The enthusiasm of Pierling, who considered Guasconi 'le pillier de

[23] Archivio di Stato di Venezia. Inquisitori di Stato. Riferite di confidenti. Busta 610. Guasconi Francesco. The text has also been reproduced in Evgenii Shmurlo (ed.), *Sbornik dokumentov otnosiashchikhsia k istorii tsarstvovaniia Imperatora Petra Velikogo*, t. I. *1693-1700*, Iur'ev, 1903, pp. 80 (where Guasconi asks for news, for the tsar, about the organization of the Venetian fleet), 93, 101, 135, 139, 146, 232.

[24] RGADA, f. 152, ed. khr. 2. *Dukhovnye dela inostrannykh ispovedanii*. The text of the interrogations is published in full by D. I. Tsvetaev, *Iz istorii inostrannykh ispovedanii v Rossii v XVI i XVII vekakh*, Moscow, 1886, 2, appendix 5 and mentioned in several other of his works.

[25] M. O. Koialovich (ed.), *Pis'ma i doneseniia iezuitov o Rossii kontsa XVII i nachala XVIII veka*, St Petersburg, 1904, pp. 279, 297.

la mission naissante' in Russia,[26] was naturally countered, on the Orthodox side, by the intensely hostile opinion of D. I. Tsvetaev, M. E. Krasnozhen and D. A. Tolstoi, who defined him outright as 'a Jesuit'.[27] So far, there is no proof of his belonging to the order; he did, however, conduct his activities in a context in which the Jesuits were doing everything in their power to start proselytizing again in Muscovy, and in which outside pressure made this prospect even more intolerable for the Orthodox hierarchy.

With the beginning of Peter's autonomous reign and with so many Russian aristocrats now travelling to Italian states, the services provided by Guasconi and his financial network were once again in great demand as the money required for such journeys was deposited abroad: P. A. Golitsyn, a member of the group of *navigatory* sent to Venice in 1697 made use of them, and he was probably not the only one. Russians visited Italian capitals showing deference for and interest in their cultural and religious life, and this aroused illusions about their possible conversion to the Catholic faith; then there were those who, like Palladii Rogovskii, returned home after having studied in Rome and were expected to be forerunners for Catholicism in Russia: Cosimo III looked to him, and to Sheremetev, with confidence, expressing his concern for them in his letters after their return to Russia.

The Grand Duke of Tuscany was particularly curious about faraway lands, and not only for economic ends: he was intrigued by Russian customs, clothes and the exotic peoples that lived there.[28] But China too came into his horizon, perhaps because he dreamed of establishing trading relations with that country. In 1682 he enquired whether Francesco Guasconi could find him some descriptions of the itinerary between Muscovy and China. On that occasion he began corresponding with Andreas Winius, who, swearing him to secrecy, sent the Grand Duke the text (which he translated into Dutch) of the report of the Russian embassy in China in 1675–78 (headed by N. Spafarii), a map of China and a portrait of the emperor Kangxi.[29] Later Winius sent other things to satisfy his illustrious petitioner's curiosity: ginseng roots, a piece of asbestos cloth and a page with drawings depicting 'various

[26] Pierling, p. 101.

[27] M. E. Krasnozhen, *Inovertsy na Rusi*, vol. 1, Iur'ev, 1902; D. A. Tolstoi, *Ob iezuitakh v Moskve i Peterburge*, St Petersburg, 1859, p. 1.

[28] During one of his visits to Hamburg a report of a Polish embassy to Russia was translated from Polish into Latin in his honour; it is now published in M. D. Buturlin, *Bumagi Florentiiskogo Tsentral'nogo Arkhiva, kasaiushchiesia do Rossii*, Part 2, Moscow, 1871, pp. 394–431. J. Reutenfels' treatise *De Rebus Moschoviticis ad Serenissimum Magnum Ducem Cosmum Tertium*, Patavii, 1680 was also dedicated to him.

[29] The letters, secretly translated into Italian, are reproduced in Bacci, pp. 329–34; 434–38. Unfortunately, the text of the report has still not surfaced in the Florence archives. In exchange for these favours, a diamond ring to be given to Winius was ordered from Holland.

nations subjected to their imperial majesties'. Winius failed, however, to procure the gift that Cosimo III yearned for and had been asking Guasconi to find him for years: a Siberian youth, in typical dress and bearing arms, or else a 'Circassian Tatar', or a 'Kalmuck', preferably 'with an easy temper and a docile nature'.[30] Despite declaring that the purchase would not have been difficult in Moscow, Guasconi had had to give up the idea because sending such a gift abroad had turned out to be impossible, and for years the Grand Duke kept pestering anyone willing to listen to him with the same request. It was Petr Golitsyn who finally made him happy in 1698, by sending him, via Palladii Rogovskii, two Kalmuck children (aged seven and five), who were then converted to Catholicism and educated by the Grand Duke; in exchange, the boyar was allowed to take a young castrato singer, Filippo Balatri, back to Muscovy with him.

Cosimo III's passion for exotica, his desire to gratify the young Tsar Peter and a brutal exchange of human flesh were thus the origins of the extraordinary fate of Filippo Balatri, shipped off to Russia, at the age of just sixteen, with Petr Alekseevich Golitsyn and a large group of craftsmen, sailors and also a number of musicians. The young man from Pisa, 'on loan' from Cosimo on condition that he preserved his Catholic faith and took note of everything he saw, arrived in Moscow in February 1699, in time to see the corpses of the *strel'tsy* hanging on the road leading to the capital. Given his young age, Balatri failed to record details of Russian political life, but his memoirs, written almost thirty years later and reinterpreted in the light of later experience, remain a valuable source for descriptions of numerous aspects of everyday life, not least in the Nemetskaia Sloboda.[31]

'Filippushka', as he was generally called, lived in the Golitsyn palace in the centre of Moscow, but attended Court several times a week and on feast days worshipped in the Catholic church in the German Quarter. He regularly lunched at Guasconi's house, where letters from Italy were addressed to him. In the space of two years he learnt to speak Russian and came into contact with people from diverse social classes; of these he left lively, though not always precise and somewhat romanticized memories. A few months after his arrival in Moscow, the tsar introduced him into the home of his young mistress, Anna Mons: according to Balatri, she lived in a 'magnificently furnished Sloboda house. There I ran into H. M. again, sitting all alone reading a Dutch book. "This is the place", he said, addressing himself to me, "where *Peter Alexieivitc* comes when he wants to leave the Tsar at Court, and this is where I usually come to take a break from my studies and my

---

[30] Villani, p. 53.
[31] For a reconstruction of the salient facts in the life of Balatri, see M. Di Salvo, '*Vita e viaggi di Filippo Balatri*: preliminari all'edizione del testo', *Russica Romana*, 6, 1999, pp. 37–57.

business affairs. Here I can while away the time satisfactorily and feel free to enjoy excellent food in the company of infidels without having to worry about ridiculous scruples or scandalizing the weak'" (*Vita e viaggi*, t. II, ll. 100–100v).

Balatri liked to let his characters speak for themselves, limiting himself to the occasional moralizing or didactic comment, so that the episodes he narrated very much resemble anecdotes, a genre that became increasingly popular when the myth of Peter the Great held sway in Russia and in Europe. On the other hand, he wrote his memoirs late in life, while preparing himself to enter a monastery, and dedicated them to a clerical friend. His positive heroes (who include the tsar) are often portrayed in a somewhat hackneyed manner, dictated by conventional clichés: he thus praised Peter's just severity, either glossing over or denying against all historical evidence the violent side of his character and any behaviour that was morally inconsistent with such models. The same is true in the case of Anna Mons,[32] with whom he even claimed to have had an innocent flirtation under the amused gaze of the tsar himself. The power of the ruler's mistress, attributed by Balatri to the prestige she had gained among the inhabitants of the Sloboda thanks to her natural virtues, can in any case be deduced from the insistent questions that even high-ranking figures such as the Golitsyns made about her, and also from their decision to remove the young castrato from Moscow as soon as his flirtation with Anna Mons became compromising.

Though we may reasonably wonder how far Balatri was actually in a position to understand what was going on — and other sources give a quite different picture of the tsar's activities in the German Quarter[33] — there is a certain verisimilitude in the young castrato's description of the evenings Peter spent into the small hours in the company of his mistress and a young girlfriend of hers: lively adolescent discussions, music and endless games of chess with the unbeatable Anna, in a homely atmosphere in which her mother ended up taking an after-dinner nap while her father was often either out or already (diplomatically?) asleep.[34]

---

[32] Balatri wrote that she was the daughter of a Calvinist English merchant who had settled in Moscow a long time before; but the language spoken in the Mons household was Dutch.

[33] One might recall the mock-marriage of his jester Filat with Princess Shakhovskaia described by Cornelius de Bruyn in Lefort's mansion, or the rumours that Anna Mons was the mistress of both Peter and Franz Lefort. Lefort was described by Boris Kurakin as a 'deboshan frantsuzskii', who introduced the tsar to all sorts of vices. See B. I. Kurakin, 'Gistoriia o tsare Petre Alekseeviche', in *Petr Velikii: Vospominaniia, dnevnikovye zapisi, anekdoty*, Moscow, 1993, p. 75.

[34] These events date to around 1700; I am not sure exactly when Anna Mons' father died, whereas her mother's complicity and avidness — demonstrated in the inheritance disputes after her daughter's death — are well documented: see M. I. Semevskii, *Tsaritsa Katerina Alekseevna, Anna i Villem Mons 1692–1724*, St Petersburg, 1884.

In general, Balatri's memoirs convey a fairly diversified picture of life in the German Quarter, portraying it as a place of cultural exchange for the Muscovites, but also, in spite of everything, of gradual integration, if it is true that 'the English, Dutch, Flemish, French and German families only know that there are other countries in the world apart from Muscovy because they have heard it from their grandparents and great grandparents; they preserve their languages, but consider their native tongue to be that of Moscow' (*Vita e viaggi*, t. I, ll. 218–19). Naturally enough, the author tends to focus on what he perceives as exotic. However, after several months in Muscovy, he cannot conceal his own delight at finding a harpsichord in Anna's house to accompany his singing, while elsewhere musical instruments were limited to organs and violins and destined for dancing (he does not, however, recall the presence of other musicians and singers). And on the occasion of a reception at the above-mentioned 'Capitano' Lominso's he introduces us to the interior of an almost excessively luxurious home, with a bed adorned with lace and ribbons, a wardrobe full of rich fabrics, pistols and carabines, a large number of clocks, a library of erotic literature and novels: all objects the mere presence of which testified to a cultural world with which Russians were just beginning to familiarize themselves (*Vita e viaggi*, t. IV, ll. 74v–76).

Among the numerous signs of the hedonism that reigned in the German Quarter — which Balatri compared with the presumed frugality of the Russians — there was also the rich variety of foodstuffs and the host of elaborate ways in which these were prepared; this might explain the presence among the foreigners of so many doctors and apothecaries, unfamiliar to the Muscovites (*Vita e viaggi*, t. III, ll. 121v–22). The Muscovites are also said to marry later than the inhabitants of the Sloboda, where 'at the age of 18 it is shameful not to be married' (ibid.); and it is worth remembering here that in his letters to his family, Franz Lefort repeatedly mentions the appropriateness of taking a wife too, 'car un ieune garson comme moy ne s'en peut pas passer pour le pays ou nous sommes [...] vous ne voyes pas un garcon qui aye seixe années qui ne soit marié ni autrement vous estes exposé a la raillerie des colonels'.[35] Unlike Balatri's claims, however, that this demonstrated the Russians' greater innocence, it was more a question of public order. As is well known, the establishment of the Sloboda itself had been justified by the brawls and the scandal that the foreigners — initially mostly soldiers, and not always with an entirely

---

[35] Lefort, p. 48.

irreprehensible past[36] — aroused in the people of Moscow; marriage was thought to curb the ardent spirits of so many single men.

Comparisons between the life of the Russians and that of the foreigners in the German Quarter were not, however, always made in terms of 'nature vs. nurture' (to the advantage of the former). More often than not, they reflected another (similar, but not equivalent) long-standing opposition: of 'barbary vs. civilization'. Shortly after his arrival in Moscow, Balatri witnessed a lavish party at the Lefort palace,[37] where, on observing the rooms prepared for dancing and card playing and windows supplied with torches to light up the outside, he 'thought that the *Slobotta* was a sister of Florence, in the sense that I felt as if I were back home' (*Vita e viaggi*, t. I, l. 233). On that occasion the tsar obliged the few Russian ladies present (to the amazement of the Sloboda's inhabitants) to dance with him and to eat in the company of the foreigners; the doors of the mansion were controlled by sentries, who, for three days, prevented the guests from leaving. This initially caused quite an outcry in town, especially among members of the church hierarchy; but Moscow's boyars and their wives, encouraged by the tsar's approval, soon began attending new parties and engaging in conversation with the foreigners. Those who had travelled appreciated this chance to brush up their languages, and thanks to such 'positive contagion', their customs became more civilized: 'in six months, it was as if *Paris* had come to *Moscow*' (*Vita e viaggi*, t. V, l. 79). The tsar's dress reform also contributed to establishing more frequent relations with the German Quarter, which 'profited enormously from this innovation, because the entire city of Moscow was obliged to procure their clothes and fashion accessories there, both for the gentlemen and the ladies' (*Vita e viaggi*, t. V, l. 76). Neither were such reforms too costly, because French fashions required much less material than the old Muscovite

[36] On 23 June 1699 Francesco Emiliani, one of the Catholic priests that settled in the Nemetskaia Sloboda, reported to his superiors that the moral situation of his flock was deplorable: most of them were steeped in sin and had found refuge in Muscovy after having fled or been hounded out of their own countries. See M. O. Koialovich (ed.), *Pis 'ma i doneseniia iezuitov o Rossii*, Latin text, p. 19, Russian translation, p. 225.

[37] Balatri reached Moscow in February 1699 and it could have been the lunch held on 12 February, also mentioned by Korb, where however, as is known, Natal´ia Alekseevna herself did not sit at table with the guests, but observed the scene hidden in another room. A three-day session of the All-Drunken Assembly is mentioned by Korb after the execution of the *strel´tsy* at the end of February, while Balatri speaks about Lefort's wedding feast; he may have confused or deliberately mixed together the marriage of Patrick Gordon's daughter he witnessed shortly afterwards with some event involving Lefort (who died at the beginning of March 1699). As is well known, Peter used the Lefort palace, later donated to Menshikov, as a stage for public ceremonies. This episode is very similar to the marriage of Peter's jester described by Cornelious de Bruyn (see above, n. 33), but Balatri was no longer in Moscow at that date (January 1702).

style of dress, and also because the tsar himself kept an eye on the prices charged by foreign tailors.[38]

To Peter's *ukazy* Balatri added the fact, also claimed by other foreign observers, that 'the Muscovites are very astute [...] and, if they can't invent something themselves, they are good at imitating what they see or what is taught to them by any foreigners that happen to be there' (*Vita e viaggi*, t. I, l. 304). As a result, Russia appeared to be headed for very rapid evolution; and in this the German Quarter played a key pedagogical role, as the depository of European cultural models and as a hub of innovation. Balatri's somewhat simplistic view — still echoed in school textbooks — basically extended Peter's individual experience to Russian society as a whole. But those who took a positive view of the tsar's activities were by no means the only ones to exaggerate the significance of the German Suburb. For opposing ideological reasons, traditionalists greatly overestimated the influence of his connections in the Nemetskaia Sloboda (just as they overestimated the number of his foreign advisors). For example, the hope expressed by Western observers that foreign settlements in the capital would spread a quick, positive contagion was met by an equal, but opposite, fear on the part of churchmen who had demanded that the foreigners should be isolated. But Balatri's memoirs also remind us that only a handful of the German Quarter's inhabitants were of the stature of Patrick Gordon or Franz Lefort, while the district was plagued by petty intrigues and gossip. Everyday life did feature objects and forms of sociability that were unusual for Russia, but was mainly marked by regular Sunday worship — and subsequent lunch — by efforts to find suitable husbands for daughters and by frequent fires, rather than by parties at the Lefort palace or by lofty diplomatic games.

As regards the relations between Russians and foreigners in the German Quarter, Balatri does not offer any new elements to clarify them; thirty years later, another Italian visitor, G. B. Venuti, still complained of the robberies that had taken place during a huge fire and the 'anger and hatred for foreigners that this country expresses'.[39] While taking the effective gravity of numerous episodes of xenophobia

---

[38] As Lindsey Hughes observed, the sources attribute a whole range of adjectives to describe the new clothes favoured by the Tsar, but this 'simply underlines the blurring of national identities in fashion as in other spheres. [...] The general outline of what Peter [...] required was clear, the precise origin unimportant'. L. Hughes, *Russia in the Age of Peter the Great*, New Haven, CT and London, 1998, p. 287.

[39] M. Di Salvo, 'Incontri russo-italiani: la famiglia Venuti e la Russia', in D. Rizzi and A. Shishkin (eds), *Archivio italo-russo II. Russko-ital'ianskii arkhiv II*, Salerno 2002, p. 18. It is the same episode (May 1729) witnessed by the duke of Liria, to whose entourage Venuti belonged; see also, Lindsey Hughes, 'Attitudes towards Foreigners in Early Modern Russia', in C. Brennan and M. Frame (eds), *Russia and the Wider World in Historical Perspective*, New York, 2000, p. 16.

into due account, here too we are faced with a stereotype; mere travellers' memoirs are obviously not enough to clarify such an issue, which would require diversified sources and more thorough analyses.[40] As Lindsey Hughes recalled in one of her last articles, 'Early modern Russian attitudes [. . .] need to be viewed in a comparative perspective; dislike of foreigners, of "the other", was (is) universal'.[41]

---

[40] See Paul Bushkovitch's poignant reflections on this subject: 'Aristocratic Faction and the Opposition to Peter the Great: the 1690s', *Forschungen zur osteuropäischen Geschichte*, 50 (1995), pp. 80–120, esp. pp. 80–81.
[41] Hughes, 'Attitudes towards Foreigners', p. 17.

Casting Mazepa's Legacy: Pylyp Orlyk and Feofan Prokopovich[1]

GARY MARKER

THE time was the early 1720s. The Ukrainian hetman Ivan Mazepa's 'betrayal' of the tsar lay firmly in the past. Charles XII of Sweden was dead, shot inadvertently by one of his own soldiers. The Great Northern War, which had consumed in a most literal sense the previous two decades, was now ended, with a victorious Russia, newly recast as an empire, standing supreme in northeastern Europe. In the Imperial capital of St Petersburg the Senate had granted Tsar Peter I the new title Emperor Peter the Great, the heroic champion of Nystadt. Hundreds of kilometres away, in the Hetmanate itself, the tumultuous events of 1708–09 had played themselves out. Mazepa, the defeated hetman, had died in 1709, shortly after the pivotal battle of Poltava, protected behind the fortress walls of Bendery, then a part of the Ottoman Empire. His risky wager-on-the-Swedes had proven a failure, and the general uprising against the Russian military presence that he had hoped to inspire among Cossack regiments along the Dnepr and Don rivers never materialized.[2] His erstwhile comrades in arms, the

Gary Marker is Professor of History at the State University of New York at Stony Brook.

The author gratefully acknowledges the John S. Guggenheim Foundation and the American Council of Learned Societies for their support of this research.

[1] On transliteration and terminology: even though most of the leading figures in this paper are Ukrainian, Russian transliteration has been employed for those, such as Prokopovich and Iavorskii, who spent most of their careers in Russia proper. For those, like Orlyk, who worked primarily in a Ukrainian milieu and for places lying within Ukraine (e.g., Kyiv and Baturyn), Ukrainian transliteration has been employed. When quoting other authors, or translations already in print, authors' own spellings have been used.

An equally complex, and potentially sensitive, issue is determining how to render the many different terms used at the time for 'Ukraine' and 'Ukrainians'. To contemporary eyes, the term 'Little Russian' is offensive, and several scholars have insisted that 'Ruthenian' is the appropriate word to encompass the people of the hetmanates, left and right bank. As several scholars have pointed out, 'Ruthenian', a Latinization of *Rus´*, rarely if ever appeared in sources written in the Cyrillic alphabet during the seventeenth and eighteenth centuries. By contrast, 'Malorossiia' and 'Ukraina' were commonplace, in both Cyrillic and Latin texts. Since this paper relies upon a close reading of the language used at the time, and since the terms used were multiple and varied in their intent, they are rendered literally as written. Hence, 'malorossiiskii' is translated as 'Little Russian,' 'ukrainskii' as 'Ukrainian,' etc. Nothing more than a literal rendering of the terminology used at the time is intended.

[2] The latest, and in many ways the best, scholarly biography of Mazepa provides a plausible explanation of the events, Mazepa's motivation, and the causes for his failure to achieve wider support. Tat´iana Tairova-Iakovleva, *Mazepa*, Moscow, 2007, pp. 218–39. Somewhat older and more overtly nationalist, but still of value is Olexander Ohloblyn, *Het´man Ivan Mazepa ta jogo doba*, New York, 1960.

so-called Mazepists, were either long dead or scattered in exile in Poland, Sweden, the Crimea, the Ottoman lands and elsewhere.[3] Ivan Skoropads'kyi, Peter's choice to replace him, had been installed successfully as hetman with relatively little overt opposition, and the old left-bank capital of Baturyn was physically gone, having been razed by Alexander Menshikov's troops at Peter's direct order.[4]

Mazepa's name, and the events he engineered, remained alive, however, in Kyiv, in the Ukrainian exile, and even in St Petersburg, a veritable unhealed wound kept raw in vivid memory, political imagination and popular lore, far too fresh for dispassionate retrospection or closure. Nevertheless, by the 1720s, interested parties, of which there was no shortage, could begin to speak of Mazepa in the past tense. If it was too soon to ask about the deeper meaning or legacy of the events (the merciless judgement of History), one could still discuss the proximate causes and short-term consequences. Why had he taken such a fateful step? What did he have in mind? Who, or what, was to blame, and for what? And, at least for the moment, how should he be remembered?

These are familiar questions for the aftermath of dramatic political events, but the competing tales and legacies of Mazepa never seem to end, and they continue to engage political and artistic imagination even now. My goal in this paper is to return to the beginnings of those legacies, not so much to draw lessons or to affix responsibility as to recapture the political and territorial identities of the time, the discursive fields that Petrine-era myth-makers endeavoured to devise. Paying attention, in particular, to rhetorical strategies, the use of carefully chosen words and images that conveyed powerful meanings at the time, and the evolution of their usage proves instructive in situating claims and counter claims. Rather than surveying the field of contemporary writing, I concentrate on two eloquent and forceful figures who stood worlds apart politically in the 1720s. One, Feofan Prokopovich, personified what might be called the triumphalist Russian/Petrine side, a view expressed in his *History of the Early Years of Peter the Great*. The other, Pylyp Orlyk, embodied the post-Mazepa Ukrainian resistance.

---

[3] There exists a very large literature about the Mazepists in exile, penned largely by Ukrainian and Ukrainian émigré scholars. The most sophisticated and judicious of these remains Orest Subtelny, *The Mazepists: Ukrainian Separatism in the Early Eighteenth Century*, New York, 1981. See also Alfred Jensen, *Les emigrants ukrainiens en Suède*, Leopol, n.d.; and the documentary collection by O. V. Kresin, *Polityko-pravova spadshchyna ukrains'koi politychnoi emihratsii pershoi polovyny XVIII stolittia*, Kyiv, 2001.

[4] On Baturyn as a capital and the contemporary archaeological expeditions around it, see Volodymyr Kovalenko, 'Baturyn — Het'mans'ka stolyttsa', in Giovanna Siedina (ed.), *Mazepa e il suo tempo. Storia, cultura, società*, Alessandria, 2004, pp. 205–29; and Volodymyr Mezentsev, 'An Archaeological and Historical Survey of Baturyn, The Capital of Hetman Mazepa', in ibid., pp. 229–56.

In July 1721 he penned a long private letter to Metropolitan Stefan Iavorskii, a senior cleric and the long-time nominal head of the Russian Church, in which he expressed his own distinctive gloss on what might be termed the Ukrainian/Mazepist view. In each case the interlocutors were Ukrainian by birth and upbringing, but their lives had long since moved in opposite directions. Prokopovich, the bishop of Pskov and later archbishop of Novgorod, stood at the tsar's right hand as the clerical voice of the new empire, while Orlyk, Mazepa's erstwhile brother in arms and his successor as hetman among the rebel Cossacks, languished in exile while still defending the cause of Ukrainian freedom to anyone who might be able to assist.

On one level the two texts are hardly comparable. Prokopovich's *History* was intended as a semi-official (albeit not eyewitness) account of the early years of Peter's reign, a secular hagiography if ever there was one. Although the Mazepa affair loomed large in the *History*, it did not dominate the text or define its themes. Although it is rough and incomplete, one assumes that Prokopovich wrote the text for publication, judging by its length (over 200 printed pages), the definitive tone, and the notations he left for himself for future — ultimately uncompleted — additions and emendations.[5] In other words, this was a text written for public consumption and for posterity, even if it had to wait until 1773 to see the light of day. Orlyk's private letter clearly was not intended for publication but, unlike Prokopovich, Orlyk did offer an eyewitness account, even if written in hindsight. Nevertheless, the two texts do share some important features, both as narrative and more importantly as artefacts. Like Prokopovich's *History*, Orlyk's letter is rich in argumentation, replete with complex personal characterizations and adorned with literary flourishes. Through this letter Orlyk was endeavouring to influence the judgement of contemporaries — perhaps including the Russian Court and religious hierarchy — every bit as much as was Prokopovich, and perhaps that of posterity. But the symmetry grows clearer when one views the two as artefacts or as texts in themselves, read primarily in retrospect (which in fact is what happened) rather than in their own day. Moreover, both authors offer complicated accounts and verdicts that at times appear to be much more alike than one might anticipate, and their worries about the future converge in unexpected ways.

---

[5] Feofan Prokopovich, *Istoriia Imperatora Petra Velikogo ot rozhdeniia ego do poltavskoi batalii*, St Petersburg, 1773, pp. 3–4. The editor of this first printing, Prince M. M. Shcherbatov, notes that the manuscript was discovered in the private papers of the emperor and was written out in Prokopovich's own hand. He describes it as a rough draft, incomplete, and littered with bad grammar, odd spellings and foreign words, but with marginal notations indicating changes he had intended to make to the text.

So far as is known, Prokopovich and Orlyk had had no direct contact after 1709, and there is no reason to suspect that they imagined each other as competing voices for the hearts and minds of contemporaries or future generations, notwithstanding their strong personalities and separate senses of destiny. This assuredly was not a corner-to-corner correspondence; the two of them were not alone in trying to pass some sort of worldly-wise judgement on the political tergiversations of the hetmanate. But in their separate realms each commanded immense authority, and they both wrote as if they were fully aware of their standing. They came from a younger generation of prominent Ukrainians than Mazepa, who was born around 1639 (Orlyk was born in 1672 and Prokopovich in 1681). Their intellectual formations followed similar tracks, and evolved within a common political and cultural environment shaped to a considerable extent by Mazepa, rather than in the time of the so-called 'Ruin' that preceded him. Both, in this particular sense, were Mazepa's fledglings (*ptentsy*), and the trajectories of their world views and subsequent careers continued to reflect those beginnings. Yet, in the 1720s, the language in which each staked these particular claims was Russian, and the audiences they sought lay preeminently in the courts and cathedrals of St Petersburg and were likely one and the same for both. Thus, if the decision to juxtapose them in this essay is entirely mine, it does correspond to real circumstances on the ground at the time.

No sensible person doubts — or doubted then — that Peter prevailed at Poltava and that his forces won the Northern War. Notwithstanding the defection of some Cossack legions to the Swedish side and their willingness to continue the fight against Peter, the hetmanate's immediate fate rested in the hands of the Russian tsar and state, which ultimately abolished the hetmanate altogether in 1764. As the victorious party at Nystadt, Imperial Russia presided over and widely disseminated the initial master narrative, in large measure through the oratorical and literary agency of Prokopovich, by this time the leading panegyrist of the last decade of the reign of Peter the Great. Prokopovich was much more than an ideologist, however. A prolific author, he penned important tracts and seminary textbooks both in Latin and in Russian, numerous sermons and serious works on a variety of religious and secular subjects. A towering presence in the early history of the Russian Empire, Prokopovich's biography is well known and need not be reviewed in detail here. Educated first at the Kyivan Academy, he subsequently attended academies in Lviv and Cracow, at which he — like a number of others of his generation — converted briefly to the Uniate faith, a conversion that led him to study at the St Athanasius Jesuit College in Rome, under the aegis of the Vatican's Department for the Propagation of the Faith (*Propaganda Fidei*), a branch of the

Vatican hierarchy that maintained a keen and well-informed interest in Kyivan affairs in hopes of moving the borders of Catholicism eastward.[6] Upon returning to Kyiv in 1702 he renounced his conversion and commenced teaching at the Kyivan Academy, whose rector he became in 1707.

Even before the fateful events of 1708–09 Prokopovich had overtly and dramatically cast his lot with Peter and the Russian state (and in this he was not alone among the Left-bank black clergy). His first contacts with the tsar during the latter's trip to Kyiv in 1706, for which he orated a sermon at the Cathedral of St Sofiia on 5 July in Peter's honour,[7] and his subsequent move to St Petersburg to become a bishop in 1717 are well known and need not be retold here.[8] Still, prior to October 1708 Mazepa had been his primary and generous patron, a role that Mazepa had filled for several clergy and religious institutions, and the two had been on amicable terms. Prokopovich's five-act play, the tragi-comedy *Vladimir* (1705), included a dedication to the hetman in its frontispiece and, because the play was publicly performed, the bond between the two was common knowledge among Kyiv's elites.[9] Most specialists are convinced that the play functioned in part as a panegyric, drawing broadly implied parallels between the tenth-century baptizer of Rus´ and the pious hetman. In short, embracing Peter did not imply turning one's back on the hetmanate or one's Ukrainian affinities. This happy state of affairs came to an abrupt end soon enough, and for Prokopovich the choice was clear. Once Mazepa's *izmena* had become known, Prokopovich vigorously condemned him, and even preached a sermon praising Menshikov for his

---

[6] Although commonly known, the Vatican's keen interest in Ukrainian and Russian affairs has been rather lightly studied. In fact, the Vatican kept voluminous records on events in the hetmanates, and it had access seemingly to an extensive list of informants. Many of these documents have been published in large, but obscure, complendia. See, for example, Augustin Theiner (ed.), *Monuments historiques relatifs aux regnes d'Alexis Michaelowitch, Feodor III, et Pierre le Grand Czars de Russie. Extraits des archives du Vatican et de Naples*, Rome, 1859, especially pp. 306–435; Atanasii Velykyi, *Literae nuntiorum apostolicorum historiam Ucrainae illustrantes, 1550–1850*, Rome, 1959–; A. H. Velykyi, *Congregationes particulares ecclesiam Catholicam Ucrainae et Bielarusjae spectantes*, Rome, 1956–57.

[7] 'Slovo privetstvitel´noe na prishestvie v Kiev ego Tsarskago Presvetlago Velichestva', *Slova i rechi*, vol. 1, pp. 1–14.

[8] Prokopovich's letter (in Latin) to the faculty of the Kyivan Academy over which he had presided, announcing his departure and expressing his continued affection for both the Academy and its city is published in Feofan Prokopovich, *Epistolae illustrissimi ac Reverendissimi Theofanis Procopowicz variis temporibus et ad varios amicos datae nunc primum in unum corpus collectae*, Moscow, 1776, pp. 13–22.

[9] The full text of *Vladimir* is widely available in several published collections. See *Vladimir. Tragedokomediia* in Feofan Prokopovich, *Sochineniia*, Moscow, 1961, pp. 148–206. The lengthy dedication read, in part, '... privetstvuiushchoi iasnevelmozhnogo ego tsarskogo presvetlago velichestva voiska zaporozhskago oboix stran Dnepra getman i slavnago chinu Sviatago Andreia Apostola kavaliera Ioanna Mazepi ...'.

brutal actions against the hetman and Swedes.[10] Like other prominent clerics in the hetmanate, he followed Peter's orders and pronounced the anathema from his pulpit in Kyiv.[11]

Among the several relevant works he authored during and after 1708–09, the one that stands out for this enquiry is his *History*. Composed well after the events he describes, few of which Prokopovich witnessed, it endeavours to put the author's own hagiographic cast on the ruler, his challenges and his opponents. The book's triumphal tone resounds as *History's* verdict, the author's definitive word on events now firmly resolved and consigned to the past. Our interest here is limited to the characterizations — of which the book offers a number — of the hetman, his personality, loyalties and identity.

Mazepa first appears at the beginning of the fourth section, and is identified as 'by family background and personal identity a Little Russian (*malorossiichik*), or, as he was called more simply, a Cherkassian (*Cherkasin*)'.[12] These rather off-hand and colloquial appellations, *malorossiichik* instead of the more formal and respectful *malorossiianin* or *ukrainets*, and the slightly odd use of 'Cherkassian',[13] served to diminish the

---

[10] 'Slovo v chest slavnykh del kniazia Aleksandra Menshikova', orated on 5 December 1709, shortly after the events at Poltava and Mazepa's death. Published in Feofan Prokopovich, *Slova i rechi*, 1, St Petersburg, 1760, pp. 51–73.

[11] Scholars currently are in disagreement as to whether Feofan's Kyivan-period political ideas changed once he moved to the Imperial capital, specifically regarding his understanding of *Rossiia*. Iurii Shevelov, writing under the pseudonym of Jurij Šerech argued long ago that the pre-Poltava Prokopovich had been something of a Ukrainian patriot. More recently, Serhii Plokhy has endorsed this viewpoint, insisting that Prokopovich's pre-Poltava *Rossiia* referred narrowly and specifically to the Ruthenian lands, whereas afterwards he employed the term with a specifically Russo-centric intention. James Cracraft has argued the opposite, i.e., for continuity of expression, maintaining that the writings before and after Poltava were much the same politically. This is a crucial issue, not just for understanding Prokopovich, but also for deciphering the complex and often subtle articulations of ethnicity, empire, and nationality in the late seventeenth and eighteenth centuries. This is far too large and complex a topic to address adequately in a few sentences, but, in brief, I tend to agree with Plokhy that Prokopovich's written works undergo a shift, first after 1708 and then again in 1717. I am less sure about Plokhy's reading of *Rossiia*, however, even though I agree that *Rossiia* is one of the key words that define Feofan's political outlook throughout his career.
Iurii (George) Shevelov, 'On Teofan Prokopovič as Writer and Preacher in His Kyivan Period', *Harvard Slavic Studies*, 2, 1954, pp. 211–13; Serhii Plokhy, *The Origins of the Slavic Nations: Premodern Identities in Russia, Ukraine, and Belarus*, Cambridge, 2006, pp. 270–83; James Cracraft, 'Prokopovyč's Kiev Period Reconsidered', *Harvard Ukrainian Studies*, 2, 1978, 2, pp. 138–57. Both Shevelov's and Plokhy's essays have been reprinted elsewhere.

[12] Ibid., p. 156.

[13] At the time 'Cherkasin' was sometimes used very loosely to mean something like 'Ukrainian', but not usually in a formal sense except in some late seventeenth-century census records when referring to Cossacks in Sloboda Ukraine. Ia E. Vodarskii, *Naselenie Rossii za 400 let (XVI–XX vv.)*, Moscow, 1973, p. 47. One would not normally expect such a piece of patois in a work of Prokopovich, whose care in language is well documented. Mazepa had no particular link to Cherkasy, and the town had never served as the hetman's headquarters, hence my suspicion that Prokopovich was using the word rhetorically in order to cast Mazepa as something of a bumpkin.

former hetman rhetorically, to paint him as a provincial, better suited to the troublesome frontier between Poland and Russia (the town of Cherkasy at the time was on the Polish side, and the borderland was known as being particularly violent and unruly, difficult to govern from either capital) than to Kyiv. Language such as this subtly telegraphed to the potential reader Prokopovich's refusal to grant political stature to Mazepa. It also provided a basic glossary, a template for the central rhetorical role of ethnic affiliations and territoriality in his subsequent denunciations of the hetman. Mazepa 'utterly despised the Great Russian people' and behaved so deceptively that even the tsar refused to give credence to the negative rumours he had heard about him.[14] Mazepa, he related darkly, intended to 'tear Little Russia asunder from Russian sovereignty' ('otorgnuti rossiiskoi derzhavi Maluiu Rossiiu') and place them under the Polish yoke, while all the time presenting himself as a zealous patron and protector of Orthodoxy by, for example, granting large sums in construction for the Kyivan Academy.[15]

Over the next several pages Prokopovich's tone grows nastier and ever more condescending. 'This blackguard (*kovarnik*) bided his time, awaiting the right moment for betrayal, and he determined that the time had come while the Swedish army was engaged in Poland and the Polish forces were divided in two.'[16]

> He then told [his forces] that the tsar hated them [. . .] slandering the monarch as if the Sovereign intended to hand over all of Malorossiia to the Poles; as if he wanted to abolish the town authorities and replace them with Great Russian voevodas; as if he wanted to force the Cossacks into the regular army; as if he wished to do harm to the common people. He spewed forth all these hostile assertions, even though the tsar had never entertained such ideas. With this [act], Mazepa pronounced his separation from service to the Sovereign, and he led his forces into opposition, either outside Russia's borders or somewhere within Russia itself.[17]

At this point Mazepa disappears from Prokopovich's account as the action shifts to the actual battle of Poltava.[18] Although Cossack regiments under Mazepa did fight along side of the Swedes, Prokopovich gives them no attention, as if to emphasize the hetman's marginality relative to the momentous events playing out around him

---

[14] Ibid., p. 156.
[15] Ibid., p. 158.
[16] Ibid., p. 159.
[17] Ibid., pp. 159–60.
[18] Interestingly Mazepa remains a minor figure in most subsequent scholarly histories of Poltava. For example, a 1989 monograph devoted entirely to Poltava mentions Mazepa only episodically, and hardly at all once the serious fighting begins. N. Pavlenko and V. Artamonov, *27 iiunia 1709*, Moscow, 1989, pp. 55ff.

between the Russian sovereign and the real enemy (*nepriatel'*, a much
more formal and neutral term that connoted an acknowledgement of
power, even a kind of parity with Peter), Charles XII. Even the Don
Cossack rebel (*buntovshchik*), Bulavin, is afforded more attention — and
by implication greater respect — in this section, as Prokopovich
recounts how the Russians took delight in annihilating his 5,000-strong
force at Azov.[19] Renowned for its evocation of decisive battles, and its
proto-nationalist invocations of *Rossiia* and *Rossiane*, Prokopovich's
account of the actual battle constitutes the final section of the *History*.
It is here that he places Peter's apocryphal exhortation to his troops,
famously recounted in numerous subsequent histories, to fight not for
Peter himself, but 'for the state, [. . .] for your own kin [*svoi rod*], for the
all Russian nation [. . .] and it was apparent that for Peter his own life
was not so dear, only that Russia and Russia's piety, glory, and well
being [triumph]'.[20] Then, at the very end of the text the defeated
Mazepa reappears in ignominy.

> And then Mazepa, shaken by his slavish fright and fleeing his deserved
> judgment, stood before the king for some hours along with a few of
> his confederates. He crossed the Dnieper, but a faction of the Cossack
> *starshyna* [the most senior members of the Cossack host] retreated and then
> approached the sovereign and pled for mercy. And, although these mag-
> nates were doing so belatedly, Peter granted these residents their wish and
> numerous other acts of mercy.[21]

Let us leave aside Feofan's fanciful account of the battle and its pre-
lude, a frothy blend of real events and vivid imagination, and instead
focus on the polemic. These words of condemnation, at once thunder-
ing and dismissive, reduce Mazepa to a sideshow, a disagreeable
footnote whose inclusion might be unavoidable but who causes barely
a ripple in the grand narrative. Here was Prokopovich's judgement
from the hindsight of the 1720s: Ivan Mazepa was a traitorous,
duplicitous *individual*, lacking in courage and moral character, fundamentally dishonest and of little significance beyond the short-term
problems brought on by his flawed and evil character. No individual
or institution bore a larger blame: not the aspirations of the Ukrainian
people, not the blandishments of the Polish court, not even the machinations of Charles XII, beyond Mazepa himself. Mazepa lied to his
own people, lied to his sovereign, for which he paid a just price. His
symbolic, if not physical, end came on 7 November 1708 as Menshikov
took Baturyn and on the following day when the Kyivan Metropolitan,
Varlaam Iasyns'kyi, arrived at nearby Glukhiv and pronounced the

[19] Ibid., p. 162.
[20] Ibid., pp. 212–13.
[21] Ibid., p. 217.

anathema in the cathedral. Mazepa's effigy was tried, convicted, hanged
and installed in the cathedral to ritually witness the anathema; his pronouncements and orders ritually shredded;[22] the captured defenders
were executed, 'and thus, as God is our witness, everything transpired
contrary to the intentions of the enemy [Charles] and the traitor
[Mazepa]. The military capital, Baturyn, was razed to the ground'.[23]
No background or context, no mitigating circumstances or biographical contingencies were needed to help the reader comprehend why
Mazepa had acted as he did. It was as if the previous half-century of
restive disobedience by numerous hetmans against both Poland and
Russia had never happened, as if Mazepa were the only hetman to be
accused of *izmena*, rather than just the most recent.

When compared to many other of Prokopovich's writings, these
passages come across as unusually blunt and heavy-handed. Even in
the absence of literary subtlety, however, Prokopovich proved adept
at conveying layered and carefully crafted meanings. It is fruitful, for
example, to read this particular air of dismissive contempt for the
individual against the backdrop of the far shriller and more ominous
condemnations that emanated loudly from court and pulpit (including
Prokopovich's own) several years earlier, while these events were still
playing out and their outcome was uncertain. Between October 1708
and the beginning of Poltava Mazepa was vilified as a dangerous
traitor to the tsar, but more importantly to Orthodoxy. During those
perilous months Peter himself joined his clerical hierarchs in painting
the hetman as one who wished to sell Orthodox Ukraine to the enemies
of Orthodoxy, who would use their position to desecrate sacred spaces
and demean holy ritual. At that moment it was essential to do whatever was necessary to turn the population against the hetman, an
imperative that put primacy on the declaration of anathema.[24]

Even after Poltava the drum beats of religious polemics rumbled on,
as one cleric after another intoned passionately in praise of Peter and
against Mazepa. For example, Iosif Turoboiskii, another prominent
Ukrainian cleric who had come into Russian service in 1701, wrote a
description of the Triumphal Gates constructed in Moscow to celebrate
Peter's victory at Poltava. Known among specialists for his essays
explaining triumphal gates and their use of carved allegorical images,
Turoboiskii includes particularly gaudy panegyrics to Peter in this one.
Here Peter is cloaked with divine blessing, 'crowned by God', 'fortified

[22] See the insightful discussion of these events in M. E. Slabchenko, *Opyti po istorii prava
Malorossii XVII i XVIII vv.*, Odessa, 1911, p. 123.
[23] Ibid., pp. 188–89.
[24] For a more detailed discussion of this subject, see Gary Marker, '30 October 1708:
A Very Bad Day for Peter', in A. Cross (ed.), *Days from the Reigns of Eighteenth-Century Russian
Rulers*, Study Group on Eighteenth Century Russia Newsletter, 2 parts, Cambridge, 2007,
1, pp. 49–60.

by God', 'made glorious by God'. Allegorically he is a Russian
Hercules, Mars, a divinely-inspired champion of his people, including
'the significant [not little] part of our fatherland that was Little Russia
('nemalaia chast' otechestva nashego Rossiia Malaia').[25] In contrast,
Mazepa was a traitor and criminal, and a veritable Judas and an
enemy of his own people, prepared to sell their blood to the hated
Norsemen (nemtsy).[26]

In Turoboiskii's telling Mazepa had betrayed his own territory, its
population and its ethnicity (his use of 'blood'), but above all he had
sinned against true faith. Mazepa's duplicity opened the door to 'a
deluge of violence and perfidies perpetrated by those defrocked Poles
and Lithuanians residing in Russia' intending to bring harm to Russia's
monarch as well as to the lands of Little Russia.[27] The Little Russian
starshyna and common people, by contrast, showed genuine repentance
in their hearts and came to their senses ('ashche ot serdtsa pokaiutsia i
v razum istinnyi pridut'), and in response the merciful tsar granted
them a new hetman without punishing them.[28]

Feofilakt Lopatinskii, an equally luminous Kyivan from the class
of 1701, employed harsher language still. In a service of thanksgiving
officiated not long after the decisive battle of 27 June 1709, he repeated
the theme of a second Judas, 'a slave and a flatterer', as Judas
commonly was called in Slavonic liturgies. But he did not stop there.
He flayed Mazepa as 'more a devil in outlook than a human being'.[29]
Mazepa, argues Lopatinskii, cajoled some of his followers to sell their
blessings for thirty pieces of silver, thereby echoing Zachariah 11:12
('so they paid me my thirty pieces of silver'). Lopatinskii then leaves
his audience to complete the thought on their own, and to ponder the
darker denouement that follows in the subsequent passage (Zachariah:
11:17): 'Woe to the worthless shepherd who deserts the flock! May the
sword strike his arm and his right eye! May his arm be completely
withered, his right eye totally blinded!'[30] The struggle against Mazepa

---

[25] Below, p. 176. The counterpoint of 'nemalaia/Malaia' seems too obvious to have been
unintended. Rossiia Malaia was definitely not *malaia*.

[26] Iosif Turoboiskii, *Politikolepnaia apofeosis dostokhvalnyia khrabrosti vserossiiskogo gerkulesa
presvetleishago i veliko derzhavneiskagi Bogom venchannogo, i Bogom ukrepiaemogo, i Bogom proslavliae-
mogo velikogo gosudaria nashego tsaria i velikogo kniazia Petra Alekseevicha . . .*, Moscow, 1709, pp. 9,
10, 23, 143–44. The text is sometimes attributed to Lopatinskii, who was a participant
in assembling some of the material. But the dedication is Turoboiskii's, as is much of
the descriptive language. See T. A. Bykova and M. M. Gurevich (comps), *Opisanie izdanii
grazhdanskoi pechati 1708–Ianvar' 1725 g.*, Moscow, 1955, pp. 95–96.

[27] Ibid., p. 49: 'po prestanii onago navodneniia buntov i kovarov pastriginykh polskikh i
litovskikh iavisia v Rossii.'

[28] Ibid., p. 144.

[29] 'vtoroi Iudi, rab i l'stets, obretesia syn pogibelnyi, diavol nravom a ne chelovek.'
Feofilakt Lopatinskii, *Sluzhba blagodarstvennaia o velikoi pobede*, Moscow, 1709 or 1710, p. 6.

[30] *Holy Bible, New International Edition*, London, 1998, pp. 868–69.

was much more than a clash between Peter and an *izmennik*. It pitted the devil against the angels, the Holy Spirit against the Kingdom of Darkness. Peter was a second Constantine, defeating the 'Swedish Maxentius', Charles; he followed in the footsteps of the Apostle Peter, who warned that the devil (Mazepa) could take the shape of a lion.[31]

Prokopovich's own orations on Poltava and on Menshikov adopted a somewhat different posture.[32] No less Manichean than the others, they praised Peter unreservedly as David defeating Goliath, a mighty Samson, a new Solomon. Faith in God and the fatherland had triumphed over faithlessness, fidelity over treachery, blessings over damnation. Prokopovich returns to the Psalms repeatedly here, leaving no doubt about the — allegorically — biblical scale of these events. Remarkably, though, Prokopovich could not bring himself to mention the name of Mazepa, or even to make explicit reference to the hetmanate. There are just two places in the Poltava text where Prokopovich speaks of 'traitors', the first a lengthy and bitter passage contrasting loyal subjects with 'traitors and criminals', whom he compares to the traitors of Troy in Virgil's *Aeneid*.[33] Here he lets everyone know to whom he refers when he alludes to the monarch's 'proclamations on the cunning Zaporozhians' ('Gramoty o lukavykh Zaporozhtsakh').[34] But he does not utter the name. The second reference several pages later ('iako sam tokmo so izmennikom izbezhe verkhovnyi vrag Tvoi') highlights Feofan's insistence that the true enemy was Sweden.[35] A more complete depersonalization of the hetman could scarcely be imagined.

The speech on Menshikov entailed an equally deft and precarious balancing act. The brutal assault on Baturyn had turned the Radiant Prince into a feared and loathed presence on the Dnepr, and Prokopovich employed all of his rhetorical gymnastics in explaining why this bloodbath had been a necessary and laudable undertaking. Menshikov's unswerving loyalty to the tsar gave him the strength to do what had to be done on behalf of the fatherland, enabling him to 'smash the contrivances of the traitor' ('siia est´ razoritel´nitsa izmennicheskikh

---

[31] Lopatinskii, pp. 21–22, 31.
[32] 'Slovo pokhval´noe o preslavnoi nad voiskami sveiskami pobede', in *Slova i rechi*, vol. 1, pp. 15–52. Reprinted in Prokopovich, *Sochineniia*, pp. 23–37. For an interesting discussion of Prokopovich's early sermons and speeches see also O. M. Buranok, *Oratorskaia proza Feofana Prokopovicha i istoriko-literaturnyi protses v Rossii pervoi treti XVIII veka*, Samara, 2002, pp. 41–50, 88–89.
[33] 'Pokhval´noe slovo', p. 29. In this passage Prokopovich uses 'traitor' and 'traitorous' repeatedly ('polchitsa izmenicheskaia', 'otstupnikov i izmennikov', 'v smushchenii sem izmenicheskom', 'kliatvoprestupnyie izmenniki') but without naming Mazepa.
[34] Ibid., p. 30.
[35] 'Pokhval´noe slovo', in *Slova i rechi*, vol. 1, p. 43.

ukhishchrenii') and to defend Orthodox tsardom.[36] Once again, Prokopovich never utters Mazepa's name, and intones instead against
'perfidious treasonous thoughts', 'the treasonous soul', etc. The outcome, he recounts, was beneficent and crowned by God. Prokopovich
does not ignore the assault on Baturyn or the carnage it entailed,
but he deems the fortress city yet one more of the unnamed traitor's
contrivances.[37] Its structures become, in essence, a material extension
of Mazepa rather than an inseparable part of the land or its people.
'Let us not rejoice at shedding the blood of our co-religionists and
fellow countrymen', let all of Russia nevertheless share in celebrating
the victory over treason.[38]

Silences, we have come to recognize, can speak as loudly as utter-
ances, and the art of the well-placed omission had been carefully
cultivated among Ukrainian hierarchs, as David Frick has elegantly
demonstrated.[39] In this instance it is difficult to imagine that Prokopovich's omissions were anything other than intended refusals to grant
Mazepa a name. Unlike Turoboiskii, Lopatinskii and several others,
Prokopovich had not moved away from the hetmanate, and one
suspects that the impact of Mazepa's abandonment of Peter affected
Prokopovich more acutely than it did those clerics who were removed
from the hetmanate by time and distance. One can only imagine the
visceral response and recognition of personal vulnerability for a relatively young monk (Prokopovich was then in his mid-twenties), highly
visible, and a rising star in Kyiv (a city where suddenly everyone's true
loyalties were open to question). He had showered both tsar and
hetman with lavish praise within a few months of each other in 1705–
06, and even recycled some of the hagiography from *Vladimir* in his
paean to the tsar. Each, he had suggested was a new Vladimir, and
each linked to Vladimir's sacred path through a historic bond with
Kyiv.[40] If the choice a mere three years later between tsar and
hetman was clear, the sense of personal betrayal and vulnerability must
nevertheless have been enormous.

By the 1720s, clearly, this fiery holy war had ceased, tempers
had cooled somewhat — even if Prokopovich's ire remained barely
suppressed — and the hetman's anathema drew barely a mention in

[36] Feofan Prokopovich, 'Slovo pokhval'noe Svetleishemu Rimskago i Rossiiskago Gosudarstv Kniaziu Izherskomu ... Aleksandru Danilovichu Menshikovu', in *Slova i rechi*, vol. 1, pp. 59–61.
[37] Ibid., p. 65.
[38] Ibid., pp. 65–66.
[39] David A. Frick, 'Misrepresentations, Misunderstandings, and Silences: Problems of Seventeenth-Century Ruthenian and Muscovite Cultural History', in Samuel H. Baron and Nancy Shields Kollmann (eds), *Religion and Culture in Early Modern Russia and Ukraine*, DeKalb, IL, 1996, pp. 158–65.
[40] See 'Slovo privetstvitel'noe,' pp. 4–5 and ff.

the *History*. The gist of his hindsight was to portray Mazepa as a small man, rejected and publicly scorned by his own people, hardly a persona at all, who deserved to be remembered only for his individual perfidy and the misfortunes he caused. In effect, he was choosing to radically dislocate and decontextualize Mazepa, to make him into villain outside of time and place. To be sure, Prokopovich continued and even extended the ethnic and territorial motifs raised in the earlier polemics, but without casting Mazepa as integral to them. He seemed to be at pains to portray the Little Russian lands and its people as innocent of the crime, and hence not in need of punishment, even if he left no doubt as to where, and to whom, Ukraine properly belonged. Much like Turoboiskii's 'significant part of the fatherland', Prokopovich's Ukraine was integral to the realm (most often referred to as *otechestvo* or *otchizna*), but one that had distinct qualities that the Prokopovich of the 1720s considered important to retail. However fictive his version of Peter's intentions toward Cossack autonomy or his characterization of the hetmanate under Skoropads´kyi, he deemed these matters sufficiently important to include in his account. In so doing he seemed to legitimate Cossack autonomy to his imagined readers, albeit within the parameters of the Russian Empire, and to acknowledge the special (i.e., negotiated) relationship between the tsar and the hetman's people.

Several possible explanations for including these thoughts in the *History* come immediately to mind. First and most obviously, this was the government's official line — if hardly its consistent practice — dating back to the *kazatskaia rada* that had elected Ivan Skoropads´kyi. A decree of 1 March 1710 that forbade insulting the people of the hetmanate had made this view official doctrine.

> No one shall dare to call 'traitors' Our Tsarist Majesty's loyal subjects the Little Russian people. For one who is not guilty of this crime should not suffer such blame vicariously for [the fault of] another person. Indeed, the people of Little Russia and the Zaporozhian Host have faithfully served us, the great sovereign, and took no part in Mazepa's treason; as for those who were traitors, they have suffered the punishment they deserved. [. . .] Should anyone disobey this injunction of [. . .] Our Tsarist Majesty and insult, irritate, or reproach any of the Little Russian people, then, if he be an officer or an official, he shall be court-martialed and suffer due punishment accordingly; if he be a private soldier or a man of low rank, he shall be severely punished after an investigation; for very grave offenses capital punishment [shall be meted out] without mercy. For all articles and carts taken without special order the offender shall pay a threefold price to the offended party.[41]

[41] Translation adopted from a University of Toronto webpage devoted to documents on Peter and Ukraine, 1708–10 <https://tspace.library.utoronto.ca/citd/RussianHeritage/6.PG/6.L/7.X.12.html>.

However pacified the hetmanate had become in the 1720s, any public suggestion from official circles of intent to curtail 'traditional Cossack liberties' could have revived armed restiveness in an instant. Regardless of whether Feofan meant the *History* primarily for audiences in St Petersburg or in Kyiv, the two cities were in constant and extensive intercourse with one another. Disquieting words could spread quickly east or west, especially through the lines of communication that connected Ukrainian clergy in the hetmanate with those in the Imperial capital. Already discomfited by the formal abolition of the Patriarchate, the clerical hierarchy did not need any more ammunition coming from Prokopovich to feed its displeasure.

Prokopovich may also genuinely have hoped to salvage the core elements of Cossack autonomy, both for narrowly pragmatic reasons — i.e., to avoid a slide back into the violence of the Northern War and the 'Ruin' before it — and in recognition of the value of that autonomy to Orthodoxy, the Empire and himself. Church and state needed Kyiv and Chernihiv to continue to be a steady source of well-educated and worldly elites to staff the dioceses and offices in the capital. Prokopovich unquestionably understood this imperative, especially given the suspicion among Muscovite traditionalists that the archbishop of Novgorod harbored dangerous Protestant sympathies.[42] He, and Peter, simply could not afford for the intellectual pipeline across the Dnepr to be shut off, or for those sent east to arrive with ready-made hostility to matters Russian. The exposure to what Feofan deemed obscurantism would have been too great.[43] When viewed in that light, Feofan's careful re-articulation of Cossack liberties neatly complemented his condemnation of Mazepa: yes, excoriate the man (who must, therefore, be named), but hold Ukraine more or less harmless. A gesture of reassurance to Ukrainian elites, simultaneously a word of caution to the Russian ones, and a carefully crafted and pragmatic strategy to sustain the reforms, this narrative juxtaposition of individual guilt and collective innocence constituted an intervention into realpolitik. More personally, it can be understood as a determined

[42] The polemics around Prokopovich's alleged Protestant sympathies were long standing and the denunciations particularly nasty. Most of the contemporary scholarship has concluded that the claim was exaggerated, and that the categories 'Protestant' and 'Catholic', much like the Latinizer-Grecophile controversy of a generation earlier, had polemical muscle but little theological insight. Nevertheless, Prokopovich's enemies among the Muscovite clergy were real enough, and they forever viewed him as an agent of alien ideas. See Max J. Okenfuss, *The Rise and Fall of Latin Humanism in Early-Modern Russia: Pagan Authors, Ukrainians, and the Resiliency of Muscovy*, Leiden, 1995.

[43] For more details on the ongoing recruitment of Ukrainian clerics, see K. V. Kharlampovich, *Malorossiiskoe vliianie na velikorusskuiu tserkovnuiu zhizn'*, Kazan, 1914, ch. 7, 'Arkhierei-malorossy; malorossiiskii element v sostave eparkhial'nogo upravleniia', pp. 505–50; and Jan Plamper, 'The Russian Orthodox Episcopate, 1721–1917: A Prosopography', *Journal of Social History*, 34, 2000, 1, pp. 6–8.

effort to reconnect the two halves of Feofan's identity and loyalty that had been abruptly torn asunder in 1708.

This interpenetration of the personal and the political emerges more vividly in Pylyp Orlyk's work. Originating from a similar social and educational background, Orlyk's life took a radically different trajectory than Prokopovich's. Born near Vilnius to a Catholic father and Orthodox mother nine years earlier, in 1672, he too pursued his education through the church, first in a Jesuit College (in Vilnius) and then at the Academy in Kyiv. A polyglot, he composed verse in Latin, including a panegyric to Mazepa, *Alcides Rossyiski* (*The Russian Alcides*), in 1695.[44] Although never tonsured, he became the secretary of the Kyivan consistory for a brief period beginning in 1698, a very important post that brought him into direct contact with leading clergy and political figures of the hetmanate. Let us recall the turbulence that had preoccupied much of Kyiv's clerical hierarchy over the previous decade. The metropolia had lost its autocephalous status in 1686, which had been maintained under the loose oversight of the Constantinople Patriarchate for several decades. In its place the metropolia was obliged to accept formal incorporation into the Moscow Patriarchate, from which it now received direction — often unappreciated — and to whom it contributed a steady flow of clergy. Although the expressed reactions to this change were far from uniform, much of the local clergy expressed unease at the loss of autonomy, especially since many felt themselves to have a superior level of culture and sophistication than their co-religionists to the east.[45] Orlyk's responsibilities put him in constant touch with these concerns, as well as with representatives from the Moscow Patriarchate, as all parties jockeyed for advantage in this new arrangement.

In 1699 Orlyk switched his service to the political hierarchy, becoming a senior member of the military council, arguably the most important constituted body in the hierarchy of the Zaporizhian hetmanate. In 1706, or more or less the time when Prokopovich was emerging as an orator of note, Mazepa appointed Orlyk to become his new chief military advisor. As such, he witnessed first hand the discussions and machinations that would result in the *izmena* of 1708, and from which experiences he drew his political lessons thereafter. During the tumultuous days of 1708–09 Orlyk remained at Mazepa's side, and

---

[44] On panegyrics to Mazepa in general, see Lidiia Sazonova, 'Getman Mazepa kak obraz panegiricheskii: iz poetiki vostochnoslavianskogo barokko', in Giovana Siedina (ed.), *Mazepa e il suo tempo Storia, cultura, società. Mazepa and His Time. History, Culture, Society*, Alessandria, 2004, pp. 462–87.

[45] The classic and most informative discussion of this issue remains Kharlampovich, *Malorossiiskoe vliianie*, p. 181 and passim.

when the hetman died a hastily-summoned *kazatskaia rada* selected Orlyk, the personal choice of the Swedish emperor, to be the new hetman in exile. It was in that capacity that he authored his most famous document, the so-called Bendery Constitution, acclaimed by some in contemporary Ukraine as the world's first modern written constitution and the foundation of Ukrainian republicanism.[46] Although little known outside the region, Orlyk has re-emerged several times during the past two centuries as a towering and memorialized figure of the Ukrainian national imaginary, in particular during the revolutionary years of 1917–21, again in the twentieth-century diaspora, and now once again in independent Ukraine. For many, his persona has come to represent a legacy of political independence, popular sovereignty, representative government and resistance to tyranny. Only Bogdan Khmel′nitskyi and Mazepa himself from the era of the hetmanate loom larger for modern Ukrainians. Little wonder, then, that a cornerstone of the recently-founded US–Ukraine Foundation is the Pylyp Orlyk Institute for Democracy, whose mission in part is 'to help revive Ukrainian democratic traditions'.[47]

Like other educated Kyivans of his day Orlyk wrote prolifically and in several languages (Latin, Polish, Russian, Ukrainian, French). While in exile he maintained a voluminous 'campaign diary' covering most of the years until his death, and he penned a number of political tracts.[48] In that sense he was more like Prokopovich and the other clerical luminaries and less like Mazepa, whose astonishing fluency in many languages (including, apparently, Turkish and Tatar) notwithstanding, limited himself largely to private letters and official documents. The 1721 letter to Iavorskii stands out, however, for its plaintive and argumentative tone, as well as for its rich detail. First printed in the journal *Osnova* in 1862[49] and subsequently published by Orest

[46] Pylyp Orlyk, *Pacta et Constitutiones legume libertatumque exercitus Zaporovienis: Inter Illustrissimum dominum dominum Philippum Orlik, neoelectum ducem exercitus Zaporoviensis, et inter generales, colonellos, nec non eundem exercitum Zaporoviensem, publico utriusque parties laudo conventa ac in libera electione formali iuramento ab eodem illustrissimo duce corroborate, anno domini 1710, Aprilis 5, ad Benderam*, Moscow, 1858. See also Oleksii Shtanko, Myroslav Trofymuk and Omeljan Pritsak, *Persha konstytutsiia Ukrainy Het′mana Pylypa Orlyka: 1710 rik*, Kyiv, 1994; S. Mazuryk, 'La Constitution de Bendery, document précurseur de la démocratie européenne', *Kačka*, 9, 2002, p. 2.

[47] See the website <http://www.usukraine.org/POID.shtml>, p. 1.

[48] Daniel Beauvois, 'Le *Journal* de Phillipe Orlyk: du mirage d'éxile au mythe identitaire ukrainien', in *Mazepa e il suo tempo*, especially pp. 148–77. Much of the diary has been published over the years, both in the original Polish and in Ukrainian translations. A facsimile of the manuscript was produced several years ago by Harvard. See, inter alia, *The Diariusz podrozny of Pylyp Orlyk, 1720–1726*, ed. Orest Subtelny, Cambridge, MA, 1989; *The Diariusz podrozny of Pylyp Orlyk, 1727–1731*, ed. Omeljan Pritsak, Cambridge, MA, 1988; *Diarii Het′mana Pylypa Orlyka*, Warsaw, 1936.

[49] 'Pis′mo Orlika k Stefanu Iavorskomu', *Osnova*, 10, 1862, pp. 3–28. I wish to thank Giovanna Brogi Bercoff for bringing this publication to my attention.

Subtelny in English translation,[50] it has received surprisingly little attention in the scholarship. The three published versions, although accurate and substantively complete, do not reproduce all of Orlyk's Latin and French expressions, and by this omission they do not convey the full flavour of his strategic self-presentation to Iavorskii. Consequently, I have in some instances gone back to the original manuscript, located in the Petrine-era papers of the Russian Archive of Ancient Acts (RGADA) in Moscow,[51] in an effort to restore some of the literary flourishes of the original.

Iavorskii had been Orlyk's instructor in both Rhetoric and Philosophy at the Kyivan Academy in the early 1690s. By some accounts Iavorskii had been instrumental in placing Orlyk in the consistory and later in his military ascendancy. Although his political star had fallen markedly since 1714, largely because of his thinly-veiled preference for a more independent church and for a restoration of the Patriarchate,[52] Iavorskii retained widespread respect, particularly among the diocesan elites and among the black clergy overall. Equally important was his standing among the educated and well-placed elites in Kyiv. His extended family had remained locally visible and active in the affairs of the Kyivan church. For example, his brother Fedor had played a central role in identifying capable Ukrainian clerics, including Turoboiskii and Lopatinskii, and had arranging for them to serve in the Muscovite church at the very beginning of the eighteenth century.[53] Born in 1658, he came from an older generation than most of the other clerical luminaries from Ukraine then living and working in St Petersburg. The Metropolitan of Riazan´ and long a resident of St Petersburg, he was the most senior of the Kyivan-trained clerics in Peter's service. He also was one of the few remaining living ties between tsarist authority in the capital and those both in Kyiv and in exile who experienced the relationship between hetmanate and the double-eagled crown as it had been before 1708.

Written while in lonely and increasingly desperate exile (since 1710 he had moved to Crimea, Sweden, Silesia and Warsaw, and was soon to be placed under guard for the rest of his life in various locales in the Ottoman Empire), Orlyk's extraordinary letter occupied a different

---

[50] 'Pylyp Orlyk's letter to Stefan Iavorskyi (1721): An Eyewitness Account of Hetman Mazepa's Defection', in Subtelny, *The Mazepists*, pp. 178–205.

[51] 'Pis´mo Orlika k Mitropolitu Stefanu Iavorskomu ob izmene Mazepy', Rossiiskii Gosudarstvennyi Arkhiv Drevnikh Aktov (RGADA), Razriad VI, no. 154.

[52] For a detailed discussion of Iavorskii's views on the Patriarchate, and on Patriarchs in general, see Viktor Zhivov, *Iz tserkovnoi istorii vremen Petra Velikogo: Issledovaniia i materialy*, Moscow, 2004, pp. 119–30.

[53] Institut rukopisei Natsional´noi biblioteki Ukrainy im. V. I. Vernads´kogo, Kyiv (hereafter, IR NBU), f. 194, no. 120, 'Vypisi i kopii arkhivnykh dokumentov', p. 66; f. II, no. 2309, 'Gramota tsarskaia Preosviashchennomu Varlaamu Iasinskomu Mitropolitu kievskomu, o ne vozbranenii vo uchat´sia v kievskoi akademii', pp. 5–6.

genre altogether. We do not know whether Orlyk intended the letter for eyes other than the metropolitan's, but the form and content were suffused with shared memories and a sense of intimacy. He expresses himself repeatedly as if writing in confidence and in pain, although much of this reads as highly instrumental prose. Nominally, he was endeavouring to place his actions during those fateful days in context, nominally to secure the tsar's forgiveness, and more fundamentally to seek salvation before God — 'I wish to confess before Your Holiness, as before the prelate who spans the heavens and knows the secrets of the heart'.[54] Needless to say, Prokopovich's text contained nothing of the sort.

Orlyk's letter needs to be situated in the specific political context of the Ukrainian exile community and its diminished security as the Northern War neared its end. The Swedes had reneged on a promise to raise the issue of Ukraine in the Nystadt negotiations, thus rendering untenable Orlyk's continued stay in Sweden. Several exiles had petitioned for pardons and had returned to the Empire, although not always back to Ukraine. Some had been relocated in Archangel, others further east, and a few had been captured abroad and been returned to the Russian state involuntarily. Orlyk's military aide and brother-in-law, Hryhor Hertsyk, had been seized while in transit in Warsaw in 1721, brought back to St Petersburg, and interrogated at length about the political activities of his confreres.[55] Hertsyk's family had shared a long personal and political history with Orlyk, and the two men were very close. Orlyk had served under Hertsyk's father, a Cossack colonel the 1690s, and in 1698 he married the elder Hertsyk's daughter, Anna. Losses such as this came uncomfortably close to home, and Orlyk was quickly exhausting his options.[56] In that light he understood that his only chance for a pardon ran through Iavorskii, and the only way to achieve it would be to denounce Mazepa retroactively.[57]

Orlyk set an early tone of individualized deference, even submission, by characterizing his relationship to Iavorskii as that of 'a pupil to one's teacher', 'a son to his father', and 'a sheep to the shepherd'.[58] In the main he employs Belorussian dialect — more or less his native tongue — as a further expression of his personal connection to Iavorskii.[59]

---

[54] Unless otherwise noted, I am relying upon Subtelny's fine English translation (hereafter, Subtelny). References to the printed Russian text are noted as *Osnova*. The original in RGADA will be referred to as 'Manuscript'. Subtelny, p. 179; *Osnova*, p. 2.

[55] RGADA, f. 6, no. 154, 'Doprosy i perepiska Grigoriia Gertsika izmenivshago vmeste s Mazepoi i Orlikom i skhvachennago v Varshave'.

[56] Subtelny, pp. 124–27.

[57] Beauvois, pp. 159–60.

[58] Subtelny, p. 178; *Osnova*, p. 3.

[59] Manuscript, p. 4. The dialect is noted by the chancellery official who inventoried the letter.

But this was no ordinary member of the flock, and Orlyk asserts his intellectual credentials by addressing Iavorskii in French ('À son Éminence Monseigneur Étienne de Iaworski, Archevêque Metropolit-ain de Resagne et Mourome'),[60] a language in which Iavorskii was apparently unlettered. He intersperses the text with Latin phraseology and recapitulations of the vernacular text, and then he comes full circle by composing the salutation once again in French: 'Monsieur. Votre tres humbles, tres affectionné et tres obeisant Frere et Serviteur, Pilip Orlik.'[61] In other words, Orlyk was establishing two planes of author-ity and intimacy, reaching out to Iavorskii as a supplicant from a shared background while simultaneously presenting himself as an intellectual equal, or more. If Mazepa's treachery and apostasy lay beyond doubt in Prokopovich's *History*, it was far less clear-cut to Orlyk, who con-structed a narrative of shadowy ambiguities and unresolved dualities (intellect and faith, mind and heart, appearance and reality, loyalty and treason, native and foreigner). The tensions between these many and varied poles guided both his argument and narrative.

Like Prokopovich, Orlyk looks at Mazepa as a discreet personality. In sharp contrast to Prokopovich, however, he situates Mazepa both temporally and spatially very precisely within the political maelstroms that defined his world, as an individual struggling unsuccessfully to control forces that perpetually threaten to consume him. He casts Mazepa's move to the Swedish side as a diabolical seduction, in which the Polish court of King Stanisław Leszczynski, specifically Princess Dolska, played the role of temptress. 'Whether, before he went into Poland with his army in the service of the Tsar and before the devil, taking advantage of the bonds of kinship, led Princess Dolska into secret conference with him, Mazepa had any inclination for the oppos-ing side and for the thoughts of betrayal, God alone [. . .] knows.'[62] He launches into a long and torturous review of meetings, correspondence, and events from the period 1705–08 in order to display the impossibil-ity of knowing exactly when or how Mazepa was turned (in retrospect Orlyk surmises that it might have been as early as 1705). Of course, most of this brief focused on Orlyk's professions of his own lack of foreknowledge, and his ignorance of secret negotiations until the fall of 1707. In the process it is important for him to set the record straight on Mazepa, if not to pronounce judgement at least to present the facts. But even the facts prove elusive in the disorienting political hall of mirrors that he depicts. On one hand, he insists that he was convinced that Mazepa had long remained faithful to the Tsar, faithful to his oath, and reverential to his faith. On the other hand, Mazepa said so

[60] *Osnova*, p. 3; Manuscript, p. 3.
[61] Manuscript, p. 36.
[62] Subtelny, p. 179.

many contradictory things, and behaved with such careful conceal-
ment, Orlyk maintained, that it often proved impossible to know what
was truth and what was artifice.

Both Orlyk and Mazepa had grown increasingly suspicious of
Menshikov and his designs on Ukraine (his opponents among the
Russian forces had whispered to Orlyk that Menshikov wanted to 'dig
a hole' under Mazepa in order to become the hetman himself). Denunciations of Menshikov recur repeatedly in Orlyk's letter, at a time when
Menshikov was being celebrated in St Petersburg as a conquering hero.
Mazepa here comes across as a man whose honour has been wounded
by the Radiant Prince's affronts and by his fear that the ongoing
wars were exhausting his forces and inexorably subordinating them to
the tsar's regiments. Simultaneously he was engaged in an extensive
ciphered communication with Warsaw, nominally about using Mazepa's
influence to try to convince the tsar to abandon August II and support
Lesczcynski, although Orlyk confesses that he knew the contents of
these letters only on those occasions when Mazepa allowed him to
decode them. Troubled by the malefactions encircling them, the
Cossack colonels worried about preserving their traditional freedoms.
'The colonel of Pryluk [said], "Just as we always prayed to God for the
soul of Khmel´nitskyi and blessed his name for freeing Ukraine from
the Polish yoke, so, on the contrary, will we and our children forever
curse your soul and bones, if, as a result of your hetmancy, you leave
us in such slavery after your death".'[63] Mazepa seemingly was being
pulled in many directions, encircled by increasingly contradictory
imperatives. Up to this point, Orlyk's version undermined the official
Petrine doctrine, of which he was well aware, that emphasized Ukraine's
collective innocence and non-involvement in the hetman's doing.
Rather than the renegade lone wolf that Prokopovich described,
Orlyk's hetman was a virtual hostage of his colonels' vocal displeasure,
at one with the land and its people in their collective aspiration to
maintain traditional freedoms.

This, however, was a tale of what Daniel Beauvois has termed 'a
theatre of shadows':[64] hints, veils and misdirection, as if to play on the
region's mystique of political inscrutability. What seemed clear in the
summer of 1707 was rendered opaque or illusory a few months later.
Orlyk describes an epiphany from 16 September 1707, when in his
presence Mazepa read a letter from the Polish king telling him to act
as planned in anticipation of the arrival of Swedish forces into Poland.
Recognizing that this amounted to opening the doors of Ukraine to
the Swedes, Orlyk now 'comprehended that Mazepa was plotting a

[63] Ibid., p. 185.
[64] Beauvois, p. 153.

betrayal'.[65] Orlyk's reaction, he tells Iavorskii, was fear — 'Frightened
by this betrayal and wishing not to perish with my wife and children
because of it, my heart had no inclination for it.'[66] What then of
Mazepa's oneness with the Ukrainian people, or Orlyk's oneness with
Mazepa? On the next day Mazepa revealed his true thoughts, or what
he maintained were his true thoughts on that day, according to Orlyk's
letter to Iavorskii written fifteen years after the fact.

> Since it can no longer be concealed from you, I swear before God that it
> is not for my own private gain, nor for higher honors, nor for greater
> wealth [...] that I act. But I do so for all of you who are under my rule
> and command, and for your wives and children, for the common welfare
> of our fatherland, unfortunate Ukraine, for the entire Zaporozhian Host
> and the Little Russian people for the expansion of the Host's rights and
> privileges [dlia podvyshinenii i razshirenii prav i volnostei voiskovykh] so
> that, with the aid of God, neither you, nor your wives and children, nor
> the fatherland together with the Zaporozhian Host might perish because
> of either the Muscovite or Swedish side.[67]

These passages, so reminiscent of Prokopovich's own language,
reveal the extent to which the two sons of Kyiv were cut from the same
literary cloth. Each interpolates heroic speeches at liminal political
moments, verbal gauntlets to inspire one's troops who are on the
threshold of committing themselves to decisive and consequential
action. In both cases the larger-than-life leaders renounce personal
glory or ambition, and instead exhort their respective followers to fight
for family, fatherland, nation/people (narod), and posterity. This is not
the only instance in which the two texts appear to echo one another.
Prokopovich's remorse at the spilling of Christian blood at Baturyn
sounds eerily similar to language Orlyk employed in describing
Mazepa's reaction to the same event.

> I swear to [...] God that I did not desire the spilling of Christian blood
> [...] I intended to declare [in a letter to Peter — G. M.] that we had
> acquiesced voluntarily [svobodne] to the sovereignty of His Tsarist Majesty
> for the sake of the unified Eastern Orthodox faith. Being a free people
> [svobodnym narodom], we now wished to withdraw freely [svobodne], expressing
> gratitude for the Tsar's protection and not wishing to raise our hands in
> the shedding of Christian blood.[68]

These are very telling soliloquies, and they reveal a great deal about
how claims to allegiance and collective solidarity had subtly shifted
since Poltava. We need keep in mind that these are fundamentally

[65] Subtelny, p. 189.
[66] Ibid., p. 190.
[67] Ibid., pp. 190–91; Osnova, pp. 13–14. Here I have made some minor revisions to
Subtelny's translation.
[68] Subtelny, pp. 201–02; Osnova, pp. 24–25.

the *authors'* (i.e., Prokopovich's and Orlyk's) words; we have no idea
whether Peter or Mazepa actually uttered them. It is the words rather
than the speakers that resonate and, it is here, in these clarion calls,
that both Prokopovich and Orlyk stake their claim to History's judgement on the momentous events of which they were a part, and
separately from the outsized personas that otherwise loom so large.
The common frames of reference reveal the extent to which strikingly
modern evocations of state, a people, blood and fatherland had moved
to the foreground of the discursive tête-à-tête, and faith or antiquity
had receded, but by no means disappeared. Implicit in this shift is
the centrality of sovereignty, political and geographic boundaries as
primary issues, and the allegiances of peoples within multi-peopled
empires, whose numbers now included Russia. In short, this switch in
terminology put the meaning of *Rossiia* at the very centre of the discussion, the contours of *Imperiia*, and the place that the *nemalaia chast'* that
was Malaia Rossiia would occupy within it. One might go so far as to
suggest that Ukraine was the main soil on which 'empire' would take
shape, the discursive and physical battleground of political allegiances.
In that context Orlyk's continued use of *svoboda* to convey Mazepa's
articulation of Ukraine's negotiated status with contiguous states,
rather than the formulaic and familiar 'traditional rights and freedoms
[*prava i volnosti*] of the Cossacks', is quite telling.

Orlyk offers a highly personal exploration of these unreconciled
issues in his accounts to Iavorskii of loyalty and the meanings of the
sacred oaths that he and others had sworn. Mazepa had demanded
that Orlyk swear an oath on the cross that he would preserve the secret
he now knew. Orlyk reluctantly complied, and then wondered aloud
about how it would all end. In his summation Orlyk returned to the
oaths in order to explain his failure to inform the Tsar.

> I knew of this secret, accidentally revealed to me, and was forced by
> Mazepa's order, by his terrible oath, and, in addition, by subversion, to
> take a mutual oath of loyalty. I did not reveal the secret to anyone and
> maintained an unscathed faithfulness, *like a servant to his master, like a
> foreigner and client to his benefactor* [*iako sluga panu, iako inozemets i kreatura svoemu
> blagodetelevi*]. (Italics added — G. M.)[69]

This bitter metaphor comes in the penultimate paragraph of the letter,
and thus offers both a striking contrast and poetic symmetry to the
metaphor with which Orlyk began — in the second paragraph! — his
supplication to Iavorskii 'like a pupil to his teacher, like a son to his
father'. The use of 'foreigner' is particularly striking, and it echoes a
phrase that Orlyk had employed earlier in describing his increasingly
conflicted sentiments and his deepening distrust of Mazepa.

[69] Ibid., p. 204; *Osnova*, p. 27.

I began to think of some means of preserving myself from impending
troubles. However I was deterred by several chilling thoughts which passed
through my mind [. . .] my Christian conscience forced me to consider the
oath by which I was bound to serve faithfully only him. Mazepa was the
Hetman and my lord [*Getmanu i panu svoemu*]. In relation to His Tsarist
Majesty I was a foreigner and newcomer to Ukraine, never having sworn
either submission or loyalty to him [*I ni na poddanstvo, i ni na vernost' nikogda
i prisiagal est'*]. Therefore I was troubled [by the thought] of the damnation
of my soul not only as an oath breaker, but also as a betrayer of my lord
and benefactor.[70]

Here Orlyk was combining the sacred inviolability of oaths and the
opacity of the loyalty/*izmena* dichotomy. He used his Vilnius origins as
doubly defining: they made him a foreigner both in the hetmanate and
in the larger realm of Russia. Orlyk seems to have chosen his words
carefully, and his deployment of 'foreigner' (in both cases *inozemets*)
referred to political spaces and boundaries, whereas his understanding
of oaths and the loyalties they encumbered was personal, spiritual and
intimate. Hence, Ukraine (and in these passages Orlyk uses 'Ukraina'
rather than 'Malaia Rossiia') is implicitly perceived as a space of dual,
or layered sovereignty, simultaneously local and imperial. Remarkably,
this is not so different from Prokopovich's articulation of Ukraine's
special status.

What, then, was the verdict on Mazepa? After all, anything short
of a personal denunciation would guarantee an unreceptive hearing.
It is here, I would argue, that rhetorical virtuosity and awareness of
audience, specifically the reader's capacity to differentiate the characterization of the persona speaking from the words of the soliloquy,
become critical in allowing Orlyk to defend the cause while condemning the man. The entire second half of the letter amounts to an unravelling of Mazepa's words and deeds, sorting out truth from falsehood,
along with conveying Orlyk's existential dilemma of what to do once
he has perceived what was really going on. Orlyk does not shy away
from the language of treason and traitor, words that he employs repeatedly to describe Mazepa. But his main point is to paint Mazepa as
being beyond duplicitous: caught between impossible alternatives he
was deceiving *everyone* (Russia, Poland, Sweden, Crimea, the starshyna,
Menshikov, his own aides), issuing misleading proclamations, negotiating
with everyone and against everyone simultaneously. In Orlyk's telling
this was less a struggle of nation against nation than a barely constrained Hobbesian nightmare, with Mazepa as both active subject and
overwhelmed victim. In the end, the fateful decision to switch sides
comes across as impulsive; the careful secret negotiations as a failing of

[70] Subtelny, pp. 196–97; *Osnova*, pp. 23–24; *Archive*, p. 73.

a deluded figure who convinced himself beyond all reason that he could control the tides, knowing full well that most of the Cossack regiments would not stand with him. Was he alone in this, as Prokopovich maintained, or was he expressing the collective will of his people? In the final analysis Orlyk tries to have it both ways, once again using the power of words and sacred oaths to make his case. Having told us of the widespread unease among the Cossacks with Mazepa's dangerous diplomacy, and of the general awareness that many of the regiments would not follow him to the Swedish side, Orlyk makes his final plea for gaining the same forgiveness that other Cossack leaders had received:

> I alone could not have done His Tsarist majesty any harm, because one man can do nothing [bo unus nullus]. Why did none of the others, sons of Ukraine, fervent of their fatherland, from [the time of] their fathers faithful subjects of His Tsarist Majesty, having discovered the secret, not reveal it? Moreover, by their oath did they not reinforce it and promise, by kissing the Holy Gospel, to stand by Mazepa to the death in defense of their rights and liberties [za prava i volnosti].[71]

In other words, they too were bound by an unbreakable oath, subservient to the power of words sworn with Scriptural witness, obliged to defend a course of action with which they did not agree. Mazepa's soaring genius and fatal sin had been to recognize the power of those words and the faiths to which they referred to control those around him and oblige them to follow through on ill-fated campaigns. Like Prokopovich, Orlyk was determined to proclaim the irreducible being and social function of language. Like Prokopovich, he was directing his readers, present and future, to be mindful of the words — in this case his words, embedded orations perhaps — as enduring beyond the immediate times or individuals to whom they were attached.

Conclusion

In the final analysis Orlyk and Prokopovich agreed that responsibility for the events of 1708–09 lay with Mazepa. Orlyk's Mazepa was fundamentally a man of politics, a figure of endless 'cunning and deceit' (*prelest´ i khitrost*), the architect of a disaster, but very much a real human being, mistaken and conflicted rather than demonic and evil. His strategic judgement was flawed and his diplomacy a tattered ruin. Nonetheless, he was acting out of motives larger than himself, motives that remained honorable. Prokopovich's Mazepa was, on the other hand, an irredeemable traitor to his faith. And for sharply different reasons they agreed that the rights and freedoms of the Cossacks were larger than the man himself and that they were important to maintain.

[71] Subtelny, p. 204; *Osnova*, p. 27.

The Summer Gardens in the Social Life of St Petersburg, 1725–61

PAUL KEENAN

DURING the late seventeenth and early eighteenth centuries, the elaborate gardens maintained by the leading European royal Courts were an important symbol of wealth and status. The celebrated and influential example of Versailles inspired a number of imitators across Europe throughout this period.[1] The regulation of nature and its inherent hierarchy were important themes in these gardens, adopted for the glorification of monarchical authority in this context.[2] However, such gardens also performed a number of important social functions for rulers and their attendant Courts. For example, in a period when social status was usually reflected in one's appearance through conspicuously opulent clothing, gardens provided a useful opportunity to see and to be seen by one's social peers.[3] Gardens also provided a suitable forum for a number of related sociable activities, such as strolling and polite conversation, that were increasingly an established part of European social interaction.[4]

Whilst the social function of gardens in this period has been examined in several other parts of Europe, the role of the Summer Gardens in the early social and cultural life of St Petersburg has been relatively understudied.[5] Whilst the Summer Gardens have been discussed by

Paul Keenan is Lecturer in International History at the London School of Economics and Political Science.

[1] T. C. W. Blanning, *The Pursuit of Glory: Europe, 1648–1815*, London, 2007, pp. 440–41.

[2] Chandra Mukerji, *Territorial Ambitions and the Gardens of Versailles*, Cambridge, 1997, pp. 8–18 and 248–72.

[3] Daniel Roche, *The Culture of Clothing: Dress and Fashion in the 'Ancien Régime'*, Cambridge, 1994, p. 130.

[4] Norbert Elias, *The Court Society*, trans. Edmund Jephcott, Oxford, 1983.

[5] Scholarship on the Summer Gardens during the eighteenth century has often followed the pattern of the more wide-ranging studies of gardens in Russia. Two loose groupings can be identified amongst these works. The first group could be described as horticultural (or technical) studies, in that the focus is primarily on the history of the physical form of the gardens, including architects and models, and certain features therein, such as the busts, statues and fountains located in the Summer Gardens. The key work in this respect remains the detailed archival work presented in T. B. Dubiago, *Russkie reguliarnye sady i parki*, Leningrad, 1963. The second group could be described as allegorical studies, in that the focus is on the symbolic significance of their design and the meanings of the overall motifs or inspirations, often drawing on Classical or contemporary European models. This approach is exemplified by D. S. Likhachev, *Poeziia sadov: k semantike sadovo-parkovykh stilei. Sad kak tekst*, St Petersburg, 1991 and, more recently, by Andreas Schönle, *The Ruler in the Garden: Politics and Landscape Design in Imperial Russia*, Bern and New York, 2007. Chronologically, there has naturally been an emphasis on the reign of Peter I in studies of the Summer Gardens, while

historians of the reign of Peter I,[6] the period from his death in 1725 to the death of his daughter, Elizaveta Petrovna, in 1761, has been largely neglected.[7] However, this was a significant period in the history of the Summer Gardens and of social life for three main reasons. Firstly, the Summer Gardens were an important symbol of the 'Europeanization' process at work in Russia during this period, both because they took a consciously European form and because European specialists were employed to carry out work there.[8] Secondly, the gardens provided an important social forum within the city for both the Court and its elite, in which they could interact in a 'new' manner similar to their European contemporaries. Thirdly, this period is crucial for addressing the issue of regular access to the Summer Gardens for members of St Petersburg society. For much of their early existence, the Summer Gardens represented a space largely reserved for the Imperial family, members of their personal retinues and a select

[5] *Continued*
    for the remainder of the eighteenth century, the focus has been mainly on the gardens outside St Petersburg, particularly at Peterhof and Tsarskoe Selo, and on the leading noble estates. See, for example, Margrethe Floryan, *Gardens of the Tsars: A Study of the Aesthetics, Semantics and Uses of Late 18th Century Russian Gardens*, Aarhus, 1996, and Priscilla Roosevelt, *Life on the Russian Country Estate: A Social and Cultural History*, New Haven, CT and London, 1995.

[6] An excellent overview of the Summer Gardens during this period is provided by the magisterial Lindsey Hughes, *Russia in the Age of Peter the Great*, New Haven, CT and London, 1998, pp. 211–15 and 217–18.

[7] A recent exception — albeit with the main focus on the palace, rather than the gardens — is the chapter 'V Letnem dvortse', in K. A. Pisarenko, *Povsednevnaia zhizn´ russkogo dvora v tsarstvovanie Elizavety Petrovny*, Moscow, 2003, pp. 138–61.

[8] The use of the term 'Europeanization', where one might equally expect to find its frequent bed-fellow 'Westernization', naturally raises the spectre of the debatable nature of such concepts (or processes) for Russia in this period. Traditionally, many historians referred to Russia's 'European turn' during the eighteenth century, mainly at elite level, without defining the concept for this particular context, beyond the broad confines of Russia becoming 'more European/Western'. However, a number of important contributions have developed the debate by questioning some of its assumptions. First, when comparing Russia to a broadly-defined region, be it Europe or 'the West', one must question what that region meant to contemporaries, rather than applying it retrospectively. For a thought-provoking discussion of 'Europe' in the early modern period, see Peter Burke, 'Did Europe Exist before 1700?', *History of European Ideas*, 1, 1980, pp. 1–29. A useful introduction for Russia and Europe in the eighteenth century is provided by Janet Hartley, 'Is Russia Part of Europe? Russian Perspectives on Europe in the Reign of Alexander I', *Cahiers du monde russe*, 33, 1992, 4, pp. 369–85 (esp. pp. 369–72). Secondly, by studying the process in more specific detail, scholars have drawn attention to very important questions about the dating of its origins, the areas that it affected and the extent of its impact. These issues, albeit with a varying focus on several conceptual frameworks, are the subject of a lively discussion in *Slavic Review*, 41, 1982, 4, pp. 611–38, with particular reference in the contribution by James Cracraft (pp. 629–33). Indeed, one of the latter author's recent contributions to this debate provides a working definition of 'Europeanization', for the purposes of this article: 'assimilation or, more appropriately, appropriation in some degree of European cultural practices and norms', in James Cracraft, *The Petrine Revolution in Russian Culture*, Cambridge, MA, 2004, p. 308.

number of other privileged individuals. However, by the middle of the century, there was a clear attempt to enable more people from a range of different social groups to make use of the Summer Gardens on a more regular basis, as distinct from the limited access to the gardens granted to certain groups during Court celebrations.

There was no real parallel between the elaborate, formal gardens associated with other contemporary European Courts and the more functional nature of the examples from Muscovite Russia.[9] Even in the gardens of the extensive estates around Moscow, notably Izmailovo and Kolomenskoe, the emphasis was on the produce of the land, rather than any inherent aesthetic qualities or social use.[10] Thus, the creation of a formally-planned, European-style garden in St Petersburg can be interpreted as an important symbol of the different direction intended for Peter I's 'new' city, his 'paradise' on the Baltic.[11] In the first place, it reflected a desire to create urban spaces in which different forms of social interaction could take place, more akin to Peter's experiences whilst travelling during the Grand Embassy.[12] Although, from the later eighteenth century onwards, Nevskii Prospekt would become the main avenue in St Petersburg for the type of informal strolling that was common in other European cities, properly-paved and indeed safe areas in which to stroll were considerably more restricted in this period of the city's development.[13] The Summer Gardens are therefore significant in that they provided one such space for this social activity within the city's limits during the first half of the eighteenth century.

However, this also highlights an important distinction between the Summer Gardens and several of the major contemporary examples, such as Versailles, Hampton Court or Schönbrunn, that might be considered comparable.[14] In the latter cases, the gardens were part of

---

[9] A. P. Vergunov and V. A. Gorokhov, *Russkie sady i parki*, 2nd edn, Moscow, 2007, pp. 21–35.

[10] James Cracraft, *The Petrine Revolution in Russian Architecture*, Chicago, IL, 1988, p. 182.

[11] *Russia in the Age of Peter*, pp. 211–12. Of course, this is not to suggest that the Court gardens ceased to have a practical function in the eighteenth century and the Court kitchens continued to use the produce of the Summer Gardens throughout this period (see below, n. 20).

[12] Lindsey Hughes, 'The Courts of Moscow and St Petersburg, *c.* 1547–1725', in John Adamson (ed.), *The Princely Courts of Europe, 1500–1750*, London, 1999, pp. 295–313 (pp. 302–04).

[13] A collection of early nineteenth-century views is presented in *Progulki po Nevskomu Prospektu v pervoi polovine XIX veka*, ed. A. M. Konechnyi, St Petersburg, 2002.

[14] Ian Thompson, *The Sun King's Garden: Louis XIV, André Le Nôtre and the Creation of the Gardens of Versailles*, London, 2006. Simon Thurley, *Hampton Court: A Social and Architectural History*, New Haven, CT, and London, 2003. A wide-ranging overview of Schönbrunn, Belvedere and other contemporaries of the Summer Gardens is provided by Thomas DaCosta Kaufmann, *Court, Cloister, and City: The Art and Culture of Central Europe, 1450–1800*, Chicago, IL, 1995.

large royal estates, distinct from their associated cities, whereas the Summer Gardens were essentially an area within St Petersburg itself.[15] This factor is certainly relevant to discussions of its role in the city's social life and the granting of access to it for certain social groups, the main subjects of this article. As such, the urban gardens of other major European cities, such as Kensington Gardens in London or the gardens of the Tuileries palace or the Palais-Royale in Paris, provide a more relevant comparison.[16] These gardens were previously exclusive Court spaces which were opened to regular and relatively open access during the eighteenth century and which formed important social spaces within the city as a result.[17] However, despite the greater degree of access in this period, compared to previous practice, the restrictions that were imposed on those individuals wishing to take advantage of this privilege in St Petersburg also had parallels across contemporary Europe.

It is worth briefly discussing the physical layout of the eighteenth-century Summer Gardens, since the modern-day version is considerably smaller and organized rather differently than its predecessors. The main territory of the initial Summer Garden was divided into two sections by the Poperechnyi canal, although they were linked by a small bridge with a fountain in the middle. From this canal to the Neva was the area later known as the 'first' Summer Garden. This garden was initially planned by Peter I and subsequently supervised by Ivan Matveev from 1705–06 onwards. It was strongly influenced by the contemporary Dutch style, no doubt drawing on Peter's experience of visiting Het Loo in 1697.[18] This influence was consolidated with his

[15] Several other examples in eighteenth-century Russia have borne comparison with these European contemporaries. For example, the gardens of the imperial residence at Peterhof claimed a direct inspiration from Versailles in a number of its features, such as the naming of certain features and its use of fountains. However, Likhachev is quick to highlight the differences between source 'text' and Russian 'translation' in his analysis: Likhachev, *Poeziia sadov*, pp. 153–87. Equally, scholars have examined the shifting influences on the extensive gardens surrounding the palace at Tsarskoe Selo, where the mid-century taste for French formal gardens was succeeded by an enthusiasm for the English style under Catherine II. A useful overview is presented by Anthony Cross, 'The English Garden in Catherine the Great's Russia', *Journal of Garden History*, 3, 1993, 3, pp. 172–81, whilst the considerable influence of the Scottish architect Charles Cameron on Russian garden design is detailed in D. O. Shvidkovsky, *The Empress and the Architect: British Architecture and Gardens at the Court of Catherine the Great*, New Haven, CT, 1996.

[16] For a lively introduction to the social use of these urban gardens in Paris, see Colin Jones, *Paris: The Biography of a City*, London, 2004, pp. 142–43 and 182–85.

[17] James van Horn Melton, *The Rise of the Public in Enlightenment Europe*, Cambridge, 2001, p. 169.

[18] *Russkie sady i parki*, pp. 46–47. For Peter's visit to Holland, see Lindsey Hughes, *Peter the Great: A Biography*, New Haven, CT, and London, 2002, p. 45. Hughes also highlights Peter's interest in the various parks and gardens he saw during his visit to London, particularly at Greenwich (as designed by Le Nôtre): ibid., p. 48.

hiring of the Dutch gardener Jan Roosen in 1712, whose project for the garden was implemented in 1713–14. Roosen's plan made a feature of Peter's stone Summer Palace (1710) in one corner of the garden and also led to the construction of the 'Grotto', a common feature in contemporary European gardens, further along the Fontanka side of the garden from the Petrine Summer Palace.[19] The presence of these two buildings meant that this area was often used to host the Court's outdoor celebrations, which will be discussed below.

The other half of the gardens, from the canal to the Moika river, later became known as the 'second' Summer Garden. It was also divided, albeit less formally, with the area on the Fontanka side housing the more functional, horticultural sections, such as the orangeries, fruit trees and herb gardens.[20] Due to the presence of the former, this area was often referred to as the Krasnyi Garden.[21] To the west, these 'first' and 'second' gardens were separated from Tsaritsyn Meadow by the Swan canal (Lebiazhaia kanavka). To the south, on the other side of the Moika lay the Tsaritsyn Garden, so-called due to its origins as a gift from Peter I to Catherine I, which later became known as the 'third' Summer Garden. There was a small wooden palace in these gardens, built for Catherine's use in 1710–11 and which survived until the end of the century.[22] This palace was subsequently overshadowed by a larger wooden Summer Palace, designed and built by Francesco Bartolomeo Rastrelli. It was initially intended for Anna Leopol´dovna, when work began in 1741, but was subsequently completed for Elizaveta Petrovna by 1743.[23] The palace and its gardens were connected to the first two gardens by a footbridge, later joined by an enclosed gallery which was used for Court celebrations.[24]

European influences on the design and layout of the Summer Gardens are reflected in the succession of foreign and foreign-trained Russian personnel involved in their development. The initial Dutch influence of Roosen was subsequently modified by French-influenced

---

[19] For details on the design and construction of this 'Grotto', see *Russkie reguliarnye sady*, pp. 70–71, and E. V. Anisimov, *Iunyi Grad: Peterburg vremen Petra Velikogo*, St Petersburg, 2003, pp. 246–47.

[20] E. I. Indova, *Dvortsovoe khoziaistvo v Rossii*, Moscow, 1964, p. 209. My thanks to Simon Dixon for this reference.

[21] T. B. Dubiago, *Letnii sad*, Moscow and Leningrad, 1951, pp. 56–58.

[22] O. N. Kuznetsova and B. F. Borzin, *Letnii sad i letnii dvorets Petra I*, Leningrad, 1988, pp. 30–31.

[23] *Russkie reguliarnye sady*, pp. 94–96.

[24] Ibid., p. 96. The celebrations held in the Summer Gardens for the Grand Duke's name-day in late June 1746 provide one such example, with dining tables set up in this gallery ('v galleree, chto chrez kanal') and extending into the gardens: *Iurnaly i zhurnaly kamer-fur´erskie, 1695–1774 godov*, ed. B. M. Fedorov, St Petersburg, 1853–55 (hereafter, *KFZh*, followed by event date and year in brackets, then page reference), (29 June 1746), pp. 66–67.

architects and engravers. For example, in 1716, a revised plan for the gardens was proposed by the architect Jean-Baptiste LeBlond, who had been a student of André Le Nôtre, the master of the Versailles gardens, and was commissioned by Peter I to work on a number of projects around St Petersburg. His proposed design consisted of a central alley running from the Neva river to the Moika, which would be lined with Classical busts and statues. The rest of the gardens were then to be arranged symmetrically on either side, featuring fountains, pavilions and a wide variety of plants and trees.[25] Although this project was not fully adopted, it was significant as the first plan that envisaged all three gardens as part of a whole ensemble. The interconnected nature of the gardens was reflected in plans for their subsequent development, as can be seen in another plan, attributed to the architect M. G. Zemtsov, dating from 1723–25, and later in the various projects of Rastrelli which dominated the development of the gardens from the 1740s to the 1760s.[26]

One final aspect of the layout of the three Summer Gardens which sees clear development in this period is the creation of specific spaces for social interaction. The intended roles of the two Summer Palaces and the 'Grotto' are the most obvious examples of this, but there were several other structures from this period that clearly played a part in the social life of the Court and which clearly link Russian developments to the rest of Europe. For example, Zemtsov's project for the gardens in 1723–25 contained plans for the creation of a labyrinth in the 'second' Summer Garden, featuring further sculptures and fountains with the overall theme of Aesop's Fables. Work on this project was begun during Peter I's reign but completed only in the 1730s.[27] Such labyrinths were a common feature of formal gardens throughout contemporary Europe and this project, physically and thematically with its use of Aesop, echoed the 'Labyrinthe' at Versailles.[28] Another labyrinth was also planned by Rastrelli as part of the extension of the 'third' Summer Garden in 1747. The 1753 map of St Petersburg shows its location to the south of the 'new' Summer Palace, toward Nevskii Prospekt. However, given the speculative nature of certain areas of the 1753 map, this particular feature may never have existed as anything more than a project, with the costs involved in its construction put forward as a plausible explanation.[29]

[25] *Iunyi grad*, p. 421 and *Russkie reguliarnye sady*, pp. 64–67 (with plan).
[26] Ibid., pp. 68–69.
[27] *Letnii sad i letnii dvorets Petra I*, pp. 36–38.
[28] *Territorial Ambitions*, pp. 283–86.
[29] P. N. Stolpianskii, *Peterburg: kak voznik, osnovalsia i ros Sankt-Piterburkh*, St Petersburg, 1995, p. 271.

Several other structures were also constructed for sociable purposes within the confines of the gardens. For example, Zemtsov was also responsible for the design and construction of the 'Hall for Glorious Celebrations' (Zal dlia slavnykh torzhestvovanii), which was built in the 'first' Summer Garden in early 1725 alongside the second stone Summer Palace (on the corner of the Swan canal and the Neva river). This was used to host part of the celebrations for the wedding of Anna Petrovna and Karl Friedrich, duke of Holstein (discussed below), before being replaced by a wooden extension to the second stone Summer Palace in 1732.[30] It has been suggested recently that this hall was relocated to beside the Karpiev pond in 1730, where it was renovated in order to host comedies during Anna Ioannovna's reign.[31] However, this role was more probably performed by the stone amphitheatre, designed by Rastrelli and built in the 'first' Summer Garden in 1736, with the audience using temporary wooden seating (perhaps taken from the former hall, hence the potential for confusion).[32] The gardens' alleys themselves were used to host certain Court events. For example, banqueting tables were set up under the covered sections near the 'Grotto' in the first Summer Garden, as noted by Mrs Jane Vigor, then wife to the English resident, Claudius Rondeau, in 1734 when she described the celebrations for the capture of Danzig.[33]

Finally, an area linked to the Summer Gardens, and deliberately intended for the purpose of 'strolling', was the so-called 'Promenade' (Promenad). This project was based on a plan proposed by Rastrelli in 1740, which was ordered to proceed in June 1744 by the Chancellery of Construction. The order notes that it was intended for 'strolling' ('dlia promenadu, dlia progulki') and the 1740 plan is dominated by its long, broad, straight alleys. However, other priorities, principally the works at the 'third' Summer Garden and Tsarskoe Selo meant that materials were diverted away from it from 1745 onwards.[34] The remainder is briefly mentioned by Bogdanov as an Imperial garden planted in the meadow alongside the Summer Palace, leading to the 'old' Postal Yard (Pochtovyi dvor) in his description of St Petersburg in 1749–51.[35] The limited information on this garden available before Dubiago's work in the archives meant that there was some confusion

---

[30] *Russkie reguliarnye sady*, pp. 70 and 74.

[31] S. V. Sementsov, O. A. Krasnikov, T. P. Mazur and T. A. Shrader, *Sankt-Peterburg v kartakh i planakh pervoi poloviny XVIII veka*, St Petersburg, 2004, p. 237.

[32] *Russkie reguliarnye sady*, pp. 76–77.

[33] Mrs William Vigor, *Letters From a Lady, Who Resided Some Years in Russia, to Her Friend in England. With Historical Notes*, London, 1775, pp. 98–104.

[34] *Russkie reguliarnye sady*, pp. 91–92 (including Rastrelli's plan).

[35] A. I. Bogdanov, *Opisanie Sanktpeterburga, 1749–1751*, St Petersburg, 1997, p. 233.

in secondary accounts about whether this garden was ever constructed or where precisely it was located.[36]

It is clear, therefore, that the continued development of the Summer Gardens during the post-Petrine period owed much to the social function of the gardens. This found physical form in the realization of certain projects, most notably the labyrinth, that were not completed during Peter I's lifetime. Other projects, including the construction of the 'new' Summer Palace and the subsequent expansion of the 'third' Summer Garden around it, were essentially extensions of the trends that he had initiated and were a clear sign of the Russian Court's commitment to develop this space for its continued use. This prompts some consideration of how these spaces were used by the Russian Court during this period.

I

As with many aspects of St Petersburg's early social life, the accounts of foreign residents of and travellers to the city help to overcome the relatively sparse material provided by contemporary Russian observers. However, many of the early eighteenth-century descriptions of the Summer Gardens tend to dwell on its physical appearance, discussing its plan, the fountains and other features, such as the 'Grotto', as well as the large variety of plants that the gardens contained.[37] An important exception is provided by the diary of Friedrich-Wilhelm von Bergholz, a member of the duke of Holstein's retinue resident in the city during the early 1720s. His work contains useful details relating both to the layout of the gardens and a number of the events hosted there during the later years of Peter I's reign, which help to illustrate the role that they played in the city's social life.

A typical example occurred in late June 1721, when the duke attended celebrations in the Summer Gardens at 5 p.m., following a military presentation by the two Guards regiments to the tsar on Tsaritsyn Meadow that afternoon. Bergholz's description of the evening's events includes mention of his strolling along the garden's alleys and conducting

---

[36] Stolpianskii's work on St Petersburg, which continues to inform some recent scholarship, suggests that it was located in the empty area between the 'third' Summer Garden and the 'new' Summer Palace, along the Moika. Stolpianskii may have been influenced by Makhaev's 1753 engraving of the empress's Summer Palace, in which strolling and other social activities are conducted in the enclosed area in front of the palace. Stolpianskii, *Peterburg*, p. 276 and 'Letnii sad', in *Tri veka Sankt-Peterburga. Entsiklopediia. Tom I – Os´mnadtstoe stoletie: kniga pervaia*, Moscow, 2003, p. 548.

[37] See, for example, the rather cursory description in the otherwise informative F.-C. Weber, *The Present State of Russia*, London, 1968, pp. 308–09.

polite conversation with women by the garden's fountains. He also notes these sociable activities, and some others (like smoking), taking place amongst the invited guests, including the Imperial family, members of the Russian elite and foreign dignitaries. Amidst this informal, 'free' gathering, the typically Petrine element of compulsion was notable through the presence of the members of the Guards regiments, who were rewarded with beer and wine by the tsar. They were then used to enforce the drinking of toasts to Peter's health in large measures by all present later in the evening. On the other hand, the limit of even the tsar's authority was demonstrated when a sudden shower forced participants to take shelter in one of the galleries in the garden, although a number were left out in the rain, and also served as a timely reminder of the fickle nature of the weather in Peter's 'paradise'.[38]

There is evidence to suggest that this pattern of use for the Summer Gardens continued under Peter I's successor, Catherine I, in much the same manner as other events from his social calendar. The wedding of Anna Petrovna to Karl Friedrich, duke of Holstein, in late May 1725 represents one of the major Court celebrations which took place within the Summer Gardens during this period. It was for this event that Zemtsov constructed his 'hall for celebrations', which was used to host the banquet held in the gardens after the wedding ceremony. In terms of the attendance for these celebrations, the implications for access to the gardens, the official account, printed by the St Petersburg Typography at the end of June 1725, initially notes that the upcoming nuptials were announced throughout the city on 18 May, accompanied by trumpets and drums.[39] However, there is little detail given on those invited to participate in the ceremony and subsequent procession, beyond broad reference to senators, the Generalitet and other 'distinguished ranks' (*znatnye chiny*), and foreign ministers. The description of those present at the banquet is only slightly more specific, noting Russian gentlemen (*kavalery*), foreign ministers and those holding up to Rank 7, as well as their respective partners.

However, more significantly, in the same section, the account also notes that 'all lowly/common people of different ranks were allowed in the garden of Her Majesty for strolling' ('i vse podlye raznykh chinov liudi pushcheny byli dlia gulian′ia v ogorode Eia Velichestva').[40] No

[38] Friedrich W. von Bergholz, 'Dnevnik kamer-iunkera Fridrikha-Vil′gel′ma Berkhgol′tsa, 1721–1725, chasti 1 & 2', in V. P. Naumov (ed.), *Neistovyi reformator*, Moscow, 2000, pp. 107–502 (pp. 135–42).

[39] 'Opisanie o brake mezhdu Eia Vysochestvom Annoiu Petrovnoiu, Tsesarevnoiu Vserossiiskoiu, i Ego Korolevskim Vysochestvom Karlom Fridrikhom, Gertsogom Golshteinogottorpskim', *Syn otechestva*, 8, 1839, 3, pp. 265–72 (p. 268).

[40] Ibid., p. 269.

further details are given and the presence of a wider group at these celebrations is not mentioned by Bergholz, who was himself a guest.[41] This is not a reference to Tsaritsyn Meadow, where the festivities for the wider populace were held, taking the traditional form of roast meat and fountains of wine, as the two areas are mentioned separately by both accounts and clearly distinguished in the text.[42] The banquet and other celebrations in the gardens were then repeated on the following day, although on this occasion only those guests invited to the wedding ceremony itself were in attendance.[43] Similarly, the diary of P. D. Apostol, son of the Cossack Hetman, notes that the anniversary of the empress's coronation on 7 May 1726 was celebrated in the Summer Gardens, which were 'open to all' (*otkryt dlia vsekh*) although there is no further detail.[44] In other respects, however, his brief notes of using the gardens — for strolling with Menshikov or meeting with members of his close circle — fits with the broader pattern of privileged access for foreign dignitaries, discussed below.[45]

The Summer Gardens continued to play a role in Court events during the reign of Anna Ioannovna. Although they are generally mentioned much less frequently in the official Court journals than during either Peter or Elizaveta's reigns, the limited nature of these sources for Anna's reign should not be taken as a indication of declining use or interest. The empress continued to use the Summer Palace as her main residence in St Petersburg from early May until mid-October each year and the gardens were thus used to host several important celebrations that occurred during these months. Prominent examples from this period include the banquets to celebrate the capture of Danzig in June 1734 (described by Mrs Vigor, as noted above) and to celebrate the capture of the Turkish fortress of Ochakov, held on 28 August 1737.[46] At the same time, the gardens continued to be used to host elements of the more regular social events of the Court calendar. For example, there was a banquet in front of the 'Grotto' for the Empress and some distinguished guests after a Court masquerade in the Summer Palace on 9 July 1739.[47]

The Summer Gardens also provided the backdrop for the last significant ceremony associated with Anna Ivanovna as empress, as the

[41] He otherwise presents his usual level of detail, particularly concerning the leading Court figures present: Bergholz, 'Dnevnik', pp. 287–91.
[42] 'Opisanie o brake', p. 269; Bergholz, 'Dnevnik', p. 290.
[43] 'Opisanie o brake', pp. 271–72.
[44] P. D. Apostol, 'Dnevnik (Mai 1725 g.–Mai 1727 g.)', in *Kievskaia starina*, 50, 1895, 7–8, p. 142.
[45] Ibid., p. 147 (on 1 and 8 July 1726).
[46] *KFZh* (28 August 1737), pp. 33–35.
[47] *KFZh* (9 July 1739), p. 38.

'old' (i.e. Petrine) Summer Palace was where her corpse was kept until the Neva had frozen over to allow the funeral procession to the SS Peter and Paul Cathedral. Her corpse lay in state in the main hall of the palace from 16 to 23 December 1740, a practice which had begun in Russia with Peter I.[48] During this period, it was possible for 'people of all ranks' to visit between 9–11.30 a.m. and 2–5 p.m. every day. Indeed the sheer number of people who came to mourn meant that the black drapery at the entrance was damaged and had to be replaced.[49] For the very short subsequent reign of the infant Ivan VI and his mother Anna Leopoldovna, the paucity of evidence makes it very difficult to discuss the social function of the Summer Gardens, although the fact that Rastrelli was commissioned to build a new wooden Summer Palace (noted above) perhaps indicates continued use in this period.[50]

During the reign of Elizaveta Petrovna, however, there is considerably more material on the Court's activities and a defined change in its use of the gardens for this purpose. Although the empress and, after 1743, the Grand Duke were officially resident in the 'new' and 'old' Summer Palaces (respectively) from May until October each year, the Court journals for the period indicate that, in both cases, they spent much of that time outside the city. This was, after all, a period of considerable investment and development of the suburban estates at Peterhof, Tsarskoe Selo and Oranienbaum. As a result, while the city continued during this period to host Court social events which involved use of the gardens, both as a means to access the summer residences and other associated buildings (the opera house), they were not in regular use by either the rulers or their heirs for much of the summer. This leads on to the question of who else was entitled to make use of the gardens during this period.

II

By the late 1730s, and certainly by the 1740s, the Summer Gardens had been firmly established as a place to host both major Court celebrations and regular events in the Court social calendar. However,

---

[48] Lindsey Hughes, 'The Funerals of the Russian Emperors and Empresses', in Michael Schaich (ed.), *Monarchy and Religion: The Transformation of Royal Culture on Eighteenth-Century Europe*, Oxford, 2007, pp. 395–420.

[49] P. N. Petrov, *Istoriia Sankt-Peterburga, s osnovaniia goroda do vvedeniia v deistviia vybornogo gorodskogo upravleniia, 1703–1782*, St Petersburg, 1885, pp. 429–30.

[50] The emphasis in one of the main examinations of the Court in this period is decidedly on the flora and fauna therein, indicating the nature of surviving records: *Vnutrennii byt Russkogo gosudarstva s 17-go oktiabria 1740 goda po 25-e noiabria 1741 po dokumentam khraniashchimsia v Moskovskom arkhive ministerstva iustitsii*, 2 vols, Moscow, 1880, 2, pp. 154–64.

for much of this period, these events relied essentially on the presence of both the empress and the Court elite. The remainder of this article will focus on the accessibility of the gardens beyond such specific Court social occasions, moving more toward the development of the Summer Gardens as a space for social interaction more akin to some of the examples elsewhere in Europe. Whilst this may have been inferred from the activities of Peter I, as noted by Bergholz and highlighted by some previous historians, it was only during the 1750s that a defined attempt was made to create this wider access through legislation.

The various groups within Russian society who were invited (or more often expected) to participate in these occasions were not generally the focus of many of the foreign descriptions and official sources used in the previous section. However, from the mid-1740s onward, the log entries in the 'Journals of the Duty Adjutant-General' ('Zhurnaly dezhurnykh general-ad"iutantov') provide a useful alternative source of information about the Court's activities which is not available for the earlier period.[51] These entries provide details about the movement of the Imperial family and the security arrangements at the Imperial residences and other key areas. For example, an entry made by Captain Shubin of the Semenovskii Guards in early May 1748 included a register of the positions of and instructions to sentries on the eve of the empress's removal to the Summer Palace, as well as referring to instructions already established for certain posts.

There were the standard sentry posts at both the 'new' Rastrelli Summer Palace, beside the Moika river, and the 'old' Petrine Summer Palace, which restricted access to the apartments of the Imperial family and service areas, such as the palace kitchens. There were also guards at the entrances to the gardens, like the gates by the 'Private Wharf' (Partikuliarnyi verf') on the Fontanka river, and at different points throughout the gardens, such as the 'Grotto' where the empress and her guests (her then-favourite, Aleksei Razumovskii, was named in this particular entry) would dine together.[52] The bridge across the Swan canal, separating the 'first' Summer Garden from Tsaritsyn Meadow, was permanently manned by a corporal and two soldiers from one of the Guards regiments, since it controlled access not only to the gardens themselves but also to the Court theatre (also referred to as an 'opera house') that had been built there in early 1750.[53] The

---

[51] These records were partially published as *Zhurnal dezhurnykh general-ad"iutantov. Tsarsvovanie imperatritsy Elisavety Petrovny*, comp. L. V. Evdokimov, St Petersburg, 1897 (hereafter, *ZhDA*, with event date and year in brackets, then page reference).

[52] *ZhDA* (1 May 1748), pp. 70–71.

[53] Bogdanov, *Opisanie*, p. 189.

Guards regiments also provided a sentry patrol for the gardens themselves, consisting of a junior officer, two corporals and twenty soldiers.[54]

It should be noted that the details of the sentries included in the register from May 1748 provide an example of the standard procedure and posting points. Further orders were usually issued to the sentries for specific Court events involving either the Summer Palace or the gardens. For example, the first five ranks of the Generalitet, foreign ministers and the nobility with their families (excluding young children) were invited to attend a 'public' masquerade in the 'new' Summer Palace in May 1755. However, whilst the members of the Generalitet were instructed to enter the Summer Palace in the usual manner — in other words, through the main 'upper' entrance on the side facing toward Nevskii Prospekt — the other guests were to approach the palace through the Summer Gardens. From Tsaritsyn Meadow, they were to enter the Summer Gardens using the bridge across the Swan Canal by the opera house, where they would have their tickets checked by a chamber servant (kamer-lakei) and a detachment of troops from the Guards regiments. They were then to proceed through the gardens as far as the Moika river and use the lower entrance, on the left-hand side of the Summer Palace.[55] For this event, the information contained in the povestki that were sent out to the ladies and gentlemen of the Court was also sent to the officers of the Guards detachment at the bridge by the opera house and to the sentry detachment patrolling the gardens, in order to avoid any confusion over the guests.[56]

However, the orders discussed above relate to relatively limited access for very specific events and, for much of this period, regular access to the gardens was still largely the preserve of the ruler and her close circle. There were exceptions, however, both privileged and practical in origin. For example, regular access to the gardens was permitted for Court personnel who had official business requiring them to pass through the gardens. They would be issued with a special ticket or seal to allow them to pass the sentries. For example, on 19 May 1748, such tickets were issued to the priests, deacons and psalm-readers serving at Court so that they could move between the 'old' and 'new' Summer Palaces, with the entry also noting that they had previously been issued on two other occasions in the same month.[57]

---

[54] *Povsednevnaia zhizn'* (see note 7 above), p. 151. This information appears to be based on the details of the *prikaz* issued to the captain in charge of these sentries on 10 May 1755 (see note 71 below).

[55] *KFZh* (17 and 21 May 1755), pp. 56–58.

[56] St Petersburg, Rossiiskii Gosudarstvennyi Istoricheskii Arkhiv (hereafter, RGIA), f. 439, op. 1, d. 10, ll. 43–430b (Journals of the Duty Adjutant-General, Entry for 17 May 1755).

[57] *ZhDA* (19 May 1748), p. 76. The two previous occasions were on 4 and 18 May.

This did not apply to all servants, however, and sentries were occasion-ally reminded that the gardens were not to be used as a short-cut by those without the necessary permission.[58]

The other notable exception was the apparently regular access granted to the foreign ministers resident in St Petersburg, along with members of their diplomatic staff. An entry in Bergholz's diary for 24 August 1721 (when the duke decides to visit the Summer Gardens, meets Anna and Elizaveta Petrovna, and spends time strolling with them) includes an interesting statement that the duke and his retinue alone had been granted the privilege to have free access to the Summer Gardens at any time.[59] Mrs Vigor mentions the Summer Gardens only briefly. In Letter XVI, sent from St Petersburg in 1733, in which she discusses the foreign ambassadors in the capital, she says in passing that, whilst she and her husband were walking 'in the garden of the Summer palace', they met the Chinese ambassadors, who were being shown the gardens.[60] Although providing no significant detail about either the gardens or other such guests, this extract nevertheless reiterates the point raised by Bergholz's earlier comment.

The account of Carl Reinhold Berch, a Swede resident in St Peters-burg in 1735–36, highlights the issue of access to the gardens in relation to certain events. He states that, for the most part, the gardens were reserved for use by the empress and her close circle, with the suggestion that they preferred the peace and quiet that this measure ensured. The only exceptions to this rule were on days when comedies were performed at the theatre by the Karpiev pond (the aforementioned amphitheatre) or when *kurtagi* were held, either in the gardens them-selves or, more usually, in the Summer Palace. Berch's account also included an important example of the restrictions present, even for those with privileged access. He notes an occasion when the minister of the Holy Roman Empire, Count Karl Heinrich von Ostein, was stopped by the guards because he had brought a servant with him to carry his cloak.[61] Although it will become clear that the issue of access to the gardens for liveried servants is not wholly clear-cut from the contemporary legislation, this incident nevertheless highlights the continued use of the gardens by certain diplomatic personnel.

The question of privileged access was also raised during the reign of Elizaveta Petrovna. The *Kamer-fur'erskie zhurnaly* mentioned that the Office for Ceremonial Affairs in May 1750 was instructed (by the Court

[58] For one such warning, in relation to the 'third' Summer Garden and servants getting through gaps in the fencing, see *ZhDA* (30 June 1751), p. 246.

[59] Bergholz, 'Dnevnik', p. 200.

[60] Vigor, *Letters*, p. 84.

[61] Carl Reinhold Berch, 'Putevye zametki o Rossii', in Iu. N. Bespiatykh (ed.), *Peterburg Anny Ioannovny v inostrannykh opisaniiakh*, St Petersburg, 1997, pp. 111–302 (p. 166).

Office) that the Imperial ambassador was to be allowed to stroll in the Empress's garden, although the entry does not specify to which of the Imperial gardens it refers.[62] The journal entry concludes with the statement that this privilege had previously been extended to other foreign ministers. Although no further details are provided, either identities or allegiances, it bears out the comments made by contemporary foreign travellers' accounts, noted above. However, an entry in the 'Journals of the Duty Adjutant-Generals' from July of the same year sheds some interesting light on this particular issue. An order to Major Gur´ev of the Life Guards stated that it had been made known to the Empress that foreign ministers and members of the Generalitet were not being allowed to walk in the Imperial gardens. As a result, the Empress ordered that anyone from amongst the foreign ministers, members of the Generalitet or other distinguished (*znatnye*) persons wishing to stroll in the Summer Gardens should be allowed to do so, but that 'common' (*podlye*) people should continue to be excluded.[63]

From the evidence of these two entries, it would seem that certain privileged groups had previously been allowed to make use of the Summer Gardens for strolling but that this practice had lapsed either through a lack of use or, more likely, by error. Given the relative dates of the two entries and the fact that the case of the Imperial ambassador was specifically dealt with in a written communication, it seems likely that this was simply an oversight on the part of the sentries which, when realized, was dealt with. It is also significant that the second entry coincided with a period when Elizaveta Petrovna and her Court were resident at Peterhof and therefore not making regular use of the Summer Gardens.[64] Nevertheless, during the latter half of her reign, there was a move toward allowing wider access to these gardens. This access was curbed by a number of important criteria, however, which provide further evidence of the empress's strict requirements for the participation of a larger group of people in social arenas that had been previously been accessible only to a small elite.[65]

Access to these gardens was initially extended beyond the foreign ministers and privileged members of the Russian elite (Generalitet and *znatnye liudi*) in late May 1752, a month after the Empress had made her

[62] *KFZh* (22 May 1750), pp. 58–59.

[63] *ZhDA* (1 July 1750), p. 208.

[64] The empress was officially resident at Peterhof that year from 6 June until 3 August, when she returned to the 'new' Summer Palace: *KFZh* (1750), pp. 63 and 85.

[65] It is interesting to note that Elizaveta Petrovna also widened access to several other Court social spaces, most notably the so-called 'public masquerades' (*publichnye maskarady*) and performances at the Court theatre. See my 'Creating a Public in St Petersburg, 1703–61', unpublished PhD thesis, University of London, 2006, pp. 128–56 (currently being prepared for publication).

annual move from the Winter Palace to her 'new' Summer Palace.[66] An *ukaz* sent from Count P. I. Shuvalov, the Empress's *dezhurnyi general-ad''iutant*, to the Police Chancellery ordered that 'subjects' (*poddannye*) of the Empress, foreign dignitaries (*inostrannye znatnye persony*) and certain other groups (detailed below) should be allowed access, with their families, to the first and second Summer Gardens by the Neva river on Sundays and 'festive days' (*torzhestvennye dni*) in order to 'stroll' (*guliat'*). The various groups are listed in the order, beginning with the junior officers, corporals and grenadiers of the Life Company, followed by the staff officers and senior officers of the Life Guards and army regiments, the Cadet Corps, the Artillery and Engineering Corps, and the Navy. The list continues with the inclusion of civil administrative posts, with rank equivalent to military officers, and all of the nobility, without exception (*bez iz''iatiia*).

The list then moves on to other prominent non-noble social groups, principally noting the inclusion of wealthy Russian and foreign merchants. It is perhaps a reflection of Elizaveta's social experiences during the reign of her father that access was also granted to foreign naval personnel, principally ships' captains and other senior crew members (described as *morskie sluzhiteli*). Common sailors (*matrozy*) were specifically excluded.[67] The *ukaz* then continued with a requirement that those admitted to the gardens should be appropriately dressed, according to their rank or status ('v pristoinykh s ikh zvaniem plat'iakh'). Ladies were not allowed to enter if they wore clothing that was considered inappropriate for the setting, such as domestic caps or dresses without crinolines, or similar under-frames. The merchantry were not permitted to have 'beards or untidy hair' ('v borodakh i raspretanykh volosakh'), where the latter may refer to the lack of a wig or appropriate styling for one's natural hair. Liveried servants (*lakei v livreiakh*) or household serfs[68] were not to be allowed into the gardens under any circumstances, with the threat of punishment specifically stated, rather than the fines mentioned in connection with transgressions at Court events. The *ukaz* was to be published and sent to the Police Chancellery, who would inform those concerned.[69]

The first thing to note about this *ukaz* is the considerable increase in both the number and type of people who were granted access to the gardens in comparison with earlier examples, which appear to have

---

[66] *KFZh* (28 April 1752), p. 34.

[67] RGIA, f. 1329, op. 2, d. 44, l. 13 (Order from the Court Office to the Main Police Chancellery, 25 May 1752).

[68] This is my interpretation of the term *kholopy* used in this context.

[69] Ibid., ll. 13–13ob. Note that this *ukaz* is omitted from the *Polnoe sobranie zakonov Rossiiskii imperii ... 1649–1825*, 40 vols, St Petersburg, 1830 (hereafter, *PSZ*, followed by volume number, then document number and date in brackets, then page reference).

been either on an occasional basis, or in response to an individual query (as appears to have been the case with the Imperial ambassador). Alongside the highest ranks of the Russian elite and foreign ambassadors, from 1752 the gardens could be used at least once a week by members of the nobility and their families, including the senior officers of all branches of the military and the civil service, and select non-noble groups, like the merchantry and ships' captains. The prominence of clothing and appearance as the key means to determine the suitability of prospective users reflects the role of the gardens as a social platform.[70]

Following this *ukaz*, wider access to the Imperial gardens does not feature in either the Court journals or in the orders issued by the Court Office, although the 'Journals of the Duty Adjutant-Generals' continue to list entries incorporating instructions to sentries when the empress was resident in the 'new' Summer Palace, and if there was an event in either the Summer Palace or the gardens. However, in May 1755, again shortly after the empress's move from the Winter Palace to her 'new' Summer Palace, she issued an order to the Court Office to inform the Guards captain in charge of the sentries that on Thursday of every week, foreign ministers, members of the Generalitet (present in St Petersburg) and other persons of 'every rank/status' were to be allowed to 'stroll' in the first and second gardens. This was possible only if they were dressed 'in a clean and tidy manner'. The order then goes on to define what is considered untidy, and therefore unsuitable, dress. For men, this meant tousled hair (as the merchantry were warned in 1752), military-style boots (*sapogi*), and grey (referring to undyed, coarse Russian cloth) kaftans. For women, specific reference was made to simple Russian dresses and 'our' (*nasha*, presumably meaning traditional Russian) shawls. The exclusion of liveried servants from the gardens was again highlighted ('i livreinykh sluzhitelei nich´ikh nepropushchat´').[71]

As earlier foreign accounts had suggested, the Imperial ambassador is specifically mentioned in this order as exceptional (*v otlichnost´*), since he was permitted to make use of these two gardens whenever he wished.

---

[70] Clothing and appearance were naturally the most visible signs of the 'Europeanization' process at work during this period amongst the Russian nobility and leading members of urban society. See my 'The Function of Fashion: Women and Clothing at the Russian Court, 1700–1762', in Wendy Rosslyn and Alessandra Tosi (eds), *Women in Russian Culture and Society, 1700–1825*, Basingstoke, 2007, pp. 125–43.

[71] RGIA, f. 439, op. 1, d. 10, l. 370b (Journals of the Duty Adjutant-General, Entry for 10 May 1755). On the use of the word 'simple' (*prostoi*) to describe a woman's dress, Pisarenko believes that it is used to refer to one which does not have the underframe (*fizhma* or *fizhbein*), a distinction that was also mentioned in the 1752 *ukaz*: *Povsednevnaia zhizn´* (see note 7 above), p. 151.

This privilege was also extended to the members of his entourage, namely his gentlemen and their attendant pages, although this still did not include their servants (*krome lakeev*). The order ends with a minor but interesting detail on the means to enter the gardens. For all of these groups, access was by means of the canal bridge at the opera house, with its permanent Guards sentry post.[72] The same information was also sent to the ladies and gentlemen of the Court, the Main Police Chancellery and the Office of Ceremonial Affairs; the latter was responsible for informing the foreign diplomats, especially the Imperial ambassador in this case.[73]

This *ukaz* is immediately followed in the 'Journals of the Duty Adjutant-Generals' by the *prikaz* sent on the same day to Guards Captain Vatkovskii, who was in charge of these sentries. This is virtually identical to the *ukaz* sent to the Court Office, except for some of the details in the clothing regulations. For example, a note about merchants with beards was included (similar to that from the *ukaz* of 1752) and the nature of the required female clothing (previously described as *prostoi*) was made more explicit by specifically mentioning the lack of the requisite crinolines or under-frames ('ne v fizhmennykh iubkakh').[74] The fact that the merchantry were mentioned in this *prikaz*, although they were not named in the original *ukaz*, indicates that they were still considered to be amongst the general group of people of 'every rank/status'.

The details contained in the two May orders proved to be a template for further developments on the issue of access to the gardens later that summer, but with a significant addition. For example, the *Chamberlain's Journals* (*Kamerfur'erskie Zhurnaly*) for mid-June 1755 included the same details about the people allowed to 'stroll' in these gardens and their required appearance. All of this information was again sent to the ladies and gentlemen of the Court, the Main Police Chancellery and the Office of Ceremonial Affairs, on the same basis as 10 May. However, the access was now permitted to all three Imperial gardens.[75] Likewise, the entry in the 'Journals of the Duty Adjutant-Generals' and the order issued by the Court Office on the following day both contained similar details about the groups of people and the dress stipulations, but with all three gardens listed as accessible on Thursdays and Sundays.[76]

---

[72] RGIA, f. 439, op. 1, d. 10, l. 38.
[73] *KFZh* (10 May 1755), pp. 54–55.
[74] RGIA, f. 439, op. 1, d. 10, l. 38.
[75] *KFZh* (16 June 1755), p. 66.
[76] RGIA, f. 439, op. 1, d. 10, l. 54 (Journals of the Duty Adjutant-General, Entry for 17 June 1755); RGIA, f. 1329, op. 2, d. 47, l. 29 (Order from the Court Office to the Main Police Chancellery, 17 June 1755).

The inclusion of the third Imperial garden coincided with the departure of the empress and her Court to Peterhof on the following day, while Grand Duke Peter and Grand Duchess Catherine had already left St Petersburg for Oranienbaum. When the empress returned to St Petersburg early on 3 August, a *prikaz* was sent to Guards Captain Ashcherin, then head of the sentries, in which it was stated that access to the third Imperial garden was no longer permitted on Thursdays and Sundays, although the first and second gardens were still open on those days.[77] This order suggests that, perhaps due to its proximity to the empress's Summer Palace, the third Summer Garden was largely reserved for use by the Imperial family and their immediate social circle during their residency in the summer months.

The effect of the presence of the empress in St Petersburg on access to the Imperial gardens was also highlighted by an *ukaz* from her *dezhurnyi general-ad"iutant* Ivan Buturlin to the Main Police Chancellery in May 1756. This stated that access to the first and second Imperial gardens was granted on Thursdays of every week when the Empress was present in St Petersburg, and on Thursdays and Sundays of every week when she was not present. The *ukaz* included all of the groups of people previously mentioned in the example above from May 1752, that is to say from both noble and non-noble social groups, and the prohibited groups were listed as ordinary sailors, personal serfs and common people. The dress stipulations were the same as those listed in the orders issued in 1755.[78] However, the *ukaz* then goes on to state that the first two ranks of the Generalitet and foreign ambassadors, especially those of the Holy Roman Empire, England and Sweden (specifically named as Count Horn), along with their entourage and one page, were permitted to make use of the first and second gardens on the above days whenever they wished. Finally, it is noted that the ladies and gentlemen of the Court would continue to have their usual privileged access, a detail which had not previously been noted in other earlier *ukazy*.[79]

The privileged nature of this smaller group was confirmed by a further *ukaz* in June 1756, when the Empress ordered that foreign ministers and members of the Generalitet from the rank of brigadier upwards were to be granted access to the third Imperial gardens on Thursdays and Sundays.[80] With the issuing of these *ukazy*, a deliberate

---

[77] *KFZh* (3 August 1755), p. 73; RGIA, f. 439, op. 1, d. 10, l. 64ob (Journals of the Duty Adjutant-General, Entry for 3 August 1755).
[78] RGIA, f. 1329, op. 2, d. 48, ll. 16-16ob (24 May 1756).
[79] Ibid., l. 16ob. NB this is also the first *ukaz* regarding access to the Imperial gardens to appear in the *PSZ*, 14 (10560: 24 May 1756), pp. 573-74.
[80] RGIA, f. 1329, op. 2, d. 48, l. 19 (Order from the Court Office to the Main Police Chancellery, 19 June 1756). See also *PSZ*, 14 (10573: 19 June 1756), p. 588.

divide was established within the social groups who were allowed to 'stroll' in the first and second Imperial gardens, dependent on the Empress's presence in St Petersburg, and those who could make use of any of the three Imperial gardens on both of the selected days. The inclusion of the third Imperial garden, previously kept closed for use by the Imperial family when they were in St Petersburg, was an important step towards creating this smaller and more select group, which consisted of the same people as attended other selective Court events, such as 'Court days' (*kurtagi*).

III

There are naturally a number of limitations on the conclusions that one can draw from the introduction of this legislation. For example, it is very difficult to gauge the extent to which the various social groups mentioned in it took advantage of this new accessibility in the absence of any substantive reference to it in contemporary accounts of the city. The Summer Gardens drew scarcely any comment in the principal memoirs of the 1750s, such as those of Grand Duchess Catherine. Similarly, there are very few accounts from foreign visitors to the city in this period and the gardens merit only brief mention (in contrast to Peterhof).[81]

Nevertheless, there are grounds to consider this legislation significant for both the gardens themselves and the city's social life. Firstly, the Summer Gardens were an important symbol of Russia's 'Europeaniza-tion' process in the first half of the eighteenth century. They provided an essentially non-Russian space (at least in form) within the city which was intended to provide a forum for various 'new' forms of interaction, hitherto unknown in Russian social life. The period following Peter I's death has been identified as one of consolidation, or refinement, and this provides a useful metaphor for the continued development of the gardens and the various elements or structures within them.[82]

Secondly, the use of contemporary European examples to provide both inspiration for layout or features and skilled personnel is also part of this process. Comparison with the leading gardens of the day, such as Het Loo or Versailles, reveals many similarities of form and content.

---

[81] For example, the account of the city in the late 1750s by Louis Alexandre Frotier, comte de la Messelière, omits to mention the Summer Gardens, but includes a (brief) description of the garden at Peterhof, which hosted a banquet for the departure of Prince Karl of Saxony: 'Zapiski M. de la Messel'era o prebyvanii ego v Rossii s maia 1757 po mart 1759 goda', *Russkii arkhiv*, 1, 1874, 4, pp. 952–1031 (p. 1008).

[82] A. B. Kamenskii, *The Russian Empire in the Eighteenth Century: Searching for a Place in the World*, trans. David M. Griffiths, Armonk, NY, 1997.

However, the location of the Summer Gardens suggests that a comparison with other urban gardens might be more instructive when considering the enabling of regular access to such gardens for groups beyond the Court elite. Importantly, the *ukazy* from the 1750s were not an attempt to create informal or unrestricted access to the gardens, as was the case with a number of the aforementioned examples.[83] They contained clear guidelines to regulate access for prospective visitors, centring on their rank or social status, their appearance (clothing and grooming), availability (by establishing specific days on which the gardens would actually be open to this wider group), and the high-profile presence of sentries (at the entrance and on patrol) to ensure orderly behaviour. At the same time, such restrictions were hardly unusual amongst other contemporary examples. Visitors to Kensington Gardens in this period commented on the importance of dress to gain entrance, and guards enforced a strict appearance policy to keep 'domestics' and the lower ranks from both the gardens of the Tuileries palace and the Palais-Royale.[84]

Finally, the significance of these measures can be seen in the opening of other, previously private gardens to wider access from the reign of Catherine II onwards. For example, in June 1759, the journal *Prazdnoe vremia v pol'zu upotreblennoe* carried a notice announcing that the gardens of the Cadet Corps were to be opened on certain days of the week to people of all ranks.[85] As with the Summer Gardens, and indeed other European examples, liveried servants and poorly-dressed individuals were not permitted to enter.[86] Similarly, from the 1780s, other gardens belonging to leading nobles were also opened for wider access, principally those belonging to Count A. S. Stroganov (on the Vyborg side) and to I. I. Elagin, Catherine II's *gofmarshal* (on Elagin island).[87] A related development was the emergence of pleasure gardens, or 'vauxhalls' after the English model, which were opened in St Petersburg by foreign

[83] For the relative ease of access to the gardens of the two leading European Courts in this period, see Jeroen Duindam, *Vienna and Versailles: The Courts of Europe's Major Dynastic Rivals, 1550–1780*, Cambridge, 2003, pp. 165–68.

[84] For London, see George Rudé, *Hanoverian London*, London, 1971, pp. 71–72. For Paris, see Duindam, *Vienna and Versailles*, p. 166, and David Garrioch, *The Making of Revolutionary Paris*, Berkeley, CA, 2002, pp. 99–101.

[85] Douglas Smith suggests that these gardens were open on Thursdays and Sundays, clashing with the Imperial gardens, in his monograph *Working the Rough Stone: Freemasonry and Society in Eighteenth-Century Russia*, DeKalb, IL, 1999. However, the announcement in the *Sanktpeterburgskie vedomosti* instead lists them as open on all days *except* Thursdays and Sundays. My thanks to Andreas Schönle for highlighting this disparity.

[86] *Prazdnoe vremia v pol'zu upotreblennoe*, 1, 1759, pp. 365–66, cited in *Working the Rough Stone*, p. 68.

[87] M. I. Pyliaev, *Staryi Peterburg*, Moscow, 1990, pp. 432–33.

entrepreneurs for a paying public, with the first examples dating to the 1770s.[88]

With any consideration of social or cultural legislation, it is important to remember the influence of the Russian context on shaping such developments, particularly in terms of the debate on assimilation versus imitation.[89] However, given that strolling was already an established part of elite and urban social life elsewhere in Europe, it is telling that the Summer Gardens proved to be an enduring and alluring element in St Petersburg's social scene for the remainder of the century, despite the setbacks posed by the extensive flooding in the 1770s.[90] The granting of regular access to the Summer Gardens in the mid-eighteenth century to a number of social groups beyond the traditional Court elite, albeit with strict regulations still in place, was an important step toward the consolidation of gardens as a space in which to socialize and the related development of strolling as a social pursuit in Russia. As such, it also represents an important development in the cultural life of Russia's European capital.

[88] Johann Gottlieb Georgi, *Opisanie Rossiisko-Imperatorskogo stolichnogo goroda Sankt Peterburga i dostopamiatnostei v okrestnostiakh onogo, s planom*, St Petersburg, 1996, pp. 454–57. For discussion of the nineteenth century, see E. D. Uvarova, 'Vokzaly, sady, parki', in E. V. Dukov (ed.), *Razvlekatel'naia kul'tura Rossii, XVIII–XIX vv. Ocherki istorii i teorii*, St Petersburg, 2001, pp. 316–49.
[89] *Russia in the Age of Peter*, pp. 462–68.
[90] It is significant that both Georgi and Heinrich Storch, writing of the city in the 1790s, identified the Summer Gardens remaining the city's leading public promenade by the end of the century: Georgi, *Opisanie*, pp. 82 and 454; Heinrich Friedrich von Storch, *The Picture of Petersburg*, London, 1801, pp. 430–31.

'Ropsha, where Peter III was murdered …': Faces and Façades of an Imperial Estate

ROGER BARTLETT

THE settlement of Ropsha, on the Izhora heights outside St Petersburg, became an Imperial estate and residence in the reign of Peter the Great. It was one of a number of estates ringing Peter's new capital, and remained in the ownership either of the Imperial family or of aristocratic favourites or agents until the 1917 revolution: we shall meet many of these personalities in the course of our investigation. However, it is most firmly associated in historical and popular lore with the death there in 1762 of the unfortunate Tsar Peter III.

After a reign of only six months, Peter III was overthrown by his wife, the future Catherine II, and her supporters in the coup d'état of 28 June (O.S.) 1762.[1] Historically, Peter's image and reputation have suffered from the self-serving account of him given by Catherine in her memoirs; during his short period in power he promulgated some serious and important legislation, and his foreign policy choices, usually derided, have been the subject of vigorous rehabilitation attempts.[2] There seems little doubt, however, that he was both socially and politically immature, naive and tactless, and despite having serious advisers around him he succeeded within months of his succession in alienating most of the influential power groups within the state. Particularly disastrous was his upsetting of the army and the guards, by making common cause with the recent enemy Prussia and — disregarding the exhaustion of both troops and treasury at the end of the Seven Years' War — planning a new campaign against Denmark which would have

Roger Bartlett is Professor Emeritus of Russian History in the Department of History at UCL SSEES.

[1] For general accounts of the coup, see S. M. Solov'ev, *Istoriia Rossii s drevneishikh vremen*, ed. L. V. Cherepnin, 15 vols, Moscow, 1959–66 (hereafter Solov'ev), 13, pp. 83–101; I. de Madariaga, *Russia in the Age of Catherine the Great*, London 1981, pp. 21–37; Carole S. Leonard, *Reform and Regicide: The Reign of Peter III of Russia*, Bloomington, IN, 1993, pp. 138–49. The ingenious and thought-provoking revisionist thesis of K. A. Pisarenko ultimately fails to convince: K. A. Pisarenko, 'Neskol´ko dnei iz istorii "uedinennogo i priiatnogo mestechka"' [i.e Ropsha], in O. A. Ivanov, V. S. Lopatin and K. A. Pisarenko, *Zagadki russkoi istorii: XVIII vek*, Moscow, 2000, pp. 253–398. I have not seen I. V. Kurukin, *'Epokha "dvorskikh bur'": ocherki politicheskoi istorii poslepetrovskoi Rossii 1725–1762 gg.*, Riazan´, 2003.

[2] For a revisionist account of Peter III and his reign, see Leonard, *Reform and Regicide*.

taken guards regiments away from the capital and possibly into front-line battle. These factors, combined with the threat posed to his wife and son by his infatuation with his mistress Elizaveta Vorontsova, whom he seemed to intend to marry, were sufficient to provoke a Court conspiracy and the coup headed by Catherine and supported by the guards. Peter, taken unawares and quickly losing courage, was deposed, in the acid words of his great hero Frederick II, 'like a child sent off to bed'. In her justificatory accession manifesto Catherine claimed to have taken power by popular demand in order to safeguard the Empire and Orthodoxy.

Under arrest and given a choice of temporary residence, Peter selected Ropsha as his initial place of confinement,[3] while permanent quarters were being prepared for him in the Schlüsselburg fortress. The Ropsha estate in fact belonged to Peter: it had been given to him by Empress Elizaveta Petrovna towards the end of her reign, and he liked the place,[4] although as Grand Duke he spent his time in his other nearby estate of Oranienbaum where there was a 'toy fortress' with which he amused himself and with which Ropsha could not compete[5] — like his grandfather Peter I and putative son Paul I, Peter III as Grand Duke loved playing soldiers. At 8.00 p.m. on 29 June, a guarded carriage brought him to Ropsha. He was lodged in a bedroom of the palace, a fairly spacious room, and left alone. Sentries were posted outside the door and in profusion around the palace. The prisoner slept badly and next day complained, asking for his favourite bed at Oranienbaum, which was duly brought for him: initially all such personal requests — for his bed, his personal valet, his doctor, his violin (but not his mistress) — were immediately granted. He was not, however, allowed out of the room, and his chamber windows were covered with green blinds.[6]

Peter's guards were under the command of Aleksei Orlov, brother of Catherine's favourite and a main mover in the coup. A. Orlov's notes to Catherine in St Petersburg in the following days, a striking mixture of formality and familiarity, show the concerns and pressures faced by the conspirators: to consolidate the new Empress's position

---

[3] Madariaga, *Russia in the Age of Catherine the Great*, p. 31.

[4] M. Pyliaev, *Zabytoe proshloe okrestnostei Peterburga*, 1889, reprinted St Petersburg, 1996, p. 332; N. V. Murashova and L. P. Myslina, *Dvorianskie usad'by Sanktpeterburgskoi Gubernii: Lomonosovskii raion*, St Petersburg, 1999, p. 140. I have found no further evidence as to exactly why Peter chose Ropsha for his temporary prison.

[5] *Perevorot 1762 goda. Sochineniia i perepiska uchastnikov i sovremennikov. Vtoroe, ispravlennoe izdanie*, Moscow, 1908, p. 116.

[6] Ibid., pp. 116, 129–30. According to another account, one of his keepers, Prince Fedor Bariatinskii, or another duty officer, stayed permanently in the room, under orders 'not to take your eyes off the prisoner': Iu. A. Duzhnikov, *Ropsha*, Leningrad, 1968, p. 22.

Peter's permanent removal was essential and his death much to be desired, but the cold-blooded murder of an anointed crowned head would be a moral and political step into the unknown. On 2 July Orlov wrote: 'We are all [. . .] well. Only our monster [Peter III — R. B.] has fallen very ill, he is seized with a desperate colic, and I'm afraid he may die this night; but I'm still more afraid that he may recover.' The guards included the body-physician Kruse, but this seemed to make little difference. Four days later Orlov wrote again to say that Peter was so ill he was unlikely to survive: 'I don't know what to do now. I fear the wrath of Your Majesty, lest you think of some furious [punishment] for us and lest we cause the death of Your enemy [*zlodeia* — i.e. Peter], the enemy of the whole of Russia and of our faith . . .' The same evening however, 6 July, Catherine received Orlov's well-known, frantic letter announcing Peter's death:

> Little Mother, most gracious lady, How can I explain or describe what happened. You will not believe your faithful servant but before God I speak the truth. Little Mother, I am ready to go to death but I know not how this happened. We are ruined if you don't show mercy. Little Mother, he is no longer in the world! But it never occurred to anyone, how could anyone think of raising a hand against our sovereign Lord! But, sovereign Lady, the disaster happened. We were drunk, and he too. He started a quarrel at table with Prince Fedor [Bariatinskii], and before we could separate them he was gone. We ourselves don't remember what we did but one and all are guilty, worthy of punishment. Have mercy, if only for my brother's sake. I have made my confession [here] and there is nothing to investigate. Forgive us, or order an end to be made quickly. Life is worthless, we have angered you and lost our souls forever.[7]

What exactly happened is uncertain. The French diplomat Claude Carloman de Rulhière claimed in his sensational *Histoire, ou anecdotes, sur la révolution de Russie, en l'année 1762* that Orlov and others had tried to poison Peter, had used force when he resisted and finally had strangled and suffocated him.[8] Catherine, in her letters of the time to her former lover Count Stanisław Poniatowski, went out of her way to deny that Peter had been poisoned — she had had an autopsy carried out, she explained.[9]

According to her semi-confidante Ekaterina Romanovna Dashkova, the new Empress was initially shocked and deeply disconcerted by the death: 'Je suis affectée, même terrassée par cette mort', she told

---

[7] Madariaga, *Russia in the Age of Catherine the Great*, pp. 29–32; E. A. Anisimov, *Zhenshchiny na rossiiskom prestole*, St Petersburg, 1998, pp. 323–24. The texts of the letters to Catherine at this time from Peter III and from Aleksei Orlov are printed in *Perevorot 1762 g.*, at pp. 142–43, 135 and 143–44 respectively.
[8] C. C. de Rulhière, *Histoire, ou anecdotes, sur la révolution de Russie, en l'année 1762*, Paris, an v. (1797), Russian version in *Perevorot 1762 g.*, here pp. 67–68.
[9] Ibid., p. 103.

her friend.[10] Probably, however, there was premeditation here on Catherine's part: the French diplomat Baron de Breteuil observed that she presented a face of sorrow and tears when the event was made publicly known, although she had had time to compose herself, having in fact received news of it the night before.[11] At any rate, she soon recovered. None of the conspirators was punished; but, unusually in eighteenth-century Russia until that date, nor were any proscriptions or persecutions subsequently undertaken against Peter's supporters. Peter was buried in the Alexander Nevsky Monastery on 10 July, without any regal pomp; at the insistent request of her advisers and of the Senate corporately, Catherine did not attend.[12]

The new ruler's position on the throne was consolidated without too much difficulty. There were dangers and uncertainties. Her Imperial manifesto announcing that Peter had died of a 'haemorrhoidal colic' was greeted with widespread scepticism. Some disaffected guardsmen had to be dealt with very firmly; and in 1764 the disgruntled Ukrainian *shliakhtich* Vasilii Mirovich sought to emulate her coup d'état by attempting to free and proclaim the imprisoned Emperor Ivan VI, incarcerated since babyhood in Schlüsselburg. Following Imperial instructions, Ivan was dispatched by his guards, leaving Catherine with another death upon her conscience. In France, Rulhière's *Histoire*, hinting strongly at Catherine's complicity in her husband's demise, circulated in manuscript and enjoyed a *succès de scandale*; Diderot had to persuade him not to publish it until after the Empress's death.[13] But despite such superficial turbulence there was no serious challenge to the new ruler. Catherine also spent lavishly to reward and conciliate supporters and potential opponents — between July and December 1762 she distributed 1.5 million roubles, and between July 1762 and March 1763 made grants of estates and serfs totalling 21,423 male souls: a greater largesse than any other dispensed after a coup at the eighteenth-century Imperial court.[14] The Ropsha affair was successfully hushed up. When in March 1763 Archbishop Amvrosii queried a Synodal instruction to perform an official office for the dead (*panikhida*) in memory of Peter III, because 'among the common people they will talk about him in a way different from that shown in the manifestos', Catherine's response

---

[10] 'Bumagi Dashkovoi', *Arkhiv kniaz′ia Vorontsova*, 40 vols, 21, Moscow, 1881, pp. 93–94; *The Memoirs of Princess Dashkov*, trans. and ed. K. Fitzlyon, London, 1958, pp. 89–90.

[11] *Perevorot 1762 g.*, p. 147.

[12] Ibid., pp. 69, 141.

[13] Madariaga, *Russia in the Age of Catherine the Great*, p. 337. There is some question as to whether or not Rulhière accepted the substantial sum of money offered to him by the Russian side; at any rate he kept to his undertaking not to publish during Catherine's lifetime.

[14] I. V. Kurukin, quoted by E. K. Wirtschafter, *Russia's Age of Serfdom 1649–1861*, Malden, MA and Oxford, 2008, p. 132.

was bullish. Confidently confirming the instruction, she declared: 'God ordered us to pray even for evil-doers, and especially for an errant soul, and if we did not pray for his soul, rumours would circulate among the people that he is alive.'[15] Nevertheless the authorities saw that an end had to be put to rumours and loose talk about the coup and the new Empress: after the discontent among the guards had been dealt with, in June 1763, an official manifesto was issued 'Concerning silence', threatening condign punishment for 'persons of debased (*razvrashchennykh*) morals and thoughts, [rumour-mongers] who do not think about the common good and tranquillity, but being themselves infected with strange conceptions of affairs which have nothing to do with them and of which they have no direct information, try to infect other equally feeble-minded people'.[16]

Ropsha itself was likewise to be surrounded with a wall of silence: the Empress, apparently, forbade any mention of it.[17] Then in 1764 Catherine gave the estate as a present to her favourite Grigorii Orlov. Orlov, it has been claimed, never liked Ropsha, and thereafter the ill-omened place was allowed to decay:

> Under [Orlov] the estate fell into neglect. The lake became overgrown, the canals were covered in slime, the fruit-trees wilted, weeds ran riot, the wooden buildings became rickety. Time wiped out the traces of Rastrelli's estate planning. Only the stone palace stood as a memorial to Ropsha's past.[18]

'Palaces too, like domestic animals, may become unserviceable [noted another, anonymous, commentator]. Sometimes they are connected with such memories that they are stamped with the seal of rejection. Such is Ropsha, which Emperor Paul called "the Field of Blood".'[19] The modern St Petersburg historian Evgenii Anisimov carried this dark picture of the estate over to the present day, writing in 1998: 'Ropsha still exists at the present time. The park is wild and neglected; the palace, fouled and abandoned, is collapsing. The accursed scene of a crime.'[20] The association with the murdered emperor remains vivid in the popular imagination, as journalist Liubov' Savosina found when

---

[15] Solov'ev, 13, pp. 211–12. In fact such an assertion was reported already in September 1763 (ibid., p. 212) — a foretaste of the extraordinary series of false Peter IIIs to come.

[16] Ibid., p. 211; Madariaga, *Russia in the Age of Catherine the Great*, p. 34.

[17] At least according to Duzhnikov, *Ropsha*, p. 23: '"O Ropshe ne vspominat'" — skazala imperatritsa. "O Ropshe pisat' zapretit'" — vtorili tsensory.' I have been unable to find evidence or a source for this statement.

[18] Pyliaev, *Zabytoe proshloe*, p. 333, paraphrased by Duzhnikov, *Ropsha*, p. 24; id., *Ropsha. Istoriko-kraevedcheskii ocherk*, Leningrad, 1973 (2nd edn of Duzhnikov, *Ropsha*), p. 59.

[19] *Perevorot 1762 g.*, p. 116. Paul apparently wished to rename Ropsha 'Field of Blood' (Krovavoe Pole), as he renamed other places associated with things he disliked about his mother's reign: Pyliaev, *Zabytoe proshloe*, pp. 333 n. 20, 598.

[20] Anisimov, *Zhenshchiny na rossiiskom prestole*, p. 326: '*Prokliatoe mesto prestupleniia.*'

she visited in 2004: 'The Lomonosov Region. Ropsha Settlement (*pose-lok*). I ask kids running past, "Where's the estate and park here?" They put me right in an offended tone: "It's not an estate, but a palace! A tsar's palace — Emperor Peter III's palace! He was even killed here!"'[21]

However, the potency of the Peter III story should not obscure the rest of Ropsha's history: if the estate today is still in a sad state of disrepair, enduring metaphysical gloom is not wholly appropriate and it has several other claims to fame besides its association with Peter III. Its succession of palaces and associated buildings has drawn the attention and admiration of architectural historians,[22] and although it is one of the former Imperial estates around Petersburg which have not yet been restored, it is included on the UNESCO list of World Heritage sites.[23] In the twentieth century it was the scene of fierce fighting around the northern capital: in 1919 it repeatedly changed hands between White and Red forces in the Civil War, and during the Great Fatherland War it was occupied by the Germans from 1941 until liberation in 1944. These military engagements and the heroism of Red Army men involved in them have been predictably celebrated in Soviet accounts:[24] the first Red Army tank to re-enter Ropsha in 1944 was set up on a pedestal in the estate as a permanent commemoration. The eighteenth-century period under Orlov is susceptible of a different interpretation, as we shall see: Ropsha has a little-known history as a site of social and economic innovation and the place where the first attempt was made to find a way of cutting the Gordian knot of serfdom and giving land to Russian peasant farmers.

I

Ropsha's origins as a Russian settlement go back to the Middle Ages; its original name was Khrapsha. But it became Swedish territory at the Treaty of Stolbovo in 1617 and its modern history begins with the reconquest of Ingria from the Swedes by Peter I in the Great Northern War. Under Swedish rule Ropsha and its villages had belonged to the Swedish General Gastfer. Now they were at the Russian Crown's

---

[21] Liubov´ Savosina, 'Usad´ba: Ropsha', in *Adresa Peterburga* no. 11/23, 2004 <http://www.adresaspb.ru/arch/adresa_11/adresa_11_main.htm> [accessed 20 November 2008].

[22] Duzhnikov, *Ropsha*; Duzhnikov, *Ropsha: Istoriko-kraevedcheskii ocherk*; id., *Po izhorskoi vozvyshennosti*, Leningrad, 1972, ch. 'Ropsha, Gorbunki, Razbegai'; Murashova/Myslina, *Dvorianskie usad´by*, esp. pp. 130–53. I have been unable to obtain Viktor Monia, *Ropsha*, St Petersburg, 2007, but see the preface to it by V. Simakov at <http://www.ipkvesti-spb.ru/predisloviyaizdatels/> [accessed 17 September 2008].

[23] Part of 'Historic Centre of Saint Petersburg and Related Groups of Monuments', UNESCO ID no. 540-009.

[24] Duzhnikov, *Ropsha*, pp. 34–42.

disposal. The foundation of St Petersburg in 1703 in this bleak north-western part of the growing empire was followed by the creation of numerous estates as Imperial and aristocratic residences at points around the new city, and especially to the west along the Gulf of Finland: notably Tsarskoe Selo (original name Sarskaia *myza* [farm-stead], now Pushkin), Oranienbaum (now Lomonosov), Peterhof, Gatchina, Strel'na, Kipen' — and Ropsha. Peter gave Ingrian estates to favoured courtiers, but initially kept Strel'na, Peterhof and the Ropsha estate for himself.

Peter first turned his attention to Ropsha in the course of arranging water sources for the proposed new residences and fountains at Strel'na and Peterhof; he was also particularly attracted by accounts of benefi-cent springs in the area. Ropsha has a multitude of springs, some of them with mineral content, the largest of them called 'The Jordan' (*Iordan'*). Peter, who took European spa waters himself at Baden in 1698 and 1708, Carlsbad in 1711–12, Bad Pyrmont in 1716 and Spa in 1717, was very interested in the medical potential of springs in Russia;[25] his body-physician and Chief Arkhiater Robert Erskine (Areskine) was also an enthusiast for balneotherapy.[26] From 1717–19 a 'spa commission' (*rodnikovaia kommissiia*) composed of Erskine and his protégé Laurentius Blumentrost was charged with examining the qualities of the water of promising springs. Principal interest was centred on sources around Peter's new Karelian foundation of Petrozavodsk, where in 1714 the virtues of local waters had been reported and in 1716 W. Henning, the Chief Inspector of Mines, had confirmed the discovery.[27] The spa Martial Waters (Martsial'nye vody)[28] was thus created; the tsar took the waters there several times in the 1720s but, as Lindsey Hughes tells us: 'After Peter's death the "native" spa of which he was so proud, far from St Petersburg and with no local interest, more or less ceased to function.'[29]

[25] Lindsey Hughes, *Peter the Great: A Biography*, New Haven, CT and London, 2002, p. 137.

[26] R. Collis, *The Petrine Instauration: Religion, Esotericism and Science at the Court of Peter the Great, 1689–1725*, Turku, 2007, pp. 135–43.

[27] Hughes, *Peter the Great*, p. 136; Collis, loc. cit.

[28] One early meaning of English 'martial' and Russian 'martsial'nyi' is 'pertaining to iron', since in early chemistry and alchemy iron was associated with the god Mars.

[29] Hughes, *Peter the Great*, loc. cit. See further Collis, loc. cit., and <http://www.conspekt. info/8628482815> [accessed 20 November 2008]: 'In 1717–19, on Peter I's instructions, his body-physicians R. Areskin and L. Blumentrost examined the composition of iron-bearing (*martsial'nykh*) waters, which they pronounced beneficent for the treatment of a number of diseases. A decree was published announcing the opening of [the spa resort] "Martial Waters", together with "Physician's rules on how to conduct oneself at the said waters". In the same years was published an article "Genuine investigations concerning the effect of the iron-bearing Konchezero waters", which contains nine short descriptions of diseases and of the outcome of their treatment with iron-rich waters. In the 1720s Peter I repeat-edly took the waters at Martsial'nye vody. At the spa special palaces were built for the tsar and his family, which however rapidly fell into disrepair after the emperor's death.' Unofficial local use of the waters continued, however, and in the Soviet period the site was revived, first as an open-air museum, then as a spa: Hughes, *Peter the Great*, pp. 136–37, 142, 189–90, 242–43.

Meanwhile Ropsha's mineral springs had also drawn Peter's attention: in July 1713 he spent some time in neighbouring Kipen´ and visited Ropsha to take the waters. It was probably at this time that the first Ropsha palace was constructed, on an eminence near the Jordan, a simple wooden structure providing travelling accommodation for the tsar and reminiscent of Peter's 'little house', famous for its small size and frugality, which is still preserved in St Petersburg.[30] A wooden church and palace outbuildings were built at the same time, and the whole surrounded by a defensive earthen rampart and ditch, a sign of the still unquiet times — the area was not safe from Swedish incursions until after the tsar's Poltava victory in 1709. The wooden palace at Ropsha survived until 1780. However, Peter's building plans at this stage were mainly concentrated on the development of Strel´na and Peterhof, for which Ropsha's many springs contributed a useful water supply: in the end the extensive Peterhof fountains were served by a well-founded 22-kilometre system of canals, dams and aqueducts drawing water by gravity from the whole hinterland.

The Ropsha estate remained relatively undeveloped, and in fact Peter soon divided it and gave the parts to two of his most trusted associates. The original farmstead, Ropshina *myza*, he granted in 1712 to a servitor of long standing, G. I. Golovkin.[31] A former gentleman of the bedchamber (*postel´nichii*) and *stol´nik* who had watched over Peter during Sophia's regency, Golovkin was a member of the Great Embassy of 1697–98, President of the Ambassadors' Chancellery and then Russia's first, long-time, Chancellor and President of the College of Foreign Affairs (although he knew no foreign languages). One foreign diplomat described Golovkin as worthy of respect on all counts: modest, cautious, a lover of the old ways but prepared to acknowledge the new if he saw their utility; attached to his country, and incorruptible in his loyalty to its rulers — a suitable neighbour for the tsar. Not all characterizations were so sympathetic, however: he was also known for miserliness. When Peter I's water supply system for Peterhof was completed in 1721, Golovkin gave a party in Ropsha to celebrate the event; but the Holstein diarist Bergholz noted that the hospitality was not splendid nor the guests well feasted, 'since he is an extremely niggardly as well as a very rich man'.[32]

---

[30] Pyliaev, *Zabytoe proshloe*, quoted by Duzhnikov, *Ropsha*, p. 10.

[31] Biographical details of G. I. and his son M. G. Golovkin in *Entsiklopedicheskii Slovar´ Brokgauz-Efron*, 9, St Petersburg, 1893, pp. 72–73. See also Duzhnikov, *Ropsha*, p. 11; Murashova/Myslina, *Dvorianskie usad´by*, pp. 132–34. G. I. Golovkin later became a member of the Supreme Privy Council, but in 1730 supported the assembled nobility against the 'oligarchs' in the confrontation with Anna Ioannovna and so escaped their fate.

[32] Cited by E. Amburger, *Ingermanland. Eine junge Provinz Russlands im Wirkungsbereich der Residenz- und Weltstadt St. Petersburg-Leningrad*, 2 vols, Cologne, 1980, 1, p. 538.

The other part of the estate, including the Jordan, the tsar presented two years later, in 1714, to his equally loyal henchman F. Iu. Romodanovskii.[33] Prince Fedor Iur´evich Romodanovskii, who traced his descent from Riurik, had already achieved high rank under Peter's father Tsar Aleksei Mikhailovich, and distinguished himself in Muscovy's wars of the Holy League with the Turks. A prominent participant both in Peter's 'toy' military activities, from which he derived the nick-name 'the King of Pressburg <Preobrazhenskoe>', and in the notorious All-Drunken, All-Joking Synod, of which he was the 'King-Emperor',[34] in the first years of Peter's reign he was a figure of the greatest importance. He enjoyed Peter's complete trust and confidence and fulfilled crucial roles in the areas of government and security; Peter left him in charge of Moscow and of the government when he went abroad. An intimidating personality, much attached to old ways but loyal and open to Peter's innovations, he was most known, and feared, as head of the Preobrazhenskii Chancellery, effectively Peter's secret police, in which capacity he showed complete ruthlessness, great cruelty, and remarkable integrity.[35] When Ropsha became the seat of the head of the Preobrazhenskii Chancellery, rumours spread that he had set up a 'torture centre' there; but he seems to have done little to develop his new property.

On Romodanovskii's death in 1717 the estate passed to his son, Ivan Fedorovich, who also inherited his father's 'play' titles, as well as his security duties and fearsome reputation, becoming head of the Secret Chancellery. In 1722 I. F. Romodanovskii's daughter Ekaterina married the son of his neighbour Golovkin, Mikhail Gavriilovich, receiving as her dowry Romodanovskii's Ropsha estate and 20,000 serfs; and when the two fathers died successively in 1730 and 1734, the young Golovkins were able formally to unite both Ropsha holdings.[36] The Ropsha estate continued to exist within these boundaries up to the present.

Already in 1725 G. I. Golovkin had begun construction of a stone house in Ropsha near the Jordan and in the 1730s his son developed the building further. The architect for the new building programme may have been Mikhail Petrovich Eropkin. Sent abroad as a student

[33] Duzhnikov, *Ropsha*, p. 13.
[34] On these aspects of Peter's reign see Lindsey Hughes, *Russia in the Age of Peter the Great*, New Haven, CT and London, 1998, ch. 4 (1), 'Monarch and Mock Sovereign' and ch. 8 (1), 'The All-Drunken Assembly and the Mock Court'; Lindsey Hughes, *Playing Games: The Alternative History of Peter the Great*, London, 2000.
[35] Biographical information on F. Iu. and his son I. F. Romodanovskii: *Russkii Biograficheskii Slovar´* (hereafter, *RBS*), vol. Romanov-Riasovskii, Petrograd, 1918, pp. 120–24, 130–39.
[36] Duzhnikov, *Ropsha*, p. 14.

by Peter to study architecture from 1716 to 1725 in Amsterdam, Venice and Rome, Eropkin later worked with distinction in several Imperial estates and was engaged in government service in St Petersburg as well as undertaking numerous private commissions there. He was on very friendly terms with Mikhail Gavriilovich Golovkin, with whom he had studied abroad. M. G. Golovkin was a member of the Construction Chancellery of St Petersburg, and well acquainted with the work of Eropkin as well as other leading architects; he also had a good knowledge of foreign and Russian park design. Eropkin was, if not the architect, at least influential in the new development. The house at Ropsha was considerably expanded: set imposingly on the hill down which streams from the Jordan ran to the lake below, its two stories were embellished with new galleries and wings to a length of 110 metres, built on a newly-constructed terrace. On the terrace to the west of the house silver fir-trees were planted on newly-fashionable turf squares and cut in the shape of pyramids, while an orangery was added on the east side. According to Iu. Duzhnikov, on its own level, as a private estate, M. G. Golovkin's Ropsha 'embodied everything that was best and typical about Russian park-construction of the first half of the eighteenth century'.[37]

This was the state of affairs at Ropsha when Mikhail Gavriilovich Golovkin fell from official favour; the building was not quite finished, and the internal decoration never completed. After the death of Empress Anna Ioannovna in 1740, Golovkin had supported her designated heir Ivan VI and the latter's mother and regent Anna Leopol'dovna of Brunswick-Wolfenbüttel, becoming Vice-Chancellor and a close adviser in the new government. Consequently, when Elizaveta Petrovna's coup d'état overthrew the Brunswick family in 1741, Golovkin was on the wrong side: he was accused of treason and put on trial together with the former minister Andrei Ivanovich Osterman (Heinrich-Johann-Friedrich Ostermann). In 1742 his property was confiscated and he himself condemned to death, commuted to Siberian exile.[38] Golovkin died fourteen years later in exile, whither his wife had followed him; Ropsha was forfeited to the Crown and became part of the Court estates.

Under Elizabeth, Ropsha became a regular stopping-point for the Imperial party when it travelled from Peterhof to Tsarskoe Selo, and increasingly a destination in its own right, for hunting and other parties; the Empress enjoyed fishing in its lake. From 1748 a major construction programme was undertaken under the supervision of

[37] Ibid., pp. 14–16; Murashova/Myslina, *Dvorianskie usad'by*, pp. 134–36.
[38] Solov'ev, 9, pp. 134–42.

Elizabeth's architect F. B. Rastrelli.[39] The Golovkin house was reconstructed according to Rastrelli's concept into an extensive palace two
hundred metres in length. On the west side the old house was widened
almost double: a row of rooms was added onto the covered promenade
gallery, whose windows looked out onto the garden with its pyramid
firs, turning the gallery into a longitudinal corridor. On the sides of the
Golovkin house appeared two new single-storey galleries, each some 26
metres long. One gallery was to end in a cross-shaped church (its base
has survived to the present) and the other in a 'refectory pavilion' or
Hermitage; however, the pavilion was never built. The church and
pavilion were to be constructed four metres forward of the line of the
main façade, a favourite device of Rastrelli's. The big central room of
the Golovkin house — called the Blue Room after the colour of
its walls — was preserved, and lavishly decorated. The Blue Room,
intended for state balls, was connected to a reception room, built on as
part of the new western section of the palace. At the same time, to the
west of the palace, four long stone corpuses were added, guest and
service blocks, parallel to each other and perpendicular to the main
building.

The park also was replanned. The Upper Park was laid out in the
'Dutch style' fashionable at the time: lawns of green turf alternated with
flowerbeds of attractive design, the alleys were paved with crumbled
brick and coloured glass. The Upper Park was broader than the new
palace, 250 metres long and 210 metres wide. To the north it was
bordered by a canal, to the south by orangeries and hothouses. The
earthen terrace to the west of the palace was significantly raised and a
stone staircase constructed, leading from it down to the Lower Garden.
Here were planted Spanish limes, and the trees were divided by alleys
laid out to form star shapes, another feature typical of Rastrelli's work.
Two lakes were included in the design, one new, the other a development of the existing lake below the house. The outbreak of the Seven
Years' War in 1756 halted the reconstruction in its latter stages, and
Rastrelli's plan was never finally completed. But Ropsha had become
part of the great architect's architectural heritage: Rastrelli's palace
remained the core of the Ropsha ensemble thereafter.

II

In 1764, as we have seen, the Ropsha palace and estate passed to
Catherine's favourite Grigorii Orlov, then at the height of his fortune.

[39] The following account is based on Duzhnikov, *Ropsha*, pp. 17–20; see also Murashova/
Myslina, *Dvorianskie usad´by*, pp. 137–40. It has been suggested that Rastrelli was distracted
by other business and the French architect and landscape engineer N. Girard was more
involved in realizing the Ropsha design.

VIEW of the PALACE and APARTMENTS at ROPSCHA.
in which PETER III was murdered

The Rastrelli palace, Ropsha: print published in 1823

The following year, on the death of Catherine's influential adviser on economic matters, Count Boris-Leontii Kurakin, Catherine bought the estate of Gatchina from his heirs, and gave that, too, to Orlov; and the year after, heaping still further bounty on him, she presented him with the estate of Lakhta.[40] Gatchina became the focus of Orlov's own attempt to create a suitable aristocratic country residence: in 1766 construction began on the very extensive Great Palace at Gatchina, from plans by the architect Antonio Rinaldi, and a 7 km^2 landscaped park was laid out in the newly fashionable English style — the first in Russia — including a stud-farm and menagery.[41] It seems likely that Orlov's concentration on the transformation of Gatchina precluded significant work on the Ropsha ensemble — the only construction work

[40] Amburger, *Ingermanland*, 1, p. 176. Orlov acquired other villages too, some in these transactions, some by private purchase.

[41] The textually vague but lavishly illustrated soft-pornographic work of 'Bernard Gip' claims that Orlov's interior decoration of the new Gatchina palace included sexually explicit figures and frescoes reflecting his liaison with the Empress: Bernard Gip, *The Passions and Lechery of Catherine the Great*, Charles Skilton Ltd (London, Edinburgh and Oslo). Copyright: Les Éditions Nagel, Geneva, 1971.

there recorded during his ownership was some renewal of the church in 1781.[42]

However, Orlov's relative neglect of Ropsha's palace and park may possibly reflect not only distaste for 'accursed' Ropsha and preoccupation with Gatchina, but a different approach to this new domain. The available modern accounts of Ropsha's history are written from the point of view of local historians interested primarily in the estate's public face, the buildings and landscape of the 'nobleman's nest'. Ropsha, however, like all such estates, was also a working community of peasants and others with a society and economy of its own, which are scarcely mentioned in the existing literature.[43] Grigorii Orlov seems to have viewed Ropsha at least in part as a working space, a place in which to pursue projects of social and economic policy. In the first decade of Catherine's reign, Orlov was not only the publicly-acknowledged official favourite, with rooms in the Winter Palace adjoining those of the Empress: he also exercised significant influence on affairs. Besides his Guards career and high military rank (by the end of his life he was General-in-Chief and Commander-in-Chief of Artillery [general-fel'dtseigmeister]), Orlov was one of the main movers in the foundation of the Free Economic Society in 1765, and a deputy in Catherine's famous 'Legislative Commission' of 1767. From 1763 as President of the new Chancellery for Protection of Foreigners (Kantse-liaria Opekunstva Inostrannykh) he was given charge of one of Catherine's first major programme initiatives, the invitation to foreigners to settle in Russia and the creation of settlements for those who came. Most of the foreigners who responded to Catherine's immigration Manifestos of 1762 and 1763 were sent on to the Volga German colonies near Saratov and other colonies elsewhere, but a few, mostly small artisans, were not; and Ropsha became the destination for some of these. A sealing-wax manufacturer, Heinrich Trüper, sent by the Chancellery for Protection of Foreigners to the Office of the College of Manufactures in 1765, was directed to Ropsha on the grounds that new manufactures had been banned in St Petersburg.[44] Two years later, in 1767, a German ribbon manufacturer, Major Johann von Gommel

---

[42] Amburger, Ingermanland, 1, pp. 413, 426; Duzhnikov, Ropsha: Istoriko-kraevedcheskii ocherk, p. 59. On Orlov's death in 1783 Catherine bought Gatchina back from Orlov's heirs and presented it to her son Paul.

[43] The exception is Amburger, Ingermanland, which however treats Ropsha as a fragment of a much larger landscape. The estate archive of Ropsha, which was one of Duzhnikov's sources but from which he presents almost no evidence on the estate's internal life in the eighteenth century, is held in the Russian State Historical Archive, St Petersburg (still closed at the time of this writing).

[44] On restriction of industry in St Petersburg, see Polnoe Sobranie Zakonov Rossiiskoi Imperii, Sobranie pervoe, 45 vols, St Petersburg, 1830, nos 10914 (1759), 11689 (1762).

(Hommel), who failed to meet immigrant criteria, was likewise referred by the Chancellery to the Manufactures Office and given permission to set up in Ropsha.[45] This would seem to suggest that Orlov wished to encourage the development of craft production or small-scale industrial activity on his estate (or possibly that Ropsha offered a useful solution to difficult settlement cases).

In 1768 Catherine II had herself and her son inoculated (strictly, variolated) against the deadly scourge of smallpox: the Empress's treatment with this often controversial procedure was a sensational event in St Petersburg. Her English physician Dr Thomas Dimsdale — created Baron in reward for his success — helped to establish an inoculation hospital in the capital, directed by Dr August Wilhelm Schulinus with the assistance of a Dr Strenge. At the same time a smallpox epidemic broke out in Ropsha, and Orlov called on the celebrity doctor for help. The St Petersburg Lutheran pastor Joachim Christian Grot, who subsequently championed the new medical procedure in annual sermons on the anniversary of Catherine's heroic deed and wrote a first history of smallpox inoculation in Russia, recorded the outcome:

> Outside of St Petersburg inoculation also had great success in some neighbouring villages. The first attempt made with it took place as early as late 1768 on the estates Ropsha and Kipen´ belonging to Prince Orlov. To this purpose Baron Dimsdale, at that time still in St Petersburg, was summoned there together with Court Counsellor Strenge. The disease had already broken out in these villages and raged with such severity that in Ropsha alone 31 people had already been snatched away. To save as many people as possible in this threatening danger, the Baron commissioned the Court Counsellor to inoculate everybody without distinction who showed no sign of the natural smallpox. The number treated was 123.

Of those inoculated, forty-seven were babies; only twelve were over twenty (including one forty-year-old); sixty-eight were male and fifty-five female. Only three, all children afflicted with other conditions, died.[46] This first mass inoculation in Russia gave the Empress's

[45] R. P. Bartlett, *Human Capital: The Settlement of Foreigners in Russia 1762–1804*, Cambridge, 1979, p. 165. Trüper failed to establish himself and went on to Saratov. Von Hommel only lasted one year.

[46] *Petersburgische Kanzelvortraege, von Joachim Christian Grot, Pastor bey der Evangelischen Katharinenkirche auf Wasiley-Ostrow*, Leipzig und Riga, 1781, pp. 371–76. Grateful thanks to Dr Karin Friedrich and to Siobhan Convery and Michelle Gait of Aberdeen University Library for help with this source. On the 1768 variolation of Catherine and her son Paul, see W. J. Bishop, 'Thomas Dimsdale, M.D., F.R.S. (1712–1800) and the Inoculation of Catherine the Great of Russia', *Annals of Medical History*, N.S., 4, July 1932, 4, pp. 321–48; P. H. Clendenning, 'Dr Thomas Dimsdale and Smallpox Inoculation in Russia', *Journal of the History of Medicine and Allied Sciences*, 28, April 1973, 2, pp. 109–25; Roger Bartlett, 'Russia in the Eighteenth-Century European Adoption of Inoculation for Smallpox', in R. Bartlett, A. Cross and K. Rasmussen (eds), *Russia and the World of the Eighteenth Century*, Columbus, OH, 1988, pp. 193–213, 681–84.

favourite an opportunity to show himself a true follower of his mistress in setting a national example, and a supporter of Enlightened rationality and modern medical practice. As landlord and serf-owner Orlov was also evidently ahead of the general game in intervening to preserve his peasants from decimation by smallpox — without consulting their wishes on the matter; and he was able to use his unique position at Court to engage the services of the best doctors available.

The most remarkable episode in Orlov's 'socio-economic' use of Ropsha, however, was the appointment as estate manager there in 1764 of the Livonian Lutheran pastor J. G. Eisen. Eisen had succeeded in gaining an audience with Catherine II in 1763 with a plan to free Russia's serfs and provide them with contractual leasehold rights to land. Catherine agreed to let Eisen run a trial on one of her own estates, and according to Eisen this was in fact the real reason for the grant of Ropsha to Orlov: Catherine, he wrote in his autobiographical notes, had given her favourite Ropsha, Kipen´ and other villages 'in order through me to get rid of serfdom and to plant colonies'.[47]

In 1764 Eisen, who had initially returned home to his parish of Torma, near Lake Peipus in Livonia (now Estonia), was summoned back to the capital

> by the Chancellery of Guardianship at the most high order of Her Imperial Majesty, and then again through Prince [Grigorii] Orlov, in order on the Orlov estates near St Petersburg really to introduce peasant property. I arranged for the ministers of the neighbouring parishes to receive my parish revenues from the [Lutheran] Higher Consistory, for locum service in Torma; I spent one and a half years in Ropsha, received the granted estates from several imperial chancelleries and began preparations on them for the great work: my plan was approved by the Empress and the hereditary leasehold charters were to be issued any day.[48]

But in 1766 the project was suddenly aborted:

> Only, as it had taken so long for me to take receipt of all the estates from the various chancelleries, all sorts of ear-benders who claimed to know better than I did how to do things had the time, with the help of the enemies of freedom in Livonia and through a hundred chicaneries, to bring me to the point where I requested permission to return home, with the promise of my services for the future.[49]

[47] On Eisen and his project, see my '30 October 1763: The Beginning of Abolitionism in Russia', in Anthony Cross (ed.), *Days from the Reigns of Eighteenth-Century Rulers. Proceedings of a Workshop, dedicated to the Memory of Professor Lindsey Hughes, held at Biblioteca di Storia Contemporanea 'A Oriani', Ravenna, Italy, 12–13 September 2007*, Study Group on Eighteenth-Century Russia Newsletter, Parts 1 & 2, Cambridge, 2007, 2, pp. 135–48; Roger Bartlett, 'Russia's First Abolitionist: The Political Philosophy of J. G. Eisen', *Jahrbücher für Geschichte Osteuropas*, 39, 1991, pp. 161–76; R. Bartlett and E. Donnert (comps and eds), *J. G. Eisen (1717–1779). Ausgewählte Schriften. Deutsche Volksaufklärung und Leibeigenschaft im russischen Reich*, Marburg, 1998.
[48] *Der Philanthrop* (1777), reprinted in *Ausgewählte Schriften*, pp. 487–88. Count G. G. Orlov became a Prince of the Holy Roman Empire in 1772.
[49] Ibid., pp. 30, 113.

Eisen's notes give no explanation of exactly what happened. Evidently no leasehold charters were issued, and his services in this field were never called upon again. Eisen's work in Ropsha, however unsuccessful, was the first step towards abolition in Russia; the latter was also a cause which he pursued throughout his life. Eisen, a man of many-sided activity, made a reputation as a pioneer of smallpox inoculation and had great success with a system of drying and preserving vegetables, whose military potential brought him recognition and medals from several European rulers. His campaign against serfdom, however, produced no results in his lifetime: no servile peasants were freed or granted land rights in Russia until the well-known 'Free Agriculturalists' law was promulgated in 1803. Grigorii Orlov's achievement in fighting bubonic plague and quelling attendant social unrest in Moscow in 1771 was commemorated by a triumphal arch in Gatchina; but his use of Ropsha as a site for social and economic experimentation seems to have ended with the mass inoculation and the outbreak of Catherine's first Turkish war. By the time of his death the palace and park were in decay.

III

Grigorii Orlov died in 1783. Two years later his four brothers and heirs sold the Ropsha estate to Ivan Lazarevich Lazarev.[50] A man of great wealth, banker and Court jeweller, entrepreneur and philanthropist, Lazarev was a native of Dzhulfa in Persia and an outstanding representative of the extensive Armenian diaspora in Russia.[51] Under Catherine, Lazarev made important purchases of land and enterprises which

[50] Biographical information: *RBS*, vol. Labzina-Liashchenko, St Petersburg 1914, p. 36; Amburger, *Ingermanland*, 2, p. 721 n. 79. Pictorial account of the Lazarev/Lazarian family: <www.geocities.com/azat10/lazar.htm> [accessed 22 January 2009] (incorrect information on Lazarev Institute).

[51] Lazarev was involved at some point in the negotiations for the purchase of the great Orlov or Amsterdam diamond, which Grigorii Orlov bought from an Armenian merchant as a gift for Catherine II and which was then set in the Imperial sceptre. The events leading up to Orlov's acquisition of the stone are the subject of much speculation and contradictory report. The Armenian merchant has even been identified with Lazarev (see e.g. http://query etc. below), though this seems highly unlikely. Duzhnikov (*Ropsha*, p. 24), and others, have adopted this hypothesis and taken it further, asserting, without providing evidence, that Ropsha was ceded to Lazarev in payment for the diamond. This seems equally improbable, and the contract (see below) contains nothing to indicate that it was not a normal sale. Ivan Lazarev died in 1801; the Lazarev family fortune made possible in 1815 the foundation of the 'Armenian Lazarev Institute', subsequently the important Lazarev Institute for Oriental Languages.
    On the diamond and its provenance see, *inter alia* <http://famousdiamonds.tripod.com/orlovdiamond.html> and <http://query.nytimes.com/gst/abstract.html?res=9804EF DA153DE533A25751C1A9609C94629FD7CF&scp=2&sq=The+Orlov+Diamond&st=p> [accessed 25 January 2009].

established him as one of the major industrialists of the time. He bought estates, factories, mines and serfs from the Stroganov, Demidov, Golitsyn, Shakhovskoi and other noble families, including in 1778 the Perm´ estate of the Stroganov family, which amounted to nearly 800,000 hectares of land with over 7,000 serfs, the largest transaction of its time.[52] The Ropsha purchase was thus one among many.

The contract of 12 June 1785, which I was recently able to study,[53] allows a closer glimpse than hitherto into the make-up of the estate and its inhabitants. It conveyed to Lazarev

> [the property] most graciously granted to [G. G. Orlov] by Her Imperial Majesty on 9 November 1764, situated in the Oranienbaum district of St Petersburg *guberniia*, viz. the *myza* Ropsha and the *myza* Kipen´, with the villages belonging to them: Mikhailovskaia, Novaia, Lipitsa, Khabania, Semsepalaia, Volkovitsa, Prokovsina, Nikisemianaia, Bol´shaia Gorka, Malaia Gorka, Bol´shoi Simogond, Malyi Simogond, Lavduga, Aliskova and Porzova.

Not surprisingly in the social and economic circumstances of the time, the contract devotes great attention to the status of the dependent population. The sale included 'according to the recent fourth revision[54] 1,090 courtyard people and peasant souls, together with their wives [and] children died and new-born of both sexes since that fourth revision, and all their families', as well as their buildings, grain, livestock, fowl and personal possessions. As usual, fugitive peasants from before and after the revision were also included, as well as any peasants illegally seized by other landowners, also peasants from other Orlov estates who had married into Ropsha, Kipen´ and their villages; but local women and their children who had married out before the sale were explicitly excluded. If the stated number of souls proved incorrect, Lazarev was to receive 110 roubles per soul compensation. A number of named peasant families, in all sixteen male and nine female souls, were excluded from the sale to be resettled in other Orlov estates.

The sale price was 118,140 roubles; in accordance with contemporary practice, the contract, signed by the four surviving Orlov brothers, was

---

[52] The Lazarev and Lazarev-Abamelek family archive, in private hands, was recently offered for sale at Christie's. See description in Christie's sale catalogue: *London, Valuable Russian Books and Manuscripts, Thursday 27 November 2008*, Lot 8, pp. 14–16 (here p. 15); the catalogue entry was researched by Prof. A. Kamenskii, Moscow. See also <http://antrakt. ng.ru/antiquare/2008-11-21/13_london.html> [accessed 25 January 2009].

[53] Lazarev archive; see also the partial facsimile in the catalogue front cover, and description p. 16. I am indebted to the anonymous owner and to Christie's Book Department for permission to consult this document.

[54] The fourth revision (tax census) of 1783 recorded 179,177 male souls in St Petersburg province (*guberniia*). The total population at the time has been estimated at some 550,000 people, of which about 220,000 were residents of St Petersburg: S. A. Lisitsyn (ed.), *Istoriia i kul´tura Leningradskoi zemli s drevneishikh vremen do nashikh dnei*, 2nd rev. edn, St Petersburg, 2005, p. 92.

witnessed by numerous members of the high nobility. It is commonly said that Lazarev was acting in this matter as a proxy for Grand Duke Paul, who revered his father's memory but could not take direct ownership of Ropsha in his mother's lifetime. New plans for remodelling the palace complex, drawn up under Lazarev by the Court architect Antonio Porto,[55] were indeed submitted for approval to the Grand Duke; though it might be supposed that if Lazarev was in fact only a front-man, Paul would have acquired the estate on or shortly after his accession in 1796, which was not the case — the Crown bought it in 1801.[56]

Porto, who was responsible for planning and constructing a number of major buildings in St Petersburg, retained Rastrelli's palace as a core but remodelled the exterior in Classical taste. The eastern side, facing the Lower Park, became the principal façade. He added to it a jutting portico with Ionic columns, resting on an arcade, above a wide granite staircase leading down to the park. The portico was surmounted by a broad, low triangular pediment, and a small round belvedere added above the central part of the building provided splendid views of the park. The interior was also remodelled and richly furnished. 'The interiors of the Ropsha palace were in no way inferior to interiors designed by such masters of Russian Classicism as Cameron or Voronikhin.'[57] Porto also began a substantial second church on the estate, but this was never completed.[58]

To remodel the park, Lazarev called upon the services of Grigorii Ivanovich Engel'mann, a young engineer trained in Germany and Holland and expert landscaper in the new English style,[59] whom he supplied with unlimited financial resources. Over many years Engel'mann radically reconstructed the grounds at Ropsha, changing and expanding the proportions of the existing parks, undertaking major earthworks and creating new plantations and numerous water features

---

[55] Also named in the literature as Porta or Della Porta.

[56] Amburger, *Ingermanland*, 1, p. 181; Duzhnikov, *Ropsha*, p. 24.

[57] Ibid., p. 27.

[58] Amburger, *Ingermanland*, 1, p. 498.

[59] Between the years 1785 and 1840 two English gardeners worked at Ropsha, Thomas Gray and Isaac Oldaker. The latter served at Ropsha 1804–12, before going on to a long and productive career in England, primarily as gardener to Sir Joseph Banks (see E. Perfect, A. L. Reiman and Yu. A. Duzhnikov, *Isaac Oldaker, The Man from Ropsha*, High Wycombe, 2001). Conflicting dates for the activities at Ropsha of Thomas Gray (1754–1840) are given by Perfect et al. (p. 17: 1804–40) and Murashova/Myslina (p. 143, from 1785, 'for half a century'). Gray worked at Ropsha for Lazarev: Iu. M Gogolitsyn and T. M. Gogolytsina, *Pamiatniki arkhitektury Leningradskoi oblasti*, Leningrad, 1987, p. 181; he also worked at Krasnoe Selo: A. L. Reiman, 'Krasnosel'skie landshafty', in *Pamiatniki istorii i kul'tury Peterburga*, St Petersburg, 1994, pp. 181–96. In 1825 Gray was summoned from Ropsha by Alexander I to lay out a garden near Taganrog: N. K. Shil'der, *Imperator Aleksandr Pervyi: ego zhizn' i tsarstvovanie*, 4 vols, 2nd edn, St Petersburg, 1904–05, 4, p. 358. I am indebted to Prof. A. G. Cross for information on Gray.

— including new shaping of the two lakes, named Ivanovskii and Artem'evskii in honour of Lazarev and his son.

It was appropriate that the entrepreneur Lazarev should introduce industrial activity into Ropsha: at the far end of the estate from the palace Lazarev had a mill built to produce paper. It was designed by the architect Iurii M. Fel'ten, famous among other things for his work in creating the granite facings of the Neva riverbank in St Petersburg; Fel'ten was an old acquaintance of Lazarev, having built Armenian churches in both Moscow and St Petersburg which Lazarev had funded. The mill, also in the Classical style, was constructed over six years, 1788–94. A dam and mill-pond were created and in its early years the mill worked on water power, employing 200 workers and producing 18–20,000 reams of paper annually.[60] The mill was managed by master paper-maker Johann Buchmeyer, who continued to rent it from the Crown after Paul's purchase and the estate's subsequent transfer to the tsar's Cabinet (private office) in 1804. Father (†1816) and son Buchmeyer ran the enterprise until 1844. It was technically unsophisticated: Buchmeyer only installed up-to-date machinery in 1839. The mill remained in operation until 1939.[61] In 1817–19 it was joined briefly by a wallpaper manufacturer under a Frenchman, J. Brochette, which, however, soon relocated to Tsarskoe Selo.[62]

In February 1801, in the fifth year of Paul's reign as Emperor, Lazarev sold the estate to the Crown, for 400,000 roubles; Paul gave him in addition an annual pension of 4,000 roubles, rank and honours, and also granted land and benefits to Lazarev's fellow-countrymen in the south-Russian Armenian colony of Nakhichevan'.[63] Paul, as already mentioned, apparently thought of renaming the estate Krovavoe Pole, Field of Blood; a few weeks after the purchase he suffered the same fate as his father.

In all, Lazarev spent some 300,000 roubles on refashioning Ropsha.[64] When the estate was finally sold, Engel'mann had still not quite completed his work. But the Porto/Engel'mann Ropsha ensemble remained basically the same thereafter.

---

[60] Duzhnikov, *Ropsha*, pp. 31–33; Murashova/Myslina, *Dvorianskie usad'by*, p. 148. Paper-making became a significant branch of industry in the St Petersburg area in the late eighteenth century: Amburger, *Ingermanland*, 1, pp. 332–33. Lazarev's mill was visited in 1796 by a group of Petersburg aristocrats who went on an excursion to visit Lazarev and his estate. Their forty-four-page account of the occasion, *Voyage de Robscha* [*sic*], written in French, details the welcome accorded them by the owners and describes the park, fields, orchards and fruit trees, and the mill. It is held in the Mss Division of the Russian State Library in Moscow: see Gos. Biblioteka SSSR im. V. I. Lenina, Otdel Rukopisei, *Vospominaniia i dnevniki XVIII–XX vv. Ukazatel' rukopisei*, ed. S. V. Zhitomirskii, Moscow 1976, p. 131, no. 271. I have not been able to consult this document.

[61] Amburger, *Ingermanland*, 1, p. 342; Lisitsyn, *Istoriia i kul'tura*, p. 96.

[62] Amburger, *Ingermanland*, 1, p. 347.

[63] Ibid., 1, p. 181; Pyliaev, *Zabytoe proshloe*, p. 333; Murashova/Myslina, *Dvorianskie usad'by*, p. 151. How far the Nakhichevan' grants were linked to Lazarev remains unclear.

[64] Pyliaev, *Zabytoe proshloe*, loc. cit.

The Porto palace, Ropsha, in 1908

Sited at four levels — the Upper Park, the terrace with the buildings, the Lower Park with the Ivanovskii lake and the factory complex with the millpond — the Ropsha ensemble presented a unique example of land-scaped parks varying in scale and character, interconnected both by their design and by the artificial water system which spread out from the main spring, the Jordan. Their artificial origins are so hidden, so veiled at Ropsha that they seem to have been made by Nature, and only specialists recognize the hand of the skilled master-craftsman who created them.[65]

During the nineteenth century various working buildings (green-houses, orangeries) were added, and repair work and some minor alterations were carried out, but nothing fundamental changed. From 1804 to 1825 Ropsha was administered by the Cabinet of His Imperial Majesty; the buildings and grounds were well looked after, and the final work left undone by Engel'mann was completed.

In the new century Ropsha became involved in the work of the St Petersburg Foundling Home, now under the jurisdiction of Paul's widow Dowager Empress Mariia Fedorovna, who controlled and actively managed a range of charitable organizations. Set up in 1772 with the laudable purpose of combating infanticide, controlling child abandonment and increasing the country's population, the Foundling Home had a terrible record of infant mortality; there were also problems in finding sufficient wet-nurses for the foundlings in the capital. This led in 1799 to the creation of Rural Sections of the Home: found-lings should now be sent to be reared by peasants in the countryside.

[65] Ibid., p. 149.

Ropsha became the centre of a Rural Section; in this connection the first systematic health care appeared on the estate, with the appointment in 1801 of a doctor from the Foundling Home. However, the new system of fostering foundlings with peasant families was no more successful than the old: mortality remained frighteningly high.[66]

On the accession of Nicholas I in 1825, the new tsar presented Ropsha to his wife, Aleksandra Fedorovna (née Princess Charlotte of Prussia), who had first visited it in 1820. Administration continued to be handled by His Imperial Majesty's Own Chancellery, Nicholas's newly reorganized private office, until the estate was placed under the Appanage Department in 1837.[67] Ropsha must have appealed to the romantically-inclined German tsarina, who had spent her honeymoon at Peterhof and been enchanted by the local countryside. In 1818 she had noted in her diary that after the distractions of public life she liked to withdraw deep within herself, and at such moments 'nature was as essential to me as a good sermon'.[68] Aleksandra Fedorovna, known for her philanthropic activities and after Mariia Fedorovna's death in 1828 in charge of the latter's charitable foundation, took a serious interest in Ropsha 'and turned the park into a flourishing garden. She settled German colonists, helped the families of local workers in the vineyards, orangeries and fishery, concerned herself with the children's education. [Under her guidance], the first school was set up in Ropsha'.[69]

The death of Nicholas I in 1855 (which was followed in 1860 by that of his widow) ushered in the period of 'Great Reforms' and the emancipation from serfdom of the Russian peasantry. With the exception of the German colony, the peasants of the Ropsha district (*volost'*) belonged to the Appanage Department and were treated in accordance with the relevant legislation. The workers in the paper-mill, however, required special consideration. On the eve of the February 1861 emancipation, the Appanage Department redesignated all non-specialist workers as peasants, and combined many of them into a separate settlement (*sloboda*), while eighty-seven families were given land in surrounding appanage villages. The specialist workers, as well as workers in the palace, received special conditions.[70] The work of the mill was unaffected.

---

[66] Amburger, *Ingermanland*, 1, pp. 454, 461–63; in general, on the Foundling Home and fostering system, see D. L. Ransel, *Mothers of Misery: Child Abandonment in Russia*, Princeton, NJ, 1988.

[67] Amburger, *Ingermanland*, 1, p. 185.

[68] Quoted by Murashev/Myslina, *Dvorianskie usad'by*, p. 152.

[69] <http://www.ropsha.ru> [accessed 22 January 2009]. On the mid-nineteenth-century settlement of German colonies in Ropsha, Oranienbaum and elsewhere, and their successful development of *gîtes* for the St Petersburg middle classes, see Amburger, *Ingermanland*, 1, pp. 265, 271–81, 564.

[70] Ibid., pp. 230, 256, 265, 377.

Under succeeding tsars, Ropsha remained an Imperial estate. Aleksandra Fedorovna's grandson Grand Duke Nikolai Nikolaevich junior became owner in 1907; his cousin Tsar Nicholas II frequently came to Ropsha to hunt in the estate grounds and the surrounding countryside, but these parties stopped in 1914.

IV

In the Soviet period the Ropsha estate became a fish-farm. Even in the Imperial period its many lakes had been known for their fish stocks, grown for the Court; a particular type of scaly carp is named after it, and Grand Duke Nikolai Nikolaevich had set up a fish-breeding station, whose traditions were continued by the Ropsha Central Experimental Station of the Soviet State Scientific Research Institute for the Lake- and River-Fish Economy (TsES GosNIORKh 'Ropsha'). The palace became a rest home for Party leaders and economic managers. Badly damaged during the Great Fatherland War and the German invasion, Ropsha's working buildings and housing were rebuilt after the war but the palace ensemble was not restored, despite some works, and was in military use until 1989. After 1991 it was leased out to various enterprises with the condition of restoring the building, which however was not honoured. In the last two decades it has suffered further, and fallen into complete decay: vivid pictures taken in 2008 of its dilapidation can be seen on the Internet.[71]

In 2003 a federal programme designed to preserve the architecture of old towns brought government money for restoration work to the Government of the Leningrad Region, which began considering the restoration of Ropsha, where it favoured a centre of tourism.[72] The St Petersburg Hermitage's Volunteer Service (HVS) became involved, with ideas of a museum dedicated to the Romanovs, and in 2006 HVS published a project to set up a Museum of the Christmas Tree (Muzei novogodnei elki) in the area of the palace and park, devoted to celebrations of the New Year, in partnership with the local secondary school. Ropsha would be appropriate to this, HVS argued, because (as with Prince Albert and the British Christmas tree) 'the appearance of the New Year fir tree in Russia is inseparably linked with the name of one of Ropsha's owners, the Empress Aleksandra Fedorovna' and the estate

---

[71] <http://seaseas.livejournal.com/212243.html> [accessed 24 January 2009]. (The 1908 photograph included here shows of course the palace as remodelled by Porto, not — as asserted — the Rastrelli buildings in which Peter III was killed.)

[72] <http://www.expert.ru/printissues/northwest/2005/18/18no-sobsh1> [accessed 24 January 2009].

was presented to her by Nicholas I on New Year's Eve 1825. The school was to be renamed in Aleksandra Fedorovna's honour:

> As it develops, the museum should become not only an exhibition space for children's work, but a pro-active centre of child creativity. The schoolchildren will take the most active possible part in the creation of the museum [. . .] In order to create a new museum display in Ropsha, it is planned to make use of the results of the competitions of children's creative work which are run in the State Hermitage on the initiative of the Volunteer Service [. . .] in cooperation with the education committees of St Petersburg and the Leningrad District.

Among other collaborators of HVS had been the Federal Breeding and Genetic Centre for Pisciculture in Ropsha, successor to TsES GosNIORKh:

> The only building on the territory of the ensemble which is being carefully preserved by staff of this extremely old scientific centre in Russia, occupied with issues of raising fish stocks since the eighteenth century, is the former building of the Paper Factory [. . .] This building has regularly been the venue for concerts and with the participation of the State Hermitage's Volunteer Service, it is where exhibitions have been arranged.[73]

This wide-ranging project combined a return to Ropsha's Imperial traditions with care for the Russian cultural heritage and with Russians' deep-laid concerns for child development. But it generated no money beyond government funds, and it came into competition with major commercial interests: also in 2006, an Italian development company leased the estate for five years, with a view to a further lease of forty-nine, with a multi-million-Euro project to develop it as a hospitality and entertainment centre:

> A project to rebuild the imperial park has been developed by a group of European companies. According to the plan, in 2009 the reconstructed Ropsha Palace will be opened as a 5-star hotel. 50 private villas are being built in the park. An international congress-centre is also to be developed on the site. An adjacent area is planned as an entertainment centre with a casino, a supermarket, and seven restaurants.[74]

All these plans, however, appear to have run into problems of property rights, ownership and competing interests. Ropsha is federal, not regional property. The vehicle for the Italian project, Ropsha Invest plc (OAO), failed in its initial attempt to register the Ropsha lease, and

---

[73] <http://www.hermitage.museum.ru/html_En/06/hm6_5_0_0_0.html> [accessed 22 January 2009].
[74] *Wikipedia*, s.v. 'Ropsha' <http://en.wikipedia.org/wiki/Ropsha> [accessed 22 January 2009]; see further <http://www.allcafe.info/news/2006/03/18/4809/print> [accessed 22 January 2009].

its director claimed that this failure reflected interest in the Ropsha
site on the part of the Administration of the President, already
responsible for the transformation of nearby Strel´na into a state
hospitality centre.[75]

The current interest in redeveloping the complex presupposes a new
identity for the palace and grounds, and investment on a vast scale.
Twenty-first-century Ropsha, once developed, will in all likelihood be
very different from its Imperial incarnations. Ropsha's Imperial past,
present dilapidation and potential future transformation are features it
has in common with a number of other unrestored estates around
St Petersburg. In all the recently published discussions, however, the
notorious fact of 1762, unique of course to Ropsha, is a constantly
repeated point of background reference.[76] Whatever the future holds,
it seems likely that Ropsha children, like those whom Savosina met in
2004, will still learn as local lore that 'It's not an estate, but a palace!
A tsar's palace — Emperor Peter III's palace! He was even killed
here!'

---

[75] *St Petersburg Business Guide*, 17 March 2008 <http://www.spbgid.ru/index.php?news=
144231> [accessed 24 January 2009].
[76] It likewise recurs, in somewhat clinical form, in the recent semi-official *Istoriia i kul´tura
Leningradskoi zemli*, ed. S. Lisitsyn, which refers on p. 105 to 'the estate at Ropsha, in whose
history are reflected events of the period of palace revolutions'.

Religion and Enlightenment in Eighteenth-Century Russia: Father Platon at the Court of Catherine II

ELISE KIMERLING WIRTSCHAFTER

THE Russian Enlightenment was at its core a lived enlightenment. As such, it centred on the pursuit of enlightenment or an enlightened way of life informed by an array of moral and philosophical principles. Inspired by the intellectual modernity of Europe, the enlightened life implied belief in the natural equality, goodness and dignity of all human beings; the efficacy of properly cultivated human reason; the moral self-reformation of the individual; and the government-led reformation of institutions. Unlike the Enlightenments of Central and Western Europe, which put forth coherent sets of ideas to be realized through social and political change, the Russian Enlightenment cannot be understood by tracing the genealogy of philosophical schools or ideological movements. The Russian Enlightenment, an enlightenment to be lived, stressed the spiritual development and moral perfectibility of the individual human being. Whether applied to the social, political, or cultural sphere, it provided a moral voice for an emergent public, a 'civil society of the educated', in search of autonomy and progress.[1]

Most studies of the Russian Enlightenment focus on the ideas, science, scholarship and arts imported into Russia from Europe beginning in the late seventeenth century. Only a handful of modern scholars look at the indigenous sources of the Russian Enlightenment,

Elise Kimerling Wirtschafter is Professor of History at California State Polytechnic University, Pomona.

[1] On educated society's search for autonomy and progress, see Marc Raeff, 'Transfiguration and Modernization: The Paradoxes of Social Disciplining, Paedagogical Leadership, and the Enlightenment in Eighteenth-Century Russia', in *Alteuropa — Ancien Régime — Frühe Neuzeit: Probleme und Methoden der Forschung*, ed. Hans Erich Bödeker and Ernst Hinrichs, Stuttgart and Bad Cannstatt, 1991, pp. 99–115; idem, *Origins of the Russian Intelligentsia: The Eighteenth-Century Nobility*, New York, 1966. On the Russian Enlightenment as a moral voice for society, see Elise Kimerling Wirtschafter, *Russia's Age of Serfdom 1649–1861*, Malden, MA, 2008, ch. 6. See also Charles Taylor regarding the dependence of the modern self or identity on the moral sense: *Sources of the Self: The Making of the Modern Identity*, Cambridge, MA, 1989.

including the traditions of Orthodox Christianity.[2] As every historian knows, however, the teachings and liturgy of the Orthodox Church played a central role in public and private life across Russii society. In addition to observances associated with feast days in the Christian calendar and with life events such as birth, marriage and death, religious ritual accompanied coronations, nameday and birthday festivities, dedications of buildings and institutions, celebrations of military victories and the passing of health crises. To mark these occasions, Russian elites not only enjoyed banquets, balls, fireworks displays and artistic performances; they also attended church services and listened to speeches and sermons delivered by prominent churchmen.

In the reign of Empress Catherine II, one of the most admired of these churchmen was the Court preacher and teacher of catechism Father Platon (Petr Georgievich Levshin, 1737–1812). Born the son of a village priest, Petr Levshin received his education first at the Kolomna Seminary and later at the Moscow Slavonic-Greek-Latin Academy, where he also began clerical service as teacher of poetics and public catechist. In 1758, at the request of his mentor and patron, Gedeon (Krinovskii), Petr was appointed teacher of rhetoric at the seminary of the Trinity-Sergius Lavra. Soon thereafter the young cleric took monastic vows and became Hierodeacon Platon. In 1761 Platon assumed the rectorship of the Trinity Seminary, and in 1763, after meeting Catherine during two imperial visits to the Lavra (in 1762 and 1763), he advanced to the post of *namestnik* (*locumtenens*). Chosen that same year to be teacher of catechism, or God's Law, to Catherine's son and heir, Tsesarevich Paul, Platon moved to St Petersburg to take up his new duties. He remained in the position of religious teacher for ten years, from August 1763 until Paul came of age and married in September 1773. Throughout this period and continuing until around 1782, Platon also regularly preached at Court. As one would expect in the case of a prominent prelate who enjoyed the monarch's patronage, prestigious appointments dotted Platon's career: archimandrite of the Trinity-Sergius Lavra (1766), member of the Synod (1768), archbishop of Tver′ (1770), archbishop of Moscow and Kaluga (1775), founder of the Vifaniia Monastery (1783) and finally, metropolitan of Moscow (1787).[3]

---

[2] Superb examples directly relevant to this discussion include Georgii Florovskii, *Puti russkogo bogosloviia*, Paris, 1937; Minsk, 2006; V. M. Zhivov, *Iazyk i kul′tura v Rossii XVIII veka*, Moscow, 1996; A. I. Esiukov, *Chelovek i mir v pravoslavnoi prosvetitel′skoi mysli Rossii vtoroi poloviny XVIII veka. Istoriko-filosofskie ocherki. Monografiia*, Arkhangel′sk, 1998; idem, *Filosofskie aspekty russkoi bogoslovskoi mysli (vtoraia polovina XVIII–nachalo XIX v.): Monografiia*, Arkhangel′sk, 2003.

[3] Biographies of Platon include: K. A. Papmehl, *Metropolitan of Moscow Platon (Petr Levshin, 1737–1812): The Enlightened Prelate, Scholar and Educator*, Newtonville, MA, 1983; Platon (Levshin), 'Avtobiografiia, ili zapiski o zhizni Platona, mitropolita Moskovskogo', in *'Iz*

Praised by contemporaries and historians for his progressive views on education and religious conformity, Platon had much to say about the aspiration to lead an enlightened life.[4] Because of his ties to the Court, visits with foreign dignitaries and personal relationships with literary figures, elite servicemen and members of the imperial family, Platon regularly encountered the Enlightenment culture of late eighteenth-century Europe and Russia. After moving to St Petersburg, the Orthodox monk taught himself French, and in his capacity as director of the Moscow Slavonic-Greek-Latin Academy (from 1775), he supported the study of Latin, French, German, history, mathematics, physics and medicine.[5] Concerned throughout his career with the role of the church in the moral development of society, Platon approached preaching as a form of conversation with fellow Christians. To that end, he composed sermons in the literary Russian of the day, and his writings in general can be said to satisfy a modern aesthetic sensibility. A churchman who incorporated social and political issues into religious instruction, Platon is a fitting subject for the study of what the Enlightenment meant in eighteenth-century Russia.

To document the impact of Platon's words on the thoughts of his listeners (and readers) is a complicated endeavour, though clearly contemporaries found his sermons eloquent and moving. After hearing Platon's 'Sermon on the Usefulness of Learning', delivered in 1765 on the occasion of Tsesarevich Paul's eleventh birthday, Empress Catherine II is said to remarked, 'Father Platon does with us all that he wants; if he wants us to cry, we cry; if he wants us to laugh, we laugh'. The 'Sermon on the Usefulness of Learning' reportedly moved Platon's listeners to tears. The preacher's eloquence is likewise attested by leading poets such as A. P. Sumarokov; by the churchmen who edited and published his Court sermons, Rector of the Moscow Academy Damaskin (Semenov-Rudnev) and Prefect of the Academy Amvrosii (Serebrennikov); and by generations of biographers and scholars. The Scottish tutor William Richardson, though he did not

[3] *Continued*
glubiny vozzvakh k tebe, Gospodi ...', ed. P. V. Kalitin, Moscow, 1996, pp. 11–70; Mitropolit Evgenii (Bolkhovitinov), *Slovar' istoricheskii o byvshikh v Rossii pisateliakh dukhovnogo china Greko-Rossiiskoi Tserkvi*, Moscow, 1995; P. A. Beliaev, *Zhizn' Platona, mitropolita moskovskago s ego portretom*, Minneapolis, MN, 1982; I. M. Snegirev, *Zhizn' Moskovskago Metropolita Platona*, 2 vols, Moscow, 1856. On Platon and the history of Russian preaching, see V. P. Zubov, *Russkie propovedniki: Ocherki po istorii russkoi propovedi*, Moscow, 2001.

[4] A. N. Pypin, *Religioznye dvizheniia pri Aleksandre I*, Petrograd, 1916; St Petersburg, 2000, pp. 118, 182; P. M. Korotkevich, 'O formirovanii vzgliadov mitropolita Platona na organizatsiiu obrazovaniia v dukhovnykh shkolakh Troitse-Sergievoi lavry', *Troitse-Sergieva lavra v istorii, kul'ture i dukhovnoi zhizni Rossii*, ed. T. N. Manushin and S. V. Nikolaeva, Moscow, 2000, pp. 209–20.

[5] On Platon's educational policies, see P. V. Znamenskii, *Dukhovnye shkoly v Rossii do reformy 1808 goda*, Kazan, 1881; St Petersburg, 2001.

speak Russian, heard Platon preach on 8 August 1768 at the laying of the foundation stone of St Isaac's Cathedral. Richardson described Platon's elocution as 'fervent' and the sound of his language as 'liquid and pleasant'. Platon himself, in an autobiography written toward the end of his life, recalled his gift for eloquence and freeness with words (*svobodnost' slov*), a quality that to his mind encouraged bold speech and repeatedly caused conflict with associates.[6] Not unlike preachers and religious leaders of today, Platon based his sermons on biblical passages, which he then interpreted to teach a moral lesson about a contemporary problem. His interest in the moral message of Holy Scripture, an interest criticized by later generations of Russian theologians, at once explicated Christian teachings, echoed the religious Enlighteners and non-confessional moral philosophers of seventeenth- and eighteenth-century Europe, and brought contemporary Enlightenment concepts into the framework of church observance.[7] By elaborating Enlightenment principles in the idiom of Orthodox belief, Platon gave to the 'modern' ideas of his listeners a 'traditional' religious meaning.[8]

Any reader of the great literary classics of Imperial Russia cannot fail to notice the strong moral voice, deeply humanistic sensibility, and pleas for social justice that define the artistic canon. One way to understand the moralistic quality of Russian literary culture, and indeed of Russia's educated classes more generally, is to explore the rich relationship between Orthodox religious teachings and

[6] Elise Kimerling Wirtschafter, '20 September 1765: Tsesarevich Paul's Eleventh Birthday and Father Platon's "Sermon on Learning"', in A. Cross (ed.), *Days from the Reigns of Eighteenth-Century Russian Rulers*, Study Group on Eighteenth-Century Russia Newsletter, 2 parts, Cambridge, 2007, 2, pp. 168–69; Anthony Cross, '8 August 1768: The Laying of the Foundation Stone of Rinaldi's St. Isaac's Cathedral', in ibid., p. 176. Damaskin and Amvrosii edited the first nine volumes of Platon's collected sermons (see n. 10 below). On their role, see Evgenii, *Slovar'*, p. 73.

[7] On moral philosophy and the religious Enlightenment, see Steven Nadler, *Spinoza: A Life*, Cambridge and New York, 1999, pp. 290–92; J. B. Schneewind, *The Invention of Autonomy: A History of Modern Moral Philosophy*, New York, 1998; Jonathan Sheehan, *The Enlightenment Bible: Translation, Scholarship, Culture*, Princeton, NJ, 2005; David Sorkin, *The Religious Enlightenment: Protestants, Jews, and Catholics from London to Vienna*, Princeton, NJ, 2008; Joris Van Eijnatten (ed.), *Preaching, Sermon and Cultural Change in the Long Eighteenth Century*, Leiden, 2009. Father Georgii Florovskii characterizes Platon as a catechist and 'enthusiast of enlightenment' who placed too much emphasis on moral instruction (*nravouchenie*) and emotional humanism and too little on faith (*vera*) and the sacramental meaning of the church community (*tserkovnost'*). In interpreting Scripture, Florovskii claims, Platon preferred to seek the literal meaning rather than the sacramental or mysterious meaning which might not be present. Florovskii, *Puti*, pp. 109–15.

[8] Like religious Enlighteners across Europe, Platon used tradition for novel purposes and 'dressed up' innovation as tradition. For a theoretical statement of this dynamic, see Eric Hobsbawm, 'Introduction: Inventing Tradition', in *The Invention of Tradition*, ed. Eric Hobsbawm and Terence Ranger, Cambridge, 1983, pp. 1–14.

philosophical modernity.[9] This essay represents an initial effort in that direction. It focuses on three sermons delivered by Platon during his tenure as teacher of catechism to Tsesarevich Paul. The first two, given in 1765, address the distinction between enlightenment (*prosveshchenie*) and learning (*uchenie*) and the third, given in 1772, discusses the relationship between the church and society. All three illustrate the way in which Platon contributed to Russia's lived enlightenment by blending Enlightenment ideas into the moral precepts of Russian Orthodoxy.[10]

Sermon on Education

In 1765 Catherine II presided over a ceremony to celebrate the laying of the foundation stone of the Imperial Academy of Arts and its church. As part of this celebration, on 7 July, Father Platon delivered a 'Sermon on Education' before the empress and Tsesarevich Paul.[11] The sermon begins by describing the Academy of Arts as a place of virtue and the Academy church as a dwelling of God, the source of virtue. Together the Academy and its church symbolize the interdependence of secular and religious education. Platon openly acknowledges that secular schools help the church in the task of moral education, yet his main

[9] Jonathan Israel, referring to the Radical Enlightenment, defines fully developed philosophical modernity as a package of interconnected concepts, principles and values which can be summarized in eight primary points: 1) mathematical-historical reason is the only criterion of truth (clearly not compatible with Christianity but also not characteristic of the moderate mainstream and religious Enlightenments); 2) rejection of all supernatural agency, magic and divine providence (partially compatible with Christianity and the moderate mainstream and religious Enlightenments, which rejected magic but upheld divine providence); 3) equality of all humankind, including racial and sexual equality (echoes Christian universalism); 4) secular universalism in ethics, which is grounded in equality and concerned with equity, justice and charity (echoes Christian universalism); 5) full toleration and freedom of thought (not possible in eighteenth-century Russia); 6) freedom of expression, political criticism and the press (not possible in eighteenth-century Russia); 7) democratic republicanism as the most legitimate form of politics (not imagined in eighteenth-century Russia); 8) personal liberty of lifestyle and sexual orientation (not imagined in eighteenth-century Russia). Obviously, it remains possible to speak of Enlightenment principles in a context such as eighteenth-century Russia where not all of Israel's points were operative. Jonathan Israel, *Enlightenment Contested: Philosophy, Modernity, and the Emancipation of Man*, New York, 2006, p. 866.

[10] The sermons are published in volumes 1–2 of Platon (Levshin), *Pouchitel'nyia slova pri vysochaishem dvore E. I. V. ... Gosudaryni Ekateriny Alekseevny i drugikh mestakh s 1763 goda po 1778 skazyvannyia ...*, Moscow, 1779. In the complete collection of twenty volumes, the titles, publication dates and publishers of individual volumes vary. Eighteen volumes (to date) are available online at <http://stsl.ru/lib/platon>.

[11] Russia's Academy of Arts began its history as a department within the Academy of Sciences founded by Peter the Great. The Academy of Arts became a separate institution in 1757, during the reign of Peter's daughter Elizabeth, and construction of its building on Vasil'evskii Island took place in the years 1764–68. G. N. Komelova, 'Catherine the Great and Her Age', in *Treasures of Imperial Russia: Catherine the Great from the State Hermitage Museum, St. Petersburg*, ed. Isabella Forbes and William Underhill, Leningrad, 1990, p. xviii, and 'The Architecture of St. Petersburg in the Time of Catherine the Great', in ibid., p. 181.

concern is to show the superiority of religious teachings. Without prayer and piety, he insists, all human endeavours are empty. Indeed, it is critical that parents, teachers and guardians prepare children for 'higher learning' by teaching them virtue. Education (*vospitanie*), Platon concludes, is 'preparation for virtue'.[12] Education allows the child 'to enter into himself through knowledge [*vzoiti poznaniem v samago sebia*], to know his Creator, and to know the purpose of creation'.

Platon next enumerates the virtues that must be instilled in the souls of young children. His is the usual eighteenth-century list: piety, loyalty to the monarch, respect for superiors, lenience toward inferiors, zeal for equals, gratitude to parents, sincerity in friendship and love for all. Consistent with these virtues, education also should teach diligence in service, thoroughness in housekeeping and hard work. In the broader sphere of social obligations, children should learn to regret the poverty of others. They also should be taught not to become conceited because of happiness and good fortune, or dejected because of misfortune. Finally, they should learn earnestness for the common good and how to be sincere, gentle, courteous and lenient in all their relationships. In the words of Platon, the 'essential power of education' lies in the teaching of virtue. Although it is true that a minimum of enlightenment is needed to identify the desired virtues, to instil them in young hearts is a much more difficult task. For while there are many ways to teach virtue, problems with the present state of education also exist. The best pedagogical method is thus to set a good example. Because children are governed more by feelings than by reason, this 'mute science', the science of setting a good example, is more effective than empty words.

After highlighting the significance of moral education, Platon goes on to discuss the contrast between different forms of learning, specifically the distinction between the lessons of Holy Scripture and the knowledge attained through modern science. What benefit, he asks, can come from learning about the movements of the heavens, if a person's heart is 'bound to earthly passions'? "For what", in the words of Jesus, prophesying the Passion, "will it profit a man if he gains the whole world, and loses his own soul?" (Mark 8: 36).[13] By no means

---

[12] *Vospitanie* is usually better translated as upbringing. In this case, however, because the sermon commemorates the dedication of a school, the use of 'education' seems more appropriate. Note, moreover, that throughout the eighteenth century, the concept of education encompassed the broader meaning of moral education or upbringing.

[13] Unless otherwise stated, the biblical passages cited in this article appear in Platon's sermons and are therefore set off by double quotation marks. In instances where Platon paraphrases or gives a partial biblical quote, I provide the full passage and therefore use single quotation marks. For translation of all passages from the New Testament, I rely on *The Orthodox Study Bible: New Testament and Psalms. New King James Version*, Nashville, TN, 1982 and 1993.

intending to denigrate the sciences, Platon nonetheless makes clear that without honest deeds and a reformed conscience, they are useless. The best science consists of action, not words, and this science is the science of the Gospel: 'it is characteristic of Christian wisdom to philosophize not with words but with deeds.' A follower of the Gospel is therefore 'a light in the world'. For as Jesus said to his disciples, "Let your light so shine before men, that they may see your good works and glorify your Father in heaven" (Matthew 5:16).

To become 'a light in the world', children must learn above all to fear God. Indeed, without fear of God, human desires, indecent thoughts and harmful intentions cannot be controlled. Only after fear of God becomes rooted in the human heart is a person ready to study the arts and sciences, based on social status, ability, interest and age. Platon repeatedly acknowledges the usefulness of the secular arts and sciences, though he distinguishes between their respective functions and appears to prefer the arts. The sciences enlighten thought, illuminate the path to goodness and teach people how to choose a good life, but they also can be used for evil purposes. The arts, by contrast, serve a purpose closer to that of the Gospel. Platon seems to imagine the artist as a kind of monk engaged in a blessed and solitary activity. The arts strengthen the soul, make use of the path to goodness and constitute in themselves a good condition of life. The arts, in a word, celebrate the Creator.

Platon ends his sermon by praising Catherine for her attention to the education of her subjects and by celebrating the promise embodied in the Academy of Arts. A child educated according to the principles set forth in the sermon will become a good Christian, honourable citizen, thrifty homemaker, true friend, trustworthy neighbour and pleasant comrade. Thanks to the actions of the monarch, who has given her subjects the Academy of Arts, goodness grounded in fear of God and the teachings of the church can spread out from secular schools into society and polity.

Appropriate to the occasion being celebrated, Platon's sermon addresses a classic eighteenth-century question: the relationship between moral education and scientific learning. That this theme resonated with Russia's educated classes is evident from a 1789 essay competition sponsored by the Society of Lovers of Learnedness at Moscow University. Echoing Rousseau, the question posed to prospective essayists reveals the conflation of morality and learning which lay at the core of the Russian Enlightenment: "With which sciences should the enlightenment of a person begin — with those that concern the heart and morality or with those that belong to the mind (*razuma*) and keenness (*ostrota*)?"[14] More than two decades earlier, at about the same

---

[14] Wirtschafter, *Age of Serfdom*, p. 152.

time that pieces of Rousseau's writings began to appear in Russian translation, Platon's 'Sermon on Education' had answered this question.[15]

Sermon on the Usefulness of Learning

Throughout his career Father Platon remained committed to the education of both clergy and laity. In his capacity as Court preacher and religious teacher to Tsesarevich Paul, he performed one of the most esteemed and time-honoured roles of the Christian churchman, that of moral instructor to monarchs. Indeed, in eighteenth-century Russia, the calendar of the Orthodox Church gave preachers numerous opportunities to teach their social and political superiors. Among the most festive and visible of these were birthday and nameday celebrations at Court. Beginning in 1721, on the anniversary of Peter I's coronation, the birthdays and namedays of members of the imperial family entered the calendar of official holidays commemorated with banquets, balls, visitations and religious services. As teacher of catechism to Paul, Platon regularly preached on the birthday (20 September) and nameday (29 June) of his pupil.

Several weeks after the 'Sermon on Education' celebrated the foundation of the Academy of Arts, Platon returned to the theme of secular and religious education in the 'Sermon on the Usefulness of Learning'. Delivered on 20 September 1765 in the presence of Empress Catherine II and Tsesarevich Paul, the sermon commemorated the heir's eleventh birthday.[16] Platon took the theme of his sermon from Luke 21:14, where Jesus says to his disciples, "Therefore settle it in your hearts not to meditate beforehand on what you will answer". In the preceding passage (Luke 21:12–13), not quoted by Platon, Jesus warns his followers that they will suffer persecution 'for My name's sake', but that this will give them the opportunity to offer testimony. They should not, therefore, decide in advance how to answer their opponents. For, Jesus continues in verse 15, 'I will give you a mouth and wisdom which all your adversaries will not be able to contradict or resist'.

The overarching message of Platon's sermon is that true wisdom comes from God. To counter 'the wisdom-loving men' (read philosophers) who argue that the moral reform of humankind derives from reason (*razum*) — that the desire for good and the rejection of evil are possible only if one possesses an enlightened concept of good and evil — Platon repeats the words of Jesus recorded in Luke 21:14: "Therefore settle it in your hearts not to meditate beforehand on what you will

---

[15] Thomas P. Barran, *Russia Reads Rousseau, 1762–1825*, Evanston, IL, 2002.
[16] This sermon is briefly discussed in Wirtschafter, '20 September 1765', pp. 165–68.

answer." He interprets these words to mean that if one first strives for 'honesty of the soul', 'enlightenment of the mind' will follow. Learning produces good morals only if a person already intends to acquire good morals through learning. That is, the intent to seek goodness has to be present before the acquisition of knowledge can bring any moral benefit. For this reason, the Gospel teaches that we must pay attention to our hearts before we learn to answer. Once again Platon proclaims the belief, traceable to biblical and patristic sources, that spiritual wisdom, centred in the heart, is superior to human learning. That said, in the Enlightenment context of Catherinian Russia, the preacher could not rely solely on religious tradition to convey this message. Thus while Platon prayed that in the course of the sermon the Lord would open up to him and his listeners the mysteries of divine wisdom, he also deliberated upon the usefulness of learning.

It is a truism of modern biblical scholarship that multiple layers of meaning are intentionally built into sermons and religious writings. Not surprisingly, then, Platon can be read as both a tradition-bound church-man and a representative of the Russian Enlightenment. Although deeply committed to church doctrine and Christian spirituality, Platon also revelled in the joys of earthly enlightenment. There is no need, he points out in the sermon of 20 September 1765, to show that learning (*uchenie*) is appropriate for human beings. Here he defines learning as 'knowledge of the truth [*istinna*]', adding that human beings are endowed by the Creator with reason (*razum*) or 'the ability to know the truth'.[17] To reject learning is therefore to reject reason, which is to reject humankind. Simply put, learning is intrinsic to being human.

But what do human beings seek through learning? First, we hope to enlighten our thoughts, which allows us to take delight in the universe created by God and visible to our eyes. Guided by learning, we gain understanding of the physical world — the heavens and the earth, the movement of heavenly bodies, the animals — and especially of our-selves, of virtue and vice, and of the good and bad consequences

---

[17] Platon is not here referring to spiritual or divine truth, but to inferior human truth or knowledge. Even so, his use of the word truth (*istinna*) is to my mind ambiguous. Orthodox Christianity draws a clear distinction between 'intellect' (*nous*) and 'reason' or 'mind' (*dianoia*). Intellect refers to the highest human faculty through which it is possible to know 'God or the inner essences or principles (q.v.) of created things by means of direct apprehension or spiritual perception'. The intellect is located in the soul and is understood to be 'the organ of contemplation'. Reason or mind refers to the 'logical faculty' in human beings. Its function 'is to draw conclusions or formulate concepts deriving from data provided [. . .] by revelation or spiritual knowledge (q.v.) or by sense-observation'. Knowledge based on reason belongs to 'a lower order than spiritual knowledge (q.v.) and does not imply any direct apprehension or perception of the inner essences or principles (q.v.) of created beings' or 'divine truth'. *The Philokalia: The Complete Text compiled by St. Nikodimos of the Holy Mountain and St. Makarios of Corinth*, trans. and ed. G. E. H. Palmer, Philip Sherrard and Kallistos Ware, London, 1983, I, pp. 362, 364.

of virtue and vice. Learning gives us the ability to move toward 'the highest truths', to approach the divine, which is never fully accessible, and to see 'uncreated beauty'. Although we understand little, this little is for us great. Through it we see the unity of all things, how we are connected to God, and how we must act in the world. Like so many thinkers in seventeenth- and eighteenth-century Europe, Platon insists on the superiority of spiritual wisdom, while also upholding reason as the means to attain deeper knowledge of God and His Creation.[18] His reconciliation of religion and science follows from the belief that scientific enlightenment is but one dimension of a higher spiritual enlightenment leading to communion with God.

Platon continues his sermon by highlighting the inner satisfaction that results when knowledge of the truth enriches human reason.[19] Precisely because earthly knowledge is an aspect of heavenly knowledge, it gives people a foretaste of the eternal enjoyment to come. Earthly knowledge also provides immediate benefits to society: good laws to guarantee justice, prosperous agriculture, flourishing trade, the invention of the arts, a strong army and effective security. Clearly, Platon recognizes the advantages produced by human learning, but he also warns against the dangers of improper learning. Our knowledge, he insists, is lowly and inadequate, burdened as it is by our bodies and passions. Without proper preparation of the heart, knowledge is useless. To highlight this message, Platon quotes a passage from the Septuagint (3 Kings 3:5–9) in which God instructs a young Solomon to make a request for himself. Solomon's answer pleases God and shows that he is ready to receive 'the spirit of wisdom': "Thou shalt give therefore to thy servant a heart to hear and to judge thy people justly, and to discern between good and evil."[20] After receiving 'the treasure of wisdom', Solomon is prepared to seek riches and glory for himself and peace (*tishina*) and prosperity for his people. When acquired and applied properly, for a moral purpose consistent with God's Law, philosophical or scientific learning constitutes a source of comfort and satisfaction for human beings.

Platon's respect for earthly learning was genuine and heartfelt, yet his call to pursue knowledge and embrace the development of the human mind also appears fraught with tension. In the 'Sermon on the

---

[18] Long before Platon ancient and medieval theologians recognized the existence of two orders of truth, the natural or philosophical and the supernatural or theological, which they assumed to be in harmony. William Turner, 'Scholasticism', *The Catholic Encyclopedia*, 13, New York, 1912 <http://www.newadvent.org/cathen/13548a.htm> [accessed 29 May 2008].

[19] Here Platon seems to refer to divine truth. See note 17.

[20] Here I rely on Sir Lancelot C. L. Brenton's translation of the Septuagint, originally published in London in 1851.

Usefulness of Learning', Platon repeatedly states that without attention to the cultivation of moral virtue the acquisition of scientific knowledge produces harmful results, including arrogance and atheism. Thus, after relating the story of Solomon, he again repeats for his listeners the theme of the sermon: "Therefore settle it in your hearts not to meditate beforehand on what you will answer." In this instance, Platon takes the biblical passage to mean that we should philosophize (mudrstvovat´) about truth with deeds, not words. For the best fruit and necessary purpose of learning is 'honesty and virtue of morals'. In the words of the Apostle Paul, "Though I speak with the tongues of men and of angels, but have not love, I have become sounding brass or a clanging cymbal. And though I have the gift of prophecy, and understand all mysteries and all knowledge, and though I have all faith, so that I could remove mountains, but have not love, I am nothing" (1 Corinthians 13:1–2).

Time and again Platon rejoices in the blessings of earthly knowledge. Still, in taking his cue from the Apostle Paul, whose epistles were among his most cherished readings, Platon also cautions that "knowledge [razum] puffs up", in contrast to love, which "edifies" (Corinthians 8:1).[21] Toward the end of the 'Sermon on the Usefulness of Learning', before the concluding panegyrics addressed to Empress Catherine and Tsesarevich Paul, Platon once again comments upon the relative harmfulness of both ignorance and inappropriate learning. Abuse of learning or the wrong learning, learning that is devoid of concern for virtue, can cause as much or more harm than ignorance. High knowledge (vysokie znaniia) can be the cause of 'empty splendour', whereas a 'pure conscience' is beneficial for all. In the words of Platon, 'Not all that glitters is gold'.

Sermon on the Birthday of Her Imperial Highness[22]

Over the course of several decades Platon preached the superiority of spiritual over human (plotskii) wisdom, doggedly trying to instil in his listeners an appreciation for the distinction between religious enlightenment (prosveshchenie) and scientific or philosophical learnedness (uchenost´).[23] His position is not surprising, but it is important to understand that it represented more than a monk's desire to uphold the authority of a church and religious tradition facing the challenge of modern thought. Toward the end of Platon's life, at a time when increasingly nationalistic church leaders began to question the value of

---

[21] Platon reports that he read the Epistles of Paul more than twenty times during his childhood. Platon, 'Avtobiografiia', in *Iz glubiny*, p. 17.

[22] The full title of the sermon is 'Slovo v den´ rozhdeniia Eia Imperatorskago Velichestva Blagochestiveishiia Gosudaryni, Ekateriny Alekseevny, Samoderzhitsy Vserossiiskiia'.

[23] In addition to the sermon under discussion, see also 'Slovo v nedeliu sed´muiu po Paskhe' (5 May 1790), in *Pouchitel´nyia slova*, 15, Moscow, 1792, pp. 658–66.

the Latin curriculum taught in Russian seminaries, he continued to defend the teaching of Latin. In universalistic Enlightenment style, Metropolitan Platon remained less concerned about the purity of the faith and the possibility of Latinist influence than about the need for Russian clergy to be broadly learned.[24] Although letters from Platon's later years express anxiety about the dangers of radicalism and un-belief, he continued to appreciate the benefits of secular learning and the contribution of human endeavours to God's greater purpose.[25] His belief in the superiority of spiritual wisdom had roots much deeper than the need to defend the Orthodox Christian tradition against Latinism, science and philosophy.

Platon's attitude toward spiritual and human wisdom, including his certainty about the superiority of the former, rested on a basic theological principle: the unity of all things, of all God's creation. In the case of knowledge, the spiritual knowledge of divine provenance, conveyed through the Gospel, transcended and enveloped the partial knowledge acquired through human activity. The two could not be contradictory, because both belonged to the same unity of God and divine truth. The principle of unity also defined Platon's view of the relationship between the church and civil society, an issue he addressed in a sermon of 21 April 1772, delivered in the presence of Catherine II and Tsesarevich Paul to celebrate the empress's birthday and, because the date fell on a Saturday, the resurrection of Christ.

Platon begins his sermon on a joyous note. The church rejoices because it is blessed by the resurrection of its saviour; the fatherland rejoices because it is blessed by the birth of the Russian sovereign. 'But why', Platon asks rhetorically, 'do I separate the inseparable?' Russia also rejoices because the 'ray of the resurrection of her Saviour' shines upon her and lights up her spirit. The church likewise celebrates the anointed ruler, 'the most faithful custodian of its dogmas and the pro-tector of its glory'. The church and Russia, distinct but one — the principle of harmonious unity precludes any fundamental difference. Assuming a conversational pose, Platon explains to his listeners that the basis for 'our discussion' is 'the harmony [soglasie] of church and society [obshchestvo] God's law and civil law, the citizen and Christian'. The concordance between church and society, faith and civil law, citizen and Christian is absolute and complete in any matter that concerns 'the wellbeing of each and all together'. For just as the human being is born to be a good citizen and worshiper of God (bogopochitatel'), our monarch

[24] P. V. Znamenskii, *Istoriia russkoi tserkvi (uchebnoe rukovodstvo)*, Kazan´, 1870; Moscow, 1996, pp. 393–95; Gregory L. Freeze, *The Russian Levites: Parish Clergy in the Eighteenth Century*, Cambridge, MA, 1977, pp. 77–82; idem, *The Parish Clergy in Nineteenth-Century Russia: Crisis, Reform, Counter-Reform*, Princeton, NJ, 1983, pp. 119–25; Florovskii, *Puti*, pp. 113–15.
[25] A sampling of these letters can be found in Platon, *Iz glubiny*, pp. 91–112.

unites in her person 'the glory of Her state and the sanctity of the faith and supports one with the other in all her actions'.

Platon's assumption of an essential unity between church and society is paradigmatic, though he also recognizes a relational separation. He describes this separation by identifying two forms or manifestations of society. 'Civil society' (*grazhdanskoe obshchestvo*) Platon defines as 'an assembly of people united by the same laws and the same form of government'. A similar definition appears in the dictionary of the Russian Academy published in 1789–94: 'a people [*narod*] living under the same laws [*zakony*], under know regulations [*ustavy*], rules [*pravila*].'[26] At the same time, the society conceived by Platon is the church, for society is united by the same form of worship and the same sacred observances. In other words, society and church cannot exist independently of each other; a citizen of society is also a Christian.

Notwithstanding the fact that Platon and his sovereign can be described as religiously tolerant for their time, the preacher's definition of society clearly excludes the non-Orthodox subjects of the vast Russian empire. Given the expansionist nature and multi-confessional makeup of the empire, his formulation is problematic. Platon did not, however, think in imperial or imperialistic terms. His was a universalistic Christian conception of a distinctly Russian society, which to his mind (and heart) could not exist without the church. Simply put, a citizen could not be such without also being a Christian. This was not because in some essentialist or racialist sense only a Christian could be a member of society. Rather it was because societal affairs (*obshchestvennye dela*) can have no power or effect, if 'they are not strengthened by the law which binds the conscience' and which requires that in all matters a report be given 'not only to man but to God'.

Having described the essential oneness of church and society, Platon goes on to discuss the origins of society, the reason why human beings decide to assemble in society in the first place. The basis for society is that people need help from each other in order to overcome their individual inadequacies. Outside society a person is alone and subject to danger. People need people, 'for every person has unlimited needs [. . .] but limited powers and gifts'. Once societies form, Platon tells his listeners, worship of God or faith reveals its power. In the 'natural state' (*sostoianie estestvennoe*), faith leads people to 'eternal happiness'. In 'the union of society', the faith that 'guides people toward the heavens' becomes the most useful and necessary means for achieving general wellbeing. Equating society with a body, Platon notes that all the members of the body must feel obligated to help each other. They must

---

[26] Quoted in Elise Kimerling Wirtschafter, *The Play of Ideas in Russian Enlightenment Theater*, DeKalb, IL, 2003, p. 84.

be sincere and honest, preserve the rules of justice, subordinate their own benefit to that of society, and be zealous in their devotion to the 'common good' (*obshchee blago*). Platon's argumentation here is a bit muddled, but he seems to be saying that the faith or religion that in 'the natural state' directs individuals to eternal happiness becomes an even more potent force in 'the union of society'. The sense of mutual obligation that binds people together in society is not possible without the church.

Orthodox Christianity teaches that the heart is the spiritual centre of the human being. Not surprisingly, then, Platon argues that the fulfilment of societal obligations depends on 'conscience' (*sovest'*), which resides in the human heart. Conscience cannot hide from punishment either in this life or in the life to come, for even in the most depraved souls, conscience effects its action. To illustrate the idea that the true fulfilment of societal obligations depends on conscience and religious faith, Platon quotes Holy Scripture. "For the word of God is living and powerful, and sharper than any two-edged sword, piercing even to the division of soul and spirit, and of joints and marrow, and is a discerner of the thoughts and intents of the heart" (Hebrews 4:12). Similarly, in Exodus 20:12–17, God commands, 'Honour thy father and thy mother . [. . .] Thou shalt not commit adultery. Thou shalt not steal. Thou shalt not kill. Thou shalt not bear false witness . [. . .] Thou shalt not covet [. . .] whatever belongs to thy neighbour'.[27] Regarding the Christian's duties to the state (and to others), God's word teaches, "Render therefore to all their due: taxes to whom taxes are due, customs to whom customs, fear to whom fear, honour to whom honour" (Romans 13:7). Finally, faith teaches, "Let no one seek his own, but each one the other's well-being" (1 Corinthians 10:24), meaning that when necessary we must be ready to sacrifice our lives for our brother. These are 'the golden chains', Platon continues, that connect any society, 'the divine veins through which flows the sacred blood that preserves in itself the life and wellbeing of society'.

Platon admits that civil laws, though distinct from divine laws, also forbid evil deeds and insults, and assign punishment in due measure. But civil laws obligate the conscience of the human heart precisely because they are based on God's Law and because the earthly lawmaker (the monarch) proclaims to his subjects 'those heavenly laws which the supreme Judge orders everyone to preserve for the wellbeing of themselves and others'. As recorded in Romans 13:2, regarding the Christian's duties to the state, "whoever resists the authority resists the

---

[27] Platon's rendering of these passages follows a slightly different order. I quote here the wording and order in Brenton's Septuagint.

ordinance of God".[28] Without the divine assistance that emanates from a human conscience connected with the power of God's Law, it is difficult for earthly judges to judge correctly. Based on what is seen externally, there is a danger that evil deeds will be celebrated and innocence overlooked. To reveal 'the interior' (*vnutrennost'*) of things, the essence of a matter or what is inside a person, it is necessary that conscience be softened by the gaze of God. The biblical story of Cain and Abel illustrates the point. Cain, the first criminal, killed his brother in a state of 'natural law' (*estestvennyi zakon*) when there were no civil laws, societies, or peoples. Cain therefore had no need to fear punishment for his crime and should have remained at peace. But this did not happen; instead Cain's body trembled and his spirit suffered torment. Although Cain had no one to fear, his conscience, 'the avenger of all-seeing God', caused him to suffer. He heard the voice of God, which 'followed him, questioned him, tortured, and judged'. "Cain! Where is Abel your brother?" (Genesis 4:9).

Platon's purpose in relating the story of Cain and Abel is to show that while a criminal might be able to hide from the civil law and avoid human judgement, he will not be able to escape the judgement of God. He 'cannot hide from the torment of conscience which is connected to the law of faith'. Even in a criminal who is not tormented by conscience, the 'divine spark' is not completely extinguished. If 'the power of faith' is instilled from a young age, it is impossible for conscience to be totally absent. If conscience ceases to affect a person, it is clear that 'fear of God' has been driven from his or her soul. Fear of God, then, is 'a useful member (*chlen*) for society'. It is not enough that crimes be punished; they also must be prevented, and faith is uniquely suited to this purpose. When implanted in a person from childhood, faith teaches 'what is pleasing to God and what is offensive to him, what brings about human wellbeing and what misfortune [*neshchastie*],[29] what attracts God's blessing and what his anger, what leads to paradise and what to eternal torment [*vechnaia muka*]'. These concepts or understandings (*poniatiia*) act on the human soul, because they represent God as 'all-seeing, all-powerful, and just'. He is 'a most merciful father and impartial judge', and while it is terrible to anger such a judge, it is more terrible to offend such a father. God sees everything, and his vengeance against the unrighteous and impious is boundless. 'There is no status (*sostoianie*), age, gender (*pol*), or person' who is not subject to God's judgement and who will not receive from him according to his or her deserts. For this reason, a society in which citizens are enlightened by

---

[28] The full passage, quoted in part by Platon, is: 'Therefore whoever resists the authority resists the ordinance of God, and those who resist will bring judgment on themselves.'

[29] The spelling '*neshchastie*' appears repeatedly in Platon's sermon.

Christian teachings will be able to forestall many crimes, whereas a society lacking God's Law will suffer from unlimited human corruption. On this basis, Platon concludes, enlightened people understand that it is impossible for a society to consist solely of atheists.

To Platon's firmly Christian mind, there can be no good or even functioning society without religious faith. Faith, 'that daughter of the heavenly Father', instilled in the human heart, can never be the cause of abuses. Abuses are caused by human depravity, and even though abuses and evil deeds can be committed under the guise of holy faith, evildoers cannot be true believers. To the contrary, they are hypocrites, and their faith is nothing more than external appearance. The fruits of genuine faith — peace, goodness, mercy, gentleness and purity of heart — preclude evil deeds. Nor can the actions of hypocrites undermine respect for religion. To the contrary, hypocrites move true believers to preserve the faith in order to prevent further abuses, thereby supporting 'their own and the common good'. For Platon, the unity of church and society, of God's law and civil law, is axiomatic and eternal. A strong society requires not only that people be united by the same laws and form of government in a 'single societal body'. They also must be united by their worship of God in 'a sacred body.' A single body, a single spirit, a single foundation, and a single end — such is the Christian society that Platon imagines Russia to be. Such also was the Russian society that excluded from membership in this body the empire's numerous non-Orthodox subjects.[30]

Toward the end of the sermon honouring Catherine's birthday Platon urges his listeners, as Christians and citizens, to heed his words. Observe the laws and preserve the faith. 'Govern Your affairs by the rule of societal regulations; govern the movement of Your heart by the rule of God's Law.' By uniting these two inseparable pledges you will find your temporal and eternal wellbeing, the purpose for which divine providence created you. Indeed, declares Platon, 'our beloved Fatherland' is the clearest example of the unity of church and society. Russia governs her affairs with laws established by the sovereign and 'governs her human conscience with God's Law'. Russia fears the punishment imposed by civil law for a crime, but even more, Russia fears a tormented conscience (*muchenie sovestnoe*). Russia celebrates together the resurrection of Christ and the birthday of the monarch, for a citizen is a Christian and a Christian is a citizen. In this harmony and unity, the body is united with the soul and heaven with earth. By

---

[30] The census of 1897, the only empire-wide census every conducted in Imperial Russia, showed 71 per cent of the population, including Old Believers, to be Orthodox Christians. Andreas Kappeler, *The Russian Empire: A Multiethnic History*, trans. Alfred Clayton, Harlow, 2001, p. 286.

giving "to Caesar the things that are Caesar's and to God the things that are God's" (Matthew 22:21), the Russian is both 'an earthly and a heavenly citizen'.

As usual, Platon concludes his sermon by directly addressing Empress Catherine II. In Catherine's person the holy union of church and society is upheld. Catherine is the head of society and the protector of the church. She is 'a divinely-inspired Lawmaker and the most faithful custodian of the worship of God'. By enlightening her subjects in the law, she prepares their souls to receive the Holy Spirit. As ruler, she guides us (Platon counts himself among her subjects) toward peaceful and successful cohabitation, and by fulfilling the obligations set forth in the Gospel, she helps us to attain eternal salvation. Through your birth, Platon explains to Catherine, 'God placed You in the theatre of this, the visible, world for the discovery [*otkrytie*] of its glory and for our wellbeing'. In the sermon celebrating Catherine's birthday, Platon submerges the distinction between church and society in the same way that in other sermons he harmonizes the tension between spiritual and human knowledge, by invoking the transcendent unity of all things, which is God.

Father Platon and the Russian Enlightenment

Platon's belief in the harmonious unity of all creation and indeed of all being accorded well with the universalism of Enlightenment thought. Across seventeenth- and eighteenth-century Europe, the spread of philosophical modernity and scientific standards of evidence led to the recognition that moral principles and religious writings, including Holy Scripture, had to be understood as the products of specific historical circumstances. At the same time, Enlightenment thinkers assumed the existence of an interlocking providential order and the validity of universal moral principles in the form of human rights granted to every person by God or nature.[31] In eighteenth-century Russia, the universalistic as opposed to the particularistic historical dimension of Enlightenment thought reigned supreme. There was no immediately apparent contradiction between historical knowledge, understood as the particular incarnation of the universal, and established Christian belief. If the Russian Enlightenment is defined as the moral voice of an emergent independent society, it is easy to see how Platon and other church intellectuals became contributors to the Russian understanding of enlightenment. Much research remains to be done, but if further study confirms that churchmen played a critical role in assimilating Enlightenment ideas into Russian culture — specifically that they

---

[31] On the interlocking harmonious order, see Taylor, *Sources of the Self*.

blended key principles associated with the moderate mainstream Enlightenment into the religious teachings of Russian Orthodoxy — then two longstanding historiographical problems can be addressed.

First is the question of Russia's reception of Enlightenment thought and European culture more broadly. This is, of course, a massive topic which to answer fully would require an army of researchers working within an extended chronological framework.[32] That said, even within the confines of individual research agendas, one cannot help but be struck by: 1) the seemingly unproblematic, and consequently rapid, absorption of European ideas, learning, and art forms in eighteenth-century Russia; and 2) the fragmentary or eclectic, though not always consciously so, nature of this absorption.[33] Russia's openness to foreign culture is well documented, yet some historians continue to deny that Russia had an Enlightenment.[34] With only a handful of exceptions — the likes, for example, of M. V. Lomonosov, A. N. Radishchev and N. I. Novikov — eighteenth-century Russian intellectuals, led by Empress Catherine II, are widely accused of not having understood the humanistic, egalitarian and democratic principles that drove Enlightenment thinkers in Central and Western Europe. As defenders of serfdom, absolutist monarchy and hierarchies of gender, age and birth, most of the educated Russians who participated in the pan-European Enlightenment are, based on modern European standards, regarded as hypocritical, superficial or naive. More akin to Counter-Enlightenment than Enlightenment figures, they are said to have abandoned ideals of human dignity, personal liberty and social justice just as soon as the radical implications of Enlightenment principles threatened their domination of society and polity.[35]

It is no doubt an historical cliché to say that the outbreak and subsequent course of the French Revolution alerted educated Russians, especially those associated with the church and monarchy, to the winds of social and political change emanating from the Radical Enlightenment and the progress of mechanistic science in Europe. The beheading of King Louis XVI in January 1793 and less than two decades later the existential threat to Russia posed by the armies of Napoleon

---

[32] The classic introduction to this problem is Raeff, *Origins*.

[33] On the assimilation of European culture, see James Cracraft, *The Petrine Revolution in Russian Architecture*, Chicago, IL, 1988; *The Petrine Revolution in Russian Imagery*, Chicago, IL, 1997, and *The Petrine Revolution in Russian Culture*, Cambridge, MA, 2004.

[34] V. M. Zhivov, 'Gosudarstvennyi mif v epokhu prosveshcheniia i ego razrushenie v Rossii kontsa XVIII veka', in *Iz istorii russkoi kul'tury. Tom 4 (XVIII–nachalo XIX veka)*, Moscow, 1996, pp. 657–83.

[35] This remains the standard textbook interpretation, though the notion of a Counter-Enlightenment has not been explicitly developed in Russian intellectual or cultural history. For treatment of the French case, see Darrin M. McMahon, *Enemies of the Enlightenment: The French Counter-Enlightenment and the Making of Modernity*, New York, 2001.

had to affect Russian perceptions of European modernity. But limited or late arriving awareness of the radical implications of Enlightenment ideas cannot explain or change the fact that educated Russians of the mid to late eighteenth century relished their status as modern Europeans and derived great satisfaction from the realization that they could count themselves among the enlightened peoples of the world.[36] Before the 1790s, as the career of Platon indicates, there existed deeper reasons for Russia's receptiveness to European Enlightenment culture.[37]

Platon's writings suggest that the strength of the Orthodox religious tradition, including its ancient associations with classical philosophy, made the early reception of modern ideas and learning relatively unproblematic for Russia. This was not because church intellectuals effectively challenged or resisted the new thinking. Churchmen and most educated Russians did, however, stand strong in their religious convictions, despite the allure of European philosophy and science. Indeed, the church father St John Chrysostom provided a holy and time-honoured model for their response. A student of the fourth-century Antiochan rhetorician Libanius, Chrysostom mastered the secular sciences, but as Platon stressed, only in order to bring them into 'the school of Christ'. Chrysostom 'sanctified' classical learning, the benefits of which he recognized, so that it served 'the great science of the law of the Lord'.[38]

The secular dimension of the patristic tradition surely worked to deproblematize Russia's openness to European culture. Perhaps more significant, the Russian church of the mid to late seventeenth century also encouraged the teaching of philosophy. Forced to confront and accept the realities of religious schism and absolutist monarchy, the church emerged from the Muscovite period institutionally weakened but culturally poised to become a conduit for the Latinist learning of contemporary Europe. The schism had rid the official clergy of many uncompromising purists and, as a result, eighteenth-century Russian churchmen, especially the prelates educated at the Kiev and Moscow Academies, became better equipped to engage with modern thought, thereby strengthening the church's ability to withstand the depredations of successive governments and intellectual generations. They did so, moreover, in the only effective way this could be done, by retaining

[36] Wirtschafter, *Play of Ideas*, pp. 47–48.

[37] I am not considering here the interest in military and other technology, which also drove the openness to European culture.

[38] Platon, 'Slovo v Den´ Sviatago Ioanna Zlatoustago', in *Pouchitel´nyia slova*, 3, Moscow, 1780, pp. 125–33. According to the text, the sermon was given on 15 November 1775 in the presence of Empress Catherine II at the Zlatoust Monastery in Moscow. It is likely that the date was 13 November, the feast day of Chrysostom. The text can be viewed at <http://stsl.ru/lib/platon3/index.php> [accessed 18 July 2007].

firm belief in the rightness of traditional religious precepts. Platon's sermons reveal a mindset for which human knowledge, including Cartesian and Newtonian science, represented not a threat to religious doctrine but proof of God's glory and goodness.[39] This was in fact a major theme of the moderate mainstream and religious Enlightenments throughout Europe.[40] Although in the early nineteenth century the revolutionary challenge of mechanistic science and philosophical materialism began to appear dangerous to many conservative Russians, and also to Platon, in the reign of Catherine II the new learning seemed to enhance what already was known from the superior spiritual knowledge accessed through Holy Scripture, church doctrine and the Orthodox liturgy.

In the Orthodox religious tradition, the concept of enlightenment carries both sacramental and spiritual meaning. In the most basic sense, church doctrine equates enlightenment with the sacrament of baptism. *The Orthodox Study Bible*, noting the biblical association of darkness with sin and death, describes baptism as illumination or enlightenment 'because in it we are delivered from sin and death and regenerated by the Holy Spirit'. Similarly, 'to be illuminated is to be shown the true path of righteousness in God, thereby being led out of the darkness of sin and death'.[41] Through the mystery and concrete ritual of baptism, the Orthodox believer seeks the path of spiritual enlightenment leading, not without struggle and suffering, toward communion with God. In the words of Bishop Kallistos Ware, man beholds the divine light not through natural perception but 'through the power of the Holy Spirit acting within him'.[42] To be enlightened means to open one's heart to the Holy Spirit, which then makes it possible to walk in the light of God's truth. Indeed, in *The Festal Menaion* Christ is called 'our Enlightenment' or 'the Enlightenment of our souls'.[43] Enlightenment, then, is an essential motif in the Orthodox liturgy, one closely associated with the goal of salvation. If historians are to understand properly the reception of European culture in eighteenth-century Russia, they must investigate the interplay between Orthodox enlightenment and Enlightenment ideas.[44] When Father Platon, a man of the Enlightenment and of Christian enlightenment, preached before the Catherinian Court, his message carried a rich and multivalent

[39] There is no evidence that Platon understood Cartesian or Newtonian science.
[40] Israel, *Enlightenment Contested*; Sorkin, *Religious Enlightenment*; Van Eijnatten, *Preaching*.
[41] *Orthodox Study Bible*, p. 800.
[42] Bishop Kallistos Ware, *The Orthodox Way*, revised edn, Crestwood, NY, 2003, p. 127.
[43] Vespers service for the Holy Theophany of our Lord and God and Saviour Jesus Christ (6 January) in *The Festal Menaion*, trans. Mother Mary and Archimandrite Kallistos Ware, South Canaan, PA, 1998, pp. 338–39.
[44] This is the goal of my current research.

symbolism that helps to unlock the meaning of Enlightenment in Russia.

The second historiographical question that can be rethought in light of Platon's contribution to the Russian Enlightenment is the notion of an eighteenth-century church and clergy that had become intellectually and spiritually sterile, and hence also socially isolated from Russia's ever more Europeanized educated classes.[45] In his classic study, *The Ways of Russian Theology*, Father Georgii Florovskii criticizes eighteenth-century churchmen for propagating a Latinist/Protestant theology that in Russia 'grew on foreign soil' and thus failed to yield intellectual or spiritual fruit.[46] It is true that in the later eighteenth century much of the philosophy and theology taught in Russia's ecclesiastical schools derived from German Protestant sources.[47] It is similarly the case that the Russian interest in catechism, a seventeenth-century Latinist import sanctioned by the official church, can be described as an innovation 'alien' to Orthodoxy.[48] Finally, Florovskii's assessment may also be correct from the perspective of patristic studies and systematic theology, neither of which developed in Russia before the second quarter of the nineteenth century. But if one situates Platon in the Enlightenment context of his time, the moralistic humanism so roundly criticized by Florovskii becomes precisely the quality that makes the metropolitan an interesting historical figure. Nor can it be said that the Latinist categories of thought built into catechisms and textbooks on philosophy and theology brought no intellectual or spiritual benefits to Russia. Father Platon, a public lecturer on catechism, the author/compiler of several published catechisms and the first self-consciously Russian historian of the Russian church, clearly enriched the lives of his listeners and readers, though the exact nature of his impact has not been fully elucidated.[49]

---

[45] Recent studies that address the importance of religion in eighteenth-century elite culture include: Raffaella Faggionato, *A Rosicrucian Utopia in Eighteenth-Century Russia: The Masonic Circle of N. I. Novikov*, trans. Michael Boyd and Brunello Lotti, Dordrecht, 2005; O. M. Goncharova, *Vlast' traditsii i 'novaia Rossiia' v literaturnom soznanii vtoroi poloviny XVIII veka: Monografiia*, St Petersburg, 2004; Ernest A. Zitser, *The Transfigured Kingdom: Sacred Parody and Charismatic Authority at the Court of Peter the Great*, Ithaca, NY, 2004, and Marc Raeff, 'Enticements and Rifts: Georges Florovsky as Historian of the Life of the Mind and the Life of the Church in Russia', *Modern Greek Studies Yearbook*, 6, 1990, pp. 201, 223–27, 230–31.

[46] Florovskii, *Puti*, p. 115.

[47] Znamenskii, *Dukhovnye shkoly*, pp. 736–47.

[48] On the Orthodox catechistic tradition, see Margarita Korzo, *Ukrainskaia i belorusskaia katekheticheskaia traditsiia kontsa XVI–XVIII vv.: stanovlenie, evoliutsiia i problema zaimstvovanii*, Moscow, 2007; Peter Hauptmann, *Die Katechismen der Russisch-orthodoxen Kirche: Entstehungsgeschichte und Lehrgehalt*, Göttingen, 1971.

[49] This is also part of my current research. For a recent Russian study that attempts to define a 'Platon school' of Russian theology, see P. V. Kalitin, *Uravnenie russkoi idei (po-sviatootecheski novaia i original'naia sistema 'mysli-postupka-sotsiuma' rossiiskikh uchenykh monakhov vtoroi poloviny XVIII–nachala XIX vekov)*, Moscow, 2002.

Judging from the content of Platon's sermons, catechisms, history of the Russian church, autobiography and letters, he played three distinct but overlapping historical roles. As teacher and pastor, Platon provided moral instruction to his flock, which included monarchs, courtiers, elite servicemen, clergy and sometimes a socially mixed urban public. In this capacity Platon tried to show his listeners and readers, based on the wisdom of Holy Scripture, how to bring the Christian striving for moral goodness into everyday life, how to act in the world in a manner pleasing to God. As serviceman and subject of the Russian monarch, Platon obeyed his sovereign and rendered unequivocal panegyric praise. At the same time, however, he also used moral instruction to restrain arbitrariness, reduce violence and encourage piety, justice and support for the church. Finally, in his role as preacher, Platon carried on the evangelical work of the prophets and apostles in spreading the Gospel and the word of God. Through preaching, and through his sacramental and eparchial duties, he worked incessantly to bring his congregants closer to the divine. By preparing them to open their hearts to receive the Holy Spirit, he guided them toward the attainment of salvation.

Platon's pastoral responsibilities encouraged his interest in moral instruction and his attention to the literary accessibility of his writings. As teacher and preacher, he effectively recast Holy Scripture and traditional religious doctrine for listeners whose minds had become attuned to modern science, secular philosophy and the national literatures being produced across Europe.[50] Although in eighteenth-century Russia the divine origin and authority of religious teachings and sacred writings faced few challenges (these would come in the nineteenth century), the church's institutional authority had been shaken by the schism of the seventeenth century and by the Petrine elimination of the patriarchate. There was then a need to present Orthodox religious teachings in a fresh mode that appealed to Russia's ever more Europeanized elites.

The effort to recast religion in an Enlightenment idiom took various, not always conscious, forms. Traces of this effort can be found in numerous religious, literary and legal texts of the time. One curious example is the 'sacred tragedy' *Jephthah*, written by Apollos (Baibakov, 1737–1801) and published in Moscow in 1778. Hoping to show that biblical stories could provide compelling material for the contemporary Russian theatre, Apollos dramatized a story from Judges 11–12:7, in which judge of Israel Jephthah vows that if God grants him a victory against the Ammonites, he will give to the Lord as a burnt offering

---

[50] For a study of how the Enlightenment Bible became a cultural monument of literary, historical and moral significance for a post-theological age, see Sheehan, *Enlightenment Bible*.

whatsoever first comes forth from his house to meet him. The 'what-soever' turns out to be Jephthah's daughter, and the story's inevitably tragic ending is recounted (or implied) in the play.[51] Although the literary and dramatic qualities of *Jephthah* hardly deserve mention, and although there is no record of the tragedy ever being staged, the very fact that the noble-born Apollos, future Bishop of Sevsk and Orel, and later of Arkhangel´sk, wrote the play suggests a desire to communicate with Russia's educated public in a familiar literary language.[52]

Apollos was not the first Russian churchman to write plays, and Platon was not the first Russian preacher to think about how to make religious teachings and sermons accessible to the laity. There were seventeenth- and eighteenth-century precedents for both of these activities.[53] Still, Platon was one of the first — along with Feofan (Prokopovich), Gedeon (Krinovskii), and Gavriil (Petrov) — to preach and write sermons in the literary Russian of the day. He also was one of the first to be praised by Europeanized and European literary figures and to reach a socially diverse audience outside St Petersburg, Moscow and the Orthodox world.[54] That Freemasons such as Novikov, dissident intellectuals such as Radishchev, and moral critics such as Prince M. M. Shcherbatov read and found enlightening non-Orthodox religious writings banned by the Russian church did not mean that the church and clergy lacked spiritual influence. The moralistic humanism of Platon, his interest in the religious enlightenment of his listeners and his trust in their ability to recognize the superiority of spiritual wisdom, while also acquiring human knowledge, may not have sparked the striving for moral self-reformation that inspired Russia's 'civil society of the educated' and the first generations of the Russian intelligentsia. But certainly it did not discourage or challenge this striving.

One can speculate, moreover, that the homiletic and devotional literature produced by the likes of Platon may have represented an important source for the moralistic humanitarian impulses of educated Russians, barred from participatory politics but nonetheless committed

---

[51] As in the Hebrew Bible and Septuagint, no burnt offering is actually described.

[52] Educated at the Moscow Slavonic-Greek-Latin Academy and Moscow University, Apollos was in 1778 serving as rector of the Trinity Seminary. I have no record of his play being performed, but it is included in the collection of Russian plays published by the Academy of Sciences beginning in 1786. Wirtschafter, *Play of Ideas*, pp. 47, 72–73, 181. Note also that Apollos wrote the poetics textbook used in Russian seminaries beginning in 1774 and that seminarians studied the works of Lomonosov, Sumarokov and Derzhavin. See Znamenskii, *Dukhovnye shkoly*, pp. 729–35.

[53] Wirtschafter, *Play of Ideas*, pp. 4–7; idem, *Age of Serfdom*, pp. 64–69, 72–73. Marcus C. Levitt (ed.), *Dictionary of Literary Biography*, vol. 150, *Early Modern Russian Writers, Late Seventeenth and Eighteenth Centuries*, Detroit, MI, 1995; Zhivov, *Iazyk i kul´tura*.

[54] On this we have translations of Platon's writings into multiple European languages and lists of subscribers to his collected works, evidence that I will present in future publications.

to the idea that social reform should be grounded in the moral development and the potential perfectibility of the individual human being. In calling people to strive for a higher moral order, not simply in heaven, but also here on earth, religion in the Enlightenment taught that the end could not justify the means. Social and political action by implication needed to be consistent with God's Law. Of course, it is impossible to prove that eighteenth-century religious teachings led directly to social action or even to the igniting of social conscience. The evidence does suggest, however, that religious education remained a near universal aspect of Russian life and that religious literature, including established church doctrine, constituted an element in the cultural mix that became the Russian Enlightenment. In the hands and mouth of Platon, one might say, the Russian Enlightenment, the foundation of modern Russian culture, became the application of a religious standard to the moral categories of everyday life.[55]

[55] A little known text, which I have not fully digested, but which illustrates this process is [A. T. Bolotov], *Chuvstvovaniia Khristianina, pri nachale i kontse kazhdago dnia v nedele, otnosiashchiiasia k samomu sebe i k Bogu. Sochinenie odnogo Rossiianina*, Moscow, 1781.

The Russian Academy of Sciences Expeditions to the Steppes in the Late Eighteenth Century

DAVID MOON[1]

THIS article considers how the scientists who led the expeditions organized by the Russian Academy of Sciences in 1768–74, and two further expeditions later in the century, viewed and tried to understand the environment of the vast grasslands of the steppes. The Academy, which had been established by Peter the Great shortly before his death in 1725,[2] organized a series of scientific expeditions to various parts of the expanding empire over the eighteenth century.[3] It gave particular emphasis to collecting empirical data and specimens for scientific research, and locating natural resources for economic exploitation. Both academic and official circles believed the promotion of agriculture to be especially important, and the steppe region with its fertile soil was a prime location for settlement and arable farming.[4] The steppes, which lay to the south of the forested heartland of the Russian state

David Moon is Professor of Russian History at Durham University.

[1] This article was written while I was Felix Gilbert Member of the School of Historical Studies at the Institute for Advanced Study in Princeton in 2008–09. I am very grateful to the Institute. The article is part of a larger research project, which has been funded by the University of Strathclyde in Glasgow, the Leverhulme Trust, the Carnegie Trust for the Universities of Scotland and the British Academy. Debts of gratitude are due also to Rostov, Stavropol´ and Samara State Universities, the Rostov botanical garden, the Rostov state steppe nature reserve (*zapovednik*), the Institute for the History of Science and Technology of the Russian Academy of Sciences in St Petersburg, and libraries and archives in those cities. Outside Russia, thanks are due to the Slavonic Library of the National Library of Finland and the Firestone Library of Princeton University. I am very grateful to Professor Susan Smith-Peter and Professor Hamish Scott, and two anonymous readers, for incisive comments on earlier versions.

[2] Lindsey Hughes, *Russia in the Age of Peter the Great*, New Haven, CT, 1998, pp. 307–09.

[3] See S. A. Kozlov, *Russkii puteshestvennik epokhy Prosveshcheniia*, St Petersburg 2003; id., 'Rossiia, otkryvshaia miru: akademicheskie ekspeditsii 1768–1774 gg.', *Sankt-peterburgskii universitet*, 2001, nos 27, 29–30, November 2001 <http://journal.spbu.ru/2001/27/16.html>, <http://journal.spbu.ru/2001/29/23.html/> [accessed 22 June 2009]; Edouard I. Kolchinsky, 'The Role of Eighteenth Century Russian Expeditions in the Development of Natural History', *Proceedings of the California Academy of Sciences*, vol. 55, supplement 2, no. 8, 19 November 2004, pp. 106–16.

[4] See Denis J. B. Shaw, 'Geographical Practice and its Significance in Peter the Great's Russia', *Journal of Historical Geography*, 22, 1996, pp. 160–76; V. F. Gnucheva, 'Geograficheskii departament akademii nauk XVIII veka', *Trudy Arkhiva Akademii Nauk SSSR*, 6, 1946, pp. 23–86; Alexander Vucinich, *Science in Russian Culture: A History to 1860*, London, 1965, pp. 46–47, 57–62, 65–74, 82, 90–92, 99–101.

and to the west of the Ural mountains, had been annexed in a number of stages. The process began with Ivan the Terrible's defeat of the Tatar Khanates of Kazan´ and Astrakhan´ on the Volga in the 1550s. It continued as cossacks spearheaded Russian expansion into the basin of the lower reaches of river Don and the north Caucasus. The process culminated in Catherine the Great's victories over the Ottoman Empire in the late eighteenth century. Catherine extended the southern border of her empire to the northern and north eastern shores of the Black Sea. Her annexations included the territory of the Tatar Khanate of Crimea, most of which became part of the province of 'New Russia'.[5]

The Academy of Sciences expeditions of the late eighteenth century conceived of the land differently from the way in which the Russian state had done so in the previous century, before the greater attention to geography initiated by Peter the Great. In 1627, Tsar Michael Romanov ordered the compilation of 'The Book of the Great Map' (*Kniga Bol´shomu Chertezhu*). It was a description of an 'Old Map' of Russia and a new map of the lands to the south: the 'Field' (*Polia*), i.e. the steppes, including the Khanate of Crimea. The book contained information about the three main roads along the watersheds between the rivers which the Tatars used for their periodic raids into Russia, as well as the valleys of the major rivers themselves. The main concern of the book was not to provide a geographical description of the land, however, but to help organize the defence of Russia's steppe frontier.[6]

How the scientists of the Academy of Sciences expeditions a century and a half later viewed the steppe environment was influenced by their backgrounds and education. The Academy relied heavily on foreign, especially German, scholars. Since there were no universities in the Russian Empire in 1725, there was little alternative to appointing foreign academicians. With the development of secular education in Russia and further opportunities for Russians to study abroad, the number of Russian scholars increased, but foreigners remained in the majority among Russian academicians at the end of the eighteenth century. There were periodic tensions, moreover, between the 'Russian' and 'German' factions. An intermediate position was occupied by Baltic Germans (from the German elite of the Baltic lands of Estonia,

---

[5] See Michael Khodarkovsky, *Russia's Steppe Frontier: The Making of a Colonial Empire, 1500–1800*, Bloomington and Indianapolis, IN, 2002.

[6] For a modern edition, see K. N. Serbina (ed.), *Kniga Bol´shomu chertezhu*, Moscow, 1950. See also Denis J. B. Shaw, 'Mapmaking, Science and State Building in Russia before Peter the Great', *Journal of Historical Geography*, 31, 2005, pp. 416–22; Valerie A. Kivelson, *Cartographies of Tsardom: The Land and its Meanings in Seventeenth-Century Russia*, Ithaca, NY, 2006, pp. 1–5, 18–19, 32.

Livonia and Kurland which Peter had conquered from Sweden in the early eighteenth century). Baltic Germans were Russian subjects, but came from a region with a quite different culture, well-established links with the Germans lands and a longer history of secular education.[7] It was people from all these backgrounds — German (also Swedish), Baltic German, and Russian — who took part in the expeditions. All had received at least part of their education at German or Swedish universities, where their studies included 'natural history'. Universities in the eighteenth century also taught cameralism — a science of government that had developed in the German states and aimed to promote the 'common good' of the state by mobilizing natural and human resources.[8] The Russian Academy's expeditions were in line with similar enterprises in the home of cameralism. Writing about the reign of Frederick the Great of Prussia, David Blackbourn has pointed out that: 'By the middle of the eighteenth century, the well-tempered state was one in which the prince had access to computations, tabulations, and classifications on everything under the sun, including those tracts of "useless" land that might, one day, produce a field of corn or support a herd of Frisians.'[9] The environment of the steppes differed sharply from the Prussian marshes that Frederick wished to drain, but the fertile land in the south of the Russian Empire offered similar opportunities to convert 'useless' land into productive fields.

Visitors to the steppes who described their reactions to the environment, and its inhabitants, did so through the lens of what they were accustomed to. Thus, many descriptions by outsiders, from antiquity to modern times, contrasted the steppe environment with their homelands: they focused on what was different.[10] In the first written source on the steppes, from the mid-fifth century BCE, Herodotus contrasted 'Scythia', its environment, and people with his Greek world of city states.[11] French structuralist François Hartog argued that Herodotus constructed his writings on Scythians as nomads without houses, towns,

[7] See S. I. Romanovskii, '"Obrusenie" Rossiiskoi nauki kak natsional´naia problema', *Voprosy istorii estestvoznaniia i tekhniki*, 3, 1999, pp. 43–50; Ludmilla Schulze, 'The Russification of the St Petersburg Academy of Sciences and Arts in the Eighteenth Century', *The British Journal for the History of Science*, 18, 1985, pp. 305–35.

[8] See Wilhelm Schmidt-Biggemann, 'New Structures of Knowledge', in Walter Rüegg (ed.), *A History of the University in Europe*, 3 vols, Cambridge, 1992–2004, 2, pp. 515–29; Keith Tribe, 'Cameralism and the Science of Government', *Journal of Modern History*, 56, 1984, pp. 263–84.

[9] David Blackbourn, *The Conquest of Nature: Water, Landscape, and the Making of Modern Germany*, New York, 2006, p. 43.

[10] For a general discussion of foreign accounts of Russia, see Charles J. Halperin, 'In the Eye of the Beholder: Two Views of Seventeenth-Century Muscovy', *Russian History*, 24, 1997, pp. 409–23.

[11] Herodotus, *The Histories*, trans. Aubrey de Selincourt, further revised edn, London, 2003, pp. 243–49, 255–58.

or ploughed fields, as a 'mirror' image of Greece.[12] While critics have
argued that Hartog took his interpretation too far, and that the 'father
of history' did not simply make up his account of 'Scythia',[13] the sense
of 'otherness' conveyed by Herodotus is undeniable. And this 'otherness' can be found in writings by later visitors to the steppes, such as
those of Friar William of Rubruck from Flanders, who journeyed right
across the Eurasian steppes from Crimea to Mongolia in the 1250s, and
Anthony Jenkinson, ambassador to Queen Elizabeth of England and
agent of the Muscovy company, who travelled down the Volga on his
way to Persia and central Asia in the 1550s.[14]

Focusing on the eighteenth century, Larry Wolff argued that
'Eastern Europe' was 'invented' as a 'project of philosophical and
geographical synthesis carried out by the men and women of the
Enlightenment'. Their 'Eastern Europe' was a mirror image of how
they perceived the 'western Europe' they came from. Thus, the enlightened men and women saw 'Eastern Europe' as uncivilized, barbaric
and backward.[15] Wolff analysed Catherine the Great's journey to
her newly-conquered steppe lands in the company of the Habsburg
emperor Joseph II and an entourage of European ambassadors in 1787.
The tour was elaborately choreographed by Grigorii Potemkin, who
was the mastermind of the project to develop 'New Russia' on the
steppes. Catherine and her fellow travellers delighted in the sights of
the 'Asiatic' steppes and 'oriental' Crimea that awaited 'civilization'.[16]
Wolff paid some attention to Peter Simon Pallas, the German organizer of the Academy of Sciences expeditions of 1768–74, but not to the
other leaders of the expeditions. Nor was the natural environment a
major component in his interpretation.[17] Klaus Gestwa has gone some
way towards this by arguing that Russian nobles of this period contrasted the manicured lands of their estates with the 'wild' and 'backward' peoples and lands of the steppes and the Caucasus.[18] Analysing

[12] François Hartog, *The Mirror of Herodotus: The Representation of the Other in the Writing of History*, trans. Janet Lloyd, Berkeley, CA, 1988.
[13] See, for example, Carolyn Dewald, book review, *Classical Philology*, 85, 1990, pp. 217–24.
[14] [William of Rubruck], *The Mission of Friar William of Rubruck: His Journey to the Court of the Great Khan Möngke, 1253–1255*, trans. Peter Jackson, London, 1990, pp. 70–71; [Anthony Jenkinson], *Early Voyages and Travels to Russia and Persia*, ed. E. Delmar Morgan and C. H. Coote, New York, 1967, p. 55.
[15] Larry Wolff, *Inventing Eastern Europe: The Map of Civilization on the Mind of the Enlightenment*, Stanford, CA, 1994 (quotation from p. 356).
[16] Ibid., pp. 126–41. See also Sara Dickinson, 'Russia's First "Orient": Characterizing the Crimea in 1787', *Kritika*, 3, 2002, pp. 3–25.
[17] Wolff's chapter on geography (*Inventing Eastern Europe*, pp. 144–94) is concerned mostly with 'political geography and cultural cartography'.
[18] Klaus Gestwa, 'Der Blick auf Land und Leute: eine historische Topographie russischer Landschaften im Zeitalter von Absolutismus, Aufklärung und Romantik', *Historische Zeitschrift*, 279, 2004, pp. 63–125.

the writings of the foreign and Russian scholars who took part in the Academy expeditions to the steppes allows us to go a stage further and to test Wolff's argument in the context of environmental history. This reveals a highly significant point: all the expeditionary scientists, regardless of their national origins and cultural backgrounds, came from lands with natural environments that were forested. Indeed, it has been argued many times that forests played an important part in the identities of both Germans and Russians.[19]

When they encountered the treeless environment of the steppes, the Russians, Germans, Baltic German and Swede of the Academy of Sciences expeditions were all in an unfamiliar world of vast, open spaces dominated by big skies. The only comparable experience they would have had was at sea, which became a common metaphor to describe the steppes. Indeed, scholars working at the intersection of art history, geography, behavioural sciences and environmental studies have suggested that there may be innate human preferences for particular landscapes that offer both 'prospect' and refuge'. More simply, it is suggested that members of the species *homo sapiens* prefer landscapes in which they can 'see without being seen' as they offer the best chance of survival. The African savannah (where *homo sapiens* evolved), which has open spaces to allow 'prospect' and clumps of trees which offer 'refuge' is one such landscape. The flat, treeless expanse of the steppe is not.[20] A connection between landscape and survival was not a purely abstract theory for travellers on the steppes. Long into the eighteenth century, Russians and other visitors who did not take precautions to defend themselves risked being kidnapped by the indigenous nomads and sold into slavery.[21] Pallas was well aware of this. In August 1769 he visited the 'Kirguese' (Kirgiz, now known as Kazakhs) on the steppe to the east of the Iaik/Ural river. He noted that they committed 'petty robberies' and 'upon the Russian frontiers, they drive away a flock of horses and seize some single men and women'. 'They commonly commit their robberies so well', Pallas continued, 'as never to be caught. It has been remarked, that their neighbourhood is most dangerous in those places where the step [...] is flat and open; not in their mountainous and woody steps, where they conceal themselves

[19] See Simon Schama, *Landscape and Memory*, New York, 1995, pp. 75–134; R. A. French, 'Russians and the Forest', in James H. Bater and R. A. French (eds), *Studies in Russian Historical Geography*, 2 vols, London, 1983, 1, pp. 23–44.
[20] For a discussion of Jay Appleton's 'prospect-refuge theory' in the context of Russian landscape painting, see Christopher Ely, 'Prospect, Refuge, Coherence, Mystery: Landscape Theory and Russian Terrain', in Arja Rosenholm and Sari Autio-Sarasmo (eds), *Understanding Russian Nature: Representations, Values and Concepts*, Helsinki, 2005, pp. 21–43.
[21] See Khodarkovsky, *Russia's Steppe Frontier*, pp. 223–24.

and lie in wait for opportunities.'[22] The steppe landscape was not just different to the participants in the expeditions, therefore, but also threatening.

The detailed writings by the leaders, which were part travelogue and part scientific study, allow a reconstruction of how they understood the natural environment of the steppes and how they viewed the potential of a region, which was still a peripheral part of the empire, with a relatively sparse population of nomadic pastoralists, cossacks and some settlers, including colonists from German lands.[23] The expeditions can serve as a lens, moreover, through which to analyse the relationship between personality and place in Russian history.

Personality

The German-born empress Catherine the Great strongly supported the Academy of Science expeditions of 1768–74. She wished to know more about her empire and its potential. The expeditions, in the words of Alexander Vucinich, 'were far more ambitious than any previous ones, not only in size but also in general planning and mobilization of scholarly interests'.[24] The leaders of the expeditions were either foreign or had received all or part of their education abroad, mostly in German universities. Peter Simon Pallas was born in Berlin in 1741. He was educated at the universities of Halle, Leiden and Göttingen, and defended his doctoral dissertation — on tapeworms — at the age of nineteen. He was recommended to Catherine by a professor from Leipzig University, and elected to the Russian Academy of Sciences in 1767. He moved to St Petersburg, where he played an important role in planning the expeditions.[25] Ivan Ivanovich Lepekhin, who was a year older than Pallas, was the only Russian expedition leader. He was born in St Petersburg, and attended the gymnasium and university of the Academy of Sciences, where he excelled. In order to continue his studies of natural history he was sent abroad, to Straßburg University, where he defended his doctoral dissertation in 1766. He was selected to take part in the expeditions after his return to St Petersburg.[26] Johann Peter Falck was Swedish, born in 1725, and educated

[22] S. Pallas [*sic*], 'Travels into Siberia and Tatary, Provinces of the Russian Empire', in John Trusler (ed.), *The habitable world described, or the present state of the people in all parts of the globe, from north to south; shewing the situation, extent, climate ...*, vols 2–4, London, 1788–89, 2, pp. 289, 310–11. The Iaik river was renamed the Ural in 1775.
[23] On the settlement of the steppe region, see Willard Sunderland, *Taming the Wild Field: Colonization and Empire on the Russian Steppe*, Ithaca, NY, 2004; Roger P. Bartlett, *Human Capital: The Settlement of Foreigners in Russia, 1762–1804*, Cambridge, 1979.
[24] Vucinich, *Science in Russian Culture*, p. 150.
[25] F. Keppen, 'Pallas, Petr Simon', *Russkii Biograficheskii Slovar'*, vol. Pav-Pet, St Petersburg, 1902, pp. 153–62. See also Folkwart Wendland, *Peter Simon Pallas (1741–1811): Materialien einer Biographie*, 2 vols, Berlin, 1992.
[26] T. A. Lukina, *Ivan Ivanovich Lepekhin*, Moscow and Leningrad, 1965, pp. 8–19.

at Uppsala University. He worked as a tutor in the home of Carl
Linnaeus, the botanist and founder of modern taxonomy. Falck went
on to defend a doctoral dissertation on botany. He was working as a
naturalist in St Petersburg when he was invited to join the expeditions.
He was unwell, probably suffering from depression, for much of the
expedition, and committed suicide in Kazan´ at the end.[27] On account
of Falck's evident indisposition, in 1770 the Academy of Sciences sent
Johann Gottlieb Georgi, a German graduate of Uppsala University and
former student of Linnaeus, to assist him.[28] Samuel Gottlieb Gmelin
was German, born and educated in Tübingen. He had family connections with Russia and the Academy of Sciences: his uncle, Johann
Gottlieb Gmelin, was an early member of Academy, and took part in
an expedition to Siberia that lasted from 1733 to 1743. Samuel Gmelin's
expedition of 1768–74, like Falck's, ended in tragedy: Gmelin was taken
prisoner in Dagestan and died of fever in captivity.[29] Johann Anton
Güldenstädt was a Baltic German, born and brought up in Riga in
Livonia. He was educated in Riga and at the College of Medicine and
Surgery in Berlin, from where he was recommended to the Academy
of Sciences by the mathematician Leonhard Euler.[30]

The expeditions all included Russian students and assistants, who
were to be educated during their travels. Vasilii Zuev, a Russian
student in Pallas's expedition, completed his formal education at Leipzig
and Straßburg universities in 1774–76. (He went to lead his own expedition to the steppes in 1781–82.)[31] During the expeditions, the Russians
acted as interpreters, since only Lepekhin and the Baltic German
Güldenstädt of the leaders spoke Russian. This created problems.

[27] Fal´k, 'Zapiski Puteshestviia Akademika Fal´ka', *Polnoe sobranie uchenykh puteshestvii po
Rossii*, St Petersburg, 1824, 6, pp. v–vii. On Falck's 'melancholy and morbid depression'
('grust´ i ipokhondriiu'), see Pallas's letter of 17 February 1770. [P. S. Pallas], *Nauchnoe nasledie
P. S. Pallasa: pis´ma 1768–1771 gg.*, compiled by V. I. Osipov, trans. V. I. Osipov and G. I.
Fedorova, St Petersburg, 1993, p. 113. In a curious parallel, it is likely that one of the
leaders of the American Lewis and Clark expedition across the lands of the Louisiana
purchase to the Pacific Ocean in 1803–06 took his own life two years after he returned. See
John D. W. Guice (ed.), *By His Own Hand? The Mysterious Death of Meriwether Lewis*, Norman,
OK, 2006.
[28] V. F. Gnucheva, 'Materialy dlia istorii ekspeditsii akademii nauk v XVIII i XIX
vekakh', *Trudy Arkhiva Akademii Nauk SSSR*, pt 4, 1940, pp. 106–07; V. V. Tikhomirov and
T. A. Sofiano, 'Dvesti dvadtsat´ piat´ let so dnia rozhdeniia akademika I. I. Georgi',
Izvestiia Akademii nauk SSSR. Seriia geologicheskaia, 5, 1954, pp. 148–49. For Georgi's account
of his expedition, which mostly concerns Siberia, but also his journey along the Volga with
Pallas, see Johann Gottlieb Georgi, *Bemerkungen einer Reise im Rußischen Reich 1772–1774*, 2 vols,
St Petersburg, 1775.
[29] 'Gmeliny', *Entsiklopedicheskii Slovar´* (hereafter, *ES*), St Petersburg, 1893, 16, p. 931.
[30] Iu. Kh. Kopelevich, *Iogann Anton Gil´denshtedt*, Moscow, 1997, pp. 9–12.
[31] V. A. Gurkin, 'Pallas i Lepekhin v Simbirskoi provintsii', *Voprosy istorii estestvoznaniia i
tekhniki*, 3, 2006, pp. 114–15; V. V. Tikhomirov and T. A. Sofiano, '200 let so dnia rozhdeniia akad. V.F. Zuev i 160 let so dnia ego smerti', *Izvestiia Akademii nauk SSSR. Seriia
geologicheskaia*, 1, 1954, pp. 120–21.

Gmelin complained to the Academy in November 1768 that none of the four Russians in his detachment could translate his reports from German into Russian, and only one could speak some German. They had to communicate in Latin, partly in writing.[32] While they did not necessarily have a common language, however, all the members of the expeditions were in an unfamiliar, flat and largely treeless environment when they reached the steppes.

Place

The steppe region formed a significant part of the itineraries of the Orenburg and Astrakhan´ expeditions of 1768–74. They were made up of separate detachments. The first detachment of the Orenburg expedition, led by Pallas, travelled to Samara on the mid-Volga on its way to Orenburg, the Ural mountains and beyond to Siberia. Its return journey took in the lower Volga. The route of the second detachment, headed by Lepekhin, took it right down the Volga to Astrakhan´ and then on to the Urals and Siberia. The third detachment, under Falck, covered some of the same ground, including the Volga, but also traversed part of the north Caucasus on the return journey. The simultaneous Astrakhan´ expedition comprised two detachments. The first, led by Gmelin, travelled the full length of the river Don to the cossack capital of Cherkassk and on to Azov, before crossing the steppes to the Volga at Tsaritsyn. The detachment continued downstream to Astrakhan´, and on to the Caucasus and Persia. Güldenstädt, who headed the second detachment of the Astrakhan´ expedition, also travelled down the Don, but crossed directly from Kalachinskaia on the Don to Tsaritsyn on the Volga (near the route of the modern Volga-Don canal). The detachment crossed the Caucasus mountains to Georgia, where it spent a year. The return journey took Güldenstädt back over the mountains and across the steppes of the north Caucasus to Cherkassk, Azov and Taganrog. The Russo-Turkish War of 1768–74 prevented him from visiting the Crimea, but he travelled instead across 'New Russia' (southern Ukraine), before returning to Moscow and St Petersburg.[33]

The Academy of Sciences gave the leaders of the detachments detailed instructions. They had been prepared with the advice of the Free Economic Society, which had been established with Catherine's encouragement in 1765 to promote economic, in particular

---

[32] Sankt-Peterburgskii filial Arkhiva Rossiiskoi Akademii Nauk (hereafter, PFA RAN), fond [f.] 3, opis´ [op.] 34, delo [d.] 15, list [list] 28. See also [Pallas], *Nauchnoe nasledie*, p. 118.

[33] Gnucheva, 'Materialy', pp. 97–108.

EXPEDITIONS TO THE STEPPES

agricultural, development.[34] The instructions were clearly influenced
by cameralist ideas, which were applied in the Russian Empire over
the eighteenth century by Peter the Great and Catherine the Great.[35]
The leaders were instructed to ensure that their research and observations conformed to the expeditions' overall aim: the common good
of the state and the spread of science. More specifically, they were
instructed to investigate: the nature of the land and water; any uncul-
tivated or unpopulated land which could be used for growing grain or
other crops, or for hay meadows or forests; the economic activities
of populated places, and how they could be improved; livestock hus-
bandry; fishing; useful minerals; manufacturing; diseases and medicines.
In addition, they were to note the weather, the customs of the population and remnants of ancient peoples. The expeditionary scientists were
further instructed to make collections of animals, birds, fish, insects,
plants and things worthy of attention they found in the ground, and to
send them to the Academy in St Petersburg. The individual expeditions
were given particular instructions: Falck, for example, was to look for
'tilling instruments', i.e. ploughs, and to make models and drawings
of them.[36] There were two further expeditions to the steppes in the
late eighteenth century. Zuev led an expedition to the newly-annexed
steppe around Kherson, near the mouth of the Dnepr to the west of
the Crimea in 1781–82. His instructions were very similar to the earlier
expeditions.[37] Pallas himself made a second trip to the steppes in 1793–
94, travelling down the Volga, across the steppes of the north Caucasus
and on to the Crimean peninsula. He made detailed observations and
noted changes since his earlier visit.[38]

The accounts by the expedition leaders very much reflected what
they were instructed to do. Their descriptions of what was different
about the steppes, moreover, can be seen as the basis for what may
be termed 'modern' scientific research into the steppe environment
by climatologists, botanists, zoologists, geographers, soil scientists and
others. In the process, the expeditionary scientists of the late eighteenth

[34] N. G. Fradkin, 'Instruktsiia dlia akademicheskikh ekspeditsii 1768–1774 gg.', *Voprosy
geografii*, 17, 1950, pp. 213–18; M. I. Sukhomlinov, *Istoriia Rossiiskoi Akademii*, 8 vols, St
Petersburg, 1874–88, 1, pp. 472–79. I am grateful to Dr Aleksandra Bekasova for these
references. See also A. I. Khodnev, *Istoriia Imperatorskogo Vol'nogo Ekonomicheskogo Obshchestva
s 1765 do 1865 goda*, St Petersburg, 1865, pp. 1–2.
[35] See Marc Raeff, *The Well-Ordered Police State: Social and Institutional Change through Law in
the Germanies and Russia, 1600–1800*, New Haven, CT, 1983, pp. 181–250.
[36] PFA RAN, f. 3, op. 35, d. 1, ll. 2 ob.–3. For further individual instructions, see ibid.,
op. 30, d. 1 (Lepekhin); op. 32, d. 1 (Pallas); op. 33, d. 1 (Gil'denshtedt); op. 34, d. 1
(Gmelin).
[37] PFA RAN, f. 3, op. 37, d. 1, l. 20b–3; d. 5, l. 1; Vasilii Zuev, *Puteshestvennye zapiski
Vasiliia Zueva ot S. Peterburga do Khersona, v 1781 i 1782 godu*, St Petersburg, 1787, p. 1.
[38] Gnucheva, 'Materialy', p. 126; Wendland, *Peter Simon Pallas*, 1, pp. 271–75.

century engaged with issues that were addressed by later generations
of Russian natural scientists, who came to develop an understanding
of the steppe environment as a distinct and integrated ecosystem. The
steppe ecosystem was the subject of detailed scientific research during
a later expedition to the steppes in the 1890s. Under the leadership
of pioneering soil scientist Vasilii Dokuchaev (1846–1903), a team of
Russian scientists studied the different aspects of the steppe environment — including the climate, vegetation, wildlife, relief and drainage
and the soil — with the aim of finding ways to make agriculture on the
steppes more sustainable in conditions of recurring droughts.[39]

Climate

The accounts of the climate seem quite subjective. What visitors
considered 'hot' or 'cold' depended to quite a large degree on what
they were used to at home. The trend was started by Herodotus, who
thought the main feature of the climate was the long, cold winters and
short summers, which he also found cold.[40] Pallas, in contrast, seems
to have been especially sensitive to the heat. In mid-May 1769, when
he was in Syzran´ on the mid-Volga, he wrote:

> The heat was unsupportable, but the flying clouds seemed to promise us
> some refreshing showers. The air was like a furnace, and the heat so
> intense, that the mercury in the thermometer stood in the most airy and
> shady place at 105 degrees [on the 'upside-down' Delisle scale = approxi-
> mately 30° C]; on the 12th of May it [rose] to 93 degrees [38° C], and
> often in the sun to 85 degrees [43° C], a heat so great, that it was impos-
> sible to continue a minute in the sun-shine. [...] All nature was languid
> and panting, and the soil on the black heath cracked [...] and the
> apertures were some inches wide.

He left Syzran´ at five in evening as it was 'too sultry to travel in the
day'.[41] A month earlier, however, Pallas had noted more favourably
the fairly quick transition from winter to warm weather in the spring,
when 'all nature looked gay'.[42]

[39] See David Moon, 'The Environmental History of the Russian Steppes: Vasilii
Dokuchaev and the Harvest Failure of 1891', *Transactions of the Royal Historical Society*, sixth
series, 15, 2005, pp. 149–74. On the expeditions' importance in the development of 'natural
history', see Kolchinsky, 'Role'.
[40] Herodotus, *Histories*, p. 249.
[41] Pallas, 'Travels', 2, pp. 133–34. Pallas used the 'upside-down' Delisle scale (ibid., 3,
p. 25), on which the boiling point of water is 0 and the freezing point 150 degrees. Thus,
in contrast to other scales, hotter temperatures are indicated by lower numbers. See Hasok
Chang, *Inventing Temperature. Measurement and Scientific Progress*, New York, 2004, pp. 105,
160–61. The French astronomer Joseph-Nicolas De l'Isle (1688–1768) devised the scale while
he was director of the Russian Academy of Sciences observatory from 1725 to 1747. See
'Delil', *ES*, 19, p. 339.
[42] Pallas, 'Travels', 2, p. 118.

The sharp differences between the seasons were taken account of in the itineraries of the expeditions. Stops were scheduled each year for the winter. At the end of the first year of his expedition, Pallas stopped in Simbirsk on the mid-Volga in the second half of October. On 21 October he crossed the Volga only with difficulty, partly by boat and partly by walking on the ice. 'The frost here had been so severe', he wrote, 'that the Wolga, near a mile broad, was almost frozen over. By mid-December, the temperature had plummeted to 190 degrees [Delisle]' (approximately −27° C). Pallas stayed in Simbirsk until 10 March 1769. The Volga further downstream near Samara, however, was free from ice only on 17 April. His expedition ended for the year on 2 October 1769, when he arrived in Ufa in the southern Urals. He did not leave until over six months later, on 10 April 1770.[43] Pallas's detachment of the Orenburg expedition travelled across the north and east of the steppe region, where climate was harsher than the route followed by the Astrakhan´ expedition.

Güldenstädt arrived in Astrakhan´, where he was due to spend the winter of 1769–70, on 4 December. He crossed the Volga with all his baggage to reach the city with some difficulty, however, as the river was partly frozen and thus treacherous. A local Kalmyk, who was equipped with high leather breaches that joined onto his boots, carried the explorers on his back across a stretch of open water as far as ice that was strong enough to walk on. Gmelin, more sensibly, had arrived in Astrakhan´ a few weeks earlier. Güldenstädt was keen to resume his expedition as soon as he could, and left Astrakhan´ for Kizliar on the Terek river in the north Caucasus on 13 January 1770.[44] He would have been better advised to wait, since his detachment had to endure storms on the open steppe between Astrakhan´ and the Kuma river. The cold was 'more severe than usual', with temperatures between 166 and 176 on the Delisle scale (approximately −11° to −17° C) . They could find little fire wood, moreover, and several members of the expedition suffered from frostbite. His student and taxidermist Semen Tarbeev lost toes from both his feet.[45] Güldenstädt should have known better: the previous summer he had been informed that there were no marmots in the vicinity of a Don Cossack settlement he visited, because they had all frozen to death in their burrows during the very severe, snowless winter of 1763.[46] The following winter, Güldenstädt stopped in Kizliar, where he considered the winter to be 'short' for just under

[43] Ibid., 2, pp. 87–90, 102, 115; 3, p. 34; [Pallas], *Nauchnoe nasledie*, pp. 73–74, 94, 118; PFA RAN, f. 3, op. 30, 1768–1772, d. 1, ll. 2–20b, 5–60b.; op. 32, d. 1, ll. 1, 3.
[44] Kopelevich, *Iogann Anton Gil´denshtedt*, pp. 32–35; PFA RAN, f. 3, op. 33, 1768–1774, d. 1. l. 3; op. 34, 1768–1774, d. 1, l. 6.
[45] Iogann Anton Gil´denshtedt, *Puteshestvie po Kavkazu v 1770–1773 gg.*, trans. T. K. Shafranovskoi, St Petersburg, 2002, p. 35.
[46] Johann Anton Güldenstädt, *Reisen durch Russland und im Caucasischen Gebürg*, 2 vols, St Petersburg, 1787–91, 1, p. 64.

two months, from 13 December 1770 to 10 February 1771, before boldly heading off into the Caucasus mountains.[47]

The rainfall in the steppe region attracted considerable comment. In antiquity, Herodotus had noted 'violent thunderstorms' in the summer.[48] Many centuries later, Güldenstädt recorded thunder and lightning several times during his time on the lower Don in the summer of 1773. Semen Tarbeev, who was still with him in spite of the loss of some of his toes, claimed that the building he had been staying in had been struck by lightning. In the ensuing fire, as he explained to his mentor, five boxes containing 200 specimens that had been collected and stuffed in Astrakhan´ had perished.[49] Pallas recorded thunder storms, with violent hail and rain, in Tsaritsyn on the lower Volga in August 1773.[50] In sharp contrast to Herodotus's statement that it never stopped raining in the summer, however, the Academy of Sciences expeditions coincided with a serious drought and heatwave in the Volga basin in 1769. Pallas wrote from Samara at the end of May (when he found the heat unbearable) that, although clouds appeared on the horizon, not a drop of rain had fallen in the whole region since the start of April.[51] He visited a Chuvash village where the 'uncon-verted' peasants were 'preparing a great sacrifice for the next day, to solicit heaven in their way, for a fertile rain'.[52] According to Lepekhin, who was nearby, all the rural inhabitants (including the converted) were praying for rain.[53] Gmelin's account showed that the drought in the lower Volga basin continued throughout the summer of 1769.[54] Pallas later wrote that the 'desart' between the Volga and 'Jaik' would be more fruitful if it 'was not [made] so very droughty by the Hills on the Westside of the Wolga attracting every cloud, that hardly one year in ten the Barley comes up'.[55]

The expeditionary scientists also noted another prominent feature of the steppe climate — the hot, dry winds that blew from the east. Pallas described the winds and one of consequences: dust storms. In Tsaritsyn on the lower Volga in the summer of 1773, he noted:

[47] Gil´denshtedt, *Puteshestvie po Kavkazu*, pp. 35, 42–43.
[48] Herodotus, *Histories*, p. 249.
[49] I. Ia. Gil´denshtedt, 'Dnevnik puteshestviia v Iuzhnuiu Rossiiu akademika S. Peter-burgskoi Akademii Nauk Gil´denshtedta v 1773–1774 g.', *Zapiski Imperatorskogo Odesskogo obshchestva istorii i drevnosti*, 1879, 11, pp. 188, 190, 192.
[50] Pallas, 'Travels', 4, p. 316.
[51] [Pallas], *Nauchnoe nasledie*, p. 79.
[52] Pallas, 'Travels', 2, p. 135.
[53] I. I. Lepekhin, 'Zapiski Puteshestviia Akademika Lepekhina', *Polnoe sobranie uchenykh puteshestvii po Rossii*, 3, St Petersburg, 1821, p. 341.
[54] Samuel Georg [*sic*] Gmelin, *Puteshestvie po Rossii dlia issledovaniia trekh tsarstv estestva, pereve-dena s nemetskogo*, 4 vols in 3 parts, St Petersburg, 1771–85, 2, p. 30. The name on the title page is a misprint for Samuel *Gottlieb* Gmelin.
[55] Peter Simon Pallas, *A Naturalist in Russia: Letters from Peter Simon Pallas to Thomas Pennant*, ed. Carol Urness, Minneapolis, MN, 1967, p. 42.

The hottest and most intolerable of all the summer months is July, when it blows constantly from the arid step and sea, S.S.E. or E. After this arise the hot winds, which, though they blow irresistibly, so as to sweep off all the dust from the step, and carry it through the air, are yet as hot as if they came from a fiery furnace. These winds usually commence about two in the afternoon, and continue till past midnight; they seldom last longer. During their blowing, sheep often drop down dead, like flies, froth, bleed at the mouth, or swell, and become so suddenly puffed, that even their skins are of no use.[56]

Thus, the features of the climate that seemed most notable were the hot summers and cold winters, the torrential downpours in the summer, as well as periodic droughts, and hot, dry winds from the east that whipped up the earth in dust storms. All these climatic phenomena contrasted to varying degrees with their previous experiences which, for most of the expeditionary scientists, were the more temperate climates of central and northern Europe. Thus, although they did not articulate it directly, the accounts of the Academy of Sciences expeditions were on the way towards an understanding of a distinctive steppe climate, an idea that was presented more clearly by climatologists in the nineteenth century.[57]

Vegetation

A more striking contrast with the previous experiences of the expeditionary scientists, indeed perhaps the most striking, was the vegetation of the steppes. From the time of Herodotus, what struck most visitors about the vegetation was not what they saw, mainly grass, but what they did not see: trees. The German, Russian and Swedish expeditionary scientists of the late eighteenth century, who were natives of forested northern and central Europe, were no different. They approached the steppes from the north. The leaders commented favourably on wooded areas they passed through. Pallas, whose route took him across the northern edge of the steppes in 1769, remarked of the countryside along the road from Samara to Orenburg:

> fancy can scarce paint a prettier district; the most beautiful woods of ash and birch, relieved in turns, with green hills and luxuriant meadows. No country surely deserves cultivation more than along the river Samara, there being plenty of arable land, no want of wood, and great extent of very rich and beautiful meadow.[58]

[56] Pallas, 'Travels', 4, p. 315.
[57] See, for example, K. Veselovskii, *O Klimate Rossii*, St Petersburg, 1857, pp. 49–52; N. Adamov, 'Meteorologicheskie nabliudeniia 1892–1894 godov', *Trudy Ekspeditsii, snaria-zhennoi Lesnym Departmentom, pod rukovodstvom professora Dokuchaeva, Nauchnii otdel*, 3, 1894, 1, pp. 1–245.
[58] Pallas, 'Travels', 2, p. 141.

The expedition leaders commented negatively, however, on the increasingly treeless environment they encountered further south. Lepekhin — a Russian from St Petersburg in densely-forested northern Russia, who was educated in Straßburg in leafy Alsace — seems particularly to have suffered from the scarcity of trees on the steppes. He began to make critical remarks on the shortage of trees before he reached steppes proper. As he travelled east and south-east from Moscow, through the forest-steppe, on his way to Simbirsk on the mid-Volga, he recorded in one place that the road was mostly steppe and large forests were no longer to be seen, just small clumps of trees. He found 'only one shortcoming' with the city of Simbirsk: that it was built on the steppe, in a treeless place, and so had to import all the timber it needed. His concern for the shortage of firewood on the 'vast Orenburg steppe' to the east of the Volga prompted him to suggest that the inhabitants grow sunflowers and use the stems for fuel. On his way to Stavropol'-on-the-Volga, he despaired that 'one could not hope that there would be anything worthy of comment', as the road went alongside the Trans-Kama defensive line, where 'the vast steppes and little-forested areas begin'. He ordered his party to stop lighting fires by trees at night to keep themselves warm as he feared it would contribute to the destruction of the woods along the river. At last, near Saratov, they stopped at a monastery in 'a pleasant place, surrounded by fine groves' of trees.[59] The other expedition leaders also commented, although not quite so regularly or critically, on the lack of trees and the consequent need for the population to import firewood and timber. Falck, the melancholy Swede, recorded that the Kuma steppe in the north Caucasus was 'dry, empty, saline, exposed, and treeless'.[60] When Catherine viewed her new southern lands in 1787, she noted with dismay the absence of trees on the steppes of New Russia. She quickly added, however, that she had taken a thousand *desiatiny* (around 2,700 acres), and ordered forests to be planted to provide timber for construction and firewood. 'After a few years', she continued, 'they will say thank you to me.'[61] If only it had been that easy to grow trees on the steppes.[62]

[59] Lepekhin, 'Zapiski', pp. 90, 119–20, 126–27, 203, 228, 314, 352, 397–98.
[60] Fal'k, 'Zapiski', pp. 43, 87 (quotation); Gmelin, *Puteshestvie*, 2, p. 344; Gil'denshtedt, 'Dnevnik', p. 207.
[61] [Catherine II], 'Pis'ma Imperatritsy Ekateriny II k Iakovu Aleksandrovichu Briusu, 1787 goda', *Prilozhenie k Kamer-Fur'erskomu Zhurnalu 1787 goda*, St Petersburg, 1889, p. 25. Thanks are due to Simon Dixon for this reference.
[62] On the difficulties of planting trees on the steppes, and how to overcome them, see G. N. Vysotskii, 'Stepnoe lesorazvedenie', *Polnaia entsiklopediia russkogo sel'skogo khoziaistva*, 12 vols, St Petersburg, 1900–12, 9, 1905, pp. 443–99.

The accounts of the expeditions indicate that trees and shrubs tended to be restricted to certain locations: river valleys, ravines and uplands. Lepekhin was no doubt happy to find forested banks of the river Volga and its tributaries as he made his way downstream in 1769. Between Saratov and Tsaritsyn he recorded: 'Along the left side towards the Volga dense and tall, dark forest is to be seen everywhere, and on the right hand, open steppe', although in places there were small groups of trees. Along the same stretch in 1793, Pallas noted trees — poplars and willows — in sandy soil on the high, right bank of the river.[63] Güldenstädt seems to have found more trees than he expected as he made his way down the Don in 1769. He noted that both the high west [right] bank and low, sandy east [left] bank of the river were covered in trees, especially oak, as far as Ust'-Medveditskaia, in the north of the Don Cossack territory, but that both banks were treeless beyond this point. Further downstream, however, he recorded that the road along the bank of the river passed through an oak forest for ten versts (just under seven miles). At the point where he left the Don to cross to the Volga, there were willows and poplars along the east [left] bank.[64] Both Güldenstädt and Pallas noted the existence of 'good' and 'abundant' forest, and a wide variety of types of trees, in the Kuma and Terek river valleys, especially along the upper reaches towards the foothills of the Caucasus mountains. There were 'oaks of considerable height' on the banks of the Kuma river.[65] In his expedition in 1781–82 across the steppes to Kherson, Zuev also noted the presence of trees and shrubs near rivers.[66]

Deep, forested ravines to the south of Saratov attracted the attention of Lepekhin, who characteristically was struck by their beauty. Further south, beyond Tsaritsyn, the landscape was 'wholly steppe, and trees were not to be seen anywhere, except in the ravines, which were full of blackthorn, hawthorn and wild apple trees, which attracted a beautiful species of bird'.[67] The ravines that cut through the steppe between the Don and the Volga were also full of trees: Falck listed birch, asp, poplar, fruit trees, as well as shrubs.[68] Güldenstädt found 'many very good oaks, linden, apple and pear trees' in the ravines and gullies in

[63] Lepekhin, 'Zapiski', pp. 310, 358, 371–73, 402 (quotation); Peter Simon Pallas, *Travels through the Southern Provinces of the Russian Empire, in the Years 1793 and 1794*, 2 vols, London, 1802, 1, p. 67.

[64] Güldenstädt, *Reisen*, 1, pp. 62, 69, 74, 86, 89, 96, 114.

[65] Gil'denshtedt, *Puteshestvie po Kavkazu*, pp. 35, 36, 290–91; Peter Simon Pallas, *Puteshestvie po raznym provintsiiam Rossiiskoi Imperii*, 3 vols, St Petersburg, 1773–88, 1, p. 198 (quoted in I. V. Bentkovskii, 'O lesakh v predelakh byvshei Kavkazskoi, a nyne Stavropol'skoi gubernii', *Stavropol'skie gubernskie vedomosti* [1876], no. 1 [3 Jan.]).

[66] Zuev, *Puteshestvennye zapiski*, p. 226.

[67] Lepekhin, 'Zapiski', pp. 408–11, 465–66, 480.

[68] Fal'k, 'Zapiski', pp. 48–50.

the basin of the upper reaches of the Mius river, near Taganrog, and commented that some of the trees were tall enough to be used for construction in the port.[69] In addition, trees grew on upland areas. Lepekhin visited a German settlement south of Saratov in a 'pleasant place', with a small river, surrounded by forested hills.[70] The foothills of the Caucasus and lower slopes of the mountains were forested. Güldenstädt noted that: 'On Mashuk [one of the five hills that surrounded the site where Piatigorsk was founded in 1780] there were many forests, especially on the northern side.' The foothills near the source of the river Gegerlik were 'covered in a forest', called 'Karagach' in Tatar, which was translated directly in Russian as Chernyi Les (Black Forest).[71]

The expedition leaders considered why there were so few trees in the steppe region, and why those that were there were limited to certain areas. Some noted that insects harmed trees. Lepekhin recorded that the oak trees he found in a ravine had been attacked by insects that had eaten all their leaves, presenting a 'pitiful sight'.[72] Gmelin wrote that, in contrast to bare steppes with no rivers, trees grew in areas that were supplied with water. Lepekhin noted the presence of trees in ravines that contained springs.[73] Pallas commented that the steppe between the Volga and Iaik, which was 'droughty', was 'as fit for' planting trees 'as the desarts of Syria or Arabia'.[74] Their discussions of the reasons for the treelessness of the steppes were early contributions to a debate that attracted great interest over the nineteenth century. Towards the end of that century, Gavriil Tanfil'ev and Grigorii Vysotskii, who were colleagues of Vasilii Dokuchaev, argued that it was the presence of alkaline salts in the sub-soil that hindered the growth of trees on the steppes. In northern Russia, however, the higher rainfall leached the salts out of the soil and created the conditions for forests to grow.[75]

Back in the late eighteenth century, the leaders of the Academy of Sciences expeditions commented critically on deforestation. Lepekhin expressed concern about the 'neglect' of forests when he was still in the forest-steppe zone on his way southeast. He noted that, as a result of

[69] Gil'denshtedt, 'Dnevnik', pp. 206, 217.
[70] Lepekhin, 'Zapiski', pp. 413–14.
[71] Gil'denshtedt, Puteshestvie po Kavkazu, pp. 286, 293, 307.
[72] Lepekhin, 'Zapiski', p. 408.
[73] Gmelin, Puteshestvie, 1, p. 201; Lepekhin, 'Zapiski', p. 408.
[74] Pallas, Naturalist in Russia, p. 42.
[75] See G. Tanfil'ev, 'Predely lesov na iuge Rossii', Trudy ekspeditsii, snariazhennoi Lesnym Departamentom, pod rukovodstvom professora Dokuchaeva, Nauchnyi otdel, vol. 2, pt 1, 1894; G. N. Vysotskii, 'Pochvennye zony Evropeiskoi Rossii v sviazi s solenosnost'iu gruntov i kharakterom lesnoi rastitel'nosti', Pochvovedenie, 1, 1899, 1, pp. 19–26.

this neglect, the peasants in one village were poor, since they had to buy wood for fuel, implements and construction.[76] Several expedition leaders noted with surprise that both peasant settlers, who were recent arrivals, and cossacks, who had lived in the region for generations, used scarce timber, rather than stone or brick, for construction. Lepekhin commented that that there were no stone buildings in Saratov, which he visited in 1769, with the exception of seven churches and two monasteries.[77] At Tsaritsyn, further down the Volga, Falck recorded that the town was 'small' and the churches and houses were all wooden.[78] Gmelin and Güldenstädt both noted that the Don cossacks built their houses mostly from wood. In the large *stanitsa* (cossack settlement) of Uriupinskaia on river Khoper, Güldenstädt counted around 300 wooden houses. It became apparent to Gmelin, as he travelled down the Don, moreover, that there were more trees on the far side of the river, where the nomadic Kalmyks lived, than the cossack side, where there were almost no trees left.[79] Later in his expedition, in 1773, Güldenstädt visited Taganrog and the nearby defensive line. All the houses in the port were made from logs and there was, he noted, a shortage of forest in the area. Settlers on the defensive line, moreover, used timber brought from 40 versts up the river Mius, as all the trees lower down had been felled.[80] The Russian predilection for timber was especially noticeable in parts of the region where Russian settlers and cossacks lived alongside other ethnic groups. Falck noted that on the Terek river in the north Caucasus, the Russians' houses were wooden, while those of other people were made out of *mazanka* (wattle daubed with clay).[81]

The expedition leaders took careful notes of attempts that were made to save timber. At Azov on the Don delta, which Güldenstädt visited in 1773, the fortress was being rebuilt from bricks, instead of timber, made from local clay fired with reeds, rather than firewood. In nearby Rostov, moreover, reeds were used for fuel.[82] Even where bricks were made, this did not necessarily conserve scarce timber. Back in 1769, Güldenstädt visited a brick works in the north of the Don Cossack territory, and wrote with evident dismay that the bricks were baked in ovens fuelled with firewood that used two cubic feet (English) per brick. The firewood, moreover, included valuable oak.[83] The situation had

[76] Lepekhin, 'Zapiski', pp. 98–99.
[77] Ibid., p. 378.
[78] Fal´k, 'Zapiski', p. 128.
[79] Gmelin, *Puteshestvie*, 1, pp. 244, 265; Güldenstädt, *Reisen*, 1, pp. 50, 60.
[80] Gil´denshtedt, 'Dnevnik', p. 212.
[81] Fal´k, 'Zapiski', p. 66.
[82] Gil´denshtedt, 'Dnevnik', pp. 183, 195–96.
[83] Güldenstädt, *Reisen*, 1, p. 54

changed little in the 1780s and 1790s when Zuev and Pallas travelled across the steppes. Both the Russian and the German commented on the wasteful use of timber, the 'unpardonable' destruction of forests, and the existence of towns, such as Belgorod, built almost entirely from wood in the midst of a largely treeless environment.[84]

The expeditionary scientists did not just concern themselves with trees, but also commented on and studied the main types of steppe flora: the grasses and wild flowers. As he made his way south from Simbirsk in the spring of 1769, Lepekhin noted that the steppe was 'greening over' with feather grass, 'the young stems of which provide succulent fodder for the grazing herds'.[85] Much further south, between the Don and Volga on his way to Tsaritsyn, Güldenstädt noted that the steppe was covered in feather grass.[86] Lepekhin, who seemed almost to suffer from the lack of trees, could appreciate the beauty and scientific importance of the steppe flora. In the spring of 1769, he described how the two-coloured iris (*iris biflora*) and anemones covered the steppe with their flowers. In the summer of that year, he wrote that he could have stayed for longer collecting plants on the steppe east of the lower Volga.[87] Making his way up the Volga, Pallas noted how 'beautiful broom' grew on the slopes of water-filled, wide ravines, while on the high, dry, hilly steppe on the right bank of the river, where all the grasses dried up in the summer, 'there is one exception a yellow flowering grass that almost alone flowers in the autumn'.[88] On his second trip in 1793, he made a very detailed study of the flora on the left side of the Volga, noting amongst other plants, the wild tulips.[89] Since many of the plants in the steppe region were new to European science in the eighteenth century, the expedition leaders devoted a great deal of effort to cataloguing, drawing and collecting specimens of the plants they found. (When Güldenstädt's student Semen Tarbeev lost five boxes of stuffed specimens of fauna, when they were apparently struck by lightning, he saved a box of dried plants and seeds.)[90] The books produced by the expedition leaders contained many very carefully executed illustrations of the plants they found.[91] Pallas became a leading authority on the flora of Russia.[92]

---

[84] Pallas, *Travels through the Southern Provinces*, 1, pp. 14, 34; Zuev, *Puteshestvennye zapiski*, pp. 49, 144, 163, 170.

[85] Lepekin, 'Zapiski', p. 306.

[86] Güldenstädt, *Reisen*, 1, p. 98.

[87] Lepekhin, 'Zapiski', pp. 306, 486, 495.

[88] [Pallas], 'Puteshestvie', pp. 247–49, 257, 259, 260–61.

[89] Pallas, *Travels through the Southern Provinces*, 1, pp. 114, 121, 131–38.

[90] Gil'denshtedt, 'Dnevnik', p. 192.

[91] See, for example, Gmelin, *Puteshestvie*.

[92] See A. K. Sytin, *Petr Simon Pallas. Botanicus*, Moscow, 1997.

Several of the expeditionary scientists noted that different plants grew in different parts of the steppe region. Especially noticeable were the particular plants that grew on the salty soils in the southeast. Lepekhin listed the 'rare plants', such as the thistle 'tatarnik', he found on the Tsaritsyn steppe on the lower Volga and had not seen in other places.[93] Pallas and Falck paid attention to the 'salt plants', especially saltwort (*solianka kustovataia, Salicornia Arabica*), which they found near salt lakes east of the Volga. Falck also found such plants on the sandy and salty Kuma steppe in the north Caucasus. He contrasted these plants with what he tellingly termed 'ordinary vegetation',[94] indicating clearly that he thought the salty soils of parts of the steppe region, with their distinctive flora, were different from the norm, which for the Swedish botanist was the vegetation of northern Europe. With the development of 'geobotany' over the nineteenth century, botanists made more direct connections between types of plants and the environments in which they grew. Franz Joseph Ruprecht, the Austrian-born pioneer of geobotany in Russia, identified a specific 'steppe flora' in his work on the black-earth region of 1866. Ruprecht cited the work of Pallas and Lepekhin as well as later specialists.[95]

Wildlife

The expeditionary scientists meticulously described and collected specimens of the fauna they encountered on the steppes as well as the flora. They were particularly interested in species that were unfamiliar to them and little known or unknown to European science. Pallas, for example, compared a 'musk rat' he found near Samara with Linnaeus's classification and suggested an alternative.[96] More dramatically, several of the expeditions dug up the remains of elephants or mammoths in the valleys of the Don, Volga and Iaik rivers.[97] The expedition leaders spent more time, however, observing, describing, catching and classifying wildlife that was not extinct.

---

[93] Lepekhin, 'Zapiski', pp. 472–73.
[94] Pallas, 'Travels', 3, pp. 8, 14; [Pallas], *Nauchnoe nasledie*, p. 89; Fal´k, 'Zapiski', pp. 50, 92–93.
[95] F. Ruprekht, *Geo-botanicheskie issledovaniia o chernozeme* (Prilozhenie k 10-mu Tomu *Zapisok Imperatorskoi Akademii Nauk*, no. 6, St Petersburg, 1866, pp. 14–20. See also A. A. Fedotova, 'Geobotanicheskie issledovaniia o chernozeme F. I. Ruprekhta', *Voprosy istorii estestvoznaniia i tekhniki*, 1, 2008, pp. 22–34.
[96] Pallas, 'Travels', 2, pp. 126–27. Pallas disagreed with Linnaeus's system see Pallas, *Naturalist in Russia*, p. 4; Wendland, *Peter Simon Pallas*, 1, pp. 562–63, 779–84.
[97] Pallas, 'Travels', 2, pp. 114–15, 128, 286–87; Gmelin, *Puteshestvie*, 1, pp. 53, 119–21; Lepekhin, 'Zapiski', p. 301; Pallas, *Travels through the Southern Provinces*, 1, p. 108. See also V. S. Bajgusheva, 'Elephants from the Delta of paleo-Don River', The World of Elephants – International Congress, Rome, 2001 <http://www.cq.rm.cnr.it/elephants2001/pdf/172_175.pdf> [accessed 11 November 2008].

They were particularly keen to find the wild horses that were believed to live on the steppes. Some contemporary naturalists, including the prominent French scholar the comte de Buffon, however, doubted their existence. When Gmelin arrived in Voronezh, on the northern edge of the steppes, he heard that twenty years earlier many wild horses had lived in the vicinity of the city, but that they had since moved around a hundred versts to the southeast to the area around Bobrovsk. When he reached Bobrovsk, however, he was told that there had been no signs of the wild horses there recently, and that they must have moved off further onto the steppe. He headed off in pursuit, and was delighted to hear news of recent sightings in the village of Chikhonka, 45 versts away: 'two versty from us we saw six horses running together, which, when they saw us, galloped away with unimaginable speed.' Over the next two days, with the help of local peasants, he snared two wild stallions and two wild mares in the interests of science. He described the specimens, noting that the biggest wild horse was barely as large as the smallest domesticated horse.[98] The expeditions saw or heard about more wild horses further south and east, where there were fewer people. While travelling from Orenburg to Samara 1773, Pallas noted that the numbers of wild horses, or *tarpany*, had increased in recent years as 'the wild country between the Jaik and the Wolga has been uninhabited for a considerable time'. He was not convinced that they were wild, however, and proposed that 'they are chiefly the produce of some bewildered Kirguese and Kalmuck horses, or of the stallions of the Nomades belonging to this district, with either single mares or whole herds which they carried off'.[99] He omitted the wild horse from a long list of 'quadrupeds of Russia and Siberia' which he sent to the British naturalist Thomas Pennant in 1779. But, he added it the following year, conceding that: 'Some of them seem really to be the original wild races.'[100] Gmelin's account and specimens convinced their contemporaries. On this basis, in 1785, the Dutch naturalist Pieter Boddaert gave it the scientific name of *Equus ferus*. It is still recognized as a living or recently extinct subspecies of horse.[101] The wild horse, or *tarpan*, which once ranged across the steppe and forest-steppe regions of western Eurasia, can serve as an example of one of the major scientific 'discoveries' of the expeditions.

The expedition leaders commented on the declining numbers of wild horses due to human activity. Güldenstädt was told that they had

[98] Gmelin, *Puteshestvie*, 1, pp. 69–72.
[99] Pallas, 'Travels', 4, p. 256.
[100] Pallas, *Naturalist in Russia*, pp. 58–95, 137.
[101] Deb Bennett and Robert S. Hoffmann, 'Equus caballus', *Mammalian Species*, 628, December 1999, pp. 1, 3.

lived in large numbers on the steppe in the north of the Don Cossack territory twenty years earlier, but that there were none left when he passed through the area in 1769.[102] Gmelin, who was more persistent, recorded that they were becoming much more elusive. The local peasants considered them to be pests: they raided their hay barns, and wild stallions killed domestic male horses with their teeth, and took the mares away with them. The peasants hunted wild horses with snares and drove them away, further off onto the steppe.[103] On the Azov steppe beyond the Don, Güldenstädt learned later in his expedition that there were large herds of wild horses, but that the local Nogai nomads were exterminating them.[104] According to Pallas, the Kalmyks hunted wild horses for food.[105] The steppe nomads, who had used domesticated horses for several millennia,[106] considered their wild cousins to be pests. By the early nineteenth century, wild horses were to be found only in the more remote south and southeast of the steppes.[107] The last *tarpan* recorded in the wild was killed in Tauride province in 1879. A wild *tarpan* caught earlier in the vicinity of nearby Kherson survived in Moscow zoo until the 1880s. At around the same time, however, the Russian explorer Nikolai Przheval'skii discovered for science another subspecies of wild horse, which was named for him as Przewalski's horse, on an expedition to the far southeast of the Eurasian steppe in Chinese central Asia.[108]

The expedition leaders were intrigued by the 'wild goats which the Tatars call *saigaki*'. Gmelin, who saw some of these strange animals when they approached Astrakhan' in the winter of 1768–69, noted that they ran very quickly, with the help of their 'broad inflatable noses', and jumped all the time. They soon tired, especially in hilly areas, where hunters waited to catch them.[109] Güldenstädt saw herds of *saigaki* grazing on the steppe in the far distance from the hilly, right

---

[102] Güldenstädt, 1, p. 50.

[103] Gmelin, *Puteshestvie*, 1, pp. 68–73.

[104] Gil'denshtedt, 'Dnevnik', p. 198.

[105] Pallas, 'Travels', 2, p. 218.

[106] See Nicola Di Cosmo, *Ancient China and Its Enemies: The Rise of Nomadic Power in East Asian History*, Cambridge, 2002, pp. 24–27, 62; Alan K. Outram et al., 'The Earliest Horse Harnessing and Milking', *Science*, 323, 6 March 2009, pp. 1332–35. I am grateful to Professor Daniel Potts for his advice on this topic.

[107] See Gmelin, *Puteshestvie*, pt 2, p. 10; *Sbornik statisticheskikh svedenii po Samarskoi gubernii. Otdel khoziaistvennoi statistiki*, pt 3, *Buzulukskii uezd*, Samara, 1885, p. 7; *Nikolaevskii uezd*, pt 6, p. 14; [F. Keppen], 'Zametki pri poezdke po Tavricheskoi gubernii, letom 1864 goda', *Sel'skoe khoziaistvo i lesovodsto*, pt 89, 1865, 2nd pagn, pp. 23–31; Fedor [Petrovich] Keppen [Koeppen], 'K istorii tarpana v Rossii', *Zhurnal Ministerstva narodnogo prosveshcheniia*, 303, 1896, 1, pp. 96–171.

[108] Bennett and Hoffmann, 'Equus caballus', p. 10. See also Peter Waldron, 'Przheval'skii in Asia' elsewhere in this volume.

[109] Gmelin, *Puteshestvie*, 2, pp. 240–41.

bank of the Don in 1769.[110] *Saigaki* seem to have been more numerous further east, on the steppe between the Volga and Iaik rivers, where Lepekhin saw 'incalculable herds' of them. They scattered at the sound of gun fire, which he found amusing.[111] Pallas saw the animals in the same area in the drought year of 1769.

> Last spring [1769], he wrote, the country was over-run with antilopes [*sic*], though this animal had not been seen here for many years before. The dryness of the season having brought them in large herds or flocks, from the southern parts. They ventured even into the low grounds, and meadows.[112]

Pallas purchased several *saigaki* to be stuffed as specimens. He also sent living animals to St Petersburg, as he thought they had not been seen there before. Two pairs of live *saigaki* were duly dispatched on carts with two soldiers as guards. They eventually arrived in the capital, where they were housed in the imperial menagerie.[113] Pallas had no hesitation in including the undoubtedly wild 'Scythian Antelope' or 'Saiga' in his list of quadrupeds.[114]

Another distinctive feature of the steppe fauna was the rodents, for example marmots (*surki*) and gophers (*susliki*), that lived in burrows. Pallas wrote that in the mid-Volga region 'Russian marmotes' were 'often met with, in whole troops or families'.[115] According to Gmelin, marmots lived on the Don steppes in very large numbers. The Kalmyk nomads ate them, and the local inhabitants kept them in their homes to catch mice. The German scientist doubted, however, they were 'as pleasing to the female sex as cats'.[116] When his expedition reached the valley of the lower Volga, he identified and described a burrowing, steppe mouse that was new to science.[117] At this time, rodents usually lived out on the steppe 'in peace away from people'. In the dry summer of 1769 in the lower Volga region, however, the heatwave dried out the steppe to the extent that gophers were forced to leave their homes and move on to the peasants' fields.[118] Massive efforts were made to get rid of them. In the drought year of 1769, Lepekhin came across children pouring water into gophers' burrows and stuffing them with straw and other inflammable material to burn them out as the rodents were ravaging the crops in the peasants' fields in the lower Volga region.[119]

[110] Güldenstädt, *Reisen*, 1, p. 93.
[111] Lepekhin, 'Zapiski', p. 495.
[112] Pallas, 'Travels', 2, p. 148.
[113] [Pallas], *Nauchnoe nasledie*, pp. 84, 87, 100, 210.
[114] Pallas, *Naturalist in Russia*, p. 92.
[115] Pallas, 'Travels', 2, p. 102.
[116] Gmelin, *Puteshestvie*, 1, pp. 46–50.
[117] Ibid., and p. 239.
[118] Lepekhin, 'Zapiski', pp. 411–12.
[119] Ibid.

He also noted the presence of vast numbers of grasshoppers and locusts on the steppe between Saratov and Tsaritsyn during the drought in the summer of 1769. Locusts were sufficiently unfamiliar for Lepekhin to produce a description of the insect. In 1781, Zuev noted that locusts flew in from 'Polish Ukraine' in certain years.[120]

To some extent, the interest of the expeditionary scientists in the wildlife was purely scientific, to identify and classify species that were not known to naturalists in Western Europe. Indeed, Pallas went on to prepare a 'fundamental work' on Russian fauna that described over 900 species.[121] The expedition leaders' interest in rodents and locusts, however, indicates a concern with pests that threatened the development of agriculture in the region. Both these strands of thought — identifying a steppe fauna and the need to exterminate pests — developed over the nineteenth century.[122]

Relief and Drainage

The feature of the relief, or topography, of the steppes that was most immediately striking to outsiders was the flatness. Falck described the steppe between the Don and Volga he crossed in November 1769 as 'boundless, level, dry, open, and without trees'.[123] Gmelin's first impression on reaching Kazanka in the north of the Don Cossack territory, was: 'Along both sides of the Don are two vast steppes; on the west, the so-called [. . .] Don steppe and on the east the Kalmyk [steppe].'[124] At around the same time, Güldenstädt described the landscape of this area as 'boundless, flat steppe'.[125] Over the years of his expedition, he became familiar with a variety of landscapes in southern Russia and the north Caucasus, and with various degrees of flatness. When he reached the river Manych, which rises half way between the Black and Caspian Seas, in July 1773, he described this part of the steppe quite simply as 'absolutely flat'.[126] (The present author, a more recent visitor to the Manych´ steppes, can concur with this description.) It would be utterly wrong, however, to characterize the steppe region as a whole as two-dimensional. The steppes rise high above the river

---

[120] Ibid., pp. 444–45; Zuev, *Puteshestvennye zapiski*, p. 229.
[121] Kolchinsky, 'Role', p. 112.
[122] See, for example, A. Silant´ev, 'Organizatsiia sistematicheskikh nabliudenii nad vrednymi i poleznymi zhivotnymi na uchastkakh Osoboi Ekspeditsii', *Trudy Ekspeditsii, snariazhennoi Lesnym Departmentom, pod rukovodstvom professora Dokuchaeva, Nauchnyi otdel*, 4, 1895, 1; id., 'Zoologicheskie issledovaniia i nabliudeniia 1894–96 godov', ibid., 4, 1898, 2; V. Morachevskii, 'Bor´ba zemstv s vragami polevodstva', *Sel´skoe khoziaistvo i lesovodstvo*, 194, 1899, pp. 193–225.
[123] Fal´k, 'Zapiski', pp. 49–50.
[124] Gmelin, *Puteshestvie*, pt 1, pp. 200–01.
[125] Güldenstädt, *Reisen*, 1, p. 50.
[126] Gil´denshtedt, *Puteshestvie po Kavkazu*, p. 303.

valleys offering striking panoramas, such as the one Güldenstädt witnessed a little later from land reaching the lofty elevation of 15 *sazheni* (over 100 feet) above the delta of the Don. 'From this height', he wrote, 'we could see Azov to the ENE [East-North-East], Taganrog to the NW and in the west the Ochakov spit, which is situtated forty *versts* [about 27 miles] from here on the Sea of Azov. The view from this height was magnificent — boundless sea and steppe.'[127] It is unlikely that he could have seen the Ochakov spit, as it is on the other side of the Crimean peninsula, but there are several spits along the north coast of the Sea of Azov that are visible. While in a similar location, the present author also struggled to judge distances. Writers on other treeless landscapes, such as Antarctica, with its 'monolithic expanses of flat white ice', have noted that the lack of trees against which to guage scale distorts humans' sense of perception.[128]

The seeming monotony of much of the steppes was broken by a number of features. Many visitors commented on the burial mounds, or *kurgany*. In the mid-thirteenth century, William of Rubruck wrote that what he called 'Coman graves' were 'visible to us two leagues off' as he headed east to the north of Sea of Azov.[129] They were still there over five hundred years later when Güldenstädt passed through the same country, heading in the opposite direction. He noted many burial mounds with stone statues of men or women on top.[130] There were similar burial mounds throughout the region. Pallas saw many on the road from Samara to Orenburg in the spring of 1769, and on the lower Volga near Cherny Iar later in his expedition. He added that a large number had been dug up as they often contained saddles and harnesses with silver mountings and other valuable items.[131] Lepekhin was told the *kurgany* contained gold and silver coins and weapons, but he saw only bones.[132] Falck saw a large number of *kurgany* of the 'previous inhabitants of the steppe' along both sides of the Ilava river, to the west of the Volga. He described what was inside: in 1752, a *kurgan* had been excavated to reveal a human skeleton mounted on a

[127] Gil´denshtedt, 'Dnevnik', p. 194.
[128] See William L. Fox, *Terra Antarctica: Looking into the Emptiest Continent*, San Antonio, TX, 2005, pp. 18–21. I am grateful to Professor Adrian Howkins for drawing this parallel to my attention.
[129] [William of Rubruck], *Mission*, p. 108. Elsewhere (p. 105), he called the 'Comans' the 'Capchac', i.e. Kipchak, a Turkic-speaking nomadic people, who lived on the steppe at the time of the Mongol conquest. They were known to the Russians as 'Polovtsy'.
[130] Gil´denshtedt, 'Dnevnik', pp. 205, 206, 219, 222.
[131] Pallas, 'Travels', 2, pp. 149–51; [Peter Simon Pallas], 'Puteshestvie po raznym provintsiiam Rossiiskoi Imperii', in V. Alekseev (ed.), *Istoricheskie puteshestviia: izvlecheniia iz memuarov i zapisok inostrannykh i russkikh puteshestvennikov po Volge v XV–XVIII vekakh*, Stalingrad, 1936, p. 249.
[132] Lepekhin, 'Zapiski', p. 415.

skeletal horse, together with gold and silver ornaments.[133] In the west of the steppe region, when Zuev travelled past the rapids on the lower Dnepr in 1781, he recorded that the 'road was level, black-earth steppe, on which only *kurgany* in very large numbers were visible'.[134] This was the very location which, over two millennia earlier, Herodotus had described as the 'burial place of the Scythian kings'. His account of their burial customs described exactly what was found when the mounds were excavated in the eighteenth century.[135]

Aside from low, often sandy hillocks,[136] there were few natural hills throughout most of the steppes. There are proper hills and mountains only on the periphery. To the north-east of Orenburg are the southern Urals. As he travelled through the Ural mountains from Ufa to Cheliabinsk in the spring of 1770, Pallas described the flora and fauna, the rock and minerals, mines and manufactories, and the inhabitants. The mountains themselves did not pose a great barrier and attracted little comment, although he did describe the descent down the east side as 'very steep'.[137] Güldenstädt, whose itinerary took him to the north Caucasus on to Georgia, described mountains on a rather different scale. In March 1770, he crossed the river Terek at Mozdok and he noted that 'the first 10 versts [we travelled] across level and then hilly, open steppe'. The following day, they encountered 'at first open, rising steppe, then [...] dense forest with large hillocks and deep rifts. [...] On one side of the forest was revealed a view of the Caucasus mountains, covered in ice'.[138] The majestic Caucasus range — the highest mountains in Europe — mark the southern boundary of the steppes between the Black and Caspian seas. On his return journey from Georgia in 1773, Güldenstädt was particularly impressed by one mountain, which was shaped like a pyramid with a flat top and was permanently covered in snow. This was Elbrus, the highest mountain in the Caucasus range. With typical energy, he wanted to climb to the 'snowy peak'. The local population (Kabardintsy) refused him permission, however, because they used the summit as a refuge if their fortunes in war turned against them, and so wanted to keep the details of location secret.[139] Güldenstädt went down from the mountains, through the foothills,

---

[133] Fal´k, 'Zapiski', pp. 46–47.

[134] Vasilii Zuev, *Puteshestvennye*, pp. 263–64.

[135] Herodotus, *Histories*, pp. 262–64. Two of the best collections of 'Scythian gold' are in a museum in Azov and in the Hermitage in St Petersburg. Azovskii kraevedcheskii muzei, 38/40 ul. Moskovskaia, Azov, 346780 Rostovskaia oblast´; <http://www.hermitagemuseum.org/html_Ru/03/hm3_2_6.html> [accessed 31 October 2008].

[136] See Gil´denshtedt, 'Dnevnik', p. 182.

[137] Pallas, 'Travels', 3, pp. 45–65.

[138] Gil´denshtedt, *Puteshestvie po Kavkazu*, p. 36.

[139] Ibid., p. 289. For a fuller description of the mountains, see pp. 206–22.

and across the less immediately spectacular landscape of the north Caucasus.[140]

Four years earlier, when he first arrived on the steppes in the north of the Don Cossack territory, Güldenstädt enquired about the relief of the land between the rivers Khoper and Don, which he was about to cross, as his map seemed to show hills. He was told that it was 'level steppe', but that in places there were deep valleys and ravines.[141] Thus, another distinctive feature of the landscape is created, not by hills rising above the steppe, but by ravines and river valleys cutting through it. Güldenstädt and others recorded the presence of many ravines perpendicular to the Don and Volga. Making his way up the left bank of the Volga near Dubovka, Pallas noted that some ravines were so steep that the road made detours to get around them.[142] Expedition leaders also noted ravines between river valleys. Crossing the steppe from the Don to the Volga, Güldenstädt came across a ravine 50 *sazheni* (about 350 feet) deep.[143] The expeditionary scientists sought to explain how the ravines had been formed. On his way down the Volga in the spring of 1769, Lepekhin began to note the existence of ravines south of Simbirsk. Further downstream, near Samara, he described a deep ravine that got larger as it approached the river. And, by the time he reached Saratov, he had worked it out, writing that the Saratov ravine had been created by water erosion. He went on to describe the different layers of soil, rock and clay that had been revealed in the process.[144] Several of the scientists reached the same conclusion that ravines were created by water flowing downhill, across the steppes, into the rivers. Pallas noted that two steep ravines near Chernyi Iar by the side of the lower Volga had been 'eroded by spring and rain water'. He had earlier written that ravines further up the Volga developed 'with time', emphasizing the continuous process involved.[145] Their conclusions anticipated those of Dokuchaev in his detailed study of the formation of ravines and river valleys a century later.[146]

The expedition leaders paid particular attention to the rivers in the steppe region as they either sailed along them or used roads that

[140] Ibid., pp. 289–307.
[141] Güldenstädt, *Reisen*, I, pp. 65–66.
[142] [Pallas], 'Puteshestvie', pp. 260–61. For a similar phenomenon on the Don, see Gil'denshtedt, 'Dnevnik', p. 202.
[143] Güldenstädt, *Reisen*, I, p. 114.
[144] Lepekhin, 'Zapiski', pp. 325, 352, 392–93, 401.
[145] [Pallas], 'Puteshestvie', pp. 249, 259–61; id., *Nauchnoe nasledie*, p. 72. Güldenstädt presented a similar argument for the development of ravines in the Don valley. *Reisen*, I, p. 76; Gil'denshtedt, 'Dnevnik', p. 184.
[146] V. V. Dokuchaev, 'Ovragi i ikh zhachenie', in id., *Sochineniia*, 9 vols, Moscow and Leningrad, 1949–61, I, pp. 103–11 (first published 1877); id., 'Sposoby obrazovaniia rechnykh dolin Evropeiskoi Rossii', in *Sochineniia*, I, pp. 113–273 (first published in 1878). (Dokuchaev referred to Pallas's work in chapter I of his study.)

followed river valleys. In 1769, Lepekhin was not able to resume his expedition down the Volga for a while 'because of the spring floods'.[147] The floods were caused by melting snow and ice filling the south-flowing rivers. Spring floods did have advantages. Gmelin recorded that the floods made the land on the left, low, bank of the lower Volga very fertile, especially for meadows.[148] The duration of the spring floods varied. In the drought year of 1769, Pallas wrote that the 'Volga has not reached its normal level, and already in mid-May has started to fall'.[149] In the summer of that year, when there was drought, Lepekhin found the Don so low that it was difficult even for small ships to pass sand banks.[150] The expeditionary scientists found examples of smaller rivers and streams drying up altogether in the summer months. Falck noted this as he travelled across the Don Cossack territory and east to Tsaritsyn on the Volga in 1769.[151] Some gullies, such as those observed by Güldenstädt during his journey across the steppes to the north of the Sea of Azov in 1773, were dry for most of the year and contained water only in the spring when the snow and ice melted.[152] Seasonal streams and rivers were most common in the more arid southeast of the steppe region, such as the eastern part of the north Caucasus. Falck noted that the Kuma river, which flows into the Caspian Sea, dis-appeared into sandy hills in the summer.[153] As Güldenstädt made his way

> from the Kuma [river] to the Don [he] noticed that rivers and streams to the left side of the Manych that flow from the northern foothills [of the Caucasus mountains] have flowing water during the cold seasons of the year, but with the exceptions of the Manych and Gegerlik, [. . .] in July and August the [other rivers] largely dry up and have water only near their sources.

Fresh water could be in short supply. The water in the lower reaches of the Gegerlik was 'bitter and undrinkable', because it flowed 'over clay saturated with common salt'.[154]

Thus, the relief of the steppe region seemed alien to most of the expedition leaders, some of whom struggled to come to terms with the flatness that distorted their judgement of distances. The *kurgany* and, in particular, the mountains of the periphery of the region afforded some relief from the monotony. Their studies of the ravines anticipated later

---

[147] Lepekhin, 'Zapiski', p. 300.
[148] Gmelin, *Puteshestvie*, pt 2, p. 100.
[149] [Pallas], *Nauchnoe nasledie*, p. 79.
[150] Lepekhin, 'Zapiski', p. 462.
[151] Fal'k, 'Zapiski', pp. 44–45, 48–50.
[152] Gil'denshtedt, 'Dnevnik', pp. 187, 207, 208, 219, 220.
[153] Fal'k, 'Zapiski', pp. 89, 92
[154] Gil'denshtedt, *Puteshestvie*, p. 307.

research into water erosion in the region. The more attention they paid to the drainage, however, the more aware they became of the shortage of water in some parts of the region and at certain times of the year. This was a problem that would pose a major barrier to the development of arable farming in a region prone to droughts. Plans for irrigation schemes, for the most part, were developed only in the nineteenth century.[155]

The Soil

Most visitors from the time of Herodotus, who noted the 'good deep soil', commented on the fertility of much of the steppe region, which was so vital for arable farming. Gmelin and Güldenstädt both noted the fertility of the black earth they encountered on the steppes in the north of the Don Cossack territory in 1769.[156] As he travelled between the Don and Volga later that year, Falck wrote that there were areas covered with 'good black earth'.[157] Four years later, when he was travelling through the low foothills of the north Caucasus, Güldenstädt noted that 'everywhere [was] covered with fertile black earth'.[158] When he reached the steppes in the vicinity of Stavropol'-on-the-Volga in 1769, Lepekhin wrote that the land was much more fertile than that immediately to the north he had just explored. He attributed this to the fact that the steppes had not been inhabited for as long, and so 'the land is still abounds with the full forces of fertility for growing grain (*khleborodiia*)'.[159] Pallas took a particular interest in the soil. In August 1768, as he travelled through the mid-Volga region in the forest-steppe, he commented on the

> rich black soil so common to the Sura, Wolga, and other rivers, which flow from the east into the Wolga. In all these parts, the happy husbandman has no occasion to manure his grounds, and commonly fallows his land but every third crop. Here are spots where the soil never fails, but, where it is diminished in richness, there is plenty of ground in the less inhabited part, plenty of lay land, which if turned up, produces the finest arable imaginable.[160]

On his second expedition in 1793–94, Pallas again commented on the 'excellent black soil' and 'most fertile soil' in the mid-Volga region and the 'good arable land' in the north Caucasus.[161]

---

[155] For a survey, see S. Kizenkov, 'Oroshenie', *Polnaia entsiklopediia russkogo sel'skogo khoziaistva*, vol. 6, 1902, cols 414–68.
[156] See Gmelin, *Puteshestvie*, pt 1, p. 134; Güldenstädt, *Reisen*, 1, p. 50.
[157] Fal'k, 'Zapiski', p. 50.
[158] Gil'denshtedt, *Puteshestvie po Kavkazu*, p. 292.
[159] Lepekhin, 'Zapiski', p. 230.
[160] Pallas, *Travels through the Southern Provinces*, 2, pp. 43–44.
[161] Ibid., 1, pp. 12–13, 33, 317.

Besides the fertile 'black earth', the accounts of the Academy of Sciences expeditions also noted less fertile soils in parts of the steppe region. In his account of the northern part of the Don Cossack territory, Güldenstädt regularly noted the existence of sandy areas and sandy soil, often in river banks and along roads, but pointed out that the soil was less sandy on the open steppe.[162] As well as the 'good black earth' on the steppes between the Don and Volga, Falck wrote that parts of the surface of the land consisted largely of sand and salty clay mixed with black earth.[163] A number of the expeditions explored the lower Volga and the steppes between the Volga and the Iaik rivers and confirmed these observations.[164] On his way down the Iaik river in the summer of 1769, Pallas reported large areas of salt flats (*solonchaki*).[165] Falck speculated that the reason why the Kuma steppe was sandy and salty, as well as level, was because it was a dried-up sea bed.[166] The sand and salt created problems for the expeditions, and posed potential problems if the sandy areas were to be settled and cultivated. Pallas wrote from Iaitskii Gorodok, in the east of the steppe region on the Iaik river, in July 1769 that sand was drifting to a depth of over a *sazhen'* (about 7 feet). Pallas's journey along roads on sandy soil down the side of the Volga to Astrakhan' was hampered by the 'uninterrupted sandy hills, some of which consisted purely of drifting sand'. The horses got stuck in the sand and the drifts partly covered buildings.[167] Salt was, of course, a valuable resource that was exploited. In the summer of 1769, Lepekhin visited lake Elton on the steppes to the east of the Volga, where salt was produced commercially, and described how it was transported in large quantities, but very slowly, on ox carts to 'inner Russia'.[168]

The leaders of the Academy of Sciences expeditions paid far more attention, however, to the fertility of the black earth that covered a large part of the steppe region. They were concerned to map the distribution of this immensely valuable resource, and to explain its origins. The expeditionary scientists put forward differing theories. Güldenstädt argued that the soil had developed in part as a result of the decomposition of steppe grasses, i.e. that the black earth had its origins in the environmental conditions of the steppes.[169] Little attention was paid to

---

[162] Güldenstädt, *Reisen*, 1, pp. 50, 77, 85, 95, 96, 97, 98.
[163] Fal'k, 'Zapiski', p. 50.
[164] See, for example, Gmelin, *Puteshestvie*, 2, pp. 46–60.
[165] [Pallas], *Nauchnoe nasledie*, p. 89.
[166] Fal'k, 'Zapiski', pp. 92–93.
[167] [Pallas], *Nauchnoe nasledie*, pp. 80, 82; id, 'Puteshestvie', p. 246.
[168] Lepekhin, 'Zapiski', pp. 423–42.
[169] Guldenstadt, *Reisen*, 1, p. 33.

this idea at the time. It could be speculated that this rejection may have reflected a notion that the treelessness of the steppes was something abnormal, and was thus unlikely to have led to the development of such fertile soil. Pallas, writing in the mid-Volga region in the 1790s, asserted the opposing, and at that time dominant, view:

> There is not the least doubt that the aforementioned black vegetable stratum of the soil, which is upwards of two feet thick, originated from the forests that formerly covered these regions. This black earth is likewise found on all the hillocks and open fields [. . .] The traces of the former oak forests are obvious.[170]

Pallas was thus seeking to come to terms with an alien, treeless landscape by seeking evidence for forests in the past.

The debate over the origins of the black earth continued for almost a century. It was only in the latter part of the nineteenth century that Ruprecht[171] and Dokuchaev demonstrated the steppe origins of the black earth. Dokuchaev devised a theory to explain soil formation that took account of all the component parts of the environment in which it was situated: soils were 'the result of the extremely complex inter-action of local climate, plant and animal organisms, the composition and structure of parent rocks, the relief of the locality, [and] finally, the age of the land'.[172] The work of Dokuchaev and colleagues presented the environment of the steppes as a distinct ecosystem.[173] The research into the individual parts of the steppe environment by the Academy of Sciences expeditions had laid a basis for later generations of Russian natural scientists to build on. Dokuchaev and his contemporaries, how-ever, went a stage further. They were prepared to accept the steppe environment on its own terms, and to appreciate its value, rather than tending to see it as a landscape that was somehow incomplete as it was largely devoid of trees. Later, over the nineteenth century, as Christo-pher Ely has argued, Russian landscape painters and writers came to value and appreciate the Russian landscape, including the steppe, rather than seeing it as somehow 'meagre' and inferior to more dramatic landscapes in Western Europe.[174]

---

[170] Pallas, *Travels through the Southern Provinces*, 1, p. 33. See also P. V. Ototskii, 'Pervaia nauchnaia teoriia proiskhozhdeniia chernozema', *Pochvevedenie*, 2, 1900, 4, pp. 325–28.

[171] Ruprekht, *Geo-botanicheskie issledovaniia*.

[172] V. V. Dokuchaev, 'Russkii chernozem', *Izbrannye sochineniia*, 3 vols, Moscow, 1948–49, 1, 'Russkii chernozem', pp. 27, 35–40, 367 (first published in 1883).

[173] For a summary of his ideas written in the wake of the drought and crop failure of 1891–92, see V. V. Dokuchaev, 'Nashi Stepi prezhde i teper'', in *Sochineniia*, 6, pp. 13–102.

[174] See Christopher Ely, *This Meager Nature: Landscape and National Identity in Imperial Russia*, DeKalb, IL, 2002.

Conclusion

The main concern of the leaders of the Academy of Sciences expeditions who travelled across the steppes in 1768–74, and also the two later expeditions, was to describe and catalogue what they encountered, both in the interests of science and of the Russian state which sought to develop the region. This was what they had been instructed to do. Thus, they collected specimens of plants and animals that were not previously known to science. Further, they stressed the prospects for the further development of agriculture on the fertile black earth of much of the region. Gmelin described the steppes as a land which the 'Providential Creator had endowed with fertility' and where there were great prospects for the development of agriculture.[175] Pallas, who returned to the steppes in 1790s, extolled the productivity of the virgin land around Taganrog. He may have been exaggerating, however, when he wrote that the land 'is so fertile that in a recently tilled soil, wheat may be sown without manure during four or five successive years; its crops frequently are from twenty to thirty fold and in good seasons, even thirty-eight grains are obtained from one'.[176] Güldenstädt made the more sober but still high estimate of grain yields of 1:10 on the Don steppes in the early 1770s.[177]

In the view of the expedition leaders, therefore, the steppes were indeed a region ripe for further development. They saw this in terms of European-style agriculture, rather than the nomadic pastoralism of the indigenous population. Thus, they praised the German colonists they encountered. In the autumn of 1769, Gmelin visited the German evangelical brotherhood settlement at Sarepta, which had been founded in 1765, on the Volga just downstream from Tsaritsyn. The German scientists considered the German settlement a 'true adornment of both Tsaritsyn district and the entire Astrakhan´ province'.[178] The nomads, in contrast, were soundly criticized. Pallas considered the Kalmyks to be distinguished by 'their idleness, want of cleanliness and knavery'. They were not entirely bad, however, for 'a love of idleness is common and natural to all nations who lead an unlimited, careless and pastoral life; yet the Kalmucks have less of it, owing to their

[175] Gmelin, *Puteshestvie*, 1, pp. 269–70.
[176] Pallas, *Travels through the Southern Provinces*, 1, pp. 498–99.
[177] Gil´denshtedt, 'Dnevnik', pp. 180–228. Grain yields around 1:10 were sometimes attained in good years, especially on land newly ploughed up, in the late nineteenth and early twentieth centuries. For such high yields in the Don region, see Gosudarstvennyi arkhiv Rostovskoi oblasti (GARO), f. 46, op. 1, d. 3222, l. 50 ob (1894), d. 3440, l. 109 (1909).
[178] Gmelin, *Puteshestvie*, 2, pp. 15–16, 234.

sprightliness'.[179] Besides the 'indolence' of the indigenous inhabitants, the expedition leaders indicated other potential problems in promoting arable farming on the steppes, such as pests and shortages of water. Perhaps the most serious, in their view, was the scarcity of trees, which agricultural setters would need for timber for construction, making agricultural implements and firewood. This scarcity was made worse, moreover, by the wanton destruction of woodland on the steppes, in particular by Russian settlers who did not, it seemed to the mostly foreign or foreign-educated leaders of the expeditions, appreciate their value.

The writings on the steppes by the Academy of Sciences expedition leaders seem to swing between objective, scientific description and subjective travelogues. In both modes, however, they were viewing and moving towards an understanding of the steppe environment through the lens of their homelands, backgrounds, education, culture, experience and personalities. By focusing on what was different about the steppe environment and, therefore, new to European science, the expeditionary scientists were laying the ground work for later Russian scientific research into the steppes as a distinct and integrated ecosystem.[180] They also made contributions to the development of science in general. The prominent Russian historian of science Edouard Kolchinsky has argued that Pallas's work on flora and fauna can be seen as 'the origin of biogeography and ecology'.[181] In so far as the writings of the expedition leaders were travelogues, they were also constructing an image of the steppes as a mirror of their homelands. In the process, they suggested additional binary opposites to Wolff's contrast between a 'civilized' 'Western Europe' and 'uncivilized' 'Eastern Europe'. The expeditionary scientists made further distinctions between forest and steppe (a recurring theme in Russian history and culture), and between arable farming and nomadic pastoralism. Their accounts suggest, moreover, the prospect that once the 'indolent' nomads had been replaced by more industrious German colonists, and by Russian settlers who had learned to respect the natural resources, then the steppes could become 'civilized', Russian, and even European. At the end of his arduous six-year expedition, Pallas returned to St Petersburg in July 1774, 'though with an infirm body, and a hoary head, at the age of 33'. He was, nevertheless, 'full of grateful acknowledgements to Providence,

---

[179] Pallas, *Travels through the Southern Provinces*, 2, pp. 207–08. For his views on the 'Kirguefe' (Kirgiz, i.e. Kazakhs), whom he considered to be lazy as well as thieves and kidnappers, see ibid., pp. 289–324.

[180] On the scientific importance of the expeditions, see Kolchinsky, 'Role', pp. 106–16.

[181] Ibid., p. 111.

who had preserved me to this day, amid the numerous dangers to which I had been exposed'.[182] The German scientist was, therefore, content to be back home in the Russian capital after his adventures in different, alien, and at times threatening environments that had included long journeys across the steppes.

---

[182] Pallas, *Travels through the Southern Provinces*, 4, pp. 330–31. On Pallas's physical state on his return, see Kolchinsky, 'Role', p. 111.

Self and Place in Life-Writings by Late Eighteenth- and Early Nineteenth-Century Russian Noblewomen

WENDY ROSSLYN

NOBLEWOMEN's everyday lives in the 'long' eighteenth century, as lived in Petersburg or away from the imperial centre, have not been extensively investigated.[1] The present article offers readings of three pieces of life-writing which throw light on everyday life, but which also, more importantly, offer noblewomen's reflections on their everyday lives and on its gender dimension. Place is a revealing factor, since as they move from one place to another or identify favourite places they communicate detail of everyday life in the new (or previous) location which is rarely produced by the day-to-day observation of normality. The differences between the familiar lifestyle and the new, or the preferred lifestyle and the rejected, afford the occasion for self-awareness and self-definition. Here I examine their constructions of self in relation to place and the everyday life lived in it, with the aim of examining A. V. Belova's statement about provincial noblewomen of this period:

> Change of 'locus' is not simply movement in space, but a change of the entirety of daily life, including such elements as arrangement of living space, type of occupation, rations and regime of eating, speech practice, fashion in clothing, and also factors influencing this sphere, amongst them climate, social environment, cultural traditions of daily life, the political setting and others.[2]

The three writers are Varvara Bakunina (1773–1840), née Golenishcheva-Kutuzova, wife of M. M. Bakunin (1764–1837), who at the time of writing was colonel of the Vladimir dragoon regiment, posted to Persia;

Wendy Rosslyn is an Emeritus Professor in the Department of Russian and Slavonic Studies at the University of Nottingham.

I am indebted to Sara Dickinson and Emilie Murphy for helpful comments on an earlier version of this article.

[1] See N. L. Pushkareva, *Chastnaia zhizn' russkoi zhenshchiny: nevesta, zhena, liubovnitsa (X–nachalo XIX v.)*, Moscow, 1997; A. V. Belova, 'Povsednevnost' russkoi provintsial'noi dvorianki kontsa XVIII–pervoi poloviny XIX v. (k postanovke problemy)', in *Sotsial'naia istoriia: ezhegodnik 2003*, Moscow, 2003, pp. 269–84.

[2] Ibid., p. 273.

Anastasiia Kolechitskaia (1800–71), née Lykoshina, wife of the then retired colonel P. P. Kolechitskii (b. 1792) who had distinguished himself in action at Borodino[3] and was now living in Smolensk province; and Varvara Sheremeteva (1786–1857), née Almazova, wife of S. V. Sheremetev (1786–1834), who had retired from the Ministry of Foreign Affairs with the rank of collegiate assessor to live on his estate near Moscow. Kolechitskaia and Sheremeteva came from the same extended family network. Kolechitskaia was a cousin of the Decembrist I. D. Iakushkin (1793–1857), whose estate in Smolensk province was, moreover, close by.[4] Iakushkin's mother-in-law Nadezhda Sheremeteva was a cousin of Varvara Sheremeteva.

I choose these memoirs because they recall the noblewomen's travels to the metropolis from the provinces (Sheremeteva to Petersburg and Kolechitskaia to Moscow) and a journey from the capital to the periphery (Bakunina through the far reaches of the empire to Derbent in Persia). In each case change of location prompted reflection on the identity of the self. The memoirs are of various but related genres. Sheremeteva, a first-time visitor to Petersburg in 1825–26, wrote home almost daily to her household (mother, sister-in-law, seven children, and French governess), in French with occasional brief passages in Russian.[5] Many noblewomen of this period, taught by French governesses from early childhood to speak French, and accustomed to using French in the home and at social occasions, were effectively bilingual, although they were often anxious about their ability to write Russian, or indeed to write grammatically correct French. Regular correspondence of this kind was a standard feature of noblewomen's routine. The letters were later translated into Russian by O. G. Sheremeteva and assembled into a diary.[6] Kolechitskaia kept a diary, intended for her daughter Anna (1818–76), over the period 1800–40. Here I discuss the entries for 1800–26, much of which she rewrote in the 1850s.[7] The entries are rather sporadic, mostly in Russian but with some passages in French, and incorporate retrospective narratives about her earlier life:

[3] E. E. Liamina and E. E. Pasternak, 'A. I. Kolechitskaia, "Moi zapiski ot 1820-go goda"', in A. I. Reitblat (ed.), *Litsa. Biograficheskii al'manakh*, St Petersburg, 1995, pp. 277–90 (p. 284).
   [4] Ibid., pp. 289–90.
   [5] One passage in Russian reads: 'I do not know why I keep on using French [*iz"iasniaius' na frantsuzskom dialekte*], I write very badly and would you believe, I sometimes stop and do not know how to write' (ibid., p. 26).
   [6] *Dnevnik Varvary Petrovny Sheremetevoi urozhdennoi Almazovoi, 1825–1826 gg.: iz arkhiva B. S. Sheremeteva*, Moscow, 1916.
   [7] A. I. Kolechitskaia, 'Moi zapiski ot 1820-go goda', in *Litsa*, pp. 291–341. Kolechitskaia's diary is discussed by Irina Savkina in her *'Pishu sebia ...': avtodokumental'nye zhenskie teksty v russkoi literature pervoi poloviny XIX veka*, Tampere, 2001, pp. 121–34.

I had the thought that many years of my life had passed and there were no notes to remind me about past events and impressions, I regret not keeping a diary from my earliest years: how many pleasant events, how many lessons taught me by experience have been blotted out from my memory or appear like unclear dreams. [. . .] I will make notes; it will be interesting to reread and to check up on my thoughts and deeds; and when I am dead these pages will, I know, be dear to my Annichka. (p. 291)

Bakunina's account of her travels in 1796, written in French, is in chronological order, which would suggest that it was based on day-to-day diary entries.[8] She wrote it after her return ('before even the tiniest details are blotted out of my memory', p. 344) for her sister:

I dedicate this account to you, my kind sister; out of friendship towards me you will read it with sympathy, and with your customary indulgence you will forgive me the failings of style and exposition. You are no greater an expert on politics than I am, and so you will not be critical of me when I speak about it or about war and military affairs. (p. 344)

Even though these were private communications intended only for the family, these genres, because they required the presentation of the self, potentially infringed the prescription for female modesty and required declarations to the contrary.[9]

I look here at constructions of the self, when necessary in relation to the addressees. The genres of the diary, autobiographical fragment, and letter involve the construction within the text of an image of the self. As Shari Benstock writes,

If the autobiographical moment prepares for a meeting of 'writing' and 'selfhood', a coming together of method and subject matter, this destiny [. . .] is always deferred. [. . .] autobiography reveals the impossibility of its own dream: what begins on the presumption of self-knowledge ends in the creation of a fiction that covers over the premises of its construction [. . .] the 'coincidence' of artist and model is an illusion.[10]

Moreover, these genres are not 'a confession to the self with only the self as auditor'.[11] The diaries and letters are private domestic documents directed to a female addressee or community, and the created self is oriented towards this audience.

[8] 'Persidskii pokhod v 1796 godu', translated by V. V. Timoshchuk, *Russkaia starina*, 53, 1887, pp. 343–74. Extracts in English translation are published in Robin Bisha, Jehanne M. Gheith, Christine Holden and William G. Wagner (comps), *Russian Women, 1698–1917: Experience and Expression: An Anthology of Sources*, Bloomington and Indianapolis, 2002, pp. 216–20. Page references to all the autobiographies are given in the text.
[9] On letters, see Anna Belova, 'Women's Letters and Russian Noble Culture of the Late 18th and Early 19th Centuries', in Wendy Rosslyn (ed.), *Women and Gender in 18th-Century Russia*, Aldershot and Burlington, VT, 2003, pp. 147–61.
[10] Shari Benstock, 'Authorizing the Autobiographical', in Shari Benstock (ed.), *The Private Self: Theory and Practice of Women's Autobiographical Writings*, Chapel Hill, NC and London, 1988, pp. 10–33, 10–11.
[11] Felicity A. Nussbaum, 'Toward Conceptualizing Diary', in James Olney (ed.), *Studies in Autobiography*, Oxford, 1988, pp. 128–40, 135.

The self is often contradictory, as is not uncommon in diary-writing: 'in the private writing of diary and journal, whole, coherent, and consistent selves did not have to be molded from the incoherence of a daily experience'.[12] Felicity Nussbaum points out that whereas auto-biography is often assumed to present a coherent self developing over time, the diary often allows contradictions to exist unreconciled. As a discontinuous recording of the thoughts, feelings and activities of the writer, it often does not assign meaning or come to conclusions.[13] Even an autobiographical narrative within diary does not necessarily 'attempt narrative closure or the formulation of a fixed or finished character'.[14]

The self manifests contradictions between individual identity and group identity, i.e. definition as woman, between 'the self as culturally defined and the self as different from cultural prescription'.[15] The diary offers an 'escape from dominant formulations of individuality', and private space in which to produce 'gendered subjectivity that did not fit established paradigms'.[16] The individual translates cultural defini-tions of gender into text.[17] There are both definitions to which she accommodates as well as those which she resists.[18] The self adopts various positionings in text and culture (nurturer, protegée) and shows her thoughts and actions in relation to them. Self-fashioning is located in a particular cultural context. As Nussbaum expresses it, 'in diary and journal, linguistic constructs of the self [...] are produced through social, historical, and cultural factors; and the "self" both positions itself in the discourses available to it, and is produced by them'.[19] Here the dearth of published textual models for women's diaries, especially in Russian, should be noted.[20]

---

[12] Felicity A. Nussbaum, 'Eighteenth-Century Women's Autobiographical Commonplaces', in *The Private Self*, p. 154.
[13] Nussbaum, 'Toward Conceptualizing Diary', pp. 130, 136.
[14] Nussbaum, 'Eighteenth-Century Women's Autobiographical Commonplaces', p. 164.
[15] Susan Stanford Friedman, 'Women's Autobiographical Selves: Theory and Practice', in *The Private Self*, pp. 34–62, 39.
[16] Nussbaum, 'Eighteenth-Century Women's Autobiographical Commonplaces', p. 154.
[17] Ibid., p. 149.
[18] Ibid., p. 154.
[19] Nussbaum, 'Toward Conceptualizing Diary', p. 129.
[20] On the earliest known women's diaries written in French, see E. Gretchanaia, 'Les écrits autobiographiques des femmes russes du 18e siècle rédigés en français', *Dix-huitième siècle*, 36, 2004, pp. 131–54. On the later diaries in French (though not on those discussed here), see Elena Gretchanaïa and Catherine Viollet, 'Journaux russes francophones du XIXe siècle: espaces littéraires', *La Licorne, revue de langue et littérature française*, 72, 2005, pp. 89–101; Eléna Gretchanaïa, 'Mémoires et journaux intimes féminins rédigés en français dans le premier quart du XIXe siècle: aspects religieux et linguistiques', *Les rencontres de l'Institut européen Est-Ouest. Premières recontres* <http://russie-europe.ens-lsh.fr/IMG/pdf/gretchanaia.pdf> [accessed 4 February 2009]. On diaries of this period, including women's diaries, see K. V'olle and E. P. Grechanaia, 'Dnevnik v Rossii v kontse XVIII-pervoi polo-viny XIX v. kak avtobiograficheskoe prostranstvo', *Izvestiia Akademii Nauk. Seriia literatury i iazyka*, 61, 2002, 3, pp. 18–36. On early women's autobiographies, see Savkina, chapter 2.

I discuss the three texts not in chronological order — indeed, the earliest to be written is discussed last — but following the rising curve of challenge to cultural constructions of femininity.

Varvara Sheremeteva: resistance and accommodation to social codes

Sheremeteva left the family's country estate near Moscow with her husband for the capital to further a legal case of her mother's which had to be brought to the attention of Alexander I via intermediaries, and to place their not-very-talented nephew in state service. As the negotiations coincided with the death of Alexander I and the Decembrist uprising, officialdom was first in paralysis and then in transition to the arrangements of the new reign, and the visit was extended, lasting from October 1825 to February 1826. It is not clear from the letters why Sheremeteva accompanied her husband, or who handled the negotiations, especially as setting up a Petersburg home was an expense which caused them anxiety. The further achievements of the visit, namely advantageous contacts for their children, and Sheremeteva's pleasure in witnessing high society at first hand, may have warranted her journey.

For Sheremeteva Petersburg was the seat of patronage, where she and her husband sought influential assistance for family members. Secondly, Petersburg was home to more distant relatives, with whom they made contact on arrival, and who provided their entrée into the social life of the capital, moreover at the highest level. Her husband's relative V. S. Sheremetev (1752–1831), governor of Volhynia, had, Sheremeteva observed, an income of 300,000 roubles (p. 101). His daughter Iuliia was a lady-in-waiting (p. 83), and the family had a glittering social circle — 'All Petersburg visits them, starting with the first minister and ending with the last senator' (p. 93). The ball they gave in 1825 was attended by Grand Duke Nicholas, who became tsar that year (p. 88). This branch of the Sheremetev family regularly invited Varvara to their home and the social events they hosted. Another relative was the immensely wealthy philanthropist Count D. N. Sheremetev (1803–71), son of Count N. P. Sheremetev and the actress Praskov'ia Kovaleva-Zhemchugova. Sheremeteva's cousin A. N. Potapov (1772–1847) was from December 1825 Adjutant-General to Nicholas I. Potapov both assisted Sheremeteva with the practicalities of settling into their Petersburg home and later served as an intermediary for messages to and from some of the arrested conspirators. Thanks largely to these relatives and their circles, Sheremeteva was able to discover the Petersburg of sophisticated social entertainments such as the ballet and the high-society ball. She perceived it as a series of social settings with defined requirements for dress and behaviour;[21] thus her Petersburg was also both a prescriptive house of fashion and an emporium offering the latest fashions and refined wares unavailable in the provinces.

Sheremeteva's letters communicate a great deal of information about a noblewoman's daily life in St Petersburg. She records the process of looking for a permanent apartment. Those she looks at are, to her embarrassment, too expensive even at a meagre 200–300 roubles a year, whereas, she discovers, an acquaintance pays 1,500 (p. 28). She settles for rooms in a building with a fine entrance on the corner of Bol´shaia Morskaia and Nevskii, but shared with ten or more families and on the second floor. Potapov helps negotiate with the landlord and undertakes to have the dirty walls whitewashed and the curtains washed (p. 25). Sheremeteva then has to buy crockery, samovar and copper saucepans, (pp. 21, 26), and hire carriage and horses (p. 24). She has three servants — cook, coachman and errand-boy — and Potapov provides a man to clean and another to open the door (p. 27). St Petersburg requires greater security than the countryside: 'here all the first rooms [in] all apartments are locked with a key, although there is a little bell both here and at home, whoever arrives rings it and a man has to sit there constantly' (p. 27). The household is modest. When the Sheremetevs (twenty guests including the Count) insist on coming to lunch she has to borrow furniture from Potapov and the food has to be cooked in his kitchen as hers is very small (pp. 120–21).

She describes the new daily routine. They rise at eight, at which time the rooms are ventilated to let out the smoke from the chimney (p. 29), after which she writes letters every morning for three hours from 9 or 10 unless prevented (p. 85), then pays calls from 2 until lunch: 'We lunched at 4 o'clock, for me this is dreadful, but in fact it is impossible to do otherwise than follow the customs. All morning visits begin only after 2 o'clock' (p. 26). Evenings 'finish extraordinarily late' (p. 126).

She notes in detail the cost of living, not only rent but also food prices: these are comparable to those in Moscow but beef is 4 kopecks per funt dearer, and wine, coffee, veal, game, fish, vegetables, eggs and oil are cheaper. The cost of feeding servants on cabbage soup and kasha is 30 kopecks per head per day (pp. 26, 31).

Sheremeteva also observes social customs: 'here English is the common language, one could say, no sooner is a child born than he

---

[21] On the link between changing dress codes and new constructions of femininity in the eighteenth century, see Lindsey Hughes, 'From Caftans into Corsets: The Sartorial Transformation of Women during the Reign of Peter the Great', in Peter Barta (ed.), *Gender and Sexuality in Russian Civilisation*, London, 2001, pp. 17–32, and her *Russia in the Age of Peter the Great*, New Haven, CT and London, 1998, pp. 280–88.

has an Englishwoman [for a nanny]' (p. 87); mourning for Alexander
I results in red sealing wax being withdrawn from sale for a whole year
to be replaced with black (p. 117); flood warnings are issued by lighting
the street lights during the night and running up white or red flags in
daytime (p. 53). In the French quadrille they do different steps from
those done in Moscow (p. 89). She notes that in this society where
appearances matter wealth is more important than birth:

> He [Telegin] is married to a very rich woman, they have just returned from
> abroad, as people say here they are *de la societé grise*, but all the same, they
> say he organizes wonderful festivities, everyone wants to go. (p. 108)

The customs of which she is most observant are those relating to
dress: 'Here you cannot move an inch without thinking about your
dress [*zanimat'sia tualetom*]' (p. 36). She comments on clothing for church
(p. 36) and for the theatre (p. 60), on the dress codes for young and
older women (pp. 48, 54, 60), on the lightness of the outdoor clothing
worn in October (p. 30), on the habit of changing fur coats several
times in the season (p. 101).

Sheremeteva records almost obsessively the adaptation of her clothing to her new circumstances, a painful process since she is endlessly
anxious about the family's inadequate finances. The letters record a
cyclical process by which she perceives a convention of the Petersburg
lifestyle, often related to dress for particular occasions, resists it for fear
of excessive expenditure, and then reconciles herself with perceived
necessity. On her first day in the city she stands by her Moscow
customs:

> We set off: imagine my dress: the brown hat which I wore [when we] went
> to Iaroslavl' and the wadded coat. The weather was fine and a mass of
> people and so decked out in finery that I was cheerful looking at them.
> I ordered myself a coat made from *drap de dames*, since everyone wears
> it here, with two plain collars with *gros de Naples* edging in Flemish taffeta
> and very thickly quilted, instead of a fur coat. This costs 135 roub., I think
> this is not dear; the tailor says to me — what colour dark red or dark
> brown; they only wear those two, I did not agree to either but chose a dark
> olive, the tailor burst out laughing — 'I've never made that [colour] up,'
> he said. Fedin´ka tried to persuade me to have a fashionable one made,
> but I stayed with the olive; then we went round the shops, the hats are very
> hideous *à la bergère* just as in Moscow, the sides are turned up so your head
> is exposed above the ears and so I ordered one of my sort, although the
> milliner was surprised, that will cost 35 roub. I will also have a dark *gros de
> Naples* made to go around in in the mornings and a white silk lace cap will
> be a necessity, and to my great regret this will cost 70 roub. I have not yet
> bought it and then that will be all that concerns my toilette, I will not do
> any more. (p. 19)

But then she becomes aware that her lack of conformity is a
constraint. She does not go for a walk with Potapov because she has

no hat, or to mass because she has no cape (pp. 22, 29). New social settings require new clothing: 'Now I need a hat for the theatre and another cap, quite elegant; because I soon have to start paying calls again, and there is also the soirée at Princess Golitsyna's and the Kikins' (p. 61). The cycle is then repeated.

Sheremeteva constructs the self by drawing the contrast with her provincial self. On arrival in Petersburg she refers to herself as a country woman [derevenskaia zhitel'nitsa] (p. 53). The self belonging to the country estate, since it is well known to the addressees, is not sketched as such. However, we know that Sheremetev had several estates and 1380 peasants.[22] The family lived on the estate at Mikhailovskoe, not far from Moscow, in relatively modest style, and had to engage in agriculture to boost income. Although they had a house in Moscow they were often too impecunious to spend the winter there.[23] Sheremeteva sends advice on looking after the estate fruit trees (p. 6). She also refers to the fact that her coat was home-made by one of the servants (p. 30), and mentions false ringlets borrowed from the French governess, an émigrée countess (pp. 65, 30). Some impression of the furnishings can be gathered from the fact that she refers to armchairs with torn upholstery (p. 179) and purchases two mattresses and three small leather cushions to send home as they have no beds (p. 9).

The temporary move to St Petersburg occasioned the most radical transformation, at least of externals. As Belova asserts, change of place entailed an entirely new everyday life, down to the details of domestic arrangements, clothing and social customs. Sheremeteva's St Petersburg self observes and learns social codes:

this morning we rose at 8 o'clock; we became accustomed to this on the way here (p. 29)

I now have much to study [mnogo zaniatii] because I am learning how to conduct myself in high society. Thank God, I am succeeding, and believe me, I find myself there just as if I had never left. (p. 51)

(Her father, P. N. Almazov was marshal of nobility in Moscow province from 1791 to 1794 and owned an enormous area of land in urban Moscow; it seems likely that he lived well and belonged to the higher circles of society.)[24] Sheremeteva then accommodates herself to the

---

[22] See Vserossiiskoe Genealogicheskoe Dvero: <http://www.vgd.ru/SH/shermetv.htm> [accessed 6 February 2009].

[23] N. I. Bednazhevskaia, O. I. Gaidamak and A. V. Kurilenko, 'Sel'tso Troitskoe — gorod Troitsk. Istoricheskie ocherki' <http://www.troitsk.ru/> [accessed 14 January 2009].

[24] Vserossiiskoe Genealogicheskoe Dvero: <http://www.vgd.ru/A/almazov.htm> [accessed 14 January 2009].

social codes, apparently continuing a process learned from moves between Moscow and the country estate.

The newly-adopted positioning is as protégée, the poor relative deserving of condescension from high society. Sheremeteva identifies the appropriately modest dress:

> I go out every day in one and the same costume, a black dress and my Moscow lace cap with white ribbons, and for particular show in another black dress and the white silk lace cap. (p. 61)
>
> I always wear black. They asked me not to, but I said directly that I cannot do otherwise because here it is the cheapest thing and then they agreed that I was right [. . .] I think that in part the fact that we do not try to live above our means disposes people to us favourably. (p. 72)

The attire is idiosyncratic, to suit her anomalous situation as someone who lays no claim to integration into high society but must function in it, marginalized and mindful of her provincial origin: 'it is necessary to be in good style [*khoroshego tona*], or in one's own, as I try to be' (p. 98). The behaviour entailed by the protegée position is to be useful in the household of her grand Sheremetev hosts. She provides the musical accompaniment for singing and dancing (pp. 34, 55: 'I was useful to society') and accompanies Iuliia on visits to the theatre (pp. 43, 60, 62). Rejecting the hosts' humiliating assumption that she will lunch with them every day, she promises to visit often in the evenings with her work and make useful items for members of the family (p. 23). Another form of appropriate behaviour is financial resourcefulness. She economizes: she asks Potapov to send off her letters to save the 4 roubles postage (p. 22), and buys false ringlets so that they can be taken away overnight for curling, thus minimizing the cost of hairdressing (p. 72). She makes over old items: 'I called into the fashion shop which is making hats for me; I took my lace cap, which had yellow ribbons; she attached white gauze ones, very elegant, and charged me 4 roubles, but after all she used 4 arshins of ribbon' (p. 23). She makes do: a cap with no flowers will be right for the theatre and, with the addition of flowers, for a grand soirée (p. 62). She borrows: 'I will ask mme Martynova for a white silk lace scarf, this does not embarrass me at all, on the contrary I thank God that there are people who show us such friendship. She told me that everything she has is at my disposal; I will make use of this' (p. 30). She shops around for a better price (p. 44), and even resorts to inspecting all the hats and caps in the best shops before refusing them all and instead buying the materials to have imitations made at half the price (p. 62).

A further positioning emerges from the coincidence of Sheremeteva's stay in St Petersburg and the Decembrist uprising. Mourning for Alexander I precluded social entertainments and thus curtailed Sheremeteva's position as protégée. But her relationship to Potapov,

who in December 1825 became a member of the commission appointed to investigate the offences of the Decembrists, gave her a more
powerful and less marginal position as dispenser of patronage, at
least by proxy. Sheremeteva became an intermediary for those sympathizers who wished to pass letters to the prisoners (notably her cousin
Nadezhda Sheremeteva, whose daughters were married to the conspirators I. D. Iakushkin and M. N. Murav´ev) (pp. 180, 185). Unlike
Kolechitskaia, Sheremeteva was hostile to the Decembrists — 'What
monsters, and what an infernal scheme! All their great plans are nothing but the desire to rob others and take all they can' (p. 161) — her
relationship to Potapov probably precluding other views, but she was
horrified by the appalling situation of her cousin and of the latter's
daughters, who were both pregnant (p. 175).

   In relation to the female community at Mikhailovskoe, the recipients
of her letters, Sheremeteva positioned herself as mediator of metropolitan culture. She informs her eldest daughter about the fashions
worn by young women (p. 50), sends her the duets played at the
Sheremetevs' (p. 33), sends presents in the form of fashionable ribbons
('now they only wear the kind I am sending', p. 98), passes on the
details of an effective medical cure (pp. 77–78), dispatches newspapers
with reports of the uprising (pp. 135, 138, 162, 170), reassures an
enquirer that her son was not caught up in the revolt (p. 152), and
responds to requests from home for special items, such as Bristol paper
made in England (p. 92). She keeps the household informed day by
day about the death of Alexander I, the uprising and its aftermath.
The enormous detail in the letters allows the family to experience St
Petersburg by proxy,[25] and to benefit from knowledge of the capital
superior to that in their neighbourhood.

   In her letters, Sheremeteva relayed to Mikhailovskoe the constructions of self occasioned by St Petersburg. But in depicting herself in her
new surroundings she became aware of the contradiction between the
new construct and her provincial self. Sheremeteva reads the letters in
which her children tell her of their 'little errors', and responds (p. 43).
But, viewing her new lifestyle from the position of her addressees, she
becomes aware that her new lifestyle seems worldly, even immoral,
and is a poor example. Looking at the morality of her behaviour she
records pangs of conscience about her retail espionage (p. 62), confesses that the ball is not at all a necessity (p. 85), and she is 'ashamed'
that she could not help an acquaintance who asks her for money,
because she has spent so much on clothes (p. 86), being so keen to take

[25] It is curious to note that Sheremeteva's oldest daughter Anna (1810–49) eventually
became the wife of Count D. N. Sheremetev. Her mother's role in the match, if any, is not
known.

up invitations to balls to be attended by members of the imperial
family, that she splashed out on a dress in white crêpe with white lace,
and a white toque with white marabou feathers (p. 72). She attempts
to reconcile the contradictions and justify her behaviour by persuading
her child addressees that her interest in high society is not for her own
pleasure but for their good (p. 41), and that they might benefit from
these contacts, though they should remember that patronage is not to
be relied upon and they must apply their own efforts (p. 64). With some
ingenuity she glosses her worldliness as maternal self-sacrifice:

> God preserve you, dear children, I am also working for you, although work
> for this world will not give us happiness for life eternal, but each has to go
> his own way according to God's will, and the circumstances in which I find
> myself are not at all to my taste and are even very exhausting; but when I
> think that papa and I will make your path less difficult by exerting ourselves
> a little I am happy and I thank God. (pp. 43–44)

When it comes to matters less delicate than morals, notably the French
language, she resorts baldly to the principle of 'do as I say, not as I
do': 'Dear Aniuta [. . .] do not be embarrassed at my bad style and
the spelling mistakes I make, may this teach you, dear friend, to pay
attention to what you are learning' (p. 73).

As procreator, nurturer, moral counsellor, organizer of the household,
careful manager of the domestic economy, enthusiastic participant in
social occasions and alert follower of fashion, Sheremeteva conforms to
contemporary assumptions about essential female roles and it is therefore not surprising that she makes no verbal comment on cultural constructions of femininity. Her desire to conform to social prescriptions is
expressed through her insistence on appropriate dress.

Sheremeteva's new selves were the direct result of her change of
location. They largely related to externals such as dress, and social
codes. For Sheremeteva the contrast between the provinces and the
top social echelon of the capital was very stark,[26] and transition from
the one to the other required radical redefinitions of self. Return to
the provinces meant that her most ordinary St Petersburg dress for
receiving calls at home would henceforth be her best for high days and
holidays (p. 99).

Anastasiia Kolechitskaia: asssertion of spirituality and family values

Like Sheremeteva, Kolechitskaia was a provincial noblewoman of
limited means. Although in her diary she records pilgrimages to holy

---

[26] On the distinction as it applied to noblewomen, see A. V. Belova, 'Oppozitsiia
"stolitsa — provintsiia" kak element kul´turnogo krugozora russkoi dvorianki', in I. G.
Seregina and N. V. Sereda (eds), *Ekonomika, upravlenie, demografiia gorodov evropeiskoi Rossii
XV–XVIII vekov*, Tver´, 1999, pp. 169–76.

places in her childhood and a visit to Moscow after her marriage (in fact, the visits were two, in 1821 and 1822), she lived in Smolensk province and only rarely travelled outside. Her construction of self in the diary is in relation to the provinces rather than to Petersburg. The Petersburg to which Sheremeteva accommodated herself more or less willingly, with its fashions, sophistication and amusements, was precisely what Anastasiia Kolechitskaia rejected, drawing upon Sentimentalist rhetoric to construct a self which is tranquil, quiet, close to nature, introspective, morally aware and bookish:

> The life of the Moravian Brethren was one of the pleasantest dreams of my youth; I felt a passionate love for the charm of a life full of quiet occupations; this manifest inclination for calm, and a certain inborn laziness, were no doubt the reason for my dislike of entertainments, noisy pleasures, in a word the high-society life of which many dream so much. I always preferred the pleasures of the mind; reading, learning, the testing of my mental and moral powers were from my earliest youth an endless source of pleasure. (pp. 312, 1825)

When her husband went to St Petersburg on family business in October 1826 she, unlike Sheremeteva, did not accompany him (p. 319).

However, Kolechitskaia's attitude to St Petersburg life was no less contradictory than Sheremeteva's. St Petersburg also represented for her a desirable life which might have been. She recounts that her husband might have had a successful career in state service — he had been personally acquainted with Alexander I between 1806 and 1811 while serving in the guards, and Alexander spoke with him when passing through Smolensk province on his way to Taganrog (p. 310). Kolechitskii was also the beneficiary of kindness from Alexander's brother Konstantin, who might have succeeded to the throne (p. 315). Kolechitskii retired from state service for health reasons, but lack of means would have prevented him from maintaining himself and his family in Petersburg had he continued; his wife regrets that he was unable to remain in service and rise to high rank and wealth like his colleagues (p. 310). Though a continued life in Petersburg as the wife of a highly-placed official would hardly have been conducive to Kolechitskaia's ideal of rural solitude, the family now had debts, resulting from the costs of state service, the death of peasants as a result of the 1812 invasion, medical expenses and the cost of governesses (p. 315).

The diary offers several constructions of self, nearly all of which are related to locations in Smolensk province, namely the family estates, estates of neighbours and relatives and the district town. The primary construction is of herself as daughter and mother, receiving and, in turn, communicating moral education [*vospitanie*]. The diary contains autobiographical fragments in which Kolechitskaia reflects on her formation by her mother and constructs former selves. Again in Sentimentalist vein, she shows herself at the age of seven or eight in mother-daughter dyad on her father's estate of Kazulino, coming to love learning and quiet domesticity:

> My mother gave us all the lessons and I have the pleasantest recollections of the hours when she sat at her bureau and made notes and I studied next to her; my exceptional love of learning began at this happy time and was developed by the example of all our family, whose life was domestic and industrious. Guests visited us but we [children] rarely appeared in their company and this way of life, so correct and appropriate to the strict upbringing that we were given, led to my preferring serious occupations to all worldly pleasures. (pp. 321, 1826)

The picture of herself she constructs as a married woman and mother at her husband's estate of Shchelkanovo is primarily as educator. She describes her daughter's education, which she understands not as mastery of social accomplishments but as religious education and 'knowledge and abilities which will aid her in all eventualities' (p. 315), as the main aim of her life (p. 292), and to depict herself draws on the image of her mother, taking notes and concerning herself with lessons:

> now I have many occupations, apart from the estate, which I have to manage as I can [...] but I also make notes out of all the books on education that I can get. (p. 292)[27]

A prime characteristic of her constructed self is love of reading and imaginative participation in books. She shows herself still at Kazulino, aged eleven, in studious solitude, reading avidly into the night and making notes, in her favourite place:

> How I loved it, this room, it was simple and modest, a bed, a few chairs, a bookcase, the keys of which were handed to me, and a window looking out on to the main road and the graveyard round the old church; how many sweet hours I spent next to this window on moonlit nights, looking at the transitoriness of life and also dreaming about life and about what lends it such charm. I was so pleased with my life of the mind that I did not dream of any amusements. (p. 323)

A year later in 1812 the women and children of the family were forced to leave Kazulino as Napoleon's Grande Armée approached Smolensk. Kolechitskaia's reading moulds her imagined future self:

> we imagined ourselves the little emigrés in Mme de Genlis' splendid novel and I dreamed, in the event of our ruination, of earning my living and supporting the family; in my inexperience I pictured the noble and dangerous actions that I would do. (p. 324)

---

[27] Kolechitskaia sold crops and kept accounts down to the smallest details (see Liamina and Pasternak, p. 285).

Just before her marriage in 1817 Kolechitskaia depicts herself at Kazulino, which survived undamaged, reading:

> the place which I loved particularly in the last year before my marriage [...] is like a little island at the very end of the garden, entirely isolated, but from it there is a view of the house, two churches surrounded by trees, the main road and the mill. In this refuge, with Zimmerman's book [on solitude] in my hands, I loved to savour the solitude which he describes with such charm. The waves on the lake, splashing at my feet, lulled me into dreams; here the dearest plans of my life, the most beautiful day-dreams, came into being. (p. 319)

The prominence of the reading self points to the construction of the self on literary models, primarily of a Sentimentalist type. Indeed, she asserts that the very desire to keep a diary was inspired in her by Richardson's *Clarissa* (p. 291).

The self devoted to the quiet cultivation of the life of the mind in rural solitude, moulded by Zimmerman and other literary texts — what may be termed the aspirational self — is in radical contradiction to the actual dutiful self. Kolechitskaia's constructions of herself as wife are as social organizer in relation to her husband's service obligations, to the extended family, and to neighbours. These constructions too are firmly located in Smolensk province. When Kolechitskii is elected marshal of nobility in 1822 they move to Krasnoi, the district centre. The diary gives a vivid picture of Kolechitskaia as marshal's spouse sharing the obligations of the post:

> ... not one of us has a quiet corner in the only apartment which I could find, and where the landlady only gave us four rooms and one porch — an extremely inconvenient thing, as poor noblemen present themselves almost every day with petitions for the marshal; our bedroom next to the entrance hall is so small that it is impossible to put up a bed and we sleep on the floor; I had to section off one window in the large room and made a room there for Hamaid [the French nanny] and my two girls and my sister Liza, who has come to visit; this leaves the sitting room where I have to receive visitors and be ready at any time — and on top of this the pleasantness of one exit! Apart from that it is impossible to get anything in Krasnoi except bread [*kalachi*] and I have to send 16 versts to Liady for meat, and to bring everything needed for the table 50 versts from Shchelkanovo; and always have lunch ready for those coming on business from the villages, and be ready to entertain Governor-General Prince Khovanskii when he is en route from Vitebsk to Smolensk. The only society in the town is old judge Engel'gardt and town governor Zakh. Vl. Shevandin, a decent young man, and our neighbours, the old Kraevskii ladies, whom Pierre took me to meet. (p. 302)

> We had to entertain the whole district, people constantly came to see my husband in the country on business and to prove their attachment to him; there were 75 and up to 100 people at festivals. Apart from that Governor-General Khovanskii [...] even came to lunch when we were in the country (p. 315).

The other constructions of self as wife are in relation to the extended family and to neighbours. Indeed, neighbours living close to the Kazulino estate and relatives were often one and the same.[28] In the diary she gives extensive surveys of these networks, with the intention of mapping them for her daughter (pp. 303–07). The intention seems to be to aid the latter in understanding the kin structure, and in maintaining the family ties with visits and celebrations. Kolechitskaia describes four households of neighbours with comments on twenty-five individuals and thirteen households of relatives, some forty individuals, headed by brothers, sisters, uncles, aunts and cousins — 'the smallest segment of our relatives' (p. 306) — together with the kind of entertainments to be expected and distances to be travelled. For example:

> Potemkino, the home of the Baraduliches, is seven versts from us, and there there is dear old lady baroness Slippenbakh, née countess Minikh, the mother of the lady of the house Mar´ia Anton., a beautiful elegant woman married to the deaf but very kind Vas. Iakov. Baradulich; his sister Elis. Iakov. is married to Pierre's older brother Iakov Petr. — Old Mar´ia Serg. is a passionate admirer of flowers and as soon as she meets Petr P. they go straight off to the garden, whatever the heat. Her elder son Konst. Ant. is in the Preobrazhenskii regiment with my brother Aleksandr. (p. 304)

One nameday celebration gathers together about one hundred guests at Shchelkanovo, of whom almost fifty spend the night, accommodated not only in the house but in the carriage shed and a marquee (p. 303). The obligations of visits to and from family and neighbours, often over large distances and several days, sometimes travelling with crockery, bedding and food (p. 304), run entirely counter to the desire for solitude and Kolechitskaia registers the contradiction between the positioning as guardian of kin relationships and the positioning as educator, regretting the waste of time needed at home for educating her daughter and her own learning (p. 305).

Kolechitskaia not only positions herself in relation to clan and neighbourhood but also presents herself chronologically in relation to family tradition. She conforms reluctantly to her husband's family tradition and custom — 'in the numerous Kolechitskii clan they observe strictly all the ancient obligations and obligatory visits on certain days in spite of distances sometimes greater than one hundred versts, and those living close by are visited as often as possible' (p. 305). She perpetuates her own family's rejection of worldliness and lack of concern for dress and appearance (pp. 293, 322) and its concern for the moral education

---

[28] Ibid., p. 279.

of children. But she does not follow her mother's lifestyle. Symbolically, the parental house at Kazulino is divided so that in one wing her
mother, Miropiia Lykoshina, can pursue her pious devotions and
household affairs, abstain from meat, and follow her own timetable for
rest and sleep, joining her children and grandchildren gathered in the
main house for coffee, tea, evening conversation and listening to 'something interesting and acceptable to her ears from our secular readings'
(p. 301).

Kolechitskaia records travel outside Smolensk province, but these
were not journeys for pleasure. As a child she was taken by her pious
mother on devotional visits to monasteries in Kiev, Tikhvin and
Moscow (pp. 292, 293). As an adult she also spent several months in
Moscow with her husband and daughter being treated for a depressive
illness after childbirth which the local doctor had been unable to cure
(p. 296). Whilst there she looked for a French nanny and a little French
girl to live with them as companion to her daughter (pp. 299–300). In
Moscow they stayed at first in the home of a priest and socialized with
members of both sides of the extended family — she names aunts,
cousins, her mother's cousin, more than ten in all (pp. 298–99) — presenting the city as an extension of her life in the provinces. Unlike
Sheremeteva, who adapts herself to the city, Kolechitskaia seeks out in
Moscow what she values at home.

The constructions of self which are not place-related are her spiritual and intellectual selves. Kolechitskaia's ideal is a soul which holds
firm to the eternal and carries out its duty (p. 301). The ideal is unaffected by such transitory factors as place. She writes with awe and
admiration of her neighbour Elizaveta Pestel'. The latter's husband, I.
B. Pestel', had been dismissed from his post as Governor-General of
Siberia for maladministration in 1822, after which they settled on her
estate in Smolensk province where they lived in very constrained circumstances on a small annual income, from which he repaid debts.[29]
Nourished by proper moral education and high culture, she is able to
cope with the fall in status and exclusion from Petersburg, adapting to
rural life and pursuing her duty:

> Mme Pestel', née Krok, is a woman of suprising intelligence, who has
> knowledge of which few women can boast. She possesses *bon ton* to the
> highest degree and the art of conducting unusually pleasant conversation,
> having spent part of her life at court, in Dresden, Paris and Italy; is it
> surprising that in her company you find so much pleasure and find out
> so much that is new. But what I value in her more than anything is her
> steadfastness, that courage thanks to which she finds in herself the source

[29] *Biografiia ru: biograficheskaia entsiklopediia*: <http://www.biografija.ru/show_bio.aspx?id=105289> [accessed 3 February 2009].

of spiritual riches, whilst living in the most remote and boring village you can imagine; and in circumstances which would break an ordinary person,[30] she has sufficient power over herself to support her husband, smooth out his life, attend to her daughter's education, and also to go attentively into all the details of the housekeeping, organize the building project, and in a word to take on herself all the burdens of painful existence; and she has moreover such good will in relation to everything on earth, and the ability to gain the love of her boring neighbours who are only capable of talking about cabbage and turnips. (p. 316)

The spiritual aspect of the writerly self is very marked. The aim of the diary is to 'check up on my thoughts and deeds'. It is impossible to tell whether the literary model here is the older Orthodox tradition of life-writing, or modern Protestant introspection. Here the addressee of the diary is the Creator, and indeed numerous passages are addressed to God and take the form of prayer, for example:

> On the 14th of this month about one hundred of the unfortunates [involved in the Decembrist revolt] were convicted; five were executed, others were sentenced to hard labour. O my God! Make my soul bow to Your inscrutable will and give the unfortunates who remain alive meekness and those who are no longer a life more happy than that which was taken from them in the flower of their existence. (p. 317)

The diary registers Kolechitskaia's inner life in trials such as poor physical and mental health, bereavement and the distress of her unhappily-married sister. Kolechitskaia builds an image of her soul as needing divine grace to discipline her will, control her attachment to transitory things, make sacrifices, be content in her situation and find the spiritual strength to bear suffering and carry out her duty. In her diary she presents herself as she stands before God, examines her thoughts and deeds in the light of Christian teaching and prays for divine aid. Although Kolechitskaia's mother is a powerful example, the two women exemplify a generational change in spirituality. Lykoshina is a devout Orthodox believer of a traditional kind who values religious ritual, devotional reading, prayer, fasts and pilgrimages and, once widowed, longs to go into a monastery (p. 296). Kolechitskaia has a more modern spirituality, possibly influenced by contemporary teaching about the inner church: she emphasizes individual experience and spiritual introspection, admires the Protestant Moravian Brethren (pp. 311–12), is a supporter of the Russian Bible Society and A. N. Golitsyn (p. 308), and has less concern than her mother for rituals and customs.

[30] Kolechitskaia writes before the involvement of her son P. I. Pestel´ in the Decembrist conspiracy had become known, and before his execution. Elizaveta Pestel´'s family name was in fact Brok.

In terms of the life of the mind Kolechitskaia draws herself as a systematic and thoughtful reader who makes the effort to acquire foreign books and journals (p. 304). She mentions Count Ségur, Richardson, Zimmerman, Maria Edgworth, Pestalozzi and Condillac, and much of her diary consists of excerpts from her reading,[31] which also characterize the self. She also shows herself liberal in outlook. In 1820 she notes, 'now new ideas are in the air, liberal endeavours, a ferment in all the world' (p. 291) and she seeks out new ideas from her neighbour and cousin the Decembrist I. D. Iakushkin:

> our dear Iakushkin, the friend of our youth, is so agreeable, intelligent, there is so much that is absorbing in his conversation, in his library there is all that is new in foreign literature, especially on social questions. I would like to be more often in such society, where you receive many new ideas. (p. 310)

She is made aware by her brother of the Decembrists' discussions of administrative abuses, the stagnation in public life and the constitutional arrangements of other countries (p. 309). When the conspirators are punished she is deeply sympathetic to the exiled Iakushkin, 'deprived of all the joys of life' (p. 318).

Kolechitskaia constructs very various selves: the soul, the reader, mother-educator, wife-hostess, educated daughter, admirer of Nature and node in the networks of family and neighbours. While most of these are culturally prescribed positions, she disputes some current assumptions about femininity: she constructs a female self which dislikes worldly social entertainments, shows no interest in physical appearance or in fashion, prefers reading to housekeeping, is interested in ideas and indeed nourished dreams of supporting her family by work. There is an ongoing conflict:

> I always preferred the pleasures of the mind: reading, studying, testing my mental and moral powers were an endless source of pleasure for me from my earliest youth, and, sitting at my writing table with a pen in my hand, I disdained the balls and entertainments which were customary for girls of my age. However, experience has taught me that a little more active character and a taste for domestic toil, which I do only grudgingly and out of duty, would be very useful to me in family life and would spare me revulsion for things which have to be done (p. 312).

Kolechitskaia's diary centres on the inner life of the mind and spirit as much as Sheremeteva's focuses on externals, and for this reason her preferred places are private and solitary, though spending time there is often only an aspiration. There is a clear conflict between the self, based on literary discourse, which pursues desires, and the self which

---

[31] Liamina and Pasternak, p. 287.

fulfils duty. Because her diary is intended to provide a guide to relatives and neighbours for her daughter she also places herself in the two extended families and in the social circle of friends and neighbours, thus locating herself definitively in Smolensk province. But though rooted there she shows herself not limited to it or by it. Her self is constructed on firm moral foundations, and whereas for Sheremeteva to travel is to refashion the self, Kolechitskaia prefers the provinces and her few changes of place do not redefine her.

Varvara Bakunina: the displaced self

Bakunina left Petersburg in 1796 to travel across the Caucasus to Persia where her husband and the Russian army were engaged in Catherine II's expedition against the Shah. The route took her to the Kizliar area, then across the Terek to Kiziliurt and across the Sulan to Derbent, then across the mountains and numerous other rivers.

For Bakunina St Petersburg is on the one hand the prime source of patronage — exercised this time in the Russian army — and on the other a place, which generates assumptions about femininity, in fact those under which she was brought up.[32] Because she finds herself following the Russian army on campaign, in an anomalous situation for which the assumptions current in St Petersburg high society could not legislate, she is able to build a self which is critical of St Petersburg culture and liberated from its constraints. The greater the cultural and geographical contrast represented by army life and Persia, the more clearly she perceives her metropolitan self.

Her diary is not a chronicle of events by a detached observer. Rather, she accompanies the description of events with moral evaluation of participants and actions, and with evaluation of her own responses. In her diary she depicts what she perceives to be the ill effects of the patronage system emanating from St Petersburg with the arrival to take up command of Count V. A. Zubov, who wielded particular power of patronage as brother of Catherine II's favourite. She notes that Zubov was spoilt by his upbringing, education and St Petersburg society:

> spoilt [...] by success and still more by the flattery which surrounded him on all sides, the Count imagined that he had deserved by his own merits the high position in which fate had placed him. Fearful of losing his dignity, he became proud; good by nature, as I have said, but weak in character, he fears like a child that those around him will think that someone is directing him, while the people who have acquired his trust were the least worthy of it and, abusing this trust, did much harm to him and the entire army. (pp. 344–45)

[32] Her father, I. L. Golenishchev-Kutuzov (1729–1802), was head of the Naval Cadet Corps in St Petersburg.

Zubov's presence, Bakunina observes, generated the 'most brilliant hopes for favour and reward' (p. 344), which distracted officers from the military task in hand: 'each of our generals wanted to have his own battery, without enquiring whether it would be useful or not, so that it would be possible to speak later of "so-and-so's battery"; some of these batteries did the Persians no harm, but served as the pretext for the distribution of rewards' (p. 355). Moreover, Zubov's custom was to reward his favourites, rather than the deserving (p. 357). She also notes the incompetence of the army command appointed by St Petersburg. Insufficient forces were sent on the expedition (p. 347), men were commanded to ford a river before its depth had been measured (p. 360), Zubov and the generals crossed with concern only for their own safety without making arrangements for the safety of the men (p. 365), a general sent his men by the wrong route, forcing them to march twice the distance (p. 367). Worst of all, the army's prize captive, Sheikh Ali, was allowed to escape (pp. 372–73). Whether or not these views were Bakunina's own, or derived from those she heard expressed, she presents the army as suffering from the incompetence of its central and local command and from the pervasive influence of patronage.

Bakunina offers several constructions of her identity in her diary. The first of these is the Petersburg self as she was before the journey to Persia. Rather little detail emerges here, possibly since the addressee of the diary, Bakunina's sister, did not require it. However, Bakunina refers to 'the fears inculcated in me by my upbringing and my sedentary life' (p. 366). And the condition on which her husband agreed to her accompanying him was, not unexpectedly, that she would not show weakness or fear (p. 351), these being aspects of her behaviour with which he was either familiar, or which he reasonably feared would manifest themselves on campaign.

A second construction is that of Zubov and his officers, for whom Bakunina is an untrustworthy, uninformed, feeble and dependent woman suited only to domestic duties, an imposition. To some extent this is realistic: when the unit is ordered to move towards Derbent with minimum transport, it is decided that Bakunina, together with the other accompanying wife and the incapacitated soldiers, should be left behind as 'the chief burden' (p. 351). She is refused information about departure times, presumably to emphasize her exclusion from the military unit. She is assumed to lack understanding of military matters. When she expresses her opinion that the captured Sheikh Ali should be sent to Astrakhan´ for greater security she is mocked and accused of reasoning like a child (pp. 357–58). The only way in which she is deemed to be useful is as society hostess. As Derbent falls, 'all the generals and colonels gathered at my place, wanting to congratulate the Count; we drank to his health, drank tea, and ate jam' (p. 356), and to celebrate its capture the Bakunins arrange a dinner for Zubov and some sixty officers, providing flowers, music, toasts and cannonade. Bakunina records that she 'tried to receive the guests as well as possible' (p. 358). When the army is camped on the banks of the Rubas, a week-long series of tea-parties with musical accompaniment is arranged by the Bakunins, Zubov and some of the generals. Bakunina complains: 'I must confess that each such picnic gave me much trouble as I always had to pour the tea' (p. 360).

Bakunina's construction of her own identity during the Persian expedition is entirely at odds with this ascribed identity. She identifies herself with the army, consistently using the pronoun 'we' for the regiment as well as for her husband and son. But from her position as an outsider to army command, writing to an addressee who is also an outsider, she does not hesitate to express critical insights. She comments on the refusal to disclose information about departure times: 'I became accustomed to such strangeness and to the eternal mystery in which the most trifling events were wrapped, probably in order to give them more importance' (p. 360). She is observant of strategy — the lack of forces necessitated retreat from Derbent which allowed the Persians to reinforce their defences (p. 347) — and of the personalities and ability of commanders:

> The former [Count A.] was the director of the office and the mind of the Count [Zubov] and, controlling both, in consequence controlled the whole army; this man was not up to his job and all the army hated him; arrogant and impertinent, he demanded that everyone bow down before him, and avenged himself on those who did not do so. M., whom you know, is a decent chap but in the wrong place; having given way to the influence of others he is a weapon in their hands and does harm involuntarily; he lacks the skill and energy required for his post. (p. 345)

She shows herself leading a life which is devoid of conventional domesticity. Her 'little home' (p. 352) is her carriage, her *kibitka* and a minimum of belongings:

> You have no grasp of what a strange way of life one has to lead on campaign; imagine perpetual movement from place to place and this for days on end; at first it is tiresome but then you become used to this life, everything has its set place in the trunk. (pp. 346–47)

The everyday life she describes is not, of course, the average commonplace life described by Sheremeteva and Kolechitskaia. Precisely because it has almost nothing in common with her everyday experience in Russia it serves to illuminate the latter by contrast. Routines such as mealtimes are dictated entirely by the progress of the day's travel (p. 362). And Bakunina revels in these rough conditions:

> you must agree that it is good to become accustomed to a nomadic life; you feel good everywhere and you do without many things and do not feel deprived. (p. 362)

Many features of this constructed self are 'masculine'. Bakunina has opinions on topics, such as military strategy, of which women are expected to be ignorant. She confronts physical dangers: fast-flowing rivers, ravines subject to attack, storms, scorpions, extreme heat, scorching winds, lack of clean drinking water. She is eyewitness to battle and learns to control her fear and squeamishness and face the sight of wounds and death:

> During one of my walks I met a wounded soldier from our Vladimir regiment, which made a strong impression on me but after a few days I became accustomed to this sight. How strange that all that strikes us on the first occasion no longer has such a strong effect on repetition; without doubt I did not become insensible to the suffering of those close to us, but later on the stories about the wounded and dead did not produce the same depressing impression on me as at first; how unhappy we would be if time and habit did not weaken our impressionability. (p. 354)

Acting out the self she promised her husband when she persuaded him to allow her to join him, she emphasizes her courage. During the siege of Derbent she remains in camp, feeling 'no fear or alarm', and has only one sleepless night due to the shooting of bullets, the shouting from the town and the noise of oxen and donkeys (p. 354). She notes her progress in self-confidence and physical robustness: 'I was pleased with myself for accomplishing the crossing without fear, and so henceforth I could count on my strength and venture on any long and dangerous journey' (p. 366). She presents a self transformed by hardship:

> I am indebted to my journey to Persia also for the fact that I became more courageous and rid myself of all the fears inculcated in me by my upbringing and my sedentary life; now no mountain, no torrent, holds fear for me; for me there is no dangerous road, and I can endure cold, damp, and searing heat without difficulty, and I can manage without many things which previously seemed to be items of prime necessity. (pp. 366–67)

Bakunina also emphasizes the exercise of reason. She is aware that fear is imparted to women by the culture of their upbringing. She has independent views — 'perhaps you read an account of the capture of Derbent in the newspapers and will be very surprised that my story does not at all agree with it; rely on me: I did not miss a single detail, and as for the forest of shining bayonets, the old man who fell to his knees and so on, all that is no more than M.'s fictions' (p. 356). She questions myths — 'these gifts were not distinguished by the much-praised asiatic luxury of which we have created for ourselves such an exaggerated idea' (p. 349). Warned that one of the camps is infested with scorpions, she becomes anxious and starts to imagine them inside her clothing, but controls her panic through reason — 'understanding that nothing can be so damaging and useless as fear, I decided to conquer it and to think in advance how to help the pain if it happened' (p. 366). Learning that the bite is not as dangerous as commonly thought, she chooses to present herself as courageous, somewhat in advance of the fact, and decides to accustom herself to the creatures:

> I had several stones lifted and began to inspect the scorpions at first from a distance and with terror, but little by little I approached closer; one can get used to anything; you remember how as a child I was afraid of spiders, now tarantulas and scorpions have entirely weaned me from that fear (p. 366).

She is aware that fearfulness is a learned response and not an essential feminine characteristic. Although she cannot do more than complain mildly about her role as hostess, Bakunina plays down those aspects of her identity which might most emphatically define her as feminine. She is in fact pregnant but makes little mention of this beyond the fact that it prevents her from riding on horseback and that being shaken by uneven roads makes travel unpleasant (pp. 348, 367). The dreadful prospect of childbirth on campaign in rough conditions is not mentioned. She also makes little reference to the fact that she is travelling with her baby son Vasia, born the previous year, who is mentioned mainly in connection with her fears for him (pp. 364, 365). The one other noblewoman who was also on the expedition hardly figures in the account (p. 352); Bakunina, underemphasizing her femininity, eschews female solidarity. For Bakunina change of place offers an opportunity for the gradual retraining of learned responses, and radical and permanent redefinition of the inner self.

The accounts which these three women give present St Petersburg as the seat of imperial government and its military and civil services, the apex of patronage networks, the acme of sophisticated social pleasures, purveyor of commodified culture in the form of theatre and balls, source of goods and services unavailable in the provinces, and the legislator of a fashionable Westernized lifestyle. They show clearly the differences in everyday life between the capital and the provinces. In the provinces traditional social interactions based on the extended family and contiguity of neighbourhood are still the norm and traditional lifestyles determined by the rituals of the Orthodox Church persist.

However, there is no categorical distinction between capital and provinces inasmuch as imperial power reaches to district centres with their culture determined by state service, modern thought reaches to the libraries of the country houses of intellectuals, even in quite modest households French is used for conversation and letter-writing, and provincial nobles spend time in the capital.

We see from these accounts that change of place, voluntary or enforced, ensured that women were aware of the selves they presented,

offered new acquaintances and situations against which to define themselves, and was one factor which allowed, or even required, psychological change and thus choices in relation to cultural constructions of
femininity. Belova's observation about its pervasive effect on noblewomen of this period is most true for Sheremeteva, who shows
how adaptation of self to circumstances, principally in respect of externals such as social occasions and clothing, is her chief occupation.
Sheremeteva remains within traditional prescriptions of femininity, and
is concerned with others' perceptions of her self rather than with its
inner essence. As a result of finding herself in a variety of circumstances, she generates a plurality of selves, some of them contradictory.
Bakunina is also powerfully affected by place, in respect both of way
of life and perception of the implications of learned codes of feminine
behaviour. But whereas change of place and new constructions of the
self are largely constricting for Sheremeteva, for Bakunina they are
liberating. In Persia she is more or less free of possessions and of conventional social situations. The culture of St Petersburg is viewed from
the new moral high ground. All of this allows her to redefine herself,
against her former self, as strong, courageous and rational, a stable
unified self. Kolechitskaia's self is cultivated to be largely immune to
changes of circumstance. She is a woman of the book whose preferred
spaces are those offering reflective solitude where she can attend
to moral issues and examine her self before God, though her more
characteristic spaces are those which impose a duty of social intercourse. Like Bakunina, she disputes the culturally imposed group
identity for women with the articulation of a single, complex, more
stable individual self with firm moral and rational principles.

General P. D. Kiselev and the Second Army HQ at Tul´chin, 1819–29

PATRICK O'MEARA

PAVEL DMITRIEVICH KISELEV ranks among the most outstanding Russian statesmen of the first half of the nineteenth century. He lived a long life (he was in his eighty-fourth year when he died in 1872) during the course of which he served three emperors successively as a military commander, a gifted administrator and a remarkable diplomat.[1] However, at an early stage of an already brilliant career he came perilously close to jeopardizing his position as a favourite aide-de-camp of Tsar Alexander I and with it his rank as adjutant-general and chief-of-staff of the Second Army at its HQ in Tul´chin (Ukraine), all of which he had achieved by the time he was thirty years old. This was because, to the consternation of his friends in St Petersburg, he allowed himself to develop close friendships and potentially compromising associations with a number of 'free-thinking' young officers under his command who were members of the Decembrists' secret societies, and especially with Pavel Pestel´, the republican ideologist of the Southern Society. He found himself obliged to distance himself rapidly from them as the

Patrick O'Meara is Professor of Russian at Durham University and Master of Van Mildert College.

[1] Kiselev's biography and service career are outlined in a substantial entry in *Russkii biograficheskii slovar´*, St Petersburg, 1897 (hereafter, *RBS*), pp. 702–17 and, more recently, in D. N. Shilov, *Gosudarstvennye deiateli Rossiiskoi Imperii*, St Petersburg, 2002, pp. 322–26. See also Henry H. Hirschbiel, 'Kiselev, Pavel Dmitrievich', *Modern Encyclopedia of Russian and Soviet History*, vol. 17, Gulf Breeze, FL, 1980, pp. 41–44. The classic biography, A. P. Zablotskii-Desiatovskii, *Graf P. D. Kiselev i ego vremia*, St Petersburg, 1882, 4 vols, has yet to be superseded. There are, however, further treatments of Kiselev's Tul´chin period in: F. Bulgakov, 'Russkii gosudarstvennyi chelovek minuvshikh trekh tsarstvovanii', *Istoricheskii vestnik*, 1882, 1, pp. 128–55; N. M. Druzhinin, *Gosudarstvennye krest´iane i reforma P D Kiseleva*, vol. 1, Moscow and Leningrad, 1946; vol. 2, Moscow, 1958; O. V. Orlik, *Gosudarstvennye liudi Rossii pervoi poloviny XIX veka: puti i sud´by*, Moscow, 2000; M. A. Davydov, '*Oppozitsiia ego velichestva'. Dvorianstvo i reformy v nachale XIX v*, Moscow, 1994; S. A. Ekshtut, *V poiske istoricheskoi al´ternativy. Aleksandr I. Ego spodvizhniki. Dekabristy*, Moscow, 1994. Kiselev also figures prominently in studies of the Decembrists' Southern Society and its leading figure, P. I. Pestel´: A. V. Semenova, 'Iuzhnye dekabristy i P D Kiselev', *Istoricheskie zapiski*, Moscow, 1975, 96, pp. 128–51; A. V. Semenova, *Vremennoe revoliutsionnoe pravitel´stvo v planakh dekabristov*, Moscow, 1982; O. I. Kiianskaia, *Pavel Pestel´. Ofitser, razvedchik, zagovorshchik*, Moscow, 2002; Patrick O'Meara, *The Decembrist Pavel Pestel: Russia's First Republican*, Basingstoke, 2003; O. I. Kiianskaia, *Pestel´*, Moscow, 2005.

net closed in on Pestel´and his confederates in Tul´chin on the eve of the uprising in St Petersburg on 14 December 1825. By focusing on Kiselev's ten years at Tul´chin from 1819, this article seeks to clarify the extent of these links and of Kiselev's own motives for them.[2] Why did an ambitious young general who had achieved so much so soon risk losing everything, just as his Decembrist associates would?

Kiselev was born in Moscow on 29 June (10 July) 1788 and, like the majority of noblemen's children at that time, was educated at home. He grew up in a middle-ranking noble family which was typical enough in most ways, though its educational attainments and its connections with the capital's political and cultural life were exceptional. It was a lively household frequented by such leading writers and historians of the day as N. M. Karamzin, P. A. Viazemskii[3] and A. I. Turgenev, who instilled in him the outlook of the contemporary intellectual elite. Kiselev thus became well versed in the European Enlightenment and the ideas of the *philosophes* whose views he broadly shared.[4]

Aged seventeen, he joined the Chevaliers Gardes Regiment whose officers were mostly drawn from the aristocracy. Among the young Kiselev's peers were not only future holders of high office under Nicholas I, such as A. A. Zakrevskii, A. S. Menshikov and V. V. Levashev, but also future Decembrists, including Pavel Pestel´, Mikhail Orlov, Pavel Lopukhin and Sergei Volkonskii.[5] Unlike other reputedly liberal high-ranking officials serving under Alexander I, such as N. S. Mordvinov and M. M. Speranskii, Kiselev belonged to the same generation as the Decembrists: Sergei Volkonskii, a close friend, was born in the same year, 1788; he was five years younger than Baron

---

[2] Kiselev is mentioned frequently in the testimony of the Decembrists: see, for example, *Vosstanie dekabristov. Materialy*, ed. A. N. Sakharov, vol. 20, Moscow, 2001, and in their memoirs, I. V. Porokh and V. A. Fedorov (eds), 'Vospominaniia N. V. Basargina', *Memuary dekabristov. Iuzhnoe obshchestvo*, Moscow, 1982; S. Ia. Shtraikh (ed.), *Zapiski, stat´i, pis´ma dekabrista I. D. Iakushkina*, Moscow, 1951. Selected correspondence from the Tul´chin period (1818–23) is published in 'Bumagi Gr. A. A. Zakrevskogo', *Sbornik Imperatorskogo Russkogo Istoricheskogo Obshchestva*, 78, St Petersburg, 1891, ed. N. F. Dubrovin, which contains sixty-one letters from Kiselev to Zakrevskii and ninety-three letters from Zakrevskii to Kiselev. See also D. A. Miliutin, 'Pis´ma k Kiselevu 1812–26', *Russkaia starina* (hereafter, *RS*), 1887, 7, pp. 226–35; A. N. Akin´shin, M. D. Dolbilov *Tul´chinksii shtab pri dvukh generalakh: Pis´ma P. D. Kiseleva A. Ia. Rudzevichu (1817–1823gg.)*, Voronezh, 1998; 'Pis´ma Pestelia k P. D. Kiselevu (1821–1823gg.)', *Pamiati dekabristov*, Leningrad, 1926, 3, pp. 150–201.

[3] The childhood friends (Viazemskii was four years Kiselev's junior) stayed in touch. In May 1827 Viazemskii wrote to him inviting him to send a contribution 'from your military or political notes' to *Moskovskii telegraf* that would pass the 'good-for-nothing' censors. Fittingly, Kiselev sent a piece entitled 'The letters and orders of Count A. V. Suvorov': M. I. Gillel´son, *P. A. Viazemskii. Zhizn´ i tvorchestvo*, Leningrad, 1969, p. 129, n. 4. I am indebted to the editor for this reference.

[4] *RBS*, p. 702; Orlik, *Gosudarstvennye liudi Rossii pervoi poloviny XIX veka*, p. 89.

[5] Druzhinin, *Gosudarstvennye krest´iane i reforma P. D. Kiseleva*, 1, p. 257.

Vladimir Shteingel', one of the oldest conspirators, and seven years older than Pavel Pestel'. Kiselev saw his first military action in 1807 aged nineteen and, like so many of his generation, he fought at Borodino in 1812. During the 1812 campaign Kiselev was appointed adjutant to General M. A. Miloradovich and participated in the taking of Paris. He thus shared much the same kind of education, upbringing, military service and war experiences central to the formation of the Decembrists' outlook, and he drew from them similar conclusions about Russia's need to reform and modernize.[6]

Although Kiselev did not become close to Miloradovich, his position as adjutant gave him privileged access to Alexander I, with whom he soon became personally acquainted, and hence also enhanced his career prospects. Indeed, as a mark of his confidence in Kiselev, Alexander appointed him his aide-de-camp in April 1814, aged only twenty-six.[7] This appointment was a defining moment in his personal development, making him a member of the Court circle and linking him indissolubly with the establishment. He was, in the view of the Soviet historian, N. M. Druzhinin: 'ambitious and authoritative, intelligent and dexterous' driven by a sense of 'obligation to make a success of his service career granted him by the tsar's grace and favour'.[8] Kiselev rapidly became a firm favourite of the tsar and was a member of his suite at the Congress of Vienna from September 1814 until May 1815 and then from June to September that year in Paris. From August to October 1816, he was among the tsar's entourage in Warsaw. From this period, Kiselev has left a rare account of an audience he had with Alexander on 4 May 1816 which gives a sense of their relationship. The young aide-de-camp's frankness reflects widespread attitudes among the Russian noble elite towards Alexander and, in turn, the tsar's own view of the challenges facing Russia. The country, he told Kiselev, 'should now be moving at the same pace as Europe' which 'we simply cannot lag behind any longer'. He complained of the lack of adequately trained personnel needed for government posts: 'I cannot even appoint 52 governors though I need thousands. [. . .] The army, the civil service — nothing is the way I'd like it to be. Russia has great potential but time is needed for everything.' According to his account of their

[6] Orlik, *Gosudarstvennye liudi Rossii*, pp. 88–89. On the political legacy of the Decembrists' military experiences in the West, see W. B. Lincoln, 'A Re-examination of Some Historical Stereotypes: An Analysis of the Career Patterns and Backgrounds of the Decembrists', *Jahrbücher für Geschichte Osteuropas*, 24, 1976, pp. 357–68.

[7] *RBS*, p. 703; Bulgakov, 'Russkii gosudarstvennyi chelovek minuvshikh trekh tsarstvovanii', p. 130. For a persuasive summary of the paramount importance of proximity to the tsar for enhanced career prospects, see S. A. Ekshtut, *Na sluzhbe rossiiskomu Leviafanu. Istoriosofskie opyty*, Moscow, 1998, p. 51.

[8] Druzhinin, *Gosudarstvennye krest'iane i reforma P. D. Kiseleva*, 1, p. 247.

exchange, Kiselev risked some home truths: 'Not everyone cares for
you, Sire. Opinion of you is hostile. [...] It is even thought that you,
Sire, do not like the nobility or even the Russian people.'[9]

Although notoriously sensitive to any criticism, Alexander seems to
have valued Kiselev's candour: at all events in 1817 he promoted his
twenty-nine-year-old aide-de-camp to the rank of general. Kiselev's
two great strengths from this early point in his career were his administrative talent and his responsiveness to the prevailing *Zeitgeist* as
seen in his determination to solve the peasant question and 'quietly
bring about the end of serfdom without damaging the state'. In 1816
he drafted for Alexander's consideration a memorandum 'on the
gradual eradication of slavery in Russia'. His main idea was the abolition of the grossest forms of the servile dependence of the peasants
which presented the greatest threat to their owners. In his paper he
urged, in terms reminiscent of the constitutional project drafted by the
Decembrist Nikita Muraviev, that 'civil liberty is the basis of national
welfare' and that 'it would be desirable to see in our state the spread
of the lawful independence of enserfed agriculturalists of which they
are unjustly deprived'.[10] It was a matter to which he would return as
Nicholas I's Minister of State Domains.[11]

On 22 February 1819 Alexander appointed Kiselev Chief of General
Staff of the Second Army in succession to General A. Ia. Rudzevich.
Kiselev had a reputation in the army for not accepting bribes which,
his obvious talents and the benefits of favouritism apart, makes Alexander's decision understandable. However, on hearing the news, the
army's commander-in-chief, Count P. Kh. Vitgenshtein, offended by
the tsar's failure to consult him, tendered his resignation. In an indig-
nant letter to Alexander (16 March) he wrote: 'The appointment of
Mr Kiselev [...] is a bitter disappointment to me and a personal insult,
not because General Kiselev does not deserve this post for I have
absolutely no doubt as to his abilities, and moreover he is the personal
choice of Your Majesty, but because his appointment is confirmation
for me of the complete loss of Your Most Merciful Sovereign's favour

[9] Bulgakov, 'Russkii gosudarstvennyi chelovek', pp. 131–34.

[10] The text of this memorandum is published in Zablotskii-Desiatovskii, *Graf P. D. Kiselev*,
4, pp. 197–99; *RBS*, p. 705; Semenova, *Vremennoe revoliutsionnoe pravitel'stvo v planakh dekabristov*,
pp. 150–51; Kiianskaia, *Pestel'*, 2005, p. 136. W. B. Lincoln asserts that 'all of Kiselev's views
on the peasant question, at least until 1856, were a series of elaborations on this first
proposal'. See W. B. Lincoln, *Nicholas I: Emperor and Autocrat of All the Russias*, London, 1978,
p. 189.

[11] In Jerome Blum's view, Kiselev 'managed to accomplish much in the eighteen years
he headed the bureau. To him, and to Nicholas who trusted and supported him, belongs
the credit for a genuine and successful effort to better the lot of the Russian peasant'. *Lord
and Peasant in Russia from the Ninth to the Nineteenth Century*, New York, 1967, p. 550.

and confidence in me.'[12] Furthermore, until he received Alexander's personal assurance that there was no hidden agenda, Vitgenshtein was convinced that Kiselev had been planted to spy on him. General I. V. Sabaneev, commander of the Tiraspol-based 6th Corps and many years Kiselev's senior, also bridled at the young general's appointment, and wrote at the time: 'As he has the Tsar's full confidence, which everyone knows, he (Kiselev) can do anything he wants [. . .] and his demands are met much faster and without any demur.'[13]

The Second Army's HQ was located in the Ukrainian village of Tul´chin, 'a little Polish town then belonging to Count Meczislaw Potocki', as the Decembrist Nikolai Basargin recalled from his posting there, 'populated by Jews and Polish *szlachta* (gentry)', where, 'apart from military personnel and HQ officials there was no society'.[14] It was located in the Bratslav district of the Podolsk region in Ukraine, 250 km south-west of Kiev, in the southern part of the Bug valley. Russia had seized it in 1793 from the Potocki family during the second partition of Poland. Here, over the next ten years, Kiselev's ascent to the highest peaks of the imperial bureaucracy began. It was to be a time of both opportunities and threats, the greatest of which was the appearance in 1825 of his name on police lists as a possible Decembrist conspirator.[15] He now occupied one of the most senior military positions in the entire Russian army, effectively the commander of hundreds of thousands of troops.[16] Crucially, it made him also for six years the immediate superior of a number of the Decembrist Southern Society's members who were among the flower of the Second Army's officer corps. Among them P. I. Pestel´, I. G. Burtsov, N. V Basargin and A. P. Iushnevskii figured particularly prominently.[17] Kiselev's friends warned him to be vigilant in Tul´chin where they knew he would encounter jealousy and intrigue. His old regimental comrade, General Zakrevskii, for example, wrote (1 May 1819) imploring him not to antagonize the commander-in-chief. On 17 May, Kiselev replied that all was well and that he was getting on fine with Vitgenshtein.[18]

Kiselev found the Second Army in a poor state and complained that his predecessors had turned it into a 'wretched poorhouse'. As he wrote

[12] Quoted in Kiianskaia, *Pavel Pestel´. Ofitser, razvedchik, zagovorshchik*, p. 99.
[13] Quoted in Davydov, '*Oppozitsiia ego velichestva*', pp. 70–71.
[14] 'Vospominaniia N. V. Basargina', *Memuary dekabristov. Iuzhnoe obshchestvo*, p. 15.
[15] O'Meara, *The Decembrist Pavel Pestel*, p. 21; *Modern Encyclopedia of Russian and Soviet History*, vol. 17, p. 42.
[16] The Russian army, in which about one million conscripts served for twenty-five years, was then the largest in Europe. See J. N. Westwood, *Endurance and Endeavour: Russian History 1812–2001*, 5th edition, Oxford, 2002, p. 57.
[17] Orlik, *Gosudarstvennye liudi Rossii*, p. 90.
[18] Bulgakov, 'Russkii gosudarstvennyi chelovek', pp. 136–37.

to Zakrevskii (13 July 1819): 'This damnable military work is killing me. I'm only doing it because I want to bring everything up to scratch and then get some rest.' From St Petersburg, Zakrevskii urged him not to rush things in Tul´chin: 'You won't be able to put everything right all at once. Just start with the most neglected aspects and you'll gradually restore order everywhere.' There was certainly a lot for the new chief-of-staff to tackle: barracks unfit for purpose, rundown hospitals, poor food, deserters, a general breakdown in discipline, a shortage of effective officers and a woeful courts-martial system.[19] Kiselev found the staff duty roster, as he informed Zakrevskii, in 'a worse than sorry state. The administrative staff is bad, the organization is even worse and it's all a terrible muddle'. However, he was soon able to report that 'the staff duty roster is now sorted out and at 0700 hours everyone is at their post'. He also sought to improve the army's hospitals, legal processes, schools and police service. The latter was needed not only to combat sedition, but also systemic corruption and widespread smuggling among senior officers.[20]

In February 1821, Kiselev wrote of the need for a more modern approach 'consistent with the spirit of the age' to discipline and correction (he was particularly opposed to cruel corporal punishment) with a corresponding reform of the administration of justice.[21] Indeed, he reviewed every aspect of his soldiers' training and welfare and achieved particularly good results in the medical arena by obtaining funding for the building of a hospital in Tul´chin in 1821. At odds with the methods and policies of Arakcheev, he sought to promote education and access to it in his army. Kiselev's personal dislike of Arakcheev, shared by many of his peers, was matched only by Arakcheev's increasing jealousy of the chief-of-staff's access to the tsar. It was a mark of Kiselev's apparent liberalism that he instead supported Denis Davydov and Mikhail Orlov's efforts to organize 'Lancaster' (mutual instruction) schools, but only for his officers: 'Education is really useful only for people who are called to command others. Those who are required to obey can do without it and they will obey even better.'[22] But he despaired of making any successful staff appointments in the absence of any 'outstanding candidates' to command his regiments. His view was reciprocated by Zakrevskii who wrote to Kiselev (1 February 1821) in equally emphatic terms about the wretched calibre of the army's officer corps, much of which was 'rubbish', and lamenting the army's

[19] Davydov, 'Oppozitsiia ego velichestva', pp. 71–72.
[20] On this see Kiianskaia, Pavel Pestel´. Ofitser, razvedchik, zagovorshchik, pp. 103–05, 109.
[21] Davydov, 'Oppozitsiia ego velichestva', p. 73.
[22] Quoted in Semenova, Vremennoe revoliutsionnoe pravitel´stvo, p. 145.

generally poor condition: 'We have to [. . .] devise ways of improving it', he concluded. 'Philanthropy won't get us anywhere.'[23]

From the start, Kiselev felt isolated at Tul'chin and missed his friends in distant St Petersburg. In a letter to Zakrevskii (13 July 1819) he complains of his dreary routine:

> I have made myself a study which I hardly ever leave: I work at papers for around ten hours and then read. There are no parties to speak of since my life, like my letters, is weighed down by dullness. I am always on my own, there are no diversions, and I am utterly despondent. Not that I'm complaining, my friend, I wouldn't dare think of doing so.[24]

Nevertheless, it was an oft-repeated refrain of his letters over the next six years. Both Kiselev and Zakrevskii, from their own different perspectives, seemed to share the same dissatisfaction with life in contemporary Russia — whether in St Petersburg or in a distant outpost of empire like Tul'chin — to which Pestel' and other Decembrists were also reacting in their own ways and in various locations. Thus, for example, a letter to Kiselev from his adjutant, the Decembrist Burtsov, contains a graphic description of rural poverty and famine in Roslavl', a town in the Smolensk province, in 1821 where he witnessed 'the despair of the nobles and of the district officials, who feared the unruliness of the peasants and all the consequences of their cruel situation'.[25] This shared dissatisfaction may be judged further from Zakrevskii's pessimistic assessment expressed to Kiselev who was then in Warsaw as a member of Alexander's suite: 'It seems to me that the state of affairs in our country will never improve, making it difficult for an honest man to serve it for the greater good and without thought of personal gain.' Knowing the sensitivity of these comments he requested Kiselev to burn his letter (31 January 1823), which the inveterate hoarder failed to do. Kiselev's response some weeks later (14 March) referred to the increasing difficulty of his own post which he hoped to resign once the imperial review of the Second Army, scheduled for September, had taken place.[26] But when it had, Alexander pronounced the Second Army to be in exemplary order and warmly commended Kiselev on his command which, ever the pragmatist, the chief-of-staff did not seek to resign after all.

There seems no doubt, as Druzhinin puts it: 'that, for all the serious political differences between them, Kiselev and progressive representatives of the noble generation were united in sincere condemnation of the existing order.' He was unquestionably an enemy of Arakcheev,

---

[23] Bulgakov, 'Russkii gosudarstvennyi chelovek', pp. 152–53.
[24] Quoted in Zablotskii-Desiatovskii, *Graf P. D. Kiselev i ego vremia*, 1, pp. 104–05.
[25] Bulgakov, 'Russkii gosudarstvennyi chelovek', p. 144.
[26] Zablotskii-Desiatovskii, *Graf P. D. Kiselev i ego vremia*, 1, pp. 172–73.

disliked Alexander's paradomania and loathed the mood of reaction and mysticism which gripped much of noble society.[27] There was indeed much he disliked both in Russia and in the army. As well as his opposition to serfdom and harsh military discipline, his letters reveal that he supported the tsar's 'splendid' speech in 1818 at the opening of the Polish *sejm* which promised to give Russia the constitutional benefits he was then granting Poland. Typically, contrary to the government's line but in accord with the view of Pestel' and the Decembrists, he advocated Russia's full military support for the Greek uprising in the principality of Moldavia in 1821.[28] His officers also knew that Kiselev shared the widespread disapproval in Russia of the military colonies. At the review of the Second Army, Alexander asked Kiselev whether he was now reconciled with them. The loyal aide-de-camp replied simply that it was his duty to accept them because this was what his Imperial Majesty wanted of him, but that he really could make no sense of them himself.[29] Kiselev's candid response suggests that he managed to retain a certain rugged independence of thought if not of action, avoiding the role of 'fawning courtier' to which so many routinely succumbed. Basargin recalled Kiselev's determination to safe-guard his independence vis-à-vis Arakcheev, unlike others at Court 'whose servility toward Arakcheev was quite ludicrous to observe'. Even in relation to the tsar, 'Kiselev did not abase himself and behaved with dignity though without forfeiting Alexander's regard for him'.[30] In fact, imperial approval was of great importance to Kiselev, as he wrote to Zakrevskii (16 July 1821): 'The sovereign [...] said so many flattering things about me that I cannot find words to express my gratitude. Such praise gives me far greater pleasure than any decoration or award.'[31] In the midst of his disillusionment and boredom in remote Tul'chin, Kiselev feared that Alexander had forgotten him. In fact, however, between 1821 and 1824 he had a number of audiences with the tsar in Moscow, Petersburg, Warsaw — and, most significantly, in Tul'chin itself.

Here Alexander spent several days in late September/early October 1823 having left Tsarskoe Selo for Moscow on 16 August to begin one of his extensive tours of empire. It took in Orel, Briansk, Brest-Litovsk and Kamenets-Podol'sk on the border with Austria, where on 25 and

---

[27] Druzhinin, *Gosudarstvennye krest'iane i reforma P. D. Kiseleva*, 1, pp. 265–66.
[28] Kiselev was prompted both by economic and religious considerations. See Theophilus C. Prousis, *Russian Society and the Greek Revolution*, DeKalb, IL, 1994, pp. 41–42.
[29] Semenova, *Vremennoe revoliutsionnoe pravitel'stvo*, p. 146; Semenova, 'Iuzhnye dekabristy i P. D. Kiselev', p. 129.
[30] 'Vospominaniia N. V. Basargina', *Memuary dekabristov. Iuzhnoe obshchestvo*, p. 31.
[31] Quoted in Zablotskii-Desiatovskii, *Graf P. D. Kiselev i ego vremia*, 1, p. 136.

26 September he had meetings with Emperor Franz I (Metternich was absent through illness), and thence across the Dniestr through Mogilev to Tul'chin for a thoroughgoing review of his Second Army. All went supremely well, except for the review of Mikhail Orlov's 16th division which Alexander was probably minded to fault anyway, primed as he was by reports of its officers' liberal tendencies. Nevertheless, Alexander's overall satisfaction was expressed in his promotion of Kiselev to adjutant-general. The tsar's visit was a happy occasion to judge from Kiselev's account to Zakrevskii of a dinner for Alexander amidst 65,000 men whose loyal toasts and cheers evinced imperial tears of joy. The chief-of-staff noted wryly: 'All shared in the joy of general celebration, most apparently forgetting their opposition five years ago to those very innovations which have raised the army to its current state of excellence.' People of Kiselev's calibre were passing rare and Alexander greatly appreciated the character and ability of his outstanding commander despite his independent streak and his undisguised hostility to Arakcheev.[32]

One further reason for Kiselev's continuing frustration with his Tul'chin posting was his losing battle against corrupt officers on his staff, one of whom was being protected by 'rogues' in St Petersburg, making it 'so hard to prove bribery when the word "loan" is used as a euphemism for robbery', as he complained to Zakrevskii. This came as no surprise to the latter who commented (2 March 1820) on the 'complete obstinacy in these matters' of one such 'rogue' and 'the astonishing indecisiveness throughout the entire state' which 'you and I are in no position to do anything about'. Zakrevskii blamed this state of affairs wholly on the malign influence of the 'unique state criminal', Arakcheev, whose actions 'are leading to the complete ruin of Russia', which will be saved only by his death.[33]

The correspondence between Kiselev and Zakrevskii on the theme of Tul'chin life culminates in 1825 with a further indication of Kiselev's state of mind. Hearing that Zakrevskii was in St Petersburg, Kiselev reminded him (18 February), 'that I am alive and living in Tul'chin. [. . .] It's hard for me to find anything new to tell you about my life. As before I am working for others and hope that I am being of some use'. The inertia of central command, however, was 'taking the shine off' his work and he was impatient 'to cast off the yoke' which he had

[32] Grand Duke Nikolai Mikhailovich, *Imperator Aleksandr I*, Petrograd, 1914 (reprint Moscow, 1999), pp. 234–36.
[33] Bulgakov, 'Russkii gosudarstvennyi chelovek', pp. 146–47, 150. For a recent study on the persistence of corruption in Russian history, see S. Lovell, A. Ledeneva and A. Rogachevskii (eds), *Bribery and Blat in Russia: Negotiating Reciprocity from the Middle Ages to the 1990s*, Basingstoke, 2000.

borne for six years. He added that after so many years in Tul´chin
he now found himself almost alone, with a negligible social life, a sick
wife lacking the treatment she needed, and grieving for the death
of their son. All in all, as he put it, 'a rather gloomy picture which
perhaps contrasts with the excitement of your life at Court'. In his
reply (6 March) Zakrevskii empathizes with Kiselev's depressed mood,
frustrated himself by the 'murderous indifference' shown to those, like
him, who try to make a difference by working effectively. Later that
year, Kiselev complains again to Zakrevskii (1 November) of his isolation in Tul´chin, 'ever more bored with each passing hour', and missing the company of friends: 'I'd like to see Volkonskii and have a
chat; I've really become stupider for lack of company because [. . .] I
see no-one and know nothing.' Kiselev's mood seemed somehow in
tune with the fateful events which were to unfold just weeks later:
Alexander's sudden death, the interregnum, the Tul´chin arrests and
the Decembrist uprisings.[34]

It was in this context and while he was in Tul´chin, where he spent
a lot of time reading and in direct contact with Decembrists, that
Kiselev's political development matured. His library included works by
the French Enlightenment writers, as well as Jeremy Bentham, Adam
Smith and Niccolo Machiavelli — a collection very similar to Pestel´'s.
The atmosphere of the officers' mess there is finely evoked in the
memoirs of Nikolai Basargin: 'We all tried to use our free time to
further our intellectual and moral education [. . .] and give each other
some account of what we were doing, reading, and thinking.'[35] Kiselev's
lively and openly trusting correspondence with Pestel´ over a four-year
period (from December 1819 to the middle of 1823) — letters which
Kiselev kept — point to an undoubted closeness between the two
men, apparently based on mutual respect and affection. They became
close collaborators sharing similar goals for the army as they strove to
improve conditions and make it a reliable battle-ready force. However,
despite his rapid promotion, Kiselev had no experience of staff work.
He had no like-minded army comrades or personal friends in Tul´chin;
on the contrary, he had numerous covert critics who remained
aggrieved by his appointment. It was no doubt his sense of isolation
that drew him to Pavel Pestel´ who, as Vitgenshtein's adjutant, was a
potentially useful ally in Tul´chin.[36]

[34] Zablotskii-Desiatovskii, *Graf P. D. Kiselev i ego vremia*, 1, pp. 236–39.

[35] 'Vospominaniia N. V. Basargina', *Memuary dekabristov. Iuzhnoe obshchestvo*, p. 15.

[36] Bulgakov, 'Russkii gosudarstvennyi chelovek', pp. 139–41; Druzhinin, *Gosudarstvennye krest´iane i reforma P. D. Kiseleva*, 1, p. 265; Kiianskaia, *Pavel Pestel´. Ofitser, razvedchik, zagovorshchik*, pp. 102–03.

Kiselev was certainly greatly impressed by Pestel''s abilities, depended increasingly on his resourceful assistance in reforming the Second Army, and entrusted him with particularly sensitive and challenging missions. For example, during 1821 he sent the young adjutant on three important missions to Bessarabia to report back to HQ on the Greek uprising in the Danube principalities of the Ottoman Empire. Kiselev soon came to include him in his personal circle at Tul'chin and over the next two years frequently spent evenings at Pestel''s quarters.[37] It seems clear that his regard for Pestel' was undiminished by his undoubted awareness from 1822 of the officer's involvement in the Southern Society, at least until after the imperial review in September 1823. In St Petersburg, however, Pestel' was regarded as highly unsuitable company for the chief-of-staff. In September 1820, Zakrevskii questioned his friend about the wisdom of this liaison: 'Rumours are reaching me that you are unpopular in the army and that you spend most of your free time with Pestel' [. . .] What exactly are the ties of friendship binding you to Pestel', knowing as you do his character and morality about which you have written to me several times?' There is no evidence that Kiselev ever responded to Zakrevskii's perfectly understandable question. At any rate, he ignored Zakrevskii's warning and in 1821 was still supporting Pestel''s case for promotion. There was clearly something about Pestel' that Kiselev found irresistible.[38] Nor was he alone in this. General Rudzevich, commander of the corps to which Pestel''s future (Viatka) regiment was attached, was similarly very taken by Pestel'. This is reflected in the affectionate tone of his letters, unusual even by the gushing standards of Romantic epistolary discourse of the age. Rudzevich was determined to outdo Kiselev's protestations of affection for Pestel': 'P. D. Kiselev has told me that he has long known you by repute and has had a lot of good things to say about you', he wrote and then proceeded unabashedly to demand of his junior officer that he accept his love and devotion as well as Kiselev's: 'A bosom friend is a great boon, and so I am also entitled to demand of you, my dear Pavel Ivanovich, that you remember who is totally devoted to you — that is your sincerely loving Rudzevich.'[39] They corresponded regularly for three years from May 1819. Rudzevich once chided Pestel' (7 October 1820) for depriving him for too long of the pleasure of hearing from him. Here again, the flirtatious tone of the reproach is striking: 'Isn't it naughty of you, my dearest Paul (*Pavlik*), to start forgetting me?' Whether this was simply a matter of overdoing

---

[37] O'Meara, *The Decembrist Pavel Pestel*. p. 21.
[38] Ibid., p. 26.
[39] S. Ia. Shtraikh, 'Dekabrist P. I. Pestel'. Novye materialy', *Byloe*, 20, 1922, pp. 106–15. See p. 111, letter of 8 May 1819.

the 'matey' tone conventionally adopted by officers in their correspondence at this time, or whether there were deeper emotions in play,
must remain a matter for conjecture. Marc Raeff is most probably right
to suggest that the intense emotional quality of such friendships at this
time may best be described as 'amitié amoureuse'; he doubts that there
was an overtly homosexual aspect to them, though this must remain
uncertain.[40]

The Decembrists Burtsov and Basargin, both Kiselev's adjutants,
also benefited from his support and goodwill, as did I. B. Avramov and
A. P. Iushnevskii. He had long-standing friendships also with Mikhail
Orlov and Sergei Volkonskii which continued after 14 December 1825.
But still, although Tul´chin is the reputed 'capital' of the Decembrists'
Southern Society, clearly not all those who took part in the life of
the Tul´chin officer corps were members of secret societies. According
to one estimate, out of forty-three officers, twenty-two never became
Decembrists.[41] Ostensibly, Kiselev was opposed to 'people with dangerous ideas' and sought to have such officers removed from his
command. On 22 January 1822, as if in anticipation of Alexander's
imminent decree banning Masonic lodges, he wrote to Zakrevskii
urging him to discharge all those out of step with the government:
'they may be harmless enough in the English Club [in St Petersburg
— P. O'M.] but in their regiments they're extremely dangerous. [. . .]
Our business is to prevent the spread of freethinking and to contain
the evil as much as we can.'[42] A key part of Kiselev's strategy was
the establishment in the Second Army of a secret police force in July
1821 which, as he informed Zakrevskii (15 March 1822), from the outset
had 'done much useful work [. . .] The spirit of the times necessitates
the strengthening of this unit and I am therefore acting accordingly'.
This initiative was given the tsar's blessing at their meeting in Slonim
(Western Belorussia) in May 1821 but Alexander made no funding
available.

Kiselev wanted to recruit agents who were 'noble people of good
education, reliable weapons against evil rather than the kind of dishonest
slanderers all too often found in the ranks of such organizations'.[43]

[40] Raeff, 'Russian Youth on the Eve of Romanticism', *Political Ideas and Institutions in Imperial Russia*, Boulder, CO, 1994, p. 49; O'Meara, *The Decembrist Pavel Pestel*, p. 22. On the culture of masculine relationships, see two recent works: B. Clements, R. Friedman and D. Healey (eds), *Russian Masculinities in History and Culture*, Basingstoke, 2002; Rebecca Friedman, *Masculinity, Autocracy and the Russian University, 1804–63*, Basingstoke, 2005.

[41] V. M. Bokova, *Epokha tainikh obshchestv. Russkie obshchestvennye ob"edineniia pervoi treti XIX v.*, Moscow, 2003, p. 101.

[42] Zablotskii-Desiatovskii, *Graf P. D. Kiselev i ego vremia*, 1, pp. 156–57.

[43] On this topic see the recent and substantial article by P. V. Il´in, 'Neizvestnyi epizod iz istorii politseiskogo nadzora nad uchastnikami tainikh obshchestv: pis´mo polkovnika Dobrovol´skogo P. D. Kiselevu (1822g.)', *14 dekabria 1825 goda*, St Petersburg, 2005, vol. 7, pp. 13–48, esp. pp. 17–18.

As is apparent from the instructions to its agents, a prime purpose was to monitor the political mood of the Second Army: 'In general, what is the mood in the regiment and are there critical views expressed about political affairs or the government?' 'Are there complaints from the troops, or any harmful ideas or secret meetings?' Following the imperial ukaz of August 1822 it is clear that Masonic lodges and other secret societies in the army were the main targets of the unit's surveillance: 'Are any of the suppressed Masonic lodges re-emerging and are there any critical views about political affairs? In whose house do any appreciable numbers of officers meet most often?' Kiselev referred in his correspondence with Zakrevskii during January and February 1822 to the presence in the army of 'free-thinkers', but confirmed that they were all under surveillance and that he knew all their activities.[44]

One of his unit's targets was V. F. Raevskii, known to Kiselev for his 'unbridled free-thinking'. The chief-of-staff's involvement in the 'Raevskii affair' highlights his propensity for double standards. Raevskii, a major in the 32nd Egerskii (Jaeger) regiment based in Kishinev, aroused his superiors' suspicions by establishing a Masonic lodge and spreading liberal ideas among his fellow officers. In February 1822 he was arrested by General Sabaneev who rightly suspected there was a secret society in the 16th division. For the same reason he was determined to get rid of General M. F. Orlov, Raevskii's commanding officer, a member of the Decembrists' Union of Welfare, and an old friend of Kiselev's. The chief-of-staff foresaw that Raevskii would 'not escape trial and exile' and, in a letter to Zakrevskii (27 February 1822), lamented the fact that Orlov not only tolerated him as a member of his staff but repeatedly defended his behaviour: 'It looks as though I'm going to have to part company with Orlov. He means no harm but he's behaved like a child and the consequences are apparent.'[45] Kiselev should not have been surprised by Orlov's behaviour. He had, after all, received a warning from Denis Davydov (15 November 1819) describing Orlov as an 'ideologist' given to time-wasting constitutional debates and burdened by a 'delusion which is both harmful to him and useless to society'. Davydov had told him repeatedly that his 'prattling would only impede his service career', and that 'he hadn't a hope [. . .] of shaking off absolutism in Russia which still has a long way to run'.[46]

Kiselev was quite prepared to be involved in the investigation of Raevskii since he really did consider him to be a dangerous individual. But it is curious that this same Kiselev, in a display of inconsistency

[44] Il'in, 'Neizvestnyi epizod iz istorii politseiskogo nadzora', pp. 19–20, 24.
[45] Zablotskii-Desiatovskii, *Graf P. D. Kiselev i ego vremia*, 1, pp. 156–57.
[46] Miliutin, 'Pis'ma k Kiselevu 1812–26', p. 228.

bordering on double-think, failed to draw self-evident parallels between Orlov's association with Raevskii and his own relationship with Pestel', whom he apparently preferred not to consider dangerous. In a telling remark in his letter to Zakrevskii, Kiselev wrote of the pain it caused him to have to take action against Orlov, his 'comrade and old friend', as his position demanded.[47] We can safely assume that he must have been similarly anguished by his eventual involvement in the arrest and subsequent execution of Pestel'. One wonders what went through his mind when, in April 1822, he read Zakrevskii's congratulations on his role in the Raevskii affair:

> You've brought the Kamchatka [regiment] case to an end, as any resolute commander should. If everyone acted like you, there'd be less nonsense and the Tsar would not be unnecessarily alarmed. I pity Orlov. *How shameful it is for a commanding officer to behave so heedlessly and defend useless and subversive members of the armed forces.*[48]

Moreover, during the Raevskii investigation Kiselev gave Burtsov the chance to destroy a list of secret society members found among Raevskii's papers. The story of its destruction reveals much about Kiselev's chosen course of action in relation to the secret society at this time and it is referred to frequently in the testimony of the Decembrists. In his memoirs, Raevskii recalled that 'Kiselev received this piece of paper in Burtsov's presence and gave it [to him] to read. Then he put it on the table and left the room. Burtsov took the opportunity to pick the list up and throw it into the stove'. Kiselev had taken the precaution of ensuring that the orderly general, I. I. Baikov, had had sight of the compromising document before conniving at its destruction. Kiselev sent it to him without comment in a bundle of documents which was delivered by his adjutant, Burtsov. Predictably, Baikov did not grasp its significance and returned it to Kiselev, assuming that it had been sent to him in error. Having made this rather feeble attempt to refer it up the chain of command, Kiselev declined to take it any further, though he must have recognized many of the names on it as officers he knew personally at Tul'chin.[49] Burtsov's own account of this episode to the Investigating Committee confirms the names of eleven members of the former Union of Welfare. He claimed that Kiselev told him that the list had been given to him by General

---

[47] Semenova, 'Iuzhnye dekabristy i P. D. Kiselev', pp. 132, 136.
[48] Bokova, *Epokha tainikh obshchestv*, p. 367. Original italics. For a critical view of Kiselev's role in the Raevskii case, see I. V. Nemirovskii, 'Pushkin i P. D. Kiselev', *Vremennik Pushkinskoi komissii*, St Petersburg, 27, 1996, pp. 18–33.
[49] Semenova, 'Iuzhnye dekabristy i P. D. Kiselev', pp. 132, 138–39.

Sabaneev, who identified all eleven as associates of Raevskii, which Kiselev did not want to believe.[50]

It is striking that, during the 'Raevskii affair', Kiselev gave interested parties every opportunity to cover the tracks leading to the secret society. As Bokova fairly comments, had Alexander specifically ordered its suppression, it seems unlikely that the wily Kiselev, who had so eagerly set about organizing a secret police force specifically to ferret out liberals and freemasons, would have turned down the opportunity to earn promotion and credit by exposing a significant political conspiracy on his doorstep.[51] Unlike Sabaneev, however, the evidence points precisely to the fact that he did indeed turn it down. This is even more puzzling, given that he was by all accounts notoriously quick-tempered and did not gladly suffer the many fools by whom, in his opinion, he had the misfortune to be surrounded. The sons of one of them, P. Ia. Kornilov, a general whom Kiselev had castigated unstintingly for his incompetence, later drew attention to passages in letters of A. S. Menshikov, A. F. Orlov and A. A. Zakrevskii purporting to show that Kiselev frequently lost his temper and that he was unpopular in the army because of his arrogance and rudeness.[52] According to the Kornilovs' account, in 1824 and 1825 Kiselev sent Alexander appraisals of thirty-two Second Army generals, which included one about himself. Their directness and acerbity was quite unusual for any document written at that time, even confidential ones, and especially those intended for the tsar. The chief-of-staff pronounced twenty-two of his generals to be incompetent and unfit for service or even detrimental to it, meaning worse than useless. Only eight of them attained a more or less satisfactory assessment. Taken at face value, Kiselev's critical comments suggest a lamentable standard of education and a mediocre calibre of Russian army generals in the first quarter of the nineteenth century. Against this, however, many of them performed outstandingly well on active service, especially in the Napoleonic Wars. In the Kornilovs' view, the glaring discrepancy had much to do with the difficult personality of Kiselev himself. His own telling self-appraisal reads provocatively:

> No previous achievements, and therefore not entitled to the post he now occupies. Intelligent and very proud, making him potentially useful. Honest and ready to sacrifice himself for the good of the cause. *But in case of the slightest dissatisfaction he is prepared to sacrifice everything to further his own ambition.*[53]

[50] The names listed included Orlov, Pestel', Volkonskii and Burtsov. See *Vosstanie dekabristov. Materialy*, ed. A. N. Sakharov, vol. 20, Moscow, 2001, pp. 198–99, 201; vol. 26, Moscow, 1986, p. 242.

[51] Bokova, *Epokha tainikh obshchestv*, pp. 387–88.

[52] Kornilovy, 'Dlia kharakteristiki russkikh generalov. P. D. Kiselev i P. Ia. Kornilov 1819–1820', *RS*, 1890, 6, pp. 727–39 (pp. 729–30).

[53] Ibid., pp. 727–28. Original italics.

Kiselev, like his friend Zakrevskii, was clearly unimpressed by the general standard of the officer corps, but how was the chief-of-staff himself perceived? Basargin's memoirs provide this contemporary view:

> Although Kiselev had no formal education he was extraordinarily clever and adroit, sociable and articulate. He had a natural ability to win the loyalty of those he commanded. [. . .] I heard him say more than once how difficult it was for him to turn a society ballroom boy [svetskii poloter], as he put it, into an effective officer, and complain of the number of sleepless nights he had, even as adjutant-general, as he sought to improve his own performance in order to be of some use.[54]

Just days after his twenty-fifth birthday, Ivan Burtsov, then a member of the Union of Welfare's directorate, wrote to Kiselev (14 December 1820) with this glowing testimony: 'I will always unfailingly respect you as one of the most honourable and rarest of people whose actions are to the enormous benefit of the country, and the period of my service under your command I will always consider the most instructive and hitherto the happiest time of my life.' Pestel´ also held Kiselev in very high regard. In a letter to him (15 November 1822) he praises the general's command of the Second Army (where he clearly eclipsed Vitgenshtein) and urges him to return from leave to rejoin his troops, 'who even in your great strictness see only evidence of your fairness and love for their general wellbeing. It gives me pleasure to say this to you because it is an expression of my feelings for you'.[55] Kiselev was clearly an impressive figure. Many years after the above evaluations, and when Kiselev was Minister of State Domains, Alexander Pushkin recorded in his diary on 3 June 1834 after meeting him (together with Zhukovskii and Viazemskii) in St Petersburg: 'He is perhaps the most remarkable of all our state officials.'[56] In fact, Pushkin had expressed a very different opinion in 1819 in a poem addressed to their mutual friend A. F. Orlov, part of which reads: 'I wouldn't rely on General Kiselev. There's no doubt he's a very nice man [. . .] but he's a courtier so his promises are worthless.'[57]

It is perhaps not surprising that the perception of Kiselev was not uniformly positive. While friends and enemies alike admired him for

---

[54] 'Vospominaniia N.V. Basargina', p. 17.

[55] Zablotskii-Desiatovskii, Graf P. D. Kiselev i ego vremia, 1, p. 94.

[56] Quoted in Orlik, Gosudarstvennye liudi Rossii, p. 91.

[57] Shtraikh (ed.), Zapiski, stat´i, pis´ma dekabrista I. D. Iakushkina, p. 542. Many years later, in 1857, A. F. Orlov was appointed chairman of the 'secret committee' formed by Alexander II to start the reform of serfdom, and was responsible in 1856 for securing Kiselev's dismissal as Minister of State Domains. See George L. Yaney, The Systemization of Russian Government. Social Evolution in the Domestic Administration of Imperial Russia, 1711–1905, Champaign, IL, 1973, p. 164.

his energy, intelligence and leadership, the historian P. V. Dolgorukov pointed to his ambivalent personality, maintaining that Kiselev was seen as 'a strange mix of liberal and courtier, a European and a Pasha; he appeared stern but was in fact supple and adroit'.[58] Kiselev could indeed be impulsive and incautious in word and deed. And this, combined with widespread envy at his rapid rise and proximity to the tsar, won him not a few enemies. Those in the Second Army circulated rumours about him designed to boost their own power and authority within it at his expense. These attempts culminated in June 1823 in Kiselev's duel with General I. V. Mordvinov. This episode in Kiselev's Tul´chin period reveals much not only about the culture of duelling, but equally about his personal relationships, especially with Alexander I, as well as the obligations of service, honour and friendship as perceived by an exceptional representative of the noble elite of the 1810s and 1820s. It also shows that, here too, Kiselev allowed his lack of aversion to risk to expose him to potentially lethal danger. The duel and the circumstances surrounding it are therefore worthy of some brief consideration.

What had started as a disciplinary procedure became a matter of honour when Kiselev felt obliged to accept his subordinate's curt challenge.[59] The prologue of the duel between the two generals was the mutinous assault of Lieutenant Rubanovskii of the Odessa Infantry regiment on its hated commander, Iaroshevitskii, who was a bully and one of Arakcheev's loyal retainers. It transpired that Mordvinov, the brigade commander, knew about the impending assault but had failed to prevent it. As Mordvinov was one those weak generals Kiselev wished to remove, he used this allegation as a convenient pretext to do so. Other senior generals now encouraged Mordvinov to seek redress and a new posting. But Kiselev turned him down, claiming that he had since received compromising information about him from the divisional commander, General Kornilov. Kiselev's opponents, led by Rudzevich and Kornilov, sought to embroil Kiselev in a duel with Mordvinov which, whether he fought it or not, was considered likely to ruin him.

Mordvinov accordingly demanded of Kiselev satisfaction for his insulting claim that he had received a damaging report about him. Although Kiselev did in fact have Kornilov's written report to hand, as

---

[58] P. V. Dolgorukov, *Peterburgskie ocherki. Pamflety emigranta. 1860–1867*, Moscow, 1934, quoted in S. A. Ekshtut, 'Cherta neprikosnoveniia: gen. P. Kiselev i dekabristy', *Rodina*, 1995, 8, pp. 47–51 (p. 47).
[59] Zablotskii-Desiatovskii, *Graf P. D. Kiselev i ego vremia*, 1, p. 182. The following account of the duel and its circumstances draws on 'Vospominaniia N. V. Basargina', pp. 24–27 and Ia. A. Gordin, *Dueli i duelianty*, St Petersburg, 1997, pp. 54–61.

a matter of honour he unhesitatingly accepted Mordvinov's challenge.
On the eve of the duel, 23 June 1823, Kiselev was hosting a dinner at
his quarters. He took Basargin and Burtsov aside and explained that
he was obliged to fight a duel with Mordivinov. He asked Burtsov to
find his pistols and accompany him to Ladyzhin, some 40 kilometres
from Tul´chin, where the duel was fought at daybreak. In the first and
only exchange of fire, Mordvinov was fatally wounded in the stomach.
As he lay dying he admitted that he had intended to take his complaint
against Kiselev to the tsar via Arakcheev. But knowing that the chief-
of-staff was a favourite of the tsar he decided this would be useless and
so yielded to Rudzevich and Kornilov's promptings to fight a duel
instead. After the duel, Kiselev handed his command over to the
orderly general, informed Vitgenshtein and wrote a letter (26 July 1823)
to Alexander which sheds considerable light on the duellist himself:

> In all the most serious circumstances of my life I have turned directly
> to Your Majesty. Permit me now to report to you an occurrence which it
> was impossible for me either to foresee or to avoid. I have duelled with
> General Mordvinov and had the grim advantage of seeing my opponent
> wounded. He challenged me and I considered it my duty not to hide
> behind the shelter of the law but to accept the challenge and thereby show
> that the honour of a serving officer is inseparable from the honour of a
> private individual.[60]

As Gordin points out, Kiselev's declaration expressed the fundamental tenet of the Russian nobility of his day: that no obligation deriving
from his service role could force a nobleman to waive the demands of
personal honour. Alexander approved Kiselev's stance partly because
he was a favourite of his and did not then suspect his closeness to the
Decembrists, and partly because his tolerant attitude to duellists was
an aspect of his complicated relationship with the nobility. Clearly, the
duel and Mordvinov's death did not cause Alexander to alter his view
of his aide-de-camp. Much to the chagrin of his enemies, Kiselev was
ordered to resume his duties as chief-of-staff and to attend the tsar
in Orel. Here, Kiselev was at first received coldly by the assembled
military elite until the arrival of the tsar who immediately engaged him
in lively conversation. As soon as Alexander had left, Kiselev found
himself surrounded by fawning generals anxious now to befriend their
far from disgraced peer.

However, as Gordin further suggests, Kiselev does not emerge
particularly well from a closer examination of the reasons for the duel.
Basargin's account relates how Mordvinov, having heard in advance
that some kind of mutiny in the Odessa regiment was being planned,

---

[60] Quoted in Zablotskii-Desiatovskii, *Graf P. D. Kiselev i ego vremia*, 1, p. 182.

decided against taking pre-emptive action, well aware that Kiselev only recently had failed to stand by his friend, the independent-minded General Orlov, and had been involved in the case against the 'first Decembrist', V. F. Raevskii, who was now languishing in prison. But while Mordvinov himself may have sympathized with his young officers' loathing of Iaroshevitskii, he certainly could not do so openly. He therefore calculated that the only way of securing Iaroshevitskii's removal was to allow Rubanovskii's imminent act of mutiny to pro-ceed. Mordvinov then revealed his true sympathies by refusing to arrest Rubanovskii which many saw as an act of considerable courage, and it aroused widespread respect. But, for his part, Kiselev made no effort to ascertain these facts and so crucially failed to realize that Kornilov and Rudzevich's support for Mordvinov was motivated primarily by their desire to exploit the hapless general to strike a blow against an unpopular chief-of-staff.

The duel between the brigade commander and the chief-of-staff became a major talking point. Most officers had little sympathy with Mordvinov since a challenge to the commander from a subordinate was considered most improper. Alexander Pushkin, however, even though he probably knew little of the circumstances which led to the duel, sided with Mordvinov, motivated chiefly in Eidel'man's view, by his dislike of Alexander I.[61] Consistent with the view many would take of the duel in St Petersburg in September 1825 between the low-born second lieutenant, K. P. Chernov, and the aristocrat and aide-de-camp, V. D. Novosil'tsev, the poet saw it in terms of the 'weak' challenging the 'strong', and a favourite of the tsar at that, and as the triumph of the code of honour and the ritual of the duel which afforded the Russian nobleman his last line of defence against the encroachment of despotism on his individual dignity. Pushkin viewed Mordvinov's act as a challenge to the unprincipled hierarchy which Kiselev so blatantly represented: any other behaviour would have run counter to his con-ception of the place of honour in the noble's sense of self.[62] In fact, Kiselev's behaviour shows us that he was considerably clearer about the obligations of honour, to the extent of duelling (and killing) to uphold them, than he was about the imperative need to avoid compro-mising associations with dangerous 'freethinkers'. Here we find a far greater ambivalence in an area where he seemed at times even to assume the role of double agent.

[61] N. Ia. Eidel'man, *Udivitel'noe pokolenie. Dekabristy: litsa i sud'by*, St Petersburg, 2001, p. 45.
[62] Gordin, *Dueli i duelianty*, p. 61. On the Chernov-Novolsil'tsev duel see Patrick O'Meara, '27 September 1825: The Funeral of Duellist K. P. Chernov', in A. Cross (ed.), *Days from the Reigns of Eighteenth-Century Russian Rulers*, Study Group on Eighteenth-Century Russia Newsletter, 2 parts, Cambridge, 2007, 2, pp. 221–33.

In view of the many contradictions and inconsistencies in Kiselev's behaviour, it is hardly surprising that historians have long debated the extent of the chief-of-staff's knowledge of his officers' participation in secret political activity without, however, ultimately reaching unanimous agreement. Thus, for example, Shilov (2002) states that Kiselev was acquainted with Pestel´ and other Decembrists but did not know of the existence of the secret society, even though the conspirators intended him to be a member of the future provisional government, while Kiianskaia (writing in 2002 and 2005) contends: 'Historians who insist that Kiselev did not know about the secret society can hardly be right. [. . .] The documents show that Kiselev not only knew about the secret organization but undoubtedly sympathized with it.'[63] Orlik (2000) occupies the middle ground in suggesting that the extent of Kiselev's personal knowledge of the conspiracy remains debatable: it is true that they belonged to the same generation and Kiselev was convinced of the need for political reform in Russia. But he most probably did not know and would not have sympathized with their radical agenda. He remained a champion of enlightened absolutism and gradual reform which took due account of the interests of the nobility and was implemented within the framework of existing political and legal processes.[64]

Be that as it may, Kiselev must surely have suspected the Southern Society's existence because he had Pestel´ and others placed under surveillance. However, even this may have been a ploy on Kiselev's part to protect a junior officer in his circle by ensuring that he alone had control over surveillance of him. It would also render Kiselev less vulnerable to charges of slack security in the event that persistent rumours of political activity in the Second Army should turn out to be true. It may be, therefore, that in return for such efforts Kiselev was indeed subsequently spared any overt probing by the Investigating Committee. A highly compromising comment was made by Vasilii Davydov who told his interrogators that Kiselev had done 'more good than harm to the society'. The same source records Mikhail Bestuzhev-Riumin's comment to Colonel Tizengauzen made in the winter of 1824–25 that Kiselev knew about Pestel´, and 'all the objectives, networks and activities of the secret society in every possible detail'. The Investigating Committee clearly had at its disposal sufficient *prima facie* evidence at the very least to charge Kiselev with connivance at a conspiracy within the Second Army.[65]

---

[63] Shilov, *Gosudarstvennye deiateli Rossiiskoi Imperii*, p. 324; Kiianskaia, *Pavel Pestel´. Ofitser, razvedchik, zagovorshchik*, p. 115; Kiianskaia, *Pestel´*, p. 135.

[64] Orlik, *Gosudarstvennye liudi Rossii*, p. 90.

[65] Ekshtut, *V poiske istoricheskoi al´ternativy*, p. 103.

Kiselev's tacit sympathy for the conspirators' outlook is reflected in the comment of his adjutant, Basargin, that 'it was perfectly natural that such a young man [as Kiselev] not only failed to oppose but actually encouraged the serious direction being taken by the youth of Tul'chin'. He recalled how Kiselev would join in their discussions and 'although sincerely devoted to the emperor, regarding him as his benefactor, he always spoke seriously and frankly, agreeing that there was much that needed to be changed in Russia, and he listened with pleasure to Pestel''s cogent and frequently blunt judgements'.[66] However, Kiselev was no revolutionary. As he wrote to Orlov and Davydov, he was opposed to political *coups d'état* which unleashed the 'madness of the mob'. Furthermore, while familiar with concepts of representative government they remained abstract and theoretical to him. Unlike Speranskii and Mordvinov, in his Tul'chin years at any rate, Kiselev never drafted any document proposing political reforms.[67] All the same, given the number of Decembrists among his staff officers, Ivan Iakushkin was certain that 'Kiselev knew beyond any doubt about the existence of the secret society but turned a blind eye to it'.[68] But Kiselev's biographer, Zablotskii-Desiatovskii (1882), roundly rejected this claim, declaring that, even though some of his most trusted officers were indeed members, Kiselev himself had no inkling of its existence. He further suggests that those involved found ways of evading the surveillance they knew they were under, though he adduces no evidence to support this claim.[69] Bulgakov responded (also in 1882) that Zablotskii-Desiatovskii deliberately played down Kiselev's knowledge of the secret organization in order to preserve the general's reputation, just ten years after his death, as an unsullied patriot. However, in view of the fact that Alexander I himself knew of its existence and that Kiselev sympathized with the widespread disaffection with the moribund Arakcheev system, as Zablotskii-Desiatovskii readily acknowledges, it is hard to believe that the chief-of-staff remained in blissful ignorance. This does not mean that he shared, or took too seriously, the views of its members which he apparently contested in his friendly discussions with them.[70] This interpretation almost certainly explains why he did not suppress the secret society and arrest Pestel' and its other members: to do so would have meant playing into the hands of the Arakcheev regime which he considered the worse of two evils. It was a risky decision which he had cause to regret as highly compromising after Pestel''s

---

[66] 'Vospominaniia N. V. Basargina', pp. 17, 20.
[67] Semenova, *Vremennoe revoliutsionnoe pravitel'stvo v planakh dekabristov*, pp. 148–49.
[68] Shtraikh (ed.), *Zapiski, stat'i, pis'ma dekabrista I. D. Iakushkina*, p. 36.
[69] Zablotskii-Desiatovskii, *Graf P. D. Kiselev i ego vremia*, 1, pp. 243–44.
[70] Bulgakov, 'Russkii gosudarstvennyi chelovek', p. 142.

exposure, arrest and execution. Years later, on 15 December 1836, Alexander Pushkin told A. I. Turgenev that Mikhail Orlov, Ermolov and Kiselev had all known about the Decembrist conspiracy: 'They knew and were waiting. They used to say: "They won't manage without us".'[71]

However, the clearest documentary evidence that Kiselev knew from early 1822 of the existence of societies of 'free-thinking' officers in his army's regiments is provided by the 'Dobrovol´skii denunciation' of 28 February. From it Kiselev learned the names of secret society members, including Pestel´ and his adjutant, P. I. Trubetskoi. Mikhailo Dobrovol´skii was one of Pestel´'s fellow officers, colonel of the Ufa infantry regiment, and his report was a product of the surveillance carried out by Kiselev's own secret police unit. The chief-of-staff certainly received at this time definite information about the existence of the Union of Welfare and also the names of officers at Second Army HQ who were closely connected to their comrade-in-arms, V. F. Raevskii, arrested that same month.[72] Despite this and despite his involvement in the Raevskii case, for months, even years afterwards, Kiselev behaved as though he knew nothing. Why? Apart from his loathing of Arakcheev, the strict obligations of friendship cannot be ruled out. For example, in January 1821 at Kiselev's request his old friend Sergei Volkonskii was transferred to the Second Army. Zakrevskii warned Kiselev to keep Volkonskii under 'special scrutiny' but Kiselev chose to ignore the advice and maintained close contact with Volkonskii right up until 1825, despite the tsar's open hint at the 1823 review to Volkonskii that he knew him to be a 'freethinker'. Kiselev was nevertheless uneasy about the dangers of expressing radically alternative political views. Volkonskii recalled his warning only months before his arrest: 'Listen, Sergei my friend, you and many of your close friends have God knows what kind of ideas running around your heads. Surely you can see that they will lead you to Siberia.' Volkonskii surmised that Kiselev had been tipped off early in 1825 by his brother-in-law, Count I. O. Vitt, commandant of the southern military colonies, about the involvement of a number of his officers in the Decembrist conspiracy. Kiselev's warning to Volkonskii confirms that by 1825 he was fully informed of the existence of the secret society.[73]

For its part, meanwhile, the Southern Society evidently considered Kiselev potentially sympathetic to its cause and had definite plans for him after the successful coup, designating him Governor-General of

[71] P. D. Dolgorukii, _Zapiski proshlogo. Vospominaniia i pis´ma_, ed. P. E. Shchegolev, Moscow, 1934, p. 47.
[72] Il´in, 'Neizvestnyi epizod iz istorii politseiskogo nadzora', pp. 14–15, 42, 46.
[73] Semenova, 'Iuzhnye dekabristy i P. D. Kiselev', p. 142.

Moscow. The Decembrist Tizengauzen claimed to have heard that Kiselev had thanked Pestel' for confiding in him the Southern Society's plans, and warned him to be more careful. Even though he affected to have no first-hand knowledge of the secret society, Kiselev well knew the personality of his young colonel, and was in a better position than most to judge the powerful influence which Pestel' exerted over his fellow officers.[74]

From February 1822, then, Kiselev had sufficient grounds to apprehend the conspirators at Tul'chin (just as Raevskii was at that time in Kishinev) but, for the reasons suggested, he opted not to. In May 1825, he received further unequivocal confirmation of the secret society's existence from Vitt, who proposed they immediately 'seize this gang of conspirators'. But Kiselev continued to play a waiting game and made no decisive move to eradicate the conspiracy.[75] On the contrary, according to one source, he immediately warned the Decembrists that they were in danger.[76] Kiselev was not alone in his wavering irresolution. When, in early November, just days before his departure for Taganrog, Alexander I received from Vitt Captain Maiboroda's report about the existence of a secret society he turned angrily to Vitt and, according to Lorer's account, asked him: 'What is going on down there [in Tul'chin]? And around you? There are conspiracies and secret societies everywhere yet you and Kiselev know nothing about them. If this is all true then the two of you will have a lot to answer to me for!'[77] Yet Alexander himself took no action either. Like Kiselev, and for his own reasons, he too preferred to play a waiting game which was, in his case, interrupted by his untimely death in Taganrog on 19 November 1825. It was only then that reports from Maiboroda and 'loyal' Shervud were followed up and the arrests started in Tul'chin on the eve of the uprising in St Petersburg. Even then, Kiselev stuck to his tactic of a double game. He warned the conspirators of the danger they were in yet unhesitatingly became General A. I. Chernyshev's loyal assistant. When Chernyshev was assigned to head for Tul'chin and arrest Pestel', General A. P. Iushnevskii, a director of the Southern Society, received a note warning him of this. The only person in a position to send this note was Kiselev himself.[78]

Chernyshev's mission was unsettling for both Vitgenshtein and Kiselev now open to charges of negligence or, in the case of Kiselev, even of connivance at the secret society's existence. Maiboroda gave

[74] O'Meara, *The Decembrist Pavel Pestel*, pp. 29, 112.
[75] Ekshtut, *V poiske istoricheskoi al'ternativy*, p. 107.
[76] Kiianskaia, *Pavel Pestel'. Ofitser, razvedchik, zagovorshchik*, p. 98.
[77] N. I. Lorer, *Zapiski dekabrista*, ed. M. V. Nechkina, Irkutsk, 1984, p. 77.
[78] Kiianskaia, *Pavel Pestel'. Ofitser, razvedchik, zagovorshchik*, pp. 281–82.

Chernyshev and Kiselev a list of forty-six members of the secret society including Volkonskii, Iushnevskii, Burtsov, Lorer and Bariatynskii, quartermaster officers of the Second Army.[79] Lorer gives a detailed account of the search of Pestel´'s quarters carried out by Chernyshev and Kiselev personally. The adjutants-general stayed in Pestel´'s quarters for three days and went through every cupboard, drawer and box, took up the floor, even searched the bath house and dug up the garden. They were looking for *Russkaia pravda*, Pestel´'s draft republican constitution, which its author had taken the precaution of concealing only days earlier. Lorer was in turn interrogated by Kiselev who told him to confess to being a member of the conspiracy. He told Lorer that he could do nothing for him as it was Chernyshev who was in charge of the investigation. Characteristically, he remarked that things might have been different had Alexander still been alive: he thought he might have interceded successfully with the tsar on behalf of his subordinates. Kiselev expressed his anger at Pestel´ and felt betrayed by a man for whose career he had done so much. He was certain that Pestel´ may even have compromised his career too as his own position as adjutant-general was now in jeopardy.[80]

Indeed, the Second Army's commanders were understandably embarrassed by the arrests and sought to exculpate themselves. Kiselev wrote to Dibich (17 December), expressing his total shock at the suspicion which, thanks to 'a few dishonourable dreamers' was now falling on the army, 'for which I answer with my head'. He implored Dibich to assure Nicholas of his complete loyalty.[81] Although Kiselev now resolutely set about arresting the Tul´chin Decembrists, his own papers were seized on the orders of Chernyshev by Staff-Captain Baron Fon-der-Khoven, a quartermaster at Second Army HQ, and brought to Vitgenshtein. When the latter had looked through them he exclaimed: 'Our poor Kiselev is doomed! He'll go to Siberia.' Khoven replied: 'He can be saved', and, taking a pile of the compromising papers, promptly threw them on the fire. Kiselev never forgot this favour and later in their respective careers afforded Khoven, who was never punished for burning Kiselev's letters, his protection when his own role as governor was under ministerial attack.[82]

On 26 December Vitgenshtein wrote to Nicholas assuring him of the Second Army's unswerving loyalty and stressing that 'this gang of criminals did not have and never could have had any influence over

[79] O'Meara, *The Decembrist Pavel Pestel*, p. 165; Kiianskaia, *Pavel Pestel´. Ofitser, razvedchik, zagovorshchik*, p. 288.
[80] Lorer, *Zapiski dekabrista*, pp. 80–81, 83.
[81] Zablotskii-Desiatovskii, *Graf P. D. Kiselev i ego vremia*, 1, p. 242.
[82] Dolgorukii, *Zapiski proshlogo*, p. 347; Kiianskaia, *Pavel Pestel´. Ofitser, razvedchik, zagovorshchik*, p. 284.

troops so accustomed to strict discipline'. The following day Kiselev wrote from Tul´chin to Dibich expressing his indignation and shock as the interrogations yielded more information:

> The admissions made to us by Major Lorer have thrown considerable light on the Pestel´ affair. [...] I cannot forgive myself for also being so grossly mistaken about a man whom I had infinitely esteemed for almost four years and of whom I had made successful use on more than one occasion. That scoundrel has deceived us most unworthily and he is not alone. But I hope that the enlightened and stern justice of our August Sovereign will eradicate the evil which for ten years has been making the most dreadful progress.[83]

Kiselev's position was not helped when he, along with Mordvinov, Zakrevskii, Golitsyn, Balashev and Ermolov were named in an anonymous letter of denunciation, fairly typical of its day, dated 26 February 1826. It is not clear to whom it was addressed and was probably written by a professional informer (*donoschik*). Its most damning lines read:

> None of these high-ups [*aristarkhi*] were themselves members of the pernicious clubs, but they knew of them and were important elements in their barbaric schemes. *Kiselev*: by general consensus he is charged with inaction and total negligence which allowed the criminals free access to meetings and gatherings over such a long period in a very small town. Many believe that a little idle curiosity on his part would have been enough to establish the reason for these meetings of people who were not serving in the army but often visited its HQ. My own opinion is that he gave tacit approval to what he chose to turn a blind eye to.[84]

This perception of Kiselev's deliberate inaction may have been representative, widespread in army circles and, indeed, largely accurate, but from this point Kiselev presented himself in letters to St Petersburg as the victim of the conspirators' brazen deceit, Pestel´'s in particular. Even so, he spoke up on behalf of Basargin, denied his involvement, and invited him to a farewell party at his quarters — in the circumstances a bold step. In his memoirs Basargin records Kiselev's parting words to him: 'My dear friend [...] there's nothing I can do to help you. I don't even know what sort of reception I'm going to get in Petersburg myself. All I can do is to assure you of my respect for you which will not change no matter what happens to you.' It was the kind of sympathetic attitude sensed by the hostile Chernyshev who had long suspected Kiselev of aiding and abetting the conspirators, a suspicion barely concealed in his pointed letter to him of 5 January 1826, urging him to put aside any personal feelings he might harbour for those implicated:

[83] Quoted in O'Meara, *The Decembrist Pavel Pestel*, pp. 167–68.
[84] 'Donos v 1826g.', *RS*, 1881, 1, pp. 187–88.

You will agree that every honest man, devoted to the tsar and who is a good citizen, and especially those who occupy important posts, should use every available means to expose all the ringleaders and participants of this vile conspiracy. [...] No personal sympathy and no deeply-held feeling should prevent the fulfilment of one's duty. [...] This is what I consider it my duty to inform you both in the interests of your service and in your capacity as commander-in-chief.[85]

Kiselev sought to exculpate himself in his letter of 4 March 1826 addressed to Vitgenshtein but clearly intended for Nicholas, claiming that he had had his first vague suspicions about Pestel' only after the tsar's military review in 1823. These were strengthened on his return to Tul'chin from abroad, 'but all his plotting was conducted with such skill that my incompetent police were unable to unearth anything definitive'. He strenuously denied any knowledge of the existence of a secret society among his officers even though he made two unsuccessful attempts, in 1821 and 1823, to fund a secret surveillance unit. Then, finally, during 1825, suspicion fell on Pestel' largely because of his association with V. L. Davydov, a retired army officer and big land-owner. Davydov was, together with Sergei Volkonskii, the leader of the Kamenka branch of the Southern Society. Notorious for his 'corrupt views', his house was full of people hostile to the government. However, in spite of increased surveillance on Pestel' and Davydov, nothing incriminating was logged. It was only in December when Kiselev had sight of Maiboroda's letter that he realized what Pestel' had been up to and so was convinced of its veracity. Kiselev then wrote an abjectly loyal letter to the tsar dated 16 January 1826, beginning 'Sire, I fall at your feet', in which he denounced the 'vile conspirators'.[86] Kiselev chose to stick to an account which was consistent with his tactic of self-denial: it conveniently ignores not only claims he had made to Zakrevskii for the successes of his secret police unit, regardless of funding difficulties, which included the investigation into the Raevskii affair and its potentially compromising ramifications (1822), but also Dobrovol'skii's denunciation (also 1822) and General Vitt's report (1825). Nor did he attempt to account for his inaction from October 1823, when he 'parted company' with Pestel'.

The evidence points to the conclusion that Kiselev played a double game. While he shared some of the Decembrists' ideas he was not certain of their success and so, as an intelligent and wily political operator, he preferred not to risk his career by joining — or exposing

[85] Semenova, 'Iuzhnye dekabristy i P. D. Kiselev', pp. 143–44.
[86] O'Meara, *The Decembrist Pavel Pestel*, p. 168.

— them. But he did risk compromising himself in the eyes of the government through his imprudent friendships. Moreover, to quote M. K. Azadovskii in relation to Sabaneev: 'It was of no advantage to him, and even dangerous to expose a nest of conspirators in the corps which had been entrusted to his command, for this would have been tantamount to an admission of his own short-sightedness and negligence pointing to a blatant lack of vigilance.' The same applies equally to Kiselev who, like Sabaneev, had personal reasons for taking action against Raevskii and 'parting company' with M. F. Orlov: he feared for his career since his earlier support of Orlov had been crucial in his promotion to divisional commander.[87] It was doubtless for precisely the same reason that he 'parted company' with Pestel´ from the autumn of 1823. Moreover, as Marc Raeff argues, 'would-be reformers' at this time, such as Kiselev and Speranskii, 'felt that success lay only in the support of the monarch' since it was the tsar's autocratic power alone that could hope to enforce reform. This would certainly help to explain the ambivalence of Kiselev's position.[88]

What kind of liberal was Kiselev if, indeed, he was a liberal at all? Druzhinin's confirmation of Kiselev's liberal credentials, that is to say his openness to ideas of political and social reform in Russia, is based on his diaries and Volkonskii's letters to him which are peppered with remarks about the political struggles in France and Germany, about the work of European parliaments and the German Tugendbund, for example.[89] But this should be set against the following passage from Kiselev's letter to M. F. Orlov written in 1819 or 1820. With its echoes of I. P. Pnin on the social power of enlightenment, it sets out his political credo and shows he could never have been a Decembrist:

> Everyone from minister to watchman, from field marshal to corporal, every rank, every profession — may be useful in their own way. [...] Be useful in deeds not in words. Leave this gang of babblers and direct your excellent qualities to real effect. It's not possible for everyone to change everything, but I repeat: everyone has a preordained role in bringing about the increased welfare of the Fatherland. What I really want to do is to convince you that glory and dreams do not add one iota to our well-being; for me

[87] Semenova, 'Iuzhnye dekabristy i P. D. Kiselev', pp. 140–41; Bokova, *Epokha tainikh obshchestv*, p. 387; S. N. Chernov, *Pavel Pestel´. Izbrannye stat´i po istorii dekabrizma*, St Petersburg, 2004, p. 238. Orlov was not actually arrested until 21 December 1825 in Moscow, a week after the uprising on Senate Square.

[88] Raeff, 'The Russian Autocracy and Its Officials', in *Political Ideas and Institutions*, p. 85.

[89] Druzhinin, *Gosudarstvennye krest´iane i reforma P. D. Kiseleva*, 1, p. 260; see also 'Pis´ma S. G. Volkonskogo k P. D. Kiselevu', *Katorga i ssylka*, 1993, no. 2 and, on liberals at Court, see J. Gooding, 'The Liberalism of Michael Speransky', *Slavonic and East European Review* (*SEER*), 64, 1986, 3, pp. 401–24, and his 'Speransky and Baten´kov', *SEER*, 66, 1988, 3, pp. 400–25.

a good chief of police is far more useful than any babbler, writer-mystic, or a member of a bible- or any other do-gooders' society.[90]

These words also show that, despite his friendship with Pestel´, Orlov and Volkonskii, and despite his shared frustration with Russia's current state, he was far removed from them not only politically and ideologically, but also strategically. His failure to make this clearer to them through his words and behaviour was part of his double game. In spite — or rather because — of this, after 14 December 1825 Kiselev was the most open of all to accusations of complicity. In St Petersburg early in 1826 he was well aware of the amount of testimony against him and, according to the secretary of the Investigating Committee, A. D. Borovkov, he was required to explain himself at a secret and rigorous interrogation.[91] He stood at the very least to be stripped of his military rank and noble status if a case brought against him alleging knowledge of the conspirators' intentions could be proved. A. V. Semenova maintains that Kiselev's fate hung on the testimony of three arrested conspirators: Burtsov, Volkonskii and Pestel´. Their combined protestations of their former commanding officer's innocence effectively saved him, as did the fact that the Investigating Committee failed to adduce any compromising evidence against him.[92]

However, in February 1826, while it was still in session, an anonymous report identified Kiselev as a 'constant critic' of the government. Semenova argues that most likely a decision was taken by the Investigating Committee not to pursue Kiselev. It was clearly felt not to be in the regime's best interests to implicate him in the conspiracy since he held a high position in the state apparatus which would be besmirched by any such suggestion. It would additionally mean attaching greater significance to the secret society than was thought advisable or desirable. Kiselev was saved also by Nicholas I's anxiety not to undermine his own authority by lending credence to the conspiracy either in Russian or European eyes by putting on trial major public figures who were not directly caught up in it. Hence Kiselev retained his prestigious Second Army post. All the same, the official attitude towards him in St Petersburg early in 1826 was distinctly chilly. Kiselev left Tul´chin

---

[90] Miliutin, 'Pis´ma k Kiselevu 1812–26', pp. 232–33. Ivan Pnin argued ('Essay on Enlightenment in Russia', 1804) that the educated individual could create 'the good society'. Man, as he put it, 'dictates his laws to the world; he is on earth what God is in the universe'. See Marc Raeff, *Origins of the Russian Intelligentsia: The Eighteenth-Century Nobility*, New York, 1966, p. 167; Patrick O'Meara, 'I. P. Pnin (1773–1805)', *Biographical Dictionary of Modern European Radicals and Socialists*, Basingstoke, 1988, 1, pp. 209–11.

[91] A. D. Borovkov, 'Iz vospominanii pravitelia del sledstvennoi komissii', *Dekabristy v vospominaniiakh sovremennikov*, Moscow, 1988, pp. 299–300.

[92] Semenova, *Vremennoe revoliutsionnoe pravitel´stvo v planakh dekabristov*, p. 173; Kiianskaia, *Pavel Pestel´. Ofitser, razvedchik, zagovorshchik*, pp. 303–04, 306.

for St Petersburg on 2 January 1826 to present to Nicholas I the Second Army's loyal oath. The new emperor made known his displeasure with him for apparently covering up a plot in which so many of his staff officers had been involved. Kiselev left the reception in the palace convinced that his reputation was in tatters. There was indeed a shadow hanging over him. Not long before Alexander's death, Nicholas had received a letter from his brother referring to rumours of 'freethinking or liberalism' spreading through both armies by way of 'secret societies or clubs' which had at their disposal 'secret missionaries: Ermolov, Raevskii, Kiselev, Mikhail Orlov and Dmitrii Stolypin'.[93]

Ultimately, however, there is nothing to suggest that Kiselev's progress to high office after 1826 at the Court of Nicholas I was impeded by his imprudent friendships in the previous reign. He was clearly at pains to demonstrate his loyalty to the new regime during the six-month investigation into the Decembrist affair. Well-placed supporters helped him in his efforts to prove that he was not implicated in the conspiracy. Just weeks after the execution of Pestel´ and four other Decembrists in St Petersburg, in August 1826 Kiselev attended Nicholas I's coronation in Moscow, where he was assured of the tsar's continuing trust and support. This was confirmed with the award of the St Vladimir order. Nicholas followed his elder brother in furthering Kiselev's career by entrusting him with senior office in the war against Turkey in 1828–29, for his successful combat role in which the tsar personally rewarded the general with a golden sword encrusted with diamonds.[94] In February 1829 Kiselev was appointed commander of the 4th reserve cavalry corps. As he handed over his old post in Tul´chin to Baron Tol´ he could take pride in the fact that, as he put it, 'every report was completed, every account closed and not one incoming paper was left pending or unanswered'.[95]

By the end of 1829 he had been invested in a second chivalric order with the award of the prestigious Alexander Nevskii order and given supreme command of Russian forces of occupation in Moldavia and Wallachia where he spent a very successful five years.[96] On a brief return visit to Tul´chin in 1834 he recorded in laconic diary entries: '27 April. Tul´chin: my quarters, emotions; 28 April: walk in the garden, emotions.'[97] Among the emotions Kiselev struggled with must surely have been the realization of how close he had come to

[93] M. K. Azadovskii, 'Vospominaniia V. F. Raevskogo', *Literaturnoe nasledstvo, Dekabristy-literatory*, 2 vols, Moscow, 1956, 1, p. 59.
[94] Ekshtut, *V poiske istoricheskoi al´ternativy*, p. 108.
[95] *RBS*, p. 709.
[96] *Modern Encyclopedia of Russian and Soviet History*, vol. 17, p. 42.
[97] Zablotskii-Desiatovskii, *Graf P. D. Kiselev i ego vremia*, vol. 2, p. 1.

jeopardizing a brilliant career through sympathizing with the dissident Decembrist officers under his command. The friendships he forged in remote Tul´chin with several of them, notably Pestel´, combined with his own perceptions of Russia's shortcomings during the *Arakcheevshchina*, the frustrations in his role as the Second Army's chief-of-staff, and his misleading 'liberal' mask, led him to risk adopting a highly danger-ous strategy of a double game. He was fortunate that, for their own different reasons, neither Alexander I nor Nicholas I chose to call their favourite to account. As it was, thanks to his connections at Court, he recovered remarkably rapidly from any shadow cast over him by his Decembrist associations during his Tul´chin years: his brush with the establishment did not prevent him from making a brilliant career under Nicholas I and Alexander II. He went on to become corps command-er, infantry general, Minister of State Domains, the principal instigator of administrative reforms for the state peasants, and lastly, from 1856 to 1862, Russia's ambassador in Paris where he spent much of his retirement until his death in November 1872.

However, had Pavel Dmitrievich finally responded to the inadequa-cies of Russia under Alexander and Arakcheev in the same way and with the same conviction as his favourite staff officer, Pavel Pestel´, and had he actually been the leading liberal hope the Decembrists took him for in nominating him the putative Governor-General of Moscow in post-autocratic Russia, his would have been a very different story indeed.

'Besy', Disorientation and the Person

ROBIN AIZLEWOOD

ONE of the emblematic representations in Russian culture of disorientation of the person — from the loss of connection between person and place to a demonic disturbance of the inner world — is Pushkin's 'Besy' (Demons).[1] The poem's narration of a journey in a snowstorm set in the Russian landscape of open country (*ravnina*) becomes a primary text/intertext in Russian literature and culture. 'Besy' is a remarkable poetic creation, and its picture of the disorientation of the person in a Russian 'landscape', understood in the broadest cultural context, is taken up by Dostoevskii for one of the epigraphs and the title of his novel *Besy* ([*The*] *Demons/ Devils/ The Possessed*),[2] itself often invoked as the most prophetic premonition of the nature of the Russian revolution and the forces at work in it. In the reaction to the revolution in the collection *Iz glubiny* (*De profundis*, 1918), a reprise in apocalyptic mode of the famous collection *Vekhi* (*Landmarks/ Signposts*) of 1909, Dostoevskii's work in general and *Besy* in particular is the most persistent point of reference.[3] But Pushkin's 'Besy' is present too. The epigraph which introduces the collection as a whole and provides its title is the cry of despair/faith from the Book of Psalms (CXXX):

> Iz glubiny vozzvakh k Tebe, Gospodi!
> De profundis clamavi ad te, Domine! (p. 208)

> Out of the depths have I cried unto thee, O Lord.

The first epigraph within the collection, the epigraph to the second essay, Berdiaev's 'Dukhi russkoi revoliutsii' ('The Spirits of the Russian Revolution'), is taken from Pushkin's 'Besy':

Robin Aizlewood is Senior Lecturer in Russian Literature and Director of UCL SSEES.

[1] A. S. Pushkin, *Polnoe sobranie sochinenii*, ed. V. D. Bonch-Bruevich, 17 vols, Moscow, 1937–59, 3, 1, 1948, pp. 226–27. For a wide-ranging and seminal collection of articles on the demon/demonic in Russian literature and culture, see *Russian Literature and Its Demons*, ed. Pamela Davidson, New York and Oxford, 2000.

[2] F. M. Dostoevskii, *Besy*, in Dostoevskii, *Polnoe sobranie sochinenii v tridtsati tomakh*, Leningrad, 1972–90, 10, 1974, p. 5. The lines quoted for the epigraph are the second four lines of stanza 2 and the second four lines of stanza 6 (see below in main text for the poem in full). The other epigraph is taken from St Luke 8: 32–35, the Gadarene swine.

[3] Both *Iz glubiny. Sbornik statei o russkoi revoliutsii* (pp. 207–499) and *Vekhi. Sbornik statei o russkoi intelligentsii* (pp. 7–199) are published together in *Vekhi. Iz glubiny*, comp. A. A. Iakovlev, notes by M. A. Kolerov, N. S. Plotnikov and A. Kelly, Moscow, 1991. Further references to this edition are given in the text citing page numbers only. Translations throughout are my own, unless otherwise indicated.

Сбились мы. Что делать нам!
В поле бес нас водит, видно,
Да кружит по сторонам.

Pushkin[4]

We have lost our way. What are we to do! / A demon, see, is leading us
round in the fields / and taking us in circles all over.

Berdiaev here takes the last three lines of the second stanza, omitting
the previous rhyming line ('Khot´ ubei! Sleda ne vidno') which features
in Dostoevskii's epigraph. In so doing, Berdiaev both highlights the first
person plural pronoun and invokes the totemic resonance of the poem's
matter-of-fact words '*Chto delat´* [nam]?' ('What are we to do?') in later
nineteenth- and twentieth-century Russian society. He thus draws the
epigraph straight into the revolutionary cataclysm and its intellectual
origins. To a significant extent this epigraph casts its shadow — the
shadow of the disorientation of the person among the demonic forces
let loose in the revolution — over the whole volume, not just Berdiaev's
essay.

The main focus of this article is on disorientation. This disorientation
may be linked to the disconnection of person and place but, as in
'Besy' which moves from external to inner landscape, from losing one's
way in a snowstorm to demons at loose in the human heart, its scope
becomes far wider than person and place more narrowly or precisely
defined. I will first chart in a broad way aspects of the philosophy
of the person in Russian thought, and consider how this may relate
person to place, albeit as a rule rather loosely, metaphorically or
peripherally. My starting point here is *Vekhi*, whose contributors highlight the question of the person — and more pointedly a fundamental
misorientation and dissolution in respect of the person among the
radical intelligentsia — in their interpretation of the Russian intellectual tradition through the nineteenth century and leading up to the
revolution of 1905 and its aftermath.[5] Then I will analyse the poetics
of disorientation in 'Besy', and conclude by returning to aspects of the
philosophy of the person in relation to this analysis.

The question of the person (*lichnost´*), as highlighted in *Vekhi*, is
indeed recognized to be a central preoccupation of the Russian philosophical tradition. The person is a principal concern for many thinkers
of all persuasions and relates to the Russian tradition's focus on the
'living truth'. We may alternatively frame this, for example, as the

---

[4] N. A. Berdiaev, 'Dukhi russkoi revoliutsii', in *Iz glubiny*, pp. 250–89 (p. 250).
[5] For a recent collection of articles on *Vekhi*, see *Sbornik 'Vekhi' v kontekste russkoi kul´tury*,
comp. E. A. Takho-Godi, Moscow, 2007. On personalism in *Vekhi*, see, for example, V. B.
Mikushevich, 'Chaianie raznomyslii. (Personalizm i sobornost´ v "Vekhakh")', pp. 50–57.

question of human nature or human consciousness, and such alternative framings will alter, subtly or more substantially, our approach to the study of Russian philosophy. For all that, the person is of course not the only concern, nor indeed in every thinker the primary object of contemplation; thus, the relative emphasis on — and the relation between — the person and/or the suprapersonal offers an insightful means to compare and contrast Russian thinkers.

In juxtaposing the worldview of the Russian intelligentsia with what the *Vekhi* contributors put forward as the authentic Russian philosophical tradition, which leads from Chaadaev through the Slavophiles to the seminal figures of Dostoevskii and Solov'ev, the focus on the person in *Vekhi* starts from Gershenzon's 'Foreword': 'Their [i.e. the contributors'] common platform is the recognition of the theoretical and practical primacy of the spiritual life over external societal forms, in the sense that the inner life of the person is the sole creative force of human existence' (pp. 9–10).[6] Berdiaev, in his critique of the intelligentsia's lack of interest in the truth (*istina*) and their low level of philosophical culture, writes that 'the intelligentsia held the personality dear and yet professed a philosophy in which there is no place for the person' (p. 28). Bulgakov, in his critique of the intelligentsia's maximalism and cult of heroism, comments: 'The concepts of *personal* morality, *personal* self-perfection, the elaboration of the *personality* are extremely unpopular among the intelligentsia (and, on the contrary, the word *social* has a special, sacramental character)' (p. 53). Frank's coruscating critique of the intelligentsia's 'ethics of nihilism' seeks to explain and reveal the defining characteristics of the classic intelligentsia type, the 'intelligentsia's consciousness' (p. 176). Most colourful in his condemnation of the intelligentsia's consciousness and attitude to the person is Gershenzon: the intelligentsia are 'cripples', their consciousness is moved 'convulsively' by 'chaotic forces' and 'torn away from the native soil [*pochva*; hereafter the Russian term will be used]' (p. 74); if only, he laments, there was in Russia 'a handful of people with a developed consciousness, i.e. those in whom an elevated structure of thought is organically transformed into a personality' (p. 81).

It may seem that neither the *vekhovtsy*, nor the intelligentsia, place much emphasis on place as having any bearing on the person. The

---

[6] Concerning the discussions among the contributors about the title of the collection, and also a difference of opinion on the part of Izgoev concerning the 'common platform', not, as Izgoev explains in a footnote to his article, in respect of its 'fundamental thesis' but rather in respect of its 'principal motivation' (p. 121), see Kolerov and Plotnikov's notes (pp. 503–04). In *Iz glubiny*, the commonality of the platform of the *Vekhi* contributors is disputed by Novgorodtsev in his essay 'O putiakh i zadachakh russkoi intelligentsii' ('On the Paths and Tasks of the Russian Intelligentsia'), pp. 424–42 (pp. 426–28): Novgorodtsev interprets the key feature to be that highlighted by Struve, namely the intelligentsia's relationship to the state, not personal consciousness.

former concentrate on the inner person, or in the case of Kistiakovskii and Struve, a consciousness of law and political process respectively. The intelligentsia, at least in the judgement of *Vekhi*, concentrate on the interests of the people (*narod*) and on the external social, economic and political order. However, perhaps implicitly, through the initial reference to the contributors' fear for their 'native country' (p. 9), through frequent reference to the tradition of Russian literature (which cannot be divorced from the sense of place, both physical geography and domestic environment, in its settings),[7] through criticism of the intelligentsia's ascetic divorce from the world or, finally, by reference, as in Gershenzon's article, to *pochva*, the possibility of some sense of place as constituent of the person is at any rate not excluded from *Vekhi* (even if peripheral). Here the polysemantic *pochva*, which was projected to the foreground of discourse on Russian identity in the early 1860s by Dostoevskii and the *pochvenniki*,[8] is most conducive to invoke contexts, frameworks or metaphors that may include a spatial dimension or more specifically a sense of place. Through its literal sense of 'soil', the term 'pochva' may draw within its copious scope a sense of the physical setting in which people are rooted, to go along with the larger dominant sense of the native cultural soil of Russia.[9] Under the rubric of native cultural soil one should also understand cultural history for, even if not always historicized, *pochva* is a concept that embodies both spatial and temporal dimensions and can aptly be considered in terms of the Bakhtinian chronotope.[10]

In Chaadaev's formulation of Russian identity in his *Filosoficheskie pis'ma* (*Lettres philosophiques*, *Philosophical Letters*, 1829–30), which sets this question in motion through the nineteenth century and beyond, the historical is all and the geographical is next to nothing. Historical consciousness links us to the realm of ideas and Providence, while

[7] For a study of landscape and national identity in nineteenth-century Russian literature and pictorial art, see Christopher Ely, *This Meager Nature: Landscape and Identity in Imperial Russia*, DeKalb, IL, 2002. As Ely points out, a key trope, notably championed by Dostoevskii, draws on Tiutchev's famous poem 'Eti bednye selen'ia' ('These poor villages') with its characterization of the 'meagre nature' of Russia as contrast/analogy to her inner spiritual nature and Christ-like humility (p. 24). This trope paradoxically works against the development of a sense of place, at least in respect of physical geography, in relation to the person.

[8] For the major study of this movement, see W. Dowler, *Dostoevsky, Grigor'ev, and Native-Soil Conservatism*, Toronto, Buffalo, NY and London, 1982.

[9] In his essay in *Iz glubiny*, Frank's final pages implicitly propose an even broader, though not imprecise, understanding of *pochva/pochvennost'*, an 'ideal of the religious understanding and the national-historical foundation of social and political culture', which calls for a special kind of spiritual 'courage [*muzhestvo*]'. S. Frank, 'De profundis', pp. 478–99 (pp. 498, 497).

[10] M. Bakhtin, 'Formy vremeni i khronotopa v romane. Ocherki po istoricheskoi poetike', in Bakhtin, *Voprosy literatury i estetiki. Issledovaniia raznykh let*, Moscow, 1975, pp. 234–407.

geography is just fact.[11] Thus, the unfinished continuation of the subsequent 'Apologiia sumasshedshego' ('Apologie d'un fou', 'Apology of
a Madman', 1837) breaks off at just this problematic 'geographical fact',
which is 'at once the essential element of our political greatness and the
true cause of our intellectual powerlessness'.[12] In answer as it were to
this problematic fact, such a broad geographical sense — and not just
the religio-cultural opposition of East and West — is incorporated into
the Eurasians' conception of Russian identity in the early twentieth
century, with their notion of the 'continent-ocean' of the Eurasian land
mass.[13]

   Chaadaev's understanding of the articulation of identity at the level
of ideas, and the historical continuity of that consciousness, can be
assimilated within a broad sense of *pochva* that includes a historical as
well as spatial dimension. That said, Chaadaev also introduces a
certain spatial metaphorization of the Russian lack of identity, disori-
ented in space as well as time, when he speaks of Russians as 'nomads'.
In amongst the litany of symptoms that demonstrate Russia's woeful
condition he also lists the absence of any 'domestic hearth' as a
focal point for personal life, so that 'we seemingly camp out in our
homes'.[14] Bearing in mind the importance of personal domestic habit
for Chaadaev, one can say that such a sense of place is at any rate
peripherally present in his critique. In the Slavophile conception of
identity, on the other hand, there is a broad romantic sense of the
Russian 'land' (*zemlia*), as in Kireevskii's utopian representation of pre-
Petrine Russia: 'Imagining to oneself Russian society of olden days [. . .]
one sees a numberless multitude of small communes, spread across
all the face of the Russian land [. . .] out of which is formed the one,
common, huge concord of the whole Russian land'.[15] No less idealized

---

[11] P. Ia. Chaadaev, *Lettres philosophiques adressées à une dame*, in Chaadaev, *Polnoe sobranie
sochinenii i izbrannye pis'ma*, ed. Z. A. Kamenskii et al., 2 vols, Moscow, 1991, I, pp. 86–205
(in Russian translation, pp. 320–440); the famous First Letter, published by mistake of the
censor in 1836, addresses in provocative terms the question of Russian identity and the lack
of historical consciousness.
[12] Ibid., p. 304 (p. 538).
[13] See *Evraziistvo. Opyt sistematicheskogo izlozheniia*, in *Puti Evrazii. Russkaia intelligentsia i sud'by
Rossii*, comp. I. A. Isaev, Moscow, 1992, pp. 347–415 (p. 377); and P. N. Savitskii,
'Geograficheskie i geopoliticheskie osnovy evraziistva', in *Kontinent Evraziia*, Moscow, 1997,
pp. 295–303. Concerning such ideological interpretation of geography, see M. Bassin,
'Russia between Europe and Asia: The Ideological Construction of Geographical Space',
Slavic Review, 50, 1991, pp. 1–17; and Bassin, 'Classical Eurasianism and the Geopolitics
of Russian Identity', *Ab Imperio*, 2003, 2, pp. 257–67. For a recent collection of articles
addressing, from a range of perspectives, the theme of Russia in the Eurasian cultural
context, see *Beyond the Empire: Images of Russia in the Eurasian Cultural Context*, ed. Tetsuo
Mochizuki, Sapporo, 2008.
[14] Chaadaev, *Lettres philosophiques*, p. 90 (p. 324).
[15] I. V. Kireevskii, 'O kharaktere prosveshcheniia Evropy i o ego otnoshenii k pros-
veshcheniiu Rossii', in Kireevskii, *Kritika i estetika*, 2nd edn, comp. Iu. V. Mann, Moscow,
1998, pp. 266–314 (p. 299).

is Kireevskii's picture of Russians in their everyday way of life or *byt*, including church-going and the domestic sphere.[16] At the same time, however, there is something more grounded that may be implicit or explicit within the Slavophile worldview: this is the landowner's socio-economic sense of the land, a patriarchal sense of the family and community, and a genuinely concrete sense of the religious life grounded in the home, the community and the church that is the other side of the coin to the utopian other-worldliness and philosophical contemplation of classical Slavophile thought. Meanwhile, in a thinker such as Herzen, the arena of personal and social activity of the individual is very much the here and now, and in that sense it incorporates a certain sense of place. This may be articulated in such broad rhetorical brushstrokes as his eulogy to the ancient Greeks whose 'thinkers, historians and poets were first and foremost citizens, people who belonged to life, to the civic council, to the public square and the military camp',[17] or in the tangible sense of location that Herzen incorporates into his self-reconstruction of the person through autobiographical writing, *Byloe i dumy* (*My Past and Thoughts*), as, for example, in the chapter 'London Fogs' that introduces his time in London.[18]

As noted earlier, the concept of *pochva* — which came to prominence in the ideology of *pochvennichestvo* — can readily, if loosely and metaphorically, incorporate a sense of place, a sense of place which can or should be understood chronotopically. Despite the tendency to essentialist organic readings, *pochva* can allow for a sense both of the construction of identity and of its historical dimension. The most famous text for the diagnosis of Russian intellectual and cultural life from the point of view of *pochva* is Dostoevskii's 'Pushkin Speech' of 1880 (referred to by Bulgakov in his essay in *Vekhi* [p. 64]), with Dostoevskii's whole *oeuvre* as backdrop. Here the spatial metaphor of the wanderer, embodied in Pushkin's Aleko, Onegin and thence in a whole series of superfluous figures, is taken up in close echo of Chaadaev (although for Dostoevskii Chaadaev was himself the epitome of the type).[19] This 'homeless wanderer' is a negative figure, located — we might say — in space but lacking a sense of place, disorientated

[16] Ibid., pp. 302–03. On the conception of the house/home in Slavophile thought, see V. G. Shchukin, 'Dom i krov v slavianofil'skoi kontseptsii. Kul'turologicheskie zametki', *Voprosy filosofii*, 1996, 1, pp. 135–46.
[17] A. I. Gertsen, *Diletantizm v nauke*, in Gertsen, *Sobranie sochinenii v tridtsati tomakh*, Moscow, 1954–58, 3 (1954), pp. 5–88 (p. 52); the translation is taken from *A Documentary History of Russian Thought: From the Enlightenment to Marxism*, trans. and ed. W. J. Leatherbarrow and D. C. Offord, Ann Arbor, MI, 1987, p. 138.
[18] A. I. Gertsen, *Byloe i dumy*, 3 vols, Moscow, 1967, 3, pp. 5–8.
[19] On Chaadaev and Dostoevskii, see Robin Aizlewood, 'To Europe and Back: Chaadaev and Dostoevskii', in *Convergence and Divergence: Russia and Eastern Europe into the Twenty-First Century*, ed. Peter Duncan, London, 2007, pp. 121–37.

since uprooted, but with possible positive potential in his truth-seeking.[20] Against this type Dostoevskii champions Pushkin's Tat'iana, who is rooted in her native culture and place. It is the theme of Tat'iana's moral integrity that Dostoevskii develops at length in characterizing how she 'stands firmly on her native soil', and the same invocation of the special Christian calling of the Russian people is what draws him to Tiutchev's poem 'Eti bednye selen'ia': the 'humble land' echoes Russian spiritual humility, close to Christ.[21] But he does eventually include some sense of place in the picture: 'her memories of childhood, memories of her native land, of the village backwoods in which her humble, pure life had begun — "the cross and shade of the branches over the grave of her poor nurse"'.[22]

Subsequently Berdiaev, in *Russkaia ideia* (*The Russian Idea*, 1946), indulges in similar vein in analogies between the vast openness of Russian space, on the one hand, and features of the Russian soul and national character, on the other:

> There is a correspondence between the vastness, the boundlessness of the Russian land and the Russian soul, between physical geography and the geography of the soul. In the soul of the Russian people there is the same vastness, boundlessness, orientation towards endlessness as in the Russian plain [*ravnina*].[23]

In his own philosophy of the person, however, Berdiaev lays absolute emphasis on the noumenal, spiritual dimension as the true realm of the person and his/her uniqueness; all that is objectified has moved into the domain of inauthentic existence, the domain of necessity rather than of freedom.[24] There is little if any room for a sense of place here. On the other hand, in the thinker whom Berdiaev recognized as in many ways his polar opposite, Rozanov, a sense of place is very much constituent of the person — the embodied person — and his/her experience of life. In prioritizing the particular over the general, Rozanov's person is located in specific time and place, hence the typical identification of time and/or place under many of the entries in his genre of *Opavshie list'ia* (*Fallen Leaves*) writings, for example:

---

[20] F. M. Dostoevskii, 'Pushkin. Ocherk', *Polnoe sobranie sochinenii*, 26, pp. 136–49 (pp. 137–39).

[21] Ibid., p. 148. Dostoevskii rewords 'nature' (*priroda*) in Tiutchev's 'meagre nature' (*nishchaia priroda*) as 'land' (*zemlia*), thereby generalizing the sense beyond physical nature/landscape, but he preserves the epithet 'nishchii' which echoes the phrase 'meek in spirit' (*nishchie dukhom*) from the beatitudes. See also note 8 above.

[22] Ibid., pp. 140, 142.

[23] N. A. Berdiaev, *Russkaia ideia. Osnovnye problemy russkoi mysli XIX veka i nachala XX veka*, in Berdiaev, *Russkaia ideia. Osnovnye problemy russkoi mysli XIX veka i nachala XX veka; Sud'ba Rossii*, Moscow, 1997, pp. 3–220 (p. 5).

[24] See, for example, N. A. Berdiaev, *O naznachenii cheloveka. Opyt paradoksal'noi etiki*, Moscow, 1993, pp. 62–67.

'at my coin collection' (a regular item)
'in a cab' (a regular item)
'going to the doctor'
'when Mama in the hammock started singing a song and I heard it as I sat
by the window working on an article'
'at morning coffee, 31st July 1912'
'when I had a stomach ache. In the garden'
'having gone out onto the stairs to have a smoke'
'on returning from the wedding of Svetozar Stepanovich'[25]

Let us turn now to the two monumental, integral projects of late
nineteenth-century thought, those of Solov'ev and Fedorov, different
as they are, and then to Bakhtin. In Solov'ev place/space is subsumed
in the large project of Godmanhood and spiritualization of matter,
while in Fedorov it may be subsumed in the regulation of nature,
although for Fedorov certain places, e.g. the cemetery, the museum,
are to be key sites in the gathering of humanity for the 'common task'
of resurrecting the dead. It is Bakhtin's early philosophical writings
(c. 1920), however, that we find — as in Rozanov but couched in quite
different discursive mode — the spatial aspect as a vital constituent
of his inter-personal philosophy of the person. The person's unique
responsibility, what Bakhtin calls my 'non-alibi' in being, derives from
the unique position that I occupy in respect of others, my 'excess in
seeing': 'For only I — the one-and-only I — occupy in a given set
of circumstances this particular place at this particular time.'[26] This
uniqueness of my position in time and space, and the axiological/
valuational ingredient of this position, makes it more than a point in
space, and qualitatively akin, perhaps, to a sense of place. No less
important in Bakhtin's philosophy of the person is the notion of 'outsideness' (*vnenakhodimost'*). It is vital that, in engaging with others, in the
Bakhtinian terms of 'author' and 'hero', I also preserve my distinction,
for in erasing this I deprive the other of my unique vantage point on
him/her that serves to bestow the gift of 'consummation':

> the author's fundamental, aesthetically productive relationship to the hero
> [...] is a relationship in which the author occupies an intently maintained

---

[25] V. V. Rozanov, *Opavshie list'ia*, in Rozanov, *O sebe i zhizni svoei*, comp. V. G. Sukach,
Moscow, 1990, pp. 165–576 (pp. 199 [passim], 199 [passim], 249, 262, 276, 418, 438, 447).
The temptation to extend the examples, from *Opavshie list'ia* and other works, is hard
to resist. On situatedness in the home, the self and the other in Rozanov, see Stephen
Hutchings, 'Breaking the Circle of the Self: Domestication, Alienation and the Question of
Discourse Type in Rozanov's Late Writings', *Slavic Review*, 52, 1993, pp. 67–86.
[26] M. M. Bakhtin, *Author and Hero in Aesthetic Activity*, in Bakhtin, *Art and Answerability:
Early Philosophical Essays by M. M. Bakhtin*, ed. Michael Holquist and Vadim Liapunov, trans.
Vadim Liapunov, Austin, TX, 1990, pp. 4–256 (p. 23). For the Russian text, see M. M.
Bakhtin, *Avtor i geroi v esteticheskoi deiatel'nosti*, in Bakhtin, *Sobranie sochinenii v semi tomakh*,
Moscow, 1997– , 1, 2003, pp. 69–263 (p. 104).

position *outside* the hero with respect to every constituent feature of the hero — a position *outside* the hero with respect to space, time, value and meaning.[27]

Bakhtin's *Avtor i geroi v esteticheskoi deiatel'nosti* (*Author and Hero in Aesthetic Activity*) is conveyed in a predominantly positive key, but the negative implications of contravention of a proper interpersonal conduct of life can be deduced. I will return to Bakhtin at the end of the article.

In summary, then, aside from a certain tendency to correlate Russian identity and geography, we can observe two main strands in respect of person and place in Russian philosophy of the nineteenth and early twentieth centuries. The first is the potent motif of *pochva*, Russian cultural soil as the ground of the person, although a sense of place is incorporated for the most part only metaphorically. The second strand traces an incipient, occasional sense of place more properly speaking, which is then developed in a substantial way in Rozanov and Bakhtin through their philosophies of the person, a person, crucially, that is thoroughly embodied.

Nine years after *Vekhi* the contributors to *Iz glubiny*, as mentioned at the outset, find the prophecy and imagery of *Besy*/'Besy' a fundamental point of reference when faced with a catastrophic sense of the disorientation of the person and of Russia now plunged into the abyss of revolution and terror. While there is some inevitable shift of emphasis from the intelligentsia's consciousness (*Vekhi*) to the unfolding catastrophe (*Iz glubiny*), one has led to the other. As Struve's foreword to *Iz glubiny* points out in the opening sentence, *Vekhi* was a 'warning', albeit maybe a 'timid' one (p. 209). Such timidity is relative, however, and in many ways Gershenzon's exaggerated discourse in *Vekhi* — with his vivid picture of 'chaotic' and 'convulsive' forces (p. 74) — best adumbrates the apocalyptic mood that pervades *Iz glubiny*. Whether in respect of the person, law or the political process, the call in *Vekhi* for a reorientation on the part of the person (and then society) has not merely not been heeded but the demonic forces of darkness, disorientation and destruction have advanced beyond measure. Dostoevskii, and

---

[27] Ibid., p. 14. (in Russian, p. 96). On 'outsideness', see, for example, Gary Saul Morson and Caryl Emerson, *Mikhail Bakhtin: Creation of a Prosaics*, Stanford, CA, 1990, pp. 180–97; Caryl Emerson, *The First Hundred Years of Mikhail Bakhtin*, Princeton, NJ, 1997 (chapter 5, pp. 207–64, and especially the section 'Outsideness: What It Is and What It Is Not', pp. 220–42); Graham Pechey, 'Philosophy and Theology in "Aesthetic Activity"', in *Bakhtin and Religion: A Feeling for Faith*, ed. Susan M. Felch and Paul J. Contino, Evanston, IL, 2001, pp. 47–62 (pp. 50–54); Craig Brandist, *The Bakhtin Circle: Philosophy, Culture and Politics*, London and Sterling, VA, 2002, pp. 44–48; Caryl Emerson, 'Shklovsky's *ostranenie*, Bakhtin's *vnenakhodimost'*: How Distance Serves an Aesthetics of Arousal Differently from an Aesthetics Based on Pain', *Poetics Today*, 26, 2005, pp. 637–64.

especially *Besy*, is present in letter or spirit throughout, and is most extensively adduced by Berdiaev in 'Dukhi russkoi revoliutsii' and by Izgoev in 'Sotsializm, kul´tura i bol´shevizm' ('Socialism, Culture and Bolshevism'), while 'Besy' itself is invoked through Berdiaev's epigraph (see p. 292 above). The imagery that has 'Besy' as an original source recurs through the essays, though of course it goes without saying that such imagery is much, if not endlessly, repeated and reworked in the intervening decades of Russian culture, not to mention in the wake of the revolution. Some interesting instances of such imagery can be seen in the opening article by Askol´dov, 'Religioznyi smysl russkoi revoliutstii' ('The Religious Meaning of the Russian Revolution'), in Berdiaev's article 'Dukhi russkoi revoliutsii', and in Frank's article that concludes the collection, 'De profundis' (a concluding position matching that of his article in *Vekhi*). Askol´dov, for example, in his analysis of the darkness, death, demonism and apocalypse of the revolution, writes of the revolutionary impulse as one that does not come from the centre of the social organism but that 'rouses chaotic forces' from a 'peripheral plurality [*mnozhestvennost´*]'. A chaotic multitude has ready demonic associations and Askol´dov's image resonates interestingly with Pushkin's massed circling demons in the sixth stanza of the poem: 'Beskonechny, bezobrazny, [. . .] Zakruzhilis´ besy razny' ('Endless, hideous [. . .] the various demons have started to circle') (see p. 302 below). The opening section of Frank's essay is a powerful account of the 'abyss', in which he recalls the 'gloomy, warped fantasy of the greatest Russian prophet — Dostoevskii' and invokes chaotic imagery of the 'demonic dancing of revolutionary phantasms', the 'last dying fires after a devils' sabbath/ orgy [*shabash*]' (pp. 478–79). Finally, Berdiaev's essay proceeds from its epigraph to employ various motifs that can have a Pushkinian reference (*inter alia*, of course) and, combining Dostoevskii and Pushkin quite explicitly, he describes Petr Verkhovenskii as follows: 'the image of revolutionary demonic fury [*besnovanie*] stood forth in all its hideousness [*bezobrazie*]. He shakes all over with demonic possession, drawing everyone into frenzied, whirling, circling motion' (p. 270).

The poetics of disorientation in 'Besy'

Pushkin's predilection for so-called 'situational rhymes' is well attested. Such a predilection may be related to his exploration, through many works, of the way we perceive, construct and experience the world around us and ourselves through similarity, association and linkages (as well as difference). An example of particular interest in relation to 'Besy' and its subsequent reworking in Russian culture is the use of situational rhyme in *Mednyi vsadnik* (*The Bronze Horseman*, 1833) and its relation to the problematics of orientation and disorientation of the person and citizen.[28] Pushkin appeals to his readers to orientate through historical awareness/memory in the political and personal space (in this the poem both echoes and answers Chaadaev). Tellingly, the hero Evgenii starts without any historical orientation or awareness, having forgotten his family's history. His plight as a result of the flood becomes distilled in his frantic attempt to orientate spatially when he tries to locate his fiancée Parasha's house. In his ensuing madness, he becomes disorientated in both inner and outer worlds, an abject wanderer round the city of St Petersburg. In this he embodies both a tragic confirmation and a complex commentary on Chaadaev's diagnosis of the Russians as homeless wanderers, taken up by Dostoevskii. However, in the climactic situational rhyme, the scene of confrontation with the statue, a chronotopic concatenation of person, place and time brings him back to his senses, refocuses him, however briefly, as a person, a consciousness: 'His thoughts clarified terribly';[29] and he recognizes who, what and where he is, including — in relation to all of these — his proximity to the statue. The outcome of the confrontation completes, rather than causes, Evgenii's tragedy.

The poetics of disorientation that Pushkin employs in 'Besy' is made all the more striking for the contrast (no doubt a knowing contrast) it offers to the description of the unfortunate Vladimir losing his way in a snowstorm in the story 'Metel'' (The Snowstorm) in *Povesti Belkina* (*The Tales of Belkin*, 1830) where the process of disorientation is recorded with bathetic objectivity in the past tense.[30] 'Besy', however, operates in a quite different mode, utilizing the heightened sense of place — residing in the structurally foregrounded positioning of words — that poetry provides. From the start, the poem foregrounds a sense of place through repetition and positioning of words in the line and the stanza to create a 'topography of landmarks', as it were. In the middle of the poem these points of recognition are then disrupted, displaced

[28] A. S. Pushkin, *Mednyi vsadnik*, *Polnoe sobranie sochinenii*, 5 (1948), pp. 131–50. For a sophisticated reading of the poem, in the light of current scholarship, see Michael Basker, 'Introduction', in A. S. Pushkin, *Mednyi vsadnik*, ed. with Introduction, Notes, Bibliography and Vocabulary, London, 2000, pp. vii–lxiv.

[29] Ibid., p. 147. The coincidence of time is not exact, but involves an indication in this direction: the flood is located in the 'autumn cold' of November, now the days of summer 'inclined towards autumn'.

[30] A. S. Pushkin, *Povesti Belkina*, *Polnoe sobranie sochinenii*, 8, 1, 1940, pp. 60–120 (pp. 79–80). Both 'Besy' and *Povesti Belkina* date from the famously prolific first Boldino autumn of 1830. In the case of 'Besy', this was a return to the poem in order to rework and complete it, the poem having been first conceived and worked on the year before in 1829 in relation to the journey to/from Arzrum. The second Boldino autumn of 1833 produced, *inter alia* and in a creative coincidence of time and place, *Mednyi vsadnik*. Compare also the blizzard at the start of Chapter 2 of *Kapitanskaia dochka* (*The Captain's Daughter*): Pushkin, *Polnoe sobranie sochinenii*, 8, 1, pp. 277–374 (pp. 287–88).

and dissolved in a poetics of disorientation.[31] This has a metapoetic dimension too, since Pushkin is thereby deconstructing his ever-favoured poetics of situational rhyme, and so by extension the poem relates to the whole Pushkinian problematics of perception and construction of the world and the person outlined above.

The poem is quoted in full and is then analysed at some length:

> Мчатся тучи, вьются тучи;
> Невидимкою луна
> Освещает снег летучий;
> Мутно небо, ночь мутна.
> Еду, еду в чистом поле;
> Колокольчик дин-дин-дин . . .
> Страшно, страшно поневоле
> Средь неведомых равнин!
>
> «Эй! Пошел, ямщик! . . .» — «Нет мочи:
> Коням, барин, тяжело;
> Вьюга мне слипает очи,
> Все дороги занесло;
> Хоть убей, следа не видно;
> Сбились мы. Что делать нам!
> В поле бес нас водит, видно,
> Да кружит по сторонам.
>
> Посмотри: вон, вон играет,
> Дует, плюет на меня;
> Вон — теперь в овраг толкает
> Одичалого коня;
> Там верстою небывалой
> Он торчал передо мной;
> Там сверкнул он искрой малой
> И пропал во тьме ночной».
>
> Мчатся тучи, вьются тучи;
> Невидимкою луна
> Освещает снег летучий;
> Мутно небо, ночь мутна.
> Сил нам нет кружиться доле;
> Колокольчик вдруг умолк;
> Кони стали . . . — «Что там в поле?» —
> «Кто их знает? пень иль волк?»

---

[31] The early variants show how in Pushkin's work on the poem he develops both the 'topography of landmarks' and its deconstruction/dissolution. For example, the repetition of 'edu' and 'strashno' in the first stanza is not present in the first versions, while the subtlest 'shadow' of orientation in the final version of line 2 of the sixth stanza ('V mutnoi mesi-atsa igre') is developed from one version to the next (see Pushkin, *Polnoe sobranie sochinenii*, 3, 2, 1949, pp. 830–37).

Вьюга злится, вьюга плачет;
Кони чуткие храпят;
Вот уж он далече скачет;
Лишь глаза во мгле горят;
Кони снова понеслися;
Колокольчик дин-дин-дин . . .
Вижу: духи собралися
Средь белеющих равнин.

Бесконечны, безобразны,
В мутной месяца игре
Закружились бесы разны,
Будто листья в ноябре . . .
Сколько их! куда их гонят?
Что так жалобно поют?
Домового ли хоронят,
Ведьму ль замуж выдают?

Мчатся тучи, вьются тучи;
Невидимкою луна
Освещает снег летучий;
Мутно небо, ночь мутна.
Мчатся бесы рой за роем
В беспредельной вышине,
Визгом жалобным и воем
Надрывая сердце мне . . .[32]

Clouds rush, clouds whirl, / The moon like a spectre / Illuminates the flying snow; / Murky is the sky, the night is murky. / I am travelling, travelling in open country; / The bell goes 'din-din-din' . . . / One can't help being terrified, terrified / In the unknown plains.

'Hey! Let's get going, driver! . . .' — 'We can't: / The horses, sir, are finding it tough; / The blizzard is blinding my eyes, / All the roads have been covered over; / I can't help it, there's no track to be seen. / We have lost our way. What are we to do! / A demon, see, is leading us round in the fields / and taking us in circles all over.

Look: there, there he's playing, / Blowing, spitting at me; / There — now into a ravine he's pushing / The crazed horse; / There like a fantastic milestone / He was sticking up in front of me; / There he flashed in a little spark / And has disappeared in the empty darkness.'

Clouds rush, clouds whirl, / The moon like a spectre / Illuminates the flying snow; / Murky is the sky, the night is murky. / There's no strength to go round in circles any longer; / The bell has suddenly fallen silent; / The horses have come to a standstill . . . — 'What's that there in the field?' — 'Who knows? A stump or a wolf?'

The blizzard rages, the blizzard weeps; / The horses, sensitive, snort; / There he is leaping further away; / Only his eyes burn in the gloom; /

---

[32] Pushkin, *Polnoe sobranie sochinenii*, 3, 1, pp. 226–27 (see note 1 above).

The horses have rushed off anew; / The bell goes din-din-din ... / I can see them: spirits have gathered / In the whitening plains. /
   Endless, hideous, / In the murky play of the moon / The various de-mons have started to circle, / As if leaves in November ... / How many there are! Where are they being driven? / Why do they sing so plaintively? / Are they burying a house-spirit, / Are they marrying off a witch?
   Clouds rush, clouds whirl, / The moon like a spectre / Illuminates the flying snow; / Murky is the sky, the night is murky. / The demons rush swarm after swarm / In the boundless height, / With plaintive shrieking and howling / Tearing at my heart ...

The opening stanza of the poem establishes a 'topography of landmarks' through repetition of key words (aside from other stylistic functions of this repetition) in no less than four of the eight lines: 'tuchi ... tuchi' in line 1, 'mutno ... mutna' in line 4, 'edu, edu' in line 5 and 'strashno, strashno' in line 7 (this repetition is also echoed in the bell-sound 'din-din-din'). Verbal repetition is reinforced syntactically ('*Mchatsia* tuchi, v´iutsia tuchi', 'Mutno *nebo, noch´* mutna'), and there is additional sound repetition, for example, the repetition with inversion in '*tu*chi'-'m*ut*no' and the strong presence of the vowel 'u' in the first four-five lines. At the same time as creating topographical familiarity and spreading this across all positions in the line through the location of repeated words, there is an underlying counter-indication of defamil-iarization: this is evident, for example, in the 'tu'-'ut' sound inversion, and the contrasting chiasmus in line 4 compared to the straightforward syntactical repetition in line 1. Equally, the most striking points of orientation — the identically placed repetition of 'edu, edu' in line 5 (indicating directionality of motion) and 'strashno, strashno' in line 7 — are in counterpoint to the disturbing indication of the emotion ('strashno') and of topographical unfamiliarity in the final line ('Sred´ nevedomykh ravnin!'). At the same time the key points of orientation are drawn towards the head of the line, where they are most noticeable but also potentially vulnerable to isolation (a tactic that recurs throughout the poem).
   The second and third stanzas, to which I will return in conclusion, relate the progress of the journey — or, rather, the travellers losing their way — through the vivid narration of the coachman. While there is an echo of the 'topography of landmarks' in the repetition at the start of the third stanza ('Posmotri: *von, von* igraet, / *Duet, pliuet* na menia'), the coachman takes the foreground in narrating, drawing on folkloric motifs and also in increasingly fantastical terms, how they are being led round and round by a demon.[33]

[33] Concerning the folkloric sources of imagery in the poem, see Faith Wigzell, 'The Russian Folk Devil and His Literary Reflections', in *Russian Literature and Its Demons*, pp. 59–86 (pp. 75–76).

After these opening stanzas, it is in the next three stanzas that the poetics of disorientation is enacted. Stanza 4 returns us to ground that is apparently familiar through the repetition of the opening four lines of the poem; but, on the other hand, this can also be read as a direct continuation of the final image of the third stanza, 'the empty darkness', a space of no orientation. The familiarity of the repeated lines is thereby unsettled. Equally, the question arises as to whether this repetition should be read as an indication of forward direction (the original movement) or circularity (the movement led by the demon). This is mirrored in what now appears more clearly as the ambiguity of the snow-clouds' movement, rushing forward ('mchatsia') or whirling ('v′iutsia').

What now follows, in this stanza and beyond, serves to effect the theme of disorientation, through disrupting, displacing and dissolving the poem's 'topography of landmarks', its points of familiarity/recognition, and moving it into 'unknown' space. Line 5 of this stanza — 'Sil nam net kruzhit′sia dole' — breaks with the repetition of the first four lines, and confirms the motif of circling, but in 'dole' carries an echo of the original rhyme in this position in the first stanza, 'pole' (which comes instead in line 7). Line 6 starts with a point of recognition — 'Kolokol′chik' in the same initial position as in line 6 of the parallel first stanza — but then continues differently ('vdrug umolk') as the horses come to a halt. Line 7 opens with 'Koni', a familiar word in a familiar initial position, but not in the equivalent line: it appeared not in the first stanza but at the start of line 2 in the second stanza. The stanza concludes with a brief return to dialogue and a brief return also to a more realistic mode, but no more familiar 'landmarks' (while the travellers are looking in vain for identifiable physical objects).

The fifth stanza takes the disorientation further. The opening line — 'V′iuga zlitsia, v′iuga plachet' — is both familiar and different: its bipartite structure repeats that of 'Mchatsia tuchi, v′iutsia tuchi', and it echoes/repeats the second 'v′iuga' in 'v′iutsia', but otherwise the line is populated with different words and the verbs and nouns appear in reverse order. Line 2 opens with the familiar 'Koni', now back in the equivalent position in the stanza, but the rest of the line continues differently — into 'unknown' space — as do lines 3 and 4. Line 5 again opens with 'Koni', a point of recognition belied by the horses' transformation from tiring, stumbling animals in the second and third stanzas to rushing ones now (which conveys also a symbolic transformation into horses of the apocalypse).[34] Line 6 — 'Kolokol′chik

---

[34] Concerning the apocalyptic equine motif in Pushkin, see David Bethea, 'The Role of the *Eques* in Pushkin's *Bronze Horseman*', in *Pushkin Today*, ed. D. Bethea, Bloomington and Indianapolis, 1993, pp. 99–118.

din-din-din' — repeats line 6 of the opening stanza in full, although as a point of recognition it is similarly belied by the quite different import of the bell's ringing. Line 7 announces the gathering of the demons, no longer a single demon. Yet in line 8 not all orientation is quite lost, since it repeats line 8 of the first stanza but with 'beleiushchikh' replacing 'nevedomykh' in the middle of the line; at the same time, however, surety of recognition is delayed due to the extensive, four-syllable occupation of the middle of the line by the unfamiliar word.

The first three lines of the penultimate stanza maintain traces of the familiar but in such a transformed context that they can no longer act as stable points of orientation to locate us in a recognizable 'landscape'; from now on, too, there is nothing grounded, the poem is in the element of the air. The opening line 'Beskonechny, bezobrazny' echoes the bipartite opening line of the first, fourth and fifth stanzas, but is otherwise transformed, and introduces the paronomastic use of the prefix 'bes-' (repeated in 'bespredel'noi' in the last stanza). Line 2 'V mutnoi mesiatsa igre' echoes two separate lines 'Mutno nebo, noch′ mutna' (line 4 of the first and fourth stanzas) and 'Posmotri: von, von igraet' (line 1 of the second stanza), with in addition the moon in alternative lexical form as 'mesiats' rather than 'luna'. Line 3 repeats the motif of circular motion ('Zakruzhilis′') from the second and fourth stanzas, but the rest of the stanza has no familiar points of reference, with the move into the unknown conveyed also by the shift into questions.

The repetition of the opening lines of the first and fourth stanzas in the seventh and final stanza can serve several functions, for example, to reinforce in the finale the motif of circularity and also the divorce from any solid ground. In the light of what has gone before, any sense of orientation regained is illusory at best. The last four lines start from the familiar 'Mchatsia' but then take us through the striking imagery of the swarming, howling demons, the disturbingly oxymoronic combination of demons and the heights in 'V bespredel'noi vyshine', and so to the most unexpected final line, 'Nadryvaia serdtse mne'. This draws us to what should be the central point of reference — the narrative and poetic 'I' — but which is rendered instead the recipient location of disorientated personhood, possessed and torn apart by demons.[35]

Suffice it to say that the poetry, and not just the poem's theme, makes this poem one of such resonance in Russian culture. Interpretations of Dostoevskii's *Besy* tend to identify the epigraph from 'Besy' as pointing towards the carnivalesque strand of the novel, and this is

---

[35] The motif of *nadryv*, of people tearing themselves apart, is of course also taken up by Dostoevskii and provides the title 'Nadryvy' of Book 4 of *Brat′ia Karamazovy* (*The Brothers Karamazov*).

clearly right.[36] But if we recontextualize the poem in Pushkin's *oeuvre* too — a recontextualization urged also by its metapoetic relation to that oeuvre outlined in advance of the above analysis — we can situate its poetics of disorientation of the person in the context of his multi-faceted exploration of the ways in which we orientate, perceive and construct ourselves and the world around us. This context too is part of the poem's resonance, and a part too of any reading, more specifically, of *Besy* or *Iz glubiny*.

In conclusion, I would like to return to Bakhtin and to the notion of 'outsideness' in his interpersonal philosophy of the person. My purpose is not to propose a full and exact imposition of Bakhtin's philosophy of the person on to 'Besy', far from it, but rather to propose a certain usefulness it may have as a pointer to reading the poem. I am well aware that in so doing I am taking Bakhtin's conception out of its primary context, of 'outsideness' as 'excess of seeing', of 'outsideness' in relation to sympathy, empathy and the proper role of the person as author and as hero.[37] Nevertheless, I think that Bakhtin's framework can serve to illuminate a further dimension to the disorientation of the person in 'Besy'.

Such a reading starts from the vivid but apparently less contentful second and third stanzas of the poem, which convey the travellers' loss of direction in the journey through the snowstorm. This is ostensibly communicated through the coachman's narration which — quite improbably — lasts all of fifteen and a half lines, in loquacious response to the narrator's tersely and realistically phrased 'Ei! Poshel, iamshchik!' at the start of the second stanza. While the coachman's opening words, 'Net mochi: / Koniam, barin, tiazhelo', are reliably and realistically his, the final four lines of the third stanza, ending with 'I propal vo t′me pustoi', are at best a contamination of the coachman's voice and that of the poet narrator.[38] Whose words are whose in the ten lines in between is a moot and irresolvable point. If the indication of direct speech were absent, one might treat this as free indirect discourse, but

---

[36] See W. J. Leatherbarrow, 'The Devils' Vaudeville: "Decoding" the Demonic in Dostoevsky's *The Devils*', in *Russian Literature and Its Demons*, pp. 279–306 (p. 304 [also pp. 281, 300]). Leatherbarrow concludes that 'the Pushkin epigraph anticipates the carnival strand of the novel and goes with the revolutionary activities of Petr Verkhovensky and his circle. [...] He is a demon, certainly, but what he creates dissolves into vaudeville. [...] the breakdown of order he orchestrates offers the freedom only to go around in circles in a dark field.' On the other hand: 'The epigraph from Saint Luke, however, anticipates the apocalyptic/redemptive theme with which Dostoevsky overlays the carnival strand of the novel' (p. 304). For Berdiaev and the other writers of *Iz glubiny*, the carnival of 'Besy'/*Besy* has turned into the cataclysmic abyss that Dostoevskii prophesied.

[37] See note 27 above.

[38] Vinogradov presents the coachman's speech as 'stylized' but with 'streams of living popular language', identifying the latter in specific examples that do not, however, go beyond line 2 of the third stanza (V. V. Vinogradov, *Iazyk Pushkina. Pushkin i istoriia russkogo literaturnogo iazyka*, Moscow, 2000, p. 476).

that is not the case here. Similarly, in the brief, not especially dramatic dialogue at the end of the fourth stanza — 'Chto tam v pole?' / 'Kto ikh znaet? pen' il' volk?' — the attribution to speakers is not quite certain. One may take the easy option of supposing that the initial question belongs to the poet narrator, but in the light of what precedes, e.g. the coachman's increasingly fantastical narration being at odds with the gruff response here, it is hard to insist. It is striking too that the presence of another, separate person — the brief dialogue comes just after the line 'Sil nam net kruzhit'sia dole' with its first person plural, echoing the use of first person plural as well as singular in the previous narration of the coachman — is completely erased in the last three stanzas. Contrariwise, it is in the last three stanzas too that the singular demon abruptly transmutes into the plurality of demons (Askol'dov's essay in *Iz glubiny* again comes to mind). In fact, from a world involving two different first persons, the first person plural and dialogue between the two persons (although no use of the second-person pronouns), as well as the third-person world in singular and plural, there is now just an isolated 'I' and the plurality of demons.[39]

All this might be interpreted functionally, as a device contributing to the effect of disorientation. That is so, but there can be more to it. For it is clearly a different disorientation from that represented spatially. This is where there may be grounds for using Bakhtin as a pointer to seeing in 'Besy' something akin to the erosion of the proper 'outside-ness' of one person from another. In psychological terms, maybe we can read it as an exploration of what happens to the person in situations of extreme panic and terror, a kind of hysteria which both erodes distinction and effects isolation. Indeed, this erosion largely or entirely precedes the poem's transition into the territory of total spatial disorientation and demonic possession. Applying Bakhtin's framework negatively, such erosion entails a fundamental disorientation of the person, properly understood. This reading of 'Besy', I would like to suggest, can add significantly to our understanding of what the poem has to say about the disorientated person, in the poem itself, in the context of revolutionary Russia and its demons, or more generally.

[39] John Bayley is alert to the question of the person in the poem, but his analysis can be taken further. He notes that the opening exchange 'springs into a natural acoustic life based on the shrill note of the order, and the deep rumble of the reply', but he does not look to the rest of the coachman's speech. He also notes that, when the original third-person 'traveller' (*putnik*) becomes a first-person subject (see Pushkin, *Polnoe sobranie sochinenii*, 3, 2, p. 830), the driver becomes a 'more realistic figure [...] as if the promotion of "traveller" to intimate "I" had drawn him into an implied contrast with his passenger'. On the one hand, he concludes that 'folklore is both dramatised and internalised', and yet in respect of the folkloric imagery in the second half of the penultimate stanza he also considers that 'we can feel that the attempt to folklorise the experience is useless' (see John Bayley, *Pushkin: A Comparative Commentary*, Cambridge, 1971, pp. 63–65). In respect of Pushkin's work on the poem, it should also be noted that the abrupt shift from singular to plural demons was not observed initially, with plural 'demons' in the second stanza (see Pushkin, *Polnoe sobranie sochinenii*, 3, 2, p. 833).

Przheval´skii, Asia and Empire

PETER WALDRON

CLOSE to the remote shores of Lake Issyk-Kul in north-east Kyrgyzy-stan, near the town of Karakol, stands a granite monument marking the grave of the explorer Nikolai Przheval´skii.[1] His death in October 1888 had occurred during his fifth major expedition to Central Asia, a journey aimed at pushing south-east over the Tien-Shan mountains to reach the Tibetan plateau and then on to Lhasa itself. Przheval´skii was determined to demonstrate the reach of Russia's power at a time when Russian expansion into Asia was being viewed as a major part of its foreign policy after failures to expand its European influence. This essay will discuss Przheval´skii's place in the development of the Russian empire and analyse how Russians conceived of their Asian domains in the late nineteenth century.

Promoted to major-general in the Russian army in 1886, Przheval´skii represented the power of the Russian state at its most rumbustious. He revelled in the arduousness of exploration and saw himself as a pioneer, not just in the physical exploration of Russia's Asian borderlands, but also in proclaiming the significance of Asia for Russia's future. Born in 1839, Nikolai Przheval´skii was brought up in the countryside near Smolensk.[2] His family was not wealthy and, while his widowed mother wanted to send him to a military college that would guarantee him an army career, the family was not rich enough and had to settle for educating him at the local grammar school in Smolensk. After six years at school, he joined the Russian army at the age of sixteen, hoping to see active service in the Crimean War. But there was no opportunity for a new junior recruit to serve on the front line, and the young Przheval´skii spent five years stationed in small towns in central Russia. He resisted, however, the temptation to follow many of his fellow junior officers into a life of drunkenness and tedium, and instead he began to

---

Peter Waldron is Professor of Modern History at the University of East Anglia.

[1] Karakol was renamed Przheval´sk after the explorer's death. In 1921 the town returned to its original name, only for it again to become Przheval´sk in 1939 to mark the centenary of Przheval´skii's birth. Finally, in 1992 the town reverted to the name of Karakol.

[2] See N. M. Dubrovin, *N. M. Przheval´skii. Biograficheskii ocherk*, St Petersburg, 1890; A. V. Zelenin, *Puteshestviia N. M. Przheval´skogo*, 2 vols, St Petersburg, 1899 and 1900; and D. Rayfield, *The Dream of Lhasa: The Life of Nikolai Przhevalsky, Explorer of Central Asia*, London, 1976, for biographical details. Przheval´skii himself published a short autobiographical sketch, N. M. Przheval´skii, 'Avtobiografiia N. M. Przheval´skogo', *Russkaia Starina*, 60, 1888, 11, pp. 528–40.

dream of leaving behind the drudgery of military life in the Russian provinces and escaping to explore the wilds of Asia or Africa. Przheval´skii was intent on turning his dreams into reality and in 1861 he succeeded in passing the entrance examination for the General Staff Academy. This proved to be a turning point in the young officer's life. Even though he left the Academy after two years without completing the course, it gave Przheval´skii the opportunity to write a dissertation on the topography and military significance of the Amur region. Newly annexed to the Russian state, this great tract of land on the Pacific coast was essentially *terra incognita* to its new Russian masters. But Przheval´skii could not extend the enthusiasm he had for writing about Russia's Asian lands to the remainder of his course, and he left the Academy to go on active service in Poland. By the time he reached Russia's westernmost lands, however, the Polish revolt was almost over and the prospect of humdrum military service again palled. Nevertheless, Przheval´skii's ambition to escape into a wider world began to take shape in the mid-1860s: he became a member of the Imperial Geographical Society and then began to work teaching geography and history at a military academy in Warsaw. He was able to persuade senior officers in the Warsaw military establishment to recommend him for a transfer to Siberia and, eventually, he was posted to Eastern Siberia late in 1866.

The remaining twenty years of Przheval´skii's life were to be dominated by Asia. He began by exploring the area along the Ussuri river in Russia's Far East, given the task of reporting on the security of Russia's frontiers with China and Korea and of carrying out scientific and cartographic research. Przheval´skii took to the work with enthusiasm and 'indescribable joy', despite the isolation and difficult conditions that working in the remote region entailed.[3] When he returned to St Petersburg at the end of 1869, Przheval´skii worked hard to bring his discoveries to the attention of the geographical and military establishment. Publishing an account of his travels at his own expense, he delivered lectures to the Geographical Society and cultivated the patronage of both officials and geographers.[4] As a result, Przheval´skii's proposal for a new expedition to Central Asia was greeted with approval, and both the Ministry of War and the Geographical Society provided funds for the journey, although they remained somewhat sceptical of Przheval´skii himself and he had to contribute a significant proportion of the cost. Setting off from St Petersburg in autumn 1870, Przheval´skii aimed to explore Mongolia and to head into the Tibetan plateau, hoping to reach Lhasa itself. Travelling for three years,

[3] Ibid., p. 536.
[4] N. M. Przheval´skii, *Puteshestvie v Ussuriiskom krae, 1867–69 gg.*, St Petersburg, 1870.

Przheval'skii did not get as far as the Tibetan capital, but he did explore great tracts of Mongolia and Central Asia that were then almost unknown to Russians.

On his return to St Petersburg in 1874, he was feted as a national hero; his collection of zoological materials was inspected by Tsar Alexander II and the visiting Austrian emperor, Franz Joseph, as well as by members of the Russian government. The success of this expedition established Przheval'skii as the most significant explorer in the Russian Empire and he then found it easy to gain support from the Geographical Society for further expeditions into Central Asia. He spent much of the next fourteen years travelling in Central Asia, crossing the borders between Russia and China with impunity: although never succeeding in attaining his goal of entering Lhasa, he got to within 250 kilometres of the city in 1879.[5] Przheval'skii was promoted to lieutenant-colonel in 1874 and in 1876 he set out on another expedition to Tibet, again approved by the Ministry of War. Further expeditions followed: he made his way back to Central Asia once more in 1879, and then spent the period between 1883 and 1885 travelling into Mongolia and Tibet. However, the explorer was careful to return to St Petersburg after each journey as he needed to ensure that he retained the favour of the Russian establishment. Przheval'skii accomplished this with spectacular success: in 1881 he was invited to meet the new tsarina, Mariia Fedorovna, at Gatchina and to talk to her son, the future Nicholas II. In 1886, he was received by Alexander III and promoted to the rank of major-general, and on what was to prove his last expedition, the young Nicholas asked the explorer to carry a photograph of himself with him and to send him regular reports about the progress of the journey. In all, Przheval'skii led five major expeditions into Asia, travelling a total of more than 30,000 kilometres. After Przheval'skii's death, the Academy of Sciences published substantial material documenting the scientific discoveries made during his travels, the Geographical Society launched a public subscription to erect a monument to the explorer in St Petersburg itself and officially-sponsored biographies were published in substantial print-runs.[6] Przheval'skii had become one of the heroic figures of late imperial Russia.

Exploring Central Asia and the Far East involved great hardships for Przheval'skii. Terrain and climate both presented substantial challenges to the explorer, and since Przheval'skii and his companions were

---

[5] N. M. Przheval'skii, *Tret'e puteshestvie v Tsentral'nuiu Aziu. Iz Zaisana cherez Khami i Tibet na verkhov'ia Zheltoi reki*, St Petersburg, 1883, pp. 386–87.

[6] For example, *Nauchnye rezul'taty puteshestvii N. M. Przheval'skogo. Otdel botanicheskii: Flora tangutica*, St Petersburg, 1889.

venturing into areas where Russians had hardly before been, they repeatedly encountered dangers and difficulties. Przheval´skii revelled in the discomfort that his expeditions involved: describing conditions to V. I. Roborovskii, a potential member of his team, he 'depicted in the most vivid colours all the difficulties that accompanied a journey in Central Asia: the frosts, the heat, the deserts and the privations of every type'. Despite this, Roborovskii could not be dissuaded from joining Przheval´skii and the expedition that set out from St Petersburg in 1879 proved to be every bit as demanding as predicted. Crossing a 'desert area devoid of water and vegetation [. . .] took two difficult and exhausting weeks. Many of our camels died from lack of nourishment and those that survived were weakened and could hardly put one foot in front of the other'.[7] It was not just pack animals that suffered: Przheval´skii himself had become seriously ill during his 1876 expedition, suffering from excruciating skin complaints but, desperate to avoid abandoning his journey, he treated himself with a bewildering mixture of remedies, including rubbing the affected area with a mixture of tar and mutton fat. The explorer used the dangers of his travels to explain why he never married, writing that 'I would set off on my travels, leaving my wife to worry about me — that would not do'.[8] Przheval´skii's image was of a man who had sacrificed himself for exploration and the greater glory of Russia: his accounts of his travels described the adversities he encountered in graphic detail, and his overcoming of the physical and personal tribulations of Central Asia did much to enhance his standing among the Russian public.

At a time when Europeans were exploring Africa, Przheval´skii gave the Russians their own heroic figure to idolize. His death in the heart of Asia gave him a particular significance, but Przheval´skii's importance in both the popular imagination and the official rhetoric of the Russian state stemmed from much more than his undeniable personal courage and determination. Przheval´skii was testing and extending the limits of Russian power in Asia and he personified a pioneering spirit that resonated powerfully in an empire that was rapidly expanding its domains. Five years after Przheval´skii's death, the American historian Frederick Turner articulated a set of ideas that emphasized the significance of the frontier and of the pioneers that explored it in the development of an American identity.[9] Turner argued that it was the encounter between the wilderness of North America and its advancing peoples that shaped the nature of American society. He

[7] V. I. Roborovskii, 'Nikolai Mikhailovich Przheval´skii v 1878–1888 gg.', *Russkaia Starina*, 1892, 1, pp. 218–19.

[8] Ibid., p. 234.

[9] F. J. Turner, *The Frontier in American History*, New York, 1921, ch. 1.

believed that the process of exploration gave the American people a sense of individualism which defined the exceptional nature of the United States. Turner argued that 'out of his wilderness experience, out of the freedom of his opportunities, [is] fashioned a formula for social regeneration — the freedom of the individual to seek his own'.[10] The process by which the Russian state expanded bore many similarities to the American case: in both cases settlers and explorers moved across often inhospitable landmasses seeking wealth and the expansion of the state. But, while economic motivations were among the reasons for Russians to advance east and south from the Muscovite heartland, the history of Russian expansion from the seventeenth century onwards bore characteristics that distinguished it from the American experience. The Russian state, and its army, played a crucial role in the process of exploration and colonization of the Russian Empire. Przheval´skii was himself a representative of this tradition, an army officer who spent almost his entire career living the life of an explorer. It was settlers who, in the main, preceded the apparatus of the state in America, but in Russia this process was reversed with the imperial regime taking control of a region — albeit often tentatively — before settlement could occur.[11]

Frontiers were of great significance for the Russian state. The great Eurasian landmass lacked significant natural boundaries in much of its space, with geographical features proving to be of little significance in defining the extent of state power.[12] The Muscovite princedom had been able to expand out from its forested fastness with relative ease in the fifteenth and sixteenth centuries, taking its cue from the Mongol invasions in earlier centuries. The flat forests and undulating grasslands of the Russian lands meant that armies — and especially cavalry — could move rapidly, so that defining the frontier was vital for the Russian state in setting the extent of its authority. This posed significant problems for the state in the West, where a vigorously expansionist Russia came into conflict with other European states in the seventeenth and eighteenth centuries, and even where geography might have been expected to help in defining the frontier, the Russian state encountered significant obstacles. The mountains of the Caucasus, 'a mighty fortress, marvellously strong by nature', as General A. A. Veliaminov described them in 1828, appeared to offer a natural frontier between Russia and the Ottoman and Persian states but, as Veliaminov went

---

[10] Ibid., p. 213.

[11] J. Hartley, 'Gizhiga: Military Presence and Social Encounters in Russia's Wild East', *Slavonic and East European Review*, 86, 2008, 4, pp. 665–84.

[12] J. P. LeDonne, *The Russian Empire and the World 1700–1917: The Geopolitics of Expansion and Containment*, New York, 1997, pp. 1–20 sets out the position.

on, they were 'artificially protected by military works and defended by a numerous garrison'.[13] The peoples of the Caucasus proved to be doughty fighters, deeply proud of their independence and unwilling to be subordinated to Russia. The process of the Russian conquest of the Caucasus presented successive Russian rulers with continuing problems and, despite the apparent presence of a 'natural' frontier, Russia was never able to establish uncontested authority in the region. Even so, this frontier region provided Russia with clear visions of what the frontier meant. In 1822, Pushkin published his poem, *The Prisoner of the Caucasus*, which the critic Belinskii described as transforming the region into 'the cherished land not only of wide, expansive freedom, but of inexhaustible poetry, the country of boiling life and bold dreams'.[14] Pushkin's portrayal of the Caucasus was echoed by other Russian writers: Lermontov's *Hero of our Time* was set in the mountains while Tolstoi's *Prisoner in the Caucasus* continued the tradition of portraying the region as one that could offer a particular freedom to Russians.[15]

While some of these portrayals were explicitly Romantic, they presented a view of the frontier that offers significant parallels with the American experience. But the freedom offered by the Caucasus — and indeed, by Russia's entire Asian lands — was also very different from that provided by the American West: the remote frontiers of Russia provided a freedom that was unobtainable in the heartland of the empire. The rigid autocracy of Tsar Nicholas I in which Pushkin and Lermontov wrote was oppressive and stifling, and the frontier gave an opportunity for adventurous Russians to explore an environment where they could exercise initiative and experience a freedom of action that was unobtainable in St Petersburg and Russia's centre. The Caucasus offered an experience that could be full of danger for Russians, but it was also an exotic environment, full of culture and life, that removed the region from the category of wilderness. The Caucasus thus gave Russians both a sense of the foreign and the Orient, without requiring them to experience the physical hardships that the exploration of Siberia and much of Asia imposed.

The frontier in Russia's eastern lands provided a very different set of challenges, and expansion eastwards into Siberia posed many diffi-culties for Russian explorers, but they did not have to face any real resistance from the indigenous peoples of the region. The harsh climate and inhospitable terrain meant that few people inhabited the great

[13] T. M. Barrett, 'Lines of Uncertainty. The Frontiers of the Northern Caucasus', *Slavic Review*, 54, 1995, p. 578.
[14] K. Hokanson, 'Literary Imperialism. *Narodnost'* and Pushkin's Invention of the Caucasus', *Russian Review*, 53, 1994, p. 336.
[15] S. Layton, *Russian Literature and Empire: Conquest of the Caucasus from Pushkin to Tolstoy*, Cambridge, 1995.

forests of the Siberian landmass, territory made even less welcoming by
an extreme climate that varied from months of sub-zero temperatures
in the winter, to hot summers that filled the forests with mosquitoes
and other insects. Russians were drawn there by two urges: first, they
wanted to exploit the very rich natural resources of the region, in particular to gain the pelts of the fur-bearing animals that roamed the
Siberian wilderness. Merchants played an important role in providing
finance for early expeditions that explored Siberia, and Siberian markets played an important role in Russian commerce in the seventeenth
and eighteenth centuries.[16] But Russian adventurers were also filling a
vacuum that existed across northern Asia. These lands were outside the
control of any real authority and it was a natural process for Russians
gradually to move eastwards in the absence of any opposition. The
remoteness of most of Siberia made its colonization a difficult task, and
Russians did not always have an easy time establishing their power.
Settlements were often abandoned, especially during the sixteenth and
seventeenth centuries, as the barren tundra and the wild forest proved
too challenging an environment for settlers from European Russia to
prosper in. By 1600, they had taken the lands between the Urals and
the River Ob, the westernmost of the three great Siberian waterways.
Within twenty years, they had reached the River Enisei and it took less
than another decade before Russians came to the banks of the River
Lena in 1629. Access to the great Siberian rivers gave explorers a less
treacherous method of travelling through Siberia and it was by taking
a water-borne expedition up the tributaries of the Lena that the
Cossack captain Ivan Moskvitin was able to find a means of reaching
the Pacific Ocean in 1639.[17]

The pace of exploration intensified during the eighteenth century.
The Dane, Vitus Bering, was commissioned in 1724 by Peter the Great
to explore the northern Pacific and to gain information about Alaska.
Returning to St Petersburg in 1730, Bering was again pressed into
service by Russia to take part in what became known as the Great
Northern Expedition. Initially focused on charting the northern
Siberian coast and exploring the possibility of the North East Passage
from the White Sea to the Pacific, the expedition expanded to gain
information about inland areas and to explore the Kamchatka peninsula.[18] Siberia also came to fulfil another role for the Romanov state:

---

[16] D. Ia. Rezun, 'O nekotorykh momentakh osmysleniia znacheniia frontira Sibiri i
Ameriki v sovremennoi otechestvennoi istoriografii', in D. Ia. Rezun et al. (eds), *Frontir v
istorii Sibiri i Severnoi Ameriki v XVII–XX vv.: obshchee i osobennoe*, Novosibirsk, 2001, p. 33.

[17] D. A. Shirina, *Letopis' ekspeditsii Akademii Nauk na severo-vostok Azii v dorevoliutsionnyi period*,
Novosibirsk, 1983, gives an introduction to the history of Russian exploration.

[18] P. U. Møller and N. O. Lind (eds), *Under Vitus Bering's Command: New Perspectives on the
Russian Kamchatka Expeditions*, Århus, 2003.

its very remoteness and inhospitability made it an ideal destination for prisoners whom the government wanted to exile far away from the centres of population in European Russia. From the seventeenth century onwards, one of the most severe punishments that the Russian state could levy was to sentence its opponents to exile and to hard labour in the Siberian wastes. After the Decembrist revolt of 1825, the numbers of political prisoners despatched in convoys along the roads eastwards from Moscow increased and they came to form a permanent feature of the Siberian population.[19] The Russian experience of the frontier was in many ways very different from that in North America, but the impetus to discover and explore new lands was potent on both sides of the Pacific Ocean.

The Russian desire to expand into Asia was motivated by a central desire to ensure the security of the state. The sparsely-populated lands of Siberia and much of Central Asia offered almost empty expanses that were open to conquest and occupation, whether by the Russians or by the Asian powers to the south. The experience of the Mongol invasions in the fourteenth century had left a deep imprint on Russian memory, and its rulers were keen to ensure that Russia could not again be overrun from the East. Seeking security in Europe was an essential part of Russian policy from the seventeenth century, but Russia's Asian borders offered a greater danger to the state, stretching for thousands of kilometres across terrain that was difficult to defend.[20] During the nineteenth century, Russia believed that it faced significant challenges in Asia. In the south, the increasing presence of the British in India and in Afghanistan suggested to some in the Russian elite that they faced a potential threat to their Central Asian domains from that quarter.[21] This threat was in some ways illusory: in 1866 the military governor of recently-annexed Turkestan reported that 'it would not be at all surprising if English officers soon appeared in Bukhara. Therefore it would be extremely useful to anticipate the wish of the Emir [of Bukhara] and provide him not only with officers, but even with Russian escorts to guard his person'.[22] The 'Great Game' that Russia and Britain played in Central Asia during the nineteenth century offered no real threat to either imperial power, but it did allow the more aggressive members of the diplomatic and military elites on both sides to make a powerful

---

[19] See L. M. Goriushkin (ed.), *Ssylka i obshchestvenno-politicheskaia zhizn' v Sibiri (XVIII–nachalo XX v.)*, Novosibirsk, 1978.

[20] A. J. Rieber, 'Persistent Factors in Russian Foreign Policy: An Interpretive Essay', in H. Ragsdale (ed.), *Imperial Russian Foreign Policy*, Cambridge, 1993, pp. 329–35.

[21] P. Fleming, *Bayonets to Lhasa*, London, 1961 and P. Hopkirk, *The Great Game: On Secret Service in High Asia*, London, 1990, both give dramatic accounts of Anglo-Russian rivalry.

[22] *Zapiska o znachenii Bukharskogo khanstva dlia Rossii i neobkhodimosti priniatiia reshitel'nykh mer dlia prochnogo vodvoreniia nashego vliiania v Srednoi Azii*, St Petersburg, 1867, p. 35.

case for expanding their military and political power in Central Asia. The British experience in the Afghan wars between 1836 and 1842 and again between 1878 and 1880 showed that it was extremely difficult for a European power to make headway in the mountainous terrain that stretched across the heart of Asia separating British India from the lands that Russia was colonizing to the north.

Russia only took control of Turkestan in 1864 and its hold on the region remained tentative right until the end of the tsarist regime.[23] In 1916, the Muslim population of Russian Turkestan rose in rebellion against their Russian masters when the Romanov regime attempted to remove their exemption from military service and require its Central Asian population to perform civilian work in support of the war effort.[24] In its public pronouncements, the Russian government avoided making much of its military and political ambitions in Central Asia. When Russia first moved into Turkestan, the veteran foreign minister, Gorchakov, announced to his fellow European powers that

> the position of Russia in Central Asia is the same as the position of any civilized state which comes into contact with a semi-barbarous people [...] the interests of frontier security and of trade relations require that the more civilized state acquires a certain power over its neighbours. [...] The United States in America, France in Africa, Holland in her colonies, England in the East Indies — they have all been trapped on this path of forward movement, motivated less by ambition than by extreme necessity, and where the greatest difficulty lies in being able to stop.[25]

This justification of imperial expansion was deliberately couched in terms that would resonate with the other European powers, but much of the impetus for Russian expansion into Asia was motivated by sentiments that were distinctively Russian. The Russian nationalism that developed during the 1830s and 1840s was predicated upon Russia having a distinctive mission in the world. The ideas encapsulated in the doctrine of 'Official Nationality' that was formulated by Uvarov, Nicholas I's long-serving Minister of Education, with its lauding of the principles of autocracy, Orthodoxy and nationality, had an application in the wider world. Uvarov defined Russian identity as unique and separate and insisted that Russia should find its own solutions to the issues that confronted it in the mid-nineteenth century. As with his

---

[23] D. Brower, 'Islam and Ethnicity: Russian Colonial Policy in Turkestan', in D. R. Brower and E. J. Lazzerini (eds), *Russia's Orient: Imperial Borderlands and People, 1700–1917*, Bloomington, IN, 1997, pp. 115–35.

[24] E. D. Sokol, *The Revolt of 1916 in Russian Central Asia*, Baltimore, MD, 1954, and D. Brower, *Turkestan and the Fate of the Russian Empire*, London, 2003, provide the best accounts of the uprising.

[25] S. S. Tatishchev, *Imperator Aleksandr II. Ego zhizn' i tsarstvovanie*, St Petersburg, 1903, pp. 115–16.

approach to education, Uvarov believed that the imperial Russian state had both the duty and the right to direct the development of each of its subject peoples. Uvarov paid considerable attention to Russia's Asian lands, and was instrumental, through his presidency of the Academy of Sciences, in encouraging scientific work on Russia's newly acquired regions. He also acted to introduce the study of eastern languages and cultures into Russian universities, primarily as a means of training the Russians who were needed to administer the growing empire.[26] It was argued that the Asian lands into which Russians were moving were backward and needed to be revitalized by an assertive Russian nationalism. A major part of this definition of Russia's mission was that Russians had a duty to disseminate the virtues of the Russian nation and the formation, in 1845, of the Imperial Geographical Society played an important part in this process.[27] While its foundation stands alongside the formation of the other geographical societies in European states, the Russian society adopted aims that set it apart from the general work of promoting the extension of geographical knowledge that characterized the establishment of similar societies elsewhere in Europe. In 1851, the society declared that it would work by 'directing all its efforts towards the benefit of Russia, devoting them primarily to the study of the Russian land and the Russian people in all of their varied relationships, striving to place even those tasks which do not relate immediately to Russia into the closest correspondence with the practical interests and needs of the fatherland'.[28]

The security of the state and the 'missionary' element of nineteenth-century colonial activity were only a part of the motivation for Russia to advance across Asia. Siberia, the Far East and Central Asia offered the opportunity for Russia to gain economic advantage. The huge natural resources of Siberia gave Russia a chance to enrich itself: the fur-bearing animals of the wild forests could be trapped by men working on their own without any need for heavy machinery, but they then required a means of transporting them to the market. It was thus vital for Russia to acquire and sustain access to the Pacific Ocean.[29] As exploration became more intense and the wider riches of Russia's Asian

---

[26] P. Waldron, 'The Legacy of Count Sergei Uvarov', in M. Branch (ed.), *Defining Self: Essays on Emergent Identities in Russia, Seventeenth to Nineteenth Centuries*, Helsinki, 2009, pp. 211–23.

[27] N. Knight, 'Sciences, Empire and Nationality. Ethnography in the Russian Geographical Society, 1845–1855', in J. Burbank and D. Ransel (eds), *Imperial Russia: New Histories for the Empire*, Bloomington, IN, 1998, pp. 108–41.

[28] 'Otchet Imperatorskogo Russkogo geograficheskogo obshchestva za 1851 god', *Vestnik Imperatorskogo Russkogo geograficheskogo obshchestva*, 1852, vol. 2, pt 4, p. 16.

[29] A. V. Remnev, 'Imperskoe prostranstvo Rossii v regional´nom izmerenii: dal´nevostochnyi variant', in B. V. Anan´ich and S. I Barzilov (eds), *Prostranstvo vlasti: istoricheskii opyt Rossii i vyzovy sovremennosti*, Moscow, 2001, p. 323.

lands came to the fore, the security of the Far East acquired substantial importance for the Russian Empire. The Amur river, draining a great swathe of north-eastern Asia, appeared to offer Russia the scope to develop its agriculture and commerce in the Far East.[30] This was part of a more general interest in the region: the nineteenth-century focus by the European powers on the declining Chinese empire accentuated Russia's interest in the area as the Romanov state was determined not to allow its rivals to dominate these parts of Asia. The weakness of China, together with the aggressive actions of the West European powers, worried the Russians as they began to believe that European expansion into China could easily result in envious eyes turning towards Russia's possessions in Eastern Siberia and an attempt to detach the region from the Russian Empire. Przheval'skii's interest in the Amur region was thus not simply a matter of geographical curiosity, but showed that he was attuned to the wider issues of power politics that were concerning Russia's rulers. The governor-general of Eastern Siberia from 1847 until 1861, Count Nikolai Murav'ev,[31] took the lead in Russia's formal annexation of the Amur region, arguing that

> it is an indisputable fact that for their complete and entire control of trade in China, the British need the mouth of the Amur and navigation on this river [...] whoever shall control the mouth of the Amur will control Siberia, at least up to Lake Baikal, and control it firmly, for it is enough to possess the mouth of this river and navigation on it as a key in order that Siberia [...] will become a permanent tributary and subject of whichever government shall possess that key.[32]

International rivalry intensified in north-east Asia during the later part of the nineteenth century with Russia's assertion of its authority in the region. But, there were significant tensions inside the Russian establishment about the ways in which Russia should express its authority in its Asian borderlands. The tradition of aggressive expansionism that Murav'ev represented permeated much of the Russian military during the nineteenth century. Przheval'skii's position as an officer attached to the Russian General Staff showed the importance that the army gave to the exploration of Asia, and the gathering of intelligence was a vital — if not, indeed, the most important — element of his expeditions.[33] Writing in 1878 to propose a journey to penetrate

---

[30] J. R. Gibson, 'Russia in the Pacific: The Role of the Amur', *Canadian Geographer*, 12, 1968, pp. 15–27.

[31] See N. P. Matkhanova, *General-gubernatory vostochnoi Sibiri serediny XIX veka*, Novosibirsk, 1998, pp. 101–244.

[32] M. Bassin, 'The Russian Geographical Society. The "Amur epoch" and the Great Siberian Expedition 1855–1863', *Annals of the Association of American Geographers*, 73, 1983, p.246.

[33] See A. Marshall, *The Russian General Staff and Asia, 1860–1917*, London, 2006, pp. 131–62.

deep into Tibet, Przheval′skii suggested that 'scientific research will camouflage the political goals of our expedition and ward off the interference of our adversaries'.[34] His travels during the 1870s and 1880s were used explicitly as a basis for the justification of war with the Chinese empire. The scientific establishment also recognized the importance of using expeditions as a means of collecting information about the political situation in Central Asia. Writing in 1870, the president of the Academy of Sciences, F. P. Litke, wrote to the Minister of War to propose collaboration over Przheval′skii's planned expedition to northern China. 'If [he] is able to reach the north-east region of China', Litke wrote, 'which is at present the scene of a muslim uprising, then there is every hope that he will be able to collect as much information as possible about this rebellion.'[35] In the mid-1880s, Russia turned its attentions very firmly towards developing its Asian policy. Frustrated by the rebuff it had suffered to its European ambitions in the Crimean War and at the Congress of Berlin following the Russo-Turkish War of 1877–78, the Russians focused on consolidating and expanding their influence in Asia. Murav′ev argued that success in the Far East would allow Russia to take revenge 'for everything that it had suffered at the hands of the West.[36] As Russia's most prominent adventurer in Central Asia, and one who was able to combine both military and scientific expertise on the region, Przheval′skii's opinions were sought on the situation and the potential for Russian expansion. He did not conceal his intentions, providing the Ministry of War with a memorandum entitled 'New Thoughts on War with China', a piece of writing that found a wider audience under the much less provocative title of 'The current situation in Central Asia' when he delivered a lecture in 1886 and was then published in the journal *Russkii Vestnik*, as well as being translated into English and appearing in the London *Asiatic Quarterly Review* in the following year.[37]

Przheval′skii was bellicose and dismissive of the Chinese, suggesting that they were inherently inferior to Russians, and that Russia should assert itself against a neighbour that was weaker than Russia itself, in moral as much as diplomatic terms. He saw the desert peoples of Central Asia as 'torpid and sluggish', without the ability for 'active or

[34] D. Schimmelpennick van der Oye, *Toward the Rising Sun: Russian Ideologies of Empire and the Path to War with Japan*, DeKalb, IL, 2006, p. 31.

[35] A. A. Visiagin et al. (eds), *Istoriia otechestvennogo vostokovedeniia s serediny XIX veka do 1917 goda*, Moscow, 1997, p. 147.

[36] A. V. Remnev, 'U istokov Rossiiskoi imperskoi geopolitiki: Aziatskie "pogranichnye prostranstva" v issledovaniiakh M. I. Veniukova', *Istoricheskie zapiski*, 122, 2001, 4, pp. 344–45.

[37] N. M. Przheval′skii, 'Sovremennoe polozhenie tsentral′noi Azii', *Russkii Vestnik*, 106, 1886, 12, pp. 472–524.

energetic exertion'. Przheval'skii disparagingly wrote that 'month-long rides on a camel at walking-pace, with their accompaniments of hunger and thirst, can only be accomplished by passive endurance', insultingly commenting that 'the life-long contemplation of the same, never-changing barren and sterile desert must have as its result a passive and inert disposition'. For Przheval'skii, as for many of his European impe-rialist contemporaries, Europeans had an innate superiority over other peoples and he demonstrated his clear disdain for the peoples of Asia by asserting that the 'unfavourable conditions' in which they lived made their intellectual development impossible. The rulers of Asia shared all the faults of their subjects, Przheval'skii argued, and he described Chinese rule in eastern Turkestan — itself an appellation that suggested that the region should be under the same control as Russian-occupied Turkestan — as 'embodying injustice, corruption, high taxes, arbitrary officials, in a word, the total absence of legality in administration or justice'.[38]

The Russian explorer argued that China was fulfilling the role in Asia that the Ottomans occupied in Europe: China was the 'weak man of Asia', and a declining empire should be subjected to military force in order to achieve stability. In one sense, this was a paradoxical view-point, given the failure of the Russian Empire to achieve its goals in the Balkans, but it did give the Russians an outlet for the imperialist ambitions that had been frustrated in Europe. Expansion into Central Asia during the 1860s and the subjugation of the Muslim khanates of Turkestan had given the Russians a greater confidence in their ability to dominate northern Asia, and Przheval'skii was determined to advance the cause of belligerence. In his memorandum, Przheval'skii proposed that newly-acquired Turkestan should act as one of the bases from which a military force could be despatched into China, with Russia's Far Eastern lands providing a second area from where troops could advance towards Peking. His plans for invasion were ambitious and largely unrealistic, suggesting that Russia would be able to despatch two substantial military forces across difficult terrain on a campaign that required an advance of well over 1,000 kilometres from the Russian border to the Chinese capital. But Przheval'skii argued that the Chinese would capitulate to the more powerful Russian forces, as the European power imposed its might on its Oriental neighbour, and that conquest would prove to be an easy matter. Russia, he argued, was admired in Central Asia because of 'the insupportable yoke of China on the one side and the renown of the humane manner in which we (Russia) treat the natives of our Asiatic possessions'. The 'good name we bear even in the depths of the Asiatic deserts' would serve

[38] Ibid., pp. 477–78, 493.

to advance the Russian cause and would make Russian domination of China an easy matter.[39]

This view of the relative positions of Russia and China was not exceptional, since there was a significant tradition of thinking in Russia that glorified Russia's traditions of conquest and expansion.[40] Nikolai Karamzin, the founder of Russian historical writing, produced a monumental *History of the Russian State* between 1818 and 1829 in which he exalted the size and power of the Russian Empire, and he identified its military prowess and tradition of imperial growth as being essential parts of the state. In particular, Karamzin praised the way in which Russia's rulers had reclaimed areas of territory that had earlier been seized by its enemies, with particular credit given to Ivan IV's acquisition of areas that had formerly been under the control of the Tatars. Imperial expansion was portrayed by Russians writing on their own history as being an essential part of the state's activity. Karamzin argued that it was essential for Russia to intervene in weaker states on its borders should they fail to maintain proper order in their own domains. 'Russia was founded on victories and centralization of authority', he wrote,[41] while writers in the second part of the nineteenth century offered explicit justifications for Russia's expansion into Asia. Sergei Solov´ev was especially influential through his monumental *History of Russia from Earliest Times* in which he traced a continuing historical conflict between Russia and Asia. Referring to Asian peoples as 'predators' and brigands', Solov´ev and his followers suggested that Central Asia had to be conquered since there was no possibility of coexisting peacefully with its Muslim population. This pragmatic view of Russia's historical mission was complemented by a view of its geographical situation. For Solov´ev, Russia's destiny was determined by its geography. Resonating with Turner's view of American development, Solov´ev argued that Russian had natural frontiers and that the state must expand to occupy all the space within them.[42] There was, in Solov´ev's view, a fundamental and historic struggle between Russia and Asia that was inevitable and intense. Russia had to keep up a continuous crusade against Asiatic barbarism if it was to survive. Once the Urals had been breached by Russians, there was an imperative on Russia to reach the Pacific coast and to secure its domination of all the lands in between. Russian influence transformed Asia.

---

[39] Ibid., pp. 492–93.
[40] D. B. Saunders, 'The Political Ideas of Russian Historians', *Historical Journal*, 27, 1984, pp. 757–71.
[41] N. M. Karamzin, *Istoriia gosudarstva Rossiiskogo*, St Petersburg, 1843, vol. 12, appendix, p. xxxix.
[42] M. Bassin, 'Turner, Solov´ev and the "Frontier Hypothesis": The Nationalist Signification of Open Spaces', *Journal of Modern History*, 65, 1993, pp. 495–510.

Kostomarov, writing in the 1870s, described how Russia had sub-jugated a variety of Tatar peoples in Siberia and had transformed it into a peaceful and prosperous land, akin to the Russian heartland itself. Kliuchevksii, professor of history at Moscow University, delivered a series of seminal lectures during the 1880s (which were to become the basis of his celebrated *Course of Russian History*) in which he argued that colonization was the central feature of Russia's development.[43] Przheval'skii thus stood within a clear tradition of Russian ideologues who pressed for the virtues of the Russian state to be expanded as widely as possible. While the explorer's plans for an invasion of China appear dramatic, much of the activity of Russia during the nineteenth century had been motivated by the same fundamental views that drove Przheval'skii to call for the conquest of the Middle Kingdom. There was little distinction between the attitudes of different monarchs to Russia's historic mission: the annexation of Turkestan had occurred under the more liberal Alexander II, while his successor Alexander III pursued a vigorous policy of Russification in the empire, at the same time encouraging a 'forward' policy in east Asia.

Przheval'skii's expeditions were also firmly in the tradition of Russian imperial expansion. The process of adventurers setting off into the wild and unexplored areas of the Russian lands was an integral part of the development of the idea of Russian nationhood. The process of exploring beyond the Urals gave Siberia a particular place in the development of Russian national identity.[44] The wild and savage Siberian lands were the source of great prosperity for Russia, but the exploitation of that wealth required huge determination and courage from the men who trapped fur-bearing animals. When the first serious explorers set out into the forested wilderness of Siberia, they encoun-tered landscapes of both great beauty and immense harshness. The physical challenge that Asian exploration presented to Russians was immense but this proved to be one of the features that attracted young men to explore its most remote regions. Exploration, however, pro-vided other opportunities for Russians. For Przheval'skii, as for many of his compatriots, the work of exploring the distant parts of the empire allowed them to escape from the constricting atmosphere that per-vaded much of official Russia. Asia offered a way of finding a degree of freedom that was not open to men who stayed working in the impe-rial bureaucracy or in the main body of the Russian army. Siberia in particular gave young Russians a means of setting distance between themselves and the imperial heartland, while allowing them still to

---

[43] See R. F. Byrnes, *V. O. Kliuchevskii. Historian of Russia*, Bloomington, IN, 1996, ch. 10.
[44] C. Weiss, 'Nash: Appropriating Siberia for the Russian Empire', *Sibirica*, 5, 2006, pp. 141–55.

demonstrate their loyalty and service to the state through embarking on journeys that were dangerous and had a direct utility to the state. Przheval'skii wrote of how 'Siberia astonished me with its wildness, its vastness and its never-ending freedom'.[45] The process of exploration was vital in binding its remote and thinly-populated regions to the European centre of Russia. The process of empire-building contributed to the development of Russian nationhood, allowing Russia to define itself as unique among the ranks of the Great Powers, a state that bestrode two continents and drew its strength as much from the wilderness of Siberia as it did from its European heart. Russia would 'gradually assimilate [the half-wild tribes of Central Asia and the Far East] to its civilization, its social life and its nationality,' wrote Peter Semenov, perhaps Russia's greatest geographer, in 1855.[46]

The scientific work of surveying and mapping provided tangible evidence of the appropriation of these new territories by the Romanov state. Explorers saw the production of maps as a vital part of their work, allowing the St Petersburg government to actually identify the extent and nature of its domains. Przheval'skii's journeys into east and central Asia gave him the opportunity to depict the lands he visited, both by sketching and by drawing maps which, if not always accurate, offered a way in which Russians could obtain a real appreciation of the expanse of their empire. It was essential for the state that it could show that the lands that it was colonizing were an extension of metropolitan Russia. The nature of Russia's empire — at once both a single, contiguous state and a collection of disparate colonies surrounding the metropole itself — made it especially important for the peripheral areas of the empire to become identified as genuinely Russian. For Przheval'skii, his position as an officer in the Russian army gave him a particularly significant role: he was both a representative of the state, and also a buccaneer who had the freedom to express opinions in a way that was not open to a member of the St Petersburg bureaucracy.

Explicitly geographical studies formed only one part of the activity of Russian explorers. The lands into which they ventured had very different characteristics from the European heartland of the Russian state, and the sheer distance between the centre of the empire and its peripheries meant that Russia's Asian lands had fauna and flora that were wholly distinctive. The emphasis on scientific work in Russia's new domains was also a part of the nineteenth-century emphasis on uncovering the characteristics of the natural environment. While the

[45] N. M. Przheval'skii, 'Avtobiografiia', p. 536.
[46] M. Bassin, *Imperial Visions: Nationalist Imagination and Geographical Expansion in the Russian Far East, 1840–1865*, Cambridge, 1999, pp. 203–04.

world of nature had been seen as largely hostile by humans until well into the eighteenth century, the development of rational thought and the ideas that became crystallized in the Enlightenment led humans to view their surroundings in a different way. As the influence of religion lessened, humans began to be persuaded of their ability to master the natural world, rather than having their lives determined by the vagaries of climate and terrain.[47] While exploration of wild and unfamiliar lands had been an important part of European culture since the fifteenth century, it was only during the nineteenth century that significant numbers of Europeans were able to venture away from their 'civilized' homelands and stamp their mark upon wild environments. But it was not simply as a result of a greater confidence in human ability that men embarked on journeys into hitherto-unexplored lands. Scientific advances provided humans with the techniques and equipment to enable them to navigate more accurately across difficult terrain, while the quality and precision of maps had improved to a level where the world could be accurately delineated and portrayed in a way that was not simply impressionistic. The explorers of Russia's Asian lands were faced with challenges akin to those that travellers into the African interior encountered during the nineteenth century, albeit those who explored Siberia were rarely met by hostile indigenous peoples.

While scientific advances made the prospect of travelling into Russia's Asian domains less daunting during the nineteenth century than it had been in earlier periods, it remained the case that Przheval'skii and his fellow pioneers found their journeys frequently to be dangerous and very uncomfortable. But, they were driven forward by the simple urge to explore, as much as they were by the imperial imperative. Even though Przheval'skii came to see his expeditions as helping to propel Russia towards greater power in Asia, he was also motivated by the excitement and challenge involved in the process of discovery itself. This was exemplified by the 1879 expedition that took his band of explorers into Tibet. Scientific equipment made up a significant proportion of the materials the explorers took with them: a variety of instruments to record weather conditions were essential, as were surveying tools, along with preserving fluid and 1,500 sheets of blotting paper for the insects and plant life that the expedition anticipated collecting.[48] Soon after leaving the expedition's Kyrgyz base of Zaisansk, local men presented Przheval'skii with the skin of an animal which he recognized as belonging to the near-fabled Mongolian wild horse, an animal which had never before been seen by a European. Przheval'skii

[47] See K. Thomas, *Man and the Natural World: Changing Attitudes in England, 1500–1800*, London, 1983.
[48] Rayfield, *The Dream of Lhasa*, p. 115.

despatched the skin back to St Petersburg for study, suggesting that it was a form of primitive horse. A month later, he was able to catch sight of a herd of these horses in the wild, writing a detailed description of them in his account of the journey, and describing the horses' exceptional caution in approaching humans. Przheval´skii saw these animals only twice during his travels, never getting within rifle range of one and suggesting that the animals were found only in a very small area of central Asia. Przheval´skii's discovery of the horse resulted in it being named *Equus przewalskii*: a live horse was not captured by Europeans until into the twentieth century. This horse is the most prominent example of Przheval´skii's scientific work, but he also achieved significant accomplishments by simply helping to define and delineate the Central Asian landscape. Przheval´skii provided definitive measurements of height for more than 225 mountains, and established the extent of the main mountain ranges of Central Asia. He was the first European to survey the northern boundary of the Tibetan plateau, and his expeditions first provided the correct locations for the major lakes of the region, along with a detailed description of the topography, fauna and flora of the Gobi desert. Przheval´skii took the first reliable sets of meteorological observations for the region, describing the dust- and sandstorms that struck the area in detail.[49] It was the novelty of the Asian landscape and its flora and fauna that were of especial interest to Przheval´skii, and he showed consistent wonderment at the discoveries that he made.[50]

He brought back very substantial numbers of specimens for examination in St Petersburg. His efforts at botanical collection resulted in him transporting more than 16,000 specimens from some 1,700 species from Asia and in 1889 the Academy of Sciences published a substantial account of his work with the flora of the area. Between 1888 and 1912, volumes dealing with every aspect of his expeditions' scientific work appeared in print, including a major analysis of the meteorological observations that Przheval´skii had recorded.[51] Exhibitions of the materials that Przheval´skii brought back from Asia proved to be a considerable draw for St Petersburg society: in 1874 the General Staff organized an exhibition of the zoological specimens that he had returned with the previous year, The Minister of War, Dmitrii Miliutin, visited the exhibition and noted that 'the whole hall was filled with

[49] I. V. Kozlov, *Velikii puteshestvennik. Zhizn´ i deiatel´nost´ N. M. Przheval´skogo, pervogo issledovatelia prirody Tsentral´noi Azii*, Moscow, 1985, pp. 139–41.

[50] David Moon similarly emphasizes the way in which eighteenth-century explorers from the Academy of Sciences focused on *difference*. See above, p. 206.

[51] *Nauchnye rezul´taty puteshestvii N. M. Przheval´skogo. Otdel meteorologicheskii. Marshruty i meteorologicheskie nabliudeniia*, St Petersburg, 1895.

countless stuffed birds and animals'.[52] Altogether, Przheval'skii's expeditions provided more than 7,500 specimens of the fauna of Central Asia: he brought back more than 700 mammals, over 5,000 birds, 1,200 reptiles and amphibians and over 600 fish. His specimens formed the heart of the Academy of Sciences' zoological collection.

Przheval'skii represented a significant strand in Russian imperial thinking. He was determined to advance Russian authority in Asia, and to transform Russia into the pre-eminent power on the continent. But he was not simply an imperialist adventurer. He recognized the vital importance of binding Russia's new domains to the state itself, and was fascinated by the environment that he experienced in Central Asia. Przheval'skii's energy was immense and his expeditions were his *raison d'être*: he never married and had no real enthusiasm for the social life of the provinces or the Russian capital. Enduring polite society as a necessity when he was seeking approval and funds for a new journey, he was at his happiest when heading into the far-off wilds of Asia. Geography, science and jingoism drew him back time and again to the harsh and difficult lands on Russia's southern border. While his plans for a Russian invasion of China were never viewed as practicable by the St Petersburg authorities, his confidence in Russian power in Asia came to form part of Russia's assertive policy in the Far East during the 1890s and the first few years of the twentieth century. The outbreak of war with Japan in 1904 was firmly in the tradition of Przheval'skii's actions and thinking.

[52] D. A. Miliutin, *Dnevnik*, Moscow, 1947, vol. 1, p. 165.

A Corner of a Foreign Field: The British Embassy in St Petersburg, 1863–1918

ANTHONY CROSS

THE sweep of the Palace Embankment from Rastrelli's immense Winter Palace as far as Rinaldi's Marble Palace provides one of St Petersburg's most famous and beloved panoramas, captured at various stages of its development in the work of many artists — and photographers.[1] Perhaps best viewed from the Peter and Paul Fortress across the wide basin of the Neva, the embankment is flanked to the west by the Palace Bridge and to the east by the Trinity Bridge, which link the 'mainland' to Vasil'evskii Island and the Petrograd Side respectively. The view was always one to enchant visitors but the buildings themselves have inevitably been subject to many changes over the city's 300-year history, while preserving the horizontal unity that would have pleased the city's founder. Peter would have been less happy that bridges now straddle the river. The bridges are a comparatively late addition, the Palace Bridge was only opened in 1916, while the Trinity was completed in 1903. The latter, however, was preceded by a pontoon bridge (*naplavnoi* or *plashkoutnyi*), which had been erected in 1803, early in the reign of Alexander I, and was originally called the Peterburgskii, linking the Summer Garden with the Petersburg/Petrograd Side. It was renamed the Suvorovskii (later Troitskii) and its position moved to the site of the present permanent bridge in connection with the replanning of the area east of the Marble Palace, best known as the Field of Mars.[2]

During the reign of Catherine the Great building along the Palace Embankment had been extended and the embankment itself faced with granite. Rinaldi had begun building the Marble Palace (near the site of the old Post Office — Pochtovyi dvor) in 1768 for Catherine's

Professor Anthony Cross is Emeritus Professor of Slavonic Studies at the University of Cambridge and a Fellow of Fitzwilliam College.

[1] The panoramic tradition was begun by Aleksei Zubov during Peter's reign and continued in the famous Makhaev album of 1753. Among foreign artists providing similar views are the Swede Benjamin Pattersen, the Englishman John Augustus Atkinson (*Panorama of St Petersburg*, 1802–03), the Scot Sir John Carr (1805), and the Italian Antonio Toselli (1817–20).

[2] M. S. Bunin, *Mosty Leningrada*, Leningrad, 1986, pp. 49–50.

favourite Grigorii Orlov, completing the row of formal palaces. The palace was finished in 1784, more or less at the same time as the elegant iron railings (attributed to Fel'ten and Egorov) which enclosed the Summer Garden along the widened and strengthened embankment by the Neva.[3] The gap, as it were, between the Marble Palace and the Summer Garden opened out inland into the Field of Mars. The Field of Mars was a large open space, which from the earliest decades of the city had been used for walks, fireworks, entertainments, military parades, activities reflected in eighteenth-century variants of the name, such as Promenad, Poteshnoe pole and Marsovo pole, although its most persistent form was then the Tsaritsa's Meadow (Tsaritsyn lug). Its military associations were to be emphasized, however, during the reign of Paul I by the erection of statues of two great army commanders, the field marshals P. A. Rumiantsev and A. V. Suvorov. The Rumianstev obelisk, 'For the Victories of Rumiantsev' ('Rumiantseva pobedam'), designed by Vicenzo Brenna, was first erected in 1799 by the River Moika in the south-eastern corner of the Field of Mars, but was replaced two years later by Mikhail Kozlovskii's statue of Suvorov, moving to a position nearer the Neva. As part of the replanning of the area undertaken by Carlo Rossi, the statue of Rumiantsev was moved again in 1818 to Vasil'evskii Island by the Cadet Corps (where the field marshal had studied), while Suvorov's statue was installed in its present position in the centre of what became known as Suvorov Square, leading from the Field of Mars towards the Trinity Bridge. The original position of the two statues (and the generally unkempt state of the Field of Mars) seen from the Moika shortly before this final reshuffle, is captured in a coloured engraving by I. A. Ivanov of 1814 (Fig. 1). The Rumiantsev obelisk is flanked on the left (the west) by the Marble Palace and on the right by two private mansions that had been built in the late 1780s. It is these two buildings, principally the more westerly, that are henceforth the object of our attention. The second of these was to become the home of the British Embassy, but only some years after the Crimean War. It is nonetheless important to trace the pre-British history of the building and its occupants in the preceding decades from the end of the reign of Catherine II.

Nos 2 and 4 Palace Embankment, to give them their contemporary postal address,[4] are associated to this day primarily with two of Catherine's grandees, Ivan Ivanovich Betskoi (1704–95), renowned for

---

[3] V. I. Kochedamov, *Naberezhnye Nevy*, Leningrad and Moscow, 1954, p. 50. (On the left-bank embankments in general, see pp. 23–72.)

[4] The 'historical' address of no. 4 was I Admiralteiskaia chast', I kvartal, 17, Dvortsovaia naberezhnaia 16 (L. I. Broitmaan, 'Adresnyi kalendar', in A. M. Gordin and M. A. Gordin, *Pushkinskii vek: Panorama stolichnoi zhizni*, St Petersburg, 1995, p. 384).

Figure 1: View of the Field of Mars (Tsaritsyn lug) from the Moika in 1814. Coloured engraving by I. A. Ivanov. The Saltykov and Betskoi mansions are on the right

his progressive educational ideas, and Nikolai Ivanovich Saltykov (1736–1816), veteran of the Seven Years' War, field marshal, senator and tutor to the Grand Duke Konstantin Pavlovich. Betskoi was the first owner of no. 2, a two-storeyed house with corner towers that enclosed a hanging garden and was built to his specifications during the years 1784–87 by an architect whose identity has never been established. After Betskoi's death, the house passed to his daughter (wife of Admiral de Ribas) and then to her daughter, before it was purchased by the state in the 1830s for the Prince of Oldenburg, who commissioned Ivan Stasov to add a third storey and effect other changes.[5] Saltykov on the other hand was not the original owner of no. 4, although the association of his family with the house was to long outlive that of Betskoi's with no. 2.

The plot on which no. 4 was to be built was initially granted to State Secretary P. A. Soimonov, but within a matter of months he

---

[5] T. E. Tyzhnenko, *Vasilii Stasov*, Leningrad, 1990, pp. 133–34. (It is worthy of note that during the years 1791–96 Ivan Krylov lived in rooms in the original building and published from there his satirical journals *Zritel'* and *Sankt-Peterburgskii Merkurii*, the second of which was closed on the orders of the empress in 1792.)

disposed of it to an obviously affluent foreign (Dutch?) merchant Philipp Grootten (1748–1815).[6] It was Grootten who commissioned the Italian architect Giacomo Quarenghi to build him the mansion whose elegant neo-classical façade today still graces the Neva embankment. Quarenghi had arrived in Russia only at the very end of 1779 and had been put to work by Catherine at Tsarskoe Selo and Peterhof. In 1784, when work began on his commission for Grootten, he was already involved in several major projects in Petersburg itself, including the Academy of Sciences, the Hermitage Theatre, the Stock Exchange and the Silver Rows on Nevskii Prospect. Relatively insignificant compared with such buildings, the new mansion nevertheless occupied an important position on the embankment and Quarenghi produced a fitting façade. As his ink and water-colour drawing, preserved in the Museum of the History of St Petersburg, clearly shows, he relied on the appeal of the symmetry of the ten windows and an unadorned pediment to convey an impression of severe dignity.[7]

There are, however, no further extant drawings by Quarenghi of the mansion and very few references in his correspondence and it is difficult to establish with any certainty what he projected for the rest of the house, the layout of the rooms and, indeed, the number of storeys. From the rear the building offered an unusual, not to say unfinished, look. The Ivanov engraving reveals that while the front of the building was four-storeyed, the sides towards the rear were as yet three-storeyed. Moreover, the rear wall itself facing the Field of Mars was only two-storeyed and provided the main carriage entrance into what was apparently a large inner courtyard. In addition, above the main block facing the Neva there was a fenestrated round tower, possibly a belvedere, that may have been above the grand staircase. It can be clearly seen not only in Ivanov's engraving but in earlier engravings by Fedor Alekseev and Benjamin Paterssen.[8] The west wall shows an unsystematic series of windows at second- and third-floor levels and, adjoining it, a large walled garden. The garden occupied the building plot that had been originally offered to, and declined by, Count A.

[6] Erik Amburger, *Ingermanland*, 2 vols, Cologne and Vienna, 1980, 1, pp. 762, 768.

[7] Al'bina L. Pavelkina, *Disegni di Giacomo Quarenghi: La raccolta del Museo statale della Storia di San Pietroburgo*, Mendrisio, 2003, p. 75. The building is mentioned, if briefly, in other studies of Quarenghi and his work, e.g. V. P. Taleporovskii, *Kvarengi*, Leningrad and Moscow, 1954, p. 16 and illustration nos. 70–71; M. F. Korshunova, *Dzhakomo Kvarengi*, Leningrad, 1977, pp. 65–66 (and photograph); V. I. Piliavskii, *Dzhakomo Kvarengi: arkhitektor, khudozhnik*, Leningrad, 1981, p. 133. See also A. N. Petrov et al., *Pamiatniki arkhitektury Leningrada*, Leningrad, 1969, pp. 114–15.

[8] See Gosudarstvennyi russkii muzei, *Zhivopis' XVIII vek. Katalog*, 1, St Petersburg, 1998, p. 44, no. 11 (Alekseev), A. M. Gordin, *Pushkinskii Peterburg*, Leningrad, 1974, illustr. 17 (Paterssen).

R. Vorontsov in the 1780s and had been acquired and developed by subsequent owners.

The house had had a series of bewildering changes in ownership. Within two years of its completion it was sold by Grootten to another merchant Thomas Sievers, who three years later, in March 1793, in turn sold it for a healthy profit to Princess Ekaterina Petrovna Bariatynskaia, née Princess Holstein-Bech, wife of Prince I. P. Bariatynskii (1738–1811), a former Russian ambassador to France. The Bariatinskiis lived in the house again for a period of three years, when at last it came into the possession of the Saltykovs, presented to Count Nikolai Ivanovich as a gift from the empress for his guardianship of Grand Duke Konstantin. It seems unlikely that any of the pre-Saltykov owners of the house had the time to effect any changes on the house as Grootten had commissioned it. It was now, however, to be passed down through generations of Saltykovs for more than a century, from 1796 until 1918, earning its name as 'the Saltykov Mansion'. During this period, but at intervals over many decades, it was to undergo a whole series of changes, both externally and internally.[9]

The garden was to disappear c. 1818 as a result of Rossi's replanning of the Field of Mars and the creation of Suvorov Square. Although a third storey was added to the façade facing the Field of Mars at about the same time, it would appear that the financial disarray in which the Saltykov family found itself subsequent to the death in 1816 of the by then Prince Nikolai Ivanovich put a brake on any ambitious building plans his heir Dmitrii Nikolaevich (1767–1826) might have had. Indeed, the family was only saved from complete ruin by the intervention of the new tsar Nicholas I in 1826, shortly before Dmitrii's death.[10] It was Dmitrii's eldest son Ivan (1796–1832) and more particularly his widow, Princess Elizaveta Pavlovna Saltykova, née Strogonova, who were responsible for the substantial additions and alterations, not least the regularizing of the fenestration facing Suvorov Square and the Field of Mars, that brought the mansion the balanced appearance it had previously lacked. There is in the Manuscript Department of the Russian State Library in St Petersburg an album of plans for the redesign of

---

[9] The most informative source for the early history of the house is S. A. Reiser, 'Dvortsovaia naberezhnaia, 4', *Trudy Leningradskogo bibliotechnogo instituta imeni N. K. Krupskoi*, 4, 1958, pp. 33–47. Reiser acknowledges his extensive use of the unpublished paper by A. N. Petrov, 'Dom b. Saltykovykh. Istoricheskaia spravka' (1953). See also Pavel Kann, *Progulka ot Letnego dvortsa do Zimnego dvortsa po Dvortsovoi naberezhnoi Sankt-Peterburga*, St Petersburg, 1996, pp. 74–82. Most guidebooks, including those devoted to the particular area, have little of value to say about any aspect of the house and nothing about the period when it was occupied by the British. See, for example, A. N. Ageev, S. A. Ageev and N. A. Ageev, *Mezhdu Bol'shoi Nevoi i Moikoi*, Moscow and St Petersburg, 2005, pp. 74–78; V. G. Isachenko, *Arkhitektura Sankt-Peterburga. Spravochnik-putevoditel'*, St Petersburg, 2008, p. 93; T. A. Solov'eva, *Dvortsovaia naberezhnaia*, St Petersburg, 2005, pp. 151–55.

[10] Reiser, 'Dvortsovaia', pp. 42–43.

the building, unsigned and undated, but obviously post-1832, since it is addressed to Princess Saltykova and her son Nikolai.[11] It comprises a general plan, plans of the four floors, and three coloured drawings of the three façades, towards the Neva (the original Quarenghi design), towards Suvorov Square, showing twenty-four windows broken at intervals by two small doors and one larger door, and towards the Field of Mars (still called here the Tsaritsa's Meadow) with six windows with two small doors and a large carriage entrance and a small balcony on the second floor that echoes Quarenghi's larger balcony overlooking the Neva.

The internal rooms were also periodically to undergo changes but parts of the building, particularly the vestibule, the grand staircase and the so-called White Hall (Belyi zal) still preserve something of the décor and detail of the first half of the nineteenth century. The vestibule has free-standing Doric columns and corresponding pilasters in the walls. Corinthian pillars alternate with high curved windows as the staircase ascends to the second floor to the White Hall, where once again Corinthian columns are found along with free-standing statuary.[12] The richly decorated White Hall in its final form was the work of the little-known German-trained architect Garal'd Bosse (1812–94), who was responsible for many private mansions in the city that reflected the eclectic tastes of mid-century.[13] It was completed in 1844, during a period when the architect was much employed in her various homes and palaces by Princess Saltykova.[14]

The Saltykovs themselves were not in a position to enjoy the delights of the White Hall. The commission that had looked into the financial affairs of the Saltykovs had recommended that the mansion should be rented out and in 1828 the *St Petersburg News* announced that it was available for rent, fully furnished.[15] It was leased by the Austrian government for its embassy in the Russian capital. So began what has been called its 'diplomatic biography'.[16]

---

[11] Manuscript Department, Russian State Library, St Petersburg, Fond 669, Saltykovy, no 157 'Dom, prinadlezhashchii kn. Elizavete Pavlovne Saltykovoi, urozhd. gr. Strogonovoi, i synu ee, kn. Nikolaiu Ivanovichu Saltykovu i Admiralteiskoi chasti i kvartala pod N 17/33, a nyne 2.3.4'.

[12] Reiser, 'Dvortsovaia', p. 39 points out there had originally been an entrance to the staircase also from the inner courtyard, the *cour d'honneur*, where guests could descend from their carriages.

[13] V. I. Andreeva, *Garal'd Bosse*, Leningrad, 2002, pp. 113, 115. Bosse also added a fourth storey to the courtyard wing on the wall adjoining the Betskoi Mansion (ibid., p. 297, note 136).

[14] Sergei Kuznetsov, *Dvortsy i doma Strogonovykh: Tri veka istorii*, Moscow and St Petersburg, 2008, pp. 170–77.

[15] *Sanktpeterburgskie vedomosti*, no. 55, 10 July 1828, p. 93.

[16] Kann, *Progulka*, p. 78.

In September 1831, after repairs and refurbishment, it became for the next eleven years the residence of the Austrian ambassador Karl-Ludwig von Ficquelmont (1777–1857).[17] More significantly, it provided the setting for two of the most famous salons of the period, reigned over by Ficquelmont's wife, Dar'ia Fedorovna (1804–63), in the evenings, and by his mother-in-law, Elizaveta Mikhailovna Khitrovo (1783–1839), the daughter of Field Marshal Kutuzov, in the mornings. The poet P. A. Viazemskii was later to recall that 'Her [Khitrovo's] mornings (which, incidentally, began at one o'clock and lasted until four) and the evenings of her daughter, Countess Ficquelmont, are indelibly inscribed in the memory of all fortunate enough to participate in them. The whole of the palpitating life of Europe and Russia, political, literary, social, was faithfully reflected in these two related salons. It was not necessary to read the papers; in the salons one could gather information about all the issues of the day'.[18] It was in salons such as the Ficquelmonts' that the *corps diplomatique* and the cream of St Petersburg high society would mingle. Pushkin was a frequent visitor and a close friend of Khitrovo and her daughter, as their letters clearly show. As behoves a man who began his civil service in the Ministry of Foreign Affairs, the poet was passionately interested in European affairs and conversed often with members from the different embassies, including the British. He is known to have met there, for instance, one of the councillors from the British Embassy, Arthur Magenis (1801–67), but it was elsewhere, at a ball in the Razumovskii mansion on Bol'shaia Morskaia, that he asked him to be his second in his duel with Georges D'Anthès.[19] Of particular interest in connection with both house and poet is the well-supported hypothesis that Pushkin, who was very well acquainted with the layout of the house, used it, rather than the real home of the Princess N. P. Golitsyna, as the setting for the Countess's mansion in his famous tale *Pikovaia dama* (1833).[20] A watercolour of one of the formal rooms in which the salon was held was discovered in the 1970s and provides a unique representation of the furnishings and decoration as Pushkin would have known them.[21]

Ficquelmont was recalled to Vienna in 1840 but the Austrians relinquished the lease on the Saltykov Mansion only in 1855, after the

---

[17] There is an engraving by L. Tumling, of the 'house of the Austrian ambassador' in the 1830s (Gordin, *Pushkinskii Peterburg*, illustr. 142).

[18] P. A. Viazemskii, *Staraia zapisnaia knizhka*, Leningrad, 1929, pp. 285–86.

[19] L. A. Chereiskii, *Pushkin i ego okruzhenie*, 2nd edn, Leningrad, 1988, pp. 257–58.

[20] First advanced by N. A. Raevskii in an article of 1971 and developed in his book *Portrety zagovorili* (1974 and five subsequent editions), the suggestion received further support from S. A. Reiser, 'Pushkin v salone Finkel'monov', *Vremennik Pushkinskoi kommissii 1977*, Moscow, 1980, pp. 36–43 (pp. 41–42).

[21] Ibid., pp. 42–43. Reproduction facing p. 49.

outbreak of the Crimean War. Following the war, rooms on the second and third floors were occupied by the Danish diplomat Baron Otten Plessen, but in 1863 the lease was taken up by the British government. For a period of fifty-five years, until the beginning of 1918, no. 4 Palace Embankment became the British Embassy.

During the Crimean War and, indeed, since 1844, the status of the head of embassy had been downgraded to envoy extraordinary and plenipotentiary. Four men had been so designated, the last of them being Sir John Fiennes Crampton (1805–86), who served from March 1858, but at a time of apparently improving Anglo-Russian relations he was made ambassador in 1860. It was during the term in office of his successor, Francis Napier, 10th Lord Napier (1819–98), that Britain obtained for the first time a building that became the British Embassy and not merely the home of the British ambassador. Previously, British representatives had rented houses in various parts of the city, but mainly on the English Embankment, near to the English Church and the heart of the British community. Sir James Harris, for instance, had lived there during Catherine's reign, as did Lord Durham, another British acquaintance of Pushkin's, in the mid-years of Nicholas I's. There was now to be in the Saltykov Mansion an unbroken line of thirteen British ambassadors.

It is possible that Lord Napier was himself renting the mansion from the beginning of his embassy in December 1860 and that it was there that Alexander II and his consort 'honoured the Embassy with their presence yesterday [10 March 1863] and charged me [Napier] with their congratulations to Her Majesty the Queen'.[22] There is nothing in the correspondence between Lord Napier and the Foreign Office that I have examined at the National Archives at Kew that sheds any light on the decision to acquire a permanent home for the embassy rather than rely, it would seem, on the unpredictable availability of suitable accommodation for each incoming ambassador. A copy of the original lease of 1863 has not been located, although files pertaining to later years when the lease on the mansion was to be renegotiated are extant and it is clear that the original lease began on 30 September 1863 for a ten-year period and was first renewed in 1873.

It is probable that even during the period the mansion was leased to the Austrians the Saltykovs never ceased to inhabit some part of it. They certainly did throughout the years it was occupied by the British. From evidence dating from the time of later leases (in 1879 and 1904) it would appear that the British leased all the rooms that faced the Neva and almost all facing Suvorov Square and sharing a party wall

---

[22] Kew, The National Archives (TNA), FO181/4, Napier to FO, 11 March 1863.

with the Betskoi Mansion. The main formal or state rooms were on the second floor (British style), the piano nobile, although confusingly, even in English documents, such as the plan reproduced here as Figure 2,[23] this is sometimes referred to as the first floor and the real first floor as the entresol or mezzanine. It was on the first floor/mezzanine, that the chancery was situated, and it is from that floor that the elegant curved staircase ascends to the state rooms on the second floor. The plan shows clearly the disposition of these rooms and the interflow from the supper and dining rooms into the ballroom and from the ballroom into the drawing and reception rooms. The Saltykovs seem to have reserved for themselves the back of the house facing the Field of Mars and partially along the wall facing the Suvorov Square. The wife of the British ambassador at the end of the 1870s refers to Princess Saltykova as 'our landlady [who] lives in the back part of this house',[24] and on another occasion, to her husband as 'our landlord and semi-detached neighbour', explaining that 'we can get through our house to his'.[25] It was in 1867 that a three-storey gallery had been built across the middle of the courtyard (a fourth storey was added in 1884) and was the de facto dividing line between the British and the Saltykovs, although, of course, the British carriages entered from the Field of Mars, driving under the gallery.[26]

The Napiers were obviously well established in their new home when they were visited by Algernon Mitford, future first Baron Redesdale (1837–1916), who had arranged to serve six months in the embassy on an exchange with the Second Secretary Locock. Arriving in the Russian capital on 30 November 1863 he was immediately driven to the embassy to introduce himself to the ambassador and present the dispatches he was bringing from London. On leaving them, he

> could think of nothing but the great charm of my Chief and Chiefess. She was certainly one of the most fascinating women I ever had the good fortune to meet. Handsome, clever, agreeable, well read, very dignified, beautifully dressed, she was delightful to look at, delightful to listen to; the type of what an ambassadress should be, doing the honours of the Queen's house on the Neva like the great lady that she was.[27]

During the winter of 1863–64 Redesdale inevitably attended many functions at the embassy. Most notably, he was present at a dinner to which Lord Napier invited a number of Russian 'men of letters', who

[23] TNA, T1/16966, Treasury 5231, registered 21 March 1879.
[24] Dowager Marchioness of Dufferin and Ava, *My Russian and Turkish Journals*, London, 1916, p. 8.
[25] Ibid., p. 71.
[26] Reiser, 'Dvortsovaia', p. 338.
[27] Lord Redesdale, *Memories*, 2 vols, London, 1915, 1, p. 206.

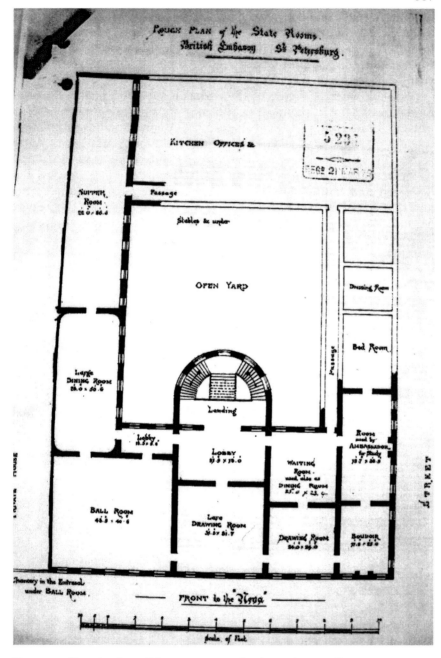

FIGURE 2: Rough plan of the state rooms in the embassy, 1879
By permission of The National Archives, Kew

but rarely made an appearance in the society of St Petersburg and included Ivan Turgenev, 'a tall, strikingly handsome man with grey hair'.[28] It is in Redesdale's memoirs that there is a reproduction of a watercolour by Adolphe Charlemagne, showing the embassy in the year following its acquisition.[29]

A decade later, a sketch of the embassy appeared in the *Illustrated London News*. One of the most significant events during the longer than usual ambassadorship (eight years) of Lord Augustus Loftus (1817–1904) was the marriage in January 1874 of the Duke of Edinburgh to Alexander II's daughter Mariia Aleksandrovna, promising a new, if false, dawn in Anglo-Russian relations. The embassy building was lavishly bedecked and illuminated for the occasion: the façade sported flags and banners of Britain and Russia and large rondels with the initials M and A on either side of the entrance and above the second-floor balcony arches with the device 'May every happiness attend them' (Fig. 3).

THE BRITISH EMBASSY AT ST. PETERSBURG ILLUMINATED FOR THE DUKE OF EDINBURGH'S MARRIAGE.

FIGURE 3: The Embassy illuminated on the occasion of the marriage of the Duke of Edinburgh, 1880 (from the *Illustrated London News*)

[28] Ibid. p. 272.
[29] Ibid. facing p. 206.

Loftus's published memoirs are extensive but with regard to Russia very disappointing. It has been noted that 'the personal element is small'.[30] Perhaps not unexpectedly, this applies to all that the ambassadors published. It is to their wives and in one unique case to a daughter that we look for glimpses of life in the embassy. Even then, sadly — at least in the present context — relatively few ambassadresses left memoirs or impressions of their sojourn in the Saltykov Mansion. A notable exception was Hariot, Lady Dufferin (1843–1936), whose husband, Frederick Hamilton-Temple-Blackwood, 1st Marquess of Dufferin and Ava (1826–1902), was ambassador from 1879 to 1881. In her preface to her diaries which were published only in 1916, she apologizes for her 'one-sided' account of embassy life — 'the business part of it is entirely left out'[31] — but it is precisely her attention to the social and domestic, which she conveys with spirit and style, that makes her book both generally and for present purposes invaluable.

The Dufferins followed the Loftuses as occupants of the 'Queen's house on the Neva', indeed, they arrived at the beginning of February 1879, when Lord and Lady Loftus were still in residence. It was at this interstice between the Loftus and Dufferin ambassadorships that the whole question of the suitability of the Saltykov Mansion and the terms of its lease became a matter of urgent discussion between the Foreign Office, the Treasury and the Office of Works on the one hand and the landlords, the Saltykovs on the other.

On 15 February a memorandum, probably drawn up by the First Secretary F. S. Plunkett with Lord Loftus's encouragement, was sent to London.[32] It opened with a very positive assessment of the house 'which is very healthily and well situated on the Quai de la Cour and is the most suitable House in St Petersburg for an Embassy; in fact there is none to be had equal to it'. The document also makes clear that the furnishing of the rooms in the mansion rented by the embassy had been the responsibility and at the expense of the incumbent ambassador. The Loftuses had furnished not only all the state rooms on the second floor but also 'the Chancery, servants' rooms and the Kitchen complete together with all the glass, China &c which is required for entertaining'. It was suggested that if everything was purchased by the government from Lord Loftus, then Lord Dufferin 'would not require anything but his own pictures, household linen, tea and breakfast services, dessert

---

[30] *Oxford Dictionary of National Biography*, 34, Oxford, 2004, pp. 307–09. See *The Diplomatic Reminiscences of Lord Augustus Loftus, 1862–1879*, 2 vols, London, 1894.

[31] Dufferin, *My Russian and Turkish Journals*, p. v. (Further references are in the text by page number.)

[32] TNA, T1/16966, Office of Works B1950/ Treasury 3431, 'Memorandum, dated St Petersburg, 15 February 1879' (Copy), 6 unnumbered pages.

services and fine glass for dinner, and his own personal property such as books'. In the event, although Lady Dufferin notes that she and her husband finished up by buying 'a good deal of Lord A. Loftus's furniture' (p. 11), much was also sold at auction. However, a Mr Boyce, a surveyor sent out from London, found the positive assessment of the state of the furniture and of the decoration and fittings of the rooms to have been exaggerated. The furniture, he concluded, 'comprised scarcely a single suite, and, with few exceptions, consisted of articles apparently purchased from time to time, inferior in quality and considerably the worse for wear'.[33] When it proved impossible to persuade the Saltykovs to undertake repairs other than agreed in the previous lease, essentially structural, then the Office of Works, in addition to providing the state rooms with more suitable furniture, undertook also to do 'the painting, colouring, and papering together with the regilding of the walls, ceilings and cornices, which are now absolutely necessary, and the cleaning and whitewashing throughout the house, which is of considerable size'.[34] The new lease was eventually signed in June 1879 at a rent of 15,000 rubles per annum for a period of fourteen years, representing in fact the remaining part of the previous lease plus a further ten years but nevertheless requiring the personal approval of the tsar.

The Dufferins initially came to Petersburg without their children. Lady Dufferin was obviously concerned to see that the embassy provided adequate accommodation and there is soon a cryptic entry in her journal about spending 'some time with the architect' (p. 34). This was at the end of May 1879 and shortly afterwards the Dufferins left for England. Although the ambassador returned a month later, it was autumn before Lady Dufferin came back, with her four children and their nurse, the venerable Mrs Hall, known within the family as Hallie. The necessary alterations to the fabric of the house had obviously been completed during her absence and she comments that 'the children's rooms have all been cleaned and painted, and are extremely comfortable and nice' (p. 53). She was soon spending much time 'in arranging furniture' and, later, hanging (unspecified) pictures (p. 56).

The great event for which the Dufferins were preparing was their 'official reception' on 30 December 1879, although they were instructed by four court officials 'what we had to do and where to stand':

[33] TNA, T1/16966, Treasury 5231, letter from Hon. G. Noel to the Lords Commissioners of the Treasury, 20 March 1879, 7 unnumbered pages.

[34] TNA, T1/16966, Treasury 10291, letter from Hon. G. Noel to the Lords Commissioners of the Treasury, dated 11 June 1879, 3 unnumbered pages.

The scene of our performance was the large, empty (unfurnished) drawing-room. It has two big doors opposite each other; the people were to come up the stairs, pass through two bright and well-lighted ante-rooms, through my drawing-room, by one door, and into the ball-room by the other. D. was placed by the first door with his two guides, and I was opposite him on the other side of the door with my two gentlemen in splendid uniforms.

When the people came in the gentlemen stopped and were presented to D., and then came on to me, whereas the ladies came straight to me and had nothing to say to the Ambassador.

The ball-room soon became a gay scene, all the gentlemen being smothered in golden uniforms, and through it people could pass into the dining-room, where a very substantial refreshment was provided them. They seemed pleased, said that they enjoyed it, and, instead of going straight away, they remained till twelve, and made quite a pleasant party of it.

On the stairs were twelve footmen wearing our liveries – at the top the two chasseurs in a costume too gorgeous for description, any amount of gold, breeches and boots, sword, etc. In the dining-room about twenty butlers who volunteered their services. I wore white brocaded satin, and my tiara, D. his Lord-Lieutenant's uniform. (pp. 58–59)

The embassy was now ready for entertaining on a grand scale, and on 8 January 1880, nearly a year after their arrival in the Russian capital, they hosted their 'first big dinner' (p. 61), when they tried out their new cook on twenty-six guests, and, three days later, were inviting a similar number of English-only guests to a dinner that was followed by a dance for 'the rest of the "[British] Colony"' and the diplomatic corps (p. 64). Their highlight was, however, the dinner in honour of the Duke and Duchess of Edinburgh in March, which was soon followed by the Dufferins' first ball. Lady Dufferin began 'a crusade against the late hours' and requested guests to come at 10.00 p.m.; to her amazement, they largely complied and soon 250 filled the ball-room. Supper was offered for the first time in the supper-room, where 147 people were seated (p. 70).

The Dufferins were in Petersburg at a time of increasing terrorist activity. Attempts on the lives on the chief of police and the tsar were followed by the latter's assassination on 13 March 1881 (NS). The embassy with its staircase 'all draped in black' (p. 116) received the Prince and Princess of Wales (the future King Edward VII and Queen Alexandra), who had attended the funeral and also invested the new tsar with the Order of the Garter. The lunch attended by the royals and numerous ambassadors was the last great event in the embassy before the Dufferins departed for Constantinople (p. 117).

The Dufferins' domestic staff, or household, consisted of 'a Swiss butler, one Russian housemaid, speaking English, one German ditto, a

Russian chasseur who always goes out with the Ambassador, and stands behind his chair at dinner, a Russian porter, a footman, a polyglot under-butler, a French cook, five moujiks (who do all the work), two servants belonging to the office, and our maid and valet, also two laundry-maids' (pp. 14–15), while the embassy staff numbered four — a First Secretary, a Second Secretary, the ambassador's private secretary, and a military attaché (pp. 16–17).

Lady Dufferin mentions in her letters all the embassy officials, including Lord Frederic Hamilton (1865–1956), a noted hunter and slaughterer of bears, who in later years published his own highly popular memoirs under the title *Vanished Pomps*. The single paragraph Hamilton devotes to the embassy at least contains details not found in other accounts:

> Our Petrograd Embassy was a fine old house, with an intimate character about it lacking in the more ornate building at Berlin [where he had previously served]. It contained a really beautiful snow-white ball-room and all the rooms fronted the broad, swift-flowing Neva [...] We had a very fine collection of silver plate at the Embassy. This plate, valued at £30,000, was the property of our Government, and had been sent out sixty years previously by George IV, who understood the importance attached by Russians to externals. We also had a small set, just sufficient for two persons, of real gold plates. These solid gold plates were only used by the Emperor and Empress on the very rare occasions when they honoured the Embassy with their presence.[35]

Writing in 1919, he finishes with the question, 'I wonder what has happened to that gold service now?' The same question might be asked about the silver service. From as far back as the 1820s embassy officials had been obliged to conduct an annual silver audit and report to the Office of Works any missing items, or indeed the need for further items. Sir Nicholas O'Conor (1843–1908), who was to be ambassador at the time of the coronation of Nicholas II, requested thirty silver soup plates for the banquet to be given in honour of the new tsar, and generated an enormous correspondence. When he retired a year or so later, it was discovered that a knife, fork and dessert spoon were missing and he was duly sent the bill for £2 3s from Garrards, the Royal Goldsmiths and Silversmiths.[36]

The Dufferins were followed by the Thorntons, Sir Edward Thornton (1817–1906) and his wife Mary. Lady Thornton soon established herself as 'the Doyenne of the Corps Diplomatique', according to Mary

[35] Lord Frederic Hamilton, *The Vanished Pomps of Yesterday*, 17th edn, London, n.d., p. 75. (The memoirs were first published anonymously in 1919 and were the first volume of a trilogy under the general title of *My Yesterdays*.)
[36] TNA, WORK 68/4.

Waddington, the American-born wife of the French Ambassador-Extraordinary William Henry Waddington, representing his country at the coronation of Alexander III in May 1883.[37] The Waddingtons subsequently spent a week in St Petersburg and visited the embassy, which Mary found 'charming' with the beautiful view of the Neva from the 'large and high' windows of the drawing room.[38] The following day they dined with the Thorntons and Lady Thornton showed Mme Waddington 'all the rooms which are charming. In all the bedrooms very thick curtains, as the light is most trying [during the White Nights]'.[39]

It was towards the end of the ambassadorship of Thornton's successor, Sir Robert Morier (1826–93), that the fourteen-year lease signed during Lord Dufferin's sojourn was again up for negotiation. In December 1892 it was argued that 'St Petersburg is one of those capitals in which it seems necessary that we should have a permanent residence for our Ambassador. Yet there is no place in which it would be less desirable to invest capital at present either by buying or building'.[40] The 'by no means unreasonable' new rent of 18,000 rubles per annum was agreed. Negotiations with Prince Nikolai Saltykov were generally amicable but protracted once more before the new lease, on this occasion for twelve years, was signed on 20 March OS 1894, by which time another ambassador, Sir Frank Lascelles (1841–1920) had been appointed.

Although the idea of finding a different home for the embassy had obviously been mooted earlier and rejected — as in the letter just quoted — by the turn of the century it had become a very burning issue.[41] In 1901 the lease had still four years to run but it is obvious that Sir Charles Scott, ambassador since 1898, and his wife were not happy with the private accommodation the Saltykov Mansion provided. At the same time, it was reported that Prince Saltykov was dying and that the emperor himself was bent on acquiring the house. Lord Esher at the Foreign Office confided to Lord Lansdowne that 'the Ch. Of the Ex. has privately agreed to the purchase of a suitable house if we can find one'.[42] Matters had been brought to a head by a report, dated 29 July 1901 and submitted to Esher by C. S. Rivers, the Principal Surveyor for Diplomatic Buildings, who had been sent out to inspect

[37] Mary King Waddington, *Letters of a Diplomat's Wife 1883–1900*, London, 1903, p. 37.
[38] Ibid. p. 124.
[39] Ibid. p. 126.
[40] TNA, WORK 10/25, letter of 15 December 1892, signed H.W.P.
[41] The classic account of the ambassadors and embassy officials in the first decades of the twentieth century is Michael Hughes, *Inside the Enigma: British Officials in Russia, 1900–1939*, London and Rio Grande, 1997.
[42] TNA, WORK 10/25, letter of Lord Esher to Lord Lansdowne, 10 August 1901.

the present embassy and to look for possible alternatives. It is a damning report, conveying a good Victorian's horror at the state of the building in general and of its plumbing and sanitation in particular. Not impressed by the landlord's inattention to necessary structural repairs, he was truly appalled to find that 'the sanitation is positively dangerous to health':

> The system of drainage is by cesspits with overflows for the liquid contents direct into the Neva. [...] None of the soil pipes are ventilated — neither are the cesspits. Under these circumstances I am not surprised to hear that sore throats of a diptheric tendency are very common in the Establishment and there have been some cases of pronounced typhoid.[43]

He provided a long list of recommendations before turning his attention to the courtyard and the buildings within it that were considered part of the embassy. The washhouse had a floor 'of wood without drainage, thoroughly rotten and there is a perfect quagmire under it'; the stable on the further side of the courtyard and facing the main building of the embassy was as bad and 'the strong effluvia from it enters the windows when they are opened'. The electric wiring was chaotic and 'excessive lengths of flexibles have been used to run round some of the rooms, held to the walls by a simple twist round glass or china buttons. The slightest pull would detach the whole'. His overall assessment was that the building 'shows evidence of decay generally':

> It is strongly suspected that some of the main timbers are badly decayed because a great increase of the vibration during heavy gun firing from the fortress on the opposite side of the River, has been noticed. All the parquet floors (with the exception of the Ball Room which the Lessor has renewed) are creaky and unpleasant to walk upon from wear and tear due to age and nail-slip. Like most of the Russian houses of that date, it is highly ornate in the reception or front portion, while the back or domestic block is of wretchedly poor construction.

His verdict was that 'if the present building were in the market I should not advise its purchase'.

The problem, however, was that alternative properties, particularly houses in such a prestigious position, were hard to come by; building a new embassy would be prohibitively expensive. Back in London, Lansdowne wondered how 'any of the inhabitants of this cloacal "Palazzo" should have survived' and agreed to widen the search for a suitable new home.[44] Over the next few months three alternative mansions were considered, two of which were on the English Embankment and had, incidentally, belonged in the eighteenth century to prominent

---

[43] TNA, WORK 10/25, Memoranda, signed C. S. R[ivers], 29 July 1901, 10 unnumbered typewritten pages.
[44] TNA, WORK 10/25, letter from Lansdowne to Esher, 14 August 1901.

British merchants, but all were ultimately rejected.[45] Sir Charles Scott's dissatisfaction with the living as opposed to the formal reception rooms they offered brought the scathing comment from Esher that 'an Embassy should in the first instance be a house of reception and the transaction of business. The comfort of the Ambassador is a secondary consideration. If Sir Charles Scott did not happen to be an Ambassador, he would be inhabiting a very ordinary house in S. Kensington'.[46] Although Esher believed that the British should seek a 'freehold building', it was ultimately decided to go along with another official's belief that there was no alternative 'but to muddle on with the old house after the drains have been put in order'.[47]

Negotiations were nonetheless protracted because of a dispute with the landlord who was, by this time, Prince Nikolai Saltykov's widow Anna Sergeevna, as to responsibility for structural repairs, such as underpinning the ballroom with steel beams.[48] A new ambassador, Sir Charles Hardinge (1858–1944) was in post before a new lease was eventually signed on 27 August 1904. The annual rent was 25,000 rubles and the lease was to run from 1 January 1905 for twelve years, with the agreement to renew for a similar term and with the British government being advised, with first option, of any proposed sale of the house.[49]

The princess was still in residence when the time came for consideration of a new lease. It was then, however, 1916 and wartime. This meant that while the purchase of a different house for the embassy was still very much the preferred British option it was inevitably to be delayed. The ambassador, who was then Sir George Buchanan (1854–1924) (Fig. 4), in post since 1910, wrote:

> The present Embassy House, though admirable for reception purposes, has many disadvantages. It is situated on one side of the noisiest thoroughfares of the town; the bedroom accommodation is bad, while, as regards the Chancery, the space is so limited that since the war began I have been obliged to place two other rooms at the disposal of the Military, Naval and commercial Attachés.[50]

---

[45] The two buildings at nos. 40 and 44 on the English Embankment are today known as the mansions of N. P. Rumiantsev and L. A. von Derviz. See T. A. Solov'eva, *K prichalam Angliiskoi naberezhnoi*, St Petersburg, 1998, pp. 129–46,150–53. The third mansion at no. 3 Gagarinskaia Street belonged to Princess Iurev'skaia, the morganatic wife of Alexander II.

[46] TNA, WORK 10/25, note, dated 16 September, added by Esher to letter of Rivers of 13 September 1901.

[47] TNA, WORK 10/25, letter of Ronald Graham, dated 10 September 1901.

[48] The Princess's architect is named as Balinskii in a letter of 8 June 1904 (TNA, WORK, 10/25).

[49] TNA, WORK 10/25, Works 6790, draft agreement in French, dated 25 July 1904.

[50] TNA, WORK 10/25, letter of Sir George Buchanan to FO, dated Petrograd 23 June 1916.

FIGURE 4: Sir George Buchanan at his desk

He would 'never recommend the eventual purchase by His Majesty's Government of the present Embassy House' and suggested a lease of only eight years and a search for an appropriate building site after the war. An eight-year lease was duly signed on 26 December 1916. It was to be the last. In June the following year Princess Saltykova asked the British Government to pay the rent to her designated heirs already in London.

Although Sir George in the year before his death published his invaluable memoirs of this period, *My Mission to Russia and Other Diplomatic Memories* (2 vols, 1923), it is to his daughter, Meriel (1886–1959), rather than to him or his formidable wife Lady Georgina (d. 1922),[51] that one turns for an evocation of embassy life rivalling that of Lady Dufferin, whose journals, coincidentally, were published during the years Meriel's parents were the last British occupants of the embassy.

---

[51] A selection of Lady Buchanan's letters to her sister-in-law in 1917 was recently published: Keith Wilson (ed.), 'From the Petrograd Embassy: Letters from Lady Buchanan', *The Historian*, 3, Summer, 1984, pp. 19–21.

Meriel believed that the mansion had been built by Catherine II for her lover Sergei Saltykov, the putative father of her son Paul, and she was not alone in that misunderstanding, but her description of the building and the layout of its rooms is detailed and invaluable:

> It was an enormous building, spacious and solidly comfortable, though not in the least beautiful. A long flight of steps led from the front door to the first-floor landing, on the left of which were the Chancery offices, and on the right the bedrooms, private sitting-rooms and bathrooms. Beyond this first landing the stairs branched in two circular flights to the second landing, which gave access to my father's study, the three state drawing-rooms, the ball-room, dining room and big supper room. All the windows of these rooms faced the square or the river, while the passages and landing looked out into the courtyard which was always stacked with huge piles of wood for the furnaces, with the stables, the kitchens, wash-houses and servants' quarters at the other end.[52]

This description appeared in 1932 in Meriel's *The Dissolution of an Empire*. A year before her death she published *Ambassador's Daughter*, a self-confessed 'attempt to silence the rumours which continue so persistently to malign my father',[53] which to a large degree repeated what she had written in her earlier book, but with sometimes unexpected changes and additions of detail. Thus, she inserts into the above description the information that the entrance porch 'with its three glass doors opened into a hall carpeted in red' and that on the second floor there was 'an ante-room hung with big portraits of Queen Victoria, King Edward VII and Queen Alexandra, King George V and Queen Mary'.[54] The latter account is in general, however, more streamlined than its predecessor and omits, not unexpectedly, other detail pertinent, for instance, to the furnishing of the various rooms in the embassy:

> All the state rooms of the Embassy were furnished by the Board of Works with very baroque gold chairs, ornate tables, copies of Louis XVI settees, huge glass chandeliers and heavy brocade curtains, which gave the rooms an air of ceremony and stiff formality. My father and mother had, however, collected old furniture in all the different countries where my father had been 'en poste' and when this arrived, and the pictures and prints had been hung up, the arm-chairs covered with bright chintzes, some of the more heavily ornate pieces removed and replaced by Queen Anne cabinets, old Dutch chests of drawers, Wedgwood or Empire chairs, the rooms took on a more homelike appearance, so that sometimes with the curtains drawn, one could almost imagine oneself in some old London Square.[55]

[52] Meriel Buchanan, *The Dissolution of an Empire*, London, 1932, p. 5.
[53] Meriel Buchanan, *Ambassador's Daughter*, London, 1958, 'Dedication', p. v. (Sir George was accused by members of the Russian aristocracy in emigration of encouraging the February Revolution and of resisting the idea of bringing the tsar to England.)
[54] Ibid., p. 91.
[55] Buchanan, *Dissolution*, p. 9. (The melancholy fate of much of this furniture and the story of the Buchanans' losses and meagre compensation from the British Treasury is recounted in *Ambassador's Daughter*, pp. 209–10.)

It is instructive and amusing to compare the staffing of the embassy, both domestic/personal and diplomatic, under the Buchanans, with the situation obtaining forty years earlier under the Dufferins. There was a similar mix of nationalities:

> besides the English butler and footmen and our own personal maids there was the Italian chef who had two or three other men under him, there were the two housemaids, the kitchen-maids and laundry-maids and a seemingly indefinite number of 'moujiks', little men in bright-coloured shirts and high boots, who swept the carpets, cleaned the windows, fed the furnaces, washed dishes and carried baskets of wood from room to room.[56]

A sign of the times was, however, the importing of a car from England complete with English chauffeur to complement the already considerable number of carriages and sleighs under the care of the colourful coachman Ivan, who 'had a sublime conviction that everything must make way for him'.[57] The head of the household was, however, William, the ambassador's butler or chasseur, 'who ruled all the others with a rod of iron'.[58] He was in constant attendance on the ambassador, equipped with a large sword and, depending on the occasion, sporting a variety of headgear, including a cocked hat with feathers that made him look like a field-marshal. No less a character, not mentioned by Meriel but appearing in other contemporary memoirs, was a Cockney named Havery, who was the chancery servant, whose sense of humour and courage was to lift the spirits of others in the embassy, particularly during the revolutionary days of 1917. He is described amusingly and with particular affection by H. J. Bruce (b. 1880), who arrived in the summer of 1913 as Head of Chancery and who, more memorably, was to woo and wed the Russian prima ballerina Tamara Karsavina.[59] Havery had in fact been appointed back in 1904 during the ambassadorship of Sir Charles Hardinge, when his predecessor, an Italian, had been caught red-handed as he attempted to take a wax impression of the key to the chancery safe. Both the ambassador's memoirs and those of Sir Nevile Henderson (1882–1942), emphasizing the increased Anglo-Russian tension at the time of the Russo-Japanese War, describe in terms worthy of John Buchan the spying activities of the Russians which included breaking into the embassy and the copying of documents but which were inevitably

---

[56] Ibid., p. 6.
[57] Ibid., p. 7.
[58] Ibid.
[59] H. J. Bruce, *Silken Dalliance*, London, 1946, pp. 159–61. (Bruce relates that 'there was much controversy as to whether his name was Avery or Havery. To settle it, the Ambassador asked him. "Avery, yer Hexcellency, with a haitch"', ibid., p. 160.)

thwarted by British vigilance.[60] This was at a time when 'it took nine keys to get from outside the house to the last drawer in the safe in the Chancery'.[61]

Henderson highlights the exacting nature of the work in the chancery and the general low level of staffing in embassies that was only addressed after World War One, when numbers were increased tenfold:

> There were no archivists and no typists. Everything except stamping and posting the letters, for which the Chancery servant was responsible, was done by the diplomatic secretaries themselves. Occasionally we were helped by so-called honorary attachés, or young men who served for a year or so abroad with a view to broadening their minds for some other future career — generally parliamentary.[62]

The chancery was the main information conduit between St Petersburg and London and the work of deciphering and encoding was intensive. Once a week a bag was sent to the Foreign Office, including a weekly summary of minor events compiled by one of the secretaries. Bruce as head of chancery under Sir George Buchanan speaks of his responsibility for 'the smooth working of the technical part of the Embassy machine' and how the work soon became 'overwhelming, staff inadequate, leave impossible'.[63] 'We spent most of the day and, in later years, much of the night in the Chancery.' There exists a wonderful photograph of Sir George in the midst of his busy chancery staff.[64] (Fig. 5) Even in pre-revolutionary days, as Henderson recalls, a previous head of chancery 'never missed coming to the office for a single day, Sundays included'.[65] The work was so unremitting that 'we seldom had an opportunity to travel in the country'.[66] Bruce's comments on the work of the chancery find support in the memoirs of another British diplomat, Richard, Viscount Cranley (1876–1945). Cranley's spell at the embassy (1904–06) antedated Bruce's, although his memoirs appeared only in 1944.[67] Cranley arrived during the last days of the ambassadorship of Sir Charles Scott and he subsequently served as private secretary to his successors, Sir Charles Hardinge and Sir Arthur Nicolson (1849–1928). It was Cranley who performed at the

---

[60] *Old Diplomacy: The Reminiscences of Lord Hardinge of Penshurst*, London, 1947, p. 107; Sir Nevile Henderson, *Water under the Bridges*, London, 1946, pp. 29–33.

[61] Ibid., p. 29.

[62] Ibid.

[63] Bruce, *Silken Dalliance*, p. 159.

[64] See I. Alekseeva, *Miriel' B'iukenen svidetel'nitsa velikikh potriasenii*, St Petersburg, 1998, between pp. 200 and 201.

[65] Henderson, *Water*, p. 28.

[66] Ibid., p. 34.

[67] Earl of Onslow, *Sixty-three Years: Diplomacy, the Great War and Politics, with Notes on Travel, Sport and Other Things*, London [1944], p. 100.

FIGURE 5: The Embassy Chancery. The ambassador is second from the left

same time the function of agent to the Office of Works and it was he who successfully negotiated the new lease in 1904 and bore the responsibility for seeing that the building's fabric was maintained.[68]

Much that Meriel Buchanan writes confirms what has already been gleaned from the diaries of Lady Dufferin, but usually in greater detail and far less guarded in her opinions: the initial official reception, totally organized by court officials, to which an estimated 3,000 guests were invited; the 'purgatory' of the 'at home' days; the endless dinners; the special occasions when visiting British delegations and dignitaries were received at the embassy; the dutiful entertaining of members of the British colony. Notable highlights were the visits of the Parliamentary delegation in February 1912 and of the British naval squadron, com- manded by Sir David Beatty, in June 1914, when formal receptions and banquets were organized in the embassy. During World War One sewing parties, hosted by Meriel's mother Lady Georgina, also took place in the Embassy (Fig. 6). Perhaps the most poignant of events was, however, the party held at Christmas 1917, when the gaiety was tinged by the doom and gloom of the historical moment:

[68] Ibid., pp. 104, 109. See also TNA, WORK 10/25, Hardinge to Lord Windsor, 30 August 1904.

Figure 6: A sewing party in the Embassy in aid of the Red Cross. The formidable Lady Georgina Buchanan sits at the end in the middle

On Christmas night we invited the members of the Chancery and of the various Naval and Military Missions, as well as some of our Russian friends who had not yet left, for a party that was to prove itself, I think, the last party ever given in the British Embassy. Luckily it was an evening when the electricity was not cut off, so the great glass chandeliers blazed with light, the big rooms were crowded and filled with laughter, and though every officer present had a loaded revolver in his pocket, though there were rifles and cartridge cases hidden in the Chancery, for the moment we tried to forget the ever-present lurking danger, the sadness of approaching good-byes, the desolation and want hidden behind the heavy red brocade curtains which were drawn across the windows.

We began the evening with a variety entertainment got up by Colonel Thornton and ended with a supper, which if it did not live up to the former meals at the Embassy, was a proof of the ingenuity and astuteness of our chef, who had somehow been able to overcome the difficulties of obtaining provisions and had managed to send up an extraordinary variety of dishes. We danced old Russian folk-dances, we sang English songs, we drank each other's health and wished each other a Merry Christmas and a happy meeting in England during the coming year. We tried to believe in the infallibility of that meeting, we tried to keep away the thought of danger or sorrow, but the shadow of death was very near some of the men who were there that night and it was impossible not to feel a chill of foreboding, a presage of tragedy, underlying the wishes for 'Good Luck' one heard on every side.[69]

The windows of the embassy had proved to be unexpectedly good vantage points for watching momentous events unfolding during 1917. Directly opposite, across the Trinity Bridge and the wide basin of the Neva, was the mansion (*osobniak*) built for the ballerina Matil'da Kshesinskaia, wife of Grand Duke Andrei Vladimirovich and former mistress of the emperor. It became the headquarters of the Bolsheviks, following Lenin's return to Petrograd and his haranguing of the crowds from its balcony on 3/16 April. Meriel watched the red flag, which had flown over the building soon after Lenin's arrival, hoisted once more on 3/16 July and witnessed during the days that followed the great crowds that surged over the bridge and swarmed in front of the embassy, the armoured vehicles racing along the embankment.[70] Bernard Pares recalls the personal courage of the ambassador, who continued to 'take his daily walk in a lounge suit undisturbed along what was practically front line' and on more than one occasion when it seemed that the embassy itself would be attacked: 'Sir George would go out on to the balcony and address them [the crowds], invariably with the best results.'[71] In the event, an attack on the embassy took place only months later.

Following the departure in January 1918 of the ambassador and his family, the embassy was left with a skeleton staff, headed by Captain F. N. A. Cromie, the naval attaché, who had originally arrived in Russia, or Russian waters, as the commander of the submarine E.19 in 1915.[72] On 31 August 1918, the day following the assassination of M. S. Uritskii, the boss of the Petrograd Cheka, in which Cromie and the British were suspected of conspiring, the embassy was invaded by a group of Red Guards. Cromie, trying to prevent their entry and shooting two of the intruders, was himself shot dead at the foot of the grand staircase. Meriel Buchanan, for whom the attaché assumed ever

---

[69] Buchanan, *Dissolution*, pp. 273–74. (See also the briefer but different account in *Ambassador's Daughter*, p. 190, particularly the reference to the ballroom 'stacked with bully beef and other provisions'.)

[70] Meriel Buchanan, *Petrograd, the City of Trouble 1914–1918*, London, 1918, pp. 130–46. (It was, incidentally, from the same spot that Sir Charles Hardinge, who was ambassador from 1904–06, saw soldiers firing into the crowds streaming over the Trinity Bridge, the first victims of 'Bloody Sunday', *Old Diplomacy*, p. 113.)

[71] Sir Bernard Pares, 'Introduction', in Meriel Buchanan, *Diplomacy and Foreign Courts*, London, [1928], p. ix.

[72] See David R. Jones (comp. and ed.), 'Documents on British Relations with Russia, 1917–1918: II–IV: F.N.A. Cromie's Letters', *Canadian-American Slavic Studies*, 7, 1973, pp. 350–75, 498–510; 8, 1974, pp. 544–62.

increasing heroic stature in her various retellings of the incident, also alleges that 'the Red guards had ransacked the Embassy from floor to ceiling, had helped themselves to furs and silver, clothes, books, ornaments, even to a certain amount of furniture, and it was only thanks to the intervention of the Dutch and Netherland Ministers that anything was saved from the general destruction'.[73]

Following the raid, the embassy was sealed. The other half of the building, however, continued to be occupied by Princess Anna Sergeevna Saltykova, who had decided not to follow other members of her family into exile and who, according to Meriel Buchanan, 'was to die of want and starvation within the year'.[74] What is more, a memorandum, dated 19 March 1918, refers to an oral agreement the princess made with the Royal Swedish Mission in Petrograd for the free use of an apartment on the second floor as a temporary refuge for German POWs and citizens waiting to be repatriated. Hence Kann's astonishment that 'in the centre of the city in the spring of 1918 there thus existed, created by the mission of a neutral country with the help of a Russian aristocrat, a refuge for the subjects of a country at war with Russia'.[75]

Kann relates a further story connected with the princess that is well worth the retelling. Later in 1918, in accordance with the Soviet decree to 'confiscate the valuables of the bourgeoisie', the art historian A. A. Voitov was sent to the Saltykov Mansion, where the old princess told him to take what he had to, as long as he also took her even older parrot. The parrot had apparently belonged to Catherine the Great's noted lady-in-waiting Mariia Savvishna Perekusikhina and had been taught by no less than Gavrilo Derzhavin to sing a song he had written in praise of the empress herself. An astonished Voitov was treated to the parrot's rendering of 'Slav´sia sim, Ekaterina, slav´sia, nezhnaia k nam mat´', but he apparently never fulfilled his promise to return and collect the bird.[76]

It is Meriel Buchanan who again provides us with a glimpse of the embassy after the raid in August 1918. In her collection of essays, entitled *Victorian Gallery*,[77] she recounts the moving story of Violet ('Parma') Froom, a member of the British colony who had become matron of the British Hospital for Wounded Russian Soldiers during the First World War until its closure in June 1917. Mrs Froom, trapped

---

[73] Meriel Buchanan, *Dissolution*, pp. 294–95.
[74] Ibid., p. 274 (see also, Meriel Buchanan, *Diplomacy*, p. 143).
[75] Kann, p. 79.
[76] Ibid., pp. 79–81.
[77] 'The Story of an Englishwoman', in Meriel Buchanan, *Victorian Gallery*, London, 1956, pp. 103–45.

for a time in the south of Russia, was obliged in September 1918 to make her way back to Petrograd, where she was to make her home in rooms in the English Church on the English Embankment and over the next two years to assist marooned, mainly sick, old and destitute members of the British community to survive by organizing a soup kitchen. On one occasion she was asked by an Englishwoman to retrieve documents which she had hidden in the British embassy. Apparently, as the situation had worsened in the city and more and more of the British colony left for England, the embassy was used virtually as a warehouse and left luggage store.[78] With great danger to herself and with the help of the ambassador's old chasseur, William, who had remained behind virtually as caretaker and was reduced to a shadow of his former self ('a thin, shivering man'), Mrs Froom managed to enter the building and make her way to the ballroom. She was confronted by a scene of chaos, belongings and furniture strewn everywhere, but she found within a piano (one of eleven!) the documents she was seeking.

The stories of possessions left in the embassy and the confiscation of valuables belonging to the Saltykovs anticipate to some degree the next phase in the history of the mansion. H. G. Wells, who had first visited Petrograd in 1914, returned for a short visit in September 1920 and stayed with his old friend Maksim Gor'kii, who had established an Expertise Commission to safeguard confiscated works of art (Fig. 7). The mansion became their repository.

> For greater security there has been a gathering together and a cataloguing of everything that could claim to be a work of art by this Expertise Commission. The palace that once sheltered the British Embassy is now like some congested second-hand art shop in the Brompton Road. We went through room after room piled with the beautiful lumber of the former Russian social system. There are big rooms crammed with statuary; never have I seen so many white marble Venuses and sylphs together, not even in the Naples Museum. There are stacks of pictures of every sort, passages choked with inlaid cabinets piled up to the ceiling; a room full of cases of old lace, piles of magnificent furniture. This accumulation has been counted and catalogued. And there it is. I could not find out that any one had an idea of what was ultimately to be done with all this lovely and elegant litter. The stuff does not seem to belong in any way to the new world, if it is indeed a new world that the Russian Communists are organising. They never anticipated that they would have to deal with such things.[79]

[78] Meriel, describing her family's departure in January 1918, stated that they were allowed only one small cabin trunk each and that most of their personal belongings were left in large trunks in the ballroom, along with the embassy furniture (*Ambassador's Daughter*, pp. 191–92).
[79] H. G. Wells, *Russia in the Shadows*, London, 1921, pp. 51–52.

FIGURE 7: Maksim Gor´kii among items requisitioned after the October
Revolution and stored in the former British Embassy

Perhaps some possessions left in the embassy by members of the fleeing British colony were also found worthy of saving by the Expertise Commission or, more probably, were simply dispersed. Reader Bullard certainly found nothing of more than curiosity value when he arrived in Leningrad in 1931 as the first British Consul-General after the resumption of diplomatic relations and was given spacious accommodation on Nevskii Prospect

> a mass of dusty stationery left behind when the Embassy left after the Revolution, cases and cases of archives going back to the earliest years of the 19th century, boxes of books belonging to a defunct English club, bound volumes of Punch, a billiard-table in bits with twenty cues, rusty fenders, a broken weighing-machine, curtain-poles without brackets and brackets without poles, tin trunks full of waste-paper and old photographs, and so on.[80]

The Saltykov Mansion was soon, however, to achieve its new identity as the home of a Soviet educational institution which with some mutations in name and direction has endured to the present day. In 1925 the N. K. Krupskaia Institute of Political Education (founded in 1918 and until 1924 known as the first Russian Institute for Extra-Mural Education) moved to its new premises which now incorporated the adjacent Betskoi Mansion, no. 4 Palace Embankment. In 1941 it became the Library Institute (Bibliotechnyi institut), but its activities were immediately curtailed by the Great Fatherland War and the ensuing siege of Leningrad, when it was transformed into a military hospital. The institute repossessed the building again in 1946 and created on the ground and third floors living accommodation for students. In 1964 it became the N. K. Krupskaia Institute of Culture, by which time Quarenghi's light green colouring had been restored to the outside walls, which had been painted red in the late nineteenth century. The end of the Soviet regime inevitably invited name changes and the institute was renamed the St Petersburg Academy of Culture in 1995. Four years later, it achieved university status and became known as St Petersburg State University of Culture and Arts.

It was early in November 2008 that I paid my first visit to the university (Fig. 8) and was given a tour of the building by Professor Svetlana Makhlina of the Department of the History of Russian Culture. The main entrance to the University is now from no. 2 and what was the dividing wall between nos. 2 and 4 has been breached in several places and on several floors to allow free access between the two buildings. Similarly, there is little sense of the former division in

---

[80] Julian and Margaret Bullard (eds), *Inside Stalin's Russia: The Diaries of Reader Bullard 1930–1934*, Charlbury, 2000, pp. 51–52.

FIGURE 8: First floor of the former British embassy, now part of the State University of Culture
Photograph: Author

the Saltykov Mansion between the rooms occupied by the British Embassy and those retained by the family. Various rooms have inevitably been divided to provide lecture halls and classrooms; the library occupies some of the former family area, looking out to the Field of Mars. Hundreds of students scurrying along narrow corridors and staircases create an impression of a rabbit warren rather than of a gracious nineteenth-century mansion. The ceilings, some of which have been restored, and the White Hall especially, are really the only reminders of former splendours, although it is still possible to enjoy the magnificent views of the Neva offered by the large windows in the former enfilade of rooms. The greatest disappointment was not being able to enter the old embassy by its main entrance and ascend the grand staircase. I was, however, allowed into the vestibule but ascending the staircase was forbidden: two chairs, on the backs of which there was written in English 'STOP', barred the way. The top of the staircase within the university precinct is encased by a glazed partition and thus also inaccessible. Turning right from the vestibule on the ground floor now takes you into a rather upmarket restaurant called the 'Seventh Guest' that runs along much of the façade onto Suvorov Square. (Incidentally, still on the ground floor but in the area formerly retained by the Saltykovs, on the corner of Suvorov Square and the Field of Mars,

FIGURE 9: The grand staircase of the embassy
Photograph: Author

there is also a student café called 'Anna'.) At least, I had stood at the foot of the staircase where Cromie fell seventy years previously (Fig. 9) and had walked through the ballroom and other state rooms where the Buchanans had received the cream of Russian aristocratic society and partied with members of the British community.

On the wall inside the entrance hall of the former Belosel'skii-Belozerskii Palace at the junction of the Fontanka and Nevskii Prospekt there is a plaque that indicates that during the First World War the palace housed the Anglo-Russian Hospital.[81] Perhaps one day the long presence of the British Embassy in the Saltykov Mansion might be similarly commemorated.

---

[81] See Michael Harmer, *The Forgotten Hospital*, London, 1982. (It was through the efforts of the author, son of the senior surgeon at the hospital in 1915–16, that the plaque was erected in 1996.)

Russian Marxism and its London Colony before the October 1917 Revolution

ROBERT SERVICE

In the early years of the twentieth century it was important for each group of Russian revolutionary emigrants to choose its geographical base with care.[1] By and large they liked to follow the flow of those thousands of students from the Russian Empire who sought a freer educational curriculum than was available to them at home. This was especially true of young middle-class women, who were frustrated by the paucity of places and narrowness of topics on the 'higher women's courses' in St Petersburg and elsewhere. Male and female students from Russia and Ukraine flocked to universities in Paris, Munich, Geneva and Zurich.[2] Quickly they formed national groups, setting up clubs and welfare facilities for new arrivals. A lot of them went already impregnated with revolutionary doctrines or at least with a sympathy for them. It made sense for revolutionaries to have an eye for where the student 'colonies' existed and to set up colonies of their own. Thus the revolutionary militants could blend into the gathering emigrant society without raising an alarm in police forces. They could take advantage of the existing facilities and expand them. They could make recruits among the student body. They could use the excellent post and telegraph services in Central and Western Europe.

London did not fit this pattern because would-be students from the Russian Empire did not go there in droves. British universities did not offer a welcome to foreigners in those years. Many of the travelling Russians, moreover, already knew German or French and the need to learn English was not an attraction. One of the exceptions was Prince Felix Iusupov who founded the Oxford University Russian Society in 1909. Iusupov's later involvement in the plot to kill Rasputin did

Robert Service is Professor of Russian History at the University of Oxford and a Fellow of St Antony's College.

[1] Lindsey Hughes had a deep interest in the history of Russians in London. As biographer of Peter the Great she loved to visit the spots he visited, and it was in this spirit that the History Department of the School of Slavonic and East European Studies undertook one of its liveliest outings to the East End.

[2] A. E. Senn, *The Russian Revolution in Switzerland, 1914–1917*, Madison, WI, 1971, chs 1–3.

not mean he belonged to radical political circles; in fact, he was an arch-conservative.[3] No city of the United Kingdom had a sizeable contingent of Russians taking or auditing courses in higher education.

What London did have were tens of thousands of poor Jewish immigrants from the Russian Empire. Crammed into the East End, they had come in search of work and to escape poverty and oppression in the northern half of the Pale of Settlement. They spoke Yiddish or else some regional variant of Russian, Polish or Ukrainian — often they could understand more than one language before taking up British residence. Usually they had been dropped off at the docks in London despite having planned to go to New York and, for one reason or another, they had stayed put. They brought their culture and their religion with them. They filled the work force in a number of trades such as tailoring, baking and carpentry; and they were the object of considerable fear and resentment among the indigenous working class since they were willing to labour for lower wages than was the current norm.[4] The Pale of Settlement was the greatest breeding ground for far-left politics in the Russian Empire before the turn of the century. Thus when the Russian Social-Democratic Workers' Party came to be formed in Minsk in 1898 it was the Jewish component — the Jewish Bund — which initially had the largest and most lively organizations. Radical socialist ideas continued to be popular among the poor working Jews of the East End.

Yet Russian 'professional' revolutionaries avoided this area of London as their habitat if they could possibly afford to find rooms elsewhere. Dickens and Conan Doyle had given the East End an international reputation for slums, insanitary surroundings and considerable physical danger for outsiders. Middle-class emigrant Marxists preferred other parts of the British capital where the lifestyle was congenial to them; and although most of them continually pleaded poverty in their letters to potential donors they frequently succeeded in finding pleasant metropolitan accommodation.

For well-heeled émigrés, the East End was primarily where they attended a public meeting in Shoreditch or used one of the printing works in the vicinity. The *Iskra* journal, for example, was based at Clerkenwell Green at the end of Farringdon Road when it was being printed at the Twentieth Century Press. (The building is now the Marx Memorial Library.) Few active Russian revolutionaries in Britain had any connection with industrial work. There were odd exceptions such as the Bolshevik Alexander Shliapnikov in the First World War. Bright

[3] Prince F. Youssoupoff, *La fin de Raspoutine*, Paris, 1927.
[4] W. J. Fishman, *East End Jewish Radicals, 1875-1914*, London, 1975; J. White, *Rothschild Buildings: Life in an East End Tenement Block, 1887-1920*, London, 1980.

and dedicated, Shliapnikov ran errands for the leadership. Always he thought for himself, and in 1920–21 he was to fall out with Lenin and Trotskii and found the Workers' Opposition to the ascendant party leadership. Shliapnikov had little time for middle-class emigrants and got less than he needed from them materially. He secured employment, as a skilled operative, in the Hendon aircraft works in the First World War. His presence in London was known to the British and Russian intelligence forces, and anyway his was only a temporary stay before he left for Scandinavia. By the time of the February 1917 Revolution he was already operating in the Bolshevik factional leadership in Petrograd. Yet even Shliapnikov was not a resident of the East End.[5]

Trotskii was one of those who had expressed an eagerness to speak in Whitechapel. Already as a young man he was convinced of the importance of oratory for modern revolutionary politics,[6] and in 1902 he was raring to prove himself on a London political platform. Lenin gave him his opportunity. Not long after arriving in England, Trotskii went with his new comrades for an open debate:

> It was at that time too that I delivered a speech in Whitechapel where I contested against the patriarch of the emigration [Nikolai] Chaikovskii and the anarchist [Varlaam] Cherkezov. I was genuinely amazed at the childish arguments with which these respected elders sought to overturn Marxism. I remember returning in a very elevated mood; my feet felt as if they were scarcely touching the pavement below me.[7]

Other comrades subsequently put in appearances and the tradition was maintained when the Bolshevik faction began to be formed in 1903. This was not a sign that Lenin and his fellow Marxist radicals were throwing themselves into the life of the British labour movement; for it needs to be taken into account that the language of communication was not English but Russian. The audience in Whitechapel consisted of people who were only too happy to hear someone speaking one of their native tongues. (Yiddish was the main language of many listeners.)

Trotskii added:

> My modest knowledge of English acquired in Odessa prison made hardly any advance in the London period. I was too much absorbed in Russian affairs. British Marxism offered no interest. The intellectual focus of the social-democracy at that time was Germany, and we intently followed the struggle between the 'orthodox' Marxists and the 'revisionists'.[8]

[5] A. Shliapnikov, *Kanun semnadtsatogo goda: vospominaniia i dokumenty o rabochem dvizhenii i revoliutsionnom podpol'e za 1914–1916 g.g.*, 2nd corrected edition, Moscow, 1923.
[6] Trotskii to A. L. Bronstein, 10 February 1903 (NS), p. 1: Arkhiv Parizhskoi Okhrany (Hoover Institution Archives), file XVIIa, folder 1a, p. 2.
[7] L. Trotskii, *Moia zhizn'*, Berlin, 1930, vol. 1, pp. 168–69.
[8] Ibid., pp. 169–70.

He did not stay long enough in London to learn the language. Lenin had less excuse since he had extended stays in 1902–03 and 1908, quite apart from several brief visits; but even so, he did not trouble to acquire much of an oral facility.

Bloomsbury, Hampstead and Highgate had always been attractive to Europe's political emigrants just as they were to British writers, thinkers and artists, and this tradition remained strong in the early 1900s. When Trotskii had arrived in London in autumn 1902 he went straight to Lenin's rented rooms at 30 Holford Square. Trotskii had come to reinforce the team, led by Lenin, which produced the *Iskra* journal. They immediately formed a political partnership. But much as he appreciated Trotskii's potential, Lenin had no intention of letting him stay with him. Instead he deposited him nearby in Sidmouth Street:

> For accommodation I was led off by Nadezhda Konstantinovna [Krupskaia, Lenin's wife] for a few blocks to a building where [Vera] Zasulich, [Iuli] Martov and [I. S.] Blumenfeld (who ran the *Iskra* press) lived. A free room was found for me there. The apartment was constructed according to the characteristic English type not horizontally but vertically: the landlady lived on the lowest floor and the inmates took rooms above each other. There was also a common room where they drank coffee and held endless conversations and where — not without some fault attachable to Zasulich and without Martov's collaboration — there reigned immense disorder. Plekhanov on his first visit named this room a den.[9]

It was with Zasulich and Martov that Trotskii spent most of his days when not engaged in political work. Lenin could not abide what he regarded as their bohemian lifestyle.[10]

Nevertheless Lenin took Trotskii on a trip to see some of the famous sights:

> He showed me Westminster and some other remarkable buildings from the bridge. I do not remember his exact words but the flavour was something like this: 'This is their famous Westminster.' The word 'their' of course referred not generally to the English but to the governing classes. This flavour was not stressed in any way but was deeply organic and was expressed in the timbre of his voice; it was always there when he was speaking about any values of culture or about new achievements, about the riches of books in the British Museum, about the information in the European press or many years later about German artillery: they know how to do something or they possess something, they have done something or have achieved something; but what enemies they are! The invisible shadow of the ruling class in his eyes had seemed to have settled on all human culture, and he sensed this shadow always with such confidence as the daylight.[11]

[9] Ibid., p. 168.
[10] Ibid., p. 170.
[11] Ibid., pp. 166–67.

Lenin had a high opinion of Trotskii; it was not often that he
so much time to his *protégés*.

Trotskii's memoir is widely taken as proof of the Bolshevi
leader's contempt for bourgeois Britain. Such an analysi
entirely convincing. Quite apart from the question of '
capacity to reproduce exact spoken words after nearly three
there is the point that Lenin made his supposed remark outside parliamentary buildings. Whereas it is credible that he despised the elected
MPs and their role in the British political system, it is less easy to accept
that central London was a zone he could not abide.

There was anyhow at least one 'bourgeois' institution for which
Lenin never had anything but praise. This was the British Museum
Reading Room, which he visited with relish under the alias of Jacob
Richter. Among the reasons why Lenin always chose to live in or near
Bloomsbury was that he could conveniently go on foot daily to the
Reading Room. The furthest place away from it that he rented were
the rooms he and Krupskaia took at Holford Square. In 1902–03 he
was mainly writing articles for the *Iskra* journal he founded with his
comrades Iuli Martov and Alexander Potresov previously. But in 1908,
when he lived at 21 Tavistock Place, he devoted himself to his
philosophical researches for an attack on fellow Bolshevik Alexander
Bogdanov.[12] The result was Lenin's crude contribution to epistemology
and ontology: *Materialism and Empiriocriticism*.[13] The Reading Room
supplied all he needed to study the works of Immanuel Kant and Ernst
Mach, if indeed he read either of them attentively at all.

Lenin was a bookish man and was seldom happier than when he
could work by himself in a well-stocked, well-run library. He was not
alone in his admiration of central London's facilities. The Menshevik
Ivan Maiskii, later to become the USSR's British ambassador, wrote of
the Reading Room:

> You will hear [...] that it is 106 feet high and the diameter of the dome is
> 140 feet, that it will hold five hundred people, that the reference library in
> it runs to many thousand volumes and the total number of books reaches
> several millions and each is noted in the catalogue, comprising a thousand
> huge folios. But no words can convey the atmosphere which reigns in this
> remarkable laboratory of the human spirit.[14]

Arriving in London in 1912, Maiskii recalled the illustrious revolutionaries who had made use of the holdings: Karl Marx, Louis Blanc,

[12] Adele Biagi corrected the Soviet account of Lenin's Tavistock Place as place of
residence: R. Service, *Lenin: A Biography*, London, 2000, p. 507, note 28. What in 1908
was no. 21 is now no. 36: see survey of *London — L.C.C.*, vol. 24, *King's Cross Neighbourhood*,
London, 1952, p. 81.
[13] V. I. Lenin, *Polnoe sobranie sochinenii*, Moscow, 1958–65, vol. 18.
[14] I. Maisky, *Journey into the Past*, London, 1962, p. 26.

Giuseppe Mazzini, Petr Kropotkin and S. M. Stepniak-Kravchinskii. He referred to the work done there by British authors such as Dickens, Tennyson, Thackeray and Shaw: 'Mighty shades from the past were all around me. I could hardly help asking myself whether I should ever prove in any way worthy of the great figures who had bent over those tables before me.' He never recalled the 'black tables' of the Reading Room except with feelings of pleasure and affection.[15]

Maiskii enjoyed wandering round the Bloomsbury area. Coming back to London in 1932 he was delighted at how little had changed:

> I strolled slowly through the adjacent streets: Bury Street, Museum Street, Montague Place, Bloomsbury Square. Everything was just the same — the second-hand booksellers with their faded volumes of old books set out on their shelves, the window displays of cheap reproductions of famous pictures, the motley shops with every kind of souvenir for foreigners. No change at all! How conservative is life in England![16]

For studious men and women from Russia the cheaply available literature in the little local shops were a powerful magnet as soon as they acquired a moderate reading competence in English.

There were plenty of restaurants and cheaper eating establishments at lunchtime. (Pubs do not seem to have been much of an attraction for the political emigrants in the middle of the day.) Maiskii remembered the scene before the First World War. Close to the British Museum was a Lyons café with its gilded letters on a white background where Maiskii had his lunch at one o'clock. He liked the free moments when, seated by himself, he could listen to 'the subdued hum of conversation' among London clerks, shop assistants and typists. His two hours away from the Reading Room were perhaps a longer break than many of his British fellow readers took, but he had a long working day — from ten in the morning till seven in the evening — before he would make his way back to Highgate. Maiskii worked intensively on nineteenth-century British Chartism, trade unionism and the labour movement in general; and when the Great War broke out in 1914 he transferred his studies to topics of international relations: 'This close look at fundamentals', he recollected, 'could be regarded as my first training and preparation for my future work as a diplomat.'[17]

Another visitor in 1913 was fellow Menshevik Alexandra Kollontai (who subsequently became a leading Bolshevik). Maiskii had met her three years previously at the International Socialist Congress at Copenhagen. Kollontai was unusual among Russian Marxists in insisting the 'woman question' ought to be no mere secondary matter

[15] Ibid., p. 28.
[16] Ibid., p. 34.
[17] Ibid., pp. 28 and 34.

for the revolutionary movement. She rushed daily to the Reading Room to deepen her researches. Her purpose was to complete a manuscript which she intended to publish as *Society and Motherhood*.[18] Unlike Maiskii, she had something of genuine novelty to say. Printed in Russian in 1915, the booklet became a founding text of Russian Marxist feminism and Kollontai went on to promote her ideas in practice when she joined the Soviet government.

By then the members of the London colony, as they called it, had become less reluctant to learn the local tongue. Several of them had no choice if they wanted to subsist. In order to secure some sort of employment it was essential to acquire a degree of fluency in English. Maxim Litvinov did a bit of Russian-language tutoring; Jacob Peters gained a job as a shipping agent for Gerhard and Hey. Litvinov was more proficient than Peters, who proved incapable of rendering Lenin's Decree on Peace into English in November 1917, but this may also have been attributable to his less than confident grasp of Russian since Latvian was his first language.[19] Not even a facility in English, though, reduced the bafflement of the Russian Marxist colony about British fellow socialists. It was not merely that the British disliked talk about a future dictatorship or aspired to making their political advance by entirely peaceful means. Nor was it just the hostility of nearly all of them to Marxism. What alienated the emigrant Marxists was the whole set of cultural and social assumptions of the indigenous comrades.

Lenin was driven to distraction by their tolerance of religious believers in their midst. Trotskii recorded their trip to the Brotherhood Church on Southgate Road N1, north of the Regents Canal, in 1902:

> One Sunday I set off with Lenin and Krupskaia to a London church where a social-democratic meeting alternated with the singing of psalms. The orator [*sic*] was a typesetter who had come back from Australia. He talked about social revolution. Then everyone got up and sang: 'Almighty God, make it so that kings and the wealthy do not exist.' I could not believe my eyes or ears. 'A multitude of elements of revolutionary ideas and socialism are spread among the English proletariat,' Lenin said in this regard once we had left the church, 'but all this is associated with conservatism, religion, prejudices and absolutely cannot find any way forward for itself and communicate itself.'[20]

If the Russians had not needed the indulgence of Revd F. R. Swann, the minister, for permission to hold occasional meetings,[21] they would hardly have troubled to set foot in the Brotherhood Church

[18] A. Kollontai, *Otryvki iz dnevnika 1914 g.*, Leningrad, 1924.
[19] B. Beatty, *The Red Heart of Russia*, New York, 1918, pp. 222–23.
[20] Trotskii, *Moia zhizn'*, 1, p. 169.
[21] A. Rothstein, *Lenin in Britain*, London, 1970, p. 23; K. Weller, *'Don't be a Soldier!' The Radical Anti-War Movement in North London, 1914–1918*, London, 1985, p. 85.

again except to conduct an anthropological survey of Britain's strange socialists.

For the Russian Marxists, as for nearly all Russian revolutionary socialists, religious faith was prioritised for elimination at the first opportunity. Priests, mullahs and rabbis were not a subject of neutral analysis. Russia's radicals regarded them as purveyors of ideological poison.

Another account comes from Ivan Maiskii, a Menshevik in the pre-war years and not a Bolshevik until 1921. He was taken to the Brotherhood Church by George Lansbury of the British Labour Party in 1914:

> We had a long walk through the dim and dirty streets if the working-class quarters before we arrived. I took in the building at a swift glance. It was like dozens of similar buildings in the capital — soot-begrimed walls, high, narrow windows, a grimy roof and a short steeple pointing to the sky. We entered through a small side door, and we were met by one of the members of the socialist group to which the church belonged. He warmly shook our hands and led us into the vestry. This was a simple, bare room which would hold about two hundred people. In one corner was a small platform and in the other a painted wooden table with a few chairs.[22]

Maiskii continued:

> I found out that the church was owned by a socialist body of considerable size, which maintained it at their own expense and held regular religious services there. Attached to it was a Sunday School which was attended by the children of its members. The purpose of the church, as indicated by its name, was to inculcate the idea of brotherhood between people of all nations, religions and convictions and to convert human society to socialist principles by peaceful means.[23]

Maiskii was no less amazed than Lenin and Trotskii had been in earlier years.

Revd Swann's hospitality, however, had been gratefully accepted in late July 1903 when the Second Congress of the Russian Social-Democratic Workers' Party had to suspend its sessions in Brussels because of pressure by the Belgian police. Delegates took a ferry to Britain and debated in the Brotherhood Church before moving to Charlotte Street on the edge of Bloomsbury.[24]

Sanctuary was again offered in May 1907 for the Fifth Congress there. The Imperial government in St Petersburg had put diplomatic difficulties in the way of holding the proceedings in Copenhagen and delegates were belatedly told to switch their travel plans to London.

---

[22] I. Maisky, *Into the Past*, pp. 136–37.
[23] Ibid., p. 137.
[24] Service, *Lenin: A Biography*, p. 152.

This had serious financial consequences for the Congress organizers, who lacked the time to raise extra funds. Where possible, the less well-off delegates were put up by British comrades or deposited in the cheapest accommodation in the East End — Stalin was among such individuals.[25] Appeals were made to wealthy English socialists in London, but still the shortfall in finance remained even if each delegate had to be satisfied with a daily subsidy of no more than two shillings. In this entire process the colony came into its own as factions banded together. Long-term Russian emigrant Fedor Rothstein contacted the left-wing liberal journalist H. N. Brailsford for help. Brailsford put them in touch with American soap manufacturer Joseph Fels, who came to the church to see what was going on. Fels was the son of Polish Jews, believed in social reforms and was no friend of the Romanov political order. He was impressed by the proceedings and made out a loan for £1,700, and the German Social-Democratic Party added a further three hundred.[26]

But the Russian political emigrants generally showed little interest in the resident 'proletariat', apart from former subjects of the Romanov dynasty, both at the time or in their memoirs. London was a haven, not a window. They did little more than temporarily accommodate themselves to London society while clinging to the comradeship of the colony. Russian Marxists repeatedly stressed their commitment to world revolution, the transformation of Europe and the annihilation of national prejudices and aspirations. When they met in gatherings of the Second (Socialist) International they were always the most strident in asserting the case for internationalism. But they lacked much curiosity about the Northampton boot maker, the Lancashire textile worker or the Birmingham lathe turner. They got their ideas about the United Kingdom largely from books. Lenin and Trotskii wrote inspiringly about Ireland and its potential for insurgency against imperial dominion without ever having departed from London. Scotland too was an occasional topic for Marxist writers from the Russian Empire.[27]

But only the Mensheviks Ivan Maiskii and Georgii Chicherin did any serious amount of travelling (although Bolshevik Litvinov did not confine himself entirely to London). Less incurious about his surroundings than his comrades, Maiskii went to Manchester and Edinburgh, as well as to 'Dodd's Socialist Camp' for a holiday at Caister-on-Sea. Maiskii enjoyed himself on his journeys. He was taken aback by what he saw and heard:

[25] R. Service, *Stalin: A Biography*, London, 2004, pp. 65–66.
[26] Maisky, *Into the Past*, pp. 139–43.
[27] Ian D. Thatcher, 'Representations of Scotland in *Nashe Slovo* during the First World War', *Scottish Historical Review*, 78, August 1999, pp. 243–52.

The English socialists with whom I came into contact every day were very different from the Russian socialists. They were a totally different intellectual, psychological and moral type, the exclusive product of a British soil which was so unlike the Russian. Three things particularly struck me about my British comrades: their peace of mind, their complete indifference to theory and their profound belief in evolutionary progress.[28]

What also disconcerted him was what he regarded as their essential frivolity:

They ate and slept well, amused themselves without a care in the world and were not afflicted by 'problems', as the Russians were. They danced morning, noon and night when they felt like it, and even grown-ups carried on in such a childish fashion that all I could do was shrug my shoulders.[29]

Maiskii was getting carried away; for the Russian Marxists too knew how to celebrate when it took their fancy.[30] But he was right that in some deep sense the Russian revolutionary traditions laid an unusual emphasis on self-sacrifice, even on what he called martyrdom.[31]

Another notable feature of the colonial existence was its lack of interest in the English intelligentsia. Their colony might just as well have been in Africa. The novelist Ivy Litvinov (*née* Low), wife of the Bolshevik Maxim, was one of the few English individuals who entered its social milieu. H. G. Wells wrote her a congratulatory letter after the appearance of her *Growing Pains*.[32] She published two novels in 1914 alone. Ivy was deeply affected by D. H. Lawrence's *Sons and Lovers* and drawn to the psychoanalytical doctrines of Sigmund Freud.[33] She adopted Lawrence as her 'party line'; she wrote to him in Italy and began a vigorous correspondence before visiting him in La Spezia in 1914.[34] Her account of her complex interaction with the colonists provides one of the most illuminating depictions of the basic assumptions of life of the Russian Marxists in London.

She repeatedly made mention of the colony's social isolation in Bloomsbury, Hampstead and Highgate. This is all the more remarkable in the light of the fact that these areas were the favoured habitat

[28] Ibid., pp. 176–77. On Chicherin, who arrived in Britain in 1914, see T. E. O'Connor, *Diplomacy and Revolution*, Ames, IA, 1988, pp. 32–35; R. K. Debo, 'The Making of a Bolshevik: Georgii Chicherin in England, 1914–1918', *Slavic Review*, 25, 1966; J. McHugh and B. J. Ripley, 'Russian Political Internees in First World War Britain: The Cases of George Chicherin and Peter Petroff', *Historical Journal*, 28, 1985, pp. 727–38.
[29] Maisky, *Into the Past*, p. 177.
[30] See below, note 42.
[31] Maisky, *Into the Past*, p. 177.
[32] I. Litvinov, 'Letters to Viola' (autobiographical fragment), pp. 2–3: St Antony's RESC Archive.
[33] Ibid., p. 3.
[34] Ibid., pp. 4 and 15.

of several prominent writers after the turn of the century. Virginia Woolf and the large 'Bloomsbury set' were denizens of the same area as the one preferred by Lenin. Goerge Bernard Shaw, Bertrand Russell as well as H. G. Wells had houses in Hampstead. When Gor´kii visited London he was greeted by many of these intellectuals; he himself liked to stay at the costly Russell Hotel on Russell Square. Gor´kii was an open supporter of the Russian Social-Democratic Workers' Party, and he put his money where his mouth was by subsidizing its activities out of his substantial royalties. The Russian political emigrants made contact with Gor´kii for ideological and financial reasons but sought no opportunity to link up with his friends in the British cultural elite of the period. Gor´kii in London was a man of two lives; the long-term resident Russian revolutionaries had only one, whose focus was directed at their homeland. London was a city to be endured until such time as the hated Romanov dynasty was overturned or the 'European socialist revolution' started.

The emigrants stressed that they were 'internationalists'. Several members of the 'colony' were not Russians; and as Jews or Latvians, such individuals felt an additional stimulus to oppose national or ethnic aspirations. The principles of their internationalism were sincerely held: they did not confect their fury when they suspected socialists of other European countries of betraying such a commitment. But it was the Russian Empire which transfixed their thoughts. They yearned for the day when they could return to the homeland and make the revolution- ary changes they had dedicated their lives to. The Romanov monarchy came close to collapse in 1905 and would surely undergo similar intense strains in the future. It was thought worth spending years abroad pre- cisely because they felt safe to assume that the contemporary political order in Russia was doomed.

The only country that fascinated them nearly as much as Russia and its borderlands was not the United Kingdom but Germany.[35] The reluctance to learn English in England or, for that matter, Italian in Italy was a sign of this skewing of interest. Once the controversy with Eduard Bernstein and the other German 'revisionists' was over, however, most radicals refrained from getting involved directly in the German Marxist discussions. Rosa Luxemburg and Karl Radek, both of them being Polish Jews belong to both the Russian Social- Democratic Workers' Party and the German Social-Democratic Party, disliked this passivity. Like Alexander Parvus-Helphand in the 1890s, they believed that the Russian Marxist leadership overlooked the

---

[35] This was true of the Russian Social-Democratic Workers Party but not of the Party of Socialist-Revolutionaries (who also thought of themselves as being basically Marxists).

German leaders' slide into 'opportunism'. But until 1914, when the German Social-Democratic Party majority supported Germany's war effort in contravention of the policy of the Second Socialist International, the foreign critics were voices crying in the wilderness. Previously Lenin, Martov and Plekhanov had refused to allow a word of criticism to alight on the head of Karl Kautskii — this was among the reasons why Lenin acquired an obsessive hostility for the rest of his career.

Their pre-war reluctance to criticise German-speaking socialism was also true of their attitude to Austria, the other country in central Europe with a substantial socialist party dedicated to Marxism. Not that Trotskii entirely avoided interfering in the Social-Democratic Party of Austria. He was outraged by the leadership's decision to establish a bakery in Vienna: 'This was the crudest adventure, dangerous in principle and hopeless in practice.' Victor Adler and his associates met him with a 'condescending smile of superiority'; they rejected his argument that they were traducing 'the position of the party of the proletariat in a capitalist society'.[36]

Trotskii also objected to the nationalist undertones of Austrian Marxists when they wrote about Austria's rivalry with Serbia. He heard directly from socialists in the Balkans, especially Serbian, how the conservative and liberal press in Belgrade quoted the Viennese *Arbeiter-Zeitung* as proof that the internationalism of the European labour movement was a mere fiction. Trotskii angrily dispatched a critical article about this to Kautskii for publication in *Neue Zeit* in Berlin. After some hesitation Kautskii complied, and the Austrian party leadership was outraged that their guest had been so vituperative. While admitting the factual accuracy of the article, they contended that no one took *Arbeiter-Zeitung*'s foreign policy editorials seriously. There was no meeting of minds. Trotskii pointed out that what was printed in Vienna had an impact in Belgrade; he called on the leadership to show greater intellectual rigour in matters of public debate.[37] Generally, though, he kept out of the internal debates of Austrian Marxism. He held rigidly to his own intellectual concerns and ignored how Otto Bauer, Karl Renner and Victor Adler were imaginatively exploring party doctrine and policy.[38]

Yet a Briton like Ivy had experiences which made her doubt that they were quite as uncomplicatedly open to foreigners as they thought they were:

[36] Trotskii, *Moia zhizn'*, 1, pp. 240–41.
[37] Ibid., p. 241.
[38] See R. Service, *Trotsky: A Biography*, London, 2009, ch. 12.

The 'Colony', more tolerant of alien tastes than I was, received me with open arms, though I think they were disappointed that their beloved 'Papasha' [one of Litvinov's other pseudonyms] had remained a bachelor so long only to fall to a daughter of the foreign bourgeoisie. There were not many spinsters among them, still if Litvinoff was going to marry at all, it was one of them he should have married. But they were all very kind to me, even affectionate.[39]

The relationship was still less understandable to Ivy's mother. Maxim was a foreigner, was Jewish and was thirteen years older than him; he was not even a well-preserved embodiment of masculinity, being taciturn and portly. Ivy, though, was determined to maintain the relationship. Her mother had continually nagged her about living 'in sin', so Ivy announced that Maxim was her chosen fiancé — and he proved a surprising success with her parent on his very first visit.[40] The wedding duly took place in the registry office at Hampstead Town Hall in 1916.[41]

Nearly all the colonists found fault with English cooking. The local dishes were a standing joke among them except for roast beef and Yorkshire pudding. The colony anyway did not need to adapt. When its members cooked for themselves they could easily run down to the 'Jewish shops in Soho' and buy pickled cucumbers, smoked salmon and other fish like dried *voblia*.[42]

Wherever in London they fetched up — Bloomsbury, Hampstead or Highgate — they turned their homes into little Russias. The colony as it existed from the years immediately before the First World War onwards, if not in Lenin's time in London, knew how to enjoy itself. They partied as if there was no tomorrow. The cry went up at the New Year's celebration held at the end of 1917: 'There's no caviar, there's no caviar!' It might be wartime in a foreign country but the colony expected to dine without compromise. Ivy, helped by Maxim's instructions and the labour of their red-faced, red-haired charlady Mrs Bristow, produced a satisfactory *borshch* (beetroot soup) followed by roast beef and an immense apple pie.[43] Normally they would have asked servants to eat with them but decided that Mrs Bristow would be linguistically out of her element. She came in for the toasts to the New Year and to the Revolution. More toasts followed, including one to Maxim as 'the First People's Ambassador of the First Socialist Republic' in the entire world.[44]

[39] I. Litvinov, 'Letters to Viola', p. 37.
[40] Ibid., p. 20.
[41] Ibid., p. 23.
[42] Ibid., p. 28.
[43] Ibid.
[44] Ibid., pp. 28a–30.

By then the Litvinovs — and no longer just Ivy as a moderately well-known novelist — were of interest to the left-of-centre British intellectuals. Soon after being confirmed as the Soviet 'plenipotentiary' in London he was invited out by the intellectual luminaries of the British political left. Maxim and Ivy dined with Bertrand Russell, the Webbs and Charles Roden Buxton. Ivy noted that her husband could at last be persuaded to go out for evenings with non-emigrants. He did not immediately flourish as a diplomat; it took months for him to surmount his stand-offishness about the British. Ivy recalled:

> It was a pity they felt obliged to invite me too. I was such a chatterbox and Maxim by nature so taciturn and glad to have others do the talking for him. Whatever the subject under discussion I generally managed to get round to psycho-analysis, and people who sincerely wished to discover what the structure of the Soviets was, found themselves diverted into acrimonious wrangles about Freud and even obliged to listen to the relation of my childhood complexes.[45]

Ivy had a tiff with Russell while Maxim Litvinov, despite being no enthusiast for English food, 'was glad to be able to enjoy his lunch in peace'.[46] (This temperamental imperturbability was to prove a decided asset when he served as the USSR People's Commissar for Foreign Affairs in Moscow.)

Ivy had often found it difficult to socialize with her husband's comrades, and she was willing to share the blame for this. For example, she committed a *faux pas* by asking Mrs Zundelevich whether her little girl's schoolteacher was 'a lady'; for in Ivy's eyes she appeared merely as 'decent working-class'. Mrs Zundelevich replied: 'Do you mean: is she an educated person?' This was not the same question, and the Zundeleviches were momentarily shocked by Ivy's snobbishness. Worse still, as Ivy Litvinov recollected:

> They judged the English 'intelligentsia' by me, for the seldom had opportunities for meeting really cultivated people in their daily life. They could not know that my Aunt Edith would have snubbed me severely for such a remark, that Catherine [Carswell] would probably have bitten my head off and that it would probably have produced an equally awkward silence in the Meynell drawing room.[47]

Ivy subsequently avoided such clumsiness.

Members of the colony did not share her capacity for self-questioning. When Ivy began her friendship with Maxim Litvinov in London, she had already begun to establish herself as a novelist and had accumulated some royalties:

[45] Ibid, p. 37.
[46] Ibid.
[47] I. Litvinov, autobiographical fragment, in ibid., pp. 17–18.

One afternoon we met a small group of Russians on our way down Hampstead to Lloyd's Bank, where I still had fifty three pounds from my last book. After a few minutes animated conversation I broke up everything by saying I must rush to Lloyds before it closed, or I wouldn't be able to cash my cheque.

Maxim didn't reproach me but I saw that he looked gloomy as I came out of the bank. The comrades had dispersed. 'Now they'll all think you're a capitalist,' he said when I asked him what the matter was.[48]

Ivy was flabbergasted:

'Where do *they* cash their cheques?', I asked. He told [*sic*] me, with his wry smile, that I couldn't imagine people living without a bank account. I asked him if there wouldn't be any more banks after the revolution. 'I could explain it to you,' he said: 'But you don't want to understand.'

With commendable patience of her own, Ivy asked him to try. He did this in a grumpy sort of way, ending with the remark: 'I shall have to explain to you certain fundamental principles. You must try to grasp what money itself is.'[49]

Apparently he did not proffer his own explanation of the essence of finance either at that time or later. What is more, the same comrades who criticized the owner of a bank account insisted on retaining all manner of comforts of the capitalist economy for themselves. Likewise Lenin drew on his mother's widow's pension; Trotskii solicited funds from his father. They used the European financial system for this purpose and bank orders were wired to them from the Russian Empire. They also received subsidies from the various party treasuries. If money still ran short, they dabbled in journalism. In London, Litvinov and Peters acquired full-time jobs. But nothing about this involved a commitment to entrepreneurship. Quite the opposite: to be a revolutionary was to choose a life that might well involve poverty, arrest, even penal servitude. None wanted to be rich. They were socially 'democratic'. Like all Russians, they liked to invite servants to eat alongside them. In London this was tricky since the servants spoke no Russian and therefore could not take part in conversation. On balance, Maxim Litvinov thought it better to leave their char lady Mrs Bristow in the kitchen.[50]

The priority for colony members was to have the freedom to work for the cause. They despised Marxists such as Alexander Parvus-Helphand who had turned himself into a millionaire trading in guns and contraceptives. Parvus, brought up in Odessa, had emigrated to central Europe as a young man after getting into trouble with the

[48] Ibid., pp. 15.
[49] Ibid., p. 16.
[50] Ibid., p. 28a.

Imperial authorities. He was bright, fluent and brash and became a flea in the ear of a German Social-Democratic Party which in his opinion was steadily losing its revolutionary impetus. Parvus replaced Lenin in 1904 as Trotskii's political and intellectual mentor. It was he who introduced Trotskii to the idea that the old Russian Marxist scheme for a two-revolution progress towards socialism was undesirable. After briefly returning to St Petersburg and being arrested in 1905–06, Parvus fled abroad and resumed his political journalism in Germany but gave most of his time to his business interests — and in the First World War he even liaised closely with the German government in the pursuit of revolutionary upheaval in Russia.[51]

Contempt for Parvus and his murky financial dealings did not prevent the Russian Social-Democratic Workers' Party — and the colony — from falling into dispute about money that came into the hands of its Bolshevik faction. Lenin's support for 'X'-s — as bank robberies were coyly known — caused an internal party scandal; and the Fourth Party Congress in Stockholm in April 1906 denounced this mode of raising funds.[52] Maxim Litvinov was intimately involved in robbery affairs. He it was who supervized the taking of the rouble notes stolen in the Tiflis 'X' of June 1907 to European bank branches in an attempt to cash them.[53] Police forces across Europe were asked to find Meir Wallach (which was Litvinov's real name).[54] The Bolsheviks also used dubious means to monopolize possession of banks accounts deriving from both a legacy from Savva Morozov and sizeable sums obtained by two Bolsheviks by seducing and marrying two naive young women. Such was the furore that the Mensheviks appealed to the German social-democratic leadership to intervene. It was only the outbreak of the First World War that saved Lenin from having to share his ill-gotten gains with the other factions or else face an official reprimand from the Second International.[55]

News of the February 1917 Revolution in Petrograd came through fast to London even though the details remained sketchy. Maxim Litvinov phoned his wife Ivy in Golders Green about what he knew. Ivy had not yet heard and was delighted: 'Darling it means we're not refugees any more.'[56] Immediately there were get-togethers

[51] Z. A. B. Zeman and W. B. Scharlau, *The Merchant of Revolution: The Life of Alexander Israel Helphand (Parvus), 1867–1924*, Oxford, 1965, chs 3–8.
[52] *Chetvertyi (ob"edinitel'nyi) s"ezd RSDRP. Protokoly. Aprel' (aprel'–mai) 1906 goda*, Moscow, 1959, pp. 401–02.
[53] R. C. Williams, *The Other Bolsheviks: Lenin and His Critics, 1904–1914*, Bloomington, IN, 1986, p. 116.
[54] Paris Okhrana (Hoover Institution Archives), file xxvii-c, folder 1.
[55] R. C. Elwood, 'Lenin and the Brussels "Unity" Conference of July 1914'", *Russian Review*, 1, 1980, pp. 40–49.
[56] I. Litvinov, 'Letters to Viola', p. 32.

of members of 'the Colony'. Litvinov contacted Rothstein, Mitrov, Berzins and Zundelevich to confer about what had to be done:

> [They] began to feel the compulsion to meet every day in each other's rooms, talking, exclaiming, surmising, looking from face to face, and their wives, unwilling to miss a word, popped the dishes into the cold oven, too impatient even to take them out to the scullery.[57]

Litvinov and Mitrov went to the House of Commons to talk with Ramsay Macdonald and found that he had no idea what 'he was going to do about the Revolution'. Next day they called in at the Russian Embassy at Chesham House, enquiring why the staff had not yet taken down the portraits of the former Imperial family.[58]

Russia's London political emigrants applied to the British government for an military convoy to take them across the North Sea to Stockholm. The Foreign Office dithered and then sent over the two veteran revolutionaries Georgii Plekhanov and Petr Kropotkin. The radicals among the Marxists were left in the cold. A second application was made and turned down. The London Russians were probably hoping to dispatch Litvinov as their delegate, but Ivy had just given birth to their son Mikhail so that Maxim was not eager to volunteer. This saved Maxim Litvinov's life because the vessel was torpedoed en route.[59]

Once the October Revolution had taken place the Soviet government had no wish for Litvinov to join others like Peters in Russia. Lenin and Trotskii needed a trustworthy, knowledgeable representative in London, and Litvinov as a veteran Bolshevik exactly fitted their requirements. At the turn of the year he was appointed as plenipotentiary to the British even though Lloyd George's cabinet rejected requests for official recognition. Lloyd George, though, was eager to maintain a line of communication between Russia and Britain. Distrusting the Foreign Office, he sent back Robert Bruce Lockhart as head of the British mission in Moscow and then Petrograd; he also allowed Litvinov to put his case for Soviet Russia to his administration. Even the treaty of Brest-Litovsk in March 1918 did not put an end to mutual overtures. The parlous situation came to an end in August 1918 when the British landed an expeditionary force at Archangel. Within weeks Lockhart had been arrested and charged with subversion. The accusation was a fair one, but Lloyd George was unwilling to leave his emissary to a grisly fate. To put pressure on Lenin, Litvinov was thrown into Brixton prison.[60]

[57] Ibid., p. 33.
[58] Ibid.
[59] Ibid., p. 36.
[60] See Litvinov's account as given to Ivan Maiskii: *Into the Past*, pp. 67–68.

The ploy worked and an agreement was made to release Litvinov as soon as Lockhart was confirmed as being safe and free. Litvinov was raging to get back to Russia. His wife had prepared herself emotionally but not yet fully in a linguistic sense. Before their marriage, Ivy wrote:

> Maxim warned me that his first duty would always be to the Revolution. 'When the drum of Revolution sounds I shall leave you,' he told me. I was not in the least alarmed. 'I shall go with you,' I said. 'Then you must learn Russian.'[61]

She did not yet go out with him. Having just months previously been delivered of their second child, she was in no physical condition to travel. Maxim and Ivy agreed, too, that Russia in the middle of its raging civil war was not an appropriate place for a young family.

Maxim was the last of the colony to go to Russia to join the Communist administration there in Moscow. Colonists had never allowed themselves to go native in London. They arrived and left with their doctrines intact. They took advantage of British residence and freedom to continue their revolutionary activity. Outwardly they were devoted to a cause which brooked no national priority and there was much sincerity in their subjective standpoint; but their assumptions, which seem to have eluded their conscious attention, were focused on the Russian Empire. Britain was a useful place to do research, publish material, send out correspondence and hold party meetings. British socialists were also useful, but they were not interesting or important in themselves. The colony kept itself to itself. From this complacent and dogmatic frame of mind came some of the outbursts of fanaticism that afflicted Soviet Russia in the early years of the October Revolution and later.

[61] I. Litvinov, 'Letters to Viola', p. 16.

The 'Mad Monk' Iliodor in Tsaritsyn

SIMON DIXON

AMONG the obstacles facing P. A. Stolypin in his attempts to renew the Russian autocracy between 1906 and 1911, none was more frustrating than the tangled relationship between Church, state and society in the aftermath of the toleration edict of 17 April 1905. Anxious to preserve 'the dignity of the Orthodox Church' in these unprecedented circumstances, the prime minister nevertheless insisted that it must operate 'in concord with the dignity of state', which was 'incompatible with unjust actions' against rival denominations.[1] Successive chief procurators of the Holy Synod realized in turn that their chances of resisting further legislation on freedom of conscience could only be jeopardized by antagonizing the temporal power. Yet their attempts to defend the Church were undermined by more intemperate forces on the Right, who condemned any concession to the heterodox as a betrayal, dismissed constitutionalism as inherently treacherous, and resorted to extra-parliamentary agitation in an effort to thwart the government.[2]

Among peasants imbued with a sense of the power of the holy, there could be no more effective messenger than a charismatic churchman, and Stolypin had no more irritating thorn in his side than the monk Iliodor (Sergei Mikhailovich Trufanov, 1880–1952), whose 'delicate, beautiful, feminine face' and 'powerful will' drew adoring crowds wherever he went.[3] Combining right-wing rhetoric with spiritual plausibility, Iliodor carved out a scandalous career that has left its mark on many histories of Russia without ever being seriously investigated. In view of the fantasies that infuse Iliodor's denunciation of Rasputin, his former patron, it is tempting to dismiss his 'adventure' as no more than

Simon Dixon is Sir Bernard Pares Professor of Russian History at UCL SSEES.

I would like to thank the British Academy, the Royal Society of Edinburgh, the former Caledonian Research Foundation and the University of Leeds for financial assistance; Richard Davies for unrivalled archival expertise; and Steve Smith, Geoffrey Hosking and Ernest A. Zitser for commenting on a draft of this article. Pre-revolutionary dates are Old Style, except in references to the *New York Times*.

[1] P. A. Stolypin, *Perepiska*, ed. P. A. Pozhigailo, Moscow, 2004, pp. 263–64, Stolypin to P. P. Izvol'skii, 27 August 1908.

[2] See P. Waldron, *Between Two Revolutions: Stolypin and the Politics of Renewal in Russia*, London, 1998, esp. pp. 139–46.

[3] P. N. Zyrianov, *Russkie monastyri i monashestvo v XIX i nachala XX veka*, Moscow, 2002, pp. 227–28, quoting *Pochaevskii listok*, 1910.

a colourful appendix to the great affairs of church and state.[4] Yet it merits close attention in its own right for three reasons: as another instance of the 'specifically Russian masculine appropriation of the feminine' highlighted by Louise McReynolds in her essay on the screen idol, Ivan Mozzhukhin;[5] as a study in celebrity at the dawn of Russian mass culture, for Iliodor's impact owed as much to a cult of personality manipulated by a variety of media as it did to his ideas; and above all as an episode in the politics of Russian religion, for no other figure in the era of Russian constitutionalism apart from John of Kronstadt was able to mobilize such a vigorous popular following, and even Father John never achieved such a disruptive effect.[6] Concentrating on the peak of Iliodor's notoriety at Tsaritsyn between 1908 and 1911, this article explores the damage inflicted on the Russian old regime when an unbalanced individual claiming to be its most loyal supporter was unleashed in an exceptionally unstable place.[7]

By the time Iliodor was appointed missionary-preacher of its makeshift monastery of the Holy Spirit on 1 March 1908,[8] Tsaritsyn had already begun to show signs of the industrial unrest that helped to make it a hotbed of revolution in 1917.[9] As the leading depot for the Volga trade in timber, fish and salt, it was one of Russia's fastest growing cities, ringed by suburban armaments factories. The population almost doubled from 56,000 to 97,000 in the decade after 1897, reaching around 130,000 by 1914.[10] Even steamship companies keen to

---

[4] *The Mad Monk of Russia Iliodor: Life, Memoirs and Confessions of Sergei Michailovich Trufanoff (Iliodor)*, New York, 1918 (hereafter, *Mad Monk*). I refer mostly to this edition rather than to Byv. Ier. Iliodor (Sergei Trufanov), *Sviatoi chort (Zapiski o Rasputine)*, with a preface by S. Mel'gunov, Moscow, 1917, because Mel'gunov omitted not only some 'really fantastic claims' and 'scabrous details' about Rasputin (p. ix), but also (less openly) details of Iliodor's early career.

[5] L. McReynolds, '"Visualizing Masculinity": The Male Sex that was Not One in Fin-de-Siècle Russia', in V. A. Kivelson and J. Neuberger (eds), *Picturing Russia: Explorations in Visual Culture*, New Haven, CT and London, 2008, pp. 133–38 (p. 136). I owe this reference to Ernest Zitser.

[6] On Father John, see Nadieszda Kizenko, *A Prodigal Saint: Father John of Kronstadt and the Russian People*, Philadelphia, PA, 2000.

[7] While Iliodor left traces in numerous central and provincial archives, the most coherent collection for this period, amply demonstrating his impact at national level, is at Rossiiskii Gosudarstvennyi Istoricheskii Arkhiv (hereafter, RGIA), f. 796, op. 191, V otd., 2 stol, dd. 143a–z. The last of these files contains the Synod's *spravka* summarizing Iliodor's career between 1905 and 1908.

[8] A. I. Mramornov, *Tserkovnaia i obshchestvenno-politicheskaia deiatel'nost' Episkopa Germogena (Dolganova, 1858–1918)*, Saratov, 2006, p. 154.

[9] See D. Raleigh, 'Revolutionary Politics in Provincial Russia: The Tsaritsyn "Republic" in 1917', *Slavic Review*, 40, 1981, 1, pp. 194–209.

[10] G. V. Khlopin, *Materialy po ozdorovleniiu Rossii: Sanitarnoe opisanie g.g. Astrakhani, Samary, Saratova i Tsaritsyna s ukazaniem mer, neobkhodimykh dlia ikh ozdorovleniia*, St Petersburg, 1911, pp. 252–54. The provincial governor exaggerated in claiming 150,000 by 1911: 'Moia bor'ba s episkopom Germogenom i Iliodorom: Iz vospominanii senatora P. P. Stremoukhova', *Arkhiv russkoi revoliutsii*, 16, Berlin, 1925, p. 19.

tempt foreign tourists to 'glide' down the 'Mother-Volga' found it hard
to praise this filthy shanty-town. Although one of their guidebooks
promised English-speaking readers 'pure balmy air free from all dust',
the accompanying Russian text admitted that Tsaritsyn's muddy streets
could boast 'neither pavements nor lighting': 'Almost all the houses are
wooden; the shops are strikingly free of any decoration.'[11] Untreated
sewage disfigured the riverbank for miles downstream, leaving the town
vulnerable to recurrent cholera epidemics from 1907 to 1910. Even
before that, Tsaritsyn was one of Europe's least healthy places: its
mortality rate of 33.6 per 1,000 inhabitants between 1903 and 1907,
though marginally lower than that of Saratov (34.2) and considerably
better than those of Samara (upwards of 42) and Astrakhan´ (43), was
worse than Hamburg's during the cholera epidemic of 1892.[12] As
Stolypin knew from his own experience as governor between 1903 and
1906, political tempers had long been high in Saratov province, which
had 'an unusually strong tradition', dating back to the 1890s, 'of coop-
eration between liberal representatives of the educated public and their
more radical counterparts among the intelligentsia and the *narod*'.[13]
Once we consider the conflicts generated by unregulated capitalist
development,[14] it will be clear that Tsarityn's turbulent frontier society
offered no shortage of targets to Iliodor, who made his first provocative
appearance in its marketplace 'crowned with the thorny wreath of a
martyr'.[15]

I

Since graduating from St Petersburg Theological Academy in summer
1905, Iliodor had rapidly established a reputation as the *enfant terrible*
of the Russian Church, having taken his first step on the ladder of
ecclesiastical preferment that autumn when he joined the staff of the

[11] *Parokhodnoe O-vo po Volge 1843g.: Putevoditel´ po r. Volge, 1903*, n.p. 'Our advice to Tourists'
(English original), p. 74 (on Tsaritsyn).
[12] Khlopin, *Materialy*, pp. 251, 255, 257, 272, 274–75; R. J. Evans, *Death in Hamburg: Society
and Politics in the Cholera Years 1830–1910*, Harmondsworth, 1987, pp. 292–96. See also
C. Henze, *Disease, Healthcare and Government in Late Imperial Russia*, London, 2010, a study of
cholera in Saratov.
[13] T. Fallows, 'Governor Stolypin and the Revolution of 1905 in Saratov', in R. A. Wade
and S. J. Seregny (eds), *Politics and Society in Provincial Russia: Saratov, 1590–1917*, Columbus,
OH, 1989, p. 161. See also A. Ascher, *P. A. Stolypin: The Search for Stability in Late Imperial
Russia*, Stanford, CA, 2001, pp. 34–96, and G. V. Skorochkina (ed.), *Saratovskii gubernator
P. A. Stolypin v zerkale dokumentov (1903–1906 gg.)*, Saratov, 2007.
[14] For an illustrated survey, see V. I. Tomarev, 'Na rel´sakh kapitalizma', in V. I.
Tomarev (ed.), *Volgograd: chetyre veka istorii*, Volgograd, 1989, pp. 53–98.
[15] *Mad Monk*, p. 50.

seminary at Iaroslavl'.[16] The choice can hardly have been accidental. As a student protégé of Arkhimandrit Feofan (Bychkov), Iliodor had been introduced not only to Archbishop Antonii (Khrapovitskii), but also to Rasputin.[17] And it was almost certainly thanks to their influence that he secured an appointment in the city where the Union of Russian People [URP] opened its first provincial branch on 26 November under the sympathetic gaze of Governor A. A. Rimskii-Korsakov, who later joined its national council.[18] Though churchmen were still expected to remain above and beyond the emergent sphere of legal party politics — St Petersburg's Metropolitan Antonii (Vadkovskii) had condemned 'agitation on the part of a clergyman' as 'criminal' as recently as April 1905 — Iliodor saw himself as 'a chosen leader in the reaction, a spokesman of Orthodoxy and the czar'.[19] He may have written *Russia is Burning* (*Gorit Rossiia*), an anonymous pamphlet distributed in an edition of 20,000 copies; certainly his diatribes against strikes among semi- and unskilled workers in the textile, tobacco and paper-manufacturing industries soon featured in *Russkii narod*, the newspaper of the Iaroslavl' URP.[20] Both the Spaso-Preobrazhenskii monastery, the thirteenth-century episcopal seat where he lived, and the seminary where he taught homiletics, overlooked the streets where right-wing thugs attacked student demonstrators and looted Jewish shops and houses for three days after the promulgation of the October Manifesto.[21] However, it was within the seminary itself that Iliodor caused his first scandal.

By November 1905, forty-three Russian seminaries had been closed in response to student protests directed largely against restrictions on their own liberty. Violence continued in the following year when rebels exploded bombs in Moscow and Tomsk, vandalized the rector's apartment at Minsk, and threw acid in the face of his counterpart at

[16] S. L. Firsov, *Pravoslavnaia Tserkov' i gosudarstvo v poslednee desiatiletie sushchestvovaniia samoderzhaviia v Rossii*, Moscow, 1996, p. 208, perpetuates the widespread misapprehension that Iliodor's first appointment was to the Pochaev lavra.

[17] Despite its bias against these former mentors, *Mad Monk*, pp. 30, 91–95, leaves little doubt of their influence over Iliodor at this time.

[18] A. Chernovskii and V. Viktorov (eds), *Soiuz russkogo naroda: po materialam chrezvychainoi sledstvennoi komissii vremennogo pravitel'stva 1917 g.*, Moscow-Leningrad, 1929, pp. 365–66. The URP was founded in St Petersburg on 8 November 1905. J. Langer, 'Corruption and the Counterrevolution: The Rise and Fall of the Black Hundred', unpublished PhD thesis, Duke University, 2007, pp. 56 ff., focuses on Odessa without discussing the church.

[19] RGIA, f. 1579, op. 1, d. 36, l. 20b., Antonii to K. P. Pobedonostsev, 4 April 1905; *Mad Monk*, p. 31.

[20] A. V. Shevtsov, *Izdatel'skaia deiatel'nost' russkikh nesotsialisticheskikh partii nachala XX veka*, St Petersburg, 1997, p. 169.

[21] 'Khronika oktiabr'skikh dnei', *Prilozhenie k 'Pravu'*, 1905, cols 171–73; *Voskhod*, 27 October 1905, pp. 44–45; 'Delo o iaroslavskom pogrome', *Rech'*, 12 January 1910.

Khar'kov.[22] At Iaroslavl', by contrast, miscreants were in a minority, and unrest was caused rather by Iliodor's campaign to undermine the respected rector, Evsevii (Grozdov). Like most of his colleagues, Evsevii scorned the URP, which was dismissed by the president of a diocesan clerical assembly in December 1905 as 'an anachronism and a misunderstanding' in the light of the October Manifesto.[23] Taunting Iliodor as a 'peasant', the seminary's three senior classes were sufficiently alienated by February 1906 to boycott his lectures for so long as he remained a member of this reactionary band.[24] Informed of events on 12 March, the Holy Synod rusticated the rebels for the remainder of the year. By the end of June, however, further investigation had persuaded them that Iliodor himself should be transferred to the seminary at Novgorod.[25]

Had he succumbed to Synodal discipline in the manner of so many contemporaries, Iliodor would doubtless have disappeared without trace. After declaring anathema on the intelligentsia, his fellow right-winger, Igumen' Arsenii, was sentenced to monastic imprisonment from which the URP proved unable to release him.[26] But Iliodor's case was different. While he threatened press revelations about 'disorders' at the Spaso-Preobrazhenskii monastery if the authorities persisted in transferring him, the first in a series of orchestrated petitions prompted the Synod to relent. They initially hoped to persuade Archbishop Iakov (Piatnitskii) to appoint Iliodor as his diocesan missionary. However, dismissing this idea as 'wholly undesirable', Iakov refused, creating an impasse resolved only when Iliodor was taken under the personal protection of Archbishop Antonii (Khrapovitskii) at the Pochaev monastery in Volhynia.

In the long term, the most significant outcome of Iliodor's departure from Iaroslavl' was a petition for his return from the president of the local URP to Nicholas II, which prompted the tsar to summon Chief Procurator P. P. Izvol'skii to Peterhof to explain the case in person on 18 August 1906.[27] A compromise was subsequently agreed allowing

[22] J. D. Morison, 'The Church Schools and Seminaries in the Russian Revolution of 1905–06', in G. A. Hosking (ed.), *Church, Nation and State in Russia and Ukraine*, Basingstoke, 1991, pp. 200, 201, 204. On Saratov, see A. I. Mramornov, *Dukhovnaia seminariia v Rossii nachala XX veka: Krizis i vozmozhnosti ego preodoleniia*, Saratov, 2007, esp. pp. 103–46.
[23] *Iaroslavskii vestnik*, 15 December 1905, quoted in S. A. Stepanov, *Chernaia sotnia v Rossii (1905–1914 gg.)*, Moscow, 1992, p. 116.
[24] RGIA, f. 796, op. 191, V otd., 2 stol, d. 143z, ll. 62–620b.; *Pravo*, 9 April 1906, col. 1305; B.V. Titlinov, *Molodezh' i revoliutsiia 1860–1905 gg.*, Leningrad, 1924, pp. 101–02.
[25] Compare *Mad Monk*, p. 31: 'as I found teaching somewhat uncongenial, I resigned my professorship', uncritically echoed in J. T. Fuhrmann, *Rasputin: A Life*, New York, 1990, p. 57.
[26] *Pravo*, 26 February 1906, col. 735.
[27] RGIA, f. 796, op. 191, V otd., 2 stol, d. 143z, ll. 63–650b. The tsar's laconic diary merely records that three ministers presented reports that day: K. F. Shatsillo et al. (eds), *Dnevnik Imperatora Nikolaia II*, Moscow, 1991, p. 329.

Iliodor to accept invitations to preach in various provincial towns, including Iaroslavl'.[28] Nor was this the last word. In January 1907, in a move widely attributed to political pressure, Iakov was translated to the less prestigious see of Simbirsk,[29] and Iaroslavl' acquired a more pliable archbishop in the future patriarch, Tikhon (Bellavin), recently returned from a nine-year spell as leader of the Russian Orthodox Church in America. Already a pattern had emerged that was soon to be repeated in Pochaev and Tsaritsyn. First, Iliodor's scandalous behaviour led to a Synodal investigation that resulted in a decision to transfer him. Then, prompted publicly by the Right and privately by highly-placed sympathizers, the tsar intervened on behalf of the rebellious monk, leaving Iliodor unscathed and emboldened, and a trail of ruined careers in his wake.

At the heart of the Pale of Settlement, he attracted further notoriety by contributing virulently antisemitic articles to *Pochaevskii listok*, the weekly journal edited by Arkhimandrit Vitalii, chairman of the Pochaev URP since its inauguration on 13 August 1906. Drawing an apocalyptic picture of Holy Russia 'fettered in Jewish chains' by capitalist speculators, Iliodor alleged that 'the race accursed of God' had condemned the Russian peasantry first to defeat in the Russo-Japanese war and then to internal revolution. Arraigned against 'the holy Black Hundred', the voluntary militias who alone stood ready to fight for faith, tsar and fatherland were 'Satan's band', a racially mixed conspiracy of workers and bourgeois intellectuals, led by the Jews, who must be killed or put to flight.[30] Although such ravings prompted Stolypin to seek the closure of *Pochaevskii listok* as a menace to political stability in the Western Provinces, the journal survived for more than two years thanks to prevarication by the Synod.[31] By contrast, it took them only a fortnight to respond to the article in the right-wing Moscow newspaper *Veche* in which Iliodor, having denounced the October Manifesto for 'inundating long-suffering Russia with blood' and demanded the death penalty for the 'traitor' Witte, urged Russians on 1 February 1907 to take the law into their own hands: 'I, the monk Iliodor, bless you in

[28] *Soiuz russkogo naroda*, pp. 374–75, shows the difficulties created by such invitations with reference to Smolensk in 1908.

[29] Noting the widespread sympathy for Iakov among his diocesan priests, a reform-minded church journal archly observed that the Synod had missed its chance to undermine critics of the hostility between black and white clergy: 'Why let slip the opportunity to have even a *single elected* bishop?' *Tserkovnyi vestnik*, 8 March 1907, cols 323–26, emphasis in the original. On this evidence, the portrait of Iakov as a grasping, cold-hearted prelate in Manuil, *Die Russischen Orthodoxen Bischöfe*, 3, Erlangen, 1984, pp. 179–81, seems unbalanced.

[30] S. M. Trufanov, *Videnie monakha*, Moscow, 1907, quoted by J. S. Curtiss, *Church and State in Russia: The Last Years of the Empire 1900–1917*, New York, 1940, pp. 264–65. See also D. C. Rawson, *Russian Rightists and the Revolution of 1905*, Cambridge, 1995, pp. 92–95.

[31] Zyrianov, *Russkie monastyri*, pp. 225–27.

the great and holy work of emancipating the dear Motherland from atheists, robbers, blasphemers, bomb-throwers, firebrands, lying journalists and slanderers — all of them cursed by God and condemned by mankind.'[32] Dismissing such incitements as 'exceedingly regrettable and unworthy of the Orthodox Church', the Synod ordered Iliodor's immediate removal from his editorial position.[33]

At first, Archbishop Antonii sprang to the defence of 'this passionate and very morbid young man', portraying his protégé as a 'completely guileless and sincere but pretentious patriot', as yet unable to realize his 'good intentions' with 'sufficient caution and the lack of wrathfulness recommended in the Gospel'.[34] Such support was only to be expected from a man who had himself privately advocated Witte's execution in the aftermath of the October Manifesto, and in February 1906 publicly attacked 'progressive' Jewish intellectuals, arguing that the Jews could never be assimilated into the Russian nation.[35] By the following spring, however, it was no secret that Antonii was losing patience with Iliodor, who had denounced Izvol´skii and the Synod in the URP newspaper *Russkoe znamia* as part of a co-ordinated campaign by the Right. On 15 April, Iliodor's Moscow ally Father Ioann Vostorgov prophesied the Russian people's deliverance from the Babylonian captivity imposed by its 'enemies' in the Duma and the bureaucracy; nine days later, monarchist leaders meeting in Kiev issued an ultimatum to the Synod condemning it as 'unrepresentative of Orthodox church-consciousness [*tserkovnost*]'.[36]

The right-wing leadership, subsequently dismissed by Iliodor's supporters as 'morally negligible',[37] was itself on the brink of discovering his subversive potential. Although Iliodor depicted autocracy as 'a lovely rose spreading its beauty and perfume over all the people', he believed that this perfume had been 'taken' by selfish intermediaries between the tsar and his *narod*, so that 'the people got only the thorns'.[38] The rich, therefore, became natural targets for his invective. Whereas

[32] *Veche*, 1 February 1907. The newspaper had itself been preserved from closure thanks to a personal appeal from Iliodor to the tsar: see P. N. Zyrianov, *Pravoslavnaia tserkov´ v bor´be s revoliutsiei 1905–1907 gg.*, Moscow, 1984, p. 143.
[33] RGIA, f. 796, op. 191, V otd., 2 stol, d. 143z, l. 66ob.
[34] Ibid., l. 67, reported speech.
[35] H.-D. Löwe, *The Tsars and the Jews: Reform, Reaction and Anti-Semitism in Imperial Russia 1772–1917*, Chur, 1993, p. 217; Arkhiepiskop Antonii, *Evreiskii vopros i Sviataia Bibliia*, Pochaev, 1907.
[36] 'Rech´ pri osviashchenii znamen-khorugvei patrioticheskikh organizatsii v Moskve, v prazdnik Vkhoda Gospodnia v Ierusalim 15 Aprelia 1907 goda', in Prot. I. I. Vostorgov, *Polnoe sobranie sochinenii*, 5 vols, Moscow, 1915, 3, pp. 168–75 (on Jeremiah, 51: 11–12); M. Agursky, 'Caught in a Cross Fire: The Russian Church between the Holy Synod and Radical Right (1905–08)', *Orientalia Christiana Periodica*, 50, 1987, pp. 181–83.
[37] See the anonymous apologia, I. L., *Pravda ob ieromonakhe Iliodore*, Moscow, 1911, p. 28.
[38] *Mad Monk*, p. 30.

the foreign ownership of many Russian enterprises made it easier for the URP 'to sound an anti-capitalist and anti-industrial note than an anti-landlord one', Iliodor never hesitated to criticize native *pomeshchiki*. As he later recalled, 'the sharpest of my attacks during the years 1906 and 1907 were directed against the landowners'.[39] Lenin, writing in 1913, looked back on him as the model of 'an extremely original and extremely important feature' of the Black Hundred: 'dark, peasant democracy of the crudest but deepest kind.'[40] A liberal journalist similarly acknowledged that Iliodor's sympathy for popular suffering had touched a genuine chord: 'democratic feelings and words' could be heard in even his most misanthropic sermons.[41] It was therefore far from implausible for Iliodor to pose as a 'true democrat',[42] even though his conception of democracy bore little relation to any conventional Western interpretation of the word.

At the fourth Monarchist Congress — held at Moscow's Hotel Continental between 27 April and 1 May 1907 amidst the full panoply of episcopal icon processions — he accused landowners of profiteering by selling land to speculators for cash instead of allowing peasants to purchase it by instalments. Inciting peasant delegates to demand the compulsory alienation of private property (with compensation), Iliodor insisted, against the advice of the URP leader, Dr A. I. Dubrovin, that they petition the tsar in person.[43] On 2 May, V. M. Purishkevich telephoned General E. V. Bogdanovich and his wife — leading URP supporters in St Petersburg whose condescending manner and negligent approach to fasting had already alienated Iliodor[44] — to warn that his behaviour threatened to split the organization. Two days later, Dubrovin confirmed in person the gravity of the crisis: in a ringing address to the congress, Iliodor had denounced not only Stolypin as Pontius Pilate, but also Dubrovin himself as Judas and V. A. Gringmut as Caiaphas. That same morning, the Bogdanovich household received the leader of a twenty-three-strong peasant delegation from Kherson province, 'prepared to follow Iliodor through fire and water' and apparently determined to destroy 'not only the people sitting in the ministries, but the walls of the ministries themselves'.[45] The Bogdanoviches were

---

[39] H. Rogger, *Jewish Policies and Right-Wing Politics in Imperial Russia*, London, 1986, p. 227; *Mad Monk*, p. 47.

[40] Quoted in A. Ia. Avrekh, *Tsarizm i IV Duma 1912–1914 gg.*, Moscow, 1981, p. 238.

[41] A. I., 'Ieromonakh Iliodor', *Rech'*, 20 May 1910.

[42] *Pravda ob ieromonakhe Iliodore*, p. 26.

[43] *Rech'*, 28 April 1907; *Novoe vremia*, 28 April 1907; Rogger, *Jewish Policies*, p. 225.

[44] *Mad Monk*, pp. 31–35.

[45] A. Bogdanovich, *Tri poslednikh samoderzhtsa*, Moscow, 1990, pp. 425–26, diary 2, 4 May 1907, misnames I. P. Fomenko, president of the Kherson URP, as Khomenko. On Fomenko, see Iu. I. Kir'ianov (ed.), 'Perepiska i drugie dokumenty pravykh (1911 god)', *Voprosy istorii*, 1998, 11–12, pp. 119–20.

not the only ones unnerved by the devotion of Iliodor's disciples. During his visit to the Second Duma in April, an American correspondent commented that 'the peasant members of the Right follow their prophet about with the implicit obedience of well-trained puppies'.[46]

By the end of March 1907, Tambov's Bishop Innokentii (Beliaev), a stalwart supporter of the URP, was convinced that Antonii (Khrapovitskii) had 'betrayed' his protégé and expelled him from Pochaev.[47] In fact, the archbishop twice recalled Iliodor from Moscow to account for his conduct and was pacified only by a signed apology. In the aftermath of the monarchist congress, however, even Antonii was persuaded that Iliodor's 'entire literary output bore witness to his hysterical insanity'. When he again berated 'the yids' in *Pochaevskiia izvestiia*, this time for sheltering revolutionaries allegedly plotting to bomb the lavra, the archbishop recommended that he be transferred to his native diocese, the Don, where he would be isolated from any 'populous centre of Russian life and thought'.[48]

Evidently concerned lest Iliodor slip the leash, the Synod instead assigned him to Antonii's personal supervision in Zhitomir. Since twenty-nine Jews had been killed and 150 wounded there in one of the first pogroms planned by the Black Hundred on 11 May 1905, the archbishop was understandably alarmed.[49] In a town whose 30,000 Russians were outnumbered by 40,000 Jews and 15,000 Poles, Iliodor's presence could only be regarded as inflammatory. Because local right-wingers were prepared for action 'at the first signal', Antonii warned, 'the very appearance of the monk Iliodor on the podium of the Russian Union' would alone 'suffice to make a pogrom, always a possibility in Zhitomir, merely a question of time'. In the event the danger was averted, for although Antonii demanded state protection for Iliodor's arrival, he was to spend no more than a day at the episcopal palace before taking two months' sick leave at the Bekrenevskii monastery in the Don province.[50]

Having sought to discredit the Second Duma from its inauguration in February 1907,[51] the Right reacted with unconcealed hostility to the new electoral system decreed on 3 June. Five days later, Rimskii-Korsakov

[46] *New York Times*, 29 April 1907.
[47] Bogdanovich, *Tri poslednikh samoderzhtsa*, p. 423, 28 March 1907.
[48] RGIA, f. 796, op. 191, V otd., 2 stol., d. 143z, ll. 68–690b.
[49] S. Lambroza, 'The Pogroms of 1903–1906', in J. Klier and S. Lambroza (eds), *Pogroms: Anti-Jewish Violence in Modern Russian History*, Cambridge, 1992, pp. 223–24.
[50] RGIA, f. 796, op. 191, V otd., 2 stol., d. 143z, ll. 70–700b. *Pravda ob ieromonakhe Iliodore*, p. 31, ranks Poles second only to Jews among Russia's 'primordial enemies'.
[51] *Obshchestvennoe dvizhenie v Rossii v nachale XX veka*, 4 vols, St Petersburg, 1909–14, 3, pp. 462–66.

complained from Iaroslavl' that 'Russian interests' under Stolypin had 'evidently become victims of the Yids'.[52] Iliodor soon joined the chorus. By 19 June, an issue of *Rech'* had been sequestrated for reporting his exhortation to peasants to march on St Petersburg to identify 'the villain who is making our autocratic tsar so indecisive'.[53] The Ministry of Internal Affairs objected to another speech at Zdolbunovo on 29 June, when Iliodor celebrated the opening of a new branch of the URP by warning that Nicholas was surrounded by untrustworthy, 'alien' ministers.[54] In such an atmosphere, it was scarcely to be expected that Iliodor's eastward trek would pass without incident. 'The people followed me by thousands and tens of thousands,' he recalled with characteristic exaggeration: 'The religious processions were miles in length.'[55]

The journey was certainly punctuated by scandal. The bishop of Ekaterinburg complained that at Rostov on 13 September, Iliodor had conducted an unauthorized service of blessing for the URP, compounding his offence next day by processing through the park, cross in hand, to deliver a 'purely political' sermon against the Jews.[56] When he continued to denounce Stolypin's treatment of the peasantry, it seemed that Iliodor had once again made himself too hot to handle. Convicting him in November of conducting services beyond the boundaries of his diocese without the local bishop's permission, the Synod instructed Archbishop Antonii that Iliodor must publish nothing further without his prior approval and that he should leave the diocese of Volhynia only in response to specific invitations. He was rescued only when Archbishop Germogen (Dolganov) petitioned for him to be transferred to the diocese of Saratov on 17 December 1907 (Fig. 1).[57] Having paid his first to Tsaritsyn in November, Iliodor wintered at Pochaev, returning to the Volga via St Petersburg after delivering a final menacing sermon in Zhitomir at Candlemas (*Sretenie*, 2 February 1908): 'Do penance, ye landowners, ere it is too late! For if you do not repent, the Germans will invade Russia like birds of prey, and will peck out the bright eyes of the Russian people.'[58]

---

[52] Quoted in M. Loukianov, 'Conservatives and "Renewed Russia", 1907–1914', *Slavic Review*, 61, 2002, pp. 770–71.

[53] D. Rayfield and O. E. Makarova (eds), *Dnevnik Alekseia Sergeevicha Suvorina*, Moscow, 1999, p. 501, 19 June 1907.

[54] RGIA, f. 796, op. 191, V otd., 2 stol, d. 143z, l. 700b; *Mad Monk*, p. 48

[55] Ibid., p. 42.

[56] RGIA, f. 796, op. 191, V otd., 2 stol, d. 143z, l. 71.

[57] Ibid, ll. 71–720b.

[58] *Mad Monk*, p. 50.

Расꙋтинъ. Епископ Гермогенъ. Иліодоръ.

FIGURE 1: Archbishop Germogen (Dolganov) of Saratov, flanked by Iliodor to his left and Rasputin to his right

II

Iliodor and Germogen were among the most extreme products of the acutely confessionalized form of Orthodoxy honed over the course of the nineteenth century in Russia's four theological academies. As the Westernized legacy of eighteenth-century scholarship was subjected to a searching critique in response to heterodox challenges both within and beyond the multinational Russian empire, students were encouraged to 'draw a clear line between that which is strictly ours and all that should be alien to us'.[59] 'Denunciatory' theology — *oblichitel'noe bogoslovie*, as comparative theology was significantly christened — became not so much a discrete discipline as a prevailing temperament.[60] In the hands of the phalanx of 'learned' monks, fostered by Chief Procurator K. P. Pobedonostsev at the theological academies from the 1880s in an attempt to purify ecclesiastical discipline, hostility to heterodoxy could take distorted forms. Even before entering the St Petersburg academy, where he was tonsured by Rector Antonii (Vadkovskii) on 2 December 1890, Germogen had castrated himself during a period of religious searching.[61] Iliodor, who was initiated into the monastic life on 29 November 1903, claimed that a fellow monk burned out one of his own eyes in a fit of ascetic extravagance.[62] Aside from his claim to have signed his renunciation from the Orthodox Church in his own blood in November 1912, Iliodor seems never to have indulged in self-mutilation.[63] Yet he too saw himself as a man apart:

> In order to harden my spirit, at the academy, I subjected myself to great privations. On one occasion I fasted three days, refusing even bread and water, and for two months I slept neither night nor day, spending the time in continuous prayers. Of course, these privations reacted detrimentally on my body, and also on my mind; so that, emaciated physically and exalted spiritually, I saw visions. I saw Christ, I saw evil spirits that grasped me by the hair, shouting: 'You shall not escape from us! You shall not escape from us!' And I saw monsters, with immense iron forks, that screamed: 'You are ours! You are ours!' In short, I brought myself to the point of mental and physical collapse.[64]

Iliodor further revealed himself as a man of heightened sensibility in a lengthy dissertation on 'The Religious-Moral Views of St Ignatii (Brianchaninov)', the renowned nineteenth-century ascetic who had

[59] S. Dixon, 'The Russian Orthodox Church in imperial Russia 1721–1917', in M. Angold (ed.), *The Cambridge History of Christianity: 5, Eastern Christianity*, Cambridge, 2006, p. 332, quoting I. A. Iakhontov's 1843 undergraduate dissertation at the St Petersburg academy.

[60] This crucial point emerges only tangentially from institutional histories by V. A. Tarasova, *Vysshaia dukhovnaia shkola v Rossii v kontse XIX–nachale XX veka: Istoriia imperatorskikh pravoslavnykh dukhovnykh akademii*, Moscow, 2005, and M. Köhler-Baur, *Die Geistlichen Akademien in Russland im 19 Jahrhundert*, Wiesbaden, 1997.

[61] Mramornov, *Tserkovnaia deiatel'nost'*, pp. 86, 81.

[62] *Mad Monk*, pp. 91, 20.

[63] Ibid., p. 265.

[64] Ibid., pp. 19–20. Excessive fasting almost certainly contributed to the intestinal constrictions and bleeding throat that first afflicted Iliodor as a student, when the probe inserted into his oesophagus during a two-month hospital confinement allegedly bequeathed a lifelong antipathy to doctors: *Mad Monk*, p. 22; *Pravda ob ieromonakhe Iliodore*, p. 91.

berated the 'spirit of the times' for generating 'sects, schisms and here-sies'. ('Must we, reborn and redeemed by Christ's suffering, work in such a spirit?' Ignatii demanded. 'No: we should stand up to it with all our heavenly strength.')[65] The germs of Iliodor's later extremism are clearly discernible in a work which concentrated, as his examiner approvingly noted, on the passions of fallen man, on Orthodoxy's exclusive powers of salvation and on monasticism as 'a form of volun-tary martyrdom'.[66] When later charged with a failure of humility, Iliodor had reason to retort that had not been 'taught to be modest and tender-hearted; I was taught to be militant'.[67] Indeed, he always insisted that he was temperamentally unsuited to contemplation. 'I sought a militant and active monastic life', he reminded his Synodal critics at the height of the crisis of 1911. 'That is my calling; that is my true life.'[68]

In contrast to Pochaev, Jews accounted for a mere 2.1 per cent of the population of Tsaritsyn, where Iliodor directed his antisemitic invective against the editors of the local newspapers.[69] Nor were jour-nalists his only targets. As relentless in his attacks on greedy entrepre-neurs as on the intelligentsia, Iliodor provoked repeated conflicts with politicians and other prominent citizens. Boasting that he would have his critics thrown into gaol,[70] he pursued them in the civil courts. In November 1910, Germogen reported 'around thirty-nine' such cases to the Synod; a year later, Iliodor's apologia listed, 'among others', thirty-five cases against newspaper editors, sixteen against timber merchants, one against the stock exchange and another against members of the Tsaritsyn municipal duma.[71] No less litigious than Iliodor, the editors in turn complained to the provincial governor, S. S. Tatishchev, who sent policemen to report on his sermons. 'It was a comical sight, I standing at the altar and preaching, the police standing at the entrance with copy-books in their hands, writing down everything I said.'[72] Since Iliodor challenged the veracity of both police and press reports, it is

[65] 'O dukhe vremeni': Slovo nastoiatelia Sergievoi pustyni Arkhimandrita Ignatiia, St Petersburg, 1874, pp. 5–6.
[66] Zhurnaly zasedanii Soveta S.-Peterburgskoi dukhovnoi akademii za 1904/5 god, St Petersburg, 1905, pp. 346–48, report by A. A. Bronzov, right-wing professor of moral theology.
[67] Mad Monk, pp. 39–40.
[68] RGIA, f. 796, op. 191, V otd., 2 stol., d. 143d, l. 35, Iliodor to Bishop Parfenii, 12 March 1911 (typed copy).
[69] Khlopin, Materialy, p. 253; Tsaritsynskaia zhizn', 7 March 1908.
[70] RGIA, f. 796, op. 191, V. otd., 2 stol., d. 143v, l. 510b., Kurlov to Luk'ianov, 30 July 1910, reporting Iliodor's speech before a crowd of 3,000 at the foundation ceremony of a new church in Tsaritsyn on 13 June.
[71] Ibid., l. 790b., Germogen to Synod, 26 November 1910; Pravda ob ieromonakhe Iliodore, p. 149.
[72] Mad Monk, p. 52.

worth emphasizing that their content was barely distinguishable from the laudatory summaries which appeared in *Bratskii listok*, a polemical mouthpiece for Germogen.[73] It was their verdicts that differed as Iliodor and his critics reached fever pitch in their attempts to besmirch one another, inadvertently exemplifying the force of Pobedonostsev's prediction about the perils of trading 'unimaginable insults' in the press.[74]

While such spiteful disputes reveal much about the fissures of provincial society in an era of aggressive urban growth, the conflicts Iliodor provoked in Tsaritsyn acquired added significance by exposing the underlying tension between the values of the pre-Petrine church and those of the post-Petrine bureaucracy. Blind to the destabilizing effect on their own dynasty, the last two tsars sponsored a return to Muscovite values intended to bring the monarchy closer to the people.[75] There was no more self-conscious epitome of medievalism than Iliodor — 'a man of the seventeenth century', as Lev Tikhomirov observed, 'not a spirit born of our own flaccid times'.[76] Yet despite condemning the iniquity of 'contemporary progress', Iliodor was by no means opposed to technological development and was noticeably more modern than Stolypin in his ability to manipulate the press.[77] As a self-confessed 'man of action' — not the least proto-fascist phrase in his vocabulary — Iliodor acknowledged that his powers of sustained argument were limited.[78] Yet although his outpourings were intellectually negligible, his central contention was subversive of both the Synod established by Peter I and the pseudo-constitutional regime established by Nicholas II. On the one hand, he saw no place in ecclesiastical administration for secular officials, whom he blamed for inculcating a bureaucratic mentality among the clergy that had paralysed their popular impact. On the other hand, 'not a single act of state, be it the publication of new laws, the declaration of war, or the participation of peasants and workers, should be managed without the preliminary advice and blessing of the church'.[79]

[73] See, for example, 'Pastyrskaia beseda ottsa ieromonakha Iliodora i dukhovnyi kontsert', reprinted from *Bratskii listok*, 1909, in Sv. A. P. Mramornov, *Sochineniia: Zapiski, eparkhial'nye khroniki, publitsistika*, ed. A. I. Mramornov, Saratov, 2005, pp. 37–42.

[74] K. P. Pobedonostsev, *Sochineniia*, St Petersburg, 1996, pp. 306–07.

[75] See R. S. Wortman, *Scenarios of Power: Myth and Ceremony in Russian Monarchy, 2: From Alexander II to the Abdication of Nicholas II*, Princeton, NJ, 2000, parts 2 and 3, esp. ch. 7.

[76] L. Tikhomirov, 'K delu ieromonakha Iliodora', *Moskovskiia vedomosti*, 4 February 1911.

[77] Compare Ascher, *Stolypin*, pp. 84, 131, 177. For Iliodor's sermon on progress, 5 April 1910, see RGIA, f. 796, op. 191, V otd., 2 stol, d. 143v, ll. 21–22, Luk'ianov to Synod, 19 May 1910.

[78] S. Kondurushkin, 'Miatushchiisia Iliodor', *Rech'*, 1, 3 April 1912. Rogger, *Jewish Policies*, pp. 212–32, is more sceptical about the proto-fascist elements in the URP.

[79] *Pravda ob ieromonakhe Iliodore*, pp. 5–7. Iliodor also wanted elections to be supervised by priests to ensure that the Duma fulfilled its true obligation, the religious and moral education of the people: ibid., pp. 5, 25–26.

So faithfully did these views reflect those of his archbishop, whose attempts to create a theocracy in the diocese of Saratov had led him to convert the local branch of the URP into an Orthodox confraternity under his own control,[80] that some commentators regarded Iliodor as a mere pawn in the 'open war' between Germogen and successive provincial governors.[81] As Stolypin warned Tatishchev's successor P. P. Stremouhkov in 1911, recalling his own experiences on the Volga, the archbishop was that most dangerous of adversaries: a master of constitutional minutiae contemptuous of bureaucracy in all its forms.[82] Determined to exploit every legal loophole to frustrate his opponents, he nevertheless ignored Synodal procedure and trampled on the sensibilities of Saratov's politicians, led at national level by a friend of the prime minister, the moderate Octobrist Count A. A. Uvarov.[83] As a leading right-wing journalist put it, in characteristically tendentious terms, the result was a volatile cocktail: 'A radical [municipal] duma, a liberal governor, a powerfully Judaized society, hypnotized by the Jewish press, a silent *narod*, and two representatives of a disappearing type: believing pastors.'[84]

III

On 10 August 1908, the simmering tensions in Tsaritsyn erupted into open violence. Police were called to break up a mass brawl after Iliodor urged his followers to defend him against the government in the wake of press insinuations about the inappropriate presence of women at his monastery.[85] As the young demagogue hit the national headlines for the first time, some observers diagnosed his antics as part of a 'spiritual plague' exemplified by the reactionary tone of the Missionary Congress held at Kiev in July.[86] Privately, the authorities in Saratov

---

[80] See Mramornov, *Tserkovnaia deiatel'nost'*, pp. 227–41 and, more generally, A. V. Posadskii, 'Chernaia sotnia v Saratovskoi derevne v 1905–1916 godakh', *Otechestvennaia istoriia*, 2007, 1, pp. 134–42.

[81] *Rech'*, 28 November 1908; Z. Vets, 'Bor'ba za vlast' (iz epopei bor'ba Germogena s gr. Tatishcheva)', *Utro Rossii*, 9 January 1911.

[82] Stremoukhov, 'Moia bor'ba', p. 16.

[83] *Otchet Izbirateliam Chlena Gosudarstvennoi Dumy Grafa A. A. Uvarova za vtoruiu sessiiu 1908/9 goda*, Saratov, 1909, pp. 97–100; *Rech'*, 20 November 1908. On Uvarov, see R. T. Manning, *The Crisis of the Old Order in Russia: Gentry and Government*, Princeton, NJ, 1982, p. 237 and passim.

[84] M. O. Menshikov, 'Radikaly i tserkov'', *Novoe vremia*, 16 September 1908.

[85] RGIA, f. 796, op. 191, V otd., 2 stol, d. 143z, ll. 74–750b. Rising levels of prurience are discussed by C. D. Worobec, 'The Unintended Consequences of a Surge in Orthodox Pilgrimages in Late Imperial Russia', *Russian History*, 36, 2009, 1, pp. 71–75.

[86] I. I. Tolstoi, *Dnevnik 1906–1916*, St Petersburg, 1997, p. 205, 18 August 1908. See also H. Coleman, 'The 1908 Missionary Congress and the Problem of Cultural Power in Late Imperial Russia', *Jahrbücher für Geschichte Osteuropas*, 52, 2004, 1, pp. 70–91.

were more alarmed by the prospect of civil unrest during the current cholera outbreak.[87] While successive consistory investigations concluded that Iliodor had been 'provoked' to make inappropriately 'sharp' remarks by the newspapers,[88] relations between Germogen and the governor were further soured by events surrounding Count L. N. Tolstoi's jubilee on 28 August. Attacks on Tolstoi by Protoierei I. P. Krechetovich in the Saratov municipal duma enraged not only Tatishchev, but also Uvarov and the Kadets, who walked out when the clerical deputy refused to accept a vote to suspend him.[89]

After the governor had travelled to the capital to petition Stolypin to remove Iliodor from Tsaritsyn, Izvol'skii, unwilling to tolerate further clerical 'wilfulness', ordered Germogen to transfer him to Saratov at the end of September and 'curtail in the most decisive manner his activities which are so dangerous to the social order and might have very serious consequences for himself'.[90] When the archbishop instead recommended his protégé as a model preacher, echoing Iliodor's offensive comparison between Tatishchev and the Tatar khans in a published telegram to the tsar, Stolypin insisted that Germogen be 'rapidly' recalled to St Petersburg, 'without the opportunity to return, even to bid farewell to his diocese, since that would inevitably lead to a new scandal'.[91] In the event, the Synod's Deputy Chief Procurator, A. P. Rogovich, a member of Countess Ignat'eva's circle sympathetic to Iliodor, was despatched to Saratov on 24 October, along with the Deputy Minister of Internal Affairs, A. A. Makarov. Unlike the Saratov police chief, who lost his job, Germogen emerged unscathed. But neither investigator seems to have been impressed by Iliodor, who claimed to have contracted tuberculosis. Under pressure from Stolypin, the Synod resolved on 27 November to transfer him to the diocese of Minsk.[92]

[87] Rech', 20 September 1908, reported 587 cases and 362 deaths at Tsaritsyn since 8 July, and a reduced level of panic by comparison with 1907. New York Times, 29 July 1908, had been more alarmist, reporting the deaths of eleven out of twelve cholera victims in the town.

[88] The investigations were led not by Prot. I. P. Krechetovich, as reported in Rech', 17, 19, 21 and 22 August 1908, but by the seminary rector, Prot. Maksimov, and Palladii, suffragan bishop of Vol'sk.

[89] Mramornov, Tserkovnaia deiatel'nost', pp. 249–54; Novoe vremia, 16 September 1908; Moskovskiia vedomosti, 28 September 1908.

[90] RGIA, f. 796, op. 191, V otd., 2 stol, d. 143z, l. 75; Rech', 13, 16 September 1908; Bogdanovich, Tri poslednikh samoderzhtsa, p. 462, 10 September 1908.

[91] Stolypin, Perepiska, p. 293, Stolypin to P. P. Izvol'skii, 9 October 1908, emphasis in the original; Rech', 8 October 1908; Mad Monk, p. 58.

[92] RGIA, f. 796, op. 191, V otd., 2 stol, d. 143z, ll. 75ob.–78ob.; Rech', 31 October, 15 and 21 November 1908.

In an emotional appeal to the tsar, Iliodor protested that this verdict was bound to mystify 'the whole Russian people'. Arguing that his sermons had been intended merely to inculcate 'strict morals among a religiously savage and corrupt people and to explain the power of the pure idea of autocracy to save the Russian realm', Iliodor accused officials of allowing his followers to be flogged 'with whips and horses' hooves' and of falsely alleging that he wanted to return to 'the era of Savonarola'.[93] Though the Synod forbade him to conduct services, he remained defiant in Tsaritsyn while Germogen pretended that his protégé was too ill to travel. Not until 24 March 1909 did the archbishop submit to pressure from St Petersburg and ban all services at Iliodor's monastery. On Germogen's advice, he travelled to the capital, where he was allowed to say mass on the first day of Easter and made a further appeal to the tsar on 28 March. While Arkhimandrit Feofan apparently refused to present this petition, 'on the pretext that it was dangerous to abuse one's privileges too often',[94] Rasputin was more amenable. The result was Iliodor's first informal audience with the tsarina, held at Anna Vyrubova's apartment at Tsarskoe Selo on 3 April, after which Nicholas II resolved, against clear ministerial advice, that out of 'pity' for Iliodor's followers, he should be allowed to return to Tsaritsyn 'on probation, and for the last time'.[95]

If this was a gesture intended to tame an unruly acolyte, it could hardly have been more counter-productive. Fortified by the tsar's reprieve, Iliodor surrounded himself with uncritical supporters. The right-wing agitator, I. D. Popov, was in regular attendance, and Iliodor's old school friend, Father Mikhail Egorov, became chaplain at the suburban Ural-Volga factory (a French-owned metalworks subsequently purchased by the British arms manufacturer, Vickers, with a workforce of over 4,000).[96] Unsympathetic clergy were either denounced to Germogen or sought transfers to another diocese.[97] Meanwhile, Iliodor forged ahead with the construction of a new monastery, modelled on the Pochaev lavra. Dismissed by Stremoukhov as 'crudely built, purely for show',[98] the place was impressive enough in scale. Its finances remain obscure, although Iliodor and his supporters, claiming a total

---

[93] *Rech'*, 12 January 1909, reprinted from *Svet* the full text of Iliodor's telegram, sent on 19 December 1908.
[94] *Mad Monk*, p. 96.
[95] RGIA, f. 796, op. 191, V otd., 2 stol, d. 143z, ll. 81–84; *Mad Monk*, pp. 57–59, 95–98, 101–03; Général A. Spiridovitch, *Les dernières années de la Cour de Tsarskoïe-Sélo 1910–1914*, 2 vols, Paris, 1928–29, 2, pp. 44–45.
[96] RGIA f. 796, op. 191, V otd., 2 stol, d. 143d, l. 190, Parfenii to Synod, 23 February 1911.
[97] Mramornov, *Tserkovnaia deiatel'nost'*, pp. 184–85.
[98] Stremoukhov, 'Moia bor'ba', p. 24.

cost of 700,000 roubles, insisted that it was funded by popular dona-
tions. The cathedral, completed in 1910 in honour of the medieval
warrior-saint, Alexander Nevsky, could accommodate 7,000 pilgrims,
though many of Iliodor's incendiary addresses were given outside in the
courtyard, surrounded by the fortress-like walls of a building designed
to accommodate more than 150 monks.[99] Within this citadel, intended
to symbolize Orthodoxy's repulsion of alien faiths, he became a self-
confessed 'monster of audacity'.[100] Following a pattern common to
many right-wing rituals, he greeted visitors at the railway station and
processed back to the monastery with miracle-working icons accompanied by a military band.[101] But no-one waged such 'indefatigable war'
against the 'cultural heathenism' that Iliodor believed was 'becoming
established in schools and in everyday life'.[102] 'I curse all atheists and
libertines and will curse them for as long as I live', he told his congregation on 14 February 1910. 'That right is given to me as a pastor of
the Holy Church by its statutes. And who gave these droopy-lipped,
carrion-crow journalists the right to be judges? No-one gave them that
right.'[103]

Dismissing the Octobrists as a 'party of self-satisfied and obese people,
incapable of idealism',[104] he continued to pour scorn on capitalist
entrepreneurs, to the consternation of the provincial authorities. 'In the
opinion of the Governor of Saratov', reported the Deputy Minister of
Internal Affairs in May 1910:

> Father Iliodor's systematic agitation against industrialists and the rich in
> general, publicly charging them with the oppression of the poor, especially
> of working people, and his constant public reminders that local stevedores
> are deprived of leisure time by the miserliness of the rich, inflame class
> hatred, incite the workers against their employers, and very probably
> will once more have an impact on the railway stevedore movement in the
> Tsaritsyn region, leading the mass of railway workers to strike again, as
> they did last year thanks to the influence of Father Iliodor.[105]

---

[99] *Pravda ob ieromonakhe Iliodore*, pp. 87, 179; *Mad Monk*, pp. 62, 67–68. According to the
modern diocese of Volgograd, there were only three celibate priests, ten lay brothers, and
four or five monks at the monastery in 1911: <http://www.vlgeparh.com/eng/cloister_eng_
1.htm> [accessed 15 August 2009].

[100] *Mad Monk*, p. 51.

[101] For example, *Russkaia zemlia*, 21 November 1910. See also H.-D. Löwe, 'Political Symbols
and Rituals of the Russian Radical Right, 1900–1914', *Slavonic and East European Review*, 76,
1998, 3, pp. 441–66.

[102] *Pravda ob ieromonakhe Iliodore*, p. 14.

[103] RGIA, f. 796, op. 191, V otd., 2 stol, 143v. l. 5–50b., report from Saratov's temporary
chief of police, 6 March 1910.

[104] *Pravda ob ieromonakhe Iliodore*, p. 27.

[105] RGIA, f. 796, op. 191, V otd., 2 stol, 143v, l. 280b., Kurlov to Luk´ianov, 20 May
1910.

Germogen countered that class conflict was more likely to be stirred up by the press than by Iliodor, and that Tsaritsyn had been strike-free in 1909 — a claim which ignored the dispute at the town's largest saw-mill, where labourers walked out at the end of June after having been compelled to work on Sundays.[106]

On 9 May 1910, when thousands gathered at the monastery to celebrate the feast of St Nicholas the Miracle-Worker, Iliodor renewed his onslaught on Russia's self-regarding governing classes, whom he accused of abandoning the people 'to the mercy of fate'.[107] This time his target was not so much the higher reaches of officialdom in St Petersburg as the local politicians who had obstructed his mission.[108] 'There was a time when they said they had no need of a monastery, and for that I called them deliberate good-for-nothings and ignoramuses with no knowledge of history. Atheists, corrupters of the Orthodox faith, blasphemers — they are mocking you, the Orthodox Russian people.'[109] Thus insulted, the municipal duma sought Iliodor's removal from Tsaritsyn. Though the provincial governor was formally obliged to protest this resolution as a breach of the Municipal Statute, nothing could have pleased him more. Egged on by Tatishchev, Stolypin once again requested the chief procurator to transfer Iliodor because he had broken the terms of the tsar's probation.[110]

Much as it detested Iliodor, the liberal press objected to the duma's request on the grounds that 'freedom of the individual from arbitrary administrative intervention should be guaranteed to all Russian citizens', whatever their politics.[111] The protracted investigations generated by his sermon certainly showed the tsarist regime at its most unpredictable. The Synod duly ordered an inquiry, to which Tatishchev, under article 200 of the Statute of Diocesan Consistories, appointed his head of chancellery. To Shul′ts, a Volga German, Iliodor's guilt seemed so obvious that the only option for his ecclesiastical patrons must be damage limitation.[112] But by entrusting the investigation to one of Iliodor's supporters in Tsaritsyn, Father Lev Blagovidov, Germogen

[106] Ibid. ll. 770b.–78, 26 November 1910; J. H. M. Geekie, 'The Church and Politics in Russia 1905–17: A Study of the Political Behaviour of the Russian Orthodox Clergy in the Reign of Nicholas II', unpublished PhD thesis, University of East Anglia, 1976, p. 217.
[107] RGIA, f. 796, op. 191, V otd., 2 stol., d. 143b, l. 4, Tatishchev to Stolypin, 20 May 1910; crowd photographed in *Pravda ob Ieromonakhe Iliodore*, p. 119.
[108] See *Rech′*, 1 October 1908, for the municipal duma's attempts to deny Iliodor land for his monastery. A plot he favoured near the river was reserved for a market.
[109] *Tsaritsynskii vestnik*, 12 May 1911.
[110] RGIA, f. 796, op. 191, V otd., 2 stol., d. 143b, ll.2–20b., Stolypin to Luk′ianov, 2 June 1910.
[111] A. I., 'Ieromonakh Iliodor', *Rech′*, 20 May 1910.
[112] RGIA, f. 796, op. 191, V otd., 2 stol., d. 143b, ll. 29–30, Stolypin to Luk′ianov, 11 August 1910; Stremoukhov, 'Moia bor′ba', p. 24.

engineered an acquittal: journalists admitted that they had reconstructed Iliodor's sermon from memory; witnesses testified that they believed nothing they read in the newspapers; and the consistory, complaining that Shul'ts had unfairly sought to broaden the scope of the investigation, concluded that Iliodor had no case to answer.[113]

However, on a charge of slander brought by Evfrosin'ia Vasil'evna Maksimova, the wife of a wealthy timber merchant, the same investigators unexpectedly reached a different verdict. When Maksimova objected to Iliodor's allegation that she had worn a low-cut dress to sing 'filthy' songs at a fundraising concert sponsored by her philanthropist husband, Stolypin instructed S. M. Luk'ianov, Izvol'skii's successor as chief procurator, to take 'rapid and decisive measures to protect the citizens of Tsaritsyn from public insults'.[114] In October, the Saratov diocesan consistory found in her favour, fining Iliodor 50 roubles and warning him that a further offence would require him to submit his sermons to preliminary censorship. Appalled by this excessively 'severe' and 'formal' verdict, which he attributed to 'pastoral conscience' and 'zeal', Germogen denounced Maksimova as 'a most unseemly woman, debauched in both thought and behaviour'. Unmoved, the Synod twice confirmed the consistory's decision, leaving the archbishop, still protesting Iliodor's 'complete innocence' in February 1911, to condemn his 'undeserved punishment' as 'offensive in the highest degree for a pastor and preacher'.[115]

IV

It is hard to imagine the prime minister of any other European Great Power becoming personally involved in the case of a singer offended by a monk's criticism of her costume at a fundraising event for a temperance society. But Stolypin had inevitably been drawn deeper into Iliodor's affairs when events took a more sinister turn. While bureaucrats and bishops squabbled behind closed doors over provincial embarrassments, public attention in the two capitals focused for the first time on Iliodor's relationship with Rasputin. Beyond the high society in which he moved, 'Grigorii' had hitherto been but a shadowy

---

[113] RGIA, f. 796, op. 191, V otd., 2 stol, d. 143b, ll. 34–55, esp. ll. 410b., 500b., 54. On the irregular conduct of consistory business under Germogen, see Mramornov, *Tserkovnaia deiatel'nost'*, pp. 121–24.

[114] RGIA, f. 796, op 191, V otd., 2 stol, d. 143a, l. 2, Stolypin to Luk'ianov, 3 June 1910.

[115] Ibid., ll. 3, Maksimova's petition; 17–19, Germogen to Synod, 10 November 1910; 15–16, same to same, 19 November 1910; 20–23, same to same, 31 December 1910; 27–28, Synod resolution, 17 January 1911; 30–350b., Germogen to Synod, 28 February 1911; 36–40, Synod resolution 26 April 1911.

figure. However, following his visit to Tsaritsyn at Christmas 1909,[116] his critics, who now included Arkhimandrit Feofan, took advantage of his open support for Iliodor to publish whispers about his lasciviousness that had been circulating in private since Anna Vyrubova's visit to his native village of Pokrovskoe during the previous Lent. The most significant attack came in *Moskovskiia vedomosti*, where Rasputin was denounced by Mikhail Novoselov on 2 March 1910 as a flagellant sectarian (*khlyst*) and 'a sex maniac'.[117] An author of popular edifica-tory books and lecturer at Moscow Theological Academy, Novoselov belonged to the circle of the ascetic Grand Duchess Elizaveta Fedo-rovna, who herself warned the tsar later that month '*that we can be mistaken and that not all who seem holy are*'.[118] Iliodor retorted with the first public defence of Rasputin on 21 March: 'I call him a holy elder [*starets*] not because he has grey hair like the old Tsaritsyn merchants, whose minds could scarcely compete with that of the most backward youth, but on account of his brain and his ascetic feats.'[119] Far from being rapacious, Iliodor insisted, Rasputin had so far sublimated his sexual instincts under the influence of prayer and fasting that he no longer slept with his own wife. Attacks on such an 'angelic soul' could only be attributed to 'yid' journalists.[120] Undeterred, Novoselov renewed his assault in the press, prompting Iliodor to urge that he be flogged.[121]

This was dangerous territory. If Rasputin really was a debauched sectarian, warned the editor of *Moskovskiia vedomosti*, then the Synod ought not to allow Iliodor to defend him since his activities risked the 'demoralization' of the *narod*: 'The personality of Grigorii Rasputin should be exposed, and the temptation should be stopped.'[122] In the light of rumours about his own female following, it was equally rash for Iliodor to mention sex since, as another journalist mordantly remarked, it was 'unnecessary to delve into the archives' to find

[116] See *Mad Monk*, pp. 129–32.
[117] M. Novoselov, 'Dukhovnyi gastroler Grigorii Rasputin', *Moskovskiia vedomosti*, 2 March 1910. Emboldened by this article, even liberal papers joined the fray: see, for example, S. V., 'Rasputin-Novykh', *Rech'*, 20, 26, 30 May 1910. On Rasputin's links with the *khlysty*, see A. Etkind, *Khlyst: sekty, literatura i revoliutsiia*, Moscow, 1998, pp. 585–630.
[118] *Materialy k zhitiiu prepodonomuchenitsy velikoi kniagini Elizavety: Pis'ma, dnevniki, vospominaniia, dokumenty*, Moscow, 1995, p. 46, Elizaveta Fedorovna to Nicholas II, 26 March 1910, emphasis in the English original.
[119] RGIA, f. 796, op. 191, V otd., 2 stol, d. 143v, ll. 11–13, Luk'ianov to Synod, 24 April 1910, forwarding the Saratov authorities' reports via Stolypin.
[120] Ibid, ll. 14–15, police report, 3 April 1910; ll 11–130b., Luk'ianov to Synod, 24 April 1910.
[121] M. Novoselov, 'Eshche nechto o Grigorie Rasputine', *Moskovskiia vedomosti*, 30 March 1910.
[122] 'O Grigorie Rasputine, Ieromonakhe Iliodore i prochikh', *Moskovskiia vedomosti*, 30 April 1910, unsigned editorial, probably by Lev Tikhomirov.

examples of Rasputin's '"bathhouse politics" among our "elders" and monks'.[123]

Alarmed by such a hostile press, the Synod demanded a report from Germogen on 4 May.[124] However, despite increasingly urgent promptings, it was not until 24 November, following a visit to Tsaritsyn, that he condescended to reply, offering a characteristically unreserved defence of his protégé.[125] In press interviews that summer, the archbishop had promoted Iliodor as an 'unimpeachable pastor' and a man of 'crystalline truthfulness' who dared to speak openly on matters about which the Saratov authorities would have preferred him to remain silent.[126] Yet news of Iliodor's unruly behaviour continued to emerge. In December, the Tsaritsyn police were summoned to prevent him and his acolytes from disrupting the Concordia Theatre's production of *Behind Monastery Walls*, itself an obvious provocation.[127] Already exasperated by Germogen's refusal to confirm when and where Iliodor would serve the month's imprisonment imposed by the Saratov circuit court a year earlier, Luk'ianov was driven to the brink by a report at the end of the month that the archbishop's own investigation had concluded that there was no case to answer. Decisive action followed when it was revealed that a judge had refused to sit in a case brought by Iliodor against three members of the municipal duma because he had 'repeatedly insulted the entire personnel of the [Tsaritsyn district] court', which now intended to bring him to account.[128]

Confronted with this information, the Synod resolved on 20 January 1911 to appoint Iliodor as abbot of the Novosil'skii monastery of the Holy Spirit, an isolated house in Tula province with only fourteen brothers, presumably chosen as an ironic shadow of his own more

---

[123] 'Eshche o Grigorie Rasputine', *Utro Rossii*, 1 May 1910.

[124] RGIA, f. 796, op. 191, V otd., 2 stol, d. 143v, ll. 17–18, Synod resolution, 4 May 1910.

[125] Ibid., ll. 25–6, 16 May; 29–31, 31 May; 37–40, 24 July; l. 59, 9 November; ll. 80–83, Germogen to Synod, 24 November 1910.

[126] M[ikhail] P[aozerskii], 'Ep. Germogen o svoem priezde v Peterburg', *Novoe vremia*, 9 June 1910, published simultaneously as 'Beseda s episkopom Germogenom' in *Utro Rossii*. Like several journalists who reported on ecclesiastical affairs, Paozerskii was a former priest (at Vasil'kovo in Novaia Ladoga *uezd*). When his pseudonymous reports on the Second Duma for *Peterburgskii listok* led to his prosecution by the St Petersburg diocesan consistory in May 1907, Paozerskii, supported by parishioners and fellow clergy, admitted writing for some eleven titles, from a 'progressive' rather than an 'anti-ecclesiastical' point of view. His request to leave the clerical estate on 23 December was seconded by an irate Metropolitan Antonii, who recommended on 9 January 1908 that the Synod accept it 'without prior application of the prescribed admonition, since it is extremely corrupting, extremely harmful and completely undesirable for this unworthy individual to remain any longer in holy orders and as part of the spiritual administration'. Three days later, the Synod agreed. RGIA, f. 796, op. 189, d. 7698, ll. 1–6.

[127] *Rech'*, 28 December 1910.

[128] RGIA, f. 796, op. 191, V otd., 2 stol, d. 143v, l. 108, Saratov consistory secretary to Luk'ianov; l. 110, Kurlov to Luk'ianov, 15 January 1911. For the resolution of the case in Iliodor's favour, see *Novoe vremia*, 2 December 1911.

pretentious establishment with the same name.[129] As the news leaked
to the press on the following day, the chief procurator sought the tsar's
approval. On 22 January, he informed the Synod that this time there
was to be no imperial reprieve.[130]

Truculent as ever, Iliodor had arrived in St Petersburg the day
before, boasting to journalists that 'there were no laws in the Empire
that could oblige him to go to Tula. They could not get him to move
to his place of exile even by force of arms'.[131] Back in Tsaritsyn,
as *Russkoe znamia* and *Zemshchina* mounted a noisy campaign in his
defence, Iliodor held the cross high above his head in the presence of
a renowned miracle-working icon, reducing his predominantly female
congregation to tearful hysteria. Another huge crowd flocked to hear
him declare war on the devil at the end of an Easter service brought
forward to Candlemas (*Sretenie*, 2 February) to create a sacrificial atmosphere. As the choir sang 'Christ is Risen', Iliodor announced a hunger
strike that would end only when he was allowed to remain in his
monastery. 'Heroes don't surrender: they die', he told the disciples who
joined him in the vow of abstinence: 'I shall not go to Tula alive!'[132]

This proved to be a false boast. Among the posse of officials who
descended on Tsaritsyn to coax him into submission was Nicholas II's
personal aide-de-camp, Captain A. N. Mandryka, a relative of one of
Rasputin's acolytes in the diocese of Saratov, the abbess of the convent
at Balashov. Bombarded by hundreds of telegrams from Iliodor's
supporters, the tsar despatched Mandryka in spite of the offence the
appointment would give to his government: 'I don't give a damn!'
Nicholas allegedly exclaimed.[133] Yet Mandryka's was not to be the
decisive voice. After frantic and apparently fruitless negotiations at
Serdobsk on 3 February, the Synod's representative, Bishop Parfenii of
Tula, reported that it was Germogen who had subsequently persuaded
Iliodor to go to Novosil´e, while ministers in St Petersburg locked
themselves into confidential discussions of his 'crimes'.[134] Arriving in

[129] RGIA, f. 796, op. 191, V otd., 2 stol, d. 143v, ll. 113–17, Synod resolution; L. I. Denisov,
Pravoslavnye monastyri rossiiskoi imperii: polnyi spisok, Moscow, 1908, pp. 872–73. Stremoukhov,
'Moia bor´ba', confuses this with Iliodor's exile to the Florishchev hermitage in Vladimir
province in January 1912.

[130] *Russkoe znamia*, 21 January 1911; *Rech´*, 21 January 1911; RGIA, f. 796, op. 191, V otd. 2
stol, d. 143v, l. 118.

[131] *Birzhevye vedomosti*, 23 and 26 January 1911.

[132] *Rech´*, 1 Feb. 1911; RGIA, f. 796, op. 191, V otd., 2 stol, d. 143g, l. 427, police report on
service on 30 January (copy); ibid., d. 143v, ll. 130–34, Iliodor's sermon on 1 February
(copy); ibid., l. 126, report of sermon on 2 February.

[133] A. N. Shvarts, *Moia perepiska so Stolypinym. Moi vospominaniia o Gosudare*, Moscow, 1994,
p. 67, 9 February 1911.

[134] RGIA, f. 796, op. 191, V otd., 2 stol, d. 143d., ll. 189–90, Parfenii to Synod, 23 February
1911; A. A. Polivanov, *Iz dnevnikov i vospominaniia po dolzhnosti ministra i ego pomoshchnika
1907–1916 g.*, ed. A. M. Zaionchkovskii, Moscow, 1924, p. 102, 10 February 1911; *Rech´*, 7
February 1911. Compare contrasting accounts of the negotiations in *Mad Monk*, pp. 60–61;
Spiridovitch, *Les dernières années*, 2, pp. 52–59.

Tula on 12 February, Iliodor petitioned the provincial governor for assistance in his new mission and delivered four approved and well attended sermons that Parfenii thought 'in general produced a good impression on the audience' though they did 'not lack his peculiar acerbity'.[135] In view of Tula's proximity to Iasnaia Poliana, Iliodor could not resist the temptation to denounce Tolstoi as 'the greatest bandit in the world'. *Russkiia vedomosti* reported that he also returned to another familiar theme, fulminating against the Jews in a sermon on 'the rivers of Babylon'.[136] 'Some disliked the hysteria into which the preacher occasionally falls', acknowledged the more sympathetic *Moskovskiia vedomosti*, 'and the sharp, high notes in his voice', but the paper found these 'fully explicable' after the 'troubles' Iliodor had experienced.[137]

From Tula, to Parfenii's relief, Iliodor finally took the train to Novosil'e on 14 February. But he was not to remain there long. No sooner had the Tula diocesan authorities judged it wise to publish a flattering account of his sermons than highly-placed sympathizers contrived to return Iliodor to the Volga, allegedly in disguise, and certainly under cover of a ministerial crisis in the second week of March.[138] The precise circumstances of this venture remain obscure. While Iliodor later acknowledged the assistance of Ol'ga Lokhtina, Stremoukhov plausibly implicated P. G. Kurlov, who had followed every step of the crisis as the Deputy Minister of Internal Affairs responsible for the police. Though Kurlov subsequently claimed to have identified Iliodor as 'a clerical careerist' and 'an obvious maniac' when Countess Ignat'eva first introduced them, he may have hoped, by conniving in the monk's escape, to cement his own connections at Court and to undermine Stolypin from within.[139] But whatever the mechanism of his retreat from Novosil'e, Iliodor once again locked himself behind the altar in his monastery, supported by Father Egorov and surrounded by emotional female acolytes.[140]

[135] RGIA, f. 796, op. 191, V otd., 2 stol, d. 143d, l. 190, Parfenii to Synod, 23 February 1911.
[136] *Russkiia vedomosti*, 13 February 1911. For a sermon on this theme at Tsaritsyn on 21 February 1910, see RGIA, f. 796, op. 191, V otd., 2 stol, d. 143v, l. 7, Kurlov to Luk'ianov, 23 February 1910.
[137] *Moskovskiia vedomosti*, 15 February 1911.
[138] *Tul'skiia eparkhial'nyia vedomosti*, 1 March 1911, chast' neoffitsial'naia, pp. 193–94; *Novoe vremia*, 15 March 1911.
[139] *Mad Monk*, p. 62; Stremoukhov, 'Moia bor'ba', pp. 33–34; P. G. Kurlov, *Gibel' imperatorskoi Rossii*, Berlin, 1923, pp. 146–47; F. S. Zuckerman, *The Tsarist Secret Police in Russian Society, 1880–1917*, London, 1996, pp. 193–97.
[140] Egorov's telegram to the tsar is at RGIA, f. 796, op. 191, V otd., 2 stol, d. 143g, l. 417, 31 January 1911. See also ibid., d. 143d, l. 670b., Stolypin to Luk'ianov, 21 March 1911.

V

The ensuing crisis dominated the national headlines for weeks, partly because it was sensational, but principally because it touched the highest levels of Russian politics. Unimpressed by Germogen's admonitory telegram to Iliodor, the Synod insisted that the archbishop travel to Tsaritsyn and if necessary subject his protégé to a psychiatric examination.[141] On arrival, Germogen replied that he had been unable to see the patient, who was confined to his cell by illness.[142] But Stremoukhov, reminding Stolypin of the archbishop's 'well-known duplicity and solidarity with ieromonakh Iliodor', confirmed that the two monks had met and that Iliodor was 'perfectly healthy'.[143] In view of Germogen's insolence, the Synod resolved not to object if the civilian authorities were to remove Iliodor from his cathedral. The prime minister, however, warned that forcible extraction would be 'extremely difficult' since Iliodor's presence 'among thousands of his followers' made it impossible for the police to risk 'an undesirable clash with the *narod*, particularly since he always kept the sacred communion bread and wine (*sviatye dary*) close to his person.[144] Yet while Stolypin advocated clerical persuasion as the best solution to the impasse, Germogen countered that his task had been complicated by the cordon of troops erected around the monastery.[145] In the face of assurances that this was merely a peace-keeping force, and that the railway carriage waiting nearby was intended only to guarantee Iliodor's safe return to Novosil´e, the archbishop insinuated that the monastery was under siege and Iliodor threatened with arrest. At the end of a meeting of the Tsaritsyn Orthodox Ecclesiastical Assembly, convened in support of his protégé by Germogen between 21 and 28 March, the errant monk himself appealed to the Synod not to treat him as 'a prisoner and a brigand'.[146]

While the crisis deepened in Tsaritsyn, Iliodor's acolytes in St Petersburg were busy whipping up support. I. A. Rodionov and Iliodor's leading parliamentary advocate, S. A. Volodimerov, defended him at

[141] RGIA, f. 796, op. 191, V otd., 2 stol, d. 143d, l. 20, Metropolitan Vladimir to Germogen, 14 March 1911.
[142] Ibid., l. 55, Germogen to Synod, 18 March 1911.
[143] Ibid., l. 42, Stolypin to Luk´ianov, 17 March 1911; l. 57, Stremoukhov to Stolypin, 19 March 1911; l. 67, Stolypin to Luk´ianov, 21 March 1911.
[144] RGIA, f. 796, op. 191, V otd., 2 stol, d. 143d, ll. 58–59, Synod resolution, 19 March; l. 65, Stolypin to Luk´ianov, 20 March 1911; l. 67, same to same, 21 March 1911.
[145] On Stolypin's predilection for siege tactics, see Ascher, *Stolypin*, p. 43.
[146] RGIA, f. 796, op. 191, V. otd., 2 stol, d 143d. ll. 77–78, Germogen to Synod, 22 March 1911; ll. 170–72, Iliodor to Synod, 28 March 1911; 'Pokhozhdenie Iliodora', *Byloe*, 24, 1924, pp. 188–91; Mramornov, *Tserkovnaia deiatel´nost´*, p. 274.

a series of public readings.[147] His principal Synodal patron, Moscow's Metropolitan Vladimir (Bogoiavlenskii), received a delegation of Iliodor's 'spiritual children' at his *podvor'e* on 24 March and six days later presented the Synod with a petition signed by Volodimerov and seven other right-wing Duma members.[148] To meet the challenge, Metropolitan Antonii (Vadkovskii) rose from his sick-bed to preside over an emergency meeting in his apartments at which the Synod resolved to relieve Iliodor of his duties in Tula and commit him to two months' monastic penance in the Crimea for leaving Novosil'e without permission.[149] In a typically theatrical gesture, Iliodor's disciples threw themselves on their knees before the metropolitan, vowing to rise only once their idol had been reprieved.[150] They were coolly told that the Synod's decision was final. But again it proved not to be so. Following an audience at Tsarskoe Selo on 1 April, Luk'ianov reported that the tsar wished Iliodor to remain in Tsaritsyn 'in view of the people's entreaties'. Next day, at an emergency session of the Synod attended only by Metropolitan Flavian and Archbishop Agafodor of Simferopol (the other bishops having returned to their dioceses for Easter), Antonii was obliged to overturn the previous resolution.[151] The strain was intolerable. On 13 April, a seizure paralysed his left side, temporarily depriving him of the power of speech.[152] Luk'ianov's fate was sealed even sooner. Fuelled by press speculation, rumours of his impending downfall had been circulating since February.[153] Only Easter delayed the inevitable: the chief procurator was dismissed on 2 May.

Regarding 'the very orientation of Iliodor's preaching as a consequence of the weakness of the Synod and the Church and as proof of the absence of ecclesiastical discipline',[154] Stolypin had long been dissatisfied with Luk'ianov. He had kept his job in February only because the prime minister feared that his sacking would be interpreted as a victory for Iliodor. That was precisely the result in May. Buoyed by his latest triumph, Iliodor appeared in the capital to be fêted by Stolypin's reactionary critics. Countess Ignat'eva's circle greeted him with open

---

[147] *Moskovskiia vedomosti*, 27 March 1911. On Volodimerov, a noble landowner and journalist from Orel province, see Iu. I. Kir'ianov (ed.), *Pravye partii: Dokumenty i materialy*, 2 vols, Moscow, 1998, 1, p. 690.

[148] RGIA, f. 796, op. 191, V otd., 2 stol, d. 143d, l. 203.

[149] Ibid., ll. 208–09, Synod resolution; *Novoe vremia*, 1 April 1911.

[150] Ibid., 2 April 1911.

[151] RGIA, f. 796, op. 191, V otd., 2 stol, d. 143d., ll. 222–23; *Novoe vremia*, 3 April 1911.

[152] Ibid., 17 April 1911.

[153] Polivanov, *Iz dnevnikov*, pp. 104–05, 24 March 1911; Tolstoi, *Dnevnik*, p. 359, 4 April 1911.

[154] 'Iz perepiski P. A. Stolypina s Nikolaem Romanovym', *Krasnyi arkhiv*, 5 [30], 1928, p. 85, 26 February 1911.

arms; flanked by Volodimerov, he made an unscheduled appearance at a session of the Russian Assembly chaired by General Shtiurmer; and at the convent founded in memory of John of Kronstadt, he posed for a photograph with Mother Angelina and her nuns, a copy of the reactionary newspaper *Kolokol* carefully displayed on his lap. As he later boasted in Tsaritsyn, he was even received by Nicholas II at Tsarskoe Selo.[155] Revelling in his renewed impregnability, Iliodor openly mocked Stolypin in the press: 'Not so long ago, they took me across Russia in a special train that had been waiting for me at the station for twenty-one days. And now, thank God, a single little ticket will suffice.'[156]

Although formally speaking Iliodor was no more than a humble *uezd* missionary — an appointment confirmed by the Saratov diocesan consistory on 9 April[157] — his ambitions ranged much wider. As Stremoukhov predicted, so far from persuading him to relent, the tsar's generosity towards Iliodor merely 'turned his head even further'. Thousands gathered for his Easter services, making an impact on even the international press:

> Telegraphic descriptions of the scenes enacted at Tsaritsin leave an impression of wonder that such extravagant adoration could be evoked by a simple priest in the twentieth century. Iliodor's exploit has appealed to the hearts and minds of millions of the humbler members of the Orthodox Church. They regard him not only as a revivalist, but as a martyr who was only saved from death by the intervention of the Czar acting as God's instrument [...] Bishop Hermogen is said to have caught the spirit of the people and to have openly declared to them, 'We are celebrating our own resurrection and that of the Little Father Iliodor'.[158]

His monastery was now effectively out of bounds to the police, who remained powerless to investigate injuries caused by a falling statue, the trampling of a youth by the crowd and the sudden death of one of Iliodor's pilgrims.[159] Even such incidents as these were made to seem trivial by comparison with the disorders that ensued on his two Volga pilgrimages later that summer.

Having converted the first-class deck of his steamer into 'a floating monastery', Germogen sailed from Saratov at 7 p.m. on Wednesday 15 June on the first stage of his journey to return the miracle-working

[155] V. S. Diakin, *Samoderzhavie, burzhuaziia i dvorianstvo v 1907–1911gg.*, Leningrad, 1978, pp. 151–52, 232–33; M. V. Shkarovskii, *Sviato-Ioannovskii stavropigial'nyi zhenskii monastyr': Istoriia obiteli*, St Petersburg, 2001, pp. 94–95; *Rech'*, 14 May 1911.
[156] *Novoe vremia*, 17 May 1911.
[157] RGIA, f. 796, op. 191, V otd., 2 stol, d. 143d, ll. 261–62.
[158] *New York Times*, 14 May 1911.
[159] 'Pokhozhdenie Iliodora', pp. 193–94, a comprehensive police memorandum, covering the period March–September 1911.

Sedmizerskaia icon of the Mother of God, which had been processed round his diocese for ten months, to the hermitage in Kazan´ province where it belonged. Iliodor and his pilgrims followed on a second crowded boat, similarly draped with patriotic banners and flags. At Vol´sk on the following day, Iliodor launched a familiar attack on the intelligentsia and the rich, interpreting Russia's recent humiliation at the hands of the Japanese as a sign that the Virgin would withhold her protection from a materialist age of unbelief.[160] The headlines, however, were dominated by his own erratic behaviour: having had the first officer removed from the steamer for questioning his sanity while sailing upstream, Iliodor publicly confronted the wife and daughter of a senior Synodal official on the way back, prompting the provincial governor to contact the chief procurator in an attempt to prevent further damaging litigation.[161]

Worse was to come when Iliodor departed on 9 July for the Sarovsk Monastery in Tambov province accompanied by some 1,700 followers including Ol´ga Lokhtina.[162] Though the pilgrimage, apparently subsidized by the tsarina to the tune of 3,000 roubles,[163] passed off peacefully at the shrine of St Serafim, it was a different matter on both the outward and return cruises. Iliodor claimed, in response to criticism from Prince Meshcherskii, that reports of his misbehaviour had been exaggerated.[164] Yet an appalled Count Uvarov protested in a parliamentary question to the Minister of Internal Affairs,[165] and police and press reports offer ample evidence of wrongdoing. As crowds of women and boys sang hymns on the upper deck of their steamer, a band of URP vigilantes disembarked in successive towns along the Volga to rough up any bystander who failed to pay sufficient respect for the Church, the tsar and Iliodor himself. 'Hats off!' went the cry: 'Rus´ is on the march!' 'Accursed yids!' screamed Iliodor at those who failed to respond: 'Anathema!' A Saratov journalist who filed critical reports was tarred and feathered for his pains. At Samara, Iliodor denounced the clergy for ignoring him, banging in disgust on the locked cathedral doors. By contrast, he was ceremonially received at Nizhnii Novgorod by the provincial governor, A. N. Khvostov, a future

---

[160] 'Velikoe palomnichestvo saratovskikh arkhipastyrei, pastyrei i mirian v Sedmizerskuiu pustyn´ Kazanskoi eparkhii', in Mramornov, *Sochineniia*, pp. 188–90, 193–94, 197.

[161] *Rech´*, 16, 17, and 26 June 1911. 'Pokhozhdeniia Iliodora', p. 195, names Tatishchev as the governor, a slip for Stremoukhov.

[162] See photograph in *Mad Monk*, p. 152.

[163] *Sviatoi chort*, pp. 62–63.

[164] In particular, he denied having anathematized Iakov (Piatnitskii) and other bishops: 'Pis´mo Iliodora k kniaziu Meshcherskomu', *Utro Rossii*, 26 August 1911.

[165] *Prilozheniia k stenograficheskim otchetam Gosudarstvennoi Dumy. Tretii sozyv. Sessiia Piataia. 1911–1912 gg. Tom 1 (№№ 1–210)*, St Petersburg, 1911, no. 159. For the reply, see ibid. *Tom III (№№ 351–500)*, St Petersburg, 1912, no. 387.

Minister of the Interior, who appeared with the monk on his balcony to popular acclamation.[166] In one sermon, Iliodor threatened to drown all Jews in the Black Sea. Accused of inciting pogroms after his return to Tsaritsyn, he replied in characteristically uncompromising terms: 'If there should be a pogrom, then it will not be Iliodor who is to blame, but the Jews and the Russian atheists.' 'Do not drink the blood [of the *narod*], or things will be hard for you, and you will suffer.'[167]

While the press buzzed with rumours that Luk'ianov's successor, V. K. Sabler, was preventing the Synod from discussing Iliodor,[168] he disappeared in early August, prompting his armed bodyguard to claim that he had flown abroad to mastermind an international conspiracy to save Russia from the bureaucrats. The truth was scarcely less fantastic. Journalists soon traced him to Moscow, where he was initially suspected of conspiring to form a new 'democratic monarchist' party in conjunction with Vostorgov. In fact, Iliodor had used his contacts at Court to persuade the city's governor-general to admit him to the transit prison to interview the thief of a renowned miracle-working icon, revered by the imperial family, which Iliodor planned to recover and carry at the head of the greatest mass pilgrimage Russia had ever seen.[169]

This extraordinary enterprise (which foundered when it emerged that the icon in question had been destroyed) was in turn intended as no more than a first step towards a new mass movement in the Volga-Don basin. As a native of the Don Cossack region, Iliodor traded on its reputation for freebooting and plain speaking, implicitly associating himself with the seventeenth-century rebel, Stenka Razin.[170] 'The Don is the river of popular anger', Iliodor's apologia proclaimed. 'If only it could speak, it would have much to say about the way that the guile-less, simple people struggled for the truth, how they were enemies of "accursed Rus'", and how, finally, they became Autocracy's best

[166] 'Pokhozhdeniia Iliodora', pp. 200, 198, 197. Having later attempted in vain to purchase the manuscript of Iliodor's memoirs, Khvostov caused a sensation at the Provisional Government's investigation of Rasputin by announcing that the author intended to shower copies from an aeroplane onto front-line troops: see S. Mel'gunov, 'Kak my priobretali zapiski Iliodora', *Na chuzhoi storone*, 2, ed. S. P. Mel'gunov, Berlin-Prague, 1923, p. 51; P. E. Shchegolev (ed.), *Padenie tsarskogo rezhima: Stenograficheskie otchety doprosov i pokazanii, dannyi v 1917 g. v Chrezvychainoi Sledstvennoi Komissii Vremennogo Pravitel'stva*, 7 vols, Leningrad, 1924–27, I, p. 40 (testimony of A. N. Khvostov).
[167] 'Pokhozhdeniia Iliodora', p. 201 and passim, catalogues complaints sent to St Petersburg by the provincial authorities.
[168] *Birzhevye vedomosti*, 5 August 1911; *Golos Moskvy*, 6 August.
[169] *Utro Rossii*, 9 August 1911; *Novoe vremia*, 18 August 1911; 'Pokhozhdeniia Iliodora', pp. 200–01; V. F. Dzhunkovskii, *Vospominaniia*, ed. A. L. Panina, 2 vols, Moscow, 1997, I, pp. 645–47; S. Karatsevtsev (ed.), *Freilina Eia Velichestva: Initimnyi dnevnik i vospominaniia A. Vyrubova*, Riga, n.d., pp. 89–90.
[170] Germogen used Razin's legacy to warn nobles of the peasantry's bandit-like tendencies: *Rech'*, 21 December 1908.

support.'[171] Even if he was not responsible for starting the popular rumour that he was Nicholas II's illegitimate brother, Iliodor did nothing to stem it: 'In the homeland of Emel'ka Pugachev', Stremoukhov remarked, 'another pretender was born'.[172]

In the grip of this 'mania for greatness',[173] Iliodor finally over-reached himself by attempting to discredit Rasputin. Precisely when he turned against his former patron remains unclear, not least because his own account is riddled with contradictions.[174] But while Iliodor was in St Petersburg to secure permission for a new newspaper, *Thunder and Lightning (Grom i Molniia)*, to be published at his monastery,[175] he and Germogen, who had been appointed to the Synod in a vain attempt to tame him, lured Grigorii to the Iaroslavl' *podvor'e* on 16 December. There, Iliodor claimed, Germogen assaulted a quivering Rasputin after Iliodor had charged him with a litany of sinful behaviour, culminating in the 'torture' of innocent women.[176] Having launched an unprecedented attack on the Synod the day before, denouncing its 'anti-canonical' approval for deaconesses and burial services for non-Orthodox Christians in a telegram to the tsar, the archbishop could expect little sympathy from Rasputin's ally, Chief Procurator Sabler. At the beginning of January, Germogen was dismissed from the Synod and exiled to the Sviato-Uspenskii monastery at Zhirovits in Minsk province.[177] Iliodor, who seems never to have been a favourite of the imperial family, having been humoured on Rasputin's advice, had lost his most influential protector.[178] He, too, was exiled, to Florishchev *pustyn'* in Vladimir province.

VI

Seasoned observers predicted that a scandal involving two such 'energetic and insolent people' could hardly be expected to end with their banishment.[179] And so it proved. At a meeting of the Union of the

---

[171] *Pravda ob ieromonakhe Iliodore*, p. 77.

[172] Quoted in Avrekh, *Tsarizm*, p. 239. See also *Mad Monk*, p. 270.

[173] *Tserkovnyi vestnik*, 1911, no. 34, col. 1057, quoting Grigorii Petrov in *Russkoe slovo*.

[174] First he claims that he had already resolved to denounce Rasputin when he defended him against Novoselov; then he says the opposite: *Mad Monk*, pp. 132–33, 217. The latter passage is omitted from *Sviatoi chort*, p. 126.

[175] *Novoe vremia*, 24 December 1911.

[176] *Mad Monk*, pp. 224–38.

[177] For the ramifications, see Prot. V. Rozhkov, *Tserkovnye voprosy v Gosudarstvennoi Dume*, Moscow, 2004, pp. 287–98, and Mramornov, *Tserkovnaia deiatel'nost'*, pp. 276–306.

[178] Though chronologically confused and presumably written with hindsight in the knowledge that Iliodor had betrayed Grigorii, *Freilina Eia Velichestva*, pp. 83–114, nevertheless gives a sense of the limited affection in which he was held by 'Mama' and 'Papa'.

[179] Tolstoi, *Dnevnik*, p. 397, 18 January 1912.

Archangel Michael on 21 January 1912, V. M. Purishkevich warned right-wing newspapers to be 'extremely cautious' in discussing Iliodor because the whole affair was 'still unravelling'.[180] His exile began with a typical piece of mystification when he duped journalists into thinking that he had set off for Florishchev on foot in the snow. Romanticized accounts of this fictional pilgrimage duly appeared in the press,[181] only to be retracted when it emerged that Iliodor had instead been smuggled to the suburban home of Dr P. A. Badmaev, a specialist in Tibetan herbal medicine well connected at Court.[182] Having helped to engineer Germogen's voluntary departure for Minsk on 22 January, in the face of police fears that he might resist deportation, Badmaev knew that Iliodor would be harder to tame.[183] Reminding the palace commandant V. A. Dediulin of both monks' thirst for martyrdom, he urged another reprieve on the grounds that 'repressive measures against them are not only harmful to the state itself, but dangerous to the Orthodox Church'. This, time, however, the tsar remained obdurate. Dediulin was no friend of Rasputin, but once he had informed Badmaev that Iliodor's pathological capacity for scandal rendered him 'harmful to any normal, so-called peaceful state structure', there was no option but to surrender the fugitive monk to the authorities.[184]

At Florishchev, Iliodor found himself confined to a 'small, damp room, with crumbling floors and with solid iron bars at the narrow windows', a humiliation he subsequently attributed to the vengeful Rasputin.[185] Sleeping on bare planks, covered by a simple cotton blanket, he had no contact with the other monks, but was permitted to write and to receive visitors, including undercover journalists and Ol'ga Lokhtina. One sympathizer found him slimmer as a result of his experiences but 'in good heart'.[186] He was, however, enraged by press reports of the closure of his Tsaritsyn monastery, where illicit hoards of cash had allegedly been discovered by the Synod's investigator,

[180] *Pravye partii*, 2, p. 106, 21 January 1912.
[181] *Rech'*, 18 and 28 January 1912; *Novoe vremia*, 19 and 28 January 1912; *Strannik*, February 1912, pp. 289–92.
[182] *Mad Monk*, p. 245, claims that Rodionov and the self-styled 'holy fool', Mitia Kozel'skii, guided him to Udel'naia. For an uncritical but informative account of Badmaev's chequered career, see T. I. Grekova, *Tibetskaia meditsina v Rossii: istoriia v sud'bakh i litsakh*, St Petersburg, 1998.
[183] C. A. Ruud and S. A. Stepanov, *Fontanka 16: The Tsar's Secret Police*, London, 1999, pp. 295–96.
[184] V. O. Semennikov (ed.), *Za kulisami tsarizma (Arkhiv tibetskogo vracha Badmaeva)*, Leningrad, 1925, pp. 3–6, Badmaev to Dediulin, undated [22 or 23 January 1912], Dediulin to Badmaev, 23 January [1912]. Compare 'Dnevnik Rasputina', in A. P. Kotsiubinskii and D. A. Kotsiubinskii, *Grigorii Rasputin:Tainyi i iavnyi*, St Petersburg, 2003, pp. 386–91.
[185] *Mad Monk*, pp. 246, 249.
[186] *Moskovskiia vedomosti*, 11 February 1912, reported that the windows had been sealed at Iliodor's own request. See also *Rech'*, 24 February 1912.

P. V. Mudroliubov.[187] 'If Mudroliubov really did give this information to *Rech'*,' Iliodor complained to the right-wing newspaper, *Groza*, 'then I am bound to say publicly that Mudroliubov is a b[lood]y slanderer! A criminal official! A servant of Satan!'[188]

Urging that he be unfrocked for such an outburst, Archbishop Nikolai of Vladimir warned the Synod that Iliodor had attended chapel only once, on arrival at the hermitage, where he had since behaved offensively. Nikolai wanted him moved to a larger monastery, since Florishchev's twenty brothers were allegedly 'too old and simple' to notice 'the cunning of unusual cellmates and pilgrims'. As Arkhimandrit Makarii complained, Iliodor had defied attempts to prevent him from receiving a delegation from Tsaritsyn, threatening 'a great scandal' if the police so much as touched a single visitor. When the Synod learned that sixty-five of the 200 pilgrims he expected had arrived in three separate groups on 22–23 April, chanting religious and patriotic songs beneath the window of his cell, Iliodor was ordered to renounce all contact with reporters, to respect the prior's authority, and to attend chapel regularly.[189] In a handwritten explanation to Makarii on 24 April, Iliodor complained that since he had stood 'as still as a statue, without saying a single word' to the crowd, Nikolai's suggestion that he had demeaned the Synod in disorderly speeches was mere slander. He continued to boycott services. Nevertheless, on 10 May he begged both the Synod and the tsar for forgiveness and requested that his telegram be published. This the Synod ignored.[190]

Among Iliodor's visitors at Florishchev was the writer Sergei Kondurushkin, who found Iliodor so 'passionate in his sincerity' that he not only published a series of flattering accounts in *Rech'*, but on 12 November delivered a paper to St Petersburg's Religious-Philosophical Society portraying Iliodor's movement as 'a popular protest against faithless democracy'.[191] It was thanks to Kondurushkin that Iliodor

[187] Mramornov, *Tserkovnaia deiatel'nost'*, pp. 114–20, confirms that Mudroliubov found the debt-ridden diocesan finances in chaos.

[188] Ierom. Iliodor, 'Klevetnikam: Pis'mo v redaktsiiu', *Groza*, 13 April 1912. See also, *Novoe vremia*, 22 January 1912; *Rech'*, 1 March 1912; RGIA, f. 796, V otd., 2 stol, d. 143e, ll. 6–7, Iliodor to Arkhimandrit Makarii, 25 April 1912.

[189] RGIA, f. 796, op. 191, V otd., 2 stol, d. 143e, ll. 1–3, 40b., Nikolai's reports, 28 April; ll. 11–14, Makarii's report, 24 April; l. 9, Synod resolution 1 May 1912. See also V. Georgievskii, *Florishcheva pustyn': Istoriko-arkheologicheskoe opisanie*, Viazniki, 1896. *Mad Monk*, p. 250, denounces Nikolai as an alcoholic.

[190] RGIA, f. 796, op. 191, V otd., 2 stol, d. 143e, ll. 119–21, Iliodor's telegram, 10 May; l. 23; Synod resolution, 15 May 1912. I have found no archival trace of the petition, dated 8 May in *Mad Monk*, p. 256, denouncing Rasputin as 'the holy devil who is desecrating Christ's church'.

[191] S. Kondurushkin, 'Miatushchiisia Iliodor', *Rech'*, 1, 3 April 1912; idem, 'Iliodorovtsy', *Rech'*, 14, 29 September. See also I. K[nizhnik], 'V religiozno-filosofskom obshchestve', *Rech'*, 14 November 1912, and D. Filosofov, 'Iliodor i Bulgakov', *Rech'*, 18 November. The quotation is from Knizhnik's manuscript notes of the meeting: see A. A. Ermichev, *Religiozno-filosofskoe obshchestvo v Peterburge (1907–1917): Khronika zasedanii*, St Petersburg, 2007, p. 129.

fell under the unlikely protection of two lifelong defenders of religious toleration and civil rights, S. P. Mel´gunov and A. S. Prugavin.[192] Their voices can be heard through the medium of his appeal to the Minister of Justice in October 1912: 'Surely the protection of the laws of the Russian empire is not denied to me alone. I cannot believe that. And so as a Russian citizen and subject of the tsar I demand the judgement of Caesar (Acts, 25: 11).'[193] By then, however, Iliodor was on the point of renouncing his faith, having refused the Synod's admonition and denounced its regime as corrupt:

> You are haughty men, madmen; you are ungodly men. By means of curses and threats of hell and eternal flames you compel the poor, timid people to worship you and to feed your insatiable stomachs. You are enemies of the true God. I do not know you, and from this time on I do not care to know you. I despise you with every fibre of my soul.[194]

When he finally submitted his renunciation on 19 November, *Rech´*, which had denounced the exile of Germogen and Iliodor as 'an anti-cultural force that not only fails to advance the moment of ecclesiastical renaissance but reinforces the perpetually low level of this country's religious system', implausibly claimed that Iliodor's text would 'remain in the history of Russian culture' as a document 'of the same calibre as Avvakum's autobiography'.[195] The Church was less impressed. Until then, there had been no move to unfrock Iliodor, perhaps, as he later claimed, because Rasputin and the imperial couple opposed the idea. Indeed, Iliodor believed that it was only his refusal to attend chapel that delayed his release from Florishchev.[196] Once he had renounced his faith, however, events moved swiftly. In the last week of November, the Vladimir diocesan consistory decreed that Iliodor should be unfrocked for continuing to publish critiques of the episcopate and refusing to attend services. The Synod confirmed their decision and on 22 December some twenty officials, led by Arkhimandrit Makarii and the local colonel of gendarmes, came to his cell to witness his signature to the deed. 'And I, who for nine years had signed my name as Iliodor, wrote Sergius Trufanoff.'[197]

---

[192] S. P. Mel´gunov, *Staroobriadcheskiia i sektantskiia obshchiny: zakon 17 oktiabria 1906 g.*, Moscow, 1907; idem (ed.), *Tserkov´ i gosudarstvo: k voprosu o svobode sovesti*, Moscow, 1907; idem (ed.), *Tserkov´ i gosudarstvo: v perekhodnoe vremia*, Moscow, 1907; A. S. Prugavin, *Monastyrskiia tiur´my v bor´be s sektantstvom*, 2nd edn, Moscow, 1906.
[193] 'Iz arkhiva Shcheglovitova', *Krasnyi arkhiv*, 2 [15], 1926, pp. 108–12, Iliodor to I. G. Shcheglovitov, 27 October 1912.
[194] *Mad Monk*, pp. 263–64.
[195] *Rech´*, 20 January 1912; 4 December 1912.
[196] *Mad Monk*, p. 265.
[197] Ibid., 267; RGIA, f. 796, op. 191, V otd., 2 stol, d. 143z, ll. 33–34, copy of Synod resolution, 13–17 December.

Iliodor's vain attempts to take revenge on Rasputin, closely moni-
tored by the police, lie beyond the scope of this essay. But Maksim
Gor´kii, then in Paris, had been delighted to learn from Kondurushkin
of Iliodor's plans to write an exposé of Grigorii and exhorted his friend
to do all he could to bring the project to fruition.[198] It was in this cause
that Prugavin spirited Iliodor into the Grand Duchy of Finland in
July 1914, delivering him into the care of Gor´kii and his fellow writer,
Evgenii Chirikov. Whereas Iliodor recalled that Gor´kii 'took a warm,
brotherly interest' in him, Chirikov, the author of a hostile account
of his Volga pilgrimage in 1911, could find 'nothing spiritual' about
Iliodor: 'An evident triumph of flesh over spirit. A man capable of forcing his way through with his fists and his elbows, but not at all by the
word of God! Not long ago, I was railing against him in the press, and
now there he is sitting in my house, on the balcony, at the tea-table!'[199]
Nevertheless, he helped Iliodor across the frontier into Sweden, and
thence to Christiana in Norway. In June 1916, he sailed to New York,
where by December he was already threatening litigation against *The
Metropolitan Magazine*, which had assumed exclusive rights to articles on
Rasputin that Iliodor had simultaneously sold to Jewish newspapers.[200]
In the following year, ever the innovative self-publicist, he inspired and
starred as himself in Herbert Brenon's silent movie, 'The Fall of the
Romanoffs', released on Broadway in September 1917.[201]

VII

Iliodor's Tsaritsyn 'adventure' was not yet over, for he returned briefly
to Russia after the Bolshevik revolution, claiming, in a characteristic
flight of fancy, to have seen the severed head of Nicholas II in a secret
chamber in the Moscow Kremlin.[202] While E. M. Iaroslavskii sought
in vain to exploit Iliodor as part of his attempt to divide the leadership
of the Orthodox Church,[203] there was no doubt about the former

[198] I. S. Zil´bershtein and N. I. Dikushina (eds), 'Gor´kii i russkaia zhurnalistika nachala
XX veka: Neizdannaia perepiska', *Literaturnoe nasledstvo*, 95, Moscow, 1988, pp. 981–85,
Kondurushkin to Gor´kii, 20 March 1912; Gor´kii to Kondurushkin, 7 November 1912.

[199] *Mad Monk*, pp. 282–90 (283); E. N. Chirikov, 'Na putiakh zizhni i tvorchestva: Otryvki
vospominanii', ed. A. V. Bobyria, *Litsa*, 3, Moscow–St Petersburg, 1993, p. 380. Compare
E. Chirikov, 'Zametki provintsiala', *Sovremennik*, August 1911, pp. 364–83.

[200] *New York Times*, 31 December 1916, 7 January 1917.

[201] Ibid., 24 September 1917. Iliodor had already been filmed preaching in the courtyard
of his monastery at Tsaritsyn.

[202] M. Ferro, *Nicholas II: The Last of the Tsars*, trans. B. Pearce, Harmondsworth, 1991,
pp. 245–46

[203] See S. G. Petrov, *Dokumenty deloproizvodtsva Politbiuro TsK RKP (b) kak istochnik po istorii
russkoi tserkvi (1921–1925)*, Moscow, 2004, pp. 34–35, 37. I am grateful to Dr Petrov for a
copy of his book and for helpful discussion. The Synod's *spravka* on Iliodor was sent to
Moscow on 14 July 1921 'for Galkin [a former Petrograd priest] and Krasikov, members of
Narkomiust, for as long as is necessary': RGIA, f. 796, op. 191, V otd., 2 stol, d. 143z, l. 1.

monk's lasting power of attraction in the city (renamed Stalingrad in 1925) where vestiges of his following survived into the 1930s.[204] Whereas Stolypin's regime had been appalled by Iliodor's 'anti-khutorist' opposition to his land reforms — a position widely shared among clergy who supported the URP[205] — the Bolsheviks in Tsaritsyn granted him facilities at his former monastery 'in view of the fact that [his] religious community [was organized] on the principles of communist life'.[206] Iliodor assured Lenin that the only path to communism was through small-scale religious communities such as his own, whose members reportedly sold their belongings to purchase two warehouses with the intention of pursuing market gardening and cattle breeding. However, Iliodor received no reply to his letter of 16 June 1921, offering to collaborate with the Soviet leader in the 'religious revolution' allegedly begun that Easter by his election as self-styled 'patriarch of Tsaritsyn', and most Soviet bureaucrats showed no more sympathetic understanding of his 'spiritual children' than the Okhrana officials deputed to support their delegations to St Petersburg a few years earlier.[207] When confronted by 'the dark masses', officials of either ideological stamp instinctively saw only benighted ignorance. 'That is the fundamental reason for the pilgrimage from Nikolaevsk to the village of Kislovo', reported the local *ispolkom* in June 1920, 'where, in his capacity as priest, Sergei Trufanov (the well-known lickspittle, the former tsarist ieromonakh Iliodor), exploiting his talent for oratory, has a really mystical effect on the masses, right up to curing them, for which the masses, out of backward religious ignorance, offer him deep gratitude and elevate him to the status of miracle-worker and healer.'[208]

Exploiting the power of superstition, Iliodor had always 'used all kinds of allegories to impress the people', and never more so than

[204] A. G. Dalgatov, *'Oppozitsionnaia religioznost'' v Sovetskoi Rossii (okt. 1917 g. – konets 1930-kh gg.)*, St Petersburg, 2002, p. 285.
[205] See *Russkoe bogatstvo*, February 1911, pp. 54–64, and E. M. Mikhailova, '"Esli tak budet idti zemel'noe delo dal'she, to milliony bednykh krest'ian ostanutsia bez kuska nasushchnogo khleba": Proshenie Glavnogo gubernskogo saratovskogo soveta Pravoslavnogo vserossiiskogo bratskogo soiuza russkogo naroda P. A. Stolypinu. 1910 g.', *Istoricheskii arkhiv*, 2004, 4, pp. 216–21.
[206] 'Protokol No 6 zasedaniia Tsaritsynskoi gubernskoi kommissii po otdeleniiu tserkvi ot gosudarstva s predstaviteliami gubChK i Zhilishchnogo otdela Tsaritsynskogo gubispolkoma', 10 April 1921, in M. M. Zagorul'ko (ed.), *Gosudarstvo i religioznye organizatsii nizhnei Volgi i Dona v XX veke: Sbornik dokumentov i materialov*, Volgograd, 2002, p. 111.
[207] *New York Times*, 20 November 1921; E. V. Buliunina and I. V. Garskova, '"Vesti russkuiu massu k politicheskoi kommune nuzhno cherez religioznuiu obshchinu": Pis'mo ieromonakha Iliodora V. I. Leninu', *Otechestvennye arkhivy*, 2005, 4, pp. 118–19. Compare, for example, A. V. Gerasimov, 'Na lezvii s terroristami', in *'Okhranka': Vospominaniia rukovoditelei politicheskogo syska*, 2 vols, Moscow, 2004, 2, pp. 301–03.
[208] 'Informatsionnaia zapiska Otdela vnutrennego upravleniia Nikolaevskogo ispolkoma v Otdel upravleniia Tsaritsynskogo gubispolkoma o religioznoi situatsii v g. Nikolaevske i uezde', 5 June 1920, in *Gosudarstvo i religioznye organizatsii nizhnei Volgi*, p. 95.

in August 1911, when he celebrated the end of the Dormition Fast by
setting light to a cardboard dragon: 'the hydra of revolution'. Placing
'children dressed as demons' inside, on the model of the Trojan horse,
he preached that 'out of this foul mouth proceeded the devils of
devastation, starvation and death'.[209] Although he denied any attempt
to 'to curry favour with the people' by cultivating a Christ-like resem-
blance, the souvenirs on sale at his monastery included crude reproduc-
tions of Mikhail Nesterov's celebrated painting 'Holy Russia', in which
the Christ-like main subject was replaced by an obvious representation
of Iliodor himself.[210] Since Iliodor dressed in white to emphasize his
saintly individuality and carried a staff to symbolize his descent from
the Prophet Moses, it is hardly surprising that critics regarded such
behaviour as a 'candidature for sainthood' and interpreted his insistence on having been three times permitted to remain in Tsaritsyn
as a claim to providential status.[211] But such charades were probably
unnecessary. As Kondurushkin discovered in 1912, there were plenty of
clean-living people in Tsaritsyn who willingly accepted Iliodor's spiritual authority. Some were still persuaded twenty years later. For once,
it was no exaggeration for him to claim that 'the people considered me
a saint, and many who were sick and suffering came to ask for healing,
attributing divine power to me'.[212]

VIII

Had Iliodor been no more than the unhinged zealot revealed by his
memoirs, he would scarcely merit sustained interest. Lost in a state of
'delusion' (*prelest'*), as Orthodox describe those who take too exalted a
view of their spiritual gifts, he was widely denounced as a maniac.[213]
Reflecting the fashion for medical vocabulary, Bishop Parfenii equated
'*prelest*' with 'psychosis'; Alexandra Bogdanovich christened it 'the
monastic disease'.[214] 'One need only talk to Father Iliodor for half
an hour to be convinced that he is abnormal', a colleague conceded:
'Even his manner of speaking — loud, hysterical, and reminiscent of
the *klikushi* — bears witness to his disturbed spiritual equilibrium.'[215]

[209] *Mad Monk*, pp. 42, 45; *Utro Rossii*, 17 August 1911; Stremoukhov, 'Moia bor'ba', p. 38;
'Pokhozhdenie Iliodora', pp. 202–03, 207.
[210] *Mad Monk*, p. 288; S. Kondurushkin, 'Iliodorovtsy', *Rech'*, 29 September 1912.
Such images were among those confiscated by police following Iliodor's disgrace: *Rech'*, 21
January 1912.
[211] M. O. Menshikov, 'Speshat v sviatye', *Novoe vremia*, 27 May 1911.
[212] *Mad Monk*, p. 45.
[213] See, among many, *Rech'*, 20 May 1910; *Tserkovnyi vestnik*, 24 March 1911, col. 372.
[214] RGIA, f. 796, op. 191, V otd., 2 stol, d. 143d, l. 190, Parfenii to Synod, 23 February
1911; Bogdanovich, *Tri poslednikh samoderzhtsa*, p. 423, 28 March 1907.
[215] M. P[aozersk]ii, 'Iz besed ob o. Iliodore', *Novoe vremia*, 17 March 1911.

However, as one of his foremost critics, Count A. A. Uvarov, remarked, Iliodor's tragedy lay not so much in his own mental imbalance as 'in the astonishing lack of resistance to evil exhibited by the clergy, and especially the civil power'.[216] It is primarily because this charismatic monk became a disruptive political instrument that Iliodor is worth studying.

The significance of time and place for his movement was confirmed when Iliodor finally sailed with his family from Libau to New York on 15 November 1922, having been allegedly arrested in June by the Riga authorities on suspicion of being a Soviet agent.[217] Recounting his erratic career shortly after his arrival in America, the *New York Times* found it 'hard to say' what he would do next, 'but whatever it is, it will be picturesque, and unexpected and well worth watching'.[218] Sure enough, customs officials soon impounded a jewelled icon and cross, which Iliodor had auctioned for $250 as gifts from the late tsar in Eka-terinburg, where he claimed to have provided the imperial family with their last satisfying meal.[219] In the longer term, however, the congrega-tion of the Russian Baptist Church on Second Avenue proved far less receptive to his oratory than had the residents of Tsaritsyn. Starved of the oxygen of publicity, Iliodor retreated into obscurity, attracting headlines only rarely. In 1936, for example, a jury took only forty minutes to dismiss his $100,000 suit for defamation against the Viking Press and the Garden City Publishing Company, publishers of *Rasputin: The Holy Devil* (1928), which accused Iliodor of antisemitism and plot-ting to assassinate Grigorii.[220] Though Iliodor had returned to the USA with the stated intention of preaching anti-Bolshevism, his political impact there was predictably nil, and while his daughter Nadezhda (Hope Morris) gave his religion as 'Russian Orthodox' and his pro-fession as 'clergyman' on the death certificate (Fig. 2) issued by Man-hattan's Bellevue Hospital on 27 January 1952, the day after his demise, it seems unlikely that his pastoral activity was vigorous in his later years, when according to unconfirmed reports he was employed as a janitor.[221]

[216] Graf A. A. Uvarov, 'Eshche ob iliodorovshchine', *Utro Rossii*, 27 August 1911.
[217] *New York Times*, 10 and 16 June 1922, 15 November 1922. Richard Davies kindly procured a copy of the passenger list of the Baltic-America Line's *SS Lituania*: Leeds Russian Archive (hereafter, LRA), MS 1829/1–2.
[218] *New York Times*, 3 December 1922.
[219] Ibid., 1 and 29 December 1922.
[220] Ibid., 19 June 1936.
[221] LRA, MS. 1829/3. I am again indebted to Richard Davies for this document. I have not seen correspondence dating from 1947–1950 between Iliodor and V. A. Maevskii, held at the Holy Trinity Orthodox Seminary, Jordanville, NY.

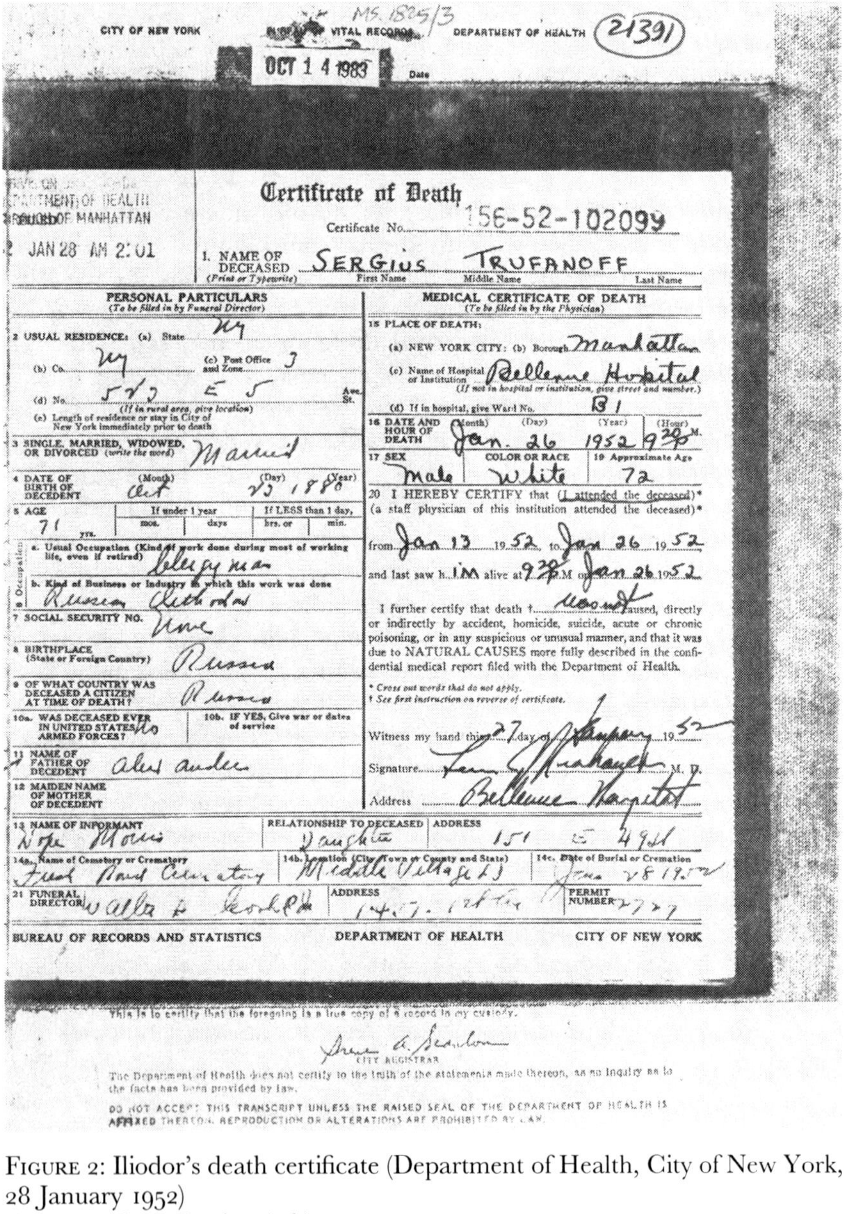

FIGURE 2: Iliodor's death certificate (Department of Health, City of New York, 28 January 1952)
Courtesy of Leeds Russian Archive

The true *raison d'être* of Iliodor and his *iliodorovshchina* lay in Russia at the end of the old regime. Although one populist critic exaggerated in proclaiming the period 1908–11 as 'the age of Iliodor in Russian history', and even in suggesting that Iliodor was 'logically inevitable' in that 'period of "vivid politics"', it was more plausible to argue that he was 'indeed only possible in such a period'.[222] This 'strange mixture of *starets* and demagogue'[223] highlighted more than one paradox at the heart of late Imperial Russia. Liberals on the Left who began by denouncing Iliodor's antisemitic ravings eventually came to champion him as a victim of religious persecution. Radicals on the Right who set out to use him to undermine Witte and Stolypin questioned the wisdom of their own judgement once it emerged that his ability to mobilize the *narod* was far greater than theirs. Hailed as a hero of the counter-revolution in 1905, Iliodor seemed a more dubious asset once he had 'transferred his denunciatory urge from the revolutionaries to the police, elected municipal politicians, the courts and the bureaucracy'.[224] Iliodor himself deployed strikingly modern tactics in the cause of his pre-modern beliefs, tolerating the violence perpetrated by his thuggish male supporters. Nevertheless, while Stolypin went to his grave permanently embittered by the support the tsar had repeatedly offered to a rebel's attempts to undermine his government,[225] Iliodor's female disciples seemed prepared to overlook all manner of base politics provided that they remained convinced of their neurasthenic idol's saintly purity.

For his part, Iliodor claimed that he had kept his monastic vow of obedience, 'but not in a way that pleased my superiors': 'I recognized no human authorities.'[226] Just as he placed himself above party discipline — 'He is, if one can put it this way, a political party in himself', his apologia declared — so he regarded himself as beyond Synodal control.[227] Ultimately, a critical journalist observed, 'nothing' existed for Iliodor 'except his own ego'.[228] Yet only in this psychological excess and the support he attracted was Iliodor truly exceptional. For in championing a theocracy in Tsaritsyn under the protection of Archbishop Germogen, he had merely taken to its logically absurd extreme the freedom of manoeuvre that Pobedonostsev had granted to his nascent phalanx of learned monks, distorting and discrediting in the process the missionary monastic revival that had seemed to promise so much at St Petersburg Theological Academy during Iliodor's boyhood years.[229]

---

[222] *Russkoe bogatstvo*, August 1911, p. 117.
[223] G. Hosking, *Russia: People and Empire, 1552–1917*, London, 1997, p. 440.
[224] *Vestnik Evropy*, March 1911, p. 386.
[225] Ascher, *Stolypin*, p. 370.
[226] *Mad Monk*, p. 21.
[227] *Pravda ob ieromonakhe Iliodore*, p. 28.
[228] *Vestnik Evropy*, August 1911, p. 419.
[229] For another product of the same milieu, scarcely less arrogant, but markedly less influential, see S. Dixon, 'Archimandrite Mikhail (Semenov) and Russian Christian Socialism', *Historical Journal*, 51, 2008, 3, pp. 689–718.

PART THREE

Lindsey Hughes: A Bibliography

SIMON DIXON

THIS bibliography lists books and articles published by Lindsey Hughes both in her lifetime and posthumously. Though all but three entries have been checked *de visu*, the list draws on notes kept in Lindsey's own papers, generously supplied by Dr James Cutshall. Reviews have not been included, though a large number of these appeared not only in leading historical periodicals, but also in the *Times Literary Supplement*, for which Lindsey reviewed Russian theatre and the arts in London for many years. Her numerous encyclopaedia articles — most notably in the *Modern Encyclopedia of Russian and Soviet History*, 59 vols and supplements, Gulf Breeze, FL, 1976 — have likewise been excluded.

ABBREVIATIONS

CASS	*Canadian-American Slavic Studies*
CSP	*Canadian Slavonic Papers*
FOG	*Forschungen zur osteuropäischen Geschichte*
OSP	*Oxford Slavonic Papers*
SEER	*Slavonic and East European Review*
SGECRN	*Study Group on Eighteenth-Century Russia Newsletter*

1976

'Moscow Baroque Architecture: A Study of One Aspect of Westernisation in Late Seventeenth-Century Russia', unpublished PhD thesis, University of Cambridge.

'Byelorussian Craftsmen in Seventeenth-Century Russia and their Influence on Muscovite Architecture', *Journal of Byelorussian Studies*, 3, pp. 327–41.

1977

'Western European Graphic Material as a Source for Moscow Baroque Architecture', *SEER*, 55, 4, pp. 433–43.

1979

'The Moscow Armoury and Innovations in Seventeenth-Century Muscovite Art', *CASS*, 13, 1–2, pp. 204–23.

1980

'The 17th-century "Renaissance" in Russia: Western Influences in Art and Architecture', *History Today*, February, pp. 41–45.

1981

'Architectural books in Petrine Russia', in *Russia and the West in the Eighteenth Century*, ed. A. G. Cross, Newtonville, MA, Oriental Research Partners, pp. 101–08.

'Ablesimov's *Mel'nik*: A Study in Success', *SGECRN*, 9, pp. 29–40.

1982

'"Moscow Baroque" — a Controversial Style', *Transactions of the Association of Russian-American Scholars in USA*, 15, pp. 69–83.

'A Seventeenth-Century Westerniser: Prince Vasily Vasil'evich Golitsyn (1643–1714)', *Irish Slavonic Studies*, 3, pp. 47–58.

'Sophia, Regent of Russia', *History Today*, July, pp. 10–15.

1983

'Russia's First Architectural Books: A Chapter in Peter the Great's Cultural Revolution', in *Russian Avant-Garde Art and Architecture*, ed. Catherine Cooke, London, pp. 4–13.

1984

Russia and the West: The Life of a Seventeenth-Century Westernizer, Prince Vasily Vasil'evich Golitsyn (1643–1704), Newtonville, MA, Oriental Research Partners, Russian Biography Series, 14, 129 pp.

1985

'Sofiya Alekseyevna and the Moscow Rebellion of 1682', *SEER*, 63, 4, pp. 518–39.

1986

'Sophia, "Autocrat of all the Russias": Titles, Ritual and Eulogy in the Regency of Sophia Alekseevna (1682–89)', *CSP*, 28, 3, pp. 266–86.

'N. A. L'vov and the Russian Country House', in *Russia and the World of the Eighteenth Century*, eds R. P. Bartlett, A. G. Cross and Karen Rasmussen, Columbus, OH, Slavica Publishers, pp. 289–300.

1988

'"Ambitious and Daring above her Sex": Tsarevna Sophia Alekseevna (1657–1704) in Foreigners' Accounts', *OSP*, New Series, 21, pp. 65–89.

'The Age of Transition: 17th-Century Russian Icon-Painting', in *Icons 88*, eds Sarah Smyth and Stanford Kingston, Dublin, Veritas Publications, pp. 63–74.

1989

Editor and translator. S. M. Soloviev, *A History of Russia*, vol. 25: *Rebellion and Reform: Fedor and Sophia 1682–1689*, Gulf Breeze, FL, Academic International Press, xxxiv + 276 pp.

1990

Sophia, Regent of Russia 1657–1704, New Haven, CT, and London, Yale University Press, xvii + 345 pp. [Awarded Heldt Prize for best book in Slavic Women's studies, 1991, by the American Association for the Advancement of Slavic Studies.]

Consultant editor and joint author with Robin Milner-Gulland and Orlando Figes. *The Russian Chronicles*, London, Century, 480 pp. [Lindsey Hughes contributed 'Britain and Russia: 1000 years of Anglo-Russian relations', pp. 12–18; 'Imperial Russia 1676–1825', pp. 144–45; 'Russian Renaissance', pp. 153–55; 'St Petersburg', pp. 169–71); 'Peter I', p. 183; 'Elizabeth', p. 193.]

'V. T. Postnikov's 1687 Mission to London: Anglo-Russian Relations in the 1680s in British Sources', *SEER*, 68, 3, pp. 447–60.

'Visions of an Imperial Capital', in *Tradition and Revolution in Russian Art*, ed. S. Causey, Manchester, Cornerhouse Publications, pp. 174–77.

1991

'The West comes to Russian Architecture', in *Russia and Europe*, ed. Paul Dukes, London, Collins and Brown, pp. 24–35. [Reprinted from *History Today*, September 1986, pp. 27–34.]

1993

Editor. *New Perspectives on Muscovite History: Selected Papers from the Fourth World Congress for Soviet and East European Studies, Harrogate 1990*, Basingstoke, Macmillan, 197 pp.

'Russia in 1689: Court Politics in Foy de la Neuville's *Relation curieuse et nouvelle de Moscovie*', in *New Perspectives on Muscovite History*, pp. 177–87.

'A Note on the Children of Peter the Great', *SGECRN*, 21, pp. 10–16.

1994

Editor and translator. S. M. Soloviev, *A History of Russia*, vol. 26: *Peter the Great: A Reign Begins, 1689–1703*, Gulf Breeze, FL, Academic International Press, xxiii + 320 pp.

Editor. Foy de la Neuville, *A Curious and New Account of Muscovy in the Year 1689*, trans. J. A. Cutshall, London, School of Slavonic and East European Studies, SSEES Occasional Papers, 23, xxxv + 78 pp.

1995

'Close Shave: a Pogonic History of Russia', *SGECRN*, 23, pp. 3–4.

1996

Editor, with Maria Di Salvo. *A Window on Russia: Papers from the Fifth International Conference of the Study Group on Eighteenth-Century Russia (Gargnano, 1994)*, Rome, La Fenice Edizioni, 317 pp.

'Between Two Worlds: Tsarevna Natal'ia Alekseevna and the "Emancipation" of Petrine Women', in *A Window on Russia*, pp. 29–36.

'Peter den store — et karaktärsporträtt', *Historisk Tidskrift för Finland*, 81, pp. 378–408.

'Peter the Great and the Fall of Communism', *Irish Slavonic Studies*, 17, pp. 1–18.

'Peter the Great's Two Weddings: Changing Images of Women in a Transitional Age', in *Women in Russia and Ukraine*, ed. Rosalind Marsh, Cambridge, Cambridge University Press, pp. 31–44.

'Did Peter the Great Abolish the Palm Sunday Ceremony?', *SGECRN*, 24, pp. 62–65.

1998

Russia in the Age of Peter the Great, New Haven, CT, and London, Yale University Press, xxx + 602 pp. [Awarded the 1998 Alex Nove Prize.]

Editor and translator, with Simon Dixon, A. G. Cross, W. Gareth Jones and others. *Britain and Russia in the Age of Peter the Great: Historical Documents*, London, School of Slavonic and East European Studies, SSEES Occasional Papers, 38, xxv + 255 pp.

'Biographies of Peter' and 'Afterword', in *Russia in the Reign of Peter the Great: Old and New Perspectives*, ed. Anthony Cross, Cambridge, Study Group on Eighteenth-Century Russia, Part 1, pp. 13–24; Part 2, pp. 187–90.

1999

'The Courts of Moscow and St Petersburg, c. 1547–1725', in *The Princely Courts of Europe: Ritual, Politics and Culture under the Ancien Régime, 1500–1750*, ed. John Adamson, London, Weidenfeld and Nicolson, pp. 295–313, 336–38.

'German Specialists in Petrine Russia: Architects, Painters and Thespians', in *The German Lands and Eastern Europe: Essays in their Historical, Political and Cultural Relations*, eds Roger Bartlett and Karen Schönwälder, Basingstoke, Macmillan, pp. 72–90.

'Restoring Religion to Russian Art', in *Reinterpreting Russia*, eds Geoffrey Hosking and Robert Service, London, Arnold, pp. 40–53.

'Peter the Great: A Hero of our Time?', *History Review*, 34, pp. 42–47.

2000

Playing Games: the Alternative History of Peter the Great, London, School of Slavonic East European Studies, SSEES Occasional Papers, 41, 32 pp. [An inaugural lecture delivered on 15 October 1998]

'Images of the Elite: A Reconsideration of the Portrait in Seventeenth-Century Russia', *FOG*, 56, pp. 167–85.

'Attitudes towards Foreigners in Early-Modern Russia', in *Russia and the Wider World in Historical Perspective: Essays for Paul Dukes*, eds Cathryn Brennan and Murray Frame, Basingstoke, Macmillan, pp. 1–23.

'The Petrine Year: Anniversaries and Festivals in the Reign of Peter the Great', in *Festival Culture in Germany and Europe from the Sixteenth to the Twentieth Century*, ed. Karin Friedrich, Lewiston, NY, Mellen Press, pp. 148–68.

'"Nothing's Too Small for a Great Man": Peter the Great's *domiki*', *SGECRN*, 28, pp. 12–15.

2001

Editor. *Peter the Great and the West: New Perspectives*, Basingstoke, Palgrave, xxiv + 280 pp.

'Images of Greatness: Portraits of Peter I', in *Peter the Great and the West*, pp. 250–70.

'Simon Ushakov's Icon "The Tree of the Muscovite State" Revisited', *FOG*, 58, pp. 223–34.

'From Tsar to Emperor: Portraits of Peter the Great', in *The Place of Russia in Eurasia*, ed. G. Szvak, Budapest, Magyar Ruszisztikai Inezet, 2001, pp. 221–32.

'From Caftans into Corsets: The Sartorial Transformation of Women during the Reign of Peter the Great', in *Gender and Sexuality in Russian Civilization*, ed. Peter Barta, London, Routledge, pp. 17–32.

'Peter the Great: a Passion for Ships', in *Scotland and the Slavs: Cultures in Contact*, 1500–2000, eds Mark Cornwall and Murray Frame, Newtonville, MA, Oriental Research Partners, pp. 3–20.

'"For the Health of the Sons of Ivan Mikhailovich": I. M. Golovin and Peter the Great's Mock Court', in *Reflections on Russia in the Eighteenth Century*, eds Joachim Klein, Simon Dixon and Martin Fraanje, Cologne, Böhlau, pp. 43–51.

2002

Peter the Great: A Biography, New Haven, CT, and London, Yale University Press, xviii + 285 pp.

'"The Crown of Maidenly Honour and Virtue": Redefining Femininity in Peter I's Russia', in *Women and Gender in Eighteenth-Century Russia*, ed. Wendy Rosslyn, Aldershot, Ashgate, pp. 35–49.

2003

'Petrine St Petersburg in the works of Pavel Svin´in (1787–1839)', in *St Petersburg 1703–1825: A Collection of Essays to Mark the Tercentenary of the City*, ed. Anthony Cross, Basingstoke, Palgrave Macmillan, pp. 148–64.

'Women and the Arts at the Russian Court from the Sixteenth to the Eighteenth Century', in *An Imperial Collection: Women Artists from the State Hermitage Museum*, eds Jordana Pomeroy et al., London, Merrell Publishers, pp. 19–49.

'Inventing Andrei: Soviet and Post-Soviet Views of Andrei Rublev and his Trinity Icon', *Slavonica*, 9, pp. 83–90.

'"Nothing's Too Small for a Great Man": Peter the Great's Little Houses and the Creation of Some Petrine Myths', *SEER*, 81, 4, pp. 634–58.

2004

With Catherine Evtuhov, David Golfrank and Richard Stites. *A History of Russia: Peoples, Legends, Events, Forces*, Boston, MA, Houghton

Mifflin, xix + 840 pp. [Lindsey Hughes contributed 'Part II. The Growth of Empire: Russia Looks West, 1613–1796', pp. 159–308.]

Editor, with Roger Bartlett. *Russian Society and Culture and the Long Eighteenth Century: Essays in Honour of Anthony G. Cross*, Münster, LIT Verlag, vii + 246 pp.

'"A Beard is an Unnecessary Burden": Peter I's Laws on Shaving and their Roots in Early Russia', in *Russian Society and Culture in the Long Eighteenth Century*, pp. 21–34.

'Secularization and Westernization Revisited: The Visual Arts in Seventeenth-Century Russia', in *Modernizing Muscovy: Reform and Social Change in Seventeenth-Century Russia*, eds J. Kotilaine and Marshall Poe, London and New York, Routledge Curzon, pp. 243–62.

'Catherine I of Russia: Consort to Peter the Great', in *Queenship in Europe, 1660–1815: The Role of the Consort*, ed. Clarissa Campbell Orr, Cambridge, Cambridge University Press, pp. 131–54.

'Monuments and Identity', in *National Identity in Russian Culture: An Introduction*, eds Simon Franklin and Emma Widdis, Cambridge, Cambridge University Press, pp. 171–96.

'The 1960s', in *A Hundred Years On: Dartford County School, 1904–2004*, Dartford, privately printed, pp. 70–88.

2006

'St Basil's Cathedral through British Eyes', in *Rossiia i Britaniia, vypusk 4: Sviazi i vzaimnye predstavleniia XIX–XX veka*, ed. A. B. Davidson, Moscow, Nauka, pp. 71–81.

'Art and Liturgy in Russia: Rublev and his Successors', in *The Cambridge History of Christianity, vol. 5: Eastern Christianity*, ed. Michael Angold, Cambridge, Cambridge University Press, pp. 276–301.

'Cultural and Intellectual Life', in *The Cambridge History of Russia, vol. 1: From Early Rus´ to 1689*, ed. Maureen Perrie, Cambridge, Cambridge University Press, pp. 640–62.

'Russian Culture in the Eighteenth Century', in *The Cambridge History of Russia, vol. 2: Imperial Russia, 1689–1917*, ed. Dominic Lieven, Cambridge, Cambridge University Press, pp. 67–91.

2007

Translator and editor. S. M. Soloviev, *A History of Russia*, vol. 28: *Peter I in Triumph and Tragedy 1707–1717: Poltava, the Pruth, Domestic Issues*, Gulf Breeze, FL, Academic International Press, xxix + 285.

'The Funerals of the Russian Emperors and Empresses', in *Monarchy and Religion: The Transformation of Royal Culture in Eighteenth-Century Europe*, ed. Michael Schaich, Oxford, Oxford University Press, pp. 395–419.

'Seeing the Sights in Eighteenth-Century Russia: the Moscow Kremlin', in *Eighteenth-Century Russia: Society, Culture, Economy (Papers from the VII International Conference of the Study Group on Eighteenth-Century Russia, Wittenberg 2004)*, eds Roger Bartlett and Gabriela Lehmann-Carli, Berlin, LIT Verlag, pp. 315–31.

2008

The Romanovs: Ruling Russia, 1613–1917, London, Continuum Books, 308 pp.

'From Tsar to Emperor: Portraits of Aleksei and Peter I', in Valerie A. Kivelson and Joan Neuberger (eds), *Picturing Russia: Explorations in Visual Culture*, New Haven, CT, and London, pp. 51–56.

'Russia', in *A Companion to Eighteenth-Century Europe*, ed. Peter H. Wilson, Oxford, Blackwell, pp. 227–43.

2009

'Petrine Russia', in *A Companion to Russian History*, ed. Abbott Gleason, Oxford, Blackwell, pp. 165–79.

2010

'The Cathedral of SS Peter and Paul', eds Robin Milner-Gulland and Simon Dixon, in *Personality and Place in Russian Culture: Essays in Memory of Lindsey Hughes*, ed. Simon Dixon, *SEER*, 88, 1–2, pp. 25–47.

ABSTRACTS

The Cathedral of SS Peter and Paul   by Lindsey Hughes

Originally intended as part of the author's unfinished study of *Landmarks in Russian Culture*, this posthumously-published article, edited by Robin Milner-Gulland and Simon Dixon, draws on a wide variety of sources ranging from the correspondence of Peter I to twenty-first-century guidebooks. The article traces the construction of the cathedral and its architectural significance, the subsequent fate of both exterior and interior, the successive roles of the cathedral as mausoleum and museum, and above all the changing resonances and responses the building has inspired in Russia and beyond since the beginning of the eighteenth century.

Bronze Tsars: Ivan the Terrible and Fedor Ivanovich in the Décor of Early Modern Guns   by Sergei Bogatyrev

This paper offers a cultural interpretation of two images of Muscovite royalty: the 'portrait' of Ivan the Terrible on a gun by Karsten Middeldorp (1559) and the image of Fedor Ivanovich on the famous Tsar Cannon by Andrei Chokhov (1586). It is argued that dynastic politics, Russia's military aggression and the growing interest in the figure of the tsar required the visualization of the tsar's power both in Muscovy and in the West. Royal portraiture expanded the cultural image of the Russian monarchy. The Muscovite tsar became a recognizable public figure who embodied the military might of Muscovy.

Printing Moscow: Significances of the Frontispiece to the 1663 Bible   by Simon Franklin

The first complete Moscow-printed Bible (1663) was designed to be impressive, starting with its opening two leaves: the illustrated title page, and — in particular — the elaborate woodcut frontispiece. The present study considers the significances of these pages on four levels, in relation to (i) the semantics of production; (ii) precedent in Muscovite and Ruthenian print culture; (iii) immediate responses; and (iv) subsequent longer-term impact. Thus, although based on just two images, the article explores a broad range of issues in Muscovite visual, verbal, technological and political culture across the seventeenth century.

The 'Italian' Nemetskaia Sloboda   by Maria Di Salvo

Italians were not so numerous in the Nemetskaia Sloboda as representatives of other nationalities, but at least two of them (the Florentine merchant Francesco Guasconi and the castrato singer Filippo Balatri from Pisa) deserve attention: the former for his involvement in the life of the Catholic minority, the latter for his close connection to Peter the Great and his mistress Anna Mons. The article aims to present as much information about life in the Sloboda as can be drawn from Italian sources, especially Balatri's as yet unpublished memoirs.

Casting Mazepa's Legacy: Pylyp Orlyk and Feofan Prokopovich   by Gary Marker

In the recently celebrated tercentenary of Poltava, no figure stirred greater controversy than Ivan Mazepa. Traitor in the eyes of some, national hero for others, his legacy remains deeply contested. As the Northern War came to an end in 1721 ideologists on all sides, with eyes turned toward posterity, began to craft their own versions of Mazepa the man and the political actor. Prominent among them were Feofan Prokopovich, archbishop of Novgorod, and Pylyp Orlyk, the hetman of the Ukrainian forces in exile. Their respective views turn out to be surprisingly ambivalent and less at odds than might be expected.

The Summer Gardens in the Social Life of St Petersburg, 1725–61 by Paul Keenan

The Summer Gardens in St Petersburg are considered symbolic of Peter I's 'Europeanizing' aims for his 'new' city. While their physical appearance naturally displays the influence and input of foreign personnel, the gardens' role as a social space for the ruler, the court and other privileged groups sheds light on another area of comparison with contemporary European practice. This article examines the social function of the Summer Gardens in the understudied period between Peter I and Catherine II and the access granted to social groups beyond the court elite in the 1750s, albeit with firm restrictions still in place.

'Ropsha, where Peter III was murdered ...' Faces and Façades of an Imperial Estate by Roger Bartlett

The article traces the history and development of the Imperial estate of Ropsha, near St Petersburg, from its incorporation into the Russian state after the Great Northern War up to the present day. It gained lasting notoriety as the place where Peter III was murdered in 1762, and had an interesting history under Grigorii Orlov (1764–83). Developed according to plans by Eropkin, Rastrelli and Porto by a succession of elite owners, it was sold back to the Crown in 1801. A centre of fish-breeding during the Soviet period, its palace now in a ruined state, it awaits redevelopment, while 1762 is not forgotten.

Religion and Enlightenment in Eighteenth-Century Russia: Father Platon at the Court of Catherine II by Elise Kimerling Wirtschafter

This article defines the Russian Enlightenment with reference to a leading figure of the religious Enlightenment. Derived from a larger study of the relationship between the Enlightenment and the Orthodox language of enlightenment, it analyses three sermons delivered by Father Platon at Catherine's court. Two of these address the distinction between enlightenment and learning, and the third discusses the relationship between the church and society. All illustrate how Platon contributed to Russia's lived enlightenment by blending Enlightenment ideas into the teachings of Russian Orthodoxy.

The Russian Academy of Sciences Expeditions to the Steppes in the Late Eighteenth Century by David Moon

In the late eighteenth century a number of scientific expeditions organized by the Russian Academy of Sciences travelled across the steppe region of the Russian Empire. The leaders were Germans (the best known was Peter Pallas), a Swede, and a Russian who received part of his education at a German university. This article interrogates the issue of 'personality' and 'place' by analysing how the expedition leaders reacted to the steppe environment — a semi-arid grassland with few trees, but fertile soil — through the lens of their backgrounds, education, and previous experience of natural environments that were forested.

Self and Place in Life-Writings by Late Eighteenth- and Early Nineteenth-Century Russian Noblewomen by Wendy Rosslyn

This article examines life-writings by Varvara Bakunina (1773–1840), Anastasiia Kolechitskaia (1800–71), and Varvara Sheremeteva (1786–1857), focusing on their constructions of self in their everyday lives in particular places. Sheremeteva remains within traditional prescriptions of femininity, concerned with others' perceptions of her self rather than with its inner essence. Bakunina is powerfully affected by place, in respect both of way of life and perception of codes of feminine behaviour. She redefines herself as strong, courageous and rational. Kolechitskaia's self is cultivated to be largely immune to changes of circumstance. Like Bakunina, Kolechitskaia disputes the culturally imposed group identity for women with the articulation of a single, complex, stable individual self with firm moral and rational principles.

General P. D. Kiselev and the Second Army HQ at Tul'chin, 1819–29 by Patrick O'Meara

Pavel Dmitrievich Kiselev (1788–1872) ranks among the most outstanding Russian statesmen of his age. During a long life he served three emperors as military commander, key administrator and distinguished ambassador. But early in his already brilliant career he risked losing everything through potentially compromising friendships with several of his staff officers who were Decembrists, in particular with Pavel Pestel', the republican ideologist of the Southern Society. By exploring Kiselev's ten years as chief-of-staff at Tul'chin from 1819, the article seeks to clarify the extent of these links, Kiselev's motives for them, and the danger they posed to his standing at court.

'Besy', Disorientation and the Person by Robin Aizlewood

This article explores disorientation of the person in Russian culture. Pushkin's poem 'Besy' — a primary text for this theme, providing one of the epigraphs of Dostoevskii's *Besy* and informing agonized reflections on the revolution in *Iz glubiny* — forms the key point of reference. The article starts from *Iz glubiny* and its predecessor *Vekhi* in order to discuss conceptualizations of the person in relation to place in Russian thought, from Chaadaev through to Bakhtin. The article then analyses the poetics of disorientation in 'Besy', placing this in the context of Pushkin's work as a whole. Finally, Bakhtin's notion of 'outsideness' is adduced to cast light on the disorientation of the person in the poem, alongside that which is conveyed symbolically through spatial disorientation.

Przheval'skii, Asia and Empire by Peter Waldron

Nikolai Przheval'skii (1839–88) was one of the most prominent Russian explorers of the nineteenth century. His journeys across Central Asia captured the imagination of the Russian public, but he also articulated a set of ideas that encapsulated how Russia perceived its Asian neighbours. Przheval'skii saw Asian peoples as inferior and he argued that Russia had a duty to extend its influence in Asia. His ideas were in the tradition of Russian nationalism that justified Russian imperial expansion, and Przheval'skii's adventures, scientific work and thinking had a substantial impact on both government policy and the public perception of Russia's empire.

A Corner of a Foreign Field: The British Embassy in St Petersburg, 1863–1918 by Anthony Cross

At the eastern end of Palace Embankment and facing the Trinity Bridge are two mansions that have been linked of recent decades to form what is now known as the St Petersburg State University of Culture and Arts. Both mansions were built during the reign of Catherine II, the first nearer to the Summer Garden was known as Betskoi's House, the second as Saltykov's and was designed by the renowned Italian architect Giacomo Quarenghi. Saltykov, tutor to the Grand Duke Konstantin, was not the first owner, but the house was to remain in possession of his descendants until the October Revolution. In 1863, however, it was leased by the British Government to become the permanent home of the British Embassy during the ensuing fifty-five years. It is to the history of the house in its various transformations and, above all, to its existence as the British Embassy that the present article is devoted.

Russian Marxism and its London Colony before the October 1917 Revolution by Robert Service

London had only a small 'colony' of political emigrants. They never went native and they arrived and left with their doctrines intact. Outwardly they were devoted to a cause which permitted no national priority; but their assumptions, which were probably unconscious, were focused on the Russian Empire. Britain was predominantly a useful place to do research, publish material, send out correspondence and hold party meetings. British socialists were also useful to the 'colony', but they were not considered interesting or important in themselves. The 'colony' kept itself to itself. From this complacent and dogmatic frame of mind stemmed some of the outbursts of fanaticism that afflicted Soviet Russia in the early years of the October Revolution and later.

The 'Mad Monk' Iliodor in Tsaritsyn   by Simon Dixon

Attracting adoring crowds with his 'delicate, beautiful, feminine face' and 'powerful will', Ieromonakh Iliodor (Sergei Mikhailovich Trufanov, 1880–1952) combined right-wing rhetoric with spiritual plausibility. Concentrating on the peak of Iliodor's notoriety at Tsaritsyn between 1908 and 1911, this article offers the first scholarly investigation of a scandalous career which threatened to undermine P. A. Stolypin. Drawing on the archive of the Holy Synod and a range of contemporary newspapers, the article touches on questions of masculinity and celebrity while concentrating on the damage inflicted on the Russian old regime when an unbalanced individual claiming to be its most loyal supporter was unleashed in an exceptionally unstable place.

INDEX

Lightning Source UK Ltd.
Milton Keynes UK
UKOW031105171011

180447UK00006B/65/P